Government and Business

Government
and Business

SECOND EDITION

BY

Vernon A. Mund

UNIVERSITY OF WASHINGTON

Harper & Brothers, Publishers, New York

To My Family

Contents

viii Contents

Illustrations

Preface to the Second Edition

The primary purpose of this book is to explain the many ways in which business and economic life are shaped and directed by government—to promote the general economic well-being, to enhance the business incomes of politically important groups, or to strengthen national defense.

As in the previous edition, the order of arrangement begins with the efforts of government to create and maintain competition in the various fields of business. Consideration is then given to the exceptions which have been made to our basic policy of competition. The study is thereupon directed to the positive forms of control which have been adopted—in place of competition—to protect the public interest.

The present volume seeks to present the latest trends and developments in the regulation and control of business. It also endeavors to take into account the comments and suggestions made by reviewers and by those using the first edition. Several reviewers suggested the desirability of including definitions of terms, especially the terms "regulation" and "control." I have accordingly integrated into the book a survey statement on the main functions of the federal regulatory commissions. In making this study, I have profited by the friendly suggestions of Professor Myron W. Watkins and Dr. W. H. S. Stevens of the Interstate Commerce Commission.

I have also prepared glossaries of basic economic terms which underlie the law on business regulation. Professors George J. Stigler, Fritz Machlup, William J. Fellner, and Edward H. Chamberlin have been particularly helpful in making critical comments on the definitions for workable competition, oligopoly, monopoly, and related terms.

A further innovation in the present book is the addition of sixteen "landmark" cases for use in classes which emphasize the case problem approach. I have found that students like to turn from the general text discussion to a consideration of "real-life" problems. My experience has been, moreover, that the resulting discussion serves to sharpen their understanding of the law and its application to business.

As teachers in the field of government and business know, it is primarily in the area of policy (or action) that differences of opinion develop. The present edition seeks to analyze governmental policy toward business in terms of alternatives. At the same time, I have included my own generalizations and summary statements.

In the preparation of the second edition, I have enjoyed the friendly help and criticisms of many persons. My thanks are especially due to officials in the regulatory commissions—federal and state—who have kindly answered my questions on the application of the laws which are analyzed in the text. In particular, I should like to mention the names of George Haddock, George P. Comer, Julius Tolton, Everette MacIntyre, Daniel J. Murphy, Corwin Edwards, Jesse W. Markham, John Blair, William S. Johnson, Joseph E. Sheehy, and Grover Ensley. My thanks are also due to Mr. Walter W. Harris, Attorney-in-charge, Seattle office, Federal Trade Commission, for his coöperation and friendly assistance in Chapters 16 and 17.

In selecting and preparing the sixteen landmark cases, I have had the assistance and counsel of Breck P. McAllister, Wendell Berge, Lee Loevinger, Kenneth S. Carlston, Everette MacIntyre, Lynn C. Paulson, Blackwell Smith, Herbert A. Bergson, Walter Adams, Robert W. Austin, George J. Stigler, George W. Stocking, and Jesse W. Markham.

Mr. P. J. Federico, U.S. Patent Office, kindly read the chapter on patents. Valuable suggestions for the chapter were also provided by Mr. Laurence I. Wood, Counsel, General Electric Co., and by Mr. Daniel G. Cullen, patent lawyer, Detroit, Michigan.

In the preparation of Chapter 5, I have profited by the critical comments of Dr. Emerson P. Schmidt (Chamber of Commerce of the U.S.); Mr. Charles M. Hackett (DuPont); and Herbert C. Morse and Willard Arant (Swift and Co.). Helpful suggestions on the case for fair trade were provided by Mr. John E. Lewis, American Fair Trade Council; and by Mr. Maurice Mermey, Bureau of Education on Fair Trade. The arguments for private power have been reviewed with Mr. Alexander M. Beebee, Rochester Gas and Electric; Mr. B. L. England, Atlantic City Electric Company; Mr. Chas. R. Landrigan, Detroit Edison; and Mr. Larry E. Karrer, Puget Sound Power and Light. The case for public power, on the other hand, has been read by Dr. John Bauer, American Public Utilities Bureau; Alex Radin, American Public Power Association; and Mr. Carlyn Anderson, Washington P. U. D. Association. Mr. Robert E. Hardwicke, Fort Worth, Texas, kindly read Chapter 28 on the use and conservation of natural resources.

I am also indebted to a number of professors in the field of government and business for suggestions and comments. Professors L. E. Traywick and Walter Adams made valuable suggestions for the improvement of the chapters on pressure groups and economic concentration. Helpful ideas were also provided by Professors E. H. Plank, Leonard J. Arrington, Charles R. Dean, Leo Fishman, and Ward S. Bowman. Professor J. K. Galbraith has kindly provided assistance on the role of antitrust policy in a system of countervailing power.

My colleagues in various fields at the University of Washington have been very helpful in providing specialized knowledge and critical comments. In particular, I should like to thank Professors Hugh A. Bone, Edward G. Brown, Philip Cartwright, N. H. Engle, J. B. Gillingham, Donald Gordon,

Earl Hald, James K. Hall, J. R. Huber, Robert Lampman, Douglas North, Calvin Schmid, and Dean Worcester.

My wife has graciously read all of the chapters. She has also made numerous suggestions and comments for their improvement.

VERNON A. MUND

Seattle, Washington
October, 1954

CHAPTER 1

The Political and Economic Functions of Government

THE APPROACH OF THE PRESENT STUDY

The essential purpose of this book is to give the reader a broad under-standing of the many ways in which business and economic life are shaped and directed by government. In developing our analysis, we shall first consider the action which government takes to create and maintain compe-tition in the various fields of business. The policy of competition, as we shall see, has proved to be uneconomic in certain areas or unacceptable to certain groups. Various exceptions accordingly have been made. We shall study these modifications, including the positive forms of control which have been adopted—in place of competition—to protect the public interest.

A study of government and business is certain to give rise to critical think-ing about the relations of government to business. What is a good economic order—both as to means and as to ends? How much government intervention should there be in the conduct of business? What forms should it take?

It is sometimes said that next to a sound digestion the most important thing for a young man or woman to have upon leaving college is a sound philoso-phy. A personal philosophy may be defined as a coherent and critical set of ideas with respect to human life and society. The phrase "critical set of ideas" is used to mean ideas and views which are subject to testing and reëxamina-tion in the light of reason and evidence. One's philosophy should also include a carefully thought out set of values—that is, criteria for judging what is sound public policy. What is it that we wish to achieve in adopting economic institutions and in regulating business?

The importance of having a workable plan for living arises from the fact that one's personal philosophy, together with the personal philosophies held by other citizens, largely determines the kind of society in which we shall live. Should government take action to dissolve large corporations? What policies should be pursued with respect to mergers? What should govern-ment do about oligopoly, basing-point and zone systems of pricing, resale price maintenance, the extension of public power, and industry-wide bar-gaining by national unions and national associations of employers? Our ideas with respect to these and other problems and the situations in which we find ourselves determine basically the way in which we shall live and work.

The purpose of the present book is not to give its readers a personal philosophy. It is rather to build up their experiences and factual background in the field of government and business so that they, themselves, will have a broader basis for developing a coherent set of ideas with respect to a desirable economic order, both as to means and as to ends.

THE DEVELOPMENT OF POLITICAL GOVERNMENT

The regulation of social and economic activity undoubtedly first took form in the rules and regulations established by individual family units engaged in self-sufficient production. Each family had its own plot of ground; and the routines of work, the division of labor, and the sharing of income were administered by the family head. The relations between parents and children, between master and slave, and between the family and property were likewise subject to a system of order and control.

With the development of exchange and commercial activity, family units entered into a growing number of new and complex social relationships. Markets came to be established, standard weights and measures were adopted, and witnesses were used to see that buying and selling were conducted openly and fairly. In the establishment of these institutions, certain individuals in the community exercised a leadership in meeting the needs of the group; and in the course of time such leadership assumed a permanence in the form of a centralized authority. This central authority came to be known as *government*.

The rules and customs which various *associations* of people—such as the family, the church, the trade association, and the labor organization—make for themselves can usually be counted upon to provide ordered relations for their own specialized group. When individuals and groups engage in community living, however, a set of rules and ordered relations becomes necessary for the social group. It is here that government arises and intervenes. The growth of private possessions, for example, occasions the need for a central authority to provide protection against theft, a means for settling disputes, and rules for the inheritance of property and the transfer of title. A further need arises in the greedy demands which organized producers make against unorganized consumers. The action of an association of bakers, for example, in agreeing that none shall sell bread below a certain price works an injury to all other citizens in the community. An important task for government in a capitalist society, accordingly, is that of making "rules of the game" for the conduct of economic activity, so that individuals in seeking their own advantage will produce results which are in accord with the public good.

Government, whether at the local, regional, or national level, is a special form of regulation for maintaining ordered relations in a community. The various types of regulation exercised by government are more vast in their scope than those of any other human association. The general authority of the state is also unique in that it is legally supreme over all other associations, as well as individuals, in its power to command obedience according to the law.

THE CONCEPTS OF COMMUNITY, STATE, AND GOVERNMENT

In considering the flow of authority in the process of government, it is desirable to differentiate the concepts of community, state, and government. The essential idea of a *community* is that of a group of people living in a certain area and having common relationships with one another. Thus, a community may be a town, a county, a regional district, or a nation. People live *in* communities, and among the relationships which they typically have with one another are those centering in their buying and selling activities. Within a community various *associations* of people arise for the pursuit of *a* common interest. They include the family, the church, the labor union, and the trade association. The most inclusive and one of the most permanent of all associations in a community is the *state*—either regional or national. The *state* may be defined as the *political* organization (or association) of a group of people living in a defined territory (a community) for the promotion of the common interest. The term "political," it may be noted, is derived from the Greek term *politikos*, which means pertaining to a "city" or to "citizens."

In the words of Professor MacIver, "We must definitely declare it [the state] to be an association belonging to the same category as the family or the church. Like these it consists essentially of a group of members organized in a definite way and *therefore* for limited ends. The organization of the state is not all social organization; the ends for which the state stands are not all the ends which humanity seeks; and quite obviously, the ways in which the state pursues its objects are only some of the ways in which within society men strive for the objects of their desire."[1]

In viewing the state as an association of people for certain ends, it is usual to define *government* as the agency or instrument of the state—and so of the people. Francis G. Wilson, for example, says that government is "the machinery of the state; it is its lever of social control, and its officers act as agents of the state."[2] Similarly, R. M. MacIver emphasizes that "when we speak of the state we mean the organization of which government is the administrative organ. Every social organization must have a focus of administration, an agency by which its policies are given specific character and translated into action. But the organization is greater than the organ. In this sense the state is greater and more inclusive than government. A state has a constitution, a code of laws, a way of setting up its government, a body of citizens. When we think of this whole structure we think of the state."[3]

THE FUNCTIONS OF GOVERNMENT

The present study is based upon an analysis of the political and economic functions of government. In the main, the general, overall functions of

[1] R. M. MacIver, *The Modern State* (London, 1926), p. 7.
[2] F. G. Wilson, *The Elements of Modern Politics* (New York, 1936), p. 55.
[3] R. M. MacIver, *The Web of Government* (New York, 1947), p. 31.

government are three: first, to protect the liberty of its citizens—from crime, foreign enemies, and personal coercion; second, to promote the social welfare; and third, to create and operate a system of economic institutions. Economic institutions are social arrangements—such as private property, freedom of contract, price competition, authoritarian price control, and compensatory fiscal policy—by means of which business and economic life are organized, directed, conducted, and regulated. It is the third function of government—the economic function—with which we shall be primarily concerned in our study of government and business.

In summary form it may be said that the main *political* functions of government are expressed as follows:

POLITICAL FUNCTIONS OF GOVERNMENT

1. *The Protection of Persons and Property.* A primary political duty of government is to provide members of the community with personal security in their daily lives, with protection to their property, and with defense against unfriendly acts or invasion by foreign states. Defense and war are enormously expensive and demand a tremendous diversion of labor and wealth from other ends. (See Fig. 1.) Expense is involved not only in direct military expenditures but also in the social cost of maintaining industries by means of tariffs and subsidies which are necessary for national security. Large quantities of goods and sums of money are also employed in building up and strengthening neighboring countries for political support in case of war. From a strictly economic point of view, controlled disarmament and the strengthening of the United Nations would make possible a substantial increase in economic well-being.

2. *The Establishment of a Fair and Expeditious System of Justice.* By providing a fair and expeditious system of justice, the government carries out its administration of the legal code of the state. The legal code is composed of civil (or private) law and public law. *Civil law* deals with the controversies which arise in the private relations of individuals. Such actions include private disputes over contractual relationships, debts, and property. A large part of the activities of the courts for civil purposes has to do with the private contractual relations of business, and the maintenance and administration of a system of civil law may also be classed as an economic task of government. *Public law*, on the other hand, deals with relations between individuals and the state and defines offenses against the common welfare. Examples of public law include the Sherman Act (1890) and the National Labor Relations Act (1935), as well as the laws against murder, theft, and treason.

3. *The Guarantee and Promotion of Human Rights.* The First Amendment of the United States Constitution provides that Congress shall make no law "respecting an establishment of religion, or prohibiting the free exercise thereof" or "abridging the freedom of speech or of the press," or the rights of assembly and petition; the Fifteenth Amendment provides that neither the

United States nor any state shall deny any citizen of the right to vote "on account of race, color, or previous condition of servitude." Increasingly, at the present time, the national government is taking steps in a positive way to protect the liberty of religious, racial, and other minority groups against the discriminatory action of other groups and persons.

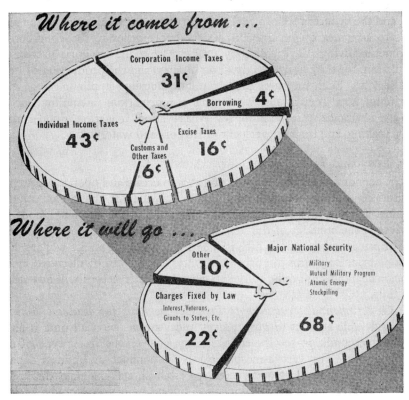

Fig. 1. Budget receipts and expenditures: fiscal year 1955 estimated. Federal budget expenditures go largely for defense, present and past. Expenditures for major national security programs constituted 68.4 percent of the 1955 budget. Interest payments, largely the result of public debts incurred during World War II, took 10.5 percent; and payments to veterans amounted to 6.4 percent. (Source: Executive Office of the President, Bureau of the Budget.)

4. *The Promotion of the General Welfare of the People.* The United States Constitution provides that Congress shall have the power to levy and collect taxes for the "general welfare of the United States"; and the individual states themselves have the power—the so-called "police power"—to promote the health, safety, morals, and general welfare of their citizens. In the exercise of the welfare function, government has engaged in a great variety of pursuits bearing directly on the well-being of the people. Activities which governments render in a cultural way include the establishment and support of public education, libraries, art galleries, museums, and public parks. Gov-

ernmental services which directly promote social and economic well-being
include public health services and social welfare benefits to aged persons, the
blind, dependent mothers, indigent persons, and homeless and neglected children.

Other activities in the general welfare group include census taking,
weather reporting, safety inspection, fire protection, city planning and zon-
ing, and the maintenance of penal and corrective agencies. Some of the social
welfare activities of government designed to ameliorate the conditions of
community living are very close to, or also within, the category of economic
regulation, for they bear directly upon business and the production of goods
and services. Such measures include public housing, minimum wage laws,
maximum hour regulations, workmen's compensation, unemployment and
old-age insurance, reforestation, soil conservation, irrigation, flood control,
canal making, and the improvement of harbors and waterways.

THE ECONOMIC FUNCTION OF GOVERNMENT

The economic function of government is to create and operate a system of
institutions (social arrangements) (1) to provide for the organization of
business activity, (2) to promote the maximum production of goods and
services in the conduct of this activity, and (3) to provide for a determination of prices and incomes which is in harmony with the public welfare. Each
of these principal forms of government intervention will be discussed in subsequent chapters, and only a brief statement of their nature will be made at
this time.

1. *Government Intervention to Provide the Basis for Business Activity.*
A considerable amount of government intervention, we shall find, is an indispensable condition for the establishment of even the freest type of economic system. The very atmosphere for the conduct of business depends
upon the intervention of government to establish and maintain the institutions of private property, freedom of contract, money and credit, weights
and measures, and a system of civil law for adjudicating the private disputes
of individuals. Such institutions make possible an elaborate system of private
planning in which individuals, rather than government, organize and direct
the production of goods and services in response to the desires of consumers.

2. *Intervention to Provide for a Maximum Production of Goods and Services.* Adam Smith in *The Wealth of Nations* (1776) declared that a principal object of political economy was that of making the production of goods
and services as large as possible. A system of "natural liberty" or freedom of
competition, he believed, would operate to make the produce of labor far
greater than it was under the then operating system of mercantilism. He gave
little attention to the problem of the distribution of the income produced.
His position appears to have been that a larger income for labor could be secured only by increasing the national income. Likewise, James Mill, in his
Elements of Political Economy (1821), stated that the object of political
economy is to ascertain by what means the objects of desire "may be pro-

duced with greatest ease and in greatest abundance, and upon these discoveries, when made, to frame a system of rules skillfully adapted to the end."

Important forms of government intervention to promote maximum production, we shall find, consist of (a) the maintenance of the right of producers to follow an occupation of their own choice (freedom of competition), (b) the prevention of monopoly and restrictive practices, (c) the use of monetary and fiscal measures to promote high-level production and price stability, (d) the adoption of public ownership and operation of certain monopolistic industries, (e) the promotion of technical improvements, and (f) the development and conservation of natural resources.

3. *Intervention to Provide Prices and Incomes in Harmony with the Public Interest.* In regulating the conduct of economic activity, government has the further duty of providing methods for the fair determination of prices and incomes. Left alone, the strong oppress the weak, and the methods of force and monopoly power come to determine prices and the sharing of the national income. In describing economic conditions in the United States around 1886, Sir Henry Maine, a British writer, declared, "There has hardly ever before been a community in which the weak have been pushed so pitilessly to the wall, in which those who have succeeded have so uniformly been the strong, and in which in so short a time there has arisen so great an inequality of private fortune and domestic luxury."[4]

In providing for a determination of prices and incomes, government intervenes in business (a) to maintain the principles of price competition and freedom of enterprise, (b) to prevent monopoly, (c) to impose public price fixing by commissions when monopoly is accepted, (d) to engage in the public ownership and operation of certain essential industries, and (e) to fix the minimum prices or incomes secured by certain groups in order to improve their economic position. Each of these forms of intervention is concerned with the prices and incomes which individuals secure.

The general principle usually followed by government in this area of control is one of eliminating, as far as possible, coercion, compulsion, fraud, arbitrariness, cheating, favoritism, monopoly, and discrimination. Such intervention, it is believed by most citizens, makes for prices and incomes more nearly in accord with the public welfare.

THE WELFARE STATE

Government not only takes action to provide for the *distribution* of the social income, but also for its *redistribution* by means of taxation. In this activity, it takes money from those who can afford it and gives it to the poorer classes in various ways as grants and subsidies. Why, it may be asked, does government go to all this trouble? Why does it not endeavor to provide for an equitable distribution in the first instance?

[4] Henry Sumner Maine, *Popular Government* (New York, 1886), p. 51.

Government action to redistribute existing income is supported by those who believe that a reform or modification of established methods for determining prices and incomes is certain to be slow and politically difficult, because of strong opposition from vested interests. Sharp differences of opinion also exist on the remedial measures which should be adopted to improve the working of our economic system. Heavy taxation, on the other hand, has become quite well established as a result of wars and depressions, and it is believed that taxation can be readily employed to promote "welfare for all."

A government which seeks to provide every citizen with minimum guarantees for material welfare—medical care, education, employment, housing, and pensions—has come to be called "the welfare state." The basic idea underlying the welfare state is the view that each individual is a human being and, as such, is entitled to a fair share of welfare, even though he does not have the necessary financial resources to secure it. Slogans expressing this idea are "fair shares for all," "welfare for all," and "a good life for all."[5]

THE GREAT EXPANSION IN SOCIAL SERVICES

During the prolonged depression which began in 1929, the social services provided by government were enormously increased. President Roosevelt proposed that national goals should include "freedom from want" and "freedom from fear." One-third of the people, he declared, were "ill housed, ill clothed, and ill fed." Under his leadership the national Congress enacted legislation providing for low-cost public housing, minimum wages, maximum hours, social security, and agricultural subsidies. At the present time, it is the desire of many individuals and social groups that the services of government be further increased to provide universal medical, dental, and nursing care, as well as a greatly expanded program of public housing.[6]

The growth of the social welfare functions of government raises the question of how far government should go in providing for the material well-being of its citizens. If the government provides care "from the womb to the tomb," as some persons currently propose, will individual initiative, ambition, and resourcefulness be dulled? One point of view is that if the government increasingly offers to take care of people they will accept the "crutch" and "lean" on government the rest of their lives. "Too much government," it is said, "means little men." It is only by struggle, adversity, and victory, many believe, that man gains self-reliance, self-confidence, and stature. In their

---

[5] Welfare legislation is frequently described as socialism. Socialists, themselves, however, declare that this is not an accurate description. Socialism, they state, is planning for the common good based upon substantial social ownership of the instruments of production. See also Norman Thomas, *Democratic Socialism* (New York, 1953).

[6] Congress appears to have a free hand to use public funds to promote the general welfare as it sees fit. In *Massachusetts and Frothingham* v. *Mellon*, 262 U.S. 447 (1923), and again in *U.S.* v. *Butler*, 297 U. S. 1 (1936), the Supreme Court held in principle that Congress may appropriate public money and authorize its use by administrative agencies for any social welfare purpose.

view man should pay the penalty for his failures and grow strong by individual effort and enterprise.

A further problem created by the social objective of welfare for all is the effect of heavy taxation, required to finance it, upon the initiative of individuals engaged in productive activity. In our present economy, financial gain is the strongest and most effective incentive for getting people to work hard, assume risks, and undertake responsibility. Without the "carrot" of money gain, many believe, individuals will be discouraged in preparing and training for executive positions, in giving managerial work the best of their ability, and in investing capital in new and uncertain ventures. If private initiative and enterprise are overburdened by taxation, it is possible that government will sooner or later be required to assume ownership and control of a growing sector of the economy.

THE NEW OBJECTIVE OF WELFARE FOR ALL HAS PROBABLY COME TO STAY

It is undoubtedly true that individuals should be given a large measure of responsibility for their own welfare if they are to become strong, self-reliant, and independent in thought and action. At the same time, however, the operation of chance, adversity, war, and the business cycle frequently leaves people in poverty through no fault of their own. From a social point of view, therefore, it is desirable and essential that some *minimum* provision should be made for the income, housing, and medical care of all individuals.

In large measure, the demand for an expanded program of social welfare activities has had its origin in the fact that the *economic system* has not been functioning effectively, so that large masses of people have found themselves without an opportunity to earn a living by the production and sale of useful goods and services. People must secure the means of livelihood, and if unemployment, unused capacity, and business depression make it impossible for millions to find work, government is forced to proceed directly to provide unemployment and old-age benefits, housing, and medical care. The impact of the great depression beginning in 1929 brought a profound change in the thinking of the American people on the social welfare function of government. The extent to which government will continue to expand its activities in this field will depend largely on the success of government in regulating the institutions of capitalism so as to provide full employment and full utilization of capacity.

IMPACT OF DEFENSE ON NATIONAL ECONOMIC POLICIES

Economists have long recognized that defense and national security are of such importance to a country that they claim priority over the aim of economic welfare. Adam Smith, for example, declared that "defense . . . is of much more importance than opulence." When defense assumes the continuing significance which it does today, it is inevitable that the defense programs will have a major impact on national economic policies.

Basically, economic policy is grounded upon considerations of economic well-being. Individual and corporate enterprises, in the main, are free to invest capital and produce goods and services without direction by government. Workers are privileged to select employments of their own choice, and consumers can choose goods of convenience and pleasure within the limits of their income.

Economic mobilization for war requires the making of drastic changes in the economy. Planning by private enterprise must be replaced by government control. Centralized control is necessary (1) to insure the maximum supplies of man power, materials, and equipment necessary for defeating the enemy; and (2) to curtail in various degrees, civilian production to vitally essential needs. Man power must be mobilized for the armed forces, and labor must be directed into war production and essential civilian activities. Materials, transportation, and capital investment must be utilized in accordance with a system of priorities, and scarce consumer goods must be rationed. Since government needs money and materials in a hurry, resort generally is made to large-scale borrowing. Inflationary pressures are created, and a system of price and wage controls must be established to retard and minimize inflation.

The economics of war is a specialized study beyond the scope of the present book. National security, however, is a *continuing* problem, and today it stands as a key factor influencing and shaping many of our national economic policies. The full impact which national security is having on our economic policies can only be surveyed and determined with time. Certain generalizations, however, appear to be warranted. We may note these briefly in order to provide a setting for our main study of economic regulation and control. In summary form, they are as follows:

1. The probable continuation of high-level defense expenditures for a decade or more (see Fig. 2). Attendant problems are high federal taxes or large budgetary deficits and an enormous public debt. Heavy tax burdens or large deficits, in turn, bear in various degrees upon economic incentives, the adequacy of private investment funds, the maintenance and expansion of social welfare programs, and the availability of funds for the efficient conduct of traditional governmental functions—such as business regulation and control.

2. A tendency toward greater economic concentration. The Army, Navy, and other defense procurement agencies follow a policy of placing major defense contracts with the dominant companies. Such a practice, they believe, saves time and centralizes responsibility for deliveries. Defense agencies also select large companies to operate government-owned plants, for such companies are the chief source of experienced personnel. Research grants, moreover, are usually made to the large companies which maintain extensive laboratories.

3. A continuing bias in the economy towards inflation occasioned (a) by high-level defense expenditures and (b) by fiscal and monetary policies

adopted to maintain maximum output and employment. (See also Chap.
27, pp. 611–612.)
4. The relaxation of antitrust law enforcement in industries closely related to
defense activity. The prosecution of antitrust cases takes the time of
corporate executives for conferences with attorneys and for court appear-
ances. Since the "interest of defense" requires adequate supplies of essential materials, it is quite unlikely that the antitrust agencies will be permitted to file cases against companies heavily engaged in defense activity.

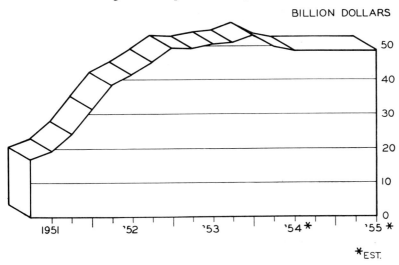

FIG. 2. Defense spending is likely to continue at high levels for many years. Expenditures
for major national security programs include those for military equipment, the support of
personnel, the operation of facilities, the purchase of equipment for our allies, the operation of atomic energy plants, the construction of air bases, the stockpiling of strategic
materials, and research. (Source: Bureau of the Budget.)

Such prosecutions, it is reasoned, might limit or handicap productive activity. Antitrust cases which involve requests for the dissolution of monopolistic enterprises also will not be brought or will be settled without
substantial remedial change, on the ground that now is no time to tinker
with industrial organization. (See also the *Alcoa* case, Appendices, pp.
695–701.)

During a period when defense considerations are paramount, government will also frequently support or tolerate the demands of organized
producers at the expense of consumers. The Interstate Commerce Commission in 1953, for example, sanctioned generous rate increases for the
railroads on the ground that the carriers must be maintained in a condition
to meet the needs of national emergency. (See also Chap. 24, pp. 536–537.)
5. A continuing program of providing economic and technical assistance to
allied nations and underdeveloped areas. Direct economic aid undoubtedly
will, and should, gradually decline. From a broader point of view, however, as Professor Howard S. Ellis has said, "It is essential in our own in-

terest that we continue and indeed intensify American aid in the sense of creating an economic milieu in which Western Europe can not only survive but increase in strength."[7] Such an "economic milieu" requires the elimination of cartel restrictions and the reduction of international trade barriers. It also calls for the prevention of large fluctuations in employment, output, and prices, in Europe as well as in the United States, by the use of appropriate domestic monetary and fiscal policies.

The economic development of underdeveloped areas also provides a means for strengthening the free world—politically as well as economically. "In the longer run—and it may extend over very many decades," says Professor Ellis, "the development of the low-income areas of the world may prove to be the most potent of all forces making for high incomes and employment in the older industrial nations."[8]

6. The development of a national policy on raw materials to promote economic growth and military security. In 1952 the President's Materials Policy Commission reported that "In area after area the same pattern seems discernible: soaring demands, shrinking resources, the consequent pressure toward rising real costs, the risk of wartime shortages, the ultimate threat of an arrest or decline in the standard of living we cherish and hope to help others to attain. If such a threat is to be averted, it will not be by inaction. . . . The United States must now give new and deep considerations to the fundamental upon which all employment, all daily activity, eventually rests: the contents of the earth and its physical environment."[9] (See also Chap. 28.)

7. The planning of expansion goals for the economy in order to insure the existence of a strong mobilization base—i.e., standby plants, adequate capacity in essential industries, and plants for producing all items needed for full mobilization. As a means of stimulating plant expansion and construction, the Office of Defense Mobilization has authority under the Internal Revenue Code to issue certificates of necessity for accelerated tax amortization. These certificates permit a company to recover the cost of a plant out of earnings over a period of five years. This heavy depreciation deduction reduces the current tax burden and allows a quick recovery of capital. The power to issue certificates of necessity for accelerated tax amortization gives government a considerable range of authority to determine *who grows and to what extent.*

THE NATURE OF INSTITUTIONS

The economic function of government, we have said, is to establish a system of *institutions* for providing (a) high-level output and employment and (b) prices and incomes in harmony with the public welfare. Although several different definitions of the term "institution" have been developed, they all seek to convey essentially the same meaning. Thorstein Veblen considered

[7] Howard S. Ellis, "American Economic Aid to Europe in Retrospect," *Kyklos*, Vol. VI, 1953, p. 15.

[8] *Ibid.*, p. 17.

[9] The President's Materials Policy Commission, *Resources for Freedom*, June 1952, Vol. 1, p. 1.

institutions to be "prevalent habits of thought."[10] In a formal definition of the term he stated, "An institution is a usage which has become axiomatic and indispensable by habituation and general acceptance."[11] Or as Francis G. Wilson has phrased it, "An institution refers not to persons, but to the form of order by which activities are directed. The family is an association, while marriage is an institution; the church is an association, while communion is an institution."[12] So likewise, R. M. MacIver says: "Institutions are the forms of order and activity consciously created by an association or community, so as to further and perpetuate some accepted principle or common interest."[13] In brief, it may be said that an institution is the *form of order* or *social arrangement* which people adopt to meet a concrete problem or to effect a common interest.

THE TASK OF CREATING A SYSTEM OF ECONOMIC INSTITUTIONS

Economic activity in the United States, in the Soviet Union, and in other countries as well, is carried on by means of *a set of institutions* which determine the way in which goods and services are *produced* and *shared* by members of the society. As Thorstein Veblen has stated, "Any community may be viewed as an industrial or economic mechanism, the structure of which is made up of what is called its economic institutions. These institutions are habitual methods of carrying on the life process of the community in contact with the material environment in which it lives."[14] The "economic system" of a nation consists of the totality of institutions by which economic activity is organized and conducted.

In large measure, the economic institutions which exist at any given time—whether in a capitalist or a socialist society—are those which have been recognized, developed, adopted, or created by government. The regulatory task of government is to give constant attention to the direction, implementation, limitation, and curtailment of these institutions so that society may enjoy (1) a growing abundance of goods and services and (2) a distribution of income which is in harmony with the public interest.

A distinguishing feature of our American political system—and of Western political tradition—is the doctrine that institutions are made and exist for men, and not that men exist for institutions. Man is the end and not the means. In so far as property rights, corporate organization, and established forms of public control promote human welfare, they find general support and maintenance. However, if experience proves that existing institutions impede welfare, they can and should be modified. Our political system—as

[10] Thorstein Veblen, *The Place of Science in Modern Civilization* (New York, 1919), p. 314.
[11] Thorstein Veblen, *Absentee Ownership* (New York, 1923), p. 101.
[12] F. G. Wilson, *op. cit.*, p. 54.
[13] R. M. MacIver, *The Elements of Social Science* (London, 1921), p. 61.
[14] Thorstein Veblen, *The Theory of the Leisure Class* (New York, 1899), 1919 edition, p. 193.

distinguished from that of communism—does not subordinate individuals to the inexorable maintenance of a fixed set of institutions. Our traditions uphold a free way of life and individual welfare; and provision is made in the democratic process for the establishment, adjustment, and change of institutions to accomplish these ends.

The origin of institutions is to be found in the thought, inspiration, ideals, and experience of people in a community with respect to the circumstances which confront them. An economic problem exists—for example, a business depression or a monopolistic industry—and this circumstance gives rise to discussion of a solution. In the solution of economic problems there are frequently alternatives, and the institution established is often a compromise or an adjustment between contending possibilities. It is also one which is broadly in line with the social philosophy currently held by politically important groups of people. Ideas may live in people's minds for decades, even centuries, before they become established in the form of an institution and also after the institution is gone.

Government, we have said, is the agency which provides laws, rules, and procedures for the establishment and operation of particular institutions. *A law, itself, is not an institution;* it is rather a means for establishing, defining, modifying, or regulating an institution. Thus, the antitrust laws seek to preserve and maintain the institutions of *free enterprise* and *price competition*. Some examples of institutions which have been created by government include standard money, a centralized reserve banking system, the business corporation, tariffs, public utilities, and social security. Although many economic institutions have become established without formal action by government—institutions such as private property, private business enterprise, marine insurance, partnerships, and collective bargaining—they are usually brought within the legal system for purposes of regulation and control. Strictly speaking, a business practice becomes an institution only when there is government recognition and acceptance of it.

Since institutions are developed to meet certain conditions in point of time, there is often a "lag" between the established institutions and the current needs of the community. The institution of "protective tariffs" to promote infant industries, for example, may have been a solution to a need of the United States a century ago, but it has little, if any, social utility today. When institutions are established, moreover, they may undergo a change which makes them socially undesirable. Thus, the protective tariffs which were instituted to build up particular domestic industries soon became perverted into a veritable spoils system of monopoly privilege.

Economic institutions are always in process of alteration and change. To a considerable degree, they flow from and reflect the interests of influential economic groups. Within a wide range of choice, economic institutions can be chosen or modified by the people as a whole. Our corporation statutes, our antitrust laws, and our agencies of regulation and control are all man-made. Such business arrangements as prohibitive tariffs, monopolistic mergers, cartels, and basing-point pricing, for example, can be replaced by competitive forms of enterprise, if the people have the insight, honest political leadership, and will to do it. Public policy, in large measure, waits upon an expression of the kind of society which we desire.

SUMMARY

Government is the *agency* or instrument of the state. The state, in turn, is an association of people living in a defined territory. Government has three main functions: (1) to protect the liberty of its citizens, (2) to promote the social welfare, and (3) to create and operate a system of economic institutions. Economic institutions are social arrangements by means of which business and economic life generally are organized, directed, conducted, and regulated. In exercising its economic function, government usually endeavors (1) to promote the maximum production of goods and services and (2) to provide methods for the determination of prices and incomes, so that the incomes which accrue to individuals will be in harmony with the public interest.

Following a survey of government as it operates in the American economy (Chapters 2 and 3), and of capitalism as the principal type of economic organization to be regulated by government (Chapter 4), we shall consider the particular ways in which business and economic life are shaped and directed by government.

Suggestions for Further Reading

Achinstein, Asher, *The Welfare State: the Case For and Against*, Library of Congress, Legislative Reference Service (Washington, 1950).

Bachman, Jules, *War and Defense Economics* (New York, 1952).

Baumol, William J., *Welfare Economics and The Theory of the State* (Cambridge, 1952).

Graham, Frank D., *Social Goals and Economic Institutions* (Princeton, 1949).

Harris, Seymour E., *The Economics of Mobilization and Inflation* (New York, 1951).

Lincoln, G. A., Stone, W. S., and Harvey, T. H. (editors), *Economics of National Security* (New York, 1950).

MacIver, R. M., *Community* (London, 1914); *The Elements of Social Science* (London, 1921); *The Modern State* (London, 1926); *The Web of Government* (New York, 1947).

Smith, Adam, *The Wealth of Nations* (1776).

Veblen, Thorstein, *Absentee Ownership* (New York, 1923); *The Place of Science in Modern Civilization* (New York, 1919); *The Theory of the Leisure Class* (New York, 1899).

Wilson, F. G., *The Elements of Modern Politics* (New York, 1936).

CHAPTER 2

The American System of Government and Business Regulation

The purpose of the present chapter is to proceed with a discussion of the American system of government as a mechanism for making and administering business regulations. What is the legal basis for the public regulation of business in the United States? How is political power divided between the federal and state governments? How much authority does the federal government have to regulate business?

THE CONSTITUTION AND THE SEPARATION OF POWERS OF CONTROL

In establishing the American government the founders provided for the federal system, with political power to be divided between the national government and the individual states. This form of government appears to have been created as a compromise between the representatives of the states then existing and the general desire of the people for a better government than the one then existing. There was general agreement that the object of a free people was to preserve their liberty and private rights, and that such preservation should be done by the imposition of constitutional restraints on the activity of government. The Constitution, accordingly, was drawn to provide (1) for the delegation of certain powers to the federal government, (2) for the reservation, in general, of other powers to the states, and (3) for the imposition of restrictions on the exercise of power by both sets of governments.

The functions delegated or assigned to the federal government include certain enumerated powers which bear directly on the operation of the economic system. These are as follows:

1. The regulation of commerce "with foreign nations, and among the several states, and with the Indian tribes."
2. The establishment of a uniform rule on bankruptcies.
3. The coinage of money, the regulation of the value of money, and the punishment of counterfeiting.
4. The fixing of standards of weights and measures.
5. The establishment of post offices and post roads.
6. The issuance of patents and copyrights on discoveries and writings.
7. The levying of taxes, duties, and excises, and the borrowing of money.

Other important powers of the national government are (1) the power to declare war and provide for the national defense, (2) the power to "make all laws which shall be necessary and proper" to carry into execution the powers vested in the national government, and (3) certain "inherent" powers which belong to a national government—such as the power to grant citizenship and the power to acquire territory.

The Constitution provides for a distribution of power among the legislative, executive, and judicial branches of government. This provision was made to prevent an undue concentration of power within the national government, and thus further to protect personal liberties and private property. A further restriction on the exercise of political power was subsequently developed in the practice of judicial review. Soon after the federal courts began to function, they faced the question of whether or not certain acts of Congress were in harmony with the Constitution. In 1803 in the famous case of *Marbury* v. *Madison*[1] the Supreme Court held that a clause of the Judiciary Act of 1789 was contrary to the Constitution. By this action the Court established a precedent for the enforcement of only those statutes passed by Congress which in its opinion are in accordance with the Constitution.

The powers not delegated to the national government or prohibited to the states were reserved to the states or to the people. The broad, residuary power reserved to the individual states by the Constitution is frequently called the "police power" of the states. Such power includes the general authority to enact legislation to promote the health, morals, education, and general welfare of the people.

THE SPECIAL PROTECTION TO PROPERTY GIVEN BY THE CONSTITUTION

At the time the Constitution was adopted many people were concerned that the government might sometime interfere with their liberty or property, and this fear led to the adoption of the constitutional provision that "no person shall be deprived of life, liberty or property without due process of law."[2] According to Professor E. S. Corwin, "originally, 'due process of law' meant simply the modes of *procedure* which were *due* at the common law." At the present time, however, he continues, " 'due process of law' means 'reasonable' law or 'reasonable' procedure, that is to say, what a majority of the Supreme Court find to be reasonable in some or other sense of that extremely elastic term."[3] Thus, in reviewing a limitation of property rights —or a restriction on freedom of contract—the Court considers whether Congress or a state legislature has exercised its powers reasonably.

The powers employed by the federal government over property include the power to regulate interstate commerce, the war powers, and the power

---

[1] *Marbury* v. *Madison*, 1 Cranch 137 (1803).

[2] The Fifth Amendment imposes this restriction on the national government, and the Fourteenth Amendment imposes it on the states.

[3] E. S. Corwin, *The Constitution and What It Means Today* (Princeton, 1947), p. 170.

to control business "affected with a public interest." These powers of the federal government resemble the police powers of the state governments, and they are sometimes referred to as the federal "police powers."[4] State governments likewise frequently interefere with property rights in exercising regulatory power at the state level. Both the federal and state governments modify or change property rights under the power of "eminent domain," which is a sovereign right of government, as such. In the exercise of this right, a government or its agency can take private property for a public use, even though the owner is unwilling, provided that just compensation for the property is paid.[5]

The doctrine of "eminent domain," it may be noted, does not mean that governments make compensation for all their acts which adversely affect the value of property. Thus, in times of revolution, when a new government takes private property, compensation is rarely, if ever, provided. Further, the action of the federal government in lowering tariffs, in destroying private monopoly power, and in declaring war does not provide grounds for compensation for those who suffer loss. The taking of such action, it is held by the courts, is a normal consequence of the exercise of lawful power.[6] Likewise, the people, themselves, by constitutional amendment can destroy private property rights in various objects without providing compensation. This was done by the Thirteenth and Eighteenth Amendments, which respectively abolished slavery and prohibited the manufacture and sale of intoxicating liquors.

THE FUNCTION OF BUSINESS REGULATION IS BASED LARGELY ON THE "POWER TO REGULATE COMMERCE"

The Constitution of 1789 gave Congress the power to regulate commerce among the several states; and in the famous case of *Gibbons* v. *Ogden* (1824) the Supreme Court held that the power to regulate such commerce was vested solely in the federal government.[7] To the claim that the term "commerce" is limited to traffic—that is, the buying and selling of commodities—

[4] See *Passenger Cases*, 7 Howard 283, 423–424, 425 (1849).

[5] The Fifth Amendment to the Constitution specifically provides, "nor shall private property be taken for public use without just compensation." Nearly all state constitutions have a similar provision limiting the power of the particular state government.

[6] *Knox* v. *Lee*, 12 Wall. 457 (1871); and *Omnia Commercial Co.* v. *U.S.*, 261 U.S. 502 (1923). In *Knox* v. *Lee* the Court held that the Fifth Amendment, which forbids the taking of private property for public use without just compensation, applies only to "a direct appropriation, and not to consequential injuries resulting from the exercise of lawful power." The Court recognized that "A new tariff, an embargo, a draft, or a war, may inevitably bring upon individuals great losses; may, indeed, render valuable property almost valueless," but held that government does not have to provide compensation for such losses.

[7] *Gibbons* v. *Ogden*, 9 Wheaton 1 (1824). According to Chief Justice Marshall, the phrase "among the states" means "that commerce which concerns more states than one" and is not "the exclusively internal commerce of a state."

Chief Justice Marshall replied: "Commerce, undoubtedly, is traffic, but it is something more—it is intercourse. It describes the commercial intercourse between nations, and parts of nations, in all its branches, *and is regulated by prescribing rules for carrying on that intercourse.*" Justice Johnson, in his concurring opinion, added: "Commerce, in its simplest signification, means an exchange of goods; but in the advancement of society, labor, transportation, intelligence, care, and various mediums of exchange become commodities, and enter into commerce; the subject, the vehicle, the agent, and their various operations, become the objects of commercial regulation."[8]

No specific guides are provided in the Constitution for the use of Congress in exercising its power to regulate commerce. Rather, the function of Congress in regulating business is to make such rules as it finds are necessary and desirable. In *Gibbons* v. *Ogden*, Chief Justice Marshall declared that the power of Congress to regulate interstate business activity is "complete" and "absolute." The discretion of Congress in selecting the ends or purposes of regulation, he stated, is subject neither to constitutional limitation nor to judicial review. The "sole restraints" on which the people must rely to protect themselves from abuse are "the wisdom and discretion of Congress, their identity with the people, and the influence which their constituents possess at elections."[9]

The term "regulate," as Chief Justice Marshall stated, has the basic meaning of prescribing rules for the conduct of business activity. Within the framework of rules prescribed by government, the law assumes, business enterprisers are free to make voluntary decisions on investment, output, prices, and wages. Subsequently, the power of Congress over commerce was interpreted by the Court to include the setting of rates on transportation from one state to another.[10] With the advent of the New Deal in 1933, the Court interpreted the power "to regulate commerce," and the power to make all laws "necessary and proper" to that end, to include the power to *control* prices, wages, and outputs in various sectors of general business activity. At present, it may be said that the power "to regulate" is the power to restrain, to encourage, to protect, to promote, to control, and to prohibit, in the furtherance of a public purpose.

FEDERAL REGULATION THROUGH TAXATION

Federal regulation of business is also exercised under the power to levy taxes. Ever since the first revenue act of 1789, Congress has from time to time enacted tax legislation for social and economic purposes rather than for the primary purpose of raising revenue. A protective tariff, for example, is a tax levied for the purpose of excluding foreign competition. Some revenue is usually secured, but revenue is not the main purpose of the tax. In uphold-

[8] *Ibid.*, pp. 189, 230. Italics added.
[9] *Ibid.*, pp. 196–197.
[10] See also Charles K. Burdick, *The Law of the American Constitution* (New York, 1922), p. 217.

ing the constitutionality of a protective tariff, the Supreme Court declared: "So long as the motive of Congress and the effect of its legislative action are to secure revenue for the benefit of the general government, the existence of other motives in the selection of the subjects of taxes cannot invalidate Congressional action."[11]

In upholding a heavy tax on the buying and selling of sawed-off shotguns, the Court declared: "Every tax is in some measure regulatory. To some extent it interposes an economic impediment to the activity taxed as compared with others not taxed. But a tax is not any the less a tax because it has a regulatory effect. . . . Inquiry into the hidden motives which may move Congress to exercise a power constitutionally conferred upon it is beyond the competency of the courts."[12] In certain situations, it is possible that a tax may be so heavy as to suppress a business activity altogether.

The Supreme Court has also held that Congress may use the power to tax as a penalty or sanction in the regulation of commerce. In the Bituminous Coal Act of 1937, for example, Congress placed a tax of 19½ percent on the market price of coal produced and sold by firms not participating in the price-fixing program. The Supreme Court upheld this use of the taxing power "in aid of the regulation of interstate commerce." According to the Court,

> Clearly this tax is not designed merely for revenue purposes. In purpose and effect it is primarily a sanction to enforce the regulatory provisions of the Act. But that does not mean that the statute is invalid and the tax unenforceable. Congress may impose penalties in aid of the exercise of any of its enumerated powers. The power of taxation, granted to Congress by the Constitution, may be utilized as a sanction for the exercise of another power which is granted to it.[13]

THE AMERICAN DOCTRINE OF LAISSEZ FAIRE

Although the Supreme Court in *Gibbons* v. *Ogden* (1824) declared that the power of Congress to regulate interstate business is complete and absolute, Congress actually did very little in the way of exercising its regulatory power prior to the advent of the New Deal in 1933. The inaction of Congress—as well as the state governments—in the field of regulation is largely to be explained by the view which early developed in politically important circles that government should exercise a minimum of interference in the conduct of economic affairs. President Van Buren, in his message to Congress on September 4, 1837, for example, declared:

> All communities are apt to look to government for too much. Even in our own country, where its powers and duties are so strictly limited, we are prone to do so, especially at periods of sudden embarrassment and distress. But this ought not to be. The framers of our excellent Constitution and the people who approved it with calm and sagacious deliberation

[11] *J. W. Hampton, Jr.* v. *U.S.*, 276 U.S. 394, 412 (1928).
[12] *Sonzinsky* v. *U.S.*, 300 U.S. 506, 513–514 (1937).
[13] *Sunshine Anthracite Coal Co.* v. *Adkins*, 310 U.S. 381, 393 (1940).

acted at the time on a sounder principle. They wisely judged that the less government interferes with private pursuits the better for the general prosperity. It is not its legitimate object to make men rich or to repair by direct grants of money or legislation in favor of particular pursuits losses not incurred in the public service. This would be substantially to use the property of some for the benefit of others.[14]

The full flowering of the American doctrine of laissez faire came with its acceptance by the Supreme Court and with the use of judicial review to set aside legislation which a majority of the Court believed meddled unnecessarily with the freedom of contract. Professor Edward S. Corwin suggests that the judicial acceptance of a doctrine of laissez faire had its origin largely in the organized efforts of the American Bar Association, which was founded in 1878.[15] The spokesmen and leaders of this organization were, and continue to be, lawyers for large business corporations, and the idea that government should pursue a "hands off" policy toward business reflected the desires of their clients. The point of view of influential business interests was well expressed by Mr. C. S. Mellen, a former president of the New York, New Haven, and Hartford Railroad Co., in testimony before a Senate committee in 1914. Said Mr. Mellen: "We did not seek so much positive legislation. . . . We could get along very well if we were let alone— very well. . . . It is not so much the things we want to do to the other fellow, as to prevent what the other fellow wants to do to us."[16] The full significance of the philosophy developed by the American Bar Association arises in the fact that from its members came a President, numerous Attorneys General, and ten future justices of the Supreme Court.

In the minds and legal briefs of corporation lawyers, the doctrine of laissez faire was a very much different policy from that advocated by Adam Smith. As urged by Smith in 1776, the idea of laissez faire was that government interference *which encourages monopoly* should be stopped. His attack centered on tariffs, exclusive trading companies, guild exclusions, and other measures confining trade and commerce to a favored few. Government intervention which promotes the general welfare was good. In a study of the exceptions which Adam Smith made to the principle of laissez faire, Professor Jacob Viner found no less than twenty-six instances in which Smith advocated government intervention to protect the public interest.[17]

In the United States, tariff favors and subsidies soon came to be widely granted by the federal government to industry groups under the influence of powerful business lobbies. It was this sort of intervention that Adam Smith so vigorously condemned. In the twisted version of "let alone" developed by the American bar, laissez faire was declared to mean that busi-

[14] *Messages and Papers of the Presidents* (New York, 1897), Vol. 4, p. 1561.

[15] E. S. Corwin, *Liberty Against Government* (Baton Rouge, 1948), p. 138.

[16] Senate Document 543, 63rd Congress, second session, 1914, p. 924. Quoted by V. O. Key, Jr., *Politics, Parties, and Pressure Groups* (New York 1952), p. 176.

[17] Jacob Viner, "Adam Smith and Laissez-Faire," in *Adam Smith, 1776–1926* (Chicago, 1928), pp. 134–155.

ness interests should be privileged to conduct their transactions as they please, without public regulation. The long tradition of the common law that economic competition should be regulated and supervised and that markets should be created and maintained for buying and selling was either forgotten or ignored. Laissez faire and competition, in the view of the leading corporation lawyers, called, in substance, for a policy of anarchy in the conduct of economic affairs.

Increasingly, the Supreme Court came to accept the doctrine of laissez faire urged by corporation lawyers in their legal briefs. This doctrine was that competition is an unregulated process, conducted without public rules or penalties, which should not be restricted as long as it is carried on in good faith to make profit. Under the banner of laissez faire and economic freedom, business was allowed to develop largely as it pleased. "Free competition" to American businessmen came to mean a freedom to conduct business affairs without government regulation or restriction. Local price cutting, rebating, and the use of "fighting" ships and brands were all looked upon as being legitimate acts of competition, even though they were morally reprehensible. Business leaders commonly declared that "competition is a state of war," to be waged without rules of fair play or without regard to moral principles of right and wrong. Such was the essential nature of laissez-faire capitalism.

THE USE OF JUDICIAL REVIEW TO LIMIT BUSINESS REGULATION

From about 1895 with few exceptions through 1935, the Supreme Court gave repeated expression to its fallacious doctrine of laissez faire and to its acceptance of competition as an unregulated, unrestricted process. By means of interpretation and judicial review, it succeeded in limiting, restricting, or nullifying a large part of the constructive legislation passed by Congress, as well as by the states, to provide rules and penalties, public administration and supervision, to keep economic competition within the bounds of public welfare. The Sherman Act of 1890, which was passed by Congress to provide for the preservation and maintenance of fair competition, was repeatedly weakened by decisions holding (1) that it did not apply to manufacturing activity and (2) that it condemned monopoly only when there were actual abuses. Further efforts of Congress to prevent monopoly and maintain competition by enacting the Federal Trade Commission and the Clayton Acts, as we shall see, were likewise limited or nullified.

In the field of social legislation, the Court similarly gave expression to its special brand of laissez faire. A state law in New York limiting the work in bakeries to ten hours per day and sixty hours per week was set aside as being an unwarranted interference with the right of free contract. Although the state presented evidence to show that bakers frequently suffer from inflammation of the lungs and bronchial tubes, running eyes, and sore legs, resulting from their long hours of work under conditions of heat and flour dust, the majority of the Court held that limitations on the hours of labor "are mere meddlesome interferences with the rights of the individual."[18] In a strong dissenting opinion, Justice Holmes declared, "This case is decided upon an economic theory which a large part of the country does not entertain. . . . A Constitution is not intended to embody a particular economic theory, whether of paternalism . . . or of *laissez-faire*. . . . I think that the word 'liberty,' in the 14th Amendment, is perverted when it is held to prevent the natural outcome of a dominant opinion."

Again, in 1923, the Supreme Court held that a minimum wage law for women passed by Congress for the District of Columbia was an unwarranted interference with the due process clause of the Constitution. According to Justice Sutherland, speaking for a majority of the Court, "But freedom of contract is, nevertheless, the general rule and restraint the exception; and the exercise of legislative authority to abridge it can be justified only by the existence of exceptional circumstances."[19]

THE PRESENT CONCENTRATION OF POWER
IN THE FEDERAL GOVERNMENT

Today, in sharp contrast with the conditions which prevailed before the great depression, the federal government has come to exercise a vast amount of direction and control over the economic life of the nation. In place of the long-held judicial theory that government intervention in the economic field should be held to a minimum, the Supreme Court beginning in 1937 adopted a positive view that Congress is entitled to exercise fully its powers to meet the needs of popular government and the growing complexities of present-day economic life. The doctrine of dual sovereignty, whereby the states and the national government were regarded as "sovereign" in their respective jurisdictions, moreover, has largely ceased to be a check on the regulatory action of the national government. "Not again for a long time," says Professor E. S. Corwin, "will the Court hold void an act of Congress against which nothing can be said by way of constitutional objection except that it invades the accustomed field of state power and tends to upset the Federal equilibrium."[20] Likewise, the principle of judicial review has been greatly weakened as a restraint on Congressional power, with the growing willingness of the Court to accept the legislation of Congress designed to meet emergent needs in the social and economic fields.

REASONS FOR THE CHANGED ATTITUDE
OF THE SUPREME COURT

Why, it may be asked, has the Court changed so completely in its interpretation of the Constitution? Why has it permitted "big government," so called, to develop? Some of the widely publicized economic facts which confronted the Court, as well as the general public, in 1937 included (1)

[18] *Lockner* v. *New York*, 198 U.S. 45, 61 (1905).
[19] *Adkins* v. *Children's Hospital*, 261 U.S. 525, 546 (1923).
[20] E. S. Corwin, *Constitutional Revolution, Ltd.* (Claremont, California, 1941), p. 108.

growing economic concentration, with 200 of the larger corporations controlling some 50 percent of all corporate wealth and exercising an even greater domination by means of interlocking directorates, formal agreements, secret understandings, and other devices for securing unity of action;[21] (2) great disparities in personal incomes, with 60 percent of American families receiving insufficient incomes to supply the basic necessities, and with 1 percent of the families receiving approximately as much total income as the 42 percent of the families at the bottom of the scale;[22] and (3) widespread economic insecurity and depression, with the estimated number of unemployed reaching a total of 10,983,000 persons in 1937.[23] When faced with these facts and many other related ones, the Supreme Court suddenly discarded its laissez-faire theory of government and adopted instead the view that the preservation of "liberty" may require the positive intervention of government. Of this change it has been said, "A switch in time saved nine!"

THE EXPANSION IN THE SCOPE OF THE COMMERCE POWER AFTER 1937

The term "interstate commerce" is not defined in the Constitution, and its meaning must be found in the decisions of the Supreme Court interpreting the scope of the power of Congress. In early decisions on the commerce clause, the Court held that interstate commerce covered only the buying and selling of goods to be shipped across state lines and the transportation of such goods. The regulation of manufacturing, mining, and agriculture was held to be beyond the scope of the power granted to Congress. Thus, in the *Sugar Trust* case decided in 1895, the Court accepted the erroneous view, urged by a combination producing 98 percent of the sugar used in the United States, that "production" is separate and distinct from "commerce."[24] Upon the basis of this view, the Court held that Congress could not regulate manufacturing, agriculture, mining, the production of oil and natural gas, quarrying, or the production of electric energy. As late as 1936, the attempt of Congress to regulate manufacturing or processing activity was set aside on the ground that production is not a part of commerce among the states.[25]

A sharp reversal in the opinion of the Court toward the scope of interstate commerce came in 1937 in a case involving the constitutionality of the

[21] A. A. Berle and Gardiner C. Means, *The Modern Corporation and Private Property* (New York, 1932), pp. 32–33.

[22] Maurice Leven, Harold G. Moulton, and Clark Warburton, *America's Capacity to Consume* (Washington, 1934), pp. 50–62.

[23] United States Government, *Census of Unemployment: 1937* (Washington 1938), Vol. 4, p. 9.

[24] *U.S. v. E. C. Knight Co.*, 156 U.S. 1 (1895). In economics commerce means *exchange* —that is, buying and selling or the making of ownership changes. Since manufacturing, mining, agriculture, and other forms of productive activity are almost always carried on for sale, it follows that they practically always involve "commerce."

[25] *Schechter Bros.* v. *U.S.*, 295 U.S. 495 (1935); *Carter* v. *Carter Coal Co.*, 298 U.S. 238 (1936).

National Labor Relations Act. This act, passed by Congress in 1935, gave workers engaged in interstate commerce the right to organize and bargain collectively through representatives of their own choosing. The Jones and Laughlin Steel Corporation, a large producer of steel with mills and other productive facilities located in many states, was accused of discharging several employees for union activity. In its reply the company took the position that the federal government had no jurisdiction because the men were engaged in *manufacturing*, which is not interstate commerce. The Court, however, upheld the application of the act upon a consideration of "the plainest facts of our national life." Since the effect of labor strife would be "immediate" and possibly "catastrophic" on interstate commerce, the Court held that Congress had "competent legislative authority" to enter the labor relations field and grant workers in the steel industry the right to organize and bargain collectively.[26]

In the case of *U.S.* v. *Darby* (1941), the Court held that Congress in the Fair Labor Standards Act of 1938 could reach directly into the sphere of manufacturing activity. By the terms of the act, Congress imposed prohibitions on (1) the shipment in interstate commerce of goods produced by labor whose wages are less than a prescribed minimum or whose compensation for overtime is at a rate less than time and one-half for hours in excess of forty a week, and (2) the employment of workmen in industrial production for interstate commerce at other than the prescribed wages and overtime rates of pay. In sustaining the act the Court held that the power of Congress "extends to those activities intrastate which so affect interstate commerce . . . as to make regulation of them appropriate means to the attainment of a legitimate end."[27] (See Landmark Cases, p. 669.)

The line between (1) interstate commerce or intrastate commerce which affects interstate commerce and (2) internal business which is subject to state control cannot be definitely drawn in advance. As the Supreme Court said in the *Consolidated Edison* case (1938), "Whether or not particular action in the conduct of intrastate enterprises does affect [interstate] commerce in such a close and intimate fashion as to be subject to federal control, is left to be determined as individual cases arise."[28] In this case, the jurisdiction of the National Labor Relations Board was extended to a public utility which made no sales outside of the state on the ground that vital interstate activity depended upon its operation.

In the case of *Wickard* v. *Filburn* (1942), the Court upheld the Agricultural Adjustment Act of 1938, which limited the amount of wheat that a farmer could grow and sell. According to the Court, "Even if appellee's activity be local and though it may not be regarded as commerce, it may still, whatever its nature, be reached by Congress if it exerts a substantial

[26] *National Labor Relations Board* v. *Jones and Laughlin Steel Corp.,* 301 U.S. 1, 41 (1937).
[27] *U.S.* v. *Darby,* 312 U.S. 100, 118 (1941).
[28] *Consolidated Edison Co.* v. *National Labor Relations Board,* 305 U.S. 197 (1938)

economic effect on interstate commerce and this irrespective of whether such effect is what might at some earlier time have been defined as 'direct' or 'indirect.' "[29]

In the case of *U.S. v. Frankfort Distilleries* (1945) the concerted action of retail liquor dealers in the state of Colorado to force producers to enter into "fair trade" price-maintenance contracts was held to be in violation of the Sherman Act. The retail dealers maintained that their business was intrastate in character and not subject to federal control. However, Justice Black, speaking for the Court, stated that the "coercive power" of the combination was "used to compel the producers of alcoholic beverages outside of Colorado to enter into price-maintenance contracts." This fact, he declared, brought the local activity within the control of the federal government.[30]

A further example of the extension of federal regulatory power is found in the case of *Mandeville Island Farms* v. *American Crystal Sugar Company* (1948). In this case, California beet sugar refiners agreed among themselves on the buying price for sugar beets grown in California. Their defense was that the purchase of sugar beets in California was a "purely local" activity and beyond the reach of the Sherman Act. The Court held, however, that "the artificial and mechanical separation of 'production' and 'manufacturing' from 'commerce,' without regard to their economic continuity, the effects of the former two upon the latter, and the varying methods by which the several processes are organized, related and carried on in different industries or indeed within a single industry, no longer suffices to put either production or manufacturing and refining processes beyond reach of Congress' authority." The test, the Court declared, for the exercise of federal power is "a showing of actual or threatened effect upon interstate commerce" which is "substantial" and "adverse" to the paramount policies of Congress.[31]

The doctrine that local activities which are a part of the flow of interstate commerce are subject to federal regulation was again affirmed in the *Lorain Journal* case (1951). This case involved an antitrust action brought by the federal government against a local newspaper, distributing local and out-of-state news. The Supreme Court held that the newspaper was engaged in interstate commerce and was subject to federal regulation. Said the Court: "There can be little doubt today that the immediate dissemination of news gathered from throughout the nation or world by agencies specially organized for that purpose is a part of interstate commerce."[32]

Upon the basis of today's brand of constitutional law, it would appear that the federal government is constitutionally entitled to regulate agriculture, manufacturing, mining (including the production of oil and gas), and retail trade, whenever the conduct of such activity has a "substantial" and

[29] *Wickard* v. *Filburn,* 317 U.S. 111, 125 (1942).
[30] *U.S.* v. *Frankfort Distilleries, Inc.,* 324 U.S. 293, 298 (1945).
[31] *Mandeville Island Farms* v. *American Crystal Sugar Co.,* 334 U.S. 219 (1948).
[32] *Lorain Journal Co.* v. *U.S.,* 342 U.S. 143, 151 (1951).

"adverse" effect on interstate business. In the present view of the Court, the sale, shipment, and transportation of products across state lines—the narrow concept of interstate commerce—cannot logically be separated (1) from the first-hand production of such products or (2) from their final distribution in retail trade.

If the federal government so desired, it would appear that it could take over most, if not all, of the antitrust activity at the state level. Likewise, the federal government would appear to be entitled to assume control of the production of oil and gas in order to conserve this highly valuable resource. Although most of the oil-producing states are now exercising control at the state level, there still continues to be much waste and needless duplication of wells which could be prevented by a more adequate system of federal control.

INTERNATIONAL CONFLICT AND THE FURTHER GROWTH OF FEDERAL POWER

The greatly increased regulatory power of the national government which came to be sustained by the Supreme Court was also increased by the "emergency" demands of World War II. Warfare has always made for a strengthening of the national political authority; and the unprecedented demands of World War II for a unified control of all resources brought forth detailed regulations setting maximum prices and rents, fixing wages and hours of work, establishing working conditions, controlling the utilization of raw materials and man power, and absorbing excess profits by means of special taxes. In considering the plea of an apartment house owner that the rentals fixed by the Office of Price Administration did not provide a "fair return" on her investment, the Court declared, "A nation which can demand the lives of its men and women in the waging of that war is under no constitutional necessity of providing a system of price control on the domestic front which will assure each landlord a 'fair return' on his property."[33] In the case of *Yakus* v. *U.S.*, the Court went even further in limiting the rights of individuals in wartime by holding that in violating the orders of a war agency an individual may even be denied the right to plead the unconstitutionality of an act of Congress.[34]

THE NEW CONCEPTION OF GOVERNMENT

Upon the basis of experiences in the great depression, organized labor, farm, and consumer groups have increasingly turned to government for assistance in improving their incomes and economic security. The satisfaction of these demands has made for a new and revolutionary conception of government. In the historical development of the United States, governmental policy was primarily a mixture of measures which provided (1) equality of opportunity for the common man (such as the public school system and the

[33] *Bowles* v. *Willingham*, 321 U.S. 503, 519 (1944).
[34] *Yakus* v. *U.S.*, 321 U.S. 414 (1944).

Homestead Act of 1862) and (2) generous favors for those who knew how to help themselves (tariff privileges, favorable corporation legislation, and ownership of the richest natural resources of the nation). With the advent of the "New Deal" in 1933—subsequently called the "Fair Deal" (1948–1952)—however, the purpose of government was shaped and directed to that of guaranteeing economic security and "fair shares" of income for all, as a necessary condition for human liberty.

An important example of the new role of government is found in the Social Security Act of 1935. This Act provides that the national taxing-spending power shall be used to support a program of financial assistance to elderly persons, to the blind, and to dependent children; unemployment insurance; old-age and survivors' insurance; maternal welfare work; vocational rehabilitation; and public health work. In upholding the Social Security Act, the Supreme Court drew upon the experiences and tragedies of the great depression, the national scope of the problem of social security, and the fact that individual states were reluctant to impose burdens on local industries when other states did not take such action.[35]

Other laws which were adopted to provide a greater measure of economic security and well-being are the Federal Deposit Insurance Act (1933), the Securities Act (1933), the Securities Exchange Act (1934), the Public Utility Holding Company Act (1935), the Wagner Act (1935), the Fair Labor Standards Act (1938), the Employment Act of 1946, agricultural price-support and subsidy legislation, and public-housing legislation.

In the main, the means employed by Congress in fulfilling its duty of guaranteeing security and welfare for all have consisted (1) of placing certain restrictions, curbs, limits, and controls upon the economically strong and wealthy groups and (2) of providing financial assistance and social services for the general public to promote economic well-being. Since the objective of welfare for all has a broad appeal in practical politics, it is probable that the new activity of government is here to stay.

SUMMARY

As a result of the stresses and strains of the great depression and World War II, and the ensuing social need for a strong national authority, there has occurred a great concentration of power in the national government. This consolidation of power, moreover, is likely to exist for an indefinite period of time. Professor E. S. Corwin observes that as a result of the changed philosophy of the Supreme Court, "the National Government is entitled to employ any and all of its powers to forward any and all of the objectives of good government."[36] Professor Corwin, in fact, declares that the concentration of power in the national government has progressed so far that "*the control over industry recently exerted by the government through priorities*

---

[35] *Carmichael v. Southern Coal and Coke Co.*, 301 U.S. 495 (1937); *Steward Machine Co. v. Davis*, 301 U.S. 548 (1937); and *Helvering v. Davis*, 301 U.S. 619 (1937).

[36] E. S. Corwin, *Constitutional Revolution, Ltd.* (Claremont, California, 1941), p. 113.

and price regulation in the name of the war power could be at any moment reasserted under the 'commerce' clause for purposes of social planning."[37]

Since the Supreme Court apparently stands ready to support Congress in its endeavors to cope with the emergent problems of our highly complex economy, an important question from the standpoint of government and business is how the enlarged powers of the national government are to be exercised *in relation to the organization and conduct of private industry.* It is in this area that the power now concentrated in the national government has yet to be applied in any sort of effective and consistent way.

Will the strengthened power of the national government be used to create a fully competitive industrial economy? Or, will the political influence of large business units cause government to adopt a laissez-faire attitude toward industrial organization and established business practices? Will private enterprise continue to play a dominant role in the production of goods and services? Or will government—federal and state—assume a greater responsibility for long-term investment and development to insure economic growth? Will the people tolerate another acute depression? Or will the federal government, in particular, by general consent, take responsibility for maintaining economic stability? Will the task of fighting depression become the major economic task of government—as important as the military task of resisting aggression?

Will organized farm groups call upon government to prosecute the monopolistic practices of business and labor? Or will they demand a continuation of present-day price assistance programs and seek new monopolistic restrictions of their own? Will the pressure of organized producers—in industry, labor, and agriculture—for special privileges force government to control prices and output in order to restrain the more powerful groups and to strengthen the weaker ones?

Will there be a continued expansion of governmental activity in the field of social welfare? Will government assume increased responsibilities for education, housing, and health? Will it be the state or federal authorities who will provide the new services?

All of the foregoing questions are in process of being answered on the floors of Congress. The major struggles in our present-day politics are the struggles of economic groups for power to determine the nature, direction, and tempo of the policies of economic regulation and control.

SUGGESTIONS FOR FURTHER READING

Anderson, William, *American Government* (New York, 1942); *The National Government of the United States* (New York, 1946).

Corry, J. A., *Elements of Democratic Government* (New York, 1947).

Corwin, E. S., *The Twilight of the Supreme Court* (New Haven, 1934); *The Commerce Power versus States Rights* (Princeton, 1936); *Court over Constitution* (Princeton, 1938); *Constitutional Revolution, Ltd.* (Clare-

[37] E. S. Corwin, *Total War and the Constitution* (New York, 1947), p. 174. Italics added.

mont, California, 1941); *The Constitution and What It Means Today* (Princeton, 1947); *Total War and the Constitution* (New York, 1947); *Liberty Against Government* (Baton Rouge, 1948); *A Constitution of Powers* (Charlottesville, Va., 1951).

Crosskey, W. W., *Politics and the Constitution* (Chicago, 1953), Vols. 1 and 2.

Dimock, Marshall E., and Dimock, Gladys O., *American Government in Action* (New York, rev. ed., 1951).

Ferguson, John H., and McHenry, Dean E., *The American System of Government* (New York, 1947).

Holcombe, Arthur N., *Our More Perfect Union* (Cambridge, 1950).

Lynch, D., *The Concentration of Economic Power* (New York, 1946).

Masse, Benjamin L., *Economic Liberalism and Free Enterprise* (New York, 1944).

Ogg, Frederic A., *Introduction to American Government* (New York, 1948).

CHAPTER 3

Democracy as a Means of Making and Administering Business Regulations

In the present chapter, we shall study democratic government as a mechanism for regulating and controlling economic activity. Government adopts a variety of measures which promote the welfare of consumers. At the same time, it also enacts legislation which increases the profits and money gains of various groups at the expense of the rest of the community. How and why do such diverse forms of intervention develop? In seeking an answer, we shall give consideration (1) to the nature of democracy and its points of strength and weakness and (2) to the growing influence of special-interest blocs, or pressure groups, on democratic government. Remedial measures for strengthening the operation of democracy will also be considered. There is a growing interest in such measures, for many believe that the existence of democracy, as we have known it, is threatened by the expansion of pressure politics.

THE MEANING OF POLITICAL DEMOCRACY

Democracy, in its political aspect, is a form of government in which ruling power is legally vested in the many, rather than in a few persons or in organized pressure groups. In a democracy the flow of authority is from the people to the state, and by means of periodic elections the government is made responsible—in varying degrees—to the prevailing ideas of the majority. There are many shortcomings and frictions in the operation of the democratic process; however, the general belief of the American people is that this system in its essentials provides the best available means for making government subject to the will of the people and for providing citizens with a measure of protection against arbitrary action.

In a dictatorship the flow of authority from the people to the state is broken. A political dictatorship is the means by which an entrenched class or political group stamps out opposition and maintains itself in power. The advantages of a dictatorship thus accrue to those in government and to the private groups closely associated with government.

Political democracy literally means "rule of the people," and in its political form is expressed in the principle of "one man, one vote." The essence of democratic government is that *all* the people through the franchise participate in governing the community and the nation. Both majority and minority groups have freedom of expression. On basic issues differences of opinion are resolved by counting votes, and thus the majority determines public policy. The minority, however, has the right "to grumble," and experience has shown that the maintenance of this right helps immeasurably in preventing extreme and arbitrary action.

To insure the operation of the democratic process, the First Amendment to the Constitution of the United States provides that "Congress shall make no law respecting an establishment of religion, or prohibiting the free exercise thereof; or abridging the freedom of speech or of the press; or the right of the people peaceably to assemble and to petition the Government for a redress of grievances." At present, advocates of social ownership of the principal means of production are clearly a minority. However, if they could persuade the majority to their way of thinking, democracy would make possible orderly and peaceful change.

The terms "democracy" and "republic" are sometimes used interchangeably. More specifically, however, a "republic" refers to a state in which the head of the government is not hereditary, but is chosen by the people. Historically, the term has been used to designate a state in which the government derives its power from the consent of the governed. Our federal system is both a democracy and a republic in its organizational form.

SOCIAL EQUALITY AND DEMOCRACY

The political rule of "one man, one vote" alone does not make for effective or successful democratic government. There are also social and economic conditions which must be fulfilled before political democracy can insure that governmental policy will reflect the interests and opinion of the majority. In addition to political equality, there must be a certain measure of social equality. An ideal is that all citizens should have a general education and be able to understand the basic issues, as well as the policies which may be pursued with respect to them. In practice, however, this condition for the operation of democracy is only partially realized. Many individuals have neither time, ability, nor interest to learn the policies which will promote national and international welfare. It is unrealistic to expect the masses to be able to solve the problems of military defense and economic prosperity. The strength of a democracy must be found in the ability and wisdom of a small part of the population. Persons in positions of influence—in business, labor, agriculture, and public life—must be relied upon to provide leadership, vision, and intelligence for the formulation of sound policies. If persons of training and ability constitute 10 percent of the population, it follows—as a practical matter—that each has the duty of informing and influencing nine other persons. With the present level of educational development, one can expect little more from the masses than an expression that they are contented or discontented with existing policies.

ECONOMIC EQUALITY AND DEMOCRACY

A further aspect of political democracy is the requirement of a certain degree of economic equality and economic opportunity. Modern democracy, and the American form in particular, developed with the rise of capitalism. With private property widely diffused and with freedom of enterprise, individuals came to enjoy a considerable measure of economic freedom. Economic freedom, in turn, made people feel free to speak and act independently in their political life. In so far as one finds himself absolutely dependent upon another person or group for a job, he usually becomes unwilling to express an independent opinion. Political freedom or its opposite thus grows out of, and is based upon, the presence or the absence of economic freedom.

THE INFLUENCE OF ECONOMIC INEQUALITY ON DEMOCRACY

As long as wealth is fairly evenly distributed, no one will tend to have preponderating political influence over others. The evil influence which wealth exerts in shaping national policies comes with the rise of great fortunes and large financial concentrations. Under monarchic and aristocratic forms of government, individuals of great wealth made gifts, contributions, and payments on the royal debts as a direct means of securing monopolistic privileges, tariffs, subsidies, and special favors. Under our political form of government indirect methods are employed. Organized wealth makes it possible for a few people to provide generous campaign funds for the support of candidates and party leaders who stand ready to grant special privileges or who promise immunity from legal prosecution or regulation.

In the American economy the rise of giant corporations, in particular, has worked to concentrate political influence in the hands of a few. From about 1890 to 1907, large corporations were the principal source of funds for the major political parties. In 1907 Congress, under pressure from the public, prohibited corporations from making campaign contributions in the national elections.[1] This legal prohibition on corporate contributions, however, did not entirely remedy the problem, for after 1907 the officers of large corporations, themselves, became generous donors to the national and state committees of the major political parties. In 1943 the Smith-Connally "Anti-strike" Act extended the prohibition on contributions to labor organizations, and in 1947 this prohibition was reënacted in the Taft-Hartley Act.

In 1940 Congress made it illegal for any "political committee" to receive more than $3,000,000 in any calendar year and limited the contributions of

[1] The statute of 1907 made it unlawful for corporations chartered under national laws to make campaign contributions, or for any corporation to make contributions in the election of President, Vice-President, senators and representatives. Many states likewise prohibit corporate contributions. The federal law of 1907 was reënacted in 1925 (Federal Corrupt Practices Act).

any person to a national committee to $5000 in any one year.[2] No limit, however, was placed on contributions to state and local committees or to other organizations which work hand in glove with the central committee. Similar loopholes exist for other regulations on campaign contributions and expenditures. Today there are no real limitations on the amount of money which a person can contribute or which a candidate or political committee can spend (see Table 1).

PRESENT-DAY SOURCES OF CAMPAIGN FUNDS

Studies made by Professor Louise Overacker show that in recent national elections the Republican party has secured its major support from bankers and manufacturers of iron, steel, autos, trucks, airplanes, food products, chemicals, textiles, cosmetics and drugs, paper, oil, public utilities, and mining. Although the Democrats have also received a substantial support from various banking and industrial interests, it has not been as large as that secured by the Republicans. The Democratic party, in particular, has had the support of public power advocates, contractors, builders, producers of materials for public works programs, brewers and distillers, organizations of the professional classes, and organized labor.[3]

The election of 1944 was the first in which a prohibition was placed on contributions by labor unions. With a little ingenuity, however, the unions were able to meet the provisions of the law by organizing political committees which raised money directly from the union members through voluntary contributions. The many gains secured under the Roosevelt administration have made organized labor increasingly conscious of the advantages to be won politically. At the present time, labor unions are cooperating with one another as never before in a program of political activity in an effort to hold their gains and possibly to increase them.

When one studies the substantial campaign contributions made by those associated with large banks, industrial corporations, and other commercial interests, he becomes vividly impressed with the great difficulty which unorganized consumers—citizens generally—face in trying to make their political voice effective. Measures which affect vested interests—such as increased appropriations for antitrust enforcement and proposals for grade-labeling

[2] These limitations are imposed by the Hatch Political Activities Act (1940). Federal laws and amendments which are currently in force are available in the *United States Code*. For the text of specific legislation as enacted by Congress see the *United States Statutes at Large* for the year in which the law was adopted.

[3] Professor Louise Overacker has published most of the significant material available bearing on this problem. Her studies are based upon a careful examination of reports filed by the Republican and Democratic parties. See the *American Political Science Review*, "Campaign Funds in the Presidential Election of 1936," June, 1937, pp. 473–498; "Campaign Funds in the Presidential Election of 1940," August, 1941, pp. 701–727; "Presidential Campaign Funds, 1944," October, 1945, pp. 899–925. For material on contributions and expenditures in the campaign of 1952—sources, donors, and amounts—see *Congressional Quarterly, Weekly Report*, July 17, 1953, pp. 915–940; and October 2, 1953, pp. 1199–1208.

TABLE 1. Federal Regulation of Campaign Contributions.

Federal Laws on Campaign Contributions	Loopholes Which Permit Laws to Be Evaded
1. Federal law makes it illegal for any national political committee to receive more than $3,000,000 in any one year.	1. (a) There may be any number of national committees to work with the central committee of each party, so long as each is nominally independent. Each can spend $3,000,000. (b) Federal law does not cover political committees confined to single-state operations. The vast majority of political committees are state and local.
2. Federal law makes it illegal for any corporation or labor union to give contributions in the election of President, Vice President, Senators, and Representatives. The prohibition covers contributions for political caucuses, conventions, primary elections, and general elections.	2. (a) The officers and directors of corporations now are important donors to national and state committees. (b) Some congressmen and candidates work for large corporations as legal counsel and consultants. (c) Corporations advocate political views in radio and newspaper advertisements and in pamphlets preceding an election. They buy whole tables of tickets at $100 per plate for political dinners. (d) Newspapers, as corporations, make "contributions of space," having cash value, in editorials supporting particular candidates. (e) Corporations spend millions of dollars for lobbying in the national conventions. They loan top-level executives to a candidate's campaign headquarters. They also make contributions to private political organizations.
889099	
3. Federal law limits the contributions of any person to any national political committee or to any candidate to $5000, in any one year.	3. (a) Contributions can be made to any number of national committees and to any number of candidates. (b) Contributions can be made through relatives and friends. (c) There is no federal limitation on contributions made to state and local committees. (d) A person can contribute as much as he desires after an election is over to make up deficits. Federal law does not cover individual contributions for conventions and primary elections.
4. Under federal law, a candidate for the Senate can spend up to $25,000 himself; and a candidate for the House can spend up to $5000 of his own funds.	4. (a) Intrastate political committees are exempt from federal regulation in raising money for candidates to federal office. (b) Each national committee can spend up to $3,000,000 for all candidates. (c) Federal law does not cover expenditures for primary elections.

legislation—stand little chance as long as our political parties are financed by the large interests rather than by the general public.[4]

THE HIGH COST OF POLITICAL CAMPAIGNS

The extensive use of radio, television, special trains, and chartered airplanes in recent campaigns has greatly increased the cost of winning votes. Estimates for the 1952 campaign place the cost to both parties at $100 million. Political campaigns, some observers remark, are becoming a contest of wallets rather than ballots.

The minimum campaign cost for a candidate to the House of Representatives, it is estimated, is around $10,000, and in closely contested races the sum is much higher. Minimum costs for the election of a senator in most states range from $150,000 to $200,000. In the Pennsylvania primary for 1950, two candidates campaigning for nomination to the U.S. Senate filed reports that each had spent over $800,000 in the primary. Senator Guy M. Gillette, in discussing this campaign, observed, "They spent over a million and a half for nomination to a job that in six years would be $75,000 in salary, and then whoever got the nomination had to bear the expense of the fall campaign for election."[5]

Why are candidates and their financial supporters willing to spend so much money to win a national election? The conservative *U.S. News* states as the reason, "The stake is control of a government that spends $79 billion a year and holds the power to grant or withhold favors of immense value. An investment of $85 million [or more in campaign costs] in that fight for control is regarded as moderate."[6] What are the favors which government can grant or withhold? They include such acts or concessions as tax adjustments, tariff favors, antitrust exemptions, government contracts, oil leases, licenses for power sites, loans, freedom from legal prosecutions, appointments for key positions, and special legislation. Organized producers are particularly interested in securing sympathetic and favorable treatment by the various regulatory agencies (see Table 9, pp. 80–81). A decision dismissing a complaint or granting a requested price or rate increase may mean millions of dollars to a large corporation or industry group.

The social and economic problems raised by large campaign expenditures are numerous. High election costs prevent many persons of ability and experience from running for important political offices. When persons of merit are nominated, they are faced with the high costs of the general election. Success may turn on wealth or access to wealth. High election costs, moreover, typically mean big gifts, and generous donors frequently expect a

[4] See also Louise Overacker, *Money in Elections* (New York, 1932), pp. 1–202; Edward M. Sait, "Campaign Expenditures," *American Political Science Review*, February, 1929, pp. 47–58; James K. Pollock, Jr., *Party Campaign Funds* (New York, 1926), pp. 111–142; and Earl R. Sikes, *State and Federal Corrupt-Practices Legislation* (Durham, 1928), pp. 188–221.

[5] *U.S. New and World Report*, October 10, 1952, p. 52.

[6] *U.S. News and World Report*, October 3, 1952, p. 15.

quid pro quo. High election costs thus greatly aggravate the problems of "political influence" and "class legislation."

INTEREST GROUPS FOCUS ATTENTION ON CONGRESS

After the elections are over, organized groups seek to bring their influence to bear directly upon members of Congress. Their goal is to shape governmental legislation along the lines of their interest. If they should lose in Congress, they appeal to the administrative agencies and then to the courts. If, by chance, they lose again, they not infrequently return to Congress in a final effort to modify the law or policy which limits their gainful activities.

The techniques of influence which interest groups use on members of Congress are numerous. They include direct contacts in offices and committee hearings, entertainment, the granting of loans, and the payment of retaining fees for legal services. Special gifts and financial favors made by known donors, in particular, serve to create a sense of obligation to private interests in the day-to-day functioning of government. Many senators and representatives, it should be noted, successfully resist the pressures of interest groups for special privileges. They stand as really great patriots in the life of our nation.

A well-known Washington correspondent has written that "property has not hesitated to corrupt government when necessary to preserve its precious advantages and to extend them. . . . We take it for granted that the property lobbies will push our legislators around whenever the interests of their principals are threatened."[7] Estes Kefauver, after many years in Congress, has declared, "It would be a startling revelation to many if figures could be obtained showing the actual and proportionate number of important bills drafted originally in the office of some lawyer or trade association."[8] Similarly, Professor D. C. Blaisdell reports in his significant study *Economic Power and Political Pressures,* "Much of the general legislation on our statute books is the result, wholly or in part, of group pressures."[9] The danger of government regulation which is directed and shaped by organized producers is that it benefits private interests at the expense of the general welfare.

ORGANIZED SPECIAL INTERESTS—THE "FOURTH BRANCH OF GOVERNMENT"

The influence exerted upon Congress by organized groups has led various writers to designate "pressure groups" as the "fourth branch of government." Strictly speaking, any association of individuals which seeks to secure or prevent specific legislation is a pressure group. Typically, however, pressure groups represent various producer and commercial interests—big busi-

[7] Kenneth G. Crawford, *The Pressure Boys* (New York, 1939), pp. ix–x.

[8] Estes Kefauver and Jack Levin, *Twentieth Century Congress* (New York, 1947), p. 156.

[9] Temporary National Economic Committee, Investigation of Concentration of Economic Power, *Monograph 26,* 76th Congress, third session, 1941, p. 57.

ness, small business, organized labor, and organized farmers. Within each major group, specialized groups—such as the oil bloc, the silver bloc, the sugar bloc, and the steel bloc—usually have selfish interests of their own, and these interests may lead them to coöperate or to compete with other groups for influence and favor.

Not infrequently the selfish interests of particular groups lead them to sponsor legislation which is in the public interest. Thus, organized exporters seeking to promote sales abroad are the source of cogent and persuasive arguments for low tariffs. Their *business interest* depends upon the ability of foreign concerns to obtain dollars by selling products within the United States. This point of view coincides with the public interest. Low tariffs promote exchange and specialization, and specialization increases productivity and enhances supplies of enjoyable goods. On the other hand, domestic producers whose products are vulnerable to import competition are the "prime movers" for our policy of restrictionism. What is it that determines whether a policy of low tariffs or high tariffs will prevail?

The congressmen who determine tariff and other public policies in their votes on the relevant laws are influenced by the factors which help to elect them to office. Making use of these factors, special interest groups apply pressure to congressmen (1) by contributing funds to their election campaigns; (2) by promising the support of large blocks of votes—such as the votes of farm and labor groups; (3) by appealing to individuals and groups of voters within a congressman's constituency—through newspaper advertising, radio broadcasts, news releases, and personal letters; and (4) by working directly with members of Congress during legislative sessions.

As in other fields money is power, and the groups with the most generous resources and the most efficient staffs are the ones most likely to be successful in gaining favorable action in Congress or with the various regulatory agencies.

In the field of tariff legislation, domestic producers fearing foreign competition have had preponderant influence in shaping public policy. Whether these groups can preserve their historical privileges, at the expense of consumers and the exporting industries, is an issue of growing political importance. At the present time, support for a policy of high tariffs comes mainly, if not entirely, from organized producers in the industries and agricultural groups listed in Table 2.

In a similar way, antitrust law enforcement secures its main support from businessmen and business groups which need protection from the monopolistic practices of other business firms. The principal organized groups in the United States which demand a strong policy of antitrust enforcement are shown in Table 3.

Many other organizations are similarly actively pressing for particular public policies. Some demand—and quite effectively—a modest program of antitrust law enforcement. Some demand favors for "private power" and increased obligations for "public power." Others are fighting for the strength-

TABLE 2. Industries and Agricultural Groups Which Demand Tariff Protection for Their Particular Production.

Almonds	Hats and millinery
Aluminum	Hothouse vegetables
Band instruments	Lace
Bicycles	
Books	Motorcycles
Carpets	Petroleum (independent units)
Cattle raising	Photoengraving
Chemicals	Pins, clips, fasteners
Citrus fruits	Pottery
Coal	
Cordage	Rubber-soled footwear
Dairy products	Scientific apparatus
	Shrimp canning and packing
Electric equipment (heavy)	Soft fibers
Fats (inedible)	Vegetables (dehydrated)
Filberts	Vegetables (Florida)
Fish canning	
Fisheries	Wallpaper
	Walnuts
Glassware	Wine
Gloves (knit)	Wood screws
	Woolens
Hard board (insulation)	Woolgrowing

(Source: *Congressional Record*, March 9, 1953, p. A1212.)

ening of resale price maintenance, the lowering of tariffs, and the reduction of taxes or their transfer to other groups. Throughout the chapters of our study we shall have frequent occasion to note the interest groups which support and oppose specific legislative action.

In most cases, congressmen want to do what is in the national interest. However, they must give first attention to the politically important groups within their constituencies. This fact causes them to reflect a less-than-national interest on many important issues of public policy. The great problem in the public regulation of business is how our representatives and administrators can work in a climate of organized private interests and at the same time maintain sufficient independence of action to provide rules and regulations which will promote the general welfare.

INTEREST GROUPS AND THE REGULATORY COMMISSIONS

Interest groups not only have a vital concern in the work of Congress and the state legislatures, but also in that of the various regulatory commissions. The commissions are daily engaged in making decisions, and these decisions are of the utmost importance to organized producers.

TABLE 3.   National Organizations Which Support
the Antitrust Laws and Their Effective Enforcement.

American Farm Bureau Federation
American Federation of Labor
Associated Retail Bakers of America

Congress of Industrial Organizations
Cooperative League of the United States
Credit Union National Association, Inc.

International Association of Machinists

National Association of Independent Tire Dealers
National Association of Retail Druggists
National Candy Wholesalers Association
National Congress of Petroleum Retailers
National Council of Farmer Cooperatives
National Farmers Union
National Federation of Independent Business
National Food Brokers Association
National Grange
National Rural Electric Co-op Association

Railway Labor Executives Association

United States Wholesale Grocers' Association

(Source: Select Committee on Small Business, House of Representatives, House Report *3237*, 81st Congress, second session,
1951, pp. 1–8.)

Very often the legislation defining the duties of a commission is expressed
only in general terms, and the commission itself is in a position to determine
the specific courses of action to be taken. The Federal Trade Commission,
for example, is charged with the duty of eradicating "unfair methods of
competition." This term is not defined, and it is within the discretion of the
Commission to proceed against certain business practices and not against
others. In most cases, too, a commission does not have enough funds to investigate and prosecute all the complaints and problems before it, so that it is
able to select some for prosecution and to reject others.

The commissions often find, moreover, that the statutes under which they
operate contain provisions which are conflicting or contradictory. In making
laws, Congress and the state legislatures commonly make concessions and
compromises in order to secure certain objectives. The resulting legislation
includes provisions and qualifications which require years for interpretation
and clarification. The Clayton Act, as amended, for example, condemns price
discrimination which injures competition. At the same time, it exempts price
discrimination made in "good faith" to meet competition. Which provision is
to control—injury to competition or a seller's privilege to discriminate to
meet competition? As will be discussed in Chapter 17, the Federal Trade
Commission has been subject to tremendous pressure from large corporations
to construe the law to permit discrimination.

The approach taken by industry groups in working with the commissions is that of getting the statutes construed *administratively* to fit the business practices which they desire to retain. The Sherman Act requires a policy of competition. *But what is competition?* Should industry be made to fit the kind of competition long established in economics and the law? Or should the concept of competition be made to fit present-day business practices and business organization? The regulatory agencies and the courts have a considerable area of discretion in answering these questions.

Today organized industry groups are actively pressing for a larger use of the "rule of reason" in the enforcement of the antitrust laws. In their view, the statutes can and should be construed—administratively and judicially— to fit the business structures and business practices which presently exist.[10] The Sherman Act contains no rule of reason, but the petroleum industry was able to get one written into the law in the *Standard Oil* decision (1911). So, likewise, the Antimerger Act of 1950 contains no provision stating that it shall be construed in "the light of reason." In applying the statute, however, the Federal Trade Commission has indicated that the rule of reason shall apply (see Chap. 16, p. 360). In this, as well as in many other examples, the decisions of the regulatory commissions reflect the values held by interest groups.

Industry groups subject to control by the various utility commissions give their utmost attention to the personnel and policies of these agencies, for the commissions have a wide range of discretion in approving rates. The rates for electricity, gas, telephone, and transportation service, it is provided, shall be "just and reasonable," but what does this phrase mean? In the *Panhandle Eastern Pipeline* case (1954), the Federal Power Commission granted the company, a pipeline company owning gas properties, an annual rate increase of over $12 million by using the "field prices," or unregulated rates, for gas rather than the actual cost of production—a standard which it had used for some fifteen years. Mr. Claude L. Draper, a member of the Commission since 1930, strongly dissented from the shift in the policy of his colleagues to favor the organized producers. In his words a large portion of the increase was "wholly unjustified." Commissioner Draper declared,

> There is, I believe, no disagreement anywhere with the statement of the Supreme Court in the signal case of *F. P. C.* v. *Hope Natural Gas Company* . . . that "Congress, however, has provided no formula by which the 'just and reasonable' rate is to be determined." But Panhandle and others have seized upon this lack of explicit Congressional directive to urge that administrative discretion has practically no limit. And the majority opinion herein seems almost eager to agree. (In the Matter of Panhandle Eastern Pipe Line Co., Docket G-1116, *et al.*, April 15, 1954, Dissenting Opinion, p. 3.)

The methods of contact with the administrative agencies are numerous.

---

[10] See, for example, the publication *Effective Competition*, a report to the Secretary of Commerce Charles Sawyer by his Business Advisory Council (Washington, 1952).

They include (1) conferences and meetings with commissioners and staff members handling cases (see Chap. 15, p. 348); (2) the provision of personnel from industry for service in governmental bureaus; (3) the sponsoring of persons for nomination and appointment to the various commissions; and (4) the official establishment of an industry committee to serve as an advisory council to the Secretary of the Interior (as in petroleum), the Secretary of Commerce, or to the President.[11]

GAINING FAVOR WITH VOTERS THROUGH PUBLIC RELATIONS

Many business firms, especially the very large ones, spend substantial amounts of money to create good relationships at the "grass-roots" level. If the people, themselves, can be induced to think kindly toward large business and its practices, it is reasoned, politicians will not attack great size. This point of view was cogently stated by a pioneer in the field of public relations as follows: "If you go direct to the people and get the people to agree with you, you can be sure that ultimately legislatures, commissions, and everybody else must give way in your favor."[12]

The forms taken by public relations activities are manifold. The National Association of Manufacturers provides lists of business leaders who will speak in colleges and universities. Many large corporations sponsor seminars for teachers, county agents, and farm representatives. Some grant university scholarships to outstanding high school graduates. Others provide teaching materials for high schools and grade schools. One large corporation has prepared a classroom unit on *Competition* for study by elementary grade school children! This unit, presented in comic book form, describes competition as "the process by which free and politically equal people coöperate with each other." In economics and the law, coöperation stands in contrast to competition. But in the view of some trade leaders, rival businessmen should engage in coöperation—especially on price.

Some large corporations hold weekly children's parties for all school children up to 16 years of age. Some work actively throughout the country in fund-raising campaigns for various charities. Others present superb plays and concerts on nation-wide TV and radio programs. General Motor's *Parade of Progress*, an elaborate traveling exhibition, sought to create public favor for General Motors as a leader in producing "more and better things for more people."

Some large corporations and their spokesmen seek to shape public attitudes—"the people at home"—by means of advertisements, articles in the daily and weekly papers, and pamphlets on such policy issues as TVA power projects, tariffs, and delivered pricing systems. In these publications, govern-

[11] For an excellent account of the relationships between interest groups and the administrative agencies, see Hugh A. Bone, *American Politics and the Party System* (New York, 1955).

[12] Ivy L. Lee, *Publicity* (New York, 1925), p. 60.

mental activity which is opposed is described as "socialism," "statism," and "the welfare state."[13] Production control in agriculture is condemned, but output curtailment by private industry to prevent price declines is approved. The antitrust laws, it is said, should be applied to labor. Their application to trade associations which promote "price stability," however, is opposed. A free enterprise economy is defined as one in which business is free from governmental regulations. Effective competition means freedom of choice of goods and services. The function of government is to promote the business interest. "What is good for business is good for the country."

Public relations activity today is an integral part of the American economy. There is much, moreover, which can be said for its use. It is important for business—or any group—to do the right thing. It is also important to let people know that you are doing what is right. The task ahead for the public is to acquire a degree of knowledge and sophistication which will enable it to learn when, and if, the private interest means the national gain.

THE REGULATION OF ORGANIZED INTEREST GROUPS

The Regulation of Lobbying Act of 1946 defines a lobbyist, in substance, as any person who receives money, or any other thing of value, for use in influencing the passage or defeat of legislation by Congress. By its terms any person "who shall engage himself for pay" for the "principal purpose" of influencing legislation must register with the Clerk of the House and the Secretary of the Senate and file quarterly reports of contributions and expenditures.[14] Some 2000 registrations have been filed under the Act of 1946. The really important lobby groups, however, probably do not exceed 500.

In a general sense, lobbying is any attempt to influence governmental decisions. It includes letter and telegram campaigns; company advertising; the distribution of books and pamphlets; the appearance of corporation executives before congressional committees; and personal contacts with members of Congress, as well as with administrators of government agencies.

Much lobbying is carried on by associations which represent individual firms and corporations. A list of representative organizations registered during 1950 is presented in Tables 4 and 7.

Lobbying is also conducted directly by the officials of large corporations and by their representatives. Among the lobby registrations of 1950 were the following large corporations or their representatives (Table 5).

Many corporations declare that they are exempt from the Lobbying Act of 1946 on the ground that their "principal purpose" is not that of influencing legislation. Accordingly, they do not register or file reports on their expenditures to influence governmental decisions. In 1950 the House

[13] See M. H. Bernstein, "Political Ideas of Selected American Business Journals," *Public Opinion Quarterly*, Summer 1953, pp. 258–267; and the *Congressional Record*, May 3, 1954, p. 5547.

[14] See also Belle Zeller, "The Federal Regulation of Lobbying Act," *American Political Science Review*, April, 1948, pp. 239–271.

TABLE 4.   Some Representative Organizations Registered Under the Federal Lobbying Act—
January 1, to October 20, 1950.

American Butter Institute	Investment Bankers Assn. of America
American Cotton Mfrs. Assn.	
American Dental Assn.	Lead Industries Assn.
American Fair Trade Council	Life Insurance Assn. of America
American Farm Bureau Federation	
American Federation of Labor	National Assn. of Mfrs.
American Hotel Assn.	National Assn. of Margarine Mfrs.
American Institute of Marine Underwriters	National Assn. of Retail Druggists
American Meat Institute	National Canners Assn.
American Medical Assn.	National Coal Assn.
American Mining Congress	National Cotton Council of America
American National Livestock Assn.	National Fertilizer Assn.
American Petroleum Institute	National Fisheries Institute
American Public Power Assn.	National Food Brokers Assn.
American Pulpwood Assn.	National Grange
American Road Builders' Assn.	National Lumber Manufacturers
American Tariff League	National Milk Producers' Federation
American Taxpayers Assn.	National Wool Growers Assn.
Anthracite Institute	National Rubber Bureau
Assn. of American Railroads	
Automobile Mfrs. Assn.	Peanut Butter Mfrs. Assn.
	Printing Industry of America, Inc.
Bureau of Education on Fair Trade	
	Rubber Mfrs. Assn.
California Almond Growers' Exchange	
California Fruit Growers' Exchange	United Mine Workers of America
Chamber of Commerce of the U.S.A.	U.S. Beet Sugar Assn.
Congress of Industrial Organizations	U.S. Brewers Foundation
	U.S. Cane Sugar Refining Assn.
Dairy Industry Committee	United Steelworkers of America
Distilled Spirits Institute	
	Wine Institute
International Assn. of Machinists	

(Source: House Report 3234, 81st Congress, second session, 1950.)

Select Committee on Lobbying Activities sent a questionnaire to 173 business corporations requesting information on expenditures actually being made to "influence, encourage, promote, or retard legislation." The corporations were asked to provide expenditures made for the travel expenses of executives, maintenance of a Washington office, printed or duplicated matter, advertising services, contributions to lobby groups, and other general expenditures.

The Committee's study revealed that "the pressure groups continue to receive large contributions, but [that] increasingly the great corporations are mounting their own major lobbying efforts." Among the leading corporations not registered under the Lobbying Act of 1946, but reporting expenditures to influence legislation, were those shown in Table 6.

What are the implications of lobbying activity conducted by organized groups and large corporations? In considering this question, the House Com-

TABLE 5.   A List of Corporations or Their Representatives Registered Under the Federal Lobbying Act—January 1 to October 20, 1950.

Allis-Chalmers Mfg. Co.	Lockheed Aircraft Corp.
Aluminum Co. of America	
American Cable & Radio Corp.	Marquette Cement Manufacturers Co.
American Export Lines, Inc.	Merck & Co., Inc.
American President Lines, Ltd.	
American Telephone & Telegraph Co.	National Lead Co.
American Tobacco Co.	New York, New Haven & Hartford R. R.
Atchison, Topeka & Santa Fe Ry. Co.	Co.
Atlantic Refining Co.	
	Ohio Oil Co.
Best Foods, Inc.	
Brown & Williamson Tobacco Corp.	Pacific Gas & Electric Co.
	Pennsylvania Railroad Co.
California Packing Corp.	Prudential Insurance Co. of America
Case Co., J. I.	
Chase National Bank	Railway Express Agency, Inc.
Chicago, Burlington & Quincy R. R. Co.	Republic Steel Corp.
	Revere Copper & Brass, Inc.
Eastman Kodak Co.	Reynolds Metals Co.
	Royal Typewriter Co., Inc.
General Electric Co.	
General Motors Corp.	Schenley Industries, Inc.
Gillette Safety Razor Co.	Sears, Roebuck & Co.
Goodrich, B. F. Co.	Sheaffer, W. A., Pen Co.
Grace Lines, Inc.	Socony-Vacuum Oil Co., Inc.
Great Northern Ry.	Southern Pacific Co.
Guaranty Trust Co.	Standard Oil Co. (Indiana)
Humble Oil & Refining Co.	Texas Gulf Sulphur Co.
International Minerals & Chemical Corp.	Union Pacific R. R. Co.
Johns-Manville Corp.	Weirton Steel Corp.
	Western Union Telegraph Co.
Kraft Foods Co.	

(Source: House Report 3234, 81st Congress, second session, 1950.)

mittee on Lobbying affirms that "We believe lobbying to be every man's right." However, it adds, "But some men are more able to make their rights meaningful than others. In practical terms, this has meant that those interests with the most to spend for protection have proclaimed 'lobbying for all men' as an almost sacred article of faith. It is not unlike the elephant shouting, 'Everybody for himself,' as he stomps up and down among the chickens."[15]

SPECIAL ECONOMIC PRIVILEGES GRANTED BY GOVERNMENT HAVE CREATED A GROWING DEMAND FOR ADDITIONAL FAVORS

The growth of great fortunes and economic inequality in the United States is largely to be explained not by the exercise of unusual technical or

[15] House Report 3138, 81st Congress, second session, 1950, p. 9.

TABLE 6. Some Large Corporations Not Reporting Expenditures Under the Lobbying Act (Jan. 1, 1947—June 30, 1950), but Making Expenditures to Influence Legislation.

Allied Chemical & Dye Corp.	Kaiser Steel Corp.
American Can Co.	Kennecott Copper Corp.
Armco Steel Corp.	
Armour & Co.	Liggett & Myers Tobacco Co.
Borden Co.	National Dairy Products Corp.
	National Distillers Products Corp.
Celanese Corp. of America	
Chrysler Corp.	Owens Illinois Glass Co.
Coca-Cola Co.	
Continental Can Co., Inc.	Procter & Gamble Co.
Deere & Co.	Shell Oil Corp.
DuPont, E. I. de Nemours	Standard Oil Co. of California
	Standard Oil Co. (New Jersey)
Ford Motor Co.	Swift & Co.
Goodyear Tire & Rubber Co.	Union Carbide & Carbon Corp.
Gulf Oil Corp.	United States Steel Corp.
International Paper Co.	Western Electric Co., Inc.
	Westinghouse Electric Corp.
Jones & Laughlin Steel Corp.	

(Source: House Report 3137, 81st Congress, second session, 1950.)

entrepreneurial ability, but rather (1) by the prodigal favors which government over the years has given to special interest groups and (2) by the laissez-faire philosophy of the Supreme Court and its acceptance of a large measure of industrial monopoly and economic concentration. The policy of extending grants of privilege to business groups had its origin in the economic ideas of Alexander Hamilton. Although Hamilton was not a member of the commercial classes of his day, he felt that the success of the national government depended upon the existence of a strong propertied class having a stake in the new government.

As a means of obtaining the support of merchants, manufacturers, and bankers, Hamilton advocated the use of protective tariffs to promote domestic industry. Once begun, the practice of granting protective tariffs soon came to be extended under the influence of powerful lobbies and generous campaign contributions to the granting of other favors and privileges. In answer to a plea for government aid in building railroads, railroad promoters and companies were given vast amounts of the nation's agricultural, forest, and mineral resources. Although the Homestead Act of 1862 was passed to encourage the settlement of public lands by individuals, fraud and maladministration gave control of great areas of the finest natural resources to large railroad, lumbering, mining, and other corporations.

In 1888 the state of New Jersey took the lead in extending the privileges

TABLE 7.   The Fifteen Largest Spenders Registered Under the Federal Lobbying Act. Expenditures reported include money spent for public relations, advertising services, salaries, fees, commissions, gifts, contributions, travel, food, lodging, entertainment, and telephone service.

	1953	1952
Natl. Assn. of Electric Companies	$547,789.32	$477,941.74
Assn. of American Railroads	235,727.73	235,977.74
Natl. Milk Producers Fedn.	233,557.84	219,837.26
American Fedn. of Labor	123,608.43	105,537.20
Natl. Economic Council, Inc.	116,477.90	106,464.66
American Medical Assn.	106,624.90	309,514.93[b]
Southern States Industrial Council	105,106.65	83,883.56
American Farm Bureau Fedn.	102,403.00	84,935.00
Chamber of Commerce, U.S.A.	90,988.05[a]	93,297.29
Natl. Assn. of Real Estate Boards	88,898.00[a]	127,893.65
American Legion, Natl. Headquarters	85,830.39	106,235.09
General Electric Co.	82,962.40	51,644.37
Natl. Fedn. of Post Office Clerks	78,252.95	97,869.16
Council of State Chambers of Commerce	70,444.17[a]	—
American Tariff League, Inc.	68,126.75	55,665.37

[a] Amount reported was for three quarters only.
[b] Included $39,340.67 for AMA Natl. Education Campaign.
(Source: *Congressional Quarterly, Weekly Report*, April 9, 1954.)

enjoyed by corporations, by providing that all corporations chartered there could own and vote the stock of other corporations. By this revolutionary act a business corporation became able to secure a control over scores of formerly independent and competing plants by the simple device of buying a majority—and sometimes only a fractional part—of their capital stock. As a result of the many mergers formed during 1897–1903, 1920–1929, and 1945 to date, and the general acceptance of mergers by the Supreme Court, most of the independent enterprises in the major fields of business have come to be owned or controlled by a few giant financial corporations.

One public privilege, it has been said, begets another. Tariff favors, mergers, fair-trade legislation, pricing formulas, and exemptions from the antitrust laws operate to moderate or restrict competition. To the extent that certain groups enjoy special privileges, other groups—such as farm and labor groups—press for measures to serve their particular interests. The determination of prices, incomes, investment, output, and employment, thereupon, increasingly comes to be determined by public authority and private monopoly. Professor O. B. Jesness sees in these activities the possible emergence of "state socialism"—that is, an economy in which government *controls* all the major segments of the economy. According to Professor Jesness,

The activities and progress of pressure groups and other combinations are interpreted by some to signify an inescapable trend toward state socialism. Such a view rests on too solid ground to be dismissed as fantastic. Those who view state control as the answer may welcome such a trend. Others who are more dubious about the blessings or efficiency of state operation may find it less cheering. If the aim of each group is to enjoy increasing monopolistic privileges, either by governmental sanction or with governmental aid, at someone else's expense, and such aim is realized, then government will be forced to assume increasing responsibility. For one thing, it will find itself pressed to do so from groups which clamor for governmental assistance in the attainment of their ends. It may be forced to assume increasing control to keep up productive activity or to protect public interest against group avarice.[16]

THE PROBLEM OF MAINTAINING A FREE PRESS

Concentration in the American economy exists not only in industry, but also in communications.[17] At the present time, large combinations control important newspapers, radio, and television stations in the principal metropolitan areas. There are also important mergers and intercompany ties in the moving picture industry and in the collection and preparation of news stories, photographs, cartoons, and special features.[18]

The evils of giant combinations in the various mediums of communication are not limited to those of economic monopoly and undue political influence. The thought of millions is shaped or at least influenced by agencies whose final purpose is profit and the attainment of greater special privileges. In 1947 a commission of leading American citizens under the chairmanship of Robert M. Hutchins made a study of the American press and concluded (1) that in the hands of gigantic business units the present-day means of mass communication do not provide a free forum for the presentation of diverse views; (2) that they do not represent the general groups and common interest of the nation; (3) that all too frequently they serve as agencies for stifling and distorting news; and (4) that their biased activities may lead to the complete frustration of political democracy.[19]

As long ago as 1815, John Adams, second President of the United States, pointed out, "If there is ever to be an amelioration of the condition of mankind, philosophers, theologians, legislators, politicians, and moralists will find that the regulation of the press is the most difficult, dangerous, and important problem they have to resolve."[20] Today, with the means of communication in the hands of giant financial combinations, the problem of regulation is rendered more complex and difficult than ever before.

NECESSARY MEASURES FOR STRENGTHENING DEMOCRACY

Governmental privileges provide economic advantages; and economic advantages, in turn, make it possible for organized groups to secure additional

[16] O. B. Jesness, "Postwar Agricultural Policy—Pressure vs. General Welfare," *Journal of Farm Economics*, February, 1946, pp. 11–12.

[17] For a detailed discussion of economic concentration in the mass communications industries, see "Local Monopoly in the Daily Newspaper Industry," *The Yale Law Journal*, June–July, 1952, pp. 948–1009.

[18] Commission on Freedom of the Press, *A Free and Responsible Press* (Chicago, 1947), pp. 30–51. See also *Congressional Record*, May 5, 1954, pp. A3268–A3269.

[19] *Ibid.*, pp. 1–19, 52–68.

[20] Charles F. Adams (ed.), *The Works of John Adams* (Boston, 1856), Vol. 10, p. 117.

and more extensive public favors. This process once begun in the American economy grew with an accelerating speed. Today a large part of government intervention in business is concerned not with regulating business activity but rather with the making of grants of special privilege to business, agricultural, and labor groups, often in an attempt to offset competitive disadvantages arising from monopoly tolerated in other areas of the economy.

It is evident that if government policy is to be turned from considerations of special privilege to a consideration of the consumer interest, political democracy must be strengthened and made to operate more effectively. As a first step, students of government agree, the American people should support a program (1) for strengthening the position and freedom of men and women in Congress, (2) for improving the educational level of the American people, (3) for promoting the dissemination of truthful information by the press, and (4) for modernizing our obsolete laws on political contributions and expenditures.

Everything should be done to make it possible for congressmen to be free from the continuing demands of organized producers for public grants of special privilege which benefit a few at the expense of the many. The independence of congressmen, it is believed, can be enhanced by the payment of adequate salaries and retirement annuities. As a supplemental measure, it has been proposed that the outside earnings and legal fees which many congressmen secure in serving private citizens and corporations be limited to $25,000 per year.

Another proposal is that all members of Congress, all federal officials receiving a salary of $10,000 or more, and all major officials of national political parties be required to make annual disclosures of their incomes by source, their assets, and their dealings in assets and securities.[21] Senator Kefauver has observed, "It is our honest conviction that the people do not often elect crooks to Congress. But there are some men grown poor in Congress who find it impossible to make ends meet and therefore, unconsciously or otherwise, hesitate to alienate groups whose support, financial and ballot-wise, they may need at the next election."[22]

Steps should also be taken to create a better social and economic base for the operation of democracy. The general level of mass education should be raised so that the people themselves will be able to discriminate against the grosser forms of propaganda. Alternative opportunities for employment in competing enterprises should also be broadened, so that individuals will feel free to speak for themselves on matters of public policy. At the same time, citizens themselves, as consumers, whose economic welfare is enhanced by a growing abundance of goods and services, will need (1) to become better informed on the basic issues of public policy and (2) to participate more actively in the nomination and election of political representatives.

[21] Report of a Subcommittee of the Committee on Labor and Public Welfare, *Ethical Standards in Government*, U.S. Senate, 82nd Congress, first session, 1951, p. 3.

[22] Estes Kefauver and Jack Levin, *op. cit.*, p. 169.

The problem of regulating the press so that the public will be given an honest and truthful presentation of facts is a difficult one. "Freedom of the press" is a basic, constitutional privilege of our nation; and it is sound policy to provide that government shall not interfere with the right of an editor to report and publish the facts as he finds them. However, "freedom of the press" does not give an editor the right to be a dictator and suppress the news or publish falsehoods as he may desire. One approach to the problem of providing the public with a measure of protection against false statements is for government to follow the rule that "there is safety in numbers." Governmental policy should seek to insure the maintenance of many independent newspapers and other news outlets. The universities should also raise their standards and levels of training for professional journalists.

MEASURES FOR REGULATING POLITICAL CONTRIBUTIONS AND EXPENDITURES

Attention needs to be given also to the regulation of campaign contributions and expenditures. This has been called by Professor James K. Pollock "one of the great unsolved problems of democracy." Experience has shown that present-day laws limiting campaign gifts and prohibiting contributions by corporations and labor organizations do not, in fact, prevent substantial gifts by important financial interests and groups. As a result of the many loopholes in existing legislation, moreover, there is at present no real limitation on expenditures in national elections.

During the past twenty-five years, numerous congressional committees have proposed remedial measures for the more serious abuses.[23] So far, however, no action has been taken. Some of the main recommendations include the following:

1. Total political contributions by any individual should be limited to $5000 (or $10,000) during any one year. This limit should apply to *total* contributions—for primary elections, party conventions, general elections, and postelection debts. Contributions should not be permitted by persons below voting age. Any person giving more than $500 should be required to sign a statement that he is the donor and not the agent of an undisclosed principal.
2. Overall, realistic limitations should be imposed on the expenditures made in behalf of candidates for federal offices by *all* organizations, partisan as well as nonpartisan, whether the committees operate in one state or in more than one state.
3. A limitation should be placed on the editorial space which any one editor or publisher can use in behalf of a candidate.

[23] For a detailed account of recent proposals, see Special Committee to Investigate Campaign Expenditures, House of Representatives, *Report 3252*, 81st Congress, second session, 1951; Hearings Before the Special Committee to Investigate Campaign Expenditures, House of Representatives, 82nd Congress, second session, 1952; and Report of the Subcommittee on Privileges and Elections, Proposed Amendments to Federal Corrupt Practices Act, U.S. Senate, 83rd Congress, first session, 1953.

4. Federal regulation of political contributions and expenditures should cover primary elections for federal offices, political party conventions, national elections, and postelection gifts.
5. Each party and each candidate for federal office should have a *single, authorized agent* who is responsible for the solicitation, collection, expenditure, and reporting of all funds used in all stages of a campaign. *The biggest difficulty in regulating campaign funds is the diffused nature of the expenditures.*
6. Federal law should provide for (a) the full reporting to a single national office of all campaign contributions and loans, showing names and addresses of each contributor or lender of $100 or more; (b) a full reporting of all expenditures, showing names and addresses of each person receiving $10 or more in any year; (c) the clear identification of each expenditure; (d) the reporting of total contributions and expenditures; (e) the publication of all records; and (f) the adoption of appropriate penalities for violations.
7. Corporations should be further restricted in their use of funds to support political parties or political creeds. Only natural persons should be privileged to participate in state or national elections.
8. The federal government itself should make some provision for financial assistance to political parties. This assistance could provide for the issuance of a publicity pamphlet at public expense on campaign platforms and issues; the granting of a limited amount of free mailing service for all candidates; and the provision of a limited amount of free radio and television time, to be granted by the stations as a condition for a federal license.
9. The 48 states should take steps to adopt uniform laws regulating campaign expenses for state offices to complement the strengthened federal legislation.

PRACTICAL OBSTACLES IN BUSINESS REGULATION

In summary, it may be said that in a political democracy, effective regulation of business is a twofold problem. First, there is the need to formulate sound measures of regulation and control. Secondly, there is the need to strengthen the democratic process, so that measures promoting the "common good" can and will be adopted.

Our study centers on the attempts of government to retain and create competition and to control monopoly when competition has been found to be ineffective. In this study, one should bear in mind that democracy operates in an environment of pressure groups. In some cases the measures of regulation themselves have been inadequate. However, in most cases the problem of ineffective public regulation arises from the fact that economic legislation has been rendered ineffective by the interest groups which it has sought to curb. Here is the crux of the matter.

If the public regulation of business is to promote "the greatest good of the greatest number," government by pressure groups must give way to a strengthened democracy. Fortunately, universal suffrage still prevails in the

United States; and there is still an opportunity to make government more responsive to the will of the majority, if we are willing to pay the price.

Suggestions for Further Reading

Bone, Hugh A., *American Politics and the Party System* (New York, 1955).

Congressional Record. Four times a year this publication carries a list of lobbyists who have registered under the Federal Regulation of Lobbying Act.

Galloway, George B., *The Legislative Process in Congress* (New York, 1953).

Harris, Joseph P. "The Senatorial Rejection of Leland Olds: A Case Study," *American Political Science Review*, September, 1951, pp. 674–692.

Hayes, Isabella M., *Financing Presidential Campaigns.* A selected bibliography (College Park, Maryland, 1953).

Key, V. O., *Politics, Parties, and Pressure Groups* (New York, 1952).

McKean, Dayton D., *Party and Pressure Politics* (Boston, 1949).

Riker, William H., Democracy in the United States (New York, 1953).

Schattschneider, E. E., *Politics, Pressures, and the Tariff* (New York, 1935).

Steiner, George A., *Government's Role in Economic Life* (New York, 1953).

Truman, David B., *The Governmental Process: Political Interests and Public Opinion* (New York, 1951).

Wilson, H. H., *Congress: Corruption and Compromise* (New York, 1951).

CHAPTER 4

The Capitalist System of Production

The purpose of the present chapter is to present an analysis of the capitalist system of production. Capitalism, in a broad sense, is the form or order of business activity which government in the United States is engaged in maintaining and regulating. More precisely, capitalism is a commercial exchanging economy based upon private property in which productive activity is organized and conducted for profit. Various amounts of government intervention are applied to capitalist enterprise—ranging from the minimum of providing a legal system to adjudicate private disputes to the maximum of "overall" economic planning. A capitalist system also invariably includes some public ownership—such as the postal system, the public school system, and public power projects. The principal alternative to capitalism is some form of socialism in which private enterprise and private property are replaced by government control and substantial amounts of public ownership.

THE PLAN OR ORDER IN CAPITALIST PRODUCTION

Although capitalism is not usually considered to involve a plan, its maintenance and effective operation actually require a great deal of government intervention. The basic institutions of private property, money and credit, weights and measures, and civil law all require public intervention and implementation. Likewise, the policies of maintaining fair competition and of preventing monopoly form a plan, a quite elaborate one, which is not self-enforcing but which requires constant and unremitting attention and enforcement by government antitrust agencies—the Department of Justice, the Federal Trade Commission, and the state attorneys general. To think of the policy of competition as planless, anarchic, and free from government regulation is a fundamental error, responsible to a large degree for its present defects.

A system of capitalism is "planless" only in the sense that, with a policy of competition, businessmen are free from the dictates of a central authority in directing and planning their investment, production, and marketing programs. The government does not determine the kind and amounts of goods to be produced or directly fix or manipulate prices. Workers, generally, moreover, are free to exercise individual initiative and choice in selecting an

53

occupation and in negotiating the terms of employment. The government does, however, have the important task of providing rules and limits for competition within which business—by voluntary decisions—can and will promote the public interest while pursuing its own.

The experience of all commercial nations indicates that when business is let alone to do what it pleases, there is a tendency toward monopoly in varying degrees, exploitation of the weak and uninformed, and extreme fluctuations in prosperity and depression. Why are some businessmen who are esteemed and respected citizens led to engage in business practices which require government interference? What reasons may be suggested for the fact that profit seeking gives rise to wide fluctuations in business activity?

THE RISE OF A COMMERCIAL EXCHANGING ECONOMY

The distinguishing feature of an incipient capitalism is the fact that a portion of productive activity changes from self-sufficient production to production for sale and for profit. A so-called "capitalist system" may be said to exist when production for sale and for profit carried on by private enterprise covers extensive and important areas of economic activity.

In the history of the Western world there have been two distinct periods in which capitalist production has developed from household production for use. The first period of capitalist activity arose in the ancient world and reached its apogee in the economies of Greece and Rome. Its decline came with the fall of the Western Roman Empire, the spread of Moslem rule, and the rise of medieval feudalism. The second distinct period of capitalism had its origins in the medieval cities which developed in western Europe during the eleventh and twelfth centuries. The commercial activity centering in these cities gradually spread to industry, finance, and eventually to agriculture; and a system of private property and free enterprise became the dominant form of economic organization in many Western countries.

Local, self-sufficient communities were usually opened to outside exchange by itinerant merchants who learned that in a certain community there was a relative abundance of one or of several commodities—wool, hides, salt, cloth, wine, and fish—in comparison with supplies available in other sections. In order to facilitate the exchange of commodities, money came into use; and the merchant's activity became one of buying and selling for the purpose of making a money profit. With the growth of commerce, the specialization of each community and of the people in the community constantly increased; and personal and household needs were increasingly met by purchase and sale in open markets established by public authorities. Gradually a large part of productive activity came to be carried on for sale rather than for use. Goods for consumption, as well as the instruments of production, became exchangeable commodities, bought and sold for a money price. Laborers, too, lost their slave or servile feudal status and sold their specialized services like a commodity for a wage.

In a commercial exchanging economy most, if not all, individuals develop an active interest in money incomes, for the goods and services which people can enjoy depend upon the money at their disposal. The entrepeneur, however, in contrast with other economic groups, has a unique interest in money. His particular *productive activity* or function is one of making a money profit. In the exercise of this function he invests money, buys raw materials, employs labor, borrows funds, and hires rentable agents to make a salable good for profit. No other economic agent has profit making as a job to do.[1] Since profit making as an end is a limitless, boundless aim, business itself became an endless search for profit.

THE INSTITUTION OF PRIVATE PROPERTY

In a capitalist economy, government does not, in the main, initiate or determine business activity. It does, however, establish, recognize, or adopt certain institutions which underlie its conduct. Basic among these is private property.

The idea of property is essentially that of rights to use and possess specific goods against the claim of others. Private property means that an object is *mine*. In economics and the law property is defined as ownership. Private property consists not of physical goods, but rather of intangible rights to control such objects. The rights of private control include the right to use, convey, or enjoy wealth as one may desire, as long as such use does not injure others or violate specific laws. At common law property rights were exercised principally over physical objects; however, today they include an ownership of valuable rights generally, such as patents, copyrights, trademarks, franchises, mortgages, stocks, and bonds.

The practice of exercising private control over certain physical objects had its origin in the activity of people themselves. Positive, *legal* rights of control, however, were, and continue to be, a creation of government. As R. M. MacIver states, "Property rights are legal rights, in other words they are dependent on government. They exist only because government recognizes and protects them."[2] Without the aid of government, one would encounter many difficulties in seeking to make effective his claims to possessions which others would like to enjoy.

Social Justification of Private Property. The acceptance of the institution of private property rests on the belief that private ownership results in the production of more and better goods. With a system of private property in a Western-type economy, owners find that there tends to be a direct relationship between their efforts and constructive planning and their personal rewards. Thus, private property tends to provide those in control of pro-

[1] In testifying before the Joint Congressional Committee on the Economic Report (March 2, 1948) Benjamin F. Fairless, president of the United States Steel Corporation, declared: "I have been in the steel business for many years. My job is to see that our business is conducted efficiently and profitably." Hearings Before the Joint Committee on the Economic Report, *Increases in Steel Prices*, 80th Congress, second session, 1948, p. 3.

[2] R. M. MacIver, *The Web of Government* (New York, 1947), p. 126.

ductive enterprises with a strong incentive to exert their best efforts to produce desired commodities in an economical way, for their income (and hence their level of living) is increased by such action. When productive wealth is given the care and attention of an owner, moreover, it is usually given careful protection and devoted to its most advantageous uses, because the resulting economic gains accrue directly to the owner who manages it. In most cases, owners take a long view and are concerned with long-time plans for improvement, for the future fruits are theirs. Saving is promoted, technology is improved, and a progressive economy is maintained.

In so far as the eagle eyes of owners do not direct the utilization of productive agents, the advantages of private ownership become weakened or nonexistent. It has long been recognized, for example, that absentee ownership of farm land and other real estate makes for inefficient production and inadequate maintenance. Disinterest replaces interest. Absentee owners commonly want quick cash returns and are frequently reluctant or unwilling to provide anything for maintenance. Since the tenants have no long-time interest in the land, they often are unwilling to make farm improvements or undertake soil conservation programs.

Many additional abuses and social evils arise in connection with a system of private property. They include a centralization of ownership of the means of production in the hands of a few people; the separation of ownership and control in large corporations, with a growing condition of absentee ownership; the development of industrial monopolies; and the wastage of natural resources. A considerable measure of governmental intervention in the business field consists of action taken to limit, regulate, change, define, or abolish private rights of control.

THE LEGAL SYSTEM OF FREE CONTRACT

When individuals are privileged to acquire a private control over economic goods, they are in a position to assemble productive agents, employ labor, and engage in producing goods for sale and profit. This activity is conducted by the system of free contract. A contract may be defined as an agreement enforceable by government whereby two or more parties bind themselves to do certain things. *The institution of contracts makes possible individual planning on a broad scale.* Individuals are free to agree to anything they desire, subject only to (a) certain rules in the public interest—such as the law against agreements to fix prices—and (b) the threat of government action to enforce all valid contracts in private suits brought in the civil courts. In the making of private contracts the force of government is ever present, for government stands ready to award damages to the person injured by the breach of the contract at the expense of the injuring party.

The Individual Proprietorship. Business activity begins with the making of contracts for the purchase and sale of goods. It expands with the making of contracts to hire labor, rent land and productive facilities, and borrow money to be repaid at a later date. Persons combining the factors of production and investing capital in productive activity are variously designated active capitalists, enterprisers, or entrepreneurs. A business enterprise owned by a single person is called an individual proprietorship. The individual proprietorship, it may be noted, was the first organizational form for business, and today it is the most widely used form of business organization in farming, retailing, and the service industries.

It is estimated that there are some 5.5 million farm units in the United States. Most of these units are individual proprietorships. The total number of business firms, on the other hand, is estimated to be around 4.2 million (see Fig. 23, p. 257). Some 69.5 percent of all business firms are individual proprietorships; 18 percent are partnerships; and 10.7 percent are corporations.

The Partnership. Since many business undertakings require more capital than a single individual possesses or can borrow, it early became common for several individuals to combine their resources and labor in a business venture. This contractual arrangement became known as a partnership. Historical records indicate that the partnership method of conducting business is of great antiquity. It was used by the Babylonians at least as early as the fourth century B.C. It was also used by the Romans and later by the medieval merchants. Today partnerships continue to be extensively used in retail trade, brokerage firms, small-scale manufacturing firms, and the professions. It is estimated that there are some 700,000 partnerships operating in the United States today.

The Corporation. Although individual proprietorship and partnership arrangements still are widely used in the conduct of business activity, they have certain defects for long-term, large-scale business operations. First, under each of these forms of organization all contracts to be performed, or in process of being performed, terminate with the death of an individual owner, and the "business" comes to a close. Secondly, the amount of capital which one person or several partners can provide is frequently not sufficient to finance large undertakings. Thirdly, individual enterprisers are personally liable for the debts and obligations incurred in the conduct of business activity, to the full extent of their private means. In the case of partnerships, the liability of each partner for the business acts of the other partner is especially serious.

In order to overcome the defects of the individual proprietorship and partnership arrangements, businessmen as early as the sixteenth century sought to adapt the corporation to their use in business activity. A corporation is a legal entity or body which is created by government and owned by an association of natural persons. It can own property, make contracts, and sue and be sued. Its life, moreover, continues without regard to the life or death of the various individuals who own it. The creation of corporations by government for business purposes has long been regarded as an act conferring special privileges and imposing certain obligations. It is for this reason that government has always required business enterprisers to secure a charter before they can use the corporate form of organization.

Today, there are approximately 450,000 active business corporations in the United States. It is estimated that these corporations account for the production of over one half of the national income (see Fig. 3).

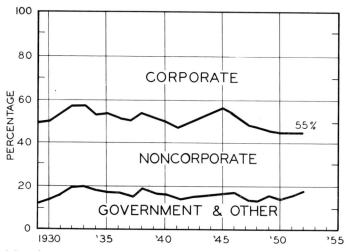

FIG. 3. Origins of national income—i.e., the aggregate earnings of labor and property during a given year. Over one-half of the national income produced each year originates in the productive activities of corporations. (Source: U.S. Department of Commerce.)

THE USE OF THE TERM "CAPITAL" IN A COMMERCIAL ECONOMY

In the rapidly expanding commercial economy of the twelfth century, the term "capital" appears to have come into use in the medieval Latin phrase *capitalis pars* to indicate the principal of a money loan as contrasted with the usury or interest. Gradually "capital" was used to designate the estimated *worth* of an enterpriser's productive agents (shops, goods, horses, wagons, ships, land, etc.), as well as the *sum* of money currently used in a business or transferred to another in the form of a loan.

During the sixteenth century various forms of the word "capital" became increasingly used in business activity as a result of the books which were then being written on the new practice of double-entry bookkeeping. A book published in 1588 in England by John Mellis, which was largely a translation of the pioneer treatise written in 1494 by the Italian Lucas Pacioli, summarized current commercial practice as follows: "Then gather together the whole summe of your ready money, debtes and goods, and therefrom subtract the totall summe of your creditours, and the remaine is the net rest, substance or capitall of the owner to be put in a trafique."[3] In an accounting

[3] Quoted by R. D. Richards, "Early History of the Term Capital," *Quarterly Journal of Economics*, February, 1926, pp. 331–332.

or business sense, capital thus came to mean that portion of a person's financial fund which is invested in business activity for a profit.

THE CAPITALIST ENTERPRISE AND ITS SPREAD IN PRODUCTIVE ACTIVITY

The investment of capital in commercial activity by merchants gradually gave rise to the idea of an abstract business unit or entity—"a capitalistic enterprise"—separate and distinct from the person or persons who invested their capital in it and having rules, aims, and policies of its own. A factor promoting this separation was the development of double-entry bookkeeping, which provides a means of accounting for capital invested and profits made separately from other possible activities of the owners. With the granting of corporate charters to business firms, the idea of a business entity separate from the persons owning it became even more apparent. The notion of a capitalistic enterprise, however, is not synonymous with corporations, for any individual business firm or partnership employing capital in business activity is a capitalistic enterprise. Profits are the impersonal return to a capitalistic enterprise, regardless of its type of ownership.

Although capitalism first appeared in the exchange of commodities, capitalist enterprisers soon extended their investment activities to an increasingly large segment of productive activity. Financial operations, such as banking, the granting of credit, security trading, and insurance, soon became organized and conducted by capitalists on a commercial basis. In agriculture, too, the growing of crops gradually came to be carried on in an organized way for profit. The most dynamic field for capitalism was industry, in which capitalist activity spread to a wide range of manufacturing operations.

THE MEANING OF CAPITALISM OR CAPITALIST PRODUCTION

Upon the basis of the capital concept from which it secured its essential meaning, capitalism may be defined as that portion of an economy in which production is organized for sale and for profit. Although all privately owned business enterprises operated for profit are a part of the capitalist system, the dynamic and characteristic features of capitalism are found in those industries in which the governmental policies of *free enterprise* and *price competition* are most completely realized. In particular, these policies are, or can be, most completely realized in mining, lumbering, fishing, construction work, warehousing, manufacturing, wholesaling, retailing, journalism, and the amusement trades.

In capitalist production there is a sizable segment of privately owned enterprises in which competition has not proved to be an effective regulator of prices and service. Such enterprises include water and gas works, electric power and light companies, railroads, streetcar lines, and telephone systems. In these fields, the physical plant facilities—such as pole lines, water mains, and rail lines—must be extended to the consumer's residence; and a duplication of such facilities proved to be wasteful or physically impossible. Price competition in these industries also proved to be unstable and chaotic. The heavy fixed investment in plant equipment makes for "decreasing costs" with large production; and the dominant companies sought to buy up or eliminate by "price wars" weaker rivals who were taking a share of the business. Since monopoly proved to be largely inevitable in such industries, public service enterprises came to be controlled by public commissions or to be publicly owned and operated.

In a system of capitalism there is also a considerable amount of government ownership of land, forests, minerals, roads, bridges, airports, shipyards, research facilities, and buildings. Varying amounts of public enterprise also exist—such as public education, fire protection, sanitary inspection, the operation of municipal utilities, the postal system, the reclamation of arid land, the improvement of rivers and harbors, the building of canals, the development of river areas, the lending of money, the manufacturing of cement and flour, the operation of railroads, and the retailing of liquor.

The federal government initiated the development of atomic energy for purposes of national defense. At the present time, it is seeking to utilize fissionable materials for peacetime pursuits. The government is undertaking this research because of the great financial risk which is involved in the application of atomic substances for use in industry, medicine, and agriculture. When knowledge for the application of atomic energy to peaceful uses has been developed, it is almost certain that the federal government will make it available without cost to private enterprise.

The military services engage in a great variety of commercial and industrial-type activities for their own use—such as the manufacturing of rope, paint, clothing, and uniforms. They also repair aircraft, tanks, trucks, engines, and ships. Military leaders report that commercial-type activity is undertaken primarily to save money and to make production fully "responsive to command."[4] As we have seen, private enterprise uses profit as the yardstick for achievement. Public enterprise, however, while desirous of having commercial success, commonly places greater emphasis on national security, economy for the taxpayers, the welfare of low-income groups, the production of highly important commodities—such as electricity—at the lowest possible prices, the maintenance of maximum output and employment, and the direct promotion of economic, social, and cultural well-being.

In general, it may be said that government undertakes the ownership and conduct of productive enterprises in a capitalist system (1) when the public stands to benefit from the service but profit prospects are insufficient—or the financial risk is too great—to attract private capital; (2) when it is believed that public ownership and operation will provide protection against private monopoly and private abuse; and (3) when considerations of national defense make essential the maintenance of publicly owned facilities. Our society is one in which there is a considerable amount of direct control and

[4] House Report 1197, 83rd Congress, second session, 1954, pp. 12–18.

public ownership, as well as a considerable area of private initiative and enterprise. It is, therefore, sometimes called a "mixed economy."

STRUCTURAL DIFFERENCES IN THE VARIOUS CAPITALIST COUNTRIES

The institutions which function in a system of "capitalism" differ considerably in the various Western nations. Cartel agreements, for example, are legalized or tolerated in the Western European countries, but not in Canada or the United States. In Western Europe, as a rule, one cannot open a new business without the approval of existing firms. Germany, in particular, has a system of licensing which restricts "freedom of entry." Such restraints on competition have no counterpart in the United States or Canada. Resale price maintenance contracts, on the other hand, are illegal in Canada, but legal in some forty-five of the American states. Compulsory grade labeling exists for canned goods in Canada, but not in the United States.

There are thus sharp and basic differences between the "capitalism" of one country and the "capitalism" of another. In some cases, capitalism is largely a cartelized, restrictive economy, and in others it is an economy with a considerable measure of price competition and freedom of entry. It is inaccurate to use the word "capitalism" alone to describe the economic systems of the Western nations. Some students distinguish between *competitive* capitalism and *monopoly* capitalism. Others speak of capitalism *with* or *without* a system of properly functioning markets.

It is also erroneous to look upon competition as a condition which existed sometime in the past. The facts are that competition existed in certain trades during the Middle Ages and that monopolistic agreements existed in others —just as is true today. The best features of capitalism have never been completely realized; and capitalism, as such, has never prevailed in all sectors of the economy.

THE PROFIT-SEEKING MOTIVE

As a consequence of the methods of contracting in business activity, workers, lenders, and owners of rentable agents secure wages, interest, and rent, respectively, as promised returns. The capitalistic enterpriser, however, receives *profits* as a resultant of the completed business process. Capitalistic enterprise, therefore, becomes an operation to secure and maximize such a profit, subject to considerations of potential competition, the presence of substitute products, and the long-run reactions of consumers. The prospect of profit is the primary motive in a capitalist society which causes businessmen to invest capital and produce desired goods and services.

The social welfare aspects of capitalism arise from the fact that the profit-seeking motive stimulates every possible effort to find activities showing the largest gain; and presumably the relative profits in different economic opportunities, in the absence of fraud, monopoly, and frictional elements, reflect the relative urgency of the desires of those consumers having money to make their desires effective. The profit-seeking motive, when spurred by price competition, also stimulates efforts to maximize profit by means of efficiency, high productivity, improved quality, the use of new methods, and careful, well-timed buying and selling. This is in sharp contrast with other productive arrangements wherein individuals have little or no motive to assume responsibility, to try innovations, to work long hours, to accommodate themselves to the desires of others, or to practice economy, for there is little if anything to gain by so doing, and there may be much to lose.

In a free-enterprise economy, the satisfying of human desires, the production of useful goods, and the practice of the economic virtues afford opportunities for profit. Since an enterpriser's purpose is the making of profit, it follows that it is possible for him to serve the public interest by pursuing his own. Adam Smith well expressed this view in his famous statement that a capitalist enterpriser, in given instances, is "led by an invisible hand to promote an end which was no part of his intention."[5] It is the ideal of capitalism that profits should be secured by prudent investment and efficient management, although in many cases they are secured by questionable, fraudulent, or even criminal methods. The opportunity of making profits carries with it the obligation to assume any losses which are incurred in productive activity. No one is entitled to obtain a profit as a matter of right. (See also Table 8).

TABLE 8.   Number of Business Failures by Size of Liabilities.[a]

Liabilities	Failures		
	1951	1952	1953
Under $5,000	1832	1428	1383
$5,000 to $25,000	4160	3884	4317
$25,000 to $100,000	1634	1769	2375
$100,000 to $1,000,000	412	512	748
$1,000,000 and over	20	18	39

[a] The ideal of capitalism is that business survival and growth shall rest upon economic efficiency and service to consumers. In the main, the broad purpose of public regulation is to maintain orderly competition and "rules of the game," so that enterprisers will have a chance to prove their superiority without being restrained or eliminated by unfair competition, discriminatory pricing, monopolistic coercion, denial of supplies, or false and mendacious advertising.
(Source: Roy A. Foulke, Dun and Bradstreet, Inc.)

THE CONFLICT BETWEEN INDIVIDUAL AND GENERAL INTERESTS AND THE NEED FOR GOVERNMENT INTERVENTION

Although profit seeking may work to organize men and materials in an efficient manner to promote the social welfare, it frequently gives rise to social evils. Profit can be made not only by producing more and better goods but also by using inferior materials, by artificially restricting supply to secure monopoly profits, by misleading and deceiving consumers, and by exploiting labor. The effects of these practices, and the manifold forms which they take,

[5] Adam Smith, *The Wealth of Nations* (1776), Book IV, chap. 2, p. 421 (4th Cannan edition, London, 1925).

moreover, are cumulative. In many ways, the profit-seeking activities of dominant capitalist groups have operated to shape a nation's economic organization along lines which contribute most to their immediate commercial interests. Thus, the destruction of open markets in Western Europe and the subsequent rise of the mercantile system were manifestations of the profit-seeking drive. In more recent times, this motive on the part of some business groups has given rise to a world-wide system of tariffs, cartels, large monopoly combinations of formerly competing plants, and frequently to an influence on representative government which forestalls effective legislation in the public interest.

The advantage of money in a capitalist economy is so great that it may color an enterpriser's standards of right and wrong. In fact, there is constant danger that the opportunity to make profit may create in some enterprisers a moral blind spot, an area in their activities which is not controlled by their usual ethical standards. Persons seeking monopoly control, employing false and mendacious advertising, or exploiting labor, for example, often include men otherwise highly esteemed and respected in public life. The making of money is a business practice, a stereotyped commercial tradition, and serves to influence decisions making for profit, even though they are against individual preferences. It is for this reason that government in a capitalist system must either maintain rules of fair competition or undertake price fixing and direct control by public commissions.

PROFIT SEEKING AND EXCESSES IN THE USE OF CREDIT AND IN SPECULATIVE INVESTMENT

A further aspect of a commercial economy which gives rise to a need for government intervention is the occurrence in its operation of cyclical fluctuations in business activity.[6] Throughout human history economic life has been marked by good and bad times, growing out of droughts, floods, wars, and epidemics. However, in a capitalist economy fluctuating periods of prosperity and depression have developed in the process of profit-seeking activity.

Since business enterprises are operated for profit, it follows that their productive activity and capital investment depend upon present and prospective profit. In a period of business expansion, profits tend to rise with rising prices. Increased borrowings occur, and the volume of outstanding debt rises rapidly. The ease of making profits tends to promote excesses in the use of credit and in speculative investment. Finally, the rate of earnings declines with rising costs, the security for outstanding credits is weakened, business failures and bankruptcies increase, prices fall, and widespread liquidation ensues.

An early example of the way in which speculative investment and the excesses of credit give rise to a money or credit crisis and a depression is

[6] Wesley C. Mitchell, *Business Cycles* (New York, 1927), pp. 75 ff., and Arthur F. Burns and Wesley C. Mitchell, *Measuring Business Cycles* (New York, 1946), pp. 3–8.

found in the tulip mania which occurred in Holland in the years 1636 and 1637.[7] The growing of tulips then, as now, was an important activity in Holland, particularly in the vicinity of Haarlem. Organized markets were established for dealing in tulips bulbs, and transactions were also conducted in contracts calling for the future delivery of bulbs.

During the years 1634 and 1635, the prices of tulip bulbs rose steadily throughout Europe. The rising prices for bulbs brought forth increased speculative investments by persons seeking to expand production and to accumulate bulbs for sale later at higher prices. By the end of 1634, more and more nonprofessional speculators—weavers, spinners, cobblers, bakers, and other tradesmen—also began to buy bulbs in the hope of making a speculative profit. The growing speculative demand for bulbs, supported increasingly by the use of credit, forced prices higher and higher; and by the autumn of 1636 it is reported that the speculation had become a "madness"! Finally, in February, 1637, a crisis developed unexpectedly, when various persons found that bulbs were not salable at the currently high prices. A drastic liquidation ensued, prices collapsed, and thousands of people suffered serious financial loss.

Causal explanations of crises and rhythmic fluctuations of business vary in the emphasis which is placed upon different aspects of the profit-seeking process. There is general agreement, however, that the major fluctuations of the business cycle have as essential elements (1) a wide variation in the quantity of money and credit used by business and (2) a large expansion and contraction in investment activity.

LAISSEZ FAIRE AN INCOMPLETE POLICY

It is frequently said that the essence of capitalism is laissez faire or a policy of letting business alone to do as it pleases. Indeed, many persons assume that if the law declares that persons are free to compete, effective competition will automatically result and society will be assured the advantages of economic abundance. These ideas, however, are in the main illusory. Experience has shown that when business is left alone to do whatever it pleases, deceptive practices, monopolistic mergers, price fixing, and speculative excesses flourish.

A policy of laissez faire undoubtedly was effective in creating competition at the time of Adam Smith when monopolistic restrictions had their origin in governmental controls and privileges. Today, however, with giant mergers, pricing formulas, and discriminating practices, laissez faire permits the exercise and continuing growth of private monopoly power.

Business organization, statute law, and governmental agencies are all man-made arrangements. The economic task we face is that of guiding and directing business practice so that it will promote and advance the public welfare. Professor J. M. Clark has wisely observed that

[7] See also N. W. Posthumus, "The Tulip Mania in Holland in the Years 1636 and 1637," *Journal of Economic and Business History*, May, 1929, pp. 434–449.

Our system must be animated by awareness of its obligation to be directed to serviceable ends, not merely tricked by an 'unseen hand' into pursuing such ends in spite of the fact that the main preoccupation of its members is with self-interested motives. . . . We can no longer rely on reaching economically correct results automatically, as an unintended by-product of what individuals do in pursuit of their private interests. We still need all we can get of such automatic adjustments; but there are growingly strategic areas in which the power of organized groups is such that, if sound terms of settlement are to be reached, people must consciously intend to reach them. This calls for some understanding of what economically correct adjustments are, and a will to promote them rather than to pursue self-interest irresponsibly.[8]

CONTINUING PLAN OF STUDY

Three principal economic imperfections of our private-enterprise system are (1) the tendency of some business enterprisers—in the drive for profits—to engage in antisocial commercial practices—such as false and mendacious advertising, adulteration of foods, misbranding of products, and the sale of harmful and dangerous goods; (2) the rise of monopoly and public grants of special privilege which benefit a few at the expense of the community; and (3) the tendency for business activity to be cyclical, with recurring periods of boom followed by periods of depression, widespread unemployment, and social distress. In succeeding chapters, we shall continue our study of government and business by considering the regulations which government has adopted (a) to protect consumers and (b) to create and maintain fair and effective competition in the principal areas of the economy. Thereupon, we shall study the activity of government in imposing positive controls in those sectors in which the policy of competition has proved to be ineffective or undesirable. In Chapter 27, we shall also give special consideration to monetary and fiscal policies adopted by the federal government to mitigate the problem of unhealthy booms and paralyzing depressions and to provide for greater economic stability.

SUGGESTIONS FOR FURTHER READING

Dean, Joel, *Managerial Economics* (New York, 1951).

Fetter, Frank A., "Reformulation of the Concepts of Capital and Income," *Accounting Review*, March, 1937, pp. 3–12; and the article on "Capital" in the *Encyclopaedia of the Social Sciences* (New York, 1937).

Friedman, Milton, *Essays in Positive Economics* (Chicago, 1953).

Haas, Francis J., *Man and Society* (New York, 1952).

Hayek, F. A. (ed.), *Capitalism and the Historians* (Chicago, 1954).

Keezer, Dexter M., *Making Capitalism Work* (New York, 1950).

Mitchell, Wesley C., *Business Cycles* (New York, 1927).

Nell-Breuning, Oswald Von, *Reorganization of Social Economy* (New York, 1936).

[8] J. M. Clark, "Aims of Economic Life as Seen by Economists," in *Goals of Economic Life* (New York, 1953), pp. 25, 50.

Marchal, Jean, "The Construction of a New Theory of Profit," *American Economic Review*, September, 1951, pp. 549–565.

Schumpeter, J. A., *Capitalism, Socialism and Democracy* (New York, 1942).

Sombart, Werner, *The Quintessence of Capitalism* (London, 1915).

Wright, David McCord, *Capitalism* (New York, 1951).

CHAPTER 5

The Public Regulation of Business

THE NEED FOR PUBLIC REGULATION

In addition to its functions of creating, adopting, and recognizing certain basic economic institutions for the establishment of a capitalist system, government has the further task of seeing that *in the conduct of business activity* the public interest is served. Not infrequently the contracts, sales methods, and organizational forms employed by individuals in productive activity conflict with the public interest. An agreement by steel producers, for example, that none shall sell their products below a certain price would be a private arrangement made in the pursuit of private advantage, but it would involve and affect adversely the welfare of the entire community. In raising prices, monopolists *restrict production* and secure *an additional income* which is without legal or economic justification. It is at this point that the political authority (government) may perform the function of intervening to regulate the private activities of individuals and corporations so that the public interest may be served.

The rules and regulations which the government makes to direct or regulate the activities of individuals in relation to the social group (the state) are called public law, and the consideration of such types or forms of intervention in the economic sphere constitutes the main field of the public regulation of business. There is agreement that the purpose of democratic government is to promote the common or general interest of the governed. *The particular aspect of the public interest with which we are concerned in our present study is that of finding and effectuating the public interest in the economic area of man's relations.*

The economic aspect of man's life is concerned with his making a living—that is, getting the goods and services which are necessary for living. In so far as individuals engage in self-sufficient production, they are concerned with land and other natural resources; and their means of living are obtained by individual or coöperative action and commonly shared according to need or status. Business activity—commercial exchange—does not exist. When, however, production for sale develops, with specialization and division of labor, most people get their means of livelihood by business dealings with others. Some of the more important *business relations* arising in commercial activity, which have been made subject to government regulation include

1. The relations among sellers or among buyers in the same line of business in the determination of price.
2. The relations between a single seller (a public utility) and the community in the determination of price.
3. The relations among employees in the determination of wages.
4. The acquisition and control of competitors.
5. Discriminatory and unfair methods of price competition.
6. The exclusion of competitors.
7. The dealings of investors and borrowers of capital.

ESSENTIAL CONDITIONS FOR THE OPERATION OF A FREE ECONOMY

In its work of public regulation, we have said, government has the duty of promoting a maximum production of goods and services and a fair distribution of income. After countless years of experience with private exchanging activity, Western governments adopted two important institutions for making capitalism an effective and desirable economic system. These institutions are (1) freedom of enterprise or the right to compete and (2) two-sided price competition as a mechanism for determining prices.

Freedom of enterprise may be defined as the right of producers to follow an occupation of their own choice without interference or dictation by other producers or by government. In establishing this right, the public authorities gave sanction and recognition to the desire and efforts of free men to make a living. They also saw and found in the right to compete an indispensable condition for the effective operation of a private enterprise economy. With a freedom of enterprise, society is given wide opportunity for having its various desires satisfied. Human and material resources tend to be allocated in places and at times where they are most urgently needed. Maximum production is promoted. At the same time, the selfish designs of individual producers are held in check by the freedom of entry for newcomers and by the opportunity of consumers to turn to alternative sources of supply.

The right to compete, it may be noted, is not a guarantee that a producer will find employment or an investment opportunity. It is rather the right to bring one's labor or productive agents into competition with those of other men. The concern of government in providing the right to compete is only that the economic field be kept open—free from restraint—for anyone who may wish to enter.

THE RIGHT TO COMPETE IN ANGLO-SAXON LAW

The legal right to compete had its origin in the common-law decisions of the English courts. An early case declaring this right was the *Schoolmaster's* case decided in 1410. In this case the Court of Common Pleas held that two schoolmasters of a grammar school at Gloucester could not secure a writ preventing another teacher from starting a second school in the same town. The plaintiffs stated in their plea that whereas they had formerly received 40 d. a quarter from each child, the entry of the other teacher had forced them to reduce their rates to 12 d. to their great damage. The court, however, declared that when "another equally competent with the plaintiffs comes to teach the children, this is a virtuous and charitable thing, and an ease to the people, for which he cannot be punished by our law." In support of this conclusion the court quoted the opinion of Chief Justice Thirning in an earlier case to the effect that "if I have a mill and my neighbor builds another mill, whereby the profit of mine is diminished, I shall have no action against him; still I am damaged."[1]

The acceptance and actual realization of the right to compete came slowly, for strongly established monopoly groups vigorously resisted any change in their established order of control. From 1410 to 1640 in particular, the courts, as well as Parliament, repeatedly reaffirmed the principle that the liberty of free men gives them the right to engage in any trade or calling of their own choice. Gradually the right to compete became a firmly established and generally accepted principle in Anglo-Saxon law.

In our economy, anyone is free to engage in business as an individual proprietor or with others in a partnership, without securing discretionary approval or permission from government. If, and when, a license is required for entry, it is usually granted to all on equal conditions. Occupational and business licenses are sometimes required for various callings or activities in which government seeks to establish minimum standards of competence. Licensing is also applied in certain lines of business to provide sanctions for the regulation or control of a business enterprise. In numerous instances, too, licensing procedures are employed as revenue measures.[2] Anyone who meets the minimum standards, complies with the appropriate rules of conduct, or pays the requisite fees, however, is privileged to engage in business. No attempt is ordinarily made by government to scrutinize, grant, or withhold entry on grounds (1) that public favors are being bestowed (such as corporate privileges or the use of public property under a franchise) or (2) that a restriction on competition is needed in the public interest (as in the case of public utility enterprises).

MARKET COMPETITION AS A METHOD OF PRICE AND INCOME DETERMINATION

In addition to its task of providing for a maximum production of goods and services, government has the function of determining whether or not prices and the incomes of individuals are in line with the general welfare.

---

[1] *The Schoolmaster's Case*, T. B. Henry IV, f. 47, pl. 21 (1410). See also Bruce Wyman, *Control of the Market* (New York, 1914), pp. 12–14.

[2] For a comprehensive review of licenses required by federal, state, and local governments, see U.S. Department of Commerce, *Small Business and Government Licenses* (Washington, 1950).

Some persons contend that "What is, is right." Throughout history, however, it has been recognized that the prices (and incomes) of some individuals or groups are not "fair" or "just" because of favoritism, bribery, private monopoly, dishonesty, ignorance, and unequal bargaining power. In an effort to bring the incomes of individuals in harmony with the general welfare, governments from earliest times have enacted rules with respect to monopoly, unfair competition, price competition, dishonest dealing, the rates of public utilities, and so forth. When certain groups—such as women and children or farmers—do not receive incomes which they or others consider to be adequate, governments frequently provide minimum wage laws, price regulations, and subsidies. If certain prices are considered to be too high—as, for example, the rates of a telephone company—maximum rates are imposed.

The notion of "fairness" or "equity" implies a standard with which we can compare or measure actual prices and incomes and declare them to be "fair" or "unfair." The standard long accepted by Western society has been that of the "market value" of the goods or services as determined by the method of price competition in open markets.

The economic principle of competition was recognized and established as a basic economic institution in the ancient societies of Greece and Rome. It was most effectively and completely realized, however, during the medieval period (800–1500) in Western Europe. An indication of the rise and growth of the market economy in England is found in the number of market grants made by the English kings. Between the years 1199 and 1483 some 2099 charters were granted for markets and some 2315 were granted for the holding of fairs. More than half of the market grants were made during the first seventy-four years of this period.[3]

It was during the period 1100 to 1500 that the market system on the Continent, as well as in England, reached its most comprehensive development. By 1500 the making of market grants had largely ceased. Indeed, the forces of monopoly were then beginning to develop, and soon after 1500 the market economy in Europe, as well as in England, began to decline.

It is important to study the medieval system of free and open markets, for the principles of market price developed there became the fundamental basis for economic regulation in the United States. When the Sherman Antitrust Act was being debated in the United States Senate in 1890, Senator Hoar, a recognized authority on jurisprudence, declared: "The great thing that this bill does, except affording a remedy, is to extend the common-law principles, *which protected fair competition in trade in old times in England, to international and interstate commerce in the United States.*"[4] The Sherman Act still stands today as the framework for our system of economic regulation, and the principles of market price provide a standard of fairness which the

[3] *Report of the Royal Commission on Market Rights and Tolls* (London, 1888), Vol. I, pp. 108–131.
[4] *Congressional Record*, April 8, 1890, p. 3152. Italics supplied.

Department of Justice, the Federal Trade Commission, and the courts seek to maintain in the sale of industrial products.

THE NATURE OF ECONOMIC COMPETITION

Economic competition is a process for the production and pricing of goods which is maintained by a system of law. It operates in two principal ways. First, in the production of goods, competition means that enterprisers freely enter a trade or calling of their own choice when profit prospects are tempting. This is made possible by the legal right of *free competition*, free entry, or free enterprise. Secondly, in the purchase and sale of goods, competition operates as a method for determining prices and incomes. *Price competition* among sellers means that sellers *lower* their "asking" prices in relation to other sellers in order to secure customers; and among buyers, it means that buyers having higher valuations *raise* their "bid" prices in order to be able to buy. Competition, in this sense, is supported by the legal freedom—and obligation—to act independently with regard to prices.

"Freedom of entry" and "freedom to act independently on prices" are the essential aspects of the term "freedom of economic enterprise." Freedom of enterprise, so described, is to be distinguished from another sort of freedom which some persons believe society should grant to the American businessman. This is the freedom of business to form financial mergers without limit, to be relieved of the antitrust laws, to follow coöperative pricing arrangements, and to discriminate in prices regardless of injurious economic effects.

Competition, by determining prices, operates also to determine the relative shares of *income* going to wage earners, owners of rentable agents, lenders, and entrepreneurs. The price of potatoes, for example, in important producing areas is determined on the Chicago Mercantile Exchange. This is a *product price*. At the same time, competition operates in various degrees to determine the *cost prices* of wages, rent, and interest incurred in the production of potatoes. These prices are *incomes* to various groups of producers. The difference between the product price and the cost price is the source of profit, and this return is the income of the entrepreneur.

In adopting the principle of competition as a rule of public policy, government has the continuous task of maintaining and strengthening it (1) by keeping the channels of production in the major lines of business open to all individuals (freedom of competition) and (2) by maintaining effective price competition in the purchase and sale of the basic commodities. This, indeed, is the fundamental purpose of the American antitrust laws. Although monopoly, status, and authority as methods of price and income determination presently operate in considerable degree, they do not form our general or basic legal pattern of economic control. The general rule is that freedom of entry and price competition shall prevail in all fields where they have not proved to be impossible of attainment.

ALTERNATIVE METHODS OF PRICE AND INCOME DETERMINATION

In general, there are four principal methods which government accepts or provides for the determination of prices and incomes. They consist of competition, which we have just discussed; force or monopoly; status; and authority. In addition to these arrangements, the distribution of income is determined in various degrees by charity and sentiment.

The Method of Force. Distribution by force means that the stronger party gets the better of the deal by the exertion of pressure, power, or compulsion. The force used to settle prices, wages, or other conditions may be based upon physical, military, or monopoly power. On the part of sellers, monopoly power is the power to get the most that buyers will pay (or some other concession) by eliminating alternative sources of supply and by withdrawing or restricting the actual supply. The advantage of industrial monopoly is the power which it gives to make more profit by controlling and curtailing supply. A principal means which groups of workers have used for improving their position has been an organization of the labor supply and the application of economic pressure by means of strikes and restrictions on membership and output. Frequently, the economic strength of organized labor is pitted against that of organized industry, and the consequences range from joint action to raise product prices to prolonged strikes and lockouts.

On the part of buyers, monopoly power is the power to depress buying prices by excluding alternative sources of demand and by withholding purchases when sellers are eager to sell. The buyer for a dominant produce company once stated to the writer "We turned down asparagus today just to make the price soft, but we think that we shall take some tomorrow."

When prices and wages are determined by the exercise of monopoly power, there is no objective standard for measuring what is "just," "fair," or "equitable." Rather the terms of settlement reflect the relative monopoly position of the two parties. In a discussion of our present-day economy, in which prices and wages over a considerable area are determined by giant corporations and giant trade unions, Dr. Jacob Viner declares:

> It is a society in which decisions are made in accordance with the principles of power politics to a large degree; and as long as we accept as inevitable and even as necessary, as I do, both the large corporation and the large trade union, power politics in part it must be. And I don't believe that in this field, as in the actual international field of power politics, power conflicts can be settled or its problems resolved by formula. I believe it is a problem of *ad hoc* pushing here and pulling there, correcting here and moderating there, as its defective working becomes apparent and as public opinion becomes aware that something has to be done. And what has to be done today may prove five years from now to have been wrong, and may then have to be undone and even reversed.[5]

[5] Jacob Viner, "The Role of Costs in a System of Economic Liberalism," in *Wage Determination and the Economics of Liberalism* (Washington, 1947), p. 19.

At the present time, a considerable part of the activity of government in the economic sphere is directed by political pressure to the granting of monopolistic privileges. As Professor M. J. Bonn has said,

> But if Government has gone into business, business has long ago gone into Government. When I use the word "business" here, I am not only speaking of capitalists. I am including the labour world as well. . . . Since people have learned that Government can be made use of as an agency for distributing the national dividend according to their liking, they all go in for politics. . . . In most countries political parties are economic groups decorated with political symbols, because these symbols had some meaning in the past. This being the case, the activities of most people in politics are economic. Governments can influence prices, and people want Governments to influence prices in the right way.[6]

The "right way" of course, it may be added, is usually one which promotes the selfish interests and profits of the special groups concerned.[7]

The Method of Status or Custom. Distribution by status means that income is determined by the acts of men not living and without reference to one's personal efforts. Feudal society in the Middle Ages was based upon status, and one's social and economic position was hereditary. A person born as a serf or as a noble continued to be one regardless of his merits or personal efforts. At the present time, certain races are not employed in various occupations because of their racial background, and their resulting incomes are frequently out of line with the value of their services. A further present-day example of income determination by status is found in the case of those who live on the earnings of inherited wealth.

In modern democracies there is a growing feeling that the principle of status or inherited position is undesirable. Each individual, it is felt, should receive a share of the total production based upon his personal contribution. Toward this end governments have adopted various measures limiting the rights of inheritance and providing that occupations shall be open to all, without regard to race, color, or creed. Some eight states and the Territory of Alaska have adopted fair-employment-practice legislation with enforcement provisions, making it illegal for an employer or a union to discriminate against any person because of such person's race, creed, color, or national origin. The states having this legislation are Connecticut, Massachusetts, New Jersey, New Mexico, New York, Oregon, Rhode Island, and Washington.

[6] M. J. Bonn, "The Relation of the State to Economics," *The State and Economic Life,* League of Nations, International Institute of Intellectual Coöperation (Paris, 1932), p. 14.

[7] R. M. MacIver emphasizes that "In approaching the functions of government it is well to remember that government is never a free agent disinterestedly engaged in adjusting its activities to the needs of the times. Every government is caught up in a complex struggle of interests, takes sides in this struggle, shifts its ground as one side or another gains, maneuvers for advantage, and strives through it all to remain in power. Every government is in some measure opportunistic." R. M. MacIver, *The Web of Government* (New York, 1947), p. 317.

The Method of Authority. The determination of prices and incomes by authority means that some person or persons in authority (family head, church official, or government agency) is accepted or chosen to assign or portion out the income produced by the group. Distribution by authority may be exercised in an arbitrary or discretionary manner, or it may be exercised according to rules. In time of war or other national emergency, it is usual for government to assume authoritarian control over prices, wages, and the allocation of supplies. Also in the case of public utilities, rates and earnings are usually controlled by government commissions. Special favors granted by government—such as subsidies and bounties—are a form of income distribution by authority, as is any action of government to favor one class of citizens at the cost of others.

The exercise of authoritarian *control* by government agencies over price is an exceedingly difficult problem, for there is no generally accepted rule on price to apply. Usually, an effort is made to find some "formula," which has the appearance of objectivity, based upon earnings in competitive industry, cost of production, or cost of living. Invariably, however, the rules of compromise and political expediency enter into the various judgments made by government agencies.

The authoritarian principle governs prices and incomes in a socialist society. In the Soviet Union, for example, the rule of work and income is "From each according to his ability, to each according to his work." In the higher states of socialist development (communism), the rule proposed is "From each according to his ability, to each according to his needs."[8] The government, of course, is necessarily the judge of one's "work" or "needs."

Charity Affects Income Distribution. In practice, the application of the principles of competition, monopoly, status, and authority are invariably modified or supplemented in varying degrees by *charity*. Charity is an expression of one's benevolence or affection. It includes gifts which are made to one's family and to one's friends. Each year an enormous amount of income is distributed to others in the charitable contributions which are made to churches and social agencies. In the purchase and sale of goods, affection and sentiment may also enter and cause one to pay more or ask less than he ordinarily would.

There is general agreement that a limited amount of charity is necessary and desirable. Too much charity, however, experience indicates, weakens the character and moral fiber of the people receiving it and causes them to want to live continuously at the expense of others. Class hatreds develop, work incentives disappear, and greater and greater demands for gifts are made upon those who have for the benefit of others. According to Professor Henry Sidgwick, "Though political economy has hardly had anything positively new to teach to experienced persons with regard to the dangers of almsgiving, it has certainly tended to make the common view of these

---

[8] V. I. Lenin, "Tasks of the Proletariat in Our Revolution," in *Collected Works* (New York, 1929), Vol. 20, p. 154.

dangers more clear, definite, and systematic. It has impressed forcibly on instructed minds the general rule that if a man's wants are supplied by gift when he might have supplied them himself by harder work and greater thrift, his motives to industry and thrift tend to be so far diminished; and not only his motives, but the motives of all persons in like circumstances who are thereby led to expect like gifts for themselves."[9] The lessons of history indicate that if democracy and a free society are to survive, public policy must be directed toward making it possible for people to secure an income by their labor and in direct relation to their own productivity.

THE STANDARD OR YARDSTICK FOR MEASURING "PUBLIC INTEREST" IN THE ECONOMIC SPHERE

In exercising the function of regulating business, how, it may be asked, is the "public interest" to be identified? What guiding rule or standard can government use in regulating the business relations of individuals and corporations?

From an economic standpoint, all citizens have a common interest in a "living." Everyone must secure each day some part of the total national stream of real income—such as food, clothing, housing, medical and dental care, automobiles, radios, furniture, and so forth. The "consumer interest" is the interest of all citizens in getting more and better goods for consumption with less time and effort. Speaking of the goal or aim of our economic system, Professor J. M. Clark states that the "most unqualified criteria of economic progress are more goods to consume and, on the side of conditions of production itself, a shorter work week and more leisure."[10] The interest of consumers in the commerce of a nation is broader than that of any group of producers or any group of sellers. It follows, therefore, that in so far as government is concerned with promoting the "common interest" in the economic sphere, its decisions should be guided by the "consumer interest."

Adam Smith has said, "Consumption is the sole end and purpose of all production; and the interest of the producer ought to be attended to, only so far as it may be necessary for promoting that of the consumer. The maxim is so perfectly self-evident, that it would be absurd to attempt to prove it. But in the mercantile system, the interest of the consumer is almost constantly sacrificed to that of the producer; and it seems to consider production, and not consumption, as the ultimate end and object of all industry and commerce."[11]

Since every producer is also a consumer, it may be asked why consumers are contrasted with producers? What is wrong about promoting the interest of producers, as such, since they are also consumers? The contrast between

[9] Henry Sidgwick, *The Principles of Political Economy* (London, 1901), pp. 591–592.
[10] J. M. Clark, "Aims of Economic Life as Seen by Economists," in *Goals of Economic Life* (New York, 1953), p. 24.
[11] Adam Smith, *The Wealth of Nations* (1776), Book IV, chap. 8, p. 159.

the interest of *consumers* and *producers* is made because an organized group of producers usually stands to gain more from a certain policy (such as legalized price fixing, a curtailment of production, an exclusion of competitors, or a protective tariff) than they stand to lose as buyers of the products of others, including their own. Producers of steel, for example, stand to gain more from a high tariff and monopolistic prices on steel than they stand to lose as consumers of the products of others which they secure in the process of exchange. Organized steel producers, therefore, even though they are consumers of steel products, can be counted upon to demand special privileges which are against the interest of consumers generally.

In so far as government grants special privileges—such as legalized price fixing, output restrictions, and exclusions on competitors—to organized groups of producers, it makes it possible for them to force others to pay more for fewer goods. The enhancement of the prices and incomes of the organized producers means a *reduction* in the incomes of others. It is easy to see the benefit of special public favors, but the concomitant injury to others is rarely seen or considered. When once started, the process of granting special privileges to pressure groups grows rapidly as more and more organized producers, including organized labor, seek to enhance their own position or to offset the disadvantages to them occasioned by the special privileges enjoyed by others. The effects of limiting output and restricting sales in a considerable area of productive activity thereupon become cumulative, and the end results are higher prices, unused capacity, and chronic or persistent unemployment in a large part of the whole economy.

The principle that it is an essential economic function of government in a capitalist economy to find and effectuate the *consumer interest* does not mean that government should never aid or favor the private interests of producers. Government, in fact, can do much to collect and disseminate reliable technical information for businessmen, laborers, farmers, and mariners. Examples of such assistance include the trade promotional activity of the Department of Commerce, the placement work of the public employment exchanges, the forecasting service of the Weather Bureau, and the soil conservation service of the Department of Agriculture. Government can also provide scientific and technical training to young men and women, and its research laboratories can be an important source of technological innovations for industry and agriculture. The point is, however, that in all these promotional activities government is also indirectly aiding the consumer interest by making it possible for individuals to produce a larger national flow of real income. The only objective standard for guiding the work of government in the economic sphere, it is suggested, is that of the consumer interest; and all plans or proposals for aiding individual producers which do not directly or indirectly meet this test cannot be said to be in the public interest.

Since government intervention in behalf of consumers—monopoly prosecution, grade-labeling legislation, and tariff reduction—is largely undertaken to protect them from the selfish designs of organized producers, it is certain that such forms of intervention will invariably be opposed by those adversely affected. In support of their position, these economic groups can be counted upon to present in a vigorous way plausible arguments showing that interference is unnecessary or undesirable *in the public interest*. Most fruit and vegetable canners, for example, are convinced that compulsory grade labeling is unsound, but consumer groups actively support the movement. Again, the United States Steel Corporation proclaims the advantages of a financial union of formerly competing steel mills, while steel consumers complain of the loss of alternative sources of supply. Whose view should prevail?

The basic and sound rule to apply as a guide for the public regulation of business is that of "the greatest good of the greatest number." Since the consumer interest is the one interest which citizens in general have in common, it follows that it is the only objective standard or yardstick for measuring or ascertaining the public interest in the economic sphere.

MEANING OF THE TERM "REGULATION"

In the present chapter, we have been considering the basic rules which government provides for the conduct of business activity. The title of the chapter is the "Public Regulation of Business." As a summary statement on the nature and meaning of *public regulation*, we shall define and distinguish the terms "regulation" and "control."

The word "regulate" has the general meaning of (a) directing or governing by rules and (b) of subjecting to guidance or restriction. In the field of government and business, the normative or usual objective of "regulation" is the provision of a *frame* within which business will and can—by voluntary decisions—do that which is socially desirable. The frame in the American economy consists of rules, decisions, and statutes designed (a) to preserve and maintain competition and (b) to prevent business from doing acts which are conceived to be socially undesirable. In providing rules for business and in deciding cases, government, in effect, declares, "If you cross this line, we shall impose penalties." Rules, decisions, and statutes serve as "warning flags" or guideposts to business firms as they otherwise pursue their own commercial interests.

A "rule" may be defined as a prescribed guide for future conduct or action. It is a specific guide—one which leaves little or no room for interpretation. The rule-making powers of administrative agencies usually provide for the making of "imperative" rules—that is, guides which must be obeyed. Imperative rules are a command.

THE FORMULATION OF RULES AND GUIDEPOSTS

Rules governing business activity usually have their origins in general statutes. Upon the basis of these statutes, various commissions have the power to formulate imperative rules (see item #4 in Table 9, pp. 80–81). Persons subject to regulation are permitted to protest the rules formulated by an agency, and all rules are subject to hearing and review. Thereupon, in supervising business behavior, a commission has only to get the facts and test them against a specific rule to determine lawful or unlawful conduct. An example of a rule governing business conduct is found in the requirement of the Securities and Exchange Commission that directors of a holding company in process of reorganization shall not trade in the securities of that company during the reorganization period.

Regulatory commissions also establish guides by initiating "cases" to restrain specific kinds of activities which appear to fall within a general statutory prohibition (see item #5 in Table 9, pp. 80–81). The Federal Trade Commission Act, for example, condemns "unfair methods of competition." It also provides for a commission (1) to get the facts on a business practice and (2) to issue complaints for testing the facts in light of the general law, subject to review by the courts. This procedure is known as the "decisional process" or the "case-by-case method." In proceeding case by case, a commission does not announce beforehand stated criteria or guides for business conduct. Rather, opposing counsel vie in developing a standard which will apply the statute and dispose of the case. At the close of the hearings, the *decision* thereupon marks out lawful or unlawful conduct. In the course of time, the decisional process operates to build up principles which serve as specific guides for future business conduct.

Imperative rules provide clear-cut, specific guides for the conduct of business activity. They make the law definite and its application consistent. Businessmen can know exactly the types of activity which they should avoid. A rule-making power also makes the task of regulation more economical and expeditious, for standards of policy can be set up in advance to guide business conduct.

The case-by-case method of regulation does not provide specific guides. The interpretation of the statutes, moreover, may vary with changes in personnel and with changes in political party. Some businessmen like to operate without definite rules, but others frequently complain that the laws regulating business are vague and uncertain. The case-by-case method, however, does give a commission a freer hand in dealing with problems. In proceeding case by case, a commission is able to construe a statute strictly or leniently (with a "rule of reason"), as long as it does not act arbitrarily or capriciously. Some agencies, it may be noted, have the power to proceed case by case and also to promulgate rules.

The absence of statutory rule-making powers may reflect a desire on the part of influential business groups to avoid specific standards for their conduct. However, it may also indicate legislative opinion that standards for regulation must be developed gradually by experience. In the case of *S.E.C. v. Chenery Corp.*, Justice Murphy presented an excellent statement on the place for the case-by-case method in business regulation. Said Justice Murphy,

Not every principle essential to the effective administration of a statute can or should be cast immediately into the mold of a general rule. Some principles must await their own development, while others must be adjusted to meet particular, unforeseeable situations. . . . In other words, problems may arise in a case which the administrative agency could not reasonably foresee, problems which must be solved despite the absence of a relevant general rule. Or the agency may not have had sufficient experience with a particular problem to warrant rigidifying its tentative judgment into a hard and fast rule. Or the problem may be so specialized and varying in nature as to be impossible of capture within the boundaries of a general rule. In those situations, the agency must retain power to deal with the problems on a case-to-case basis if the administrative process is to be effective. There is thus a very definite place for the case-by-case evolution of statutory standards.[12]

Government regulations are usually expressed negatively. They tell business enterprisers what they may *not* do; not what they must do. Regulatory agencies rarely prescribe *positive courses of conduct*—such as a rule requiring companies to quote f.o.b. mill prices, uniform to all persons at the mill; or a rule providing that basic commodities shall be offered three times on a public exchange before being sold privately. Present-day economists and lawyers, in fact, have done little to develop positive standards for use in regulating the conduct of business activity.

Regulatory policies are expressed in basic statutes (such as the Sherman Act, the Clayton Act, and the Securities Exchange Act); in the decisions, prohibitions, determinations, rules, and other prescriptions of administrative agencies; and in the interpretations and decisions of the courts.

Government "regulations" are also called "indirect controls" because their purpose is to govern by providing guideposts rather than by directly determining entrepreneurial decisions. *Within the frame provided by government*, prices, output, and investment are determined by the voluntary decisions of private enterprisers and by market forces, instead of by governmental directives.

THE NATURE OF CONTROL

The word "control" is used in a general way to mean directing the action of others. In the study of government and business, the term "direct control" has the functional meaning of governmental action (a) to place limits on prices and wages and (b) to impose restrictions on quantities used, output, and investment. In "controlling" business, government takes specific action to decide how much one can get, the maximum one can produce, and the maximum or minimum one can pay. Direct or positive controls include minimum and maximum prices or wages, rationing, restrictions on entry and new construction, subsidies, and production quotas. Customarily, "controlled" enterprises initiate their own rates and charges and file them with

[12] *S.E.C.* v. *Chenery Corporation*, 332 U.S. 194, 202–203 (1947).

TABLE 9. Main Pillars of Public Regulation

	ICC
1. Power to make findings of fact in connection with the decisional process. In proceedings for judicial review, such findings have a legal presumption of correctness if supported by substantial evidence.	Yes
2. Power to require reports by persons subject to its jurisdiction.	Yes
3. Power (and duty) to conduct investigations, require (or debar) testimony, and examine records with respect to matters within its jurisdiction.	Yes
4. Power to make rules governing business conduct subject to its jurisdiction and in accordance with basic statutes.	Yes
5. Power to restrain violations of basic statutes or orders and rules issued thereunder (cease-and desist orders, court injunctions, revocation of licenses or certificates).	Yes
6. Power to require publication of rates and charges in a prescribed manner.	Yes
7. Power to make rules covering procedures before it.	Yes
8. Power to make studies of business practices with reference to the public interest.	Yes
9. Power to publish findings, reports, and decisions.	Yes
10. Power to recommend legislation to Congress.	Yes

TABLE 10. Main Pillars of Public Control

1. Power to prescribe and require observance of uniform accounting systems and statistical regulations, including in certain instances prescription of amounts recorded on a utility's books (i.e., the classes of property for which depreciation charges may be included in operating expenses and the percentages of depreciation to be included on such property).	Yes
2. Power to place valuations on property of a utility for use in prescribing fair and reasonable rates.	Yes[a]
3. Power to prescribe rates and charges—maximum, minimum, or actual—after full opportunity for hearings.	Yes
4. Power to control entrance into or abandonment of service.	Yes
5. Power to pass on applications to acquire or control the facilities of another company operating in the same line of business.	Yes

[a] Railroads and pipelines.
[b] Refers to subsidized lines only. In so far as service is set by subsidy contract, change without permission would be violation of contract.
[c] Maximum and minimum rates may be prescribed for carriers from U.S. to territories, and between territories. Rates may be modified in all cases where they are shown to be unduly prejudicial or discriminatory.
[d] Ownership may be controlled only as between U.S. citizens and foreigners. Control over management of subsidized lines must be satisfactory to Board.
[e] There are no convenience and necessity requirements for opening a stockyard or packing plant; however, the Secretary is authorized to prescribe the conditions under which persons may register and may suspend, and as to certain classes of registrants revoke, for violations.
[f] If the effect is to create a monopoly, manipulate, or control prices, etc.
[g] The authority of the C.A.B. is limited to valuations made in the course of exercising its authority to prescribe fair and reasonable rates of compensation for the transportation of mail.
[h] For a detailed description of this power, see 47 United States Code, 221(a) and 222.
[i] The F.C.C. has the power to control entrance into and abandonment of interstate and foreign service by common carriers subject to its jurisdiction. Entrance into service by noncommon carriers is also controlled by the F.C.C. in the sense that a station license must be obtained before a radio station can be legally operated. Such licenses, however, may

Table 9 (Continued)

FPC	FCC	CAB	PSA	FMB	SEC	FTC	AD	CEA	NLRB
Yes	Yes	Yes	Yes	Yes	Yes	Yes	No	Yes	Yes
Yes	Yes	Yes	Yes	Yes	Yes	Yes, of corporations	No	Yes	Yes
Yes	Yes	Yes	Yes	Yes	Yes	Yes	Yes	Yes	Yes
Yes	Yes, in the case of common carriers	Yes	Yes	Yes	Yes	No	No	Yes	No
Yes	Yes	Yes	Yes	Yes	Yes	Yes	Yes	Yes	Yes
Yes	Yes, in the case of common carriers	Yes	Yes	Yes	No	No	No	No	No
Yes	Yes	Yes	Yes	Yes	Yes	Yes	No	Yes	Yes
Yes	Yes	Yes	Yes	Yes	Yes	Yes	No	Yes	No
Yes	Yes	Yes	Yes	Yes	Yes	Yes	No	Yes	Yes
Yes	Yes	Yes	Yes	Yes	Yes	Yes	Yes	Yes	Yes

Table 10 (Continued)

FPC	FCC	CAB	PSA	FMB	SEC	FTC	AD	CEA	NLRB
Yes	Yes	Yes	Yes	Yes[b]	Yes, under Holding Company Act	No	No	No	No
Yes	Yes	Yes[a]	Yes	Yes[b]	No	No	No	No	No
Yes	Yes	Yes	Yes	Yes[c]	No	No	No	No	No
Yes	Yes[i]	Yes	Yes[e]	Yes[b]	No	No	No	No	No
Yes	Yes[h]	Yes	Yes[f]	Yes[d]	Yes, under Holding Company Act	No	No	No	No[j]

be surrendered and the service abandoned without permission of the Commission.

[j] The regulatory powers listed in the chart do not entirely fit the operations of the National Labor Relations Board. However, the answers given describe important aspects of the Board's work in regulating a significant business relationship.

Key to Column Heads

ICC—Interstate Commerce Commission
FPC—Federal Power Commission
FCC—Federal Communications Commission
CAB—Civil Aeronautics Board
PSA—Packers and Stockyards Act (U.S.D.A.)
FMB—Federal Maritime Board
SEC—Securities and Exchange Commission
FTC—Federal Trade Commission
AD—Antitrust Division (Dept. of Justice)
CEA—Commodity Exchange Authority
NLRB—National Labor Relations Board

the governmental commissions. The commissions thereupon approve or disapprove the rates in accordance with statutory legislation. (See also
Chap. 24.)

As we shall see in Chapters 23, 24, 25, 26, and 27, direct, positive controls
are typically used by government for three purposes: (1) to protect users
and consumers from unreasonable charges made by public utilities; (2) to
strengthen groups having weak bargaining power—e.g., subsidies, "price
floors," and minimum wages; and (3) to restrain price inflation during
periods of war and rearmament.

The terms "planning," "economic planning," and "centralized planning"
are used to designate an *extreme* form of control in which government
actually takes over the crucial entrepreneurial decisions. "Planning" means
that prices and quantities produced are determined by or through governmental organisms rather than (1) by the decisions of private enterprisers and
competition or (2) by the concerted action of private industry groups. In
planning the use of economic resources, government deliberately seeks to
alter the results of the market system in order to achieve certain definite
ends, which in turn are different according to the prevailing ideology and
the interests of influential groups. Economic planning may be partial or
total; it is partial when it is limited to one or a few sectors of the economy,
and total or overall if it is extended to all sectors.[13]

At the present time, socialist and labor groups in a number of Western
nations declare that planning should be utilized (1) to improve the incomes
of workers, generally; (2) to insure full employment; and (3) to give
workers a greater share in the management of industry. Such economic
planning, it is usually said, should be based upon increased public ownership—especially in industries in which price competition is ineffective. Economic planning, moreover, it is believed, should be applied to both the
publicly owned and privately owned sectors of the economy in order to
achieve abundant production and a more just distribution of income.

MAIN PILLARS OF PUBLIC REGULATION AND CONTROL

The regulatory authority exercised by the various federal commissions
varies greatly from one agency to another, depending upon the authority
given to a particular agency by the Congress. There are certain common
elements of regulation and control, however, which are exercised by the
several agencies. In summary form, these main pillars are listed in Tables
9 and 10.

It may be noted that in some cases the key provisions of the basic statutes—
such as the Interstate Commerce Act and the Civil Aeronautics Act—are
almost identical. However, in other instances, there are important differences
which are to be explained (1) by the characteristics and nature of the industries subject to federal jurisdiction, (2) the different objectives which

[13] For an illustration of "partial" economic planning by the federal government, see
the section on price control in sugar under the Sugar Act of 1948, Chap. 23.

Congress seeks to achieve through regulatory action, and (3) the influence of interest groups dominant at the time the basic statutes were adopted. The powers of a given agency, also, do not always apply uniformly to all types of companies subject to regulation. The Interstate Commerce Commission, for example, has control over entrance into business for motor, water, and rail carriers and for freight forwarders, but not for pipe lines. In the main, however, the powers shown are generally applicable to the types of business subject to the jurisdiction of the respective agencies.

The powers of *regulation*, it may be noted, relate mainly to (1) the provision of publicity, (2) the conduct of investigations and hearings, (3) the making of findings of fact and law, (4) the issuance of orders, subject to judicial review, and (5) the prosecution of violations of basic statutes or orders and rules issued thereunder.

The Department of Justice (Antitrust Division), unlike the other agencies, has no power to issue regulations or interpretations, to conduct hearings, to make findings, to issue orders, to direct, to prohibit, or to punish. It is a prosecuting agency, not an administrative agency. It can only institute proceedings under which *the courts* may exercise their constitutional and statutory powers. The Antitrust Division decides in its own mind that certain activities of businessmen violate the law (the Sherman Act and various provisions of the Clayton Act). It thereupon brings cases, and the resulting court decisions serve as "warning flags" for competitive enterprise.

The powers of *control*, it will be seen, are exercised primarily with respect to "public utilities" subject to the jurisdiction of each particular commission. These powers are expressed, in the main, (1) in prescribing rates and charges, (2) in controlling entrance into a field or the abandonment of service, and (3) in approving or disapproving applications to expand facilities or to acquire and unify other facilities.

As a general rule, the basic purpose of commission control is to prevent extortion and to keep rates of return down to levels which presumably would exist if competition prevailed. In controlling the rates of public stockyards, for example, the Secretary of Agriculture limits charges to those which will provide a "fair return" on the value of the stockyard facilities. The provisions of the Civil Aeronautics Act, on the other hand, require a different approach. In fixing mail pay, the Civil Aeronautics Board has the duty to subsidize the industry to the extent necessary for the development of a sound air transportation industry. The Board also has the obligation to promote and develop such an air transport system not only for the purposes of commerce, but also for the national defense.

The main pillars of regulation and control are shown in summary form in order to provide a bird's eye view of regulatory authority. A more detailed analysis will be provided in succeeding chapters. Students desiring additional material for term papers and reports will find it profitable to consult the basic statutes and the annual reports of the various commissions and agencies.

In studying regulatory authority, it is useful to consider not only the powers exercised, but also the types of companies or business activities subject to regulation. Summary statements on the types of business which are within the jurisdiction of the several federal agencies are presented in Table 11. In studying the types of business subject to various agencies, it may be noted that governmental policy in the economic field is largely expressed in creating and maintaining effective competition. If and when the policy of competition has been found to be ineffective or undesirable, governmental policy is usually changed to provide price fixing by public commissions. In a democracy, such as ours, the public ultimately can be expected to demand positive governmental controls to keep private monopoly in check.

THE DECLINING "INDEPENDENCE" OF REGULATORY AGENCIES

The principal regulatory agencies, I.C.C., F.P.C., F.C.C., S.E.C., C.A.B., N.L.R.B., and F.T.C. were established by Congress as independent agencies. This means that they were created as bipartisan commissions responsible to Congress and not to the President. As "arms of Congress," the commissions are required to report to Congress and to give expression to the statutes enacted by Congress. In making the main regulatory commissions subject to Congress and not to the President, Congress desired to provide regulation which would be impartial, nonpartisan, and as free as possible from political dictation and intimidation.[14] The President serves not only as Chief Executive, but also as head of his political party. Persons in government responsible to the President give expression to his direction and will; and the President, himself, it is believed by many, may be swayed by the seductive influence of large campaign contributions and the pressure of party supporters.

In recent years, the independent agencies have increasingly become subject to the will of the President. A principal factor shaping this trend was the Reorganization Act of 1949. By the terms of this legislation, the President was given authority to coördinate and improve the functioning of the regulatory commissions. In support of the law, it was urged in Congress that the President should be given power to reduce overlapping efforts and duplicating activities in the interest of greater economy and efficiency. Upon the basis of this legislation, the President now names the chairman for each regulatory commission, except in the case of the Interstate Commerce Commission. The chairmen serve at the will and pleasure of the President. By terms of the reorganization plans, important powers formerly exercised by the commissions themselves were transferred to the chairmen of the com-

---

[14] The position of independent commissions as arms of Congress was well described in *Humphrey's Executor* vs. *U.S.*, 295 U.S. 602, 625–626, 628 (1935). Said the Court: The FTC was established as "a body which shall be independent of executive authority, *except in its selection,* and free to exercise its judgment without the leave or hindrance of any other official or any department of government. . . . Such a body cannot in any proper sense be characterized as an arm or an eye of the executive. Its duties are performed without executive leave and, in the contemplation of the statute, must be free from executive control."

missions. Such powers include (1) the appointment and supervision of personnel, (2) the distribution of business among such personnel, and (3) the use and expenditure of funds. Only in the appointment of the heads of major administrative units, must a chairman secure the approval of other commission members.

As a result of the changes under the Reorganization Act, in particular, numerous experts on government believe that the functioning of the regulatory commissions is becoming more and more subject to executive direction and control. The members of a commission, other than the chairman, moreover, are finding that they have little influence in shaping policy or in deciding upon the work to be done. Their equality in administering the law, it is felt, is becoming seriously impaired.

To the extent that the regulatory commissions are "arms of the Executive," their policies and decisions become directly subject to political change and to the prevailing political climate. It is said that even the Supreme Court, whose members have life tenure, give consideration to the election returns! Perhaps no agency of government can be entirely "independent." The historical view and judgment of Congress, however, in the problem of regulation, has been that economic regulation should be based upon facts, principles, and rational deliberations, and not upon political expediency and outside pressures.

TABLE 11. Types of Business or Business Relations Which Are Subject to the Jurisdiction of Federal Agencies.

Interstate Commerce Commission	Jurisdiction over all forms of interstate public transportation; except air carriers and pipe lines for gas and water. Controls rates for railroads; oil pipe lines; sleeping car service; express service; motor carriers; water carriers in coastwise, intercoastal, and inland-water service; and freight-forwarding companies.
Federal Power Commission	Controls licensing of hydroelectric projects on federal lands or on navigable waters of the U.S.; jurisdiction over transmission and wholesale sales of electric energy in interstate commerce and public utilities engaged therein; transportation and sale of natural gas in interstate commerce for resale and natural gas companies engaged therein.
Civil Aeronautics Board	Broad powers over interstate air commerce, generally. Jurisdiction over interstate rates (a) for the transportation of mail by aircraft and (b) for the transportation of persons and property.
Packers and Stockyards Act (U.S.D.A.)	Jurisdiction over (1) the rates and charges on stockyard facilities and by market agencies (livestock commission men), (2) the business practices of meat packers, and (3) the charges, services, and facilities for handling live poultry in large cities.
Federal Maritime Board	Broad powers of control over (1) American and foreign flag carriers engaged in foreign commerce and (2) the offshore common carriers which serve U.S. territories. Authority to modify or disapprove rates, charges, fares, and trade practices.
Federal Communications Commission	Jurisdiction over interstate and foreign commerce in communications by telephone, telegraph, and radio. The Commission exercises various powers of control over standard AM, FM, and

TABLE 11 (*Continued*)

	television broadcast stations, communications common carriers by wire or radio in interstate commerce (including telephone, telegraph, and cable companies), and the operators of maritime, aeronautical, land transportation, industrial, and certain other special radio services.
Federal Trade Commission	Power to prosecute unfair methods of competition and unfair or deceptive acts or practices; price and other discriminations; exclusive-dealing arrangements; corporate stock or asset acquisitions promotive of monopoly; interlocking corporate directorships promotive of monopoly—in all types of business engaged in interstate or foreign commerce, *except* banks, common carriers, air carriers, meat packers, and industries specifically exempted from the antitrust laws.
Commodity Exchange Authority	Regulatory powers over trading activity on all commodity exchanges designated as contract markets.
National Labor Relations Board	Regulates collective bargaining by unions with an employer or employers engaged in interstate commerce or in activities affecting such commerce, to prohibit unfair labor practices, to designate appropriate bargaining units, and to conduct elections for determining representatives of employees.
Securities and Exchange Commission	Regulatory powers over national securities exchanges and all brokers and dealers using the mails or other instrumentalities of interstate commerce. Regulates disclosures as to issuance of new securities sold in interstate commerce; the trading of securities on national stock exchanges; the provision of public information on listed securities; the borrowing of brokers, dealers, and members of security exchanges; the activities of investment trusts and investment advisers; the operations and conduct of all electric and gas *holding* companies.
Antitrust Division (Dept. of Justice)	Power to bring civil or criminal proceedings in the courts to maintain competition in all types of business, including banking, which are engaged in, or whose activities directly affect, interstate or foreign commerce, with the exception of activities specifically exempted from the antitrust laws.

SUGGESTIONS FOR FURTHER READING

Baumol, William J., and Chandler, Lester V., *Economic Processes and Policies* (New York, 1954).

Clark, John M., *Social Control of Business* (New York, 2d ed. 1939).

Cushman, Robert E., *The Independent Regulatory Commissions* (New York, 1941).

Dimock, Marshall E., *Business and Government* (New York, 1953).

MacIver, R. M., *The Web of Government* (New York, 1947).

Mill, James, *Elements of Political Economy* (London, 1821).

Mill, John Stuart, *Principles of Political Economy* (1848), ed. by W. J. Ashley (London, 1923).

Sidgwick, Henry, *The Principles of Political Economy* (1883) (3rd ed., London, 1901).

Simons, Henry C., *Economic Policy for a Free Society* (Chicago, 1948).

CHAPTER 6

Price Competition as a Price-Making Mechanism

The essential purpose of the various antitrust statutes is to create and maintain, as far as possible, (a) freedom of entry and (b) the rule or principle of price competition as the basic price-making mechanism. In most fields of business, competition results in performance which is better than that which develops under conditions of monopoly or direct public control. More and better goods at lower prices and economic power curbed by the opportunity to turn to independent sellers or buyers—these are the essential ends or reasons for competition.

The purposes of the present chapter are (1) to explain the nature and operation of price competition and (2) to illustrate the regulation which government exercises over competition in central markets. The conditions of market competition do not now widely exist; however, the type of competition which operates in central markets still serves as a standard for the kind of "workable," "effective" or "practically attainable" competition (never perfect) which is called for by the antitrust laws.

DISTORTED VIEW OF COMPETITION

There is a great deal of misunderstanding and confusion on what price competition is and how it operates. Some businessmen and some economists assert that price competition exists when there are several sellers actively seeking orders, even though prices are *identical* and *fixed*. Thus, one economist presented by industry in the *Cement* case testified that "price competition" exists among gasoline stations which offer goods at the same price but which offer other inducements for patronage, such as free air and water. In his words, "It seems to me there is competition whether that rivalry takes the form of a lowering of the price or whether it takes the form of an attempt to give better service or cleaner stations. . . . I think there is no logical difference between competition in price and any other kind of competition."[1]

A second economist appearing for the cement industry was asked whether or not "price competition" prevails in the sale of gasoline when the sellers "have agreed on the price of 18 cents per gallon that they quote and charge, and they do charge it as agreed upon." The economist replied that price competition still prevails if the sellers do not agree to standardize the quality of

---

[1] *Cement Institute et al.* v. *F.T.C.*, *Transcript of Testimony*, U.S. Court of Appeals for the Seventh Circuit, Vol. 18, pp. 42958, 42998 (filed September 1, 1943).

their products. In his words, "There is just as much opportunity for competition in the case where they have agreed upon price but let the quality of the product vary as there is where they have agreed upon a quality of the product and let the price vary."[2] Under the assumptions as given, this economist saw no restrain upon price competition even though the sellers had agreed on price.

The position of the federal antitrust agencies is that the foregoing concepts of price competition are incomplete and erroneous. In the view of the government, the price competition required by the antitrust laws is independent rivalry between two or more sellers with respect to price itself. Business firms are not excused from price competition because there is quality competition. The notion that either one is a substitute for the other is unsound. Both price competition and quality competition are required by the antitrust laws.

CENTRAL MARKETS THE IDEAL IN THE ANALYSIS OF COMPETITION

The economic basis, norm, or standard for the concept of price competition is the price competition which is found to operate in central and primary markets—such as the Chicago grain market, the Boston wool market, and the produce markets in large consuming centers. It is in central or primary markets that *price competition* operates most *effectively* and *fairly* as a price-making mechanism for the basic commodities. An essential purpose of the antitrust laws is to preserve and maintain price competition which is *effective* and *fair*, and students of our antitrust laws can learn much about fair competition by studying the operation of competition in central markets.

In central or primary markets, price competition among *buyers* and among *sellers* typically develops automatically. The very number of traders tends to prevent collusion on either side. When demand exceeds supply, bid prices are *independently* raised to bring about an equilibrium between the forces of demand and supply. On the other hand, when supply exceeds demand, asking prices are *independently* lowered to provide a price at which business can be done. The market price of each seller, moreover, is uniform (nondiscriminatory) to all buyers at a given time.

When a market concourse is not fully realized—as in the case of geographically separate sellers—it is possible for the law to require an independent, spontaneous, nondiscriminatory type of price competition analogous to that which is found in primary or central markets. This approach and point of view were taken by Congress in the enactment of the Federal Trade Commission and Clayton Acts, as well as by the Federal Trade Commission itself, in its attack on basing-point delivered pricing systems. (See Chaps. 17 and 18.) The main purpose of the Robinson-Patman Act, moreover, is to require a seller to treat his customers on more or less equal terms—as in a central market. Since the concept and characteristics of prices as determined

[2] *Ibid.*, pp. 44394–44395.

in central markets underlie basic legislation and orders regulating business, it is important to study the distinctive features of market price.

PRICE COMPETITION PROVIDES AN IMPERSONAL RULE FOR DETERMINING PRICE

Experience has shown that trade between two persons, isolated and removed from other buyers and sellers, does not make for fair and equitable prices. A buyer in desperate need can be forced to pay a very high price, and an anxious seller can be compelled to sell at an extremely low price.

In order to remove conditions of monopoly power and to provide buyers and sellers with information and alternative opportunities, public authorities from earliest times have taken measures to provide for competition on the side of buyers, as well as on the side of sellers. During the medieval period (800–1500) in particular, the public authorities in Western Europe established formal markets and concentrated all buying and selling in them. Henry of Ghent (1220–1295), a distinguished medieval philosopher, characterized the "just price" as the price at which goods are commonly sold in a market ("in fore").[3] Likewise, St. Antoninus of Florence (1389–1459) who studied closely the commercial life of that city, held that the just price is the market price.[4] Another writer identifying the just price with the market price was the Cardinal Cajetan (1469–1534) who wrote, "the just price is that which can now be obtained from purchasers, supposing common knowledge and the absence of all fraud and compulsion."[5]

A market concourse provides the essential conditions for the operation of two-sided price competition. The forces of demand and supply are centralized; and buyers and sellers conduct their exchanges with a common knowledge of supplies available, deliveries, and current prices. Each trader must independently estimate the worth of goods in their various uses, for that is the only standard by which he can be at all certain of being able to do business.

Although individual judgment is brought to bear in determining competitive price, it is not a coercive or arbitrary judgment, as it is under conditions of monopoly or authoritarian control. Under conditions of market competition, for example, various buyers attempting to pay the lowest possible prices find their efforts frustrated by the bids of other buyers willing to pay more. Likewise, sellers who seek to charge the most that anyone will pay find that their grasping demands are limited by the lower offers of other sellers who want to do business and make a modest profit. In the law, as well as in economics, competitive prices have long been looked upon as being "fair," "just," and "equitable" prices, because they are largely free from personal coercion, arbitrariness, discrimination, and favoritism.

[3] Henry of Ghent, *Quodlibeta Quaestiones*, xiv, 14.
[4] Lewis Watt, "The Theory Lying Behind the Historical Conception of the Just Price," in V. A. Demant, ed., *The Just Price* (London, 1930), p. 68.
[5] *Ibid.*, p. 69.

THE ESSENTIAL CONDITIONS FOR EFFECTIVE COMPETITION

In many cases markets have been established and maintained voluntarily by individuals in important commercial centers at which supplies are concentrated for subsequent shipment or fabrication (as the wool market in Boston, Massachusetts). In most cases, however, experience has shown that markets will not often be created or function effectively without positive assistance and regulation by government.

The essential conditions for the existence and functioning of two-sided price competition as a price-making mechanism are as follows:

1. A centralization of the forces of demand and supply. Market forces may be centralized either in a formally organized exchange or in an informal gathering in a particular district or area of a town. Price thereupon comes to reflect a balancing of the forces of supply and demand.
2. Publicity on prices, transactions, stocks available, and deliveries. Common knowledge is essential for informed, intelligent dealing and the effective operation of price competition.
3. Freedom of anyone to buy and sell. This is an aspect and a continuation of the right to engage in a business of one's own choice—the right to compete. The potential competition of other sellers also serves to provide buyers with an additional measure of protection against unfair prices.
4. Independent action among a number of buyers and sellers in making bids and offers, with no one in a position to influence the price intentionally and as he pleases. Any given firm, that is, should not control such a large percentage of the supply of a certain class of goods that it is able to make the "going price" which as an actual fact will be largely observed in the industry. (See also Glossary of Terms at the end of this chapter.)

With the essential conditions of open markets fulfilled, two-sided price competition will develop from the desire of buyers and sellers to be able to deal. In maintaining competition, the task of government *is to maintain the conditions* which make for effective competition. As a Senate Committee stated in 1913, in recommending the creation of a trade commission, "It is frequently declared that the law cannot compel men employed in like business to compete with each other. There is a sense in which this is true, but it is only technically true. What is meant when we use the phrase 'maintaining competition' is maintaining competitive conditions. We can both create and maintain competitive conditions, and, until human nature is revolutionized, when competitive conditions exist there will be actual competition."[6]

COMPETITION INVOLVES MORE THAN SUBSTITUTION OF GOODS

Price competition *plus* freedom of entry for potential competitors are described by various economists and antitrust experts as "effective competi-

[6] *Control of Corporations, Persons, and Firms Engaged in Interstate Commerce*, Senate Report 1326, 62nd Congress, third session, February 26, 1913.

tion," "complete competition," "market competition," or "practically attainable competition." In its essential nature, *effective competition analogous to that found in open markets is the type of competition called for by the antitrust laws.* (See also Fig. 22, facing p. 226.)

The so-called "new," "modern" definition of "effective competition," proposed by the Business Advisory Council of the U.S. Dept. of Commerce, Mr. D. E. Lilienthal, and others, differs from the concept of effective competition adopted in this book and long used by economists and the antitrust agencies. According to the Council, "effective competition is defined as that business rivalry, existing and potential, which tends over a period of years to serve the public interest in (a) providing alternatives and thus giving opportunities for freedom of choice of goods and services; and (b) not restricting the opportunity for others to engage in such competition."[7] In a similar way, Mr. Lilienthal describes competition as rivalry "between different ways of meeting the same or a similar need or demand for goods and services."[8] Upon the basis of these definitions, competition is seen to be provided through the choices of aluminum or copper, cigarettes or sweets. In so defining "effective competition," the Council and others omit an essential feature for the determination of prices—namely, independent price competition among sellers of a given class of goods. This omission nullifies the idea of competition as a price-making mechanism. In economics, as well as in the law, independent price competition has long been recognized as an essential condition (a) for moderating "all the traffic will bear" and (b) for providing a selling outlet at which business can be done.

In a broad sense, competition of some sort is universal and everywhere. Always there are limits and restraints on the willingness of consumers to continue buying certain goods at higher prices. Substitute competition is an important moderating force. The competition afforded by substitutes, however, does not prevent the placing of undue burdens on the public. Everyone entering a market *to buy* prefers *price competition* among sellers. Similarly, a seller prefers to have competition on the buying prices for his products.

Various industry groups and their spokesmen seek to make *substitute competition* the standard called for by the antitrust laws because in numerous segments of the economy open, aboveboard price competition does not exist.

A PRICE MECHANISM FOR BASIC COMMODITIES

The principles of market competition can be applied to the determination of the price of any commodity the units of which are standardized or physically homogeneous. Market goods must be alike in kind (as cocoa beans) and approximately the same in quality, for otherwise buyers will not be willing to shift to other sellers who may offer a better price, and a uni-

[7] *Effective Competition*, Report to the Secretary of Commerce Charles Sawyer by his Business Advisory Council, Washington, D.C., December 22, 1952, p. 11.

[8] D. E. Lilienthal, *Big Business* (New York, 1953), p. 58.

form or "going" price will not develop. It is sometimes said that in market exchange the "principle of indifference" must apply. This principle means that the various lots of a market good must be equally fit or suitable for meeting the needs of a substantial part of the buyers. It is not necessary that the goods be "perfectly homogeneous."[9] Most, if not all, parcels of natural products—such as grains, fibers, minerals, and animals—as well as semiprocessed goods—such as hides, tallow, cheese, and molasses—differ somewhat in quality. This fact, however, does not exclude the possibility of market exchange. As long as the various lots can be used interchangeably in meeting the needs of a substantial group of buyers in a given market (and a considerable power of substitution exists), there is sufficient similarity for competitive pricing. A "going" price will be established for a given class of products—Hard Red Spring Wheat, for instance—and quality differences will find expression in price differentials.[10]

Market competition is a price-making mechanism which is primarily applicable to the sale of the basic commodities—iron, steel, copper, lead, zinc, tin, petroleum, gasoline, sugar, molasses, rice, tallow, linseed oil, naval stores, tobacco, wheat, coffee, cocoa, wool, cotton, crude rubber, cement, lumber, cheese, and canned foods. It is at this level, moreover, that the establishment of fair and equitable prices is particularly important. If all individuals can secure the basic materials of production at fair prices and without restraint, the very number of fabricating users will ordinarily insure consumer protection in the sale of highly processed, specialized articles. Various types of toothpaste, for example, are substitute products; and the competition offered by substitutes (substitute competition) is an important factor serving to prevent excessive demands by single sellers whose trademarks may give them elements of monopoly power.

TYPES OF MARKETS

Markets in which the forces of supply and demand find their greatest centralizing are called "primary" markets. These markets are "funnels" through which supplies from a large area—or even the nation—are concentrated for shipment to hundreds of local markets. In such cases the general level of prices for a commodity is determined by a balancing of the centralized forces of demand and supply. Prices in the local and lesser markets—in production as well as in consumption areas—are largely a reflection of the

[9] The concepts of "pure" and "perfect" competition are useful as norms for theoretic and assumptive reasoning. However, they contain elements of perfection which do not make them practically attainable.

[10] The use of official standards for grain and cotton is now mandatory in interstate commerce. No. 1 Hard Red Spring Wheat, for example, must weigh at least 60 lb. per bushel; and it cannot contain more than 2 percent damaged kernels, 1 percent foreign material, and 5 percent wheats of other classes. U.S. Department of Agriculture, *Handbook of Official Grain Standards of the United States* (Washington, 1947), p. 3. Specific lots of Hard Red Spring Wheat which are better in quality bring slight premiums; lots which are inferior sell at a discount.

prices established in a primary market. Examples of primary market centers include the Chicago Board of Trade, the Chicago Union Stock Yards, the Boston wool market, and the New York Stock Exchange.

In many cases the products of a large production area are concentrated at a central point—as a large city—for local fabrication or use. New York City, for example, is a great consuming center for fruits and vegetables. Such market gatherings are called "central" or "terminal" markets. The concentration of supplies in a central market is usually sufficient to give it a primacy in determining prices, and prices at the various collection points or local markets are adjusted to the going price in the central market.

A market concourse may be either (1) a formally organized market—as a commodity exchange—or (2) an informal gathering of buyers and sellers. An example of a "formal" market is the Chicago Board of Trade, in which buyers and sellers are formally brought together on a trading floor (see Fig. 4). Examples of "informal" markets, on the other hand, are the wool market on Summer Street in Boston, the cotton textile market on Worth Street in New York City, and the fruit and vegetable market on Washington Street in New York City (see Fig. 5).

Primary and central markets are sometimes called "wholesale" markets, since the goods are bought and sold in large quantities for resale. In "retail" markets, on the other hand, sales are made in small quantities to the ultimate consumers. The best examples of retail markets are to be found in the municipal markets which most large cities maintain for the sale of local farm produce. A group of retail stores and shops in a town may be said to constitute a local market if the goods are sold under substantially the same conditions. If, however, the shops differ widely in the type of business done (such as cash and carry, credit and delivery), in the surroundings and facilities offered, or in location, buyers will not be able to compare and choose with indifference. Under such conditions, some sellers can charge more than others and still retain a substantial group of customers, and the various retail stores and shops may be said to constitute a market only in a partial and limited sense.

GOVERNMENT REGULATION OF MARKETS

The term "free market" is frequently used to designate trading activities in which there is an absence of *direct* governmental controls on prices, sales, or credit. This concept is partially correct, but it is not complete. The idea of free markets also includes a freedom of persons to enter the market, to have access to supplies, and to buy and sell on the same conditions as anyone else. Free markets, in this complete sense, are not self-realizing institutions. The lessons of history indicate clearly that if markets are to be free and open, government must provide rules and regulations for trading activity.

Government regulation of central and primary markets has largely taken the form of prohibiting various manipulative abuses which arise when the volume of trading is small or when market information is inadequate or misleading. Thus, the *Grain Futures Act*, passed by Congress in *1922*, was de-

Fig. 4. The trading floor of the Chicago Board of Trade showing the wheat pit in the foreground and the corn pit in the background. The wheat and corn markets are primary markets of a "formal" type. (Courtesy of the Chicago Board of Trade.)

Fig. 5. The New York City wholesale produce market located on Washington Street in lower Manhattan. This photograph illustrates a central market of an "informal" type. The Washington Street market handles about one-eighth of all the fresh fruits and vegetables marketed in the United States. It represents the type of central produce market existing in most large eastern cities. (Courtesy of U.S. Department of Agriculture.)

signed to prevent manipulative and misleading practices on the organized commodity exchanges. This legislation was amended in *1936* and was given the title of the *Commodity Exchange Act*. It is applicable to twenty-one commodities. It also creates a Commodity Exchange Authority to supervise trading in the eighteen principal commodity markets located throughout the country (see Table 12). The commodities covered by the act include wheat, corn, oats, barley, rye, flaxseed, grain sorghums, cotton, rice, mill-feeds, butter, eggs, Irish potatoes, wool tops, cottonseed meal, cottonseed, peanuts, soybeans, soybean meal, and fats and oil. All "futures transactions" in these commodities must be made on an exchange designated as a contract market. This rule, it may be noted, is equivalent to the medieval law against "forestalling"—that is, the purchase or sale of goods before they had reached the open market. Provision is also made for the registration of all commission men, brokers, and merchants dealing on the exchanges, and the Commodity Exchange Authority itself is clothed with numerous regulatory duties.

The Commodity Exchange Authority exercises constant watch over daily trading activities in the designated terminal markets to preserve and insure their open and competitive status. This supervision stands in sharp contrast to the absence of supervision which government exercises over the sale of primary *industrial* commodities—such as iron and steel, cement, and the nonferrous metals. In supervising the futures markets, C.E.A. employees go to the trading floors and watch for any activity which might indicate price manipulation, corners, or "squeezes." Their objective is to prevent the development of undesirable practices and transactions, if possible. When illegal acts do occur, they collect evidence and initiate administrative or criminal proceedings.

In summary form, the chief regulatory activities of the Commodity Exchange Authority consist of the following functions: (1) to prevent price manipulation and corners, (2) to prevent the spreading of false and misleading information, (3) to protect hedgers against fraud and cheating, (4) to insure the benefits of exchange membership to coöperatives, (5) to require trust fund treatment of margin deposits, and (6) to provide information to the public on the volume of trading and open contracts to be fulfilled by delivery and acceptance. The Commodity Exchange Authority maintains five field offices, and its accountants and auditors conduct regular and special investigations to see if the provisions of the act are being observed. If violations appear to exist, charges may be filed; and the Authority is empowered to revoke "registration" as a penalty for noncompliance. If the violations are found to be criminal in nature, the evidence is turned over to the Department of Justice.[11] (See also Table 9.)

In 1934 Congress passed the Securities Exchange Act to protect investors and the public against various abuses practiced by certain corporations,

---

[11] For additional material on the Commodity Exchange Act, see *Commodity Exchange Act and Commodity Exchange Authority*, U.S. Department of Agriculture, Leaflet 330, 1952; and the annual reports of the Commodity Exchange Authority.

TABLE 12.   Principal Commodity Markets Under Federal
Regulation.

Chicago Board of Trade
Chicago Mercantile Exchange
Chicago Open Board of Trade
Duluth Board of Trade
Kansas City Board of Trade
Los Angeles Grain Exchange
Memphis Merchants Exchange Clearing Association
Milwaukee Grain Exchange
Minneapolis Grain Exchange
New Orleans Cotton Exchange
New York Cotton Exchange
New York Mercantile Exchange
New York Produce Exchange
Portland Grain Exchange
San Francisco Grain Exchange
Seattle Grain Exchange
St. Louis Merchants Exchange
Wool Associates of the New York Cotton Exchange, Inc.

---

brokers, and dealers on the national securities exchanges and in the over-the-counter (informal) markets for securities. The act provides for the registration with the Securities and Exchange Commission (1) of the national securities exchanges and of all companies whose securities are listed and registered on the exchanges, (2) of all brokers and dealers who are engaged in over-the-counter dealings, and (3) of the national associations of security brokers and dealers. Provision is made in the act for the filing of periodic reports by all companies whose securities are listed on the exchanges, and rules are established for the disclosure of information to stockholders on proposals upon which they are asked to vote. Regulations are also established to curb the improper use of "inside" information by corporate officers and directors. The act provides for the formulation of just and equitable rules of trading and prohibits misrepresentation, market manipulation, deception, and other fraudulent practices in the sale of securities. (See also Chap. 19.)

THE PROVISION OF PRICE PUBLICITY

The principal regulatory measure which Congress has adopted in relation to the informal markets for commodities is found in the market news service provided by the U.S. Department of Agriculture. In response to complaints from farmers and farm organizations that bids for farm products were being artificially reduced, that quoted prices were not the "going" prices, and that market supplies were being manipulated to produce gluts and low prices, Congress in 1913 provided funds for the Department of Agriculture to collect and publish useful information on the marketing of farm products. As a result of this legislation, the Department began in 1915 to issue daily market reports on fruits and vegetables, covering shipments to market centers, supplies on hand in market centers, and current market prices. In 1916 a market news service was established for the marketing of meats; in 1918, for live-stock, dairy, and poultry products, as well as for hay, feed, and grain; in 1919, for cotton; in 1924, for wool; and in 1931, for tobacco.

Staff members in the market news offices secure price and sales data by checking sales slips, by interviewing buyers and sellers, and by securing reports on shipments from the railroads and trucking companies. A great deal of effort is made to get the news out to the public while it is timely. Local and central market information is transmitted to some 87 market news offices by a leased wire system. It is then released to the public through mailed reports, newspapers, radios, bulletin boards, personal contact, telephone, and telegraph. Market reports on various commodities are sent free of charge to persons requesting them.

At the present time, the Department of Agriculture collects and disseminates market information on prices, supplies, demand, and shipments for all major agricultural commodities in the principal central markets and producing areas. The commodities covered include livestock, meats, wool, fresh fruits and vegetables, dairy and poultry products, grain, hay, feed, cotton, cottonseed, tobacco, rice, honey, blackstrap molasses, and naval stores.[12]

The provision of publicity on prices, sales, and supplies is an indispensable condition for the effective functioning of price competition. It is only when buyers and sellers are well informed on market conditions that they can objectively analyze market forces and buy and sell in an intelligent manner. If government is to fulfill its declared policy of maintaining competition and preventing monopolistic practices, it should provide an adequate price- and sales-reporting system for *all* the basic commodities—industrial as well as agricultural. Various trade publications and trade associations are engaged in price-reporting activities in the industrial field, but in many instances the data either are not for public use or are not completely reliable. Since trade members and trade associations are interested parties, the reporting of price and sales statistics should be handled by some quasi-public organization—such as a commodity or securities exchange—or by the government itself. (See also Chap. 11.)

THE DETERMINATION OF MARKET PRICE

True market price under competitive conditions is a price whose level is determined by the balancing of the forces of demand and supply—that is, the quantities of goods demanded and supplied. Its determination depends upon a centralizing of these forces as they exist over a considerable area. The centralization may be expressed either by a concourse of buyers and sellers in an exchange or by the informal grouping of dealers, brokers, and other trade interests in a certain district or along a certain street.

Before engaging in buying or selling, each trader carefully studies the

[12] Further data on the Federal Market News Service may be secured by writing to the Production and Marketing Administration, U.S. Department of Agriculture, Washington 25, D.C.

statistics of demand and supply, the market news, and the prices of the last transactions. Some buyer and seller thereupon strike a bargain, and market exchange begins. The first transactions, it may be assumed, are made at $4 per unit. This fact will quickly become known to all traders either by means of a ticker tape or by some other means of price publicity. If more units are offered at $4 than will be taken at that price, some anxious seller or sellers—having lower asking prices—will thereupon decrease their offers *in order to be able to deal.* Thereupon a series of bargains will be made at a series of individual prices which are uniform to the customers of each seller. Between sellers, moreover, the prices tend to be uniform in any certain brief period. No one will bid above the "going price" or offer to sell below it, unless a preponderance of demand or of supply develops at that figure. The market price is said to be the "going price" because it consists of a continuing series of prices on transactions *currently* being made.[13]

The prices established in a market concourse are for the commodity in and at the central market. Market price is a freightless price. If delivered prices are quoted, they are f.o.b. shipping point prices plus actual freight from the place of sale to destination.[14]

THE MEANING OF THE TERM "PRICE COMPETITION"

Price competition means independent rivalry on price between two or more persons in selling or buying certain goods, each being governed by his own valuations and not restrained in his actions by any agreement or coercion. The operation of price competition *among sellers* can be observed most vividly when there is a preponderance of supply over demand at the going price. Sellers having lower latent valuations decrease their offers because they want to be able to deal. They act independently and as individuals in quoting a price at which they can sell. The price so established tends to become the current price (or equilibrium price) at which transactions by other sellers are made. Price competition *among buyers*, on the other hand, can be observed when there is a preponderance of demand over supply. Some

[13] Actual data on the transactions and prices which occur in a particular market during the course of a given day may be found by consulting the reports of various organized markets. The following data from a daily report of the Chicago Mercantile Exchange are typical: "Eggs—in cents a dozen; cars of 600 cases each. Refg. U.S. Ex. No. 2—October delivery: *9:00 to 9:25 a.m.*—2 cars at 40.75; 2 at 40.80; 2 at 40.85; 5 at 40.75. *9:25 to 9:30 a.m*—9 cars at 40.60; 5 at 40.65; 5 at 40.70. *9:30 a.m.*—20 cars at 40.75. *9:35–9:45 a.m.*—4 cars at 40.75; 1 at 40.70; 6 at 40.75," and so on during the trading period.

[14] In making delivery of a commodity purchased in a formal market—such as the Chicago Board of Trade—the usual practice is to tender warehouse receipts issued by approved warehouses located in the market center. The buyer then has to pay the actual freight to destination. In informal markets prices are quoted f.o.b. the central market or f.o.b. the mill if direct delivery is made. The term "f.o.b." stands for "free on board." It means that a seller will place the product "on board" a freight car, truck, or other means of conveyance at the site of his mill or warehouse. It means also that it is up to the buyer to pay the freight. The f.o.b. price is one which is equal and open to all customers of a given seller at the same time and under the same conditions.

buyer or buyers having higher latent valuations raise their "bid" prices in order to be able to buy, and the going price moves upward to a new equilibrium level.

Price competition, in open markets, it may be noted, is not a fierce, brutal, fatal, blind, vicious, discriminatory sort of activity; nor is it a coöperative, price-matching procedure, in which rivals compete only by means of sales effort or advertising. Market competition is rather an open, aboveboard, independent, nondiscriminatory sort of rivalry *on price* which sellers or buyers engage in without fear of "retaliation." In initiating a price reduction, a seller not only secures a temporary advantage in making sales but also contributes to the making of a price at which business can be done. In the words of a long-established metal dealer, "The best of us may be wrong, but of what use to be right if we cannot deal?" Price competition operates to make a price which will equilibrate demand and supply, and promote a full employment of productive facilities.

Sellers or buyers in an open market do not exercise an influence upon market price intentionally and arbitrarily as they please, for it is determined by a balancing of market forces. Sellers, for example, cannot make some buyers pay more than the "going price" to other buyers as they can when they enjoy monopoly control in certain areas.

Competition may occur not only on price but also with respect to quality, service, advertising, and sales effort. Rivalry to give better quality or service is clearly in the public interest. It is important, however, to have both quality *and* price competition. Quality or service competition operates to give consumers a choice of qualities and enables them to put pressure on sellers to improve the qualities offered. Price competition, on the other hand, serves to protect buyers (or sellers) from extortion and coercion by providing alternative sources of supply (or demand) and independent action with respect to price quotations. Price competition also serves to increase the total number of units of goods sold for the same dollar expenditure by consumers. With price competition, the gains of technological progress are passed on to consumers in the form of more and better goods at lower prices. The competitive activities of railroads in offering free pillows or bigger baked potatoes do not permit the general public to travel more widely; nor do free post cards, free air, water, and other services enable motorists to buy more gasoline. Quality and service competition are incomplete forms of market competition. They should be considered only as partial characteristics of a complete competition in which price competition, as well as quality and service competition, reflects and represents the changing forces of demand and supply.

SOME FEATURES OF MARKET PRICE

The price which is established by market competition may be characterized as the "going" price on actual transactions, the highest price at which market supplies find a selling outlet, and as a price whose level is influenced by supply and demand factors. Some of the features of market price which account for its being the norm and standard for public price policy are the following:

1. *A market price is one which makes trade mutually advantageous to both parties.* A merchant's saying, although loosely expressed, is that there is at least a 20 percent difference between the lowest amount that a seller would take and the most that a buyer would pay. This represents an advantage which an anxious seller in isolated exchange can be forced to forego, or a necessitous buyer can be forced to pay. In an open market, however, buyers and sellers reach a compromise between their fundamentally opposite interests and establish a basis on which they may exchange to their mutual advantage. When price competition exists among sellers, excessive prices which leave buyers almost no motive to buy cannot long exist, for only a small amount of business can be done at such prices. Some sellers are willing to take less in order to be able to deal. On the other hand, when there is competition among the buyers, prices which are "too low" are quickly bid up in the scramble to make purchases.

2. *The market price of each seller is uniform to all buyers at a given time, and the prices of various sellers tend toward uniformity.* In isolated trading, with inadequate price publicity, or under monopolistic conditions a particular commodity is commonly sold at the same time at a variety of prices. The resulting price variations may reflect differences in the urgency to buy or sell, in the ability of the various parties to pay, as well as in the importance of the uses to which the good may be put. In a market, however, buyers and sellers are approximately informed of demand and supply conditions and of the prices at which transactions are being made. Since transactions are made openly, no buyer will pay a given seller more than other buyers are paying. A seller, moreover, will have no reason to ask less from one buyer than from another (unless he is motivated by charity or sentiment). *The price of each seller is thus uniform to all buyers at a given time in an open market.* When a seller in an open market *meets* the lower offers of other sellers (made when there is a preponderance of supply over demand), he does so in order to be able to deal *at all;* and the new price so established *nets him* the same amount on *all* transactions currently being made.[15]

The principle of indifference may be applied to the behavior of a seller in a competitive market. All sales at any one time *net* a competitive seller the same amount, and any given seller is thus indifferent as to whose money he will take. When shipping goods into a central market, a given seller in a

---

[15] Under monopolistic conditions, a geographically separate mill with local monopoly power may charge a high mill net price in its adjacent territory and take a lower mill net on sales made in another sales area. Matching or "meeting" the price of a distant seller by absorbing freight—and taking a lower mill net *on a part* of one's sales—should be carefully distinguished from the action of a seller *acting competitively* in a market in quoting a lower price *on all of his sales* in order to meet the lower quotations which are being made by a rival. Regular and systematic price matching by absorbing freight is a special device of monopoly. See also chap. 17.

supply area will not take less from one prospective buyer than from another. As one country shipper of wheat expressed it, "Why would I sell at divergent prices?" The highest bids attract the product; and if the offerings exceed demand, the bids will decline until supply and demand tend toward equality. Although a country shipper of wheat may ship it to several central markets, the sales all *net* him the same amount at his shipping point at the same time. Even a difference of a quarter of a cent in the net returns will mean that the grain is sent to one market center rather than to another. Thus it is that in shipping into a competitive market a given seller *in an area of supply* receives the same net f.o.b. price on all of his sales at any one time.

In the hearings of the Federal Trade Commission on the use of the basing-point plan in the cement industry, Professor Edward A. Duddy of the University of Chicago testified that he did not know of any agricultural producer who received different net prices at his shipping point at the same time from different purchasers. In his words, "The producer typically and always, so far as I know, sells at the price which will yield him the highest net return."[16] Likewise, Professor Benjamin H. Hibbard of the University of Wisconsin testified that a wheat producer or dealer will send his products "to the point where he has reason to believe he will get the highest price and will not parcel it out here and there at differing prices."[17]

In an open market at a given time, *the prices of the various sellers tend toward uniformity*. It is sometimes said that the prices of various sellers in a market are *identical*. This is rarely, if ever, true. Slight differences in quality, reputation, and service rendered, especially in informal markets, may make for small price differentials among the various sellers. Within a given physical market, moreover, the location of sellers in separate shops or stalls may result in incomplete market information, and prices of the various sellers may not be fully and completely uniform. The prices of all sellers in a given market, however, are constantly tending toward uniformity because of publicity and the action of buyers in quickly turning to other sellers when prices appear to be out of line. A commercial maxim states, "There are no friends in the grain business for a quarter of a cent."

The concept of a uniform price in a market applies to a particular moment of time. Over a period of time, the current price or prices vary in a succession like a cinematic picture, with changes in the forces of demand and supply.

The complete and absolute identity of prices among sellers is generally considered by economists to reflect "managed pricing" or "managed competition" (a monopolistic condition). Other indicators of monopoly or ineffective competition are price rigidity (absolute constancy) over a period of weeks or several months, and variations in the mill-net prices received by an individual seller. (See also Chap. 9.)

[16] *Cement Institute et al.* v. *F.T.C., Transcript of Testimony*, U.S. Court of Appeals for the Seventh Circuit, Vol. 7, pp. 15269, 15284, 15326 (filed September 1, 1943).

[17] *Ibid.*, Vol. 8, p. 15427.

3. *Market price is a price at which transactions can actually be made.* The presence of many buyers and sellers in a primary or central market gives rise to a continuous series of transactions, and current prices are the resultant of current forces of supply and demand. At a moment's notice, any buyer can actually buy and any seller can actually sell at a price which approximates the prevailing level. Any preponderance of supply is corrected by lower offers, and any preponderance of demand is quickly offset by higher bids. With market competition, prices so high that little can be sold or prices so low that nothing can be bought simply do not exist.

The management of prices by monopoly control—rather than by a balancing of market forces—invariably results in overproduction or in unused capacity. The interest of a private monopoly group is not in moving all available supplies, but rather in curbing sales or production in order to enhance profits. Only those quantities will be produced which can be sold at the fixed prices. Under such conditions, society is denied the full fruits of technological progress. When government manages price, moreover, it must justify its sales policies to the producers; and political good will inevitably requires the maintenance of high prices, at the cost of unsold surpluses or restrictions on production.

THE ECONOMIC LAW OF MARKET AREAS

The uniform, "going" price in an open market prevails at the market place —a street, a district in a town, a trading floor, or a terminal point where buyers and sellers are formally or informally congregated. First-hand producers located away from a central market (as wheat farmers in North Dakota and Montana) must stand the cost of transporting goods to the market, and delivery charges on shipments away from a central market are an addition to the market price which must be paid by the scattered buyers. In a market, commodities are always bought and sold on the basis of their location at the market center. *Net realized prices* at various points of production (at a farm or mill) are less than the price in the primary or central market by an amount equal to the cost of transportation to the market. Likewise, *delivered prices* at various destination points are higher than the central market price by the actual costs of delivery.

Every market center has a contiguous area from which the market goods are drawn and a natural sales area into which they flow. In some instances, the centralized supply is used locally (as produce in a large city like New York); in other cases the market supplies move outward to scattered destination points or local markets (as wheat from the primary market in Chicago).

The fact that every market center has a natural sales area (or buying area) has given rise to a formalized statement on the appropriate market areas of two or more markets. Thus, the boundary line between the sales areas of two geographically separated markets is a curve or line of indifference. At any point on this line the delivered costs from the two markets are equal. The economic law of market areas is the principle that two or more geographically separate market centers have a natural sales (or buying) area which is determined by prices in the separate markets and freight costs.

Assuming that market prices at A and B in Fig. 6 are $30 per unit and that freight rates are proportional to distance, the boundary line between the respective *sales areas* is the perpendicular bisector of a line between A and B. At each point on this line, the delivered costs from A and B are equal. If the

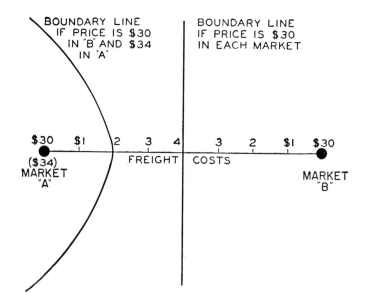

Fig. 6. A bird's-eye view of the sales area of two geographically separate markets. Assuming that freight costs are proportional to distance, the boundary line between two geographically separate markets is a series of points at which delivered costs from the two markets are equal. If the market price in A rises from $30 to $34 per unit, the delivered cost at the margin will be $36 from each market; and sellers in B will serve customers in a wider area. Shipments cannot profitably be made all the way from B to A, however, and producers at A will continue to have an advantageous sales area.

market price in one market rises in relation to the market price in another locally separate market, its natural sales area will be reduced in size. In Fig. 6, for example, if it is assumed that the market price rises to $34 per unit, the boundary line will shift toward A as shown on the diagram. At each point on the new boundary line, the difference in freight costs from the two markets is just equal to the difference in the market prices. If, by chance, the price in A should rise to $38 per unit, sellers in B would ship all the way into A and sell on equal terms with those in A.[18]

[18] Businessmen have long recognized that market areas are limited spheres separate from, but related to, each other by the prices prevailing in adjoining market centers plus the respective freight rates therefrom. In the action brought by the Department of Justice to dissolve the United States Steel Corporation (1912–1920) Elbert H. Gary, chairman of the corporation, testified, "Freight rates are very largely the determining elements in

SUMMARY

Competition is the established economic and legal policy for most kinds of business activity. In economics, as well as in the law, the term means (1) freedom of entry and (2) independent price competition in buying and selling. The standard or ideal for competition is the kind of competition found in open markets—such as the Chicago grain market or the Boston wool market. In central markets, competition is nondiscriminatory, open, and aboveboard.

When there is no legal restraint on a person's activity in offering (or buying) goods of a given class, and no private agreement or coercion—actual or implied—among sellers (or buyers), there is possible the kind of "workable" or "effective" competition (never "perfect") called for by the antitrust laws.

Every seller, in a degree, is competing with every other seller of goods and services for the buyer's money. The universal substitution of goods, which is constantly going on, is best described as *substitute competition*. The fact that a given product (such as aluminum) touches in some directions the competition of a substitute (such as copper) does not insure protection against extortion. *Price* competition *among* sellers of a given class of goods (such as aluminum) operates more fully to moderate all that the "traffic will bear" and holds sellers to a moderate profit.

Competition among sellers in a given industry may occur not only on price, but also with respect to quality, service, advertising, sales effort, and so forth. Rivalry to give better quality or service is clearly in the public interest. There is error, however, in identifying most quality and service competition with *price* competition. Quality or service competition tends to change the relative quantity of sales going to each seller; it does not operate to increase *total* sales—or provide a selling outlet for large supplies and expanding outputs. Free post cards, air, and water do not enable motorists to buy more gasoline. From the standpoint of public policy, the desired type of competition is (1) freedom of entry and (2) price competition of an individual, spontaneous, independent type, among sellers, as well as buyers, within a given industry.

Glossary of Terms Used with Reference to Competition in Public Policy

Effective Competition; Practically Attainable Competition: (a) independent rivalry on price among numerous sellers; (b) the freedom and capability of others to enter the market whenever producers for any considerable period maintain a margin between price and cost which is more than enough to afford a moderate profit; and (c) market information, as accurate and complete as possible. The same conditions apply *mutatis mutandis* on the side of buyers.

---

markets (sales areas) for any commodity, and those markets are susceptible of mathematical demonstration by reason of the freight rates." Quoted in Federal Trade Commission, *Report to the President on Steel Sheet Piling* (Washington, 1936), p. 36.

Effective competition may occur when sellers (and buyers) are few, but it is more likely to occur when they are numerous. When rivals are few in number, parallel action on prices is likely to result, with or without explicit agreement. See also Edward H. Chamberlin, *The Theory of Monopolistic Competition* (Cambridge, 1942), pp. 46–55. Under conditions of effective competition, any given firm does not control such a large percentage of the supply of a certain class of goods that it is able to make the "going price" which as an actual fact will be largely observed in the industry.

Freedom of Competition; Freedom of Enterprise: The right of producers to follow a line of business of their own choice without interference or dictation by other producers or by government.

The terms are used to designate the freedom of enterprisers to choose a line of business, to have access to supplies, and to buy and sell on the same conditions as anyone else.

Refusal to sell supplies to enterprises which exercise any degree of independence on sales policies and prices, cutthroat or predatory competition, or any pressure from others restraining an enterpriser from acting in accordance with his interests, is an interference with freedom of enterprise. Licenses and other legal interferences (such as bounties and subsidies) imposed for *restrictive* purposes, rather than for revenue or for insuring competence, are a limitation on freedom of competition.

Freedom of enterprise does not mean that business firms are free to compete as they please, without rules and penalties. If competition is to be a contest of efficiency in the public interest, experience shows, there must be government intervention (1) to insure freedom of entry and (2) to prescribe and police ground rules for the conduct of competitive activity.

Perfect Competition: This term assumes perfect knowledge, perfect homogeneity, and other elements of perfection which are conceivable, but never perfectly realized. *Pure competition* is similar to perfect competition, but assumes limited market information. Both terms are useful in assumptive reasoning, but they do not provide a practically attainable standard or model for public policy. As J. M. Clark has said, we must start with the "recognition that all practicable forms of competition are 'imperfect,' and that the 'perfect competition' of economic theory is academic. Doctrinaire insistence on perfection, in competition or in antitrust policy, is a mistake." *Guideposts in Time of Change* (New York, 1949), p. 143.

Price Competition: Independent rivalry on price between two or more persons in selling or buying certain goods, each being governed by his own valuations and not restrained in his actions by any agreement or coercion—actual or implied.

Sellers' competition moderates "all the traffic will bear," and the competitive price is lower than the price when competition among sellers is ineffective or restrained. Price competition results in a tendency on the part of sellers to sell at lower prices than their competitors, and a tendency on the part of buyers to buy at higher prices than competing buyers—each in an effort to increase his sales or purchases.

Workable Competition: This phrase is frequently used to designate the concept of "Effective Competition" as discussed above. Professor Edward S.

Mason defines the phrase as follows: "Workable competition is considered to require, principally, a fairly large number of sellers and buyers, no one of whom occupies a large share of the market, the absence of collusion among either group, and the possibility of market entry by new firms." *Harvard Law Review*, June, 1949, p. 1268.

George J. Stigler gives the following definition: "An industry is workably competitive when (1) there are a considerable number of firms selling closely related products in each important market area, (2) these firms are not in collusion, and (3) the long-run average cost curve for a new firm is not materially higher than that for an established firm." *American Economic Review*, Supplement, June 1942, pp. 2–3.

SUGGESTIONS FOR FURTHER READING

Battin, Charles T., "The Competitive Position of the Chicago Potato Market," *Journal of Business of the University of Chicago*, April, 1935, pp. 111–142.

Demant, V. A. (ed.), *The Just Price* (London, 1930).

Duddy, E. A., "The Potential Supply Area of the Chicago Livestock Market," *Journal of Farm Economics*, October, 1932, pp. 586–598.

Fellner, William, *Competition Among the Few* (New York, 1949).

Machlup, Fritz, *The Economics of Sellers' Competition* (Baltimore, 1952).

McIsaac, Archibald, *Elements of Economic Analysis* (New York, 1950).

Stigler, George J., *The Theory of Price* (New York, 1952).

Waite, Warren C. and Trelogan, Harry C., *Agricultural Market Prices* (New York, 1948).

Weintraub, Sidney, *Price Theory* (New York, 1949).

Worcester, Dean A. Jr., *Fundamentals of Political Economy* (New York, 1953).

CHAPTER 7

Business Corporations and Financial Mergers

A striking characteristic of the American economy is the fact that a few thousand corporations dominate the principal industries. Actually, it has been estimated that some 113 of the larger industrial corporations own nearly one-half of all the net capital assets used in manufacturing. The leading corporations also exercise an even greater control over other firms by means of interlocking directorates, personal ties, agreements, and other arrangements for securing unified action. Under such conditions, it is obviously impossible for government to maintain individual, independent, spontaneous price competition of the type found in central and primary markets.

What have been the causes of the vast growth of giant corporations in the American economy? One view holds that large corporations have come about as a result of a natural evolution, and that they reflect the growing demands of modern technology and national methods of distribution. Upon the basis of this view, it is held that government can or should do little or nothing to decentralize or dissolve the corporate giants. Spokesmen for large corporations have done much to foster the acceptance of the natural-evolution, technological theory of the corporation problem.

Another view with respect to giant corporations is that they have come to replace the many thousands of independent, competing, single-plant corporations because of deliberate changes in our corporation laws. These changes have made it possible for a corporation with large financial resources (1) to hold and vote the stock of other corporations, (2) to combine scores of locally separate, formerly competing plants, (3) to engage in many diverse kinds of business operations, (4) to form subsidiaries without limitation, and (5) to utilize the special powers of corporate organization without assuming specific obligations and responsibilities in the public interest. This view looks upon giant corporations as being largely the artificial result of unwise legislative action taken under the guidance of corporation lawyers for clients seeking greater corporation privileges. Persons taking this view believe that our present corporation laws should be changed (a) to limit the powers granted and (b) to require specific responsibilities, both corporate and personal, to stockholders and the public, to match the powers conferred by charter.

The purpose of the present chapter is to analyze the nature of business corporations and to survey the action which has been taken by the state and federal governments with respect to their creation. Consideration will also be given to the factors which have made possible the present-day situation of financial mergers and supercorporations.

CORPORATIONS A CREATION OF THE LAW

A corporation is a legal entity or body which is formally created by government. Such a legal body, it has been observed, "exists only on paper" and "is a mere conception of the legislative mind."[1] As a mental conception, a corporation is clothed with such powers and privileges as the legislature may give it. The main rights granted to a corporation are the power to own property, to make contracts, to sue and be sued, to own and vote the stock of other corporations, and usually, to have perpetual existence. A corporation itself is a very useful institution and has many advantages, both private and public. Like other human institutions, however, it may be abused by men whose final purpose is maximum business profit.

A group of persons seeking a corporate charter can now secure one through the secretary of state, of a state government, by paying the requisite fees and by complying with the laws of the state. Usually, the laws of the various states provide that a minimum of three persons must join in applying for a corporate charter and that a minimum of three must serve as directors. The owners of a corporation furnish the necessary capital and receive transferable shares in proportion to their contribution. Strictly speaking they—and not the corporation—are the capitalists.

A corporation is sometimes described as an artificial entity, having "neither a body to be kicked nor a soul to be damned." This description, in considerable degree, reflects the special legal status which has largely been given to corporations in the past.

At the present time, the narrow, legalistic view of corporations is coming to be replaced by a more realistic view which looks upon the persons who direct the corporation as being responsible for its acts. A corporation, it is beginning to be seen, cannot be separated from the individuals who conceive it and who will its acts, for the legal entity itself cannot will that anything be done. A corporation is simply a legal cloak for the people who do the willing. "All its power," a federal judge has declared, "resides in the directors. Inanimate and incapable of thought, action, or neglect, it cannot hear or obey the voice of the legislature except through its directors. It can neither act nor omit to act except through them."[2]

The stock of a corporation may be held by a few persons who are usually active in the conduct of the corporation's business ("close corporations"); by numerous, outside, public stockholders (publicly owned corporations); or by the government, itself (government-owned corporations). The great majority of the nation's 450,000 corporations are in the category of "close corporations." Corporations whose securities have a quoted market are clearly in the group of publicly owned corporations. An indication of the

[1] *People* v. *Knapp,* 99 N.E. 841, 844 (1912).
[2] *Ibid.*

number of such corporations may be found in the fact that some 3000 corporate stocks are traded on organized stock exchanges and some 5400 corporate stocks are bought and sold in over-the-counter markets.

COMPARATIVELY FEW BUSINESS CORPORATIONS CHARTERED PRIOR TO 1850

In granting the early corporate charters, public officials were much concerned about the privilege of continuity of existence. Individuals are mortal, and their personal accumulations of wealth and power are short-lived. Corporations, on the other hand, usually have a perpetual life. Their acquisitions of monopoly power, accordingly, may increase progressively and give them an undue political influence detrimental to the public welfare. It was for this reason that business corporations, when permitted at all, were regarded with suspicion and granted sparingly to certain types of business activity—such as banking and insurance—which required continuity of existence for their safe and successful operation. The common law also provided that corporate stock could be held and voted only by "natural persons."

In 1800 there were some 335 corporations in the United States, and most of these were enterprises engaged in operating banks, insurance companies, canals, turnpike roads, waterworks, and toll bridges. Only a few charters were granted to enterprises in general lines of business activity. The view of the legislators was that the possession of corporate charters was a privilege and not a right, and that they should be granted only to business firms having a close relationship to the public welfare.

Increasingly, enterprisers in general business came to see many advantages in the corporate device, and more and more requests were made to the state legislatures for corporate charters. The principal advantages which businessmen saw in the corporation were continuity of life, the opportunity to raise large sums of capital, and the privilege of limited liability. In business corporations the capital invested by the owners is represented by transferable "shares" or units of ownership, and the sale of shares to investors makes it possible to raise large sums of money for business purposes. An important privilege usually granted to business corporations, moreover, is that of limited liability. In general, this privilege means that a shareholder has no personal liability for the debts of the corporation, and that he stands to lose only the amount of his investment.

THE GRANTING OF CORPORATE CHARTERS BY THE STATES

Since most of the early companies requesting corporate charters were local enterprises, the state legislatures—rather than Congress—assumed the function of granting the charters. By 1850 the requests for charters had become so numerous that many states had made provision for general incorporation laws. These statutes made it possible for any group of businessmen to obtain a corporation charter simply by submitting certain information and paying a fee. The many applications for charters provided the states with a growing source of income; and in order to enhance this income, various states soon entered into a rivalry with one another for charter fees by granting increasingly liberal corporation privileges to all comers. The corporate charter—once a privilege which was conferred only to promote the public welfare—thereupon came to be sold by some states like a commodity for a price.[3]

Since business corporations, particularly with the extension of railroad lines after 1860, increasingly came to conduct an *interstate* business, Congress had a definite responsibility to provide rules and standards for all corporations operating in interstate commerce, by requiring either federal licenses or federal incorporation. As early as 1904 the Commissioner of Corporations recommended the adoption of a "federal franchise or license system for interstate commerce," so that standards could be imposed on corporate enterprises engaged in interstate or foreign commerce.[4] Some form of federal incorporation law has also been proposed by Presidents Theodore Roosevelt, Taft, and Wilson, and by many congressmen, especially Senators Borah and O'Mahoney. There is no doubt that Congress has the power to charter or license all companies operating in interstate commerce, but to date it has enacted only special incorporation laws, as for the national banks. The strong opposition of large business corporations to any legislation which would curb their privileges has been the principal factor preventing the adoption of this form of public regulation.

In describing the need for a federal incorporation statute, Dr. Charles A. Beard declared in 1937:

> I should like to emphasize the fact that our state and national governments have a responsibility for the corporate abuses and economic distress in which we now flounder. It is a matter of common knowledge that corporations are not natural persons. They are artificial persons. They are the creatures of government. Only on the authorization of government can they come into existence. Only with the sanction of government can they perform any acts, good or bad. The corporate abuses which have occurred, the concentration of wealth which has come about under their operations, all can be laid directly and immediately at the door of government. There is no escape from this responsibility. The states of the American Union and the Congress of the United States, by their actions and their inaction, have made possible the situation and the calamities in which we now find ourselves.[5]

CORPORATIONS AND THE FORMATION OF TRUSTS

The widely increased use of the corporate device as a means for conducting business activity soon after 1860 came at a time when the sales areas for business were rapidly being increased. Between 1850 and 1860 the rail lines of the country were extended at an unprecedented pace. In a very short

[3] W. Z. Ripley, *Main Street and Wall Street* (Boston, 1927).
[4] Federal Trade Commission, *Utility Corporations*, 70th Congress, first session, Senate Document No. 92, 1934, Part 69–A, pp. 4–5.
[5] Hearings Before a Subcommittee of the Committee on the Judiciary on S. 10, *Federal Licensing of Corporations*, 75th Congress, first session, 1937, Part 1, p. 72.

time it became possible for producers in various areas—such as Pittsburgh, Chicago, St. Louis, and Philadelphia—to sell not only in their own area but also in the "back yards" of other groups of producers. Increasingly, local producers who had been acting monopolistically in their local areas used their local monopoly power as a "cushion" for "cutting" prices in other sales areas to eliminate local producers or to bring them "in line" on price. Very often the larger companies or associations of producers were also able to secure discriminatory, preferential freight rates from the railroads, and these favors gave them an additional advantage over their competitors. Thus, the rapid growth of the Standard Oil Company between 1870 and 1880, it is reliably reported, was largely made possible by the rebates and preferential freight rates which it was able to secure from the railroads.[6]

As a result of the growth of discriminatory pricing in industry, as well as by the railroads, competition after 1870 became increasingly "cutthroat" and "chaotic." In an effort to escape the disastrous consequences of discriminatory pricing, and also to secure the private advantages of a wider monopoly control, business enterprises in various production centers formed "pools," "associations," and "loose-knit" combinations, in which they joined hands and made agreements with respect to prices and output. Continuous efforts were made to strengthen this unified action, and corporation lawyers seeking to promote the commercial interests of their clients hit upon the idea of making "trust" agreements. By this plan, the voting stock of competing corporations was assigned to a group of trustees in exchange for trust certificates. Thereupon, the trustees—a single agency—became able to hold the various enterprises securely in line on price, for a control of the corporate stock made it possible for the trustees to remove any recalcitrant plant manager at will.

The first use of the "trust" device appears to have been made by the Standard Oil Company. In 1882 John D. Rockefeller and associates formed a trust agreement with about forty companies which gave a group of nine trustees a control of 90 to 95 percent of the oil-refining capacity in the country. This control worked most effectively from their point of view. High prices and profits were secured; and with the coming of a business depression there was no price cutting or chaotic competition. Prices were maintained, although employment and production had to be sharply reduced. In competitive industry, on the other hand, prices and wages declined, production was maintained, and widespread unemployment did not develop. Similar "trusts" were formed in the production of cottonseed oil (1884), linseed oil (1885), whiskey (1887), sugar (1887), lead (1887), and cordage (1887).

THE CORPORATION BECOMES A STOCKHOLDER

The trusts had not been long in operation before legal proceedings were brought against them, and the threat of unfavorable court decisions forced corporation lawyers to search for a new method of monopoly control. This

[6] *Report of the Industrial Commission, Digest of Evidence* (Washington, 1900), Vol. 1, Part 1, p. 146.

was found in the idea that corporations could be given the right to purchase and vote the stock of competing enterprises. A corporation was created by the state; and if it were authorized by law to hold the securities of other companies, it was believed that the arrangement might escape public attack. The plan was presented to the New Jersey legislature, and in May, 1888, legislation was adopted providing that any corporation chartered in New Jersey could own and vote the stock of other corporations and issue its own stock in payment therefor. By this revolutionary act every corporation acquiring the stock of other corporations became in effect a "holding company."[7]

As was then expected, trust agreements were held by the courts to be illegal arrangements, and soon after 1890 business enterprises increasingly turned to New Jersey to secure corporate charters granting the holding company privilege. Some of the trust leaders which had escaped prosecution reorganized and formed corporations to hold the stock of competing companies, and other business concerns set about to control competition by buying up the stock of their competitors. The new trust movement was temporarily halted by the action of the federal government in applying the Sherman Act of 1890 against the American Sugar Refining Company, a New Jersey corporation, which had acquired a control of some 98 percent of the refined-sugar capacity in the United States. A decision of the Supreme Court was rendered in 1895. In it the Court held that manufacturing was not commerce; and that, therefore, industrial monopolies could be prosecuted only by the states. "The effect of this holding," Professor Corwin states, "was to put the Antitrust Act to sleep for a decade, during which period most of the great industrial trusts of today got their start."[8]

THE FIRST GREAT PERIOD OF CORPORATE MERGERS
(1897–1903)

With the general banning of the trust device as a means for securing monopoly control, and with the decision of the Supreme Court declaring that it was up to the states to deal with industrial monopolies, business leaders quickly resumed their use of the holding company device to secure a control over the prices and output of former competitors. The depression of 1893–1896 brought about a general collapse of the pools and informal agreements and gave emphasis to this movement. During the short period of 1897 to 1903, one or more corporations—usually chartered in New Jersey—were formed to acquire a control over important competing plants in the principal lines of industry. In some cases, the assets of competing plants were purchased outright, but usually a control was secured by purchasing their common stock. The use of the holding company privilege had the advantage of ena-

[7] In a strict legal sense, the term "holding company" is usually limited to a corporation which holds stock in one or more corporations and which actually exercises a control over those companies. James C. Bonbright and Gardiner C. Means, *The Holding Company* (New York, 1932), p. 8.
[8] E. S. Corwin, *The Constitution and What It Means Today* (Princeton, 1947), p. 37.

bling a corporation to secure control of other corporations without changing their organization and sometimes by acquiring only a fractional part of their stock.[9]

The industries chiefly affected by mergers during the period of 1897 to 1903 were petroleum, iron and steel, copper, lead, sugar, paper, linseed oil, starch, salt, powder, cans, whiskey, cottonseed oil, and coal. Some of the combinations secured a control over an unbelievably large number of separate plants. The United States Steel Corporation, for example, chartered by New Jersey in 1901, is reported to have secured a direct or indirect ownership interest in some 785 plants. In 1904 John Moody estimated that seventy-eight corporations controlled 50 percent or more of the production in their respective fields, and that twenty-six of them controlled 80 percent or more. Eight of the corporations—the American Can Company, the American Sugar Refining Company, the American Tobacco Company, the Corn Products Refining Company, the International Harvester Company, the National Cash Register Company, the Standard Oil Company, and the United Shoe Machinery Company—went so far in buying up competitors that they controlled some 90 percent of the output of their respective products.[10]

By 1903 the big wave of merger activity largely came to a close. Most of the then important industrial concerns had been brought within the control of large financial units; and the mounting public opposition to the formation of the industrial giants and the extinction of independent enterprise also caused business leaders for the time being to proceed more slowly. The formation of mergers was continued, however, though at a lesser pace, with the greatest activity centering in banking, finance, and the public service industries. In 1913 a special Congressional committee reported that leaders in finance had secured a "money trust," largely by the use of the holding company privilege and the device of interlocking directorates. According to the committee, the "money trust" which it found had come to dominate the financial life of the country, was defined as "an established and well-defined identity and community of interest between a few leaders of finance which has been created and is held together through stock holdings, interlocking directorates, and other forms of domination over banks, trust companies, railroads, public-service and industrial corporations, and which has resulted in a vast and growing concentration of control of money and credit in the hands of a comparatively few men."[11]

[9] A number of different terms have come into use to designate the various forms of combination. In our present study, the terms "merger" and "combination" will be used interchangeably to mean the acquisition of an ownership interest in former independents by a given corporation—a financial center—which gives it a complete control over the prices charged by the constituent units. A "loose-knit" combination is an association of producers which acts "as one" by agreement. See also Glossary of Terms at the end of the chapter.

[10] John Moody, *The Truth About Trusts* (New York, 1904), pp. 453, 486–487.

[11] *Report of the Committee to Investigate the Concentration of Control of Money and Credit*, House of Representatives, 62nd Congress, third session, Report No. 1593, 1913, p. 130.

The large investment banking companies early took an active interest in promoting mergers. Sales of securities constitute a principal source of their income, and the combination of independent corporations usually provides an opportunity for the flotation of new stock or bond issues. A representative of the banking firm is usually placed on the board of directors of the corporations which are financed, and this representative serves as a powerful influence in coördinating the price and output policies of a given corporation with those of other corporations financed by the same banking firm. In 1946 the Department of Justice reported, "Industry's silence on banker influence is mute testimony to its strength, not a sign of its absence. As long as they are dependent on a particular banking group for their financing, they dare not protest against such influence, even if it means that a particular company does less business than it would if it were free to compete more vigorously."[12]

THE CORPORATION AS A STOCKHOLDER

An example will serve to illustrate the typical way in which "big business" has developed in the United States. A leading merger in the nonferrous metals industry is the American Smelting and Refining Company.[13] This company is reported to refine and sell one-fourth of the world's output of lead. The company was organized in April, 1899, by a consolidation of seventeen smelters, eight refineries, and a number of mines (see Fig. 7). In 1901 it acquired the interests of M. Guggenheim and Sons, a merger of important smelting interests, and thereafter embarked on a program of acquiring additional independents whenever they became important competitors (see Fig. 8). The assets and stock which the company secured in 1905 in the American Smelters Securities Company gave it a control over five additional smelting works and some twenty-seven mining concerns (see Figs. 9 and 10). As of January 1, 1944, the company controlled 38.78 percent of the voting stock of the General Cable Corporation, an important merger of copper and brass fabricators, and this ownership interest gave the company a control over that concern (see Figs. 8 and 9). The American Smelting and Refining Company and the General Cable Corporation in turn jointly control the Revere Copper and Brass Company (see Figs. 8 and 10) a company which is itself a merger of important copper and brass fabricators.[14]

THE SECOND GREAT PERIOD OF CORPORATE MERGERS

The efforts of the federal government, as we shall discuss in subsequent chapters, have been largely ineffective in checking the growth of corporate

[12] *United States Versus Economic Concentration and Monopoly*, Staff Report of the Monopoly Subcommittee of the Committee on Small Business, House of Representatives, 79th Congress, 1946, p. 239.

[13] Hearings Before Subcommittee No. 3 of the Committee on the Judiciary on H.R. 2357, House of Representatives, 79th Congress, first session, pp. 108–120.

[14] For further concrete examples of mergers, see Report of the Federal Trade Commission, *The Merger Movement* (Washington, 1948), pp. 1–134.

mergers. In 1920, in particular, the government lost its suit against the United States Steel Corporation, in which it had sought a court order dissolving that industrial merger. The view of the Supreme Court was that the mere size of a corporation is not condemned by law. The Sherman Act, the Court declared, only punished illegal acts—such as injuring competitors or making agree-

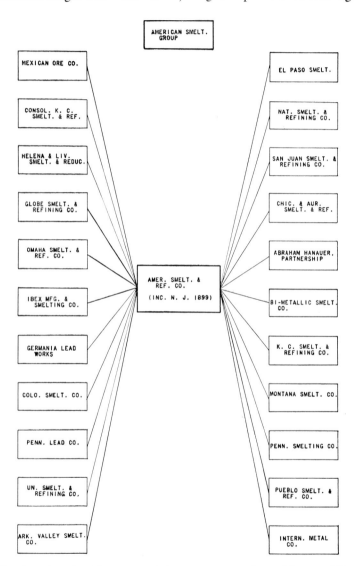

FIG. 7. The American Smelting and Refining Company as formed in 1899. The control over formerly independent firms was secured in some cases by an acquisition of all or a substantial fraction of the stock and in other cases by an acquisition of the assets. (Source: Statement by the Federal Trade Commission in Hearings Before Subcommittee No. 3 of the Committee on the Judiciary, *To Amend Sections 7 and 11 of the Clayton Act*, House of Representatives, 79th Congress, first session, 1945.)

ments with them. In the eyes of the Court, there was no restraint on legitimate price competition in the combination of scores of former independents
into a single financial and price-controlling unit.

The effect of the *Steel* decision in 1920 was to usher in a second great wave
of mergers, based upon the acquisition of the stock of competitors and increasingly upon an acquisition of their assets (see Fig. 11). This second

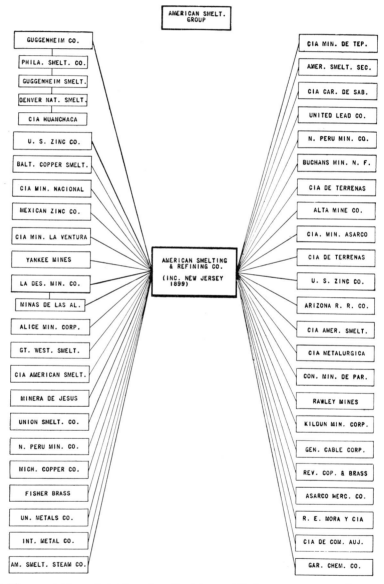

Fig. 8. The acquisitions of the American Smelting and Refining Company after its formation.

period of feverish merger activity continued until 1929, when the stock-market collapse largely brought it to a close. The industries affected by the second merger movement were very much wider in scope than in the first. They included, in particular, motion pictures, petroleum, salt, fabricated copper, whiskey, automobile parts, biscuits and crackers, electrical devices,

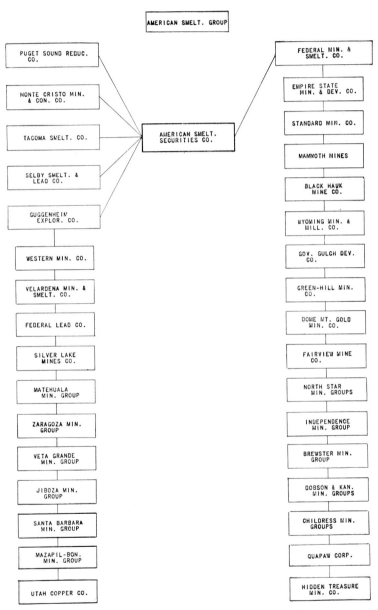

Fig. 9. Enterprises controlled by the American Smelters Securities Company, a unit of the American Smelting and Refining Company.

glass, glass containers, gypsum products, heavy chemicals, paper and fiber-board boxes, roofing materials, steel, meat, dairy products, bread, groceries, and drugs. Many corporate acquisitions were also made of retail stores, hotels, restaurants, movie theaters, banks, and public utilities.

During the period 1920–1929, the formation of mergers in the public utility field was especially extensive. By 1930, it is reported, about one-half of all the public utility enterprises in the country were controlled by three large holding company groups—the United Corporation, the Electric Bond and

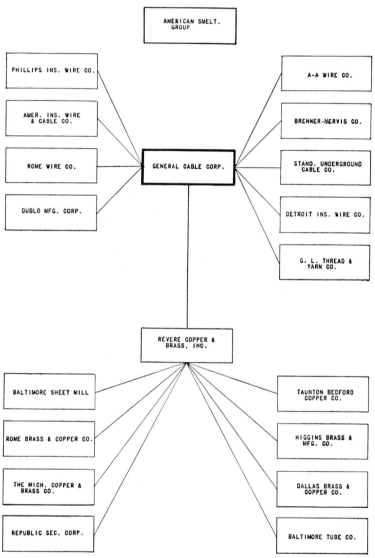

Fig. 10. Copper-fabricating enterprises controlled by the American Smelting and Refining Company.

Share Company, and the Insull companies—and another 30 percent of the industry was controlled by some ten holding companies.[15]

Studies of the merger movements of 1897–1903 and 1920–1929 show that they reached their peaks during a period of rapidly rising security prices. Such periods provided a ready opportunity for selling new securities, and merger activity itself provided a means for stimulating speculative interest in securities. Many mergers, the records show, were formed by promoters—

FIG. 11. Merger movement: number of manufacturing and mining concerns acquired or merged. (Source: Federal Trade Commission.)

persons in a given industry and from the outside—for the purpose of securing promotional profits. In combining the various plants, the promoters increased the asset valuations and secured for themselves substantial amounts of securities for the time and assets which they contributed. The general rule on such mergers was that the whole was greater than the sum of its parts.

THE THIRD IMPORTANT PERIOD OF CORPORATE MERGERS

Although the number of acquisitions fell off sharply after 1929, the process of corporate acquisition slowly but steadily continued (see Fig. 11). During the period 1939 to 1944, the Federal Trade Commission reports, some 832 companies were acquired by 430 corporations. A special study prepared for the Senate found that the formation of mergers was continued throughout

[15] Charles S. Tippetts and Shaw Livermore, *Business Organization and Control* (New York, 1932), pp. 508–509.

the course of World War II. "Taking manufacturing as a whole," the report states, "the giants expanded greatly, while all other firms, especially small business, suffered a substantial decline."[16]

Following V-J Day in 1945, the number of corporate acquisitions increased rapidly. Starting with the increasing trend toward mergers which began in 1940 and continuing through 1947, the Federal Trade Commission reports the disappearance of more than 2450 formerly independent manufacturing and mining companies. These firms, it states, owned assets in excess of 5.2 billion dollars, or more than 5 percent of the total assets of *all* manufacturing corporations in the country.

> The recent merger movement [the Commission states] has extended to virtually all phases of manufacturing and mining, but has been most conspicuous in such industries as food and beverages, textiles and apparel, and chemicals (including drugs). Together, these three groups accounted for over one-third of the total number of acquisitions. Other industries in which numerous acquisitions have taken place were non-electrical machinery, petroleum, and transportation equipment. . . . The new wave of mergers and acquisitions which set in as the war drew to a close has, of course, been superimposed upon the plateau of economic concentration which already prevailed in this country.[17]

In the main, the firms acquired during the period 1940–1947 were small firms; and the acquisitions were a less important source of growth for large acquiring firms than for small acquiring firms.[18]

Since 1951, the Federal Trade Commission reports, corporate merger activity again resumed its upward trend (see Fig. 12). Motives for the continuing growth of mergers are varied. As in the past, a principal reason is the hope on the part of large companies to secure increased profits by eliminating medium-sized and small competitors. Today, the emphasis continues to be on "horizontal" acquisitions of companies producing the same or closely related products. Other important reasons are the desire to secure an assured source of supply or a strategic selling outlet. In some cases, additional firms have been purchased in order to diversify operations and obtain a greater stability of earnings. Owners of closely held corporations frequently have had a tax incentive to sell out to others. In some cases, their desire has been to lessen the impact of estate taxes; and in other cases, their purpose has been to take accumulated profits as capital gains.[19] Influential stockholders and directors also have had a strong incentive to use corporate surpluses for acquiring additional plants rather than for paying dividends, in order to avoid

[16] *Economic Concentration and World War II*, Report of the Smaller War Plants Corporation, Senate Committee Print No. 6, 79th Congress, second session, 1946, p. 25.

[17] Federal Trade Commission, *Summary of the Report on "The Merger Movement"* (Washington, 1948), p. 3.

[18] John Lintner and J. Keith Butters, "Effect of Mergers on Industrial Concentration, 1940–1947," *The Review of Economics and Statistics*, Vol. 32, February, 1950, pp. 30–48.

[19] J. K. Butters, J. Lintner, and W. L. Cary, *Effects of Taxation—Corporate Mergers* (Boston, 1951), pp. 1–36.

higher personal income taxes.[20] In other cases, corporate managements, themselves, have taken the lead in expanding operations. Profits paid out as dividends, they reason, are gone forever; but retained in the business, they can be used to increase the size of the company—and the earning power of management.

KINDS OF MERGERS

The rise of large corporations reflects two types of growth—internal and external. Internal growth means the expansion of existing facilities, the building of new branches, or the creation of subsidiaries. External growth, on the other hand, means the combining of formerly independent companies under one central ownership. The building of new branches and the creation of subsidiaries by a parent company has been, and continues to be, an important source of "bigness" in the American economy. In the main, however, the concern of economists has centered on growth by means of mergers, for mergers mean the absorption of existing competition, the control of essential raw materials, and the consolidation of economic power.

The acquisition of smaller corporations by a larger one takes several forms. A "horizontal" merger is one which unites under one ownership *like plants*—such as cement mills—producing like products. A "vertical" merger, on the other

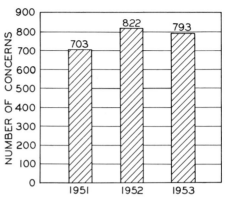

FIG. 12. Merger movement 1951 through 1953: number of concerns in the fields of manufacturing, mining, and wholesale and retail trade acquired or merged. In 1951 the Federal Trade Commission extended its recording of acquisitions to include those in wholesale and retail trade. It also began recording acquisitions of specific assets, such as plants, as well as cases in which less than 50 percent of a company's stock was acquired. The Commission's merger list is prepared from reports in the *Commercial and Financial Chronicle*, the *Wall Street Journal*, the *Journal of Commerce*, *Moody's Industrials*, *Standard Corporation Records*, *The New York Times*, and other trade papers. The data secured are incomplete and only approximate. (Source: Federal Trade Commission.)

hand, brings under one ownership a control over *unlike plants*, engaged in various stages of production from raw materials to the end product. The term "integration" is frequently used to designate a vertical merger. A third type of merger, and one which has been gaining in importance in recent years, is the "conglomerate" or circular merger. The conglomerate merger unites plants producing diverse and unrelated product lines in which the end products bear no similarity. An example of a conglomerate merger is the

[20] James K. Hall, *The Taxation of Corporate Surplus Accumulations*. A study prepared for the Joint Committee on the Economic Report. 82nd Congress, second session, 1952, pp. 19–20.

American Home Products Co. which has acquired control of many diverse products lines—BiSoDol, Kolynos, Anacin, Old English Wax, Three-in-One Oil, Clapp's Baby Foods, G. Washington Coffee, and so forth.

Each of the several types of mergers presents special economic problems. A horizontal merger results in the complete elimination of price competition among formerly independent and competing plants. The public is thus faced with a control over price which is stronger than that attained by conspiracy. A horizontal merger also makes it possible to exercise geographic discrimination by offsetting low prices in one area with high prices in other areas. In large measure, the problem of mergers centers in those of the horizontal type.

Vertical mergers frequently give a dominant concern a control over essential raw materials, such as iron ore, pig iron, and semifinished steel, which can be used to thwart or limit unintegrated firms making finished products. The producer possesses the basic products, and he can take whatever action he desires in their disposition. In exercising this power, the dominant concern may (1) refuse to sell to unintegrated firms or (2) take a high markup on the basic materials and a very low markup on the finished products which are sold in competition with others.

The diverse and incoherent product lines and financial size of a conglomerate merger give it a substantial power of control over single-line competitors. If a firm in a given field refuses to accept its price leadership, the combination may sell below cost in that field and offset its losses with profits from other product lines. In most, if not all cases, the dominant concern publishes only consolidated financial statements, and the practice of cutthroat discrimination may be pursued with slight fear of detection. It is reported that the antitrust agencies receive numerous complaints from specialized producers that various diversified firms are using a given speciality as a "loss leader."

THE PRIVILEGE OF FORMING SUBSIDIARIES

A further factor making for corporate concentration—in addition to the acquisition of competitors—is the right of a corporation to charter new corporations to conduct operations which are being done, or which could be done, by others in the field. Such operations include those conducted by sales companies, export companies, service companies, trucking companies, processing companies, and research companies. The right to create subsidiaries is essentially an *implied* right growing out of (1) the right to own and vote the stock of other corporations and (2) the right to engage in any field of operations.

A principal advantage in creating and owning a subsidiary corporation—rather than in owning a branch plant outright—is limitation of risk and civil liability. The damage liability which may be placed against a corporation in treble damage suits is limited to the amount of its assets; and a large corporation can reduce the risk of antitrust claims by having operations conducted by subsidiary corporations with comparatively small capitalizations. In the liquor industry, the loss of a license to a parent company is serious, but the loss to a subsidiary restricts only one outlet. Another advantage of creating and owning subsidiaries is the reported preference of some executives to work as *president* of a subsidiary corporation rather than as branch manager or divisional head! A further advantage in having subsidiaries is the fact that the controlled plants can be masked as "independents." In maintaining geographically separate plants as separate entities with different names, a parent company can avoid the public antagonism which sometimes attaches to great size. It can also use the subsidiary plants as "price-cutting" outlets for fighting local competition without openly revealing its own hand. An example of the ownership of multiple-subsidiary corporations is shown in Table 13.

If the federal government should desire to limit or restrict economic concentration, it could provide that corporations engaging in interstate commerce shall be restricted to a single main purpose and kind of business. Until about 1850, the corporate powers granted to business enterprises were, in fact, narrowly restricted to a specific purpose. With the coming of general incorporation statutes, however, various states in their scramble for incorporation fees relaxed all precaution and granted powers to corporations to conduct practically any kind of business operation. A number of economists and legal authorities believe that corporate powers should again be more narrowly restricted in a program for reducing corporate concentration.

THE EXTENT OF ECONOMIC CONCENTRATION

In 1932 A. A. Berle and Gardiner C. Means, of the Columbia Law School, published their highly significant study on *The Modern Corporation and Private Property*. Their investigations at that time revealed a growing corporate concentration with 200 of the largest corporations controlling some 50 percent of all corporate wealth (other than banking) and exercising an even greater domination by means of interlocking directorates, trade associations, formal agreements, secret understandings, personal ties, and other arrangements for securing unity of action on price and sales policies.[21] In most of the large corporations, Berle and Means observe, there has also come to be a separation of ownership from control. The authors distinguished five types of control: (1) control based upon complete or almost complete ownership, (2) majority control, (3) control by minority ownership, (4) control by legal devices—such as nonvoting stock—without majority ownership, and (5) management control without appreciable ownership (see Fig. 13). In the vast majority of cases, it was found, control is now exercised either by minority ownership or by management which holds no appreciable amount of stock.

The very size of the corporations which have been formed, Berle and Means declare, has given rise to a condition of absentee ownership which is weakening and destroying the virtues of private property. Since stockholders are numerous and widely scattered, it is possible for management to maintain

[21] A. A. Berle, Jr., and Gardiner C. Means, *The Modern Corporation and Private Property* (New York, 1932), pp. 32-33, 40.

TABLE 13.   Subsidiaries of the United States Steel Corporation in 1948.

	Percentage of Voting Power Including Director's Qualifying Shares Where Applicable
Agawam Iron Mining Co.	100
American Bridge Co.	100
The American Steel & Wire Co. of New Jersey	100
Standard Fence Co.	100
Washburn & Moen Manufacturing Co.	100
Angus Land Co.	100
Apollo Gas Co.	100
Bessemer & Lake Erie R. R. Co.	100
Bessemer-Union Improvement Co. (balance of shares owned by Union R. R. Co.)	50
The Meadville, Conneaut Lake & Linesville R. R. Co.	100
Birmingham Southern R. R. Co.	100
Bradley Transportation Co.	100
Central Radio Telegraph Co.	100
Carbon County Ry. Co.	100
Carnegie-Illinois Steel Corp.	100
Bessemer Electric Power Co.	100
Carnegie Natural Gas Co.	100
Chapin Mining Co.	100
Columbia Iron Mining Co.	100
Columbia Steel Co.	100
Companhia Meridional de Mineração	99.95
Connellsville & Monongahela Ry. Co.	100
Consolidated Western Steel Corp.	100
Consolidated Steel Corp. of Texas	100
Consolidated Western Constructors, Inc.	100
Consolidated Western Steel Corp., Philippines	100
Cyclone Fence Co.	100
Donora Southern R. R. Co.	100
Duluth, Missabe & Iron Range Ry. Co.	100
Elgin, Joliet & Eastern Ry. Co.	100
Essex Iron Co.	100
Etna & Montrose R. R. Co.	100
Federal Shipbuilding & Dry Dock Co.	100
H. C. Frick Coke Co.	100
Gary Land Co.	100
Geneva Steel Co.	100
Gerrard Steel Strapping Co.	100
The Gerrard Co., Inc.	100
Gerrard Pan-American, Ltd.	100
Gunnison Homes, Inc.	70
Hannibal Connecting R. R. Co.	100
Hemlock Land Co.	100
Illinois Steel Co.	100
Isthmian Steamship Co.	100
Johnstown & Stony Creek R. R. Co.	100
The Lake Terminal R. R. Co.	100
McKeesport Connecting R. R. Co.	100
Michigan Limestone & Chemical Co.	100

TABLE 13 (*Continued*)

	Percentage of Voting Power Including Director's Qualifying Shares Where Applicable
National Tube Co.	100
The Newburgh & South Shore Ry. Co.	100
Northampton & Bath R. R. Co.	100
Ohio Barge Line, Inc.	100
Oil Well Supply Co.	100
Oil Well Supply Co., Ltd.	100
Oliver Iron Mining Co.	100
The Cartier Mining Co., Ltd.	100
Pennsylvania & Lake Erie Dock Co.	88.03
Piloto Mining Co.	85
The Pittsburgh, Bessemer & Lake Erie R. R. Co.	82.64
The Pittsburgh & Conneaut Dock Co.	100
Pittsburgh Limestone Corp.	100
Pittsburgh Steamship Co.	100
Scully Steel Products Co.	100
Seventy-one Broadway Corp.	100
Tennessee Coal, Iron & R. R. Co.	100
Trotter Water Co.	100
Union Railroad Co.	100
Bessemer-Union Improvement Co. (balance of shares owned by Bessemer & Lake Erie R. R. Co.)	50
Union Supply Co.	100
United States Coal & Coke Co.	100
United States Steel Corp. of Delaware	100
United States Steel Export Co.	100
Brazaço S. A.	100
Compania de Acero:	
United States Steel Export Co. (Chile), S.A.	100
United States Steel Export Co. (Peru), S.A.	100
Compania de Representaciones Mercantiles, Cubaçero S.A.	100
Isthmian Steamship Co., Ltd.	100
Metalurgica Exportadora Estadounidense de la Argentina, S.A.	100
United States Steel Export Co. de Mexico, S.A.	100
United States Steel Export Co. of China, Inc.	100
United States Steel Export Co. (Puerto Rico), Inc.	100
United States Steel Products Co.	100
Bennett Manufacturing Co., Inc.	100
Boyle Manufacturing Co.	100
The Petroleum Iron Works Co. (Ohio)	100
The Petroleum Iron Works Co. (Texas)	100
United States Steel Supply Co.	100
Universal Atlas Cement Co.	100
Universal Exploration Co.	100
Virginia Bridge Co.	100
Warrier & Gulf Navigation Co.	100
The Youngstown & Northern R. R. Co.	100

(Source: Joint Committee on the Economic Report, *Basic Data Relating to Steel Prices,* 1ST Congress, second session, 1950, pp. 35–37.)

control by sending them proxy slips for use in authorizing two or three of the officers to vote their stock. At the present time, in large measure, the authors state, giant corporate enterprises are run by hired managers just as in the case of a government undertaking. With the separation of ownership from control, however, the top managers in industry are largely responsible to themselves alone. Berle and Means conclude that the great problem of government regulation is now one of making the hired managers in industry responsible not only to the owners but also to the community as a whole.

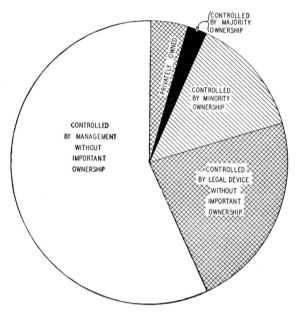

FIG. 13. Ownership and control in the 200 largest corporations, by assets. Total assets $81 billion. This figure shows how ownership and control are separated in the giant corporations (nonbanking). It indicates the prevalence of private control without appreciable ownership. Today an important problem of public regulation is that of making management responsible (a) to the owners and (b) to consumers. (Source: Berle and Means, *The Modern Corporation and Private Property*, New York, 1932.)

ADDITIONAL STUDIES ON CONCENTRATION OF CONTROL

A study of economic concentration for the year 1947 by the Federal Trade Commission revealed (a) that the 113 largest manufacturing corporations each had assets in excess of $100 million and (b) that these corporations owned nearly one-half (46 percent) of all the net capital assets (resources, plants, and equipment) used in manufacturing.[22] A further study published by the Commission in 1954 presented data on concentration expressed in terms of "value of product" accounted for by the 200 largest manufacturing concerns. According to this study, "in 1935 the 200 largest manufacturing

[22] Federal Trade Commission, *The Concentration of Productive Facilities, 1947* (Washington, 1949), p. 14.

corporations accounted for 37.7 percent of the total value of product of all manufacturing enterprises; by 1950 the proportion had risen to 40.5 per-cent."[23]

A summary of the degree and character of concentration in twenty-six industries for the year 1947 is shown in Table 14. The facts show (1) that in

TABLE 14.   Concentration in Twenty-Six Selected Industries, 1947.

	Percent of Net Capital Assets Owned by—						
	1 Com-pany	2 Com-panies	3 Com-panies	4 Com-panies	8 Com-panies	15 Com-panies	All Com-panies
1. Linoleum	57.9	80.8	92.1	93.6	......	......	100.0
2. Tin cans and other tinware	55.2	92.1	95.3	96.4	......	......	100.0
3. Aluminum	55.0	85.0	100.0	......	......	......	100.0
4. Copper smelting and refining	46.8	73.5	88.5	94.6	100.0	......	100.0
5. Biscuits, crackers and pretzels	46.3	57.0	67.7	71.4	......	......	100.0
6. Agricultural machinery	45.3	56.8	66.6	75.4	82.1	......	100.0
7. Office and store machines and devices	42.0	56.3	69.5	74.3	85.3	89.6	100.0
8. Motor vehicles	40.9	62.8	68.7	70.7	77.3	86.1	100.0
9. Cigarettes	36.6	64.4	77.6	87.8	......	......	100.0
10. Plumbing equipment and supplies	33.2	64.9	71.3	74.3	......	......	100.0
11. Distilled liquors	29.0	53.3	72.4	84.6	94.3	......	100.0
12. Meat products	28.8	54.7	64.0	69.3	77.6	81.6	100.0
13. Primary steel	28.6	42.0	49.2	54.5	69.3	77.2	100.0
14. Rubber tires and tubes	27.8	49.9	70.3	88.3	94.8	......	100.0
15. Dairy products	27.5	48.9	55.8	59.6	71.3	......	100.0
16. Glass and glassware	24.9	49.1	57.4	62.2	73.9	......	100.0
17. Carpets and rugs	24.1	36.8	48.9	57.9	......	......	100.0
18. Footwear (except rubber)	23.6	39.6	43.4	46.8	53.1	57.5	100.0
19. Industrial chemicals	21.5	36.5	45.5	51.8	70.2	80.2	100.0
20. Woolen and worsted goods	16.7	23.5	28.1	30.3	36.4	......	100.0
21. Electrical machinery	15.8	28.8	41.7	47.5	55.2	60.7	100.0
22. Grain-mill products	15.6	23.5	30.2	36.3	48.6	56.6	100.0
23. Aircraft and parts	13.6	25.4	35.2	44.0	73.7	86.2	100.0
24. Bread and other products (excluding biscuits and crackers	13.0	20.0	25.4	30.6	38.2	......	100.0
25. Canning and preserving	10.7	21.4	32.0	39.4	51.0	59.2	100.0
26. Drugs and medicines	8.4	16.5	23.5	30.0	47.7	......	100.0

(Source: Federal Trade Commission, *The Concentration of Productive Facilities, 1947*, p. 21.)

each of the selected industries a single leader is dominant and (2) that four or fewer corporations control a substantial part of the productive facilities in their respective industries. A significant section of American industry is thus characterized by oligopoly rather than by numerous independent firms. This means that the essential economic base for a policy of effective competition is lacking.

[23] Federal Trade Commission, *Changes in Concentration in Manufacturing 1935 to 1947 and 1950* (Washington, 1954), p. 17.

When sellers are few, we have observed, they are likely to act as one on prices. The extent to which the "Big Three" and "Big Four" companies in each of the concentrated industries supplement their control by the use of pricing formulas, resale-price maintenance schemes, agency arrangements, export associations, and interlocking directorates is an important area for further research and study.

Additional facts on economic concentration are reviewed in a study made by the Department of Commerce for the Celler Committee on the proportion of total shipments in each of 452 industries in 1947 which was supplied by the top four companies. The study shows that in 150 of the industries studied four companies produce more than one-half of the total shipments in each industry. A summary of the Department of Commerce data is presented in Table 15.

INTERLOCKING DIRECTORATES AS A DEVICE FOR RESTRICTING COMPETITION AND ARM'S LENGTH BARGAINING

Interlocking directorates are a major device used in business for restricting competition and for securing preferred access to customers or supplies. The term itself means that a given person serves as a director on the boards of two or more corporations. In this capacity, he "interlocks" the deliberations of the two concerns.

Interlocking relations between corporations also result when an *officer* of a given corporation (not a director of that corporation) serves as a director of a concern which is a rival, customer, or supplier. Frequently, moreover, corporate enterprises are tied together by "indirect" interlocks—that is, by directors (or officers) who meet together on the board of a third corporation (see Fig. 14).

Interlocking directorates (or relationships) are a much more effective device for securing unified selling and commercial favors than dinners, telephone conversations, or trade association meetings. In attending the board meetings of another corporation, a particular executive can listen, hear, and examine closely its procedures. He has a ringside seat which permits him to learn the most intimate details of the other's business at the very time that crucial decisions are being made.

A person serving on two or more boards frequently owns little stock in the various concerns which he interlocks. He gets his position, in other words, for reasons other than the number of shares which he votes at a stockholder's meeting. How is the interlock effected if not by substantial stock ownership? Usually, a director (or officer) of a given concern is elected to serve by the dominating person on the other board. The dominating person or key executive promotes the interlock for a number of reasons. In electing a person to serve on the board, and in giving him a ringside seat, the key executive surrounds himself with men whom he can control. In meeting and working intimately with them, moreover, he and they are in a position to effect re-

TABLE 15. Concentration of Output in Largest Manufacturing Companies Measured by Value of Shipments in 1947.

Industry	No. of Companies	First 4 Companies (percent)
Primary aluminum	3	100.0
Small arms ammunition	7	99.9
Aircraft propellers	12	98.0
Telephone and telegraph equipment	50	95.7
Aluminum rolling and drawing	15	94.2
Botanical products	13	92.1
Electric lamps	35	91.8
Files	34	91.6
Locomotives and parts	33	90.7
Coal-tar crudes	13	90.6
Cigarettes	19	90.4
Electrometallurgical products	10	88.3
Petroleum and coal products	11	88.2
Flat glass	15	88.1
Tobacco stemming and redrying	93	88.0
Steam engines and turbines	15	87.6
Carbon and graphite products	36	87.1
Softwood distillation	28	85.8
Pulp goods, pressed and molded	19	85.5
Gypsum products	33	84.6
Reclaimed rubber	14	83.8
Leavening compounds	39	83.4
Matches	18	82.7
Compressed and liquefied gases	69	82.6
Safes and vaults	26	82.4
Cork products	34	81.9
Rubber footwear	20	80.7
Salt	25	80.5
Explosives	35	80.4
Hard-surface floor coverings	14	80.3
Primary copper	9	80.0
Typewriters	23	79.4
Soap and glycerin	223	79.0
Phonograph records	96	78.8
Synthetic fibers	22	78.4
Carbon black	13	78.3
Tin cans and other tinware	102	77.8
Organs	27	77.6
Graphite: ground or blended	10	77.4
Corn products	47	77.2
Sewing machines	69	77.1
Tires and inner tubes	35	76.6
Primary batteries (dry and wet)	23	76.4
Wool-felt hats and hat bodies	45	76.3
Textile goods	24	74.9
Cereal preparations	55	74.9
Linseed oil mills	12	74.7
Distilled liquors, except brandy	144	74.6
Electronic tubes	32	73.2

TABLE 15 (*Continued*)

Industry	No. of Companies	First 4 Companies (percent)
Metal foil	38	73.2
Transformers	134	72.9
Hardwood distillation	22	72.3
Window shades	103	71.7
Biscuits, crackers, and pretzels	249	71.5
Aircraft engines	54	71.5
Primary nonferrous metals	13	70.9
Piano and organ parts	34	70.6
Alkalies and chlorine	18	70.1
Chewing gum	35	70.1
Cane-sugar refining	17	69.9
Computing and related machines	50	69.0
Jute (except felt) and linen goods	30	69.0
Medicinal chemicals	88	68.5
Beet sugar	17	68.4
Chocolate and cocoa products	31	67.9
Fatty acids	15	67.7
Reed and rattan furniture	29	67.5
Tractors	86	67.3
Blast furnaces	33	67.3
Household furniture	18	67.1
Engine electric equipment	100	66.8
Excelsior mills	48	66.5
Animal oils	14	66.2
Hand saws and saw blades	81	65.5
Thread mills	83	65.3
Nonmetallic mineral products	66	64.3
Small arms	32	64.0
Margarine	17	63.7
Inorganic color pigments	57	63.6
Glass containers	41	62.9
Elevators and escalators	108	62.7
Essential oils	40	62.6
Nonclay refractories	42	62.1
Special dairy products	97	62.1
Ball and roller bearings	78	61.9
Storage batteries	205	61.8
Yarn mills, silk system	42	61.4
Photographic equipment	346	61.2
Silverware and plated ware	221	61.2
Vacuum cleaners	34	61.0
Chewing and smoking tobacco	65	61.0
Electric measuring instruments	150	60.9
Natural tanning and dyeing materials	24	60.6
Copper rolling and drawing	56	60.1
Cooperage stock mills	102	59.4
Shortening and cooking oils	68	59.2
Rattan and willow ware	53	58.8
Laundry and dry-cleaning machinery	119	58.6
Motors and generators	224	58.6

TABLE 15 (*Continued*)

Industry	No. of Companies	First 4 Companies (percent)
Straw hats	38	58.5
Surgical appliances and supplies	593	58.4
Beauty and barber shop equipment	69	58.2
Nonferrous metal rolling	41	58.0
Vitreous plumbing fixtures	26	57.9
Ophthalmic goods	175	57.8
X-ray and therapeutic apparatus	114	57.8
Pens and mechanical pencils	180	57.6
Fiber cans, tubes, drums, etc.	109	57.6
Asbestos products	85	57.5
Electrical products	112	57.4
Printing ink	151	57.0
Industrial trucks and tractors	191	56.6
Mineral wool	73	56.5
Felt goods	37	56.4
Truck trailers	107	56.2
Artists' materials	59	55.9
Railroad and street cars	68	55.9
Motor vehicles and parts	779	55.7
Knit glove mills	41	55.6
Vitreous-china food utensils	26	55.5
Dehydrated fruits and vegetables	120	55.5
Optical instruments and lenses	114	55.3
Furniture and fixtures	29	55.0
Mechanical stokers	46	55.0
Cigar boxes	34	54.9
Communication equipment	101	54.9
Fuel briquets and packaged fuel	90	54.9
Soda-fountain and bar equipment	65	54.0
Scales and balances	73	53.9
Primary zinc	14	53.3
Hatters' fur	45	53.2
By-product coke ovens	49	52.9
Knitting mills	44	52.8
Textile bags	198	52.7
Aircraft	47	52.6
Collapsible tubes	19	52.6
Tobacco pipes	74	52.4
Work shirts	60	52.4
Metal barrels, drums, and pails	49	52.1
Wool carpets, rugs, and carpet yarn	85	51.7
Public building furniture	117	51.6
Floor and wall tile	34	50.9
Lead pencils and crayons	46	50.8
Pressed and blown glassware	107	50.8
Professional furniture	75	50.8
China decorating for the trade	65	50.8
Candles	54	50.8
Lasts and related products	40	50.6

ciprocal trading favors, such as the exchange of "inside" information on investment opportunities.

Interlocking directorates are sometimes used among rival firms to work out the details of a price-fixing plan. The periodic meetings of directors thereupon provide an effective means for supervising its operation. Interlocking

COMMON MEETING PLACES FOR THE "BIG FOUR" IN COPPER

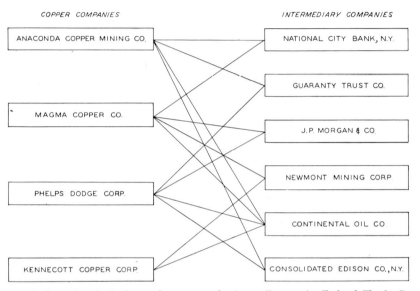

FIG. 14. Indirect interlocks in nonferrous metals. According to the Federal Trade Commission, the "big four" in copper find common meeting places in key banking and investment companies. (Source: *Report of the Federal Trade Commission on Interlocking Directorates*, Washington, 1951, p. 166.)

arrangements are also used between suppliers and customers. A dominant seller (industrial concern or bank) may find an advantage in electing a director from an important *customer* in order to secure preferred access in selling, in placing loans, or in unifying the relations of customers who are competitors. The director of the customer concern, on the other hand, finds an interest in the personal favors and corporate advantages which may be secured in working on the other board. Likewise, an important buyer may seek out a director from a key supplier (to insure supplies), and the invitee may accept the directorship for personal trading purposes, inside information, and personal financial power.

Interlocking relationships have long been condemned by socially minded lawyers, businessmen, and economists (1) as restrictive of competition between and among competitors and (2) as inconsistent with arm's length dealing which permits free choice and equal access for other concerns. Mr. Louis D. Brandeis, later Justice of the United States Supreme Court, was a leading critic of business interlocks, and his writings during the years 1913–

1914 were an important factor in leading to the adoption of federal legislation limiting—but not preventing—their use. (See Chap. 16, p. 361.) In an article entitled "The Endless Chain: Interlocking Directorates," Mr. Brandeis declared:

> The practice of interlocking directorates is the root of many evils. It offends laws human and divine. Applied to rival corporations, it tends to the suppression of competition and to the violation of the Sherman Law. Applied to corporations which deal with each other, it tends to disloyalty and to violation of the fundamental law that no man can serve two masters. In either event, it tends to inefficiency; for it removes incentive and destroys soundness of judgment. It is undemocratic, for it rejects the platform: "A fair field and no favors"—substituting the pull of privilege for the push of manhood.[24]

In a subsequent article, Mr. Brandeis further declared:

> Ordinarily in business the value of a thing or service is determined through the agreement reached by an intelligent seller and an intelligent purchaser—each looking out for his own interest to the best of his ability. Where interlocking directorates . . . exist, this protection is lost. . . .
> For the proper exercise of the functions of director, it is essential that he be disinterested; that is, be free from any conflicting interest. But it is also essential that he have knowledge. Facts, facts, facts, are the only basis on which he can properly exercise his judgment. It is as necessary that he know intimately the facts concerning the business, as that he have only one interest to subserve. Now, no man can have such detailed knowledge of the facts of many enterprises. This is due to the limitations of time and place and to those other limits set by nature upon human intelligence. How can one man know in respect to many large corporations the facts which a director needs to know in order to insure efficient management?[25]

The Clayton Act (1914), in particular, imposes various limits and restrictions on interlocking directorates. However, as we shall discuss in Chapter 16, the law is incomplete and is largely evaded or violated with impunity.

THE PYRAMIDING OF CONTROL IN INTEREST GROUPINGS

Control over other corporations, we have seen, can be secured by the ownership of all or a part of their stock or assets and by interlocking arrangements. Other "relations of dependency" can be effected through investment trusts, trade associations, personal ties, and especially banking affiliations. The National Resources Committee found that the use of various methods of alliance gives rise to what is known as an "interest group"—that is, a group of large industrial corporations which is controlled by a central interest in the form of one or several banking companies, as J. P. Morgan and Company and

---

[24] Louis D. Brandeis, "The Endless Chain: Interlocking Directorates," *Harper's Weekly*, December 6, 1913, p. 13.
[25] Louis D. Brandeis, "Interlocking Directorates," *The Annals*, January, 1915, pp. 46–48.

the First National Bank of New York, or various family groups, as the Rockefellers, Mellons, or Du Ponts. The findings of the Committee indicated that eight interest groups control at least 106 of the 250 largest corporations in the country, including banking corporations. The Morgan–First National banking interests, for example, were found to exercise control over 13 large industrial corporations (including U.S. Steel and General Electric), 12 utility corporations (including the American Telephone and Telegraph Co. and power companies controlling 37 percent of the electric generating capacity in the U.S.), 11 major railroads or railroad systems (including the New York Central and the Great Northern), and 5 large banking firms.

The top of the pyramid of economic control, the Committee concluded, rests in the hands of the few persons who control an "interest grouping." These few persons use their alliances to select the personnel of the corporate giants, and the personnel of the large corporations, in turn, control the personnel and policies of the underlying corporations which they control by means of an ownership of stock or assets. A supercorporation or merger in each industry thereupon plays a dominant role as a "price leader" in setting the price or prices which the independent corporations typically follow because of fear or favor. Thus it is that interest groupings exercise control over the policies of the larger corporations and through them a control over business activity in the basic American industries.[26]

Speaking of the many devices used by business leaders in curbing effective competition, Professors Stocking and Watkins declare:

> Out of this network of financial interconnection, commercial interdependence, and social cohesion has evolved a climate of opinion in American business that is hostile to a genuinely free market. However eager the captains of industry may be to display their prowess in forthright competition, the generals of finance set the outlines of strategy. Competition is a disturbing factor, opposed to their interests. . . .
>
> The new canons of business behavior approved a variety of specific devices designed to prevent price competition and standardize business practices. Business groups resorted to price leadership, resale price maintenance, competitive advertising, trade association activities, basing-point and other delivered pricing systems, and the like in an effort to prevent the readjustments that economic progress entails and effective competition compels. Whether legal or illegal, these practices tended to free business from the control of the automatic forces of the market and to subject the market to the deliberate guidance of businessmen.[27]

---

[26] National Resources Committee, *The Structure of the American Economy* (Washington, 1939), Part 1, pp. 160–163. For a summary of the findings on interest groupings and the corporations controlled, see Smaller War Plants Corporation. *Economic Concentration and World War II*, 79th Congress, second session, Senate Document 6, pp. 17–20, 353–356.

[27] George W. Stocking and Myron W. Watkins, *Monopoly and Free Enterprise* (New York, 1951), pp. 130–131.

SUMMARY

Vast financial size in corporations has come about largely through (1) the merger of formerly independent plants, (2) the building of branch plants, and (3) the creation of subsidiaries. Extreme corporate concentration has been greatly facilitated by the action of state governments in granting charters which contain holding company privileges. It has also been accentuated by the willingness of the states to grant charters permitting corporations to engage in more than one kind of business and to form subsidiaries without limitation. There is error in identifying the rise of giant corporations with the needs of modern technology and mass production. Corporate concentration and financial bigness, the evidence indicates, have arisen primarily (1) from the drive of various business groups for the added profits of centralized control and (2) from the failure of the federal and state governments to establish standards for the operation and conduct of business corporations.

Very few public problems arise in the case of single-plant corporations which are managed or controlled by their owners. It is rather in the existence and operation of supercorporations (or giant mergers), acting in unison through interlocking arrangements, and other ties, that the principal social, economic, and political evils arise. With the separation of ownership from management, it is possible for small minority groups, responsible to no one but themselves, to control immense aggregations of "other people's money." In many cases, these centralized powers of control have been used against the interests and rights of the actual owners, as well as against the welfare of the public. Over vast areas, moreover, corporate concentration has meant the elimination of price competition among scores of formerly independent plants.

GLOSSARY OF TERMS USED WITH REFERENCE TO BUSINESS ORGANIZATION

Amalgamation: This term is used to mean (a) the proprietary union—or the fusing of ownership—of two or more enterprises into a *new* corporation and (b) the dissolution or liquidation of the formerly existing corporations.

Combination: The terms "combination" and "merger" are commonly used interchangeably.

Consolidation: A broad term which is used to mean (1) the acquisition of one or more smaller corporations by a larger one (merger) or (2) the proprietary union of two or more enterprises into a *new* business organization or corporation (amalgamation).

Coöperative marketing association: A group of producers associated together to process, handle, and sell their products (and also to purchase supplies) without competing against one another. A producers' coöperative usually provides for a sharing of "patronage refunds" (net margins above expenses and reserves) in accordance with the amount and quality of products sold by each member through the association. Approximately 80 percent of the coöperative marketing associations are organized as corporations.

136

Coöperative marketing associations (1) of agricultural producers and (2) of producers of aquatic products are exempted from the antitrust laws. All other associations of business enterprises for marketing their products "as one" are illegal under the antitrust laws as a restraint on competition. Coöperative *purchasing* agencies (including "consumer" coöperatives) owned by a number of individuals or business firms embrace the coöperative principle. They are not, however, coöperative associations for marketing the products of their members. Coöperative purchasing arrangements are a legal form of organization.

Holding company: In principle, any corporation which owns stock in other corporations is a holding company. In a strict legal sense, however, the term is usually limited to a corporation which holds stock in one or more corporations and which actually exercises a control over those companies.

Loose-knit combinations: Various forms of associations with respect to prices and output based upon agreement rather than ownership. They range from simple agreements to formal "pools" which provide for a sharing of output, sales, or earnings. An association of firms for the purpose of agreeing on price and controlling supply is also called a "cartel." Loose-knit combinations are illegal, *per se,* under the federal antitrust laws.

Merger: The acquisition of one or more smaller corporations by a larger one —that is, the union of two or more enterprises under one ownership. In some cases, the acquired corporation is permitted to keep its identity; and in other cases, it is dissolved and its assets are transferred to the corporation which survives. The ownership interest possessed by the acquiring corporation may be complete or fractional—the essential degree of ownership is that which gives control over the constituent units.

Subsidiaries: A "subsidiary" corporation is a corporation controlled by another corporation through complete or fractional stock ownership. A corporation secures subsidiaries (1) by acquiring the stock of a formerly independent corporation or (2) by chartering an entirely new corporation.

SUGGESTIONS FOR FURTHER READING

Concentration of Banking in the United States, Staff Report to the Board of Governors, Federal Reserve System, for the Select Committee on Small Business, U.S. Senate, 82nd Congress, second session, 1952.

Economic Concentration and World War II, Report of the Smaller War Plants Corporation, 79th Congress, second session, Senate Committee Print No. 6, 1946.

Federal Trade Commission, *The Merger Movement* (Washington, 1948); *The Concentration of Productive Facilities, 1947* (Washington, 1949); *The Divergence Between Plant and Company Concentration, 1947* (Washington, 1950); *Interlocking Directorates* (Washington, 1951); *Changes in Concentration in Manufacturing 1935 to 1947 and 1950* (Washington, 1954).

Heflebower, Richard B., "Economics of Size," *Journal of Business of the University of Chicago,* October, 1951, pp. 253–268.

Lynch, David, *The Concentration of Economic Power* (New York, 1946).

National Association of Manufacturers, *Studies on Concentration: The Fed-*

eral Trade Commission Versus the Facts. No. 43, July, 1951; *The FTC's Defense of Its Research and NAM's Reply.* No. 49, May, 1952.

United States Versus Economic Concentration and Monopoly, Staff Report to the Monopoly Subcommittee of the Committee on Small Business, House of Representatives, 79th Congress, 1946.

Weston, J. Fred, *The Role of Mergers in the Growth of Large Firms* (Berkeley, Calif., 1953).

Wilcox, Clair, *Competition and Monopoly in American Industry* (Temporary National Economic Committee, *Monograph 16,* 1941).

CHAPTER 8

The Economics of Size and Public Policy

Much confusion has arisen in the discussions of business size and efficiency because various persons have divergent ideas on the meaning of the terms "large business," "bigness," "size," "mass production," and "efficiency." Do the "economies of size" relate (1) to a single physical unit—as a sugar mill at a single definite location, or (2) to various kinds of combination in which a single corporation owns or controls a number of separate plants, dispersed in geographical location, and differing in size, technical equipment, and kinds of goods produced? What is the "efficiency," "economy" or "advantage" of *large size* in physical plant or in company size?

Some declare that efficiency is measured by the size of profits. It is true that functional efficiency makes for larger profits, but so do monopoly, extortion, coercion, and misrepresentation. From a public point of view "economic efficiency" should be taken to mean the production of more and better goods with less time and effort, lower prices to buyers, the development of new products, and technological advance and innovation. With this concept of efficiency in mind, let us analyze the advantages and disadvantages of big business. A consideration of these factors is basic in determining public policy toward large corporate size.

THE ECONOMY OF MASS PRODUCTION

In studying the economies of size it is essential to distinguish between (1) large *technological* size in a single factory, plant, or works—such as a steel mill, oil refinery, or chemical works—at a specified location, and (2) large *financial* size in the centralized ownership or control of a collection of geographically separate plants.

Economists have long observed that *up to a certain limit* increasing the size *of a single plant* brings lower average unit costs. (See Fig. 15.) The main advantage of large size in a single factory arises in the mass production of one or a few products. Mass production means turning out a large quantity of a particular kind of product, such as assembled automobiles, rubber tires, or cement. In summary form, the source of the economies of mass production may be listed as follows:

1. Division of labor and specialization in particular operations. Economies include increase of skill, saving of time in changing from one operation to another, and the use of workers having limited experience and training. In a

large meat-packing plant the various labor tasks are divided into as many as 1100 different jobs.

2. The continuous use of large, specialized machines and facilities, and assembly-line methods of production. It is reported that a forge shop in the United States will produce up to 400 percent more forgings per hour than a shop in England because American shops are more spacious, the furnaces are larger and better, and mechanical handling is more highly developed.[1]

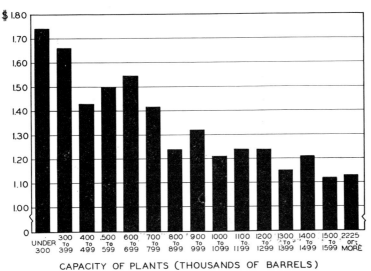

CAPACITY OF PLANTS (THOUSANDS OF BARRELS)

FIG. 15. Unit production costs of cement. The vertical scale shows costs per barrel, and the horizontal scale shows the capacity (in thousands of barrels) of 126 cement mills, grouped into 15 class intervals, arranged from the smallest to largest. Plants in the smallest size group produced cement at a cost of $1.73 per barrel, whereas plants in the largest size group produced cement at a cost of $1.12 per barrel. (Source: John Blair, "The Relation Between Size and Efficiency," *Review of Economic Statistics*, August, 1942, p. 129.)

Petroleum engineers estimate that the cost of transporting crude oil 250 miles is 24 cents a barrel in a 10-inch pipe line, and 12 cents a barrel in a 20-inch pipe line. Within certain limits, the larger the diameter of a pipe line, the lower the unit cost of operations.

3. The economies of large-scale buying and selling. Savings arise (a) in the purchase of carload and shipload quantities, and (b) in spreading selling and advertising costs over a larger output.

4. Economies secured in the physical integration, i.e., the adding or uniting of successive processing steps within a factory. A steel fabricating mill or forge works, for example, may find economies in adding an electric furnace to produce its own ingots. A steel mill making basic products likewise may expand by adding facilities for producing finished products and specialities. The uniting of several processes—or shops—in a single factory yields econ-

[1] International Labour Organization, *Factors Affecting Productivity in the Metal Trades* (Geneva, 1952), p. 32.

omies in the continuity of productive operations, in the saving of fuel and transportation costs, in buying and selling in larger quantities, and in having more assured buying and selling outlets.

LIMITS TO THE ECONOMY OF SIZE

Beyond a certain point, greater size in a single plant brings disadvantages and results in higher unit costs. The limits to the economical size of *a plant* are governed by a number of factors:

1. Maximum economies in a single plant are usually secured when a plant utilizes fully the best available, most efficient machines, processes, and assembly techniques. Little, if any, additional economy can be secured by a duplication of such facilities.
2. Auxiliary processes which a plant might add, such as power generation, may be more economically conducted as a separate large-scale operation by another company.
3. Labor tasks for a given operation, such as meat packing, cannot be continuously and indefinitely subdivided.
4. Available supplies of raw materials, livestock, labor, power, and water resources may not justify a larger operation.
5. Experience shows that management itself finds it increasingly difficult to supervise, coördinate, and control the diverse phases of a business enterprise whenever it grows beyond a certain size. Management's efforts become diluted and relatively inefficient. Personal initiative and responsibility are replaced by red tape, mechanical channels, and formalized ways of doing things. Small business can avoid this inflexibility, delay, frustration, and expense. A centralized office, further, cannot effectively win and maintain personal contacts with distant customers. Local, on-the-spot companies have an advantage in dealing with nearby customers.

    When there are many variables in a line of business—such as style changes, unstable conditions of demand or supply, ease of entry for competitors, and the need for close supervision—the problems of management in a single plant increase rapidly, and limits on the ability of a final authority to make necessary decisions are reached in relatively small plants. This is true with most farming enterprises, as well as with enterprises making fur goods, blouses and shirts, dresses, knitted outerwear, jewelry, and millinery.
6. The increasing costs—freight, icing, shrinkage, spoilage—of transporting finished products to scattered buyers at greater distances directly limits the size and output of a given plant. In general, the farther that products are shipped, the higher the delivered costs. Every plant, it has long been observed, is a "zoned business," that is, a business which has a natural sales area beyond which it cannot economically ship.
7. Large, single-product plants are particularly vulnerable to changes in local conditions of supply and demand. A farming region currently producing substantial supplies of hogs, for example, may suddenly shift to the production of sugar beets, fruits, or vegetables.

THE ECONOMY OF MASS PRODUCTION IN SINGLE PLANTS SHOULD BE PERMITTED TO DEVELOP FULLY

There are many large single factories in the American economy which undoubtedly develop in marked degree the advantages of mass production—or the economy of large production. These plants are illustrated by some of the large automobile assembly plants, airplane establishments, oil refineries, steel mills, cement mills, and chemical works. Engineers estimate that without the economies of mass production, a 1955 automobile would cost over $50,000.

No critic of big business proposes or advocates that the size of a single physical plant be limited, restricted, or reduced in any way. Indeed, it is clear to all that governmental policy should accommodate itself to the largest *plant* which is necessitated by the existing or prospective technology.

The only suggestion for a limit on the size of a plant, interestingly, comes from business itself! Thus, the president of one of our largest corporations declares, "The greatest contribution to effective organization would be the reduction of our plants to a maximum size of 2500 men." The ideal which this person has in mind is a plant in which the manager would know his men and in which each worker could fully utilize his abilities.[2] The morale of workers, it has been found, tends to deteriorate as plants become very large in size.[3]

THE CONCEPT OF BIG BUSINESS

The term "big business" is used to mean a financially large corporation (a) which owns outright or controls many geographically separate plants, *and* (b) which produces a substantial share of the output in a given industry, such as aluminum, cigarettes, or electric machinery. The term is also applied collectively to the one hundred or more largest corporations which own or control a substantial part of all corporate assets (see Table 16). Business concerns which do not meet these tests need not, in fact, be small in terms of assets or specialized operations. For example, a "small" company operating blast furnaces in the iron and steel industry is, of necessity, a large multimillion-dollar company. Likewise, many companies are small in comparison with many big concerns, but they are big in their own speciality fields. Concepts of "small business" and statistics on the total business population in the United States are presented in Chap. 12, pp. 257–258.

THE CASE *FOR* BIG BUSINESS

In the main, the advantages of large centralized management arise (1) in unifying the buying, financing, and selling activities of a group of plants; (2) in organizing and conducting joint research; (3) in developing and implementing the most advanced technology; and (4) in providing supplies and selling outlets through the integration of plants. The general practice of the

[2] Ernest Dale, *Planning and Developing the Company Organization Structure* (New York, 1952), p. 170.

[3] *Size and Morale: A preliminary study of attendance at work in large and small units,* The Acton Society Trust (London, 1953).

TABLE 16.   Total Assets, 100 Largest Manufacturing Corporations as Reported at End of 1953, in Millions.[a]

Allied Chem. & Dye Cp.	$ 703
Allis-Chalmers Mfg. Co.	402
Aluminum Co. of Amer.	906
Amer. Can Co.	432
Amer. Cyanamid Co.	443
Amer. Smelt. & Ref. Co.	364
Amer. Tobacco Co.	801
Amer. Viscose Corp.	268
Anaconda Cop. Min. Co.	836
Armco Steel Corp.	465
Armour & Co.	474
Atlantic Refining Co.	571
Avco Mfg. Corp.	223
Bendix Aviation Corp.	329
Bethlehem Steel Corp.	1,783
Boeing Airplane Co.	232
Borden Co.	296
Borg-Warner Corp.	260
Burlington Mills Corp.	301
Caterpillar Tractor Co.	261
Celanese Corp. of Amer.	322
Chrysler Corp.	898
Cities Service Co.	1,103
Coca-Cola Co.	236
Colo. Fuel & Iron Corp.	215
Continental Can Co.	321
Continental Oil Co.	409
Crown Zellerbach Corp.	243
Deere & Co.	431
Distillers Cp.—Seagrams	458
Douglas Aircraft Co.	274
Dow Chemical Co.	769
E. I. duPont de N. & Co.	1,846
Eastman Kodak Co.	524
Firestone Tire & Rub. Co.	567
Food Mach. & Chem. Cp.	223
Gen. Amer. Trans. Cp.	226
Gen. Electric Co.	1,697
Gen. Foods Corp.	353
Gen. Motors Corp.	4,405
B. F. Goodrich Co.	437
Goodyear Tire & Rubber Co.	666
Gulf Oil Corp.	1,766
Inland Steel Co.	$ 433
Inter. Bus. Mach. Corp.	520
Inter. Harvester Co.	973
Inter. Paper Co.	507
Jones & Laughlin Stl. Cp.	579
Kaiser Alum. & Chem. Cp.	320
Kaiser Steel Corp.	267
Kennecott Copper Corp.	748
Liggett & Myers Tob. Co.	497
Lockheed Aircraft Corp.	260

TABLE 16 (*Continued*)

Mathieson Chem. Cp.[b]	$ 260
Monsanto Chemical Co.	362
Philip Morris & Co.	255
Nash-Kelvinator Corp.[c]	233
Natl. Dairy Prod. Corp.	425
Natl. Distillers Prod. Cp.	422
Natl. Lead Co.	295
Natl. Steel Corp.	528
Ohio Oil Co.	313
Owens-Illinois Glass Co.	222
Phelps Dodge Corp.	345
Phillips Petroleum Co.	1,039
Pitts. Plate Glass Co.	442
Procter & Gamble Co.	444
Pullman Inc.	229
Pure Oil Co.	383
Radio Corp. of Amer.	494
Republic Steel Corp.	741
R. J. Reynolds Tob. Co.	599
Reynolds Metals Co.	432
Richfield Oil Corp.	262
Schenley Industries	414
Shell Oil Co.	985
Sinclair Oil Corp.	1,141
Singer Mfg. Co.	405
Skelly Oil Co.	275
Socony-Vacuum Oil Co.	2,154
Sperry Corporation	259
Stand. Oil Co. of Calif.	1,535
Stand. Oil Co. (Ind.)	2,036
Stand. Oil Co. (N.J.)	5,372
Stand. Oil Co. (Ohio)	296
J. P. Stevens & Co.	257
Sun Oil Co.	469
Swift & Co.	533
Texas Company	1,805
Tide Water Assoc. Oil Co.	362
Union Carbide & Car. Cp.	1,191
Union Oil Co. of Calif.	476
United Aircraft Corp.	298
U.S. Rubber Co.	489
U.S. Steel Corp.	3,248
Western Electric Co.	877
Westinghouse Elec. Cp.	1,265
Weyerhaeuser Timber Co.	323
Wheeling Steel Corp.	234
Youngstown Sh. & Tube Co.	514

[a] Total assets are shown after deducting reserves for depreciation. Table does not include Ford Motor Company, with total assets of $1,758 million on Dec. 31, 1952, or United Fruit Company, with total assets of $386 million on Dec. 31, 1953, which companies do not publish detailed income accounts.
[b] To merge with Olin Industries, Inc., as Olin Mathieson Chemical Corp.
[c] Merged with Hudson Motor Car Co. as American Motors Corp.
(Source: National City Bank, *Monthly Letter*, July, 1954.)

controlling corporation is to permit the management of each subsidiary or branch plant to operate the establishment as a separate entity, subject only to an overall control on matters of pricing, financing, and general administration.

Persons presenting the case *for* big business typically marshal their arguments to develop two main theses: (1) that big business is the indispensable dynamic factor in the preservation and continued improvement of our high level of living; and (2) that bigness in business is an inherent factor in certain types of business and is here to stay.

In stating the case for big business, it is said that the presumed "power" of large enterprises over prices is unrealistic. Large size carries with it no possible immunity from the antitrust laws. Beyond this, the character of competition today is such that it is *the customer* rather than the producer who exercises any measure of control over price. This is so because the alternatives from which he may choose have been multiplied by technical developments. If a producer should be unmindful of his customers' needs, he would soon face competition from unexpected sources *in unlike materials performing the same function.* The whole matter of substitute competition, it is emphasized, becomes increasingly important as our technology advances.

The principal advantages which are said to accrue to large business units owning or controlling many separate plants may be summarized as follows:

1. THE ECONOMY OF LARGE-SCALE MANAGEMENT

Greater efficiency is secured through superior and large-scale management. A multiplant company is financially able to employ the very best managerial talent to supervise, guide, and counsel the heads of subsidiary plants. In the view of Professor J. A. Schumpeter, the "better brains" which are available to large units are the "outstanding feature" of large business size.[4] A large firm, moreover, can divide managerial functions into numerous specialized operations and employ experts for each department. Further, the services of a specialized department, such as sales forecasting, can be utilized by the several branches of a multiplant firm. The per-unit cost of large-scale management in multiplant companies is typically low because management overhead can be spread over a large output.

An advantage is likewise secured in large companies in the training, broadening, and testing of junior executives by giving them a variety of experiences. An integrated company typically has a wider range of positions of responsibility to offer employees interested in advancement. Openings develop with greater frequency, and persons with ability find a strong demand for their services.

2. ADVANTAGES IN LARGE-SCALE BUYING AND SELLING

Big companies have advantages in large-scale buying. Quantity buying makes possible numerous savings in manufacturing, selling, packaging, pack-

[4] J. A. Schumpeter, *Capitalism, Socialism, and Democracy* (New York, 1947), p. 101.

ing, shipping, billing, and collecting. Many large buyers are able to secure substantial quantity discounts as a result of such savings, and these discounts are passed on to the public in the form of lower prices. Lower costs may also be obtained through better performance in the market in ferreting out "good buys," i.e., in finding where prices are out of line and in taking advantage of special buying opportunities.

Large company size likewise brings advantages in large-scale marketing. Such advantages arise (1) in having a more complete product line, such as regular cigarettes, filter-tip cigarettes, pipe tobacco, and chewing tobacco, and (2) in having a bigger volume of each item within a line to sell. When the volume of sales of a given item is large, a company is able to engage in national advertising which *may* be the cheapest form of selling. The large volume of sales makes it possible to decrease the overhead advertising expense per unit of sale. Unit costs of marketing can also be substantially reduced by spreading the cost of a sales organization over numerous products. Some of the large meat packers have acquired additional plants in order to build up a line of products—fresh meats, poultry, dairy products, margarine, and peanut butter—for their sales units and distribution facilities to handle.

Large companies are able to engage in large-scale mass advertising to introduce new products, as well as established products made from new sources, such as hydrogenated shortening made from lard. Experience has shown that a concern must spend from ten to fifteen million dollars in national advertising over a period of two to three years to gain consumer acceptance for a new product. Small and medium-sized companies do not have the financial resources necessary to engage in this kind of merchandising.

3. Large Size Makes Possible the Most Advanced Technology

Large companies, representing a large and varied organization, and having a great number of scientific specialists, are in a position to develop and implement the most advanced technology. One of the more important innovations in the chemical industry, for example, has been the development of the continuous process, operating 24 hours a day, based upon *automatic control*. Automatic control is a complex of instruments which assembles information and transmits "instructions" to devices which regulate the various processes of production. Today, an entire chemical process, such as the making of nylon, can be largely regulated by automatic controls which govern the temperatures, pressures, constituents, and flow of materials (see Fig. 16).

To an increasing extent, automatic controls are serving to transform industrial production. They make it possible to produce high-quality products, in large volume, with very much less labor, with less hazard (as in atomic energy units), and with far greater precision, than is possible with human control. Competent engineers believe that only a beginning has been made in the technology of automatic control. Its full potential, they say, rests with the future.

The development and implementation of automatic control programs in

Fig. 16. Control panel for the automatic control of an intricate chemical plant. The control devices in this room largely regulate the complete chemical process for the making of dimethyl terephthalate at Du Pont's plant in Repauno, New Jersey. (Courtesy of E. I. du Pont de Nemours.)

146

large-scale production are dependent upon a large organization which has great numbers of scientific specialists, as well as vast amounts of capital. Modern processes, as in synthetic fiber and atomic energy installations, are exceedingly complicated and complex. In developing technology for these processes, and in applying automatic controls to it, knowledge and experience must be drawn from many branches of science. At the present time, Du Pont employs technical people in some 160 different branches of science. This vast reservoir of knowledge, it has been found, is a necessary basis for developing and implementing continuous-process production based upon automatic control.

4. ADVANTAGES IN CONDUCTING RESEARCH

Big business units are financially able to support large research laboratories. Industrial research is expensive—it costs at least $20,000 per year for each scientist employed. A concern is lucky, moreover, if one research project out of ten actually results in increased sales revenue. Some large companies, such as Du Pont, suggest that a ratio of one to twenty is much more realistic. Large companies have an advantage over small companies to the extent that they can afford this sort of investment. Large companies can support research teams which permit an efficient attack on complicated problems. The research work, moreover, can be directly tied to the needs of the operating departments.

In the research field, the element of diversification has become increasingly important. Experience in a number of fields broadens the commercial background against which new developments can be evaluated. Du Pont reports, for example, that it is highly unlikely that its research in the high polymers would have produced a synthetic textile fiber if the company had not previously entered the rayon business and acquired a working knowledge of the textile field. A diversified structure helps to diminish the long odds of successful research operation. It also provides a broader base for developing discoveries which are not consciously sought (serendipity).

In most cases, research cannot be hurried, and frequently a number of years must be spent in developing a new product or process. It took twenty-five years, for example, to develop the production of aluminum on a practical basis. Eleven years were required from the beginning of fundamental research on giant molecules to the first commercial production of nylon. In developing nylon, the Du Pont Company invested not only great effort and patience, but also vast sums of money. Formal research on the production of titanium metal was begun in 1946. Although this metal has great military significance, only a small output has thus far been secured. Swift and Company spent nearly ten years of time and much money in developing a process for converting lard into a bland, hydrogenated shortening which can be used for cakes and pastries. In the oil and chemical fields, it is reported that if the research staffs of large companies are able to get a basic development once every five years, the top management believes that its research expenditures are fully justified.

At the present time, large corporations do not use their laboratories to "fence in" or "block" new fields of enterprise. Many large firms, such as Du Pont, deliberately grant favorable licenses to promote competition with their own business. Such concerns are now in so secure a position that they are becoming more, rather than less, liberal in sharing their ideas and developments.

5. ADVANTAGES IN UNITING SUCCESSIVE PROCESSES IN THE PRODUCTION OF GOODS

The acquisition or ownership of plants at successive stages—such as production, refining, and marketing in the oil industry—may be highly desirable in order to get (a) an assured source of supply, or (b) an assured selling outlet, as the case may be. It is very difficult, for example, to justify the investment of large sums of money required for a modern oil refinery, pulp mill, or aluminum works, unless one has reasonable assurance of a substantial proportion of his raw materials and of an outlet for his finished products.[5] Integration saves much time, effort, and expense, in buying and selling between divisions; gives the company an opportunity to plan ahead with some confidence; and minimizes fluctuations in earnings. The quality of products, from raw materials to finished items, can be carefully controlled. Also, an integrated company can make sounder decisions as to where new capital is most needed than a company which sees only one angle of the whole picture.

Provision of adequate transportation facilities, such as pipe lines and tankers, can be planned more efficiently and intelligently if one is reasonably certain about where his supply is coming from and where his products are likely to be sold over the next decade or two. Ownership of raw materials and transportation facilities, moreover, makes it possible for a company to protect itself against unwarranted price increases and monopolistic action by suppliers. "Historically," concludes Ward S. Bowman, "the expansion of steel firms into the raw material and transportation business is principally to be explained by fear of being 'caught short' or of being exploited by others."[6]

Perhaps the greatest advantage of integrated buying and selling lies in the control which centralized management exercises over the flow of products from primary plants to consumer outlets. In exercising this control, large-scale management performs the traditional functions of merchants.

Historically, independent dealers and jobbers contacted scattered plants and mills to buy supplies for sale to processing firms and consumer outlets. The broad contacts of merchants gave them knowledge of the types and

[5] See also J. W. Boatwright, "Vertical Integration in the Petroleum Industry," *Vertical Integration in Marketing*, Bureau of Economic and Business Research, University of Illinois, *Bulletin 74*, 1952, pp. 136–147.

[6] Ward S. Bowman, "Toward Less Monopoly," *University of Pennsylvania Law Review*, March, 1953, p. 604.

qualities of products desired by various users and of the places where such items could be secured. They knew, in brief, where to buy and where to sell. Merchants, as well as speculators, also performed the valuable service of accumulating inventories at a time when consumer demands were declining, to sell again when business conditions improved. This activity helped to "make a market" and also served to check extreme price advances when demand increased.

Today, large multiplant concerns themselves typically exercise the traditional functions of the merchant. Centralized management now serves as "merchant-distributor-speculator" for the multiple plants under the common ownership. Large companies find profit and economy in exercising the traditional activity of merchants for several reasons. First, in keeping supplies in their own hands until sold to fabricators or consumer outlets, they are able to avoid a substantial amount of the competition among merchants which traditionally operated at the distribution level. At the same time, in controlling a substantial flow of products, a central management is able to coördinate intracompany sales and purchases with a minimum of sales effort and handling cost. The flow of products is regularized, and extremes in local gluts and shortages are avoided. Centralized integrated control likewise makes it possible to avoid the payment of tribute to racketeers and monopolistic elements which sometimes operate in the distribution trades.

6. ADVANTAGES IN MEETING CAPITAL NEEDS

Bigness in corporate size simplifies the problems of new financing for expansion, modernization, and the development of new products. A principal function of a multiplant firm is to provide its various plants with funds for working capital or plant expansion. Earnings from one branch may be used to help finance some other branch of the business. When large corporations need to borrow, they usually can do so with greater ease and on a low-cost basis.[7]

Large corporate units also have an advantage in financing the development of new products or in improving old ones. In the automobile industry, for example, the cost of designing an engine from scratch, building prototypes, and giving these both laboratory and road tests, will be approximately the same whether the company intends to build three or three million cars of the final design. The larger automobile companies and the larger divisions of those companies have an advantage in being able to spread such development costs over a larger number of cars.

Many investors favor the securities of large corporations. Such securities have a broad and ready market. They also make it possible for an investor to diversify his risk over the several lines of business usually conducted by a large enterprise.

[7] See also Richard B. Heflebower, "Economics of Size," *Journal of Business of the University of Chicago*, October, 1951, p. 263.

7. ADVANTAGES IN DIVERSIFICATION

Large company size makes possible the reduction of risk and the offsetting of losses through diversification. With the central ownership of numerous separate plants, a company is able to reduce the risk of cyclical fluctuations in various lines of business. The impact of seasonal variations likewise can be minimized by acquiring additional plants in other lines or in other areas of production. Effects of mistaken judgment or operating losses in one division can similarly be offset by the group ownership of separate plants. The introduction of new products, such as canned meats for babies, may require a company to incur a loss on operations for as many as three to five years.

The advantage of bigness in offsetting losses—fortuitous or planned—was emphasized by Mr. Crawford H. Greenewalt, President of E. I. Du Pont de Nemours, in a Congressional hearing. The following questions were asked of Mr. Greenewalt:

> *Chairman:* Is it not true that you have two or three departments, and you can compensate yourself for your losses in department A by your profits in departments B and C? Is that not correct?
> *Mr. Greenewalt:* That is quite correct, sir.
> *Chairman:* And, if an individual goes into business and he has one department, he has to sustain his entire losses and cannot get compensation for those losses in any of the other departments. That is the advantage—that is one of the advantages of bigness, is that not true?
> *Mr. Greenewalt:* Indeed, yes.[8]

8. BIG BUSINESS IS ESSENTIAL FOR DEFENSE

Large-scale business has advantages in serving the needs of defense. It can take big defense contracts and fill them in the shortest possible time. It also has the organizational ability and know-how for filling large orders. Defense agencies lack experience for the effective allocation of production assignments. The experience of World War II and the Korean War showed the advantage of giving contracts to large companies to subcontract and to administer. The coördinating skills of big business management are of vital importance in national defense.

Big business, moreover, has the skill to develop, implement, and coördinate large defense operations. The development of atomic energy during World War II was undertaken by such large companies as Du Pont and General Electric which had large and varied organizations with diverse skills and great numbers of scientific specialists. Large organizations with staffs trained in time of peace stand ready to serve in emergencies. They cannot be hastily assembled for a defense need.

[8] Hearings before the Subcommittee of the Committee on the Judiciary, House of Representatives, 81st Congress, first session, Serial No. 14, Part 2A, 1950, p. 565.

THE CASE *AGAINST* BIG BUSINESS

According to the critics of big business, the claims (1) that big business is responsible for our high level of living, and (2) that big business is inevitable are delusions. All available evidence points to the conclusion that extreme corporate concentration has been the artificial result (1) of a drive for higher profits and dividends by promoters and business leaders; (2) of changes in our corporation laws which have made it possible for corporations to engage in more than one kind of business, to form subsidiaries, and to own and vote the stock of other corporations; and (3) of the failure of the executive, legislative, and judicial branches of government to give vigorous support to the antitrust laws.

The critics of large multiplant companies recognize that there undoubtedly are economies to be secured in joint research, large-scale management, centralized financing, and mass advertising. They point out, however, that there are always limits to such gains. Beyond a certain point, the economies of large-scale operations diminish and are offset by the disadvantages of large size—in particular, the difficult managerial problems of coördinating and directing diverse, geographically separate operations. Large, multiplant size thereupon may survive and be profitable because of monopoly control. In the opinion of the critics, the public needs (1) proof of noteworthy economies in mergers and multiplant operations, and (2) concrete evidence that such economies have been, and are being, passed on to consumers in the form of lower prices, high-level output, and better service. The burden of proof rests with big business, they affirm, and thus far specific proof has not been given.

The main arguments which are made against very large business combinations are the following:

1. BIG BUSINESSES ACT MONOPOLISTICALLY

Large business units—by combining scores of formerly independent and competing plants—have secured a unified control over price in many of the principal industries. Monopolistic control is typically evidenced (a) by unity of action on price, i.e., the quoting of *identical* delivered prices; (b) by "price leadership" in which a dominant seller makes the going price—in a given sales area or for a certain product—which is largely observed by others; and (c) by the use of discriminatory pricing to limit or injure independent competitors. Many economists believe that unified selling and centralized control are important factors preventing a full and continuous utilization of our productive capacity. These business arrangements, it is observed, result in, or contribute to, price rigidity and restrictions on economic freedom. Rigid or inflexible prices in turn serve to prolong and aggravate depressions by keeping up prices in the face of idle factories and idle groups of workers.

The exercise of control over price, it may be noted, does not depend upon the complete control of all sellers in a given industry. Mr. Charles M. Schwab, as President of the United States Steel Corporation, declared in 1901, "it does not require over 30 percent in any kind of capital or business, I think, to control, because a man owning 30 percent or 40 percent of that [the volume of production] can usually collect about him enough people who think as he does to direct the policy."[9] This, of course, is the familiar problem of oligopoly.

The main problem of unified selling in the American economy is expressed in the "Big Threes," "Big Fours," and "Big Fives" which have come to dominate the various industrial fields. As a result of mergers and the building of additional plants, a few large concerns now produce the bulk of the output in each industry. No one concern enjoys a single monopoly control, but the very fewness of the dominant concerns makes possible concerted action through a "wink and a nod" and a close identity of interests. The pattern of concerted action is further strengthened by the long-continued common use of basing-point and zone-delivered pricing systems, a concerted policy of refusing to sell to independent dealers, by trade association activities, interlocking directorates, and by a realistic fear of the disastrous effects of discriminatory price cutting.

As a general rule, it appears that the large firms in a national industry do not follow a single leader or jointly act as one throughout the nation. Rather, the practice is for one large firm to make the "going price" in a given geographic area or for a given product line and for another leading firm to manage the prices in another area or product line. Lesser, local firms thereupon observe the established prices, as do the leaders from other areas or in other product lines. In the sale of cement, for example, there is evidence that a leader in one area makes the delivered prices in its area which are largely observed by others, while on sales in distant areas, it adopts the delivered prices which are made by dominant firms in those areas.

The problem of oligopoly and reciprocal price leadership is one which has not as yet been reached by the antitrust laws. Typical industry patterns are those in which there is no single-firm monopoly. Formal conspiracies are absent or impossible to prove. A dozen or more salesmen compete for orders, and the competition for business is characterized by business spokesmen as "vigorous," "tough," and "plenty tough." In the eyes of many economists, however, when there is no rivalry *on price*, there is monopoly which should be condemned by the law, even though consumers have a choice of competing salesmen or a choice of substitute products.

2. ALLEGATIONS OF GREAT ECONOMIES UNPROVED

There is no conclusive evidence to indicate that the unit costs of large companies are typically below those of small and medium-sized firms. In a study of costs in the steel industry, Professor George Stigler found that costs

[9] Report of the Industrial Commission, *Testimony*, Washington, 1901, Vol. XIII, p. 465.

of the U.S. Steel Corporation ranged about in the middle of the costs of other steel firms.[10] Upon the basis of numerous cost studies in various industries, another authority reports: "As a generalization from the inadequate data available, it may be said that there is little evidence to support the conclusion that the largest enterprises are relatively inefficient. Nor, on the other hand, has it been proved that they have a superiority on a cost basis."[11]

It is possible that multiple-plant ownership may bring economies in financing, research, lobbying, advertising, and selling, because expenditures for such activities can be shared jointly by the various plants under a central control. Large companies, on the other hand, are particularly vulnerable to public criticism, and much money must be spent in maintaining public relations departments, and in public relations activity. This is a cost burden which small and medium-sized companies do not need to incur. Beyond a certain point, moreover, large-scale operations bring a decrease in efficiency. Large buying of supplies creates problems of warehousing and aggravates the risks of change in price, style, and product composition.

In many cases sellers do not offer a lower price for buying more than one carload, so that the economies of large-scale buying are soon exhausted. Usually low buying prices secured by certain chain buyers frequently are discriminatory and stand condemned by the Robinson-Patman Act.

Increasing corporate size, it has been found, creates numerous managerial difficulties. The top management of a large concern cannot know all the details of the business and must rely upon the reports of subordinates. Such persons are frequently reluctant to prejudice their careers by taking risks or by trying uncertain methods. Company heads who make decisions are remote from those who execute them. Bureaucracy develops, and business becomes organized and operated by rules and committees rather than by individual judgment. According to a well-known management expert:

The big firm may well be a series of wheels within wheels, an elaborate hierarchy in which every decision requires the consulting of this man, the

[10] Statement of George J. Stigler, Committee on the Judiciary, House of Representatives, *Study of Monopoly Power: Steel*, Serial No. 14, Part 4A, 81st Congress, second session, 1950, p. 122.
[11] Richards C. Osborn, "Efficiency and Profitability in Relation to Size," *Harvard Business Review*, March, 1951, p. 92. For further studies on costs and the size of plants and companies, see "Relative Efficiency of Large, Medium-Sized, and Small Business," *T.N.E.C. Monograph 13*, 1941; John M. Blair, "The Relation Between Size and Efficiency of Business," *Review of Economic Statistics*, August, 1942; J. L. McConnell, "Corporate Earnings by Size of Firm," *Survey of Current Business*, May, 1945; National Bureau of Economic Research, *Cost Behavior and Price Policy* (New York, 1943); S. R. Dennison, "The Problem of Bigness," *The Cambridge Journal*, November, 1947; John M. Blair, "Does Large-Scale Enterprise Result in Lower Costs?," *American Economic Review*, May, 1948 (Supplement); Federal Trade Commission, *The Divergence between Plant and Company Concentration, 1947* (1950); National Association of Manufacturers, *Business Size and the Public Interest*, 1949; Richards C. Osborn, *Effects of Corporate Size on Efficiency and Profitability* (Urbana, 1950); and Walter Adams, "The Dilemma of Antitrust Aims: A Reply," *American Economic Review*, December, 1952, pp. 895–900.

referring to that man, the permission of a third, the agreement of a fourth, and informing a fifth—so that decisions may become endlessly delayed. Where decisions must be reached frequently and quickly, such an organization, unless despotically controlled, may find itself paralyzed—and, if it is in fact a despotism, much of the benefit of specialist services and advice may be lost.[12]

Small business has the very real advantage of being able to establish effective team work with much less fuss and bother than big business. A small company enjoys the advantage of having its top management know details of current operations at first hand. Decisions can be reached quickly and effectively. Managerial efforts are linked more closely to results, and junior executives are given opportunity to secure all-round development. Many young men are often explicit in their preference for a small concern, citing as a reason a feeling that "you get lost in a big company."

In a number of fields, central buying has made it possible for independent retailers to secure buying prices comparable with those paid by large chains. At the same time, independents have advantages in management, in timing their activities, and in knowing their local communities.

3. CLAIMS THAT EXTREMELY LARGE MULTIPLANT CORPORATIONS ARE NECESSARY FOR PROGRESSIVENESS IN RESEARCH UNSUBSTANTIATED BY FACTS

Money for research in the United States comes from the federal government (60 percent in 1952), from private industry (38 percent), and from the universities (2 percent) (see Table 17). Although the federal government pays for a large part of the research work, much of the work (68 percent) is actually done by private industry. In conducting research, many business corporations utilize the facilities of private nonprofit research institutes (such as Mellon, Armour, Midwest, Stanford, and Battelle), commercial laboratories (some 600 in the United States), and the laboratories of certain trade associations.

The federal government, universities, and private nonprofit research institutes largely engage in long-range research in the pure and applied sciences. Most of the industry funds, on the other hand, are used for exploratory field work, the control of operations, and for development purposes.

The "outstanding fact" about research in industry, states the Paley Commission Report, is its concentration in a few industries. Four groups—chemicals, communications, petroleum (including coal products), and aircraft—in 1950 accounted for fully 50 percent of the total industrial research activity. The entire mining industry, by contrast, contributed less than one half of 1 percent.[13]

In each of the four industries designated in the Paley Report, there is a

[12] Ernest Dale, *Planning and Developing the Company Organization Structure* (New York, 1952), p. 111.

[13] President's Materials Policy Commission, *Resources for Freedom* (Washington, 1952), Vol. 1, pp. 140–141.

high concentration of output in the four largest companies (see Table 15, pp. 129–131). Large companies in these areas are clearly important factors in research. But large companies in other segments of the economy do not spend vast sums on research. It appears that factors other than extremely large multiplant size are responsible for causing *an industry* to spend substantial amounts on research.

TABLE 17.   Trend of Research and Development in the U.S., 1942–1952, in Millions.

	Total	Government Expend.[a]	Government Perform.	Industry Expend.	Industry Perform.	University Expend.	University Perform.
1942	1070	490	240	560	780	20	50
1944	1380	940	390	420	910	20	80
1946	1780	910	470	840	1190	30	120
1948	2610	1390	570	1150	1820	70	220
1950	2870	1610	570	1180	1980	80	320
1952	3750	2240	800	1430	2530	80	420

	% of Expenditure by Govt.	Ind.	Univ.	% of Performance by Govt.	Ind.	Univ.
1942	46	52	2	22	73	5
1944	68	30	2	28	66	6
1946	51	47	2	26	67	7
1948	53	44	3	22	70	8
1950	56	41	3	20	69	11
1952	60	38	2	21	68	11

[a] "Expenditure" indicates who pays for the work; "performance" indicates who does the work.
(Source: Research and Development Board, Department of Defense, Washington, D.C.)

Basic factors stimulating applied research are critical human needs and problems, e.g., remedies for cancer, polio, heart disease, and geriatrics; critical shortages of raw materials; and the existence of burdensome surpluses, waste materials, and by-products. With these underlying conditions present, a further factor making for intense research activity is competition—that is, an incentive to hold one's place in the industry, to develop new products, and to find new uses, before a rival captures the field. Examples of research pioneered to meet shortages or to conserve natural resources are found in the development of aluminum; nylon; titanium; new fertilizers, insecticides, and weedkillers; ethyl alcohol and methanol; synthetic products such as synthetic glycerine, rubber, camphor, nitrates, and amino acids; plastics; silicones; and atomic fission. Critical shortages and urgent needs have a greater impact on certain industries than on others. Research thrives on problems, not because of company size.

Where small and medium-sized companies (units producing up to 5 percent of the total output) continue to be a significant factor in an industry, they actively support research (see Fig. 17) and account for a steady stream of new methods and products. Indeed, in some fields it appears that medium-sized companies are much more likely to pioneer new processes and products than the big companies. Medium-sized companies, experience has shown, enjoy a certain freedom and flexibility of action in matters of research and engineering developments. By employing a few high caliber technical men, by operating in a specialty field, and by developing one or two general lines of products, they can usually overcome any advantage a large company may have, and can frequently develop, expand, and prosper in relation to large business. Large companies tend to improve and apply that which is already in existence, rather than to pioneer new processes and products. Their rule

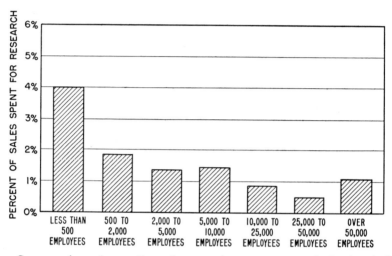

Fig. 17. Company size and expenditures for research as a percentage of sales (1951). Companies with less than 500 employees spent 3 to 4% of their sales income for research; those with 500 to 2000 employees, 1.9%; 2000 to 5000, 1.4%; 5000 to 10,000, 1.5%; 10,000 to 25,000, 0.9%; and 25,000 to 50,000, 0.5%. (Source: *Chemical and Engineering News*, Dec. 7, 1953, p. 5080. Based upon a survey conducted by the Division of Research, Graduate School of Business, Harvard University.)

is commonly "Be not the first by whom the new are tried, nor yet the last to lay the old aside." Large concerns are organized to make uniform products which will satisfy most of the people. Frequently, they will not try a new method, process, or product until it appears that consumers are readily accepting the innovation of an independent.

A considerable number of small and medium-sized companies have testified that they do not feel handicapped by their size in developing new products and methods. Almost any research problem from sales analysis to chemical study, they report, can be solved in an independent laboratory, if not in their own laboratories. Through the use of independent research laboratories, a broad cross section of talent and experience can be brought to bear on any given problem at a minimum of cost. At a research institute—such as the Battele or Mellon Institute—it is possible for a small company to carry out a research program at an annual cost of $10,000 to $25,000 per project. If the company had to equip and staff its own laboratory to accomplish the same end result, capital outlay for equipment alone might run over one-half million dollars. Virtually all corporations resort to the independent laboratories for studies beyond the capabilities of their own people or for those of non-recurring nature. Very few of the big companies have laboratories and research organizations so complete as to carry on all their research needs.

In steel it is almost axiomatic that the small companies come forth with the greatest metallurgical and technological advancements. There is a logical reason why this is true. In high alloy steel, for instance, a new product almost always begins in a small way. It has to find its place in industry; therefore in the beginning it is a small-tonnage, small-profit item. Large steel companies are not set up to manufacture at a single time a few hundred pounds of steel of some new type. The smaller companies, which are able to tailor make their products, create new business for themselves by producing such new materials. Eventually when a particular alloy matures to the extent that it can be considered a tonnage product, the larger companies begin making it. The same thing is true of many processes for steel production. Smaller companies are usually better equipped to make technological changes than the larger organizations where facilities are standardized.

The National Steel Corporation, having some 5.3 percent of the industry's net capital assets and about 5 percent of the ingot capacity, has made many notable innovations in the steel industry. In 1926 it installed the first fully continuous, four-high rolling mill; in 1938 it pioneered the development of the electrolytic line for producing tin plate; and in 1950 it began construction on one of the largest oxygen plants in the United States. During Congressional hearings on bigness and technology in the steel industry, Mr. Ernest Weir, chairman of the National Steel Company was asked, "Do you think your firm is too small to be able to effectively do research or to develop these new processes and methods?" Mr. Weir replied, "Not at all, no, sir."[14]

The history of many of our large corporations, with respect to technical progressiveness, stands in sharp contrast to that of smaller companies. In 1935, for example, the United States Steel Corporation employed Ford, Bacon and Davis, an industrial engineering firm, to survey the firm's productive efficiency. The results of this private study were publicly revealed in 1950 during the course of Senate hearings on monopoly power. Summarizing the findings at the hearings, Professor George W. Stocking stated that the engineering firm

> . . . pictured the Steel Corp. as a big sprawling inert giant, whose production operations were improperly coördinated; suffering from a lack of a long-run planning agency; relying on an antiquated system of cost accounting; with an inadequate knowledge of the costs or of the relative profitability of the many thousands of items it sold; with production and cost standards generally below those considered everyday practice in other industries; with inadequate knowledge of its domestic markets

[14] Hearings Before the Subcommittee of the Committee on the Judiciary, House of Representatives, 81st Congress, second session, Serial No. 14, Part 4A, 1950, pp. 808–809, 835.

and no clear appreciation of its opportunities in foreign markets; with less efficient production facilities than its rivals had; slow in introducing new processes and new products.

Specifically, according to the engineers, it was slow in introducing the continuous rolling mill; slow in getting into production of cold-rolled steel products; slow in recognizing the potentials of the wire business; slow to adopt the heat-treating process for the production of sheets; slow in getting into stainless steel products; slow in producing cold-rolled sheets; slow in tin-plate developments; slow in utilizing waste gases; slow in utilizing low-cost water transportation because of its consideration for the railroads; in short, slow to grasp the remarkable business opportunities that a dynamic America offered it. The corporation was apparently a follower, not a leader, in industrial efficiency.[15]

In a similar way, Arthur A. Bright, Jr., concludes that General Electric, as the industry leader in the electric lamp industry, has been slow in developing new contributions in lighting. According to Mr. Bright,

> For the most part, General Electric concentrated its efforts on improving the filament lamp and production methods. It resisted the growth of neon-type tubing for general illumination. Outside inventors conducted almost all the work on electric-discharge lamps early in the century, and the industry leader was slow in undertaking to improve the old carbon filament. It also lagged in developing fluorescent lighting to a commercial stage. When General Electric did bring out the hot-cathode fluorescent lamp, the new lamp was initially promoted only for decorative and supplementary lighting. The lack of strong competitive pressure at most times permitted General Electric to concentrate its attention on improving the older incandescent lamp, which would not endanger its established interest in the *status quo*. My own conclusion, therefore, is that General Electric's control over the lamp industry has not provided an ideal environment for the rapid development and introduction of major new *light sources*.[16]

Today leading scientists emphasize that *basic* research can most effectively be done by individuals working independently on ideas which they themselves believe should be explored.[17] Large teams, it is stated, are useful for *development* purposes and for the *application* of research. Generally, however, these teams build upon knowledge "carved out" by individuals in the universities, in government, and in independent laboratories. According to Dr. Detlev Bronk, a leading American scientist, "The most important discoveries of scientific research have come from the intellectual adventures of individual scientists." Mr. Henry Allen Moe, a long-time student of scientific work, likewise declares that, ". . . all knowledge and all understanding in

[15] Hearings Before the Subcommittee of the Committee on the Judiciary, House of Representatives, 81st Congress, second session, Serial No. 14, Part 4A, 1950, pp. 966–967.

[16] Arthur A. Bright, Jr., *The Electric-Lamp Industry* (New York, 1949), p. 456.

[17] The ensuing two paragraphs are based upon material presented by Dr. Roger D. Reid, Office of Naval Research, Washington, D.C., in "Freedom and Finance in Research," *American Scientist*, April, 1953, pp. 286–292.

the present depend upon what the individual men have had a chance to think and do in the past; their knowledge and understanding are the results of the intellectual processes only of individuals. Whatever the results, good or evil, they all start with an individual."

Dr. Roger Reid, a scientist in the Office of Naval Research, similarly stresses the need for individual research. According to Dr. Reid, "No one can tell the investigator what he is to discover. Did Newton enact the law of gravity by edict, or Einstein explain the relation of mass to energy on order? No one suggested to Fleming that he discover penicillin. These and many others, through their own intellectual instincts and imagination and with adequate time and resources, have made important discoveries for which we are grateful."

H. Stafford Hatfield, in a special study of inventions, declares "It is frequently said . . . that advance in the future will come exclusively from the magnificently equipped research laboratories of the great Trusts and Corporations. There is no evidence of this except the *ipse dixit* of the Corporations themselves." In reviewing the "outstanding inventions" made since 1889, Mr. Hatfield observes that very few have been produced by "corporation research." He states, "Into this period falls the invention by independent individuals of such first-rate things as monotype, casehardening of steel, photogravure, moving pictures, dial telephones, calcium carbide, Diesel engines, carborundum, wireless telegraphy and telephony, electric train control, electric car starters, submarines, safety razors, aeroplanes, flotation process, Bakelite, gyrocompasses . . . the autogyro, the triode valve, Haber's ammonia synthesis, Bergius's hydrogenation of coal, television, gaslight papers (offered by their inventor, Baekeland, to the greatest photographic corporation in the world, and refused by them only to be afterwards purchased at great expense when Baekeland had made a success of them). . . . The very latest example of the victory of individualism in invention is television, worked out by a young Scotsman with the slenderest resources, in a cellar in Soho."[18]

4. Technical Gains from Mergers Are Unlikely

The claim that mergers contribute to the economies of large-scale mass production is largely unproved. As a general rule, the acquired plants continue to be operated with little or no change in their physical size or methods of operation. The advantages of combinations are primarily commercial, not technical. They include an assured source of supply and an assured outlet, as well as the possibility of reducing risks and offsetting losses through diversification. They also include greater bargaining power in forcing down costs, greater control over selling prices, greater ease in securing loans, and a power to engage in coercive and predatory practices against smaller rivals. Such

[18] H. Stafford Hatfield, *The Inventor and His World* (New York, 1933), pp. 37, 45. See also W. R. Maclaurin, *Invention and Innovation in the Radio Industry* (New York, 1949), pp. 242–243.

advantages, it may be noted, are frequently secured at the expense of other persons and do not represent real savings.

The antitrust agencies have had many complaints that integrated companies (vertical mergers) charge high cost prices on sales of primary products to independent fabricators, for example, on the sale of pig aluminum to producers of sheets. Thereupon, these integrated companies sell their own finished products (sheets) in competition with independents at very low prices.[19] Since there are no published data on intercorporate transfer costs, a large rival is able to operate one subsidiary at a profit and another at a loss, to the great disadvantage of unintegrated firms. Competition between integrated and unintegrated firms is frequently characterized by cutthroat discrimination of this type. The importance of this problem to independent single-product firms can be recognized by considering that there is hardly a line of business today which one can enter without being in direct competition with a subsidiary or branch of a giant corporation.[20]

Closely related to the business practice of price squeeze is the problem of denial of supplies. This problem takes two main forms. First, there is the refusal of an integrated firm to sell basic materials to unintegrated firms which compete with the former in the sale of finished products. Usually this refusal occurs during periods of rising business activity, when an integrated firm expands its production and undertakes to meet its own needs first. However, it may occur at any time, if the integrated company desires to limit or restrict the expansion of its rivals in the finished-products field. The denial or cutting off of supplies may also be employed by certain integrated firms against independents who exercise any degree of independence with respect to sales policies and prices.[21]

Secondly, there is the further problem arising in the practice of large integrated firms—controlling basic materials—*to sell only* to fabricating "consumers" and not to independent dealers or speculators. Wholesale merchants typically accumulate heavy inventories during periods of low prices and then offer them for sale as demand increases. In order to prevent primary materials of their own production coming back into competition with them, integrated firms typically refuse to sell anything at all to non-consuming trade interests.

5. THE POWER TO LOSE MONEY

A principal advantage of large financial size and multiple-plant ownership, we have seen, is the power to take losses—fortuitous or planned—in one

[19] For concrete examples of the power of integrated companies to impose a price squeeze on smaller rivals, see *Monopolistic Practices and Small Business*, Staff Report to the Federal Trade Commission for the Select Committee on Small Business, U.S. Senate, 1952, pp. 39–57.

[20] A suggested remedy for this corporate abuse is discussed in Chap. 19, p. 441, item 9.

[21] For examples of the direct refusal of integrated companies to sell to smaller rivals, see *Monopolistic Practices and Small Business*, Select Committee on Small Business, U.S. Senate, 1952, pp. 21–37. The legal status of refusal to sell is discussed in chaps. 11 and 16.

operation (or on certain sales) and offset them with gains in other areas of the business. This power may arise from sheer financial strength, but more often it reflects multiplant operations and the power to discriminate in prices. The power to offset losses with profits elsewhere has definite *private* advantages. From a social point of view, however, it provides large business with a club which can be—and is—used to suppress independent price competition.

The U.S. Industrial Commission in 1900, after hearing voluminous testimony on large combinations in many fields, including sugar, salt, oil, copper, lead, tobacco, iron, and steel, concluded that, "The large establishments, by cutting prices in certain localities, while maintaining the prices in the main, have a decided advantage over the smaller competitors whose market is limited to the one field in which the prices are cut, and consequently can often succeed in driving their rivals out of the business."[22]

A further statement on the advantage which large companies have in being able to take "planned losses" is found in the final report (1935) of the Federal Trade Commission on chain stores. According to the Commission, "The chain has an inherent advantage over the independent retailer in price competition because the chain is able to average the profit results obtained from its stores in various localities, the low prices in one or more localities being offset by the higher prices obtained at other points. . . . All the resources represented by the profits of other stores may be thus utilized by the chain for price cutting in any particular locality."[23]

Continuing studies made by the Federal Trade Commission show that price discrimination is still a major weapon of advantage for large combinations. "Among unfair business practices," declares the Commission, "price discrimination most directly denies to small business an equal opportunity to live and grow on the basis of efficiency. . . . What is relevant, but what must remain unknown until price discrimination is eliminated, is how successful small business can be when their large rivals cannot exercise their monopolistic power to grant and receive price discriminations. Small business is entitled to the opportunity of showing what it can do in the absence of the crippling handicap of discriminatory prices."[24]

6. BIG BUSINESS AND DEFENSE

It is true that large defense orders are essential, and that defense agencies can place such orders with large corporations in a very short time. It is also true that a feature of large-scale business is skill in administration and co-

---

[22] U.S. Industrial Commission, *Trusts and Industrial Combinations* (Washington, 1900), Vol. 1, p. 34.

[23] Federal Trade Commission, *Final Report on the Chain Store Investigation*, 74th Congress, first session, 1935, pp. 37–38.

[24] *Monopolistic Practices and Small Business*, Staff Report to the Federal Trade Commission for the Select Committee on Small Business, U.S. Senate, 1952, p. 57. A summary of recent commission proceedings against price discrimination is also presented in this report.

ordination. Large corporations, however, do a vast amount of subcontracting, and the task of spreading orders is thus largely performed by private business rather than by government agencies. The defense agencies, it is believed, could perform this task of spreading orders with a little extra work, experience, and patience. Many persons, moreover, believe that they *should* do it in order to give small and medium-sized companies a fair opportunity to survive. Big business has capacity for large orders chiefly because it controls many plants. A dissolution of large combinations would not change the size of the nation's productive capacity, for the separate plants would still remain in operation.

7. SOCIAL AND POLITICAL ASPECTS OF BIG BUSINESS

Many persons are opposed to large industrial combinations because they believe that centralized financial control is giving rise to social and political developments which are detrimental to the well-being of our nation. Today, basic decisions on business policy are centered in a few executives at the top, and vast numbers of employees must spend their lives as salesmen and clerks subservient to the order of those at higher levels of management. In controlling important areas of employment, big business is also able to exercise much influence over the economic and political views of its white-collar employees. It is possible for such persons to work independently in politics, but most of them appear to find an advantage in playing it safe. The political thinking of many thus comes to be shaped by influential economic interests.[25]

Concentrated economic power also means concentrated political and social power. With large financial means, big business is able to exert undue influence in political campaigns and in the day-to-day functioning of Congress and the state legislatures. In this environment, government tends to become an agency for strengthening certain groups in relation to others and for redistributing incomes upon the basis of political pressures.

Big business is likewise able to shape public opinion along the lines of its interests by sponsoring nation-wide radio and television programs, by advertising extensively in newspapers and national magazines, and by producing privately distributed motion picture films which develop appropriate ideas on the competitive economy. Mr. Charles E. Wilson, former head of General Motors, told a congressional committee that "What is good for General Motors is good for the country." Millions of Americans appear to believe this thesis, not realizing that high prices and profits for General Motors can mean that consumers will have less money left for other things.

SOME GENERALIZATIONS ON LARGE SIZE IN BUSINESS

1. Large, medium-sized, and small companies will undoubtedly continue to exist side by side in given industries for many years to come. Each has

[25] See also C. Wright Mills, *White Collar: The American Middle Class* (New York, 1951); and "Is Big Business a Career?" in *The Literature of Business* (New York, 1928), A. G. Saunders and H. L. Creek, editors.

certain advantages in relation to the other. Numerous disabilities—such as shortage of capital, high interest costs, and limited managerial talent—may be associated with small business. At the same time, various disabilities may be characteristic of big business. Inefficiency and the lack of enterprise are not the property of any one type of business organization. To suggest that big business is sometimes inefficient does not demonstrate that small business is efficient.

2. In many situations, large company size reflects large-scale ownership and management rather than large technological size. The numerous geographically separate plants owned by the 100 largest corporations are frequently *smaller* in size than adjacent plants owned by independents.

3. Many large corporations support sizable and highly productive research laboratories. This activity contributes substantially to the development of new materials and processes. "Small" business firms also actively engage in research in their particular fields of interest. Smaller companies have an advantage in being more flexible in their research programs and more able to apply new ideas and inventions rapidly. Available evidence indicates that many small and medium-sized concerns in using their own research facilities and those of the independent chemical and engineering laboratories are able to keep up with or lead in the parade of research and development.

4. A principal advantage of large companies which own many diverse and geographically separate plants is the control which centralized management is able to exercise over the flow of products from primary plants to consuming outlets. Businessmen call this the "integration of the market." Whether or not large-scale management can perform the "merchant's function" more effectively—in the public interest—than independent dealers and jobbers operating in central markets is a problem which warrants additional research and investigation.

5. A significant advantage of large corporate size is the power to spend, lose, or invest large sums of money. This financial power takes the form of an ability (a) to introduce new processes, methods, and specialized products which may be unprofitable for a period of years; (b) to engage in long-range, costly research programs to develop products in short supply from basic materials in large supply; (c) to secure funds for expansion and modernization with greater ease and at lower cost; (d) to use mass advertising in developing a demand for particular branded products; and (e) to finance lobbying and public relations activities with respect to measures or attitudes which affect their interests.

6. Some of the advantages of large financial power are clearly in the public interest. Others, however, reflect an ability to "throw one's weight around" at the expense of someone else. These include financial power (a) to coerce, injure, and thwart small specialized producers by cutting prices in one area, or on one product, and recouping losses on sales elsewhere; (b) to force price and other concessions from suppliers by proposing to construct one's own facilities or to transfer large orders to other suppliers; (c) to exercise a greater

control over buying and selling prices by eliminating or restraining competition; (d) to impose restrictive agreements on customers, requiring them to buy the seller's full line of products ("full-line forcing") or to refrain from dealing with competitors (exclusive dealing arrangements); and (e) to engage in prolonged and expensive law suits, protecting patents of doubtful legal validity, contesting patents of smaller concerns, and pressing legal claims against others.

7. The main economic problems of large size in business are (1) the prevention of mergers of larger firms with smaller ones where the effect is to injure competition; (2) the curbing of predatory practices and discriminatory pricing by large companies where the effect is to limit, restrict, or injure other competitors; and (3) the eradication of monopolistic power in industries where sellers are few (oligopoly) (a) by the imposition of direct public controls, (b) by the extension of public ownership, (c) by the creation of "countervailing power," or (d) by dissolution and divestiture suits.

To what extent are large, multiplant companies required and made necessary by given levels of economic efficiency? Would a substantial reduction in the size of large firms have a favorable or unfavorable effect on technological progress? Should there be a direct limitation on the size of multiplant companies? Can oligopoly be eliminated without sacrificing managerial and technological economies? An attempt to develop an intelligent opinion with respect to these questions would clearly require detailed industry-by-industry study. Some economic experts believe that corporate mergers claiming economies of large-scale organization should assume the burden of proving public benefits (see Chap. 21). Thereupon, the advantages can be weighed against the disadvantages. Numerous economists also point out that if it is found that oligopoly in a given industry results from economies of scale, there is need for *public control* to limit the exercise of monopolistic power. Public control is necessary because unified selling usually enables a group of producers to charge higher prices and to maintain their position by unfair and discriminatory practices instead of by individual efficiency.

PUBLIC POLICY AND BIG BUSINESS

At present, conservatives and liberals alike are giving increasing attention to the policies which government should adopt with respect to large corporations and unified pricing methods. The attitudes developed by various groups are highly important, for in our American democracy public opinion is basically responsible for the actions taken by the President and Congress.

The principal alternatives in public policy will be studied in subsequent chapters. In summary form, however, the main policies which might be adopted are as follows:

1. *The acceptance of the status quo and the abandonment of the competitive standard expressed in the antitrust laws.* Persons holding this view declare that the "ceaseless striving" among the giants for business, the competition in advertising and salesmanship, and the competition of substitutes make for

a workable kind of competition. "Effective competition," it is said, means (a) "freedom of choice of goods and services" and (b) "the opportunity for others to engage in such competition" even though there is no independent rivalry among sellers on price. Effective competition (in the foregoing sense), they believe, makes for "the creation of new and better products and new and cheaper methods." Buyers enjoy "alternatives among goods and services as well as among sellers."[26]

Persons embracing the so-called "new" concept of competition usually state that *formal* conspiracies on price and predatory competition should be condemned. In their view, however, nothing should be done to modify oligopoly or prevent the continuing growth of large business size by mergers and the formation of subsidiaries. Application of the antitrust laws against the "Big Threes" and "Big Fours," it is declared, would strike at the very basis of our business prosperity, defense strength, and economic well-being. No action, it is added, should be taken against "administered prices" which exist in important sectors of the economy. Identical delivered pricing and price matching, indeed, are considered to be aspects of a normal competitive economy.

The "new" concept of competition is primarily held by leaders in big business. In their view, "effective" competition exists when there is rivalry in sales effort and when buyers have a choice of substitute products. The objectives they desire are (1) a suspension of the antitrust laws with respect to oligopoly, identical delivered pricing, and large business size; and (2) a freedom from public price control.

2. *The extension of public price fixing by government commissions to oligopolistic industries.* Powers of public price fixing are presently exercised by a number of governmental commissions—state and federal—in industries which have the status of public utilities. In exercising direct control, it is usual to require that all rates and charges be filed with the appropriate commission. Thereupon, the commission, either upon complaint or upon its own motion, is empowered (1) to investigate any and all rates, (2) to set aside proposed rates, and (3) to prescribe rates which it believes will meet legislative standards.

It is frequently said that public price control should be extended to additional industries in which price competition is found to be ineffective. A proposal has been made, for example, that the steel industry be required (a) to file notices of proposed price increases and (b) to defend such increases in public hearings. Presumably, a government commission would thereupon be given authority to approve or disapprove the proposed prices or to prescribe actual prices. Legislation has also been introduced in Congress to impose rigid price controls on gasoline, fuel oil, natural gas, and kindred products in order to prevent "unwarranted increases."

The general opinion of economists is that an extension of public price

[26] See *Effective Competition*, Report to Secretary of Commerce Charles Sawyer by his Business Advisory Council (Washington, 1952), p. 9.

control to cover the products of oligopoly would impose insuperable burdens on public agencies. One reason for this view is the difficulty involved in estimating and distributing fair overhead costs and fair rates of return over the wide range and variety of products produced by the dominant industrial enterprises. Another arises in the probability that increased price fixing by government will lead to still greater lobbying and political activity by the major interest groups. It may be necessary in certain areas for the public to protect itself with price fixing by public commissions. In most fields of business, however, the more practical and promising remedy for monopolistic control, it is generally believed, is one of dissolution, divorcement, and divestiture—to increase competitive forces *within* an industry.[27]

3. *The adoption of public ownership in industries characterized by oligopoly and ineffective competition.* In Chapter 25, we shall consider government ownership as an alternative to commission control. Some economists believe that it is unlikely that steps will be taken to create effective competition in oligopolistic industries, such as the steel industry, through dissolution proceedings. They are also discouraged with the effectiveness of commission control in protecting the public interest. As a constructive alternative, they propose that public corporations, such as the Tennessee Valley Authority, be created to own and operate the basic, primary producing plants whose ownership has become centralized in the hands of a few. Arguments for and against this proposal will be considered in Chapter 25.

4. *The development and promotion of "countervailing power" to limit, offset, or restrict the economic power of oligopoly.* The existence of "private economic power" on one side of the market, Professor J. K. Galbraith believes, tends to bring into being "countervailing power" on the other side. In his view, *new* restraints or checks on oligopoly have appeared to replace the traditional price competition *among* sellers of a given class of goods. These restraints on the power of oligopoly are the pressures exercised by *large customers* or *organized suppliers* (including labor unions). This offsetting power is what he calls countervailing power.[28] Countervailing power, Professor Galbraith believes, has done much to make *oligopoly* tolerable.

Professor Galbraith shares the view of those who hold that collusive arrangements and single-firm monopoly are peculiarly dangerous to the economy. In arguing that countervailing power has made oligopoly tolerable, *he does not argue that it has made the antitrust laws unnecessary.* He would continue to exclude trade unions from the application of the Sherman Act, but otherwise he would not designate any parts of the economy which should be excluded from antitrust action. He would urge, however, that there be no

[27] See also the testimony of Professors Ward S. Bowman, Arthur R. Burns, George J. Stigler, George W. Stocking, and Kenneth Hunter in Hearings before the Subcommittee on Study of Monopoly Power, Committee on the Judiciary, House of Representatives, *Steel*, 81st Congress, second session, Serial No. 14, Part 4A, 1950.

[28] J. K. Galbraith, *American Capitalism: The Concept of Countervailing Power* (Boston, 1952), p. 118.

attack on a countervailing position which leaves another position of power intact.

The actual business structure of the American economy, Professor Galbraith points out, has grown increasingly apart from the competitive standard. In place of numerous sellers, with prices and outputs governed by market forces, there is now a small number of giant sellers, with prices and outputs controlled in large measure by the deliberate action of producers themselves. In such an environmental setting, the competitive pressures of the economists' model operate most imperfectly, if at all, either to promote efficiency or to limit private power. "The incentives in the typical American industry," Galbraith states, ". . . do not in fact work in the direction of maximum output at lowest prices. . . . In consumers' goods industries, great energy is without doubt channeled into one or another form of selling effort, which is of no perceptible benefit to the public and which is not in response to any recognizable public demand."[29]

Although the rise of oligopoly has brought certain losses, it has also brought compensating gains, Galbraith declares. The losses, he believes, are "more than offset by large gains from technical development." In his view, technical innovation "can be carried on only by a firm that has the resources associated with considerable size. . . . The net of all this is that there must be some element of monopoly in an industry if it is to be progressive."[30]

In Galbraith's view, government should give countervailing power freedom to develop and also assist and participate in its development. Indeed, he observes that perhaps the major domestic function of government has become that of promoting the development of countervailing power by granting special favors to organized producers, such as the coal producers, organized labor, and farm groups. By strengthening one group in relation to another, he believes that the need for overall government control or planning is lessened.

The major weakness of countervailing power, Professor Galbraith states, arises during periods of inflationary pressures. During such periods, he observes, "it does not function at all as a restraint on market power," for employers and sellers are willing to pay higher cost prices and pass them on to consumers.

TYPES OF COUNTERVAILING POWER

Professor Galbraith has made a notable contribution in bringing to light the idea of countervailing power and in explaining its role in limiting the power of oligopoly. Labor unions, consumer and producer coöperatives, publicly owned utilities, and other forms of countervailing arrangements have an important and essential function in capitalist countries. Professor Galbraith's analysis provides a theoretical base for understanding the place of such institutions in an economic system.

[29] *Ibid.*, pp. 90–91.
[30] *Ibid.*, pp. 92–93.

Price competition among sellers in a given industry, it may be noted, has long had, and still has in many areas, the highly important task of limiting "all the traffic will bear." The basic question raised by Professor Galbraith's analysis is whether the government should (a) accept oligopoly or (b) take steps to dissolve it and create numerous competitors as a form of counter-vailing power.

Galbraith himself counsels that large companies should be accepted and that other economic groups should be strengthened to offset concentrated private power. This thesis appeals to many people. Those favoring it view with dismay the weak enforcement of the antitrust laws during the past decades, the destruction and elimination of thousands of smaller business enterprises, and the growing power and influence of business executives from giant corporations in our political and social life. In their view, efforts to maintain a genuinely competitive economy have largely failed. If oligopoly is to be curbed, they reason, persons disadvantaged must take direct action themselves, or secure governmental privileges to counterbalance established power.

The plan for building up units of countervailing power by public and private action, some economists believe, involves serious dangers for con-sumers and small business. The creation of additional special privileges for disadvantaged producers—to control production and fix prices—would un-doubtedly give them greater bargaining power in dealing with an oligopolis-tic industry. Big business, it is believed, however, will most likely still be able to look out for its own interests; and the end result will be that consumers, unorganized workers, and small business will suffer in relation to the monop-olistic groups. Further, it is said, there is the danger that labor groups and organized producers will join hands to fix and raise product prices even when inflationary pressures are not present.

Numerous economists also question the thesis that big business is the in-dispensable condition for a progressive economy. In their opinion, there is a considerable amount of evidence indicating that the vast financial size which presently exists in American industry is not essential for technical advance or for productive efficiency. There is also much evidence showing that giant size has not been the inevitable result of the economics of large-scale organi-zation. Monopolistic coercion, discrimination, denial of supplies to competi-tors, and public favors have often played an important role in the develop-ment of large size. Economists taking this view hold that if monopolistic mergers and competitive evils were effectively curbed by antitrust action, the need for government action to support and promote the growth of countervailing pressures would be significantly reduced.[31]

5. *A final type of policy which may be employed with respect to monop-*

[31] See also Walter Adams, "Competition, Monopoly, and Countervailing Power," *Quarterly Journal of Economics*, November, 1953, pp. 487–491; and George J. Stigler, "The Economist Plays With Blocs," *American Economic Review, Papers and Proceedings*, May, 1954, pp. 7–14.

olistic *mergers and oligopoly is that of changing the company structure of such industries by dissolution, divorcement, and divestiture proceedings* (see chap. 11, pp. 234–235 for an analysis of these terms). Federal action, it is proposed, should be taken against oligopolistic industries under the antitrust laws or by authority of new legislation. The objective should be the creation of as many independent enterprises *as is consistent with the economies of scale and mass production.* When sellers are numerous, independent price competition is much more likely to occur. "Effective competition" means *price competition,* not merely the freedom of buyers "to choose and to change."

The belief of a number of economists and legal experts is that the Sherman Act *can* and *should* be applied to *unified selling* by a few dominant concerns who allegedly are acting "innocently and independently." The situation of oligopoly, it is believed, can be attacked (a) on the principle of implied conspiracy or (b) under Section 2 of the Sherman Act as a condition of monopoly.

The antitrust agencies declare that they have never brought an action against a business firm solely upon the issue of size. The Sherman and Clayton Acts, they add, place no limitations upon the size of a particular plant or company. It is only when monopoly power has been attained, or attempted, that the law is applicable. In their view, the claim that the antitrust laws are opposed to bigness is a gross misstatement.

The policy of competition (or antitrust) looks at the economy from a different point of view than that of countervailing power. The social purposes of competition are (1) to protect consumers—more and better goods at lower prices—and (2) to insure enterprisers a fair and open field in buying and selling. A policy of creating countervailing power groups, on the other hand, seeks to give a trade group greater bargaining power in dealing with an oligopolistic industry. The possession of enhanced bargaining power is advantageous to organized producers, intent upon their own commercial interest and safety, but it provides no assurance of protection to smaller business firms or to the buying public.

The alternative to a system of competitive markets, economists have long emphasized, is a regime of unified selling, unless the public protects itself with commission price fixing. In the following chapter we shall study private monopoly, oligopoly, and unified selling. Following that chapter we shall consider in additional chapters the efforts of government to prevent monopolistic power; and, when this has been found to be ineffective in particular industries, to adopt public price fixing.

SUGGESTIONS FOR FURTHER READING

Chamber of Commerce of the United States, *Small Business* (Washington, 1953).

Galbraith, John Kenneth, *American Capitalism: The Concept of Countervailing Power* (Boston, 1952).

Griffin, C. E., *An Economic Approach to Antitrust Problems* (New York, 1951).

Lilienthal, David D., *Big Business: A New Era* (New York, 1953).

Mason, Edward S., "The New Competition," *Yale Review*, Autumn 1953, pp. 37–48.

Ord, Lewis C., *Secrets of Industry* (New York, 1945).

Purdy, Harry L., Lindahl, Martin L., and Carter, William A., *Corporate Concentration and Public Policy* (New York, 1950).

Quinn, T. K., *Giant Business: Threat to Democracy* (New York, 1953).

Robinson, E. A. G., *The Structure of Competitive Industry* (New York, 1932).

Stigler, George J., "The Case Against Big Business," *Fortune*, May, 1952.

Whitney, Simon N., "Errors in the Concept of Countervailing Power," *Journal of Business of the University of Chicago*, October, 1953, pp. 238–253.

CHAPTER 9

The Economic Nature of Monopoly and Monopoly Power

The purpose of the present chapter is to analyze the nature of private monopoly and monopoly power. It is this economic condition which gives rise to the principal types of government intervention in the business field. The basic regulatory policy employed by the federal and state governments is that of preventing monopoly and creating competition. When this approach fails or proves to be ineffective, government usually adopts direct price control or public ownership. Following an analysis of private monopoly power, we shall consider in successive chapters (1) the efforts of government to prevent monopoly, and (2) the acceptance of monopoly in various fields and the attempts of government to control it (a) by public price fixing or (b) by public ownership.

THE TENDENCY TOWARD MONOPOLY IN A COMMERCIAL SOCIETY

Historical studies indicate that monopoly, in the main, arises out of human action and human volition, rather than from impersonal, technological forces. Business enterprisers like to sell without competition, for it enables them to control their prices and increase their incomes. With monopoly power, a single seller or a group of sellers acting as one is in a position to raise prices to the valuations of the most urgent buyers by curbing production or by withholding a part of the supply. Monopolistic buying, on the other hand, makes it possible for a group of buyers acting in unison to force prices down to the least that sellers will take, without fear of losing the goods to a higher bidder. The very real *private* advantages of monopoly in buying and selling led Josiah Tucker, an English economist of the eighteenth century, to declare, "All men, whether natives or foreigners, would be monopolists if they could."[1]

In his famous study on the *Wealth of Nations* (1776), Adam Smith reported, "People of the same trade seldom meet together, even for merriment and diversion, but the conversation ends in a conspiracy against the public, or in some contrivance to raise prices."[2] At the present time, close observers of the behavior of businessmen find that the same situation prevails today. Thus, the editor of a leading trade journal reports that two of the most fre-

---

[1] Josiah Tucker, *A Letter to a Friend Concerning Naturalization* (London, 1753), p. 24.

[2] Adam Smith, *The Wealth of Nations*, Vol. 1, Book 1, chap. 10, p. 130.

quently discussed subjects at the many trade association meetings which he has attended are (1) "price fixing" and (2) how "to keep competition out or new competitors from starting."[3]

The economic problem of monopoly has existed in commercial societies from earliest times. The ways of attaining monopoly have changed from period to period, but the nature and problem of monopoly have remained essentially the same. The lessons of history clearly indicate that competition is effectively realized only when government takes steps to create and maintain it. When the efforts of government to preserve and restore competition are weak, the profit-seeking interest of enterprisers gives rise to an amazing variety of restrictions, restraints, and collusive actions designed to avoid competition and exclude competitors.

THE NATURE OF PRIVATE MONOPOLY

Monopoly means unity of action on price in the sale of a commodity for which there is no close substitute. This unity may be exercised by a single person or by a group of persons acting as one. The purpose of having unified selling is to insure that there will be no price competition (sometimes called "chiseling") in the monopoly action of *raising* prices above the level which would exist under conditions of price competition. The source of private monopoly power—the power to raise prices above the competitive level—arises in the ownership or control of all or a large part of the supply of a distinctive class of goods. By controlling supply a monopolist is able to increase the prices received (1) by restricting the amount of goods offered for sale and (2) by charging various groups of customers different prices on the basis of "what the traffic will bear." In restricting or curbing supply to secure higher prices, a monopolist adds a measure of *artificial* scarcity to whatever scarcity exists from other sources.[4]

From an economic point of view, the essence of monopoly is the power to manage price to make more profit by selling less. When there is no rivalry *on price*, there is monopoly in defiance of the law even though a dozen salesmen are "competing" in the field for orders. Many businessmen and their legal counsel fail to understand the nature of monopoly. The Antitrust Division of the Department of Justice, for example, reports the story of a corporation president who affirmed his innocence of monopolistic action by declaring "I want you to know that our company does not want to monopolize this industry. We have intentionally kept prices high enough to permit our principal competitor to exist"!

[3] W. A. Cyr, "What an Association Can't Do—And What It Can," *Electrical West*, April, 1948, pp. 65–68. See also *Trade Association Survey*, Monograph No. 18, Temporary National Economic Committee, 76th Congress, third session, 1941, pp. 71–103.

[4] The raising of prices only slightly may be very profitable. Textron, a leading textile firm, stated in 1954 that if it could raise its prices one cent a yard, it would gain $2.5 million per year in revenue. If the oil companies were to increase the price of Diesel oil one cent per gallon, it is estimated that it would cost the railroads alone about $30 million a year.

In economic analysis, the term "monopoly" is sometimes defined as a control over supply exercised by *one seller*. When there are two sellers of a homogeneous product, the condition is called duopoly; and when there are a few sellers—but not many—the case is one of oligopoly. Duopoly and oligopoly usually involve (1) a condition in which a dominant seller, acting as a price leader, establishes or makes the going price which is largely observed in the industry, or (2) a situation in which several large firms act as one through fear of the chaotic price competition which might result from independent action. Since the several sellers in each situation "act as one on price"—usually according to a formula—duopoly and oligopoly are also described as cases of "multiple-seller" monopoly or simply as "monopoly." In our present study, we shall use the term "monopoly" to include situations usually characterized as oligopolistic. See also Glossary of Terms at end of this chapter and Fig. 22, facing p. 226.

MONOPOLY AS A LOCAL AND LIMITED POWER

Since the sale of goods is always conducted at a place, private monopoly power comes into being as a local power—relative to a place. This means that the sales territory in which private monopoly power is exercised in the first instance is a regional area or zone. A cement mill, for example, rarely ships its product beyond a distance of 500 miles. Within a sales territory of this radius, buyers may have the choice of only one seller—or of several in collusion; and such a seller may charge a series of prices shading downward to the prices which he finds at the boundary line of his sales area. The exercise of local monopoly is thus limited by the presence of another seller located at a distance. In Fig. 18, for example, it is assumed that there is unified selling at A and at B—one seller or several sellers acting as one at each point of production. The alternative source of supply for buyers at A (or B) is at the competitive market at C. Monopoly action at A (or B), therefore, can raise the price of a product at A to $38 per unit (the price at C plus $8 freight). At *d* mill A can quote a price of $37 and secure a net price of $36 ($37 less the actual freight); and at *g* mill A will quote $34 and secure a mill net price of $30, the former competitive price at A. The exercise of local monopoly power in this example, it may be noted, shades off from a maximum at the mill at A to zero at the boundary line of its natural sales territory.

The monopoly power exercised by a locally separate mill (or several mills acting as one), it may be observed, is relative to space and limited by distance. Since the charging of local monopoly prices may bring a new mill into operation (the prospect of potential competition), private monopoly power may also be limited in time. The power to raise prices is further limited by the action of buyers in turning to goods of different quality or kind, i.e., *substitute* competition.

It is said that "appetite grows with eating," and the taste of monopoly profits may induce the enterpriser at A to acquire the mill or mills at B by merger. In this way the price leader can extend the size of the sales territory in which his monopoly power can be exercised. Private monopoly thus grows like a snowball. One advantage gained by the price leader at A (a private advantage and not a public one) in acquiring the mills at B is that with monopoly profits in the areas of A and B delivered prices can be "cut" on sales in the area of C, in a discriminatory way, to "meet" competition there.[5]

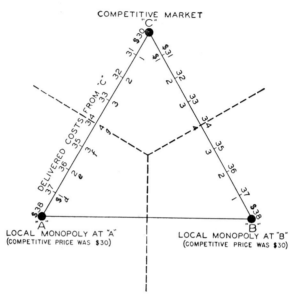

Fig. 18. The exercise of local monopoly power. In the figure it is assumed that monopolistic control over price is exercised at A and at B. The alternative source of supply for customers in the natural sales territories of A and B is at C. Unified selling at A and B can result in prices being raised in their local areas to the level of prices at C ($30) plus freight from C. The delivered prices quoted by A, for example, will yield mill net prices varying from $38 at A to $30 at g. Divergent or variable mill net prices are an example of local or geographic price discrimination.

By "cutting" his prices in the area of C—while maintaining them elsewhere —the price leader can keep the mills at C from expanding and becoming stronger competitors. This sort of competition is a *limited* kind of competition—that is, limited to those places where there are rivals. The other customers of the dominant seller are required to pay monopoly prices. Discriminatory pricing of this type is not the uniform, aboveboard sort of price competition found in open markets.

A price leader may also cut prices on sales in the area of C in a discriminatory way expressly to injure or destroy the mills operating in C. This is

[5] The terms "price cut" and "price cutting" may mean a uniform reduction in mill prices, but usually they mean a reduction of the mill price in one area while maintaining it on sales made elsewhere.

known as *cutthroat* competition.[6] As an alternative, however, he may just threaten to engage in cutthroat competition and by this means induce the mills at C to join hands in a policy of following the leader on price. The resulting concerted action may involve either actual or tacit agreement on the part of the mills at C, based upon the prospect of added profits or the fear of cutthroat competition.

The foregoing example of concerted action on price—based on price leadership and price following—is an illustration of the fact that it is not necessary for a single seller to control *all* of the supply—either in a given locality or in the Nation—in order to exercise monopoly power. Monopoly begins as a local power; and as a locally separate mill extends its area of control and influence, it may be able to establish or make the going price, or prices, which as an actual fact will be largely observed in a given sales area.

WAYS OF ATTAINING PRIVATE MONOPOLY POWER

I. COLLUSION (AGREEMENT) WITH COMPETITORS

Monopoly power is frequently exercised by rival sellers operating in one or more sales territories by agreeing one with another that no one will sell for less than a certain price—or pay more than a certain price, in the case of a buyers' monopoly. Such agreements or understandings have long been known as gentlemen's agreements, since their observance is based upon the word or pledge of each seller. Collusion is most effectively secured and maintained when the number of sellers is small. In price-fixing arrangements the problem is *the other fellow's price*. If there are only two sellers, there is only one price to worry about and one other seller to convince; and if there are three sellers, only two individuals have to be kept in line. In some cases, agreements on price have been strengthened by written compacts, as well as by the deposit of sums of money to be forfeited by any member who breaks the agreement. Since direct evidence of agreement in such cases is easy to prove, monopoly leaders nowadays typically use more subtle methods of collusion. These include collective activity in trade associations, the use of basing-point and zone-delivered pricing systems, common affiliations with the same legal, banking, or accounting firms, interlocking directorates, and intangible personal ties of various sorts.

In several European countries where collusion is tolerated or accepted by government, businessmen openly engage in collective action on price and production. An association of independent firms in the same line of business for the purpose of agreeing on price and controlling supply is called a *cartel*. The word "cartel" comes from the Latin word *charta*, meaning a sheet of paper. Its application to price-fixing associations is to be found in the fact

[6] Cutthroat competition may be defined as the reduction of price in a discriminatory way in one sales area while maintaining it elsewhere, expressly to injure an independent seller.

that agreements on price are frequently strengthened by means of a written covenant.

In the United States, collective action on price has long been held to be illegal, *per se*, and price-fixing activity is not openly discussed or admitted. As a consequence, the term "cartel" has not been widely used in this country. Mergers, on the other hand, have been looked upon with favor by the courts, and business leaders have turned to the acquisition of competitors as the principal means of securing monopoly control.

It may be added that, since collusion or conspiracy on price is illegal under the antitrust laws, businessmen closely guard any agreements on price which they may make. Price understandings are usually reached in secret meetings and implemented by telephone conversations. In some instances, business executives instruct their secretaries in filing letters to destroy any which might reveal evidence of an agreement to a government investigator. In other cases, letters to be destroyed are expressly marked, "Please note this memorandum and destroy."[7] In consequence, direct evidence of an agreement on price is usually exceedingly difficult to secure.

2. Monopoly Power Exercised and Increased by Means of Cutthroat Competition

During the early period in the United States (1870–1903), cutthroat competition was a widely used device for eliminating rival sellers in a drive to expand private monopoly power. With local monopoly in one sales territory, multiple-plant companies slashed prices ruthlessly in another territory in which rivals were operating to drive them out of business. In a review of the methods employed by the large companies in oil, sugar, salt, copper, lead, tobacco, iron, and steel, to expand their monopoly position, the United States Industrial Commission in 1900 reported that the combinations "cut prices to an unreasonable extent in certain localities, and even to individuals at certain times, for the sake of driving out their rivals."[8] Often the dominant companies also secured discriminatory, preferential freight rates from the railroads, and these rates gave them a further advantage over competitors. The growth of the Standard Oil Company of New Jersey between 1870 and 1880, it is reported, was due in large measure to railroad rebates and preferential freight rates.

The unfavorable attitude of the courts toward the use of cutthroat competition caused monopoly leaders in time to adopt a policy of "live and let live" with respect to the remaining independents. The United States Steel Corporation formed in 1901, in particular, pioneered this practice. In accordance with this new policy, if independents follow the leader on price

[7] *In the matter of Rigid Steel Conduit et al.*, Before the Federal Trade Commission, Docket No. 4452, *Brief in Support of the Complaint*, September 30, 1942; and *The Cement Institute et al. v. Federal Trade Commission, Brief for Respondent*, in the United States Court of Appeals for the Seventh Circuit, 1946, pp. 36–38.

[8] Report of the Industrial Commission, *Review of Evidence* (Washington, 1900), Vol. 1, Part 1, p. 20.

and "coöperate faithfully," they are permitted to stay in the field. However, if the independents become recalcitrant and show a price independence, prices may be cut in a discriminatory way for disciplinary purposes. The modern monopoly policy is thus said to be one of inclusion rather than exclusion.

3. MERGERS OF FORMERLY INDEPENDENT AND COMPETING PLANTS AS A METHOD OF RESTRICTING COMPETITION

The most effective way of restricting price competition which monopoly leaders in the United States have hit upon is the method of corporate merger or combination. (See also Glossary of Terms, p. 135.) This method came to be widely used soon after 1895. The acquisition of competitors may include those in processing and fabricating lines, as well as those owning supplies of natural resources and engaged in first-hand production. When formerly independent plants are owned and controlled, the management of the separate plants is rendered completely subservient on all matters pertaining to production, output, and prices. In the formation of the United States Steel Corporation, for example, Mr. Charles Schwab declared on this point, "That is the idea in our being the holders of this stock, in order that we may elect officers and directors who will be in sympathy with our policy."[9]

It may be noted that a merger of formerly competing plants in a particular section of the country which actually accounts for less than 5 percent of the sales in a given field in the entire country *may give the merger a control over all or a large part of the productive capacity in its area of practical shipment.* There is always an area of practical shipment for a mill or group of local mills, based upon f.o.b. mill prices and actual delivery charges; and in considering the monopoly power secured by a particular merger, one must examine the percentage of production or sales which it controls in its natural sales area.

4. MONOPOLY ATTAINED BY ECONOMIC EFFICIENCY

It is possible for private monopoly power to be attained by the efficiency and natural growth of a single company. This condition is rare and is likely to occur only in the case of manufactured specialties. In most cases, patents, tariffs, mergers, and other devices for restricting competition are employed along with efficiency and natural growth in the attainment of private monopoly power.

It may be added that, even though monopoly is secured by means of economic efficiency, there is still a need for public regulation to restrict the exercise of its power. The attainment of monopoly enables a producer to sell his products at discriminatory prices; and by selling in certain areas or to certain customers at extremely low prices, a monopolistic seller can stifle the development of new competitors and maintain its position without regard to economic efficiency.

[9] Report of the Industrial Commission, *Testimony* (Washington, 1901), Vol. 13, p. 453.

PUBLICLY CREATED MONOPOLIES

In addition to the monopolies secured by the action of private individuals, there are the monopolies publicly and legally granted by government. These latter may be called public or legal monopolies. They include monopolies based upon patents, copyrights, and franchises, as well as monopolistic enterprises owned and operated by government itself. The monopoly power exercised by a public or legal monopoly is usually an absolute power in one or more important respects. A national match monopoly, for example, is absolute in respect to time, place, and the kind of product. No one else may enter the field, anywhere in the nation, to produce any kind of match. So, likewise, a franchise gives an electrical utility an absolute right to sell electricity in the local community. The potential power of the company to manage prices as its own interests dictate, however, is limited by public control. By way of contrast, private monopoly power is always a relative and limited power. It is relative to space—a local or regional sales area; and its exercise is always limited by the presence of other sellers at a distance, by substitutes, and by the possibility of potential competition.

The granting of legal monopolies to authors and inventors is based upon the constitutional authority of Congress "to promote the progress of science and useful arts by securing for limited times to authors and inventors the exclusive right to their respective writings and discoveries" (Art. 1, Sec. 8). The essential idea behind the granting of copyrights and patents is that the privilege of exclusive use will stimulate and encourage authors and inventors to exert themselves in creative work. By granting an exclusive control over innovations, moreover, it is believed that there will be a greater willingness to disclose trade secrets which might otherwise be kept from public knowledge. Patents provide a monopoly right to inventors of new products, processes, or designs for a period of seventeen years. Copyrights are closely related to patents and give an author exclusive rights to musical or literary compositions for a period of twenty-eight years. An analysis of patent problems and of various proposals which have been made to remedy them will be made in Chapter 14.

TRADEMARKS AND THE CREATION OF PRODUCT DIFFERENTIATION

An early practice of merchants was to identify their merchandise with symbols or marks, and in time the common law came to protect individuals in their use of particular marks. In doing so, the law sought to protect a seller, *as well as the public*, against the "passing off" of other goods as his products. Its purpose was not to exclude others from the field, for anyone was still free to make the same products. The true function of trademarks, legal authorities agree, is to show the *origin* or *ownership* of a product.

Today trademarks are used chiefly to *differentiate* products rather than to identify their source. Thousands of people, for example, who prefer

"Camel" cigarettes or "Del Monte" canned peaches do not know the identity of the producer. In differentiating a product, a seller seeks to get consumers to buy it without comparing it with the products of other sellers.
With product differentiation *and an absence of quality guides to inform
consumers about the product*, extensive advertising may be used to educate
consumers into believing that the product has a halo around it and is superior
to all others. A seller is thereupon able to charge a substantial group of
buyers a few cents more for his product without having them turn to
another seller. Since no one else can sell the branded product, a trademark
thus gives a seller various degrees of monopoly power.

In discussing the use of trademarks, it is important to note that the issue
is not one of trademarks or no trademarks, but rather one of standardization
versus product differentiation. If staple consumer goods—such as canned
fruits and vegetables, women's hosiery, and tobacco products—were graded
as to quality and grade-labeled, sellers could still use trademarks to designate
origin or ownership—the true legal purpose of trademarks. They would not,
however, be able to use advertising to exploit the technical ignorance of
consumers by leading them to believe that a particular product is better than
it really is. Critics of grade labeling justify brand labeling by stating that it
protects consumers from inferior products. One can count, it is said, on the
quality of a highly advertised, branded product. The testing experiments of
consumer agencies, however, indicate that the quality of highly advertised
products is frequently grade B or C rather than grade A. Brand labeling and
advertising prepared by a seller necessarily reflect *his commercial interest*.

LANHAM ACT OF 1946 AUTHORIZES REGISTRATION
OF DISTINCTIVE MARKS

In the development of trademark law, Congress and the courts have constantly yielded to the pressure of producers for rights to differentiate their
products rather than to standardize them. The political power of the large
national advertisers has been used not only to prevent the adoption of grade
labeling in the sale of staple consumer goods but to extend the legal means
by which sellers can differentiate such products. "In all these cases," Professor Chamberlin has said, "there can be no question as to what the law is
doing. It is preserving, not competition, but monopoly."[10]

The common law protected the right of an owner to identify his product
with a mark showing ownership or origin. In large measure, the purpose of

[10] Edward H. Chamberlin, *The Theory of Monopolistic Competition* (Cambridge,
1942), p. 219. In a report on the Lanham Act, which was enacted in 1946, the Department of Justice stated, "The drive for the bill comes not from the thousands of small
businesses which rely on . . . common law protection . . . but from a limited group of
large companies which have failed to impress the courts with the rationales incorporated
in the bill. The philosophy of the bill is inconsistent with the recommendations of the
Temporary National Economic Committee and any program to strengthen the competitive position of small business." Hearings Before a Subcommittee of the Senate Committee on Patents on H.R. 82, *Trade-Marks*, 78th Congress, second session, 1944, p. 59.

our early statute law on trademarks was simply to provide for their public recording. The registration of a particular product mark under the Trade Mark Act of 1905 gave a person *prima-facie* evidence of the ownership of the mark. The act of 1920 extended the privilege of registration to certain types of descriptive, geographic, and surname marks which were not registrable under the act of 1905. In 1946 the efforts of large national advertisers to secure a legal right to register any mark which has become distinctive won complete success with the passage of the Lanham Act.[11]

Trademarks

KODAK
CAMEL
OLD GOLD
CHESTERFIELD
FORD
CHEVROLET
WESTINGHOUSE
GENERAL ELECTRIC
HART, SCHAFFNER & MARX

Certification Marks

The Community of Roquefort, Aveyron, Roquefort, France

Service Marks

Collective Mark

N·A·P·A

National Automotive Parts Association, Detroit, Mich.

FIG. 19. Some well-known trademarks, service marks, certification marks, and collective marks. (Source: U.S. Patent Office.)

In the Lanham Act of 1946, a "trademark" is defined as "any word, name, symbol, or device, or any combination thereof adopted and used by a manufacturer or merchant to identify his goods." Some examples of well-known

[11] Certain types of marks cannot be registered. These include marks which are immoral, scandalous, or deceptive. Otherwise, the act provides for the registration of any mark "which has become *distinctive* of the applicant's goods in commerce." Such marks include names, words, figures, letters, symbols, devices, and the like.

trademarks which have been registered with the Patent Office are shown in Fig. 19.

The act of 1946 also makes provision for the registration of "service marks," "certification marks," and "collective marks" (see Fig. 19). Service marks are essentially trademarks which are used in connection with a service business. Certification marks consist of seals of approval or union labels which indicate that the designated goods are union-made. Collective marks, on the other hand, are marks used by members of an association or other collective groups.[12]

A company registering distinctive marks under the Lanham Act strengthens its exclusive use of them. It is privileged also to enjoy their use indefinitely, provided that it renews the registration at the end of each twenty-year period. Moreover, the act provides that registered trademarks after "continuous use for five consecutive years" shall be largely incontestable. This means that a registered trademark cannot, in most cases, be attacked in cancellation or infringement suits after the first five years of registration.[13]

PRICE DISCRIMINATION AND THE EXERCISE OF MONOPOLY POWER

In an open market, we have seen, the price of each seller is uniform to all his customers at a given time. Although a seller might like to charge an urgent or well-to-do buyer a higher price, he is not in a position to get away with it. He is held in line by price publicity and the opportunity of buyers to turn to other sellers willing to sell at a more moderate profit. Under conditions of monopoly, however, a seller (or a unified group of sellers) has the power to make some buyers pay more than the price to others, for the group of buyers is unable in varying degrees to turn to another seller and get a better price. The making of a difference in the prices charged various buyers for the *same goods* without a corresponding difference in quality, service, or conditions in the terms of sale is known as *price discrimination*. Price discrimination may also exist when a seller does not make a difference in prices for a difference in the quality or service rendered. The phrase "conditions in the terms of sale" is concerned with whether the product is sold for cash or credit, in large or small quantities, and at retail or wholesale. Price differences which make only due allowance for difference in cost or value received—such as one price for cash and another for credit—are

<hr />

[12] "Trade-Mark Act of 1946" in *Rules of Practice in Trade-Mark Cases*, Patent Office, U.S. Department of Commerce (Washington, 1947), pp. 81–116. The Lanham Act also provides for registration on a *Supplemental Register* of "any trade-mark, symbol, label, package, configuration of goods, name, word, slogan, phrase, surname, geographical name, numeral, or device or any combinaton of any of the foregoing." This registration serves only as a basis for registration in foreign countries. Many foreign countries permit Americans to register marks if they are registered in the United States.

[13] According to Walter J. Derenberg, a trademark authority, "the outstanding purpose of the new Act was to vest trade-marks on the principal register with an unprecedented degree of security, dignity, and ultimate incontestability." Walter J. Derenberg, *The Lanham Trade-Mark Act of 1946* (Washington, 1948), pp. 6–7.

not considered to be discriminatory. See also Glossary of Terms at the end of this chapter.

The concept of price discrimination is usually applied to the making of a difference in the prices charged for *goods of like grade and quality* without a valid reason. A related discriminatory practice is the one in which a seller, handling many different products or product lines, cuts prices on a single product or product line, with small loss to himself, but with serious loss to small competitors who specialize in the product being subjected to price cutting. This is called the "loss leader" practice.

Price discrimination, economists have long observed, can be exercised by a seller only when he has some degree of monopoly power or when competition is substantially lessened or incomplete.[14] In open markets *with price publicity* a seller cannot ordinarily make some buyers pay more than the "going" price to other buyers *for the same commodity*. The existence of price discrimination is thus a sign and an indicator of some degree of monopoly or of incomplete competition.

KINDS OF DISCRIMINATION

1. DISCRIMINATION BETWEEN INDIVIDUALS

Price discrimination may be exercised (1) as to persons, (2) as to places, and (3) as to kinds of uses or commodities. A monopolist may, in the first place, endeavor to charge prices which approximate the reserve valuations of various individual buyers. Physicians, surgeons, and lawyers, having unique or specialized abilities, for example, frequently discriminate among their customers upon the basis of their individual capacities to pay. In the industrial field, buyers who are in a position to render certain services or to produce certain goods for themselves are sometimes able to demand rebates or preferential treatment from an established seller. Buyers with tremendous purchasing power are likewise often able to secure more favorable prices than others by threatening to shift their business to another supplier.

Discrimination as to individuals was widely employed by the railroads to win the business of large shippers. In many cases, moreover, large shippers themselves brought pressure on a railroad company to secure special rates or rebates on the threat of transferring their business to another carrier. As a solution to this problem of special advantage, Congress provided in the Interstate Commerce Act of 1887 that all railroad rates should be publicly posted and uniform to all persons.

A related problem of personal discrimination arose in a consideration of the rates granted to large shippers *as a quantity discount*. Large companies offering several carloads of business maintained that they were entitled to a

---

[14] A. T. Hadley, *Transportation* (New York, 1903), pp. 101, 108; F. W. Taussig, *Some Aspects of the Tariff Question* (Cambridge, 1915), p. 208; Jacob Viner, *Dumping* (Chicago, 1923), pp. 1–3, 94–95; and Frank A. Fetter, *The Masquerade of Monopoly* (New York, 1931), pp. 300, 411, 417.

lower carload rate than shippers having only one carload of business. Thus, in one of the first cases before the Interstate Commerce Commission there was presented the problem of whether it was sound policy for a railroad company to grant a lower rate than the carload rate for the shipment of more than 30,000 tons of coal a year (about 750 carloads). In a decision condemning the lower rates as an unjust discrimination, the chairman of the Commission stated, "A discrimination which should so limit the offer that a part of those who could and might desire to accept it would be excluded from its benefits, would for that very reason be unjust and indefensible. . . . A distinction in rates as between car loads and smaller quantities is readily understood and appreciated; but no such distinction is made in this offer. . . . The discrimination . . . cannot be supported by the circumstance that the offer is open to all; for although made to all, it is not possible that all should accept . . . and competition by those who could not get the discount would obviously be then out of the question."[15]

The Interstate Commerce Commission has long been willing to grant a lower rate for a carload of business than for a less-than-carload amount. Such a preferential rate, it believes, can be defended not only on the basis of the economies involved in handling larger orders but also on the ground that the offer is reasonably available to all who might want to accept it. The line of reasoning taken by the Interstate Commerce Commission with respect to quantity discounts has served as the basis for a growing economic belief that price differences made for quantity purchases should be related not only to cost but also to the possibility that all buyers may have an opportunity to secure them. (See also Chap. 16.)

2. DISCRIMINATION AS TO PLACES—GEOGRAPHIC DISCRIMINATION

In the second place, a monopolist may discriminate between purchasers in different localities. An early practice of the railroads was to charge customers at noncompetitive points more for a short haul than they charged those living at competitive points (water or other railroad competition) for a longer haul over the same line. In 1910 the Interstate Commerce Commission began to correct this evil, and since that time it has worked constantly to bring railroad rates into a closer relationship with distance. The practice of domestic producers to discriminate between buyers in the United States and those in foreign nations—foreign "dumping"—has long been carried on in various monopolistic industries without government control or prohibition. A far more prevalent form of geographic discrimination is found in the practice of domestic producers to charge higher net prices on local sales than they receive on shipments into distant sales areas. This practice is known as domestic dumping.

The terms "local price cutting" and "cutthroat competition" came into use around 1900 to designate the practice of dominant firms in cutting prices in one area while maintaining them elsewhere *expressly to injure or kill off a competitor.* The shocking use of these practices by such firms as the American Tobacco Company and the Standard Oil Company brought growing demands for their abolition. In 1914, the House committee studying proposed legislation to prohibit unfair competition declared,

> In the past it has been a most common practice of great and powerful combinations engaged in commerce—notably the Standard Oil Co., and the American Tobacco Co., and others of less notoriety, but of great influence—to lower prices of their commodities, oftentimes below the cost of production in certain communities and sections where they had competition, with the intent to destroy and make unprofitable the business of their competitors, and with the ultimate purpose in view of thereby acquiring a monopoly in the particular locality or section in which the discriminating price is made.
>
> Every concern that engages in this evil practice must of necessity recoup its losses in the particular communities or sections where their commodities are sold below cost or without a fair profit by raising the price of this same class of commodities above their fair market value in other sections or communities.
>
> Such a system or practice is so manifestly unfair and unjust, not only to competitors who are directly injured thereby but to the general public, that your committee is strongly of the opinion that the present antitrust laws ought to be supplemented by making this particular form of discrimination a specific offense under the law when practiced by those engaged in commerce.[16]

Following the decisions of the Supreme Court in the *Standard Oil* and *American Tobacco* cases (1911), the large combinations turned increasingly to the use of a policy of "live and let live" in their relations with competitors. The few independents remaining in the field are generally permitted to continue, and geographic price discrimination has largely taken the form of systematic and coöperative discrimination, practiced according to a formula. (See Chap. 17.)

3. DISCRIMINATION BETWEEN CLASSES OF GOODS—
ONE-COMMODITY PRICE CUTTING

Discrimination may be practiced, in the third place, as to kinds of uses or commodities. A monopolistic seller of salt, for example, may make a difference in prices by selling the same salt under a "table brand," a "commercial brand," and a "livestock brand." A seller having monopolistic power in one line of goods may also cut prices on other kinds of goods in an effort to destroy the business of a competitor. The brand or product on which the price is cut is commonly called a "fighting brand" or a "loss leader."

[16] Committee on the Judiciary, Antitrust Legislation, 63rd Congress, second session, *House Report 627*, May 6, 1914, pp. 8–9.

The American Tobacco trust was one of many large combinations which used one-commodity price cutting to advance its monopoly position. This company had a dominating position in the cigarette business, but its plug business was small. As a weapon to crush out rival plug producers, the trust used its profits on cigarettes to slash prices on plug tobacco. A special brand of plug tobacco called "Battle Ax" was offered for sale, and prices to selected dealers were cut from 50¢ to 7¢ per pound. During a period of four years, the company suffered a net loss of some $3,300,000 on the sale of chewing tobacco, but this plan of discrimination enabled it to secure a monopolistic control of the chewing tobacco field.

It is common for monopolistic associations of milk producers to use "multiple-price plans" or "use plans" for the sale of milk. The uses for milk—such as milk for fluid use, milk for cream separation, milk for cheese production, and so forth—are classified, and distributors are charged a different price for each class of use. All classes of milk are the same in quality, but the traffic will bear a higher price in some uses than in others. (See also Chap. 13, pp. 282–283.)

In 1944 Wendell Berge, then Assistant Attorney General of the United States, reported that methyl methacrylate, one of the best-known plastics, controlled monopolistically by Du Pont and Rohm and Haas, was being sold for industrial purposes at 85¢ a pound and for dental use at $45 a pound. In order to prevent dentists from purchasing their supplies from industrial users, Berge found that the monopoly sellers were considering the addition of a small amount of arsenic to the material sold to industrial users.[17]

Railroads and public utilities, especially, employ price discrimination as to kinds of commodities in their rate making. A shipper of canned salmon, for example, must pay a higher price per hundred pounds for rail transportation than a shipper of coal. Public utility commissions usually regard discrimination between kinds of commodities as being more defensible than the other types (as to persons and places) on the ground that it is applied *uniformly* to all persons and areas *under public supervision* to provide a utility with a fair return on its investment.

REASONS FOR PRICE DISCRIMINATION

A business enterprise practices discrimination, when it can do so, because it can gain much more than it can by treating its customers alike. In Fig. 20, for example, if one unit were sold at $7, one additional at $6, another at $5, and another at $4, the total receipts would be $22 rather than the $16 secured at a uniform f.o.b. mill price. Moreover, if all the seven units were sold at discriminatory prices ranging from $7 for the first unit, $6 for the second, $5 for the third, $4 for the fourth, $3 for the fifth, $2 for the sixth, and $1 for the seventh unit, the total receipts would be $28 rather than the $7 secured at a uniform price. In view of the greater profits which price discrimination

[17] Wendell Berge, *Cartels* (Washington, 1944), pp. 28–30.

brings, monopolistic sellers invariably try to work out some plan for classifying customers so that each group can be charged all that it is willing and able to pay.

An incentive to discriminate typically develops when a manufacturer finds that he cannot sell all he can produce at the top prices he would like to get. Instead of cutting prices to all his distributors (as is done in an open market), the manufacturer finds an advantage in giving certain preferred buyers a

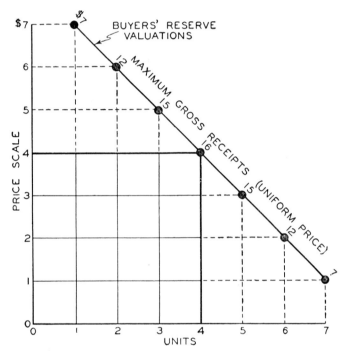

FIG. 20. Market demand schedule. A seller possessing monopoly power is often in a position to sell at a series of discriminatory prices instead of at a uniform price. When discrimination is possible, it is usually practiced, because it yields more profit.

lower price. A selling outlet is thus secured, and it is unnecessary to take lower prices on all sales.

Discrimination is also practiced geographically to secure local monopoly gains. By charging high prices in areas where competition is "in its place" or nonexistent, and by cutting mill-net prices only where necessary to meet competition, a monopolistic seller can collect local monopoly profits. Nonuniform price reductions—limited to a few—do not reduce the net returns on all sales. Geographic discrimination also enables a seller to ship into distant areas, by cutting mill-net prices on such sales, to keep distant competitors from growing bigger.

THE EVILS OF PRICE DISCRIMINATION

The granting of discriminatory lower prices to large chains is sometimes defended on the ground that the chains pass the advantage on to their customers in the form of lower prices. Many persons believe, however, that such preferential cuts are indefensible because they give the favored distributors an unfair cost advantage. If small firms are treated differently without valid justification, they are denied an equal start in the competitive game. Regardless of their efficiency, small business firms cannot compete with cost burdens ranging—in actual cases—from 25 to 35 percent higher than the costs of favored distributors.

The use of mass buying power by large chain distributors to secure discriminatory lower prices was the principal reason for the enactment of the Robinson-Patman Act (discussed in Chap. 16). This legislation makes price discrimination *between purchasers* illegal where the result may be "to injure, destroy, or prevent competition." In essence, this means that prices made by a single seller must be reasonably equal to different buyers. Each seller has the obligation to treat all his buyers on more or less equal terms.

Geographic or local price discrimination has long been condemned by economists on the grounds (1) that it denies customers located near a mill the advantage of their location, (2) that it enables a company enjoying local monopoly power to cut prices in a distant area expressly to injure a small firm which is trying to get established, and (3) that it is frequently carried on in a coöperative and systematic manner by many sellers using a basing-point or zone-delivered pricing system. In an effort to cope with the evils of *geographic* price discrimination, in particular, Congress passed the Clayton Act in 1914. This act, as amended, condemns price discrimination where the effect "may be substantially to lessen competition." Its application and adjudication will be discussed in Chap. 16.

At the present time, the antitrust laws do not place restraint on discrimination between different products or different product lines. A principal evil in this category is the "loss leader" practice. This is the practice in which a seller, handling many different products or product lines, cuts prices on a single product, with insignificant loss to himself, but with serious loss to small sellers who specialize in the sale of that product. As a remedy for this discriminatory practice, various experts have proposed that certain restraints be placed on price cutting, particularly at the retail level (see Chap. 21, pp. 481–482).

The view is sometimes advanced that price discrimination permits a seller to get additional business which he might not otherwise secure. The additional business, it is said, permits him to spread his overhead costs and reduce his unit expenses. This may be true from *his* point of view. Consumers and users, however, have no assurance that the discriminatory *higher* prices are fair and reasonable; and experience has shown that independents are thwarted and injured by the discriminatory *lower* prices. It is fallacious to argue, moreover, that price discrimination is justifiable because it permits a dominant seller to get greater profits.

ENLARGED OR GROUP MONOPOLIES

The principle of competition, we have said, consists (1) of freedom of entry and (2) of two-sided price competition in the pricing of goods. The essence of monopoly, on the other hand, is unity of action on price and the withholding of supply to make more by selling less. In a broad sense, monopoly may also be said to include any restriction or limitation which serves to exclude newcomers from a business field.

At the time of Adam Smith, the legal limitations on freedom of enterprise were very numerous. They included the navigation acts, the restrictions on imports and exports, and the exclusive regulations of the guilds and foreign trading companies. Adam Smith called all of these laws "enlarged monopolies." In his words, "All those laws which restrain, in particular employments, the competition to a smaller number than might otherwise go into them . . . are a sort of enlarged monopolies, and may frequently, for ages together, and in whole classes of employments, keep up the market price of particular commodities above the natural price, and maintain both the wages of the labour and the profits of the stock employed about them somewhat above their natural rate."[18]

It may be noted that restrictions on the entry of newcomers into a field do not, in themselves, give the established firms a monopoly position in pricing their goods. The favored, *included* sellers may actively compete against one another in the making of prices. However, since a restriction on the right of entry—such as restrictive tariff or the threat of discriminatory, cutthroat competition—keeps out other enterprisers, it is monopolistic in its nature. The excluded sellers who would be willing to sell for less are not available to moderate the demands of the established firms; and the included sellers are given an opportunity to get higher prices and incomes than they could secure if others were free to enter.

PRIVATE LIMITATIONS ON THE RIGHT TO COMPETE

Restrictions or limitations on freedom of entry may consist either of *private* or of *public* restraints. In the category of private restraints there are, first, the agreements which individual producers sometimes make in selling their business not to resume their business activity so as to compete with the buyer. These agreements early came to be known as contracts in restraint of trade, since they restrained a person in the exercise of his trade. Toward these restraints, the early common law of England showed no sympathy. In the *Dyer's* case (1415), for example, the court refused to enforce a contract held by one John Dyer against a rival who had agreed not to use his art of a dyer's

---

[18] Adam Smith, *op. cit.*, chap. 7, pp. 63–64.

craft in the plaintiff's town for a period of six months. The court, in fact, was so incensed at such a restriction that it declared, "Per Dieu, if the plaintiff were here, he should go to prison till he paid a fine to the king."[19] Subsequently, with the growth of commercial activity, the English courts held that a contract to refrain from exercising a trade made by a person upon selling or leasing his business is valid if it is (1) limited as to time and place and (2) based upon a proper consideration.[20] The American courts, following the English common law, adopted a similar rule of law. (See also Chap. 10.)

A second type of private interference with freedom of enterprise grows out of environmental factors which handicap, discourage, or defeat the efforts of independents to get established or to remain in business. Such factors may take several forms of which the following are typical:

1. Physical violence, the destruction of property, and other criminal acts are sometimes used to discourage the establishment or continued operation of a new enterprise. The cleaning and pressing and gasoline service station industries in some communities, especially, have been dominated by "goon squads" or "racketeers" who keep out new firms or injure established ones. In some instances, labor unions coöperate with organized employers to keep out new firms by the use of force or by refusing to supply them with workers. All such restrictions on enterprise are illegal and can largely be eliminated by an adequate enforcement of the law against criminal acts and conspiracies.

2. The use (or threat) of local price cutting in the area in which a new enterpriser seeks to get established is an important means of restricting freedom of enterprise. As long as large companies have this power and are not denied the right to discriminate, they have a powerful tool for discouraging new rivals or for keeping small ones from acting independently. It is reported that the fear of discriminatory competition by the large steel companies has been an important factor restricting the development of the steel industry in the West.[21]

3. The entry of new concerns into a given field may be restrained by the large cost of getting established. The cost burden or barrier may arise because of (1) the large investment which is required to establish a plant—such as a steel mill or an automobile plant—(2) the cost of getting one's product before the public and winning consumer acceptance, and (3) the high cost of raising equity capital on the part of little-known producers.

Although the growth of large-scale plants has greatly decreased the opportunities available for individual enterprise, technical size in many cases is not a factor limiting free enterprise or potential competition. A principal problem faced by new industrial enterprises is one of getting raw materials. With raw material supplies controlled by established firms, and with their policy of selling essential commodities only to firms of their own choice,

---

[19] *The Dyer's Case*, Y. B. 2 Henry V, pl. 26 (1415).
[20] *Mitchell* v. *Reynolds* (1711), 1 P. Wms. 181, 24 Eng. Rep. 347.
[21] Wendell Berge, *Economic Freedom for the West* (Lincoln, 1946), pp. 24–27.

there is often little opportunity for a manufacturer or fabricator to get started.

Elaborate advertising expenditure and high-pressure sales efforts, carried on by financially large companies, frequently build up consumer preference for branded products and make it costly for a new firm to get established. A trademark only gives a person the exclusive right to use a distinctive name or symbol, but with extensive advertising a large number of people can be taught to buy the name rather than the product itself. It is reported in the soap trade that an established company would need to spend from ten to fifteen million dollars in national advertising over a period of three years to introduce and gain consumer acceptance for a new brand of soap. Few companies are financially able or willing to embark on such ventures. It is possible that the required use of federal grades and grade labeling would help to give the public greater confidence in the products of new and unknown producers.

4. The close relations between established firms and banking agencies may result in the denial of credit to new competitors. In 1913 the House Committee to Investigate the Concentration of Control of Money and Credit reported that banking houses which have organized a large industrial corporation assume a certain guardianship over it, and that "if competition is threatened it is manifestly the duty of the bankers from their point of view of the protection of the stockholders, as distinguished from the standpoint of the public, to prevent it if possible. If they control the sources of credit, they can furnish such protection. . . . This power standing between the trusts and the economic forces of competition is the factor most to be dreaded and guarded against by the advocates of revived competition."[22]

It is common practice today for an investment or commercial bank to arrange for the placing of one or more of its officers on the board of directors or on the nominating committee of the corporations it is financing. In principle, a bank is an intermediary between the investing public and the borrowing enterprises, and in making loans it takes the position that it wants to be as certain as possible that they will be repaid. A bank, therefore, frequently does have an immediate interest in preventing the entrance of newcomers into a particular line of business activity. Moreover, when faced with the question of financing a little-known enterpriser or a long-established one, a bank will invariably choose the company which has a proved and profitable record.

5. Labor unions and professional societies frequently impose restrictions on the number of persons who can enter a given field. The craft unions, in particular, have frequently restricted entrance into a trade by apprenticeship regulations or by closing the union to new members. Similar action is sometimes taken by associations of professional people in their administration of entrance requirements.

[22] *Report of the Committee to Investigate the Concentration of Control of Money and Credit*, House of Representatives, 62nd Congress, third session, Report 1593, 1913, p. 160.

6. A final and highly important type of private restraint on freedom of enterprise is found in the action of one or several large companies—controlling a large part of the total supply of a basic commodity—in refusing to sell to independents who may subsequently resell in competition with them. Under competitive conditions, the right to select one's own customers imposes no injury on buyers, for there are numerous alternative sources of supply. In the hands of dominant enterprisers, however, it has become a most potent device for restricting freedom of enterprise. (See also Chap. 11, pp. 231–232; and Chap. 16, pp. 354–356.)

PUBLIC OR LEGAL INTERFERENCE WITH FREEDOM OF ENTERPRISE

In addition to the private restrictions on freedom of enterprise, there are many restrictions imposed by government itself. The principal varieties of public interferences consist of (1) restrictive tariffs which relieve domestic producers of the competition of foreign products and (2) regulatory measures enacted by state and local governments which confine internal trade or commerce in designated areas to a favored few.

All protective or restrictive tariffs, except those on infant industries, have as their continuing purpose and result the shutting out of foreign supplies which would serve to decrease domestic prices. Since tariffs relieve domestic producers wholly or partly from the competition of foreign products, they may be classed as a monopolistic measure. In the same category as protective tariffs may be placed our coastwise shipping laws which restrict cargo and passenger transportation between ports in the United States, as well as between ports in the United States and Alaska, Hawaii, and Puerto Rico, to ships under the American flag.

Subsidy payments, as well as tariffs, provide higher incomes to a favored class. As a general rule, subsidy programs involve restrictions on entry or on the amounts which may be produced; and producers, consequently, are not free to follow the occupation of their choice without interference and dictation by the government. It is for this reason that subsidies are classed as an interference with freedom of enterprise. In the case of subsidies, the taxpayers are burdened with higher taxes, whereas in the case of tariffs, the consumers of the protected articles are burdened by the higher prices, and thus all other industries are to that extent burdened.

INTERNAL TRADE RESTRICTIONS

In the same category as restrictive tariffs and subsidies may be placed all state and local regulatory legislation—enacted under the police powers—which confines internal trade or commerce in a designated area to favored producers. The principal types of internal trade restrictions which are designed or frequently administered to enhance the income of certain producers at the expense of the public include the following:

1. *Legislation Sponsored by Various Trade Groups Which Places Re-*

strictions on the Sale of Certain Products, as Such. Numerous states still impose a tax of 5¢ to 20¢ per pound on yellow and white margarine, respectively. City building codes and fire laws also frequently operate as barriers to the use of particular types of materials that are actually superior to those which are approved.

2. *State or Local Regulations Which Favor Home Industries or Laborers.* Laws in Ohio and Minnesota, for example, require that all printing done for state agencies must be done within the state; and an Illinois law provides that state agencies are required to use coal produced in Illinois unless the cost is 10 percent greater than out-of-state coal. In the same category may be placed state inspection, nursery, and quarantine laws which are administered to exclude wholesome or healthy products from other states. The Territory of Alaska places a tax on nonresident fishermen of $10 per year while resident fishermen pay only $5 per year. Numerous states impose a higher license fee on wholesalers of out-of-state alcoholic beverages than on those distributing only local products. Some states also require brewers and distillers using out-of-state materials to pay a very much higher annual license fee than those using home-grown materials. The gallonage tax on out-of-state wines and liquors is frequently substantially more than on local products.

3. *Restrictions Placed on Certain Types of Merchandising Organizations.* Various states impose special taxes and restrictions on chain stores (on existing units as well as on new stores) and on itinerant salesmen and merchants. A number of states have outlawed the new-type, self-service gasoline stations on the ground that they are a "fire hazard." With adequate precautions, however, fire prevention authorities report that the new stations are as safe as the conventional type. Some states permit native wines to be sold in all types of outlets, but restrict the sale of out-of-state wine to state stores or package liquor dealers.

4. *Restrictions Imposed on Entry into an Established Line of Business Activity.* Sanitary laws and regulatory measures providing standards for those entering certain occupations—such as barbers, physicians, dentists, lawyers, pharmacists, and ship pilots—are frequently administered so that persons of competence cannot comply. Laws requiring new firms to secure certificates of public convenience or necessity, or tradesmen to secure licenses, are often used to restrict entry into a given line of business—such as the trucking industry—in order to maintain high incomes for those already established.

From an economic point of view, all trade restrictions are undesirable in so far as (1) they exclude competent and reliable enterprisers, (2) they enable established producers to secure higher prices and incomes than they otherwise could, and (3) they penalize and injure consumers by causing higher prices and a smaller supply of goods or services. The enactment of tariffs, taxes, and regulatory laws which operate as restrictive barriers, it may be noted, is an aspect of the determination of prices and incomes by governmental authority.

If government is to support and effectuate a policy of competition, it must maintain not only (1) two-sided price competition in the pricing of goods but also (2) the freedom of producers to follow the occupation of their choice without interference or dictation. Freedom of enterprise assures to the public the entry of new methods, new products, and additional supplies of goods at lower prices. It also serves as a stimulus to established concerns to act competitively and progressively. Although restrictions on entry do not provide individual sellers with monopoly power, they do enable the established firms to secure higher incomes than they otherwise would.

GLOSSARY OF TERMS USED WITH REFERENCE TO MONOPOLY AND COMPETITION IN PUBLIC POLICY

Monopoly: Unity of action on price in the sale of a class of products for which there is no close substitute. This unity may be exercised by a single firm or by a group of firms acting as one. Monopoly may be achieved by agreement (conspiracy) or by mutual restraint on individual action which is tantamount to agreement.

Monopoly is based upon unified control over the supply of certain goods in a sales area. It gives the power to peg prices at higher levels than would prevail with effective competition. The essence of monopoly is sales only at managed prices, and the restriction of production when supplies do not move at the fixed prices.

The economic concept of monopoly includes the situation in which a dominant seller, acting as a price leader, establishes or makes the going price which is largely observed in the industry. It also includes many situations usually characterized as oligopolistic.

Oligopoly: Fewness of sellers *and* unified selling in which no one firm makes a decision without considering (a) his rivals' prices and sales policies and (b) his rivals' reactions to his own contemplated policies, because of a fear of retaliation, the threat of cutthroat or discriminatory competition, "like-mindedness," a doctrine of "live and let live," or business ethics which make price cutting taboo.

Economists using the term "oligopoly" usually designate "monopoly" as a situation in which productive facilities are owned by a single unit or are fully pooled. Oligopoly, on the other hand, is considered to be *unified selling by a few sellers* based (a) upon actual agreement (express, spoken), or (b) upon a mutual restraint on individual action which is tantamount to agreement. Acquiescence in unified selling may arise from the prospect of larger profits or from a fear of retaliatory action.

The pricing policy which results from monopoly and oligopoly are in most cases similar. Both designate a situation in which there is an absence of independent price competition. From the standpoint of public policy, both require the same remedial treatment, namely, (1) the creation and maintenance of numerous competitors, not too greatly unequal in size; and (2) the enforcement of existing laws against conspiracy and injurious discrimination.

Discrimination: The making of a difference in prices charged various buyers for the same class of commodities without a corresponding difference in quality, service, or conditions in the terms of sale. Price discrimination also means the sale of the same class of goods at uniform prices in spite of differences in quality, service, or conditions in the terms of sale.

Price differences due to differences in the cost of manufacture, sale, or delivery which are applicable to each product, are not considered to be discriminations.

The Accounting Division of the Federal Trade Commission identifies price discrimination as price differentials which are greater than the difference in the costs of manufacture, sale, or delivery which are applicable to each product.

Cutthroat Competition; Predatory Competition: A uniform or a discriminatory cutting of prices expressly to injure a competitor. In cutting prices locally, a dominant firm usually keeps up or raises prices elsewhere. Thereupon, when the smaller competitor has been disciplined or put out of business, prices are raised in the area of local cutting.

SUGGESTIONS FOR FURTHER READING

Bain, Joe S., *Pricing, Distribution, and Employment* (New York, 1953).

Chamberlin, Edward H., *The Theory of Monopolistic Competition* (Cambridge, 1942).

Derenberg, Walter J., *Trade-Marks*, American Bar Association (New York, 1946).

Edwards, C. D., *Maintaining Competition* (New York, 1949); "Types of Differential Pricing," *Journal of Marketing*, April, 1942, pp. 156–167.

Fellner, William, *Competition Among the Few* (New York, 1949); and "Collusion and Its Limits Under Oligopoly," *American Economic Review*, Papers and Proceedings, May 1950, pp. 54–62.

Hearings Before the Temporary National Economic Committee, *Interstate Trade Barriers*, 76th Congress, second session, Part 29, 1940.

Machlup, Fritz, *The Political Economy of Monopoly* (Baltimore, 1952).

Mason, Edward S., "Monopoly in Law and Economics," *Yale Law Journal*, November, 1937, pp. 34–49.

Stigler, George J., *The Theory of Price* (New York, 1952).

Trade Barriers Affecting Interstate Commerce in Alcoholic Beverages (1952). Joint Committee of the States to Study Alcoholic Beverage Laws, 270 Broadway, New York 7.

United States Versus Economic Concentration and Monopoly, Staff Report to the Monopoly Subcommittee of the Committee on Small Business, House of Representatives Committee Print (Washington, 1946).

CHAPTER 10

The Sherman Act of 1890 and Its Judicial Interpretation

THE BASIC LAW ON MONOPOLY AND COMPETITION

The Sherman Act of 1890 is the Magna Carta which dedicates the federal government to the economic policy of preventing monopoly and maintaining competition. In the three ensuing chapters, we shall study the background of the act, its essential provisions, its application to business, and its administration by the Antitrust Division, Department of Justice.

The original law in the United States with regard to monopoly and competition came from the English common law on markets and freedom of enterprise. The English common law, in turn, was developed by judges in hearing the complaints of people on the evils of private monopoly. Agreements among sellers on price were held to be criminal conspiracies, punishable by fines and imprisonment. In 1300, for example, the candle dealers in Norwich, England, were fined for making an agreement among themselves "that none shall sell a pound of candle at less than another."[1] Price-fixing agreements were condemned because they worked "to the great impoverishment of the people." Similarly, the action of one or several sellers in buying up the whole or a large part of a commodity (engrossing) was held to be a market offense because it made for a withholding of supplies and higher prices.

The term "restraint of trade" was applied in the common law to designate restraint on the freedom of a producer to exercise a trade of his own choice. The term "trade" was used to mean a person's craft, business, or profession. At first, the common law forbade *any* restraint on the freedom of a person to exercise his trade. Gradually, however, the rule was developed that partial restraints on trade made by a person in selling his business are valid if they are reasonable and based upon a consideration.[2]

THE SPECIAL MEANING ATTACHED TO THE WORD "MONOPOLY" IN THE ENGLISH LAW

Although all aspects of the efforts of sellers—as well as buyers—to control prices were held to be illegal in the common law, the control of price secured

---

[1] *Leet Jurisdiction in the City of Norwich*, p. 52, in Selden Society Publications, London, 1822.

[2] The leading case establishing this rule was *Mitchell* v. *Reynolds* (1711), 1 P. Wms. 181, 24 Eng. Rep. 347.

by *private* acts was not designated as monopoly. This resulted from the fact that the Greek word "monopoly" did not find its way into England until about 1516. Du Cange reports that the term *monopolium* was current in Medieval Latin by the thirteenth century, and that it was then used to designate a public grant as well as "illegal conspiracies" with respect to prices and the control of supply.

It appears that "monopoly" was first introduced into England in 1516 by Sir Thomas More in his book *Utopia*. More used the word at that time to describe the price-fixing activity of the financially dominant guildsmen. He declared: "Suffer not these rich men to buy up all, to engross and forestall, and with their monopoly to keep the market alone as please them."[3] The original edition of *Utopia* was in Latin, but the term "monopoly" soon was introduced into popular use and came to be widely employed in England to designate the action of one person or a group of persons "acting as one" in controlling supplies, limiting production, and enhancing prices.

In 1602 the term "monopoly" was added to the English law to describe the patents which Queen Elizabeth had been granting to her favorites for the exclusive manufacture and sale of many products other than new inventions. This abuse of the prerogative of government to encourage and reward inventors, designers, and writers led to widespread protests not only by consumers who were injured by high prices but also by enterprisers and workmen who were excluded from a common calling. The validity of the queen's grants was appealed to the high court in the case of *Darcy* v. *Allen* (1602).[4] In its decision the court held that a public grant restricting a trade to one or a few persons was void because it was a *monopoly*. Monopoly, the court stated, makes for higher prices, cheaper quality, and the loss of employment by persons formerly engaged in the trade. Since acts which have these consequences were against the common law, the court reasoned that monopoly was contrary to the common law.

The ruling of the court in *Darcy* v. *Allen* was embodied in statute law in the famous Statute of Monopolies (1624). The purpose of this legislation was to strengthen the control of Parliament over the granting of patents by the king. Its preamble declared that "all grants of monopoly are against the ancient and fundamental laws of this kingdom." A monopoly was defined in the law as an exclusive grant from the king for the doing of something which was before of common right. Exceptions in the statute were made for patents on new inventions, special charter rights, and other designated privileges which were not regarded as monopolies.

Thus it was that the term "monopoly" in the English law came to have a very narrow and restricted meaning—namely, a *public grant* which restrained the exercise of a lawful trade to one or a few people. The English law already had the terms "forestalling," "engrossing," and "conspiracy on price"

[3] Thomas More, *Utopia* (1516), Book 1, p. 18 (Lupton edition, 1895).
[4] *Darcy* v. *Allen*, King's Bench, 1602. 11 Co. Rep. 84; Moore, K. B. 671, Noy, 173, 77 Eng. Rep. 1260.

to designate the exercise of monopoly power by private acts, and "monopoly" was added to take care of a special political situation in which the power of government was used to restrict competition.

THE USE OF THE TERMS "MONOPOLY" AND "RESTRAINT OF TRADE" IN THE AMERICAN LAW

The peculiar meaning attached to the term "monopoly" in England was transferred to America, and for many decades the American courts used the word in its specialized, restricted sense. Justice Story in the *Charles River Bridge* case (1837), for example, defined monopoly as "an exclusive right granted to a few, of something which was before of common right."[5] Subsequently, the term was also used to describe a public franchise granted by the legislature for a public benefit.[6]

The common-law doctrine of restraint of trade was likewise introduced into the American law. In the earliest reported case on this subject (1811) the defendant had agreed not to run a stage between Boston and Providence in opposition to the plaintiff's stage. The court held this restraint to be valid, saying that "bonds to restrain trade in particular places may be good if executed for a sufficient and reasonable consideration."[7] In the next reported case on restraint of trade (1837), a craftsman bound himself never to carry on, or to be concerned with, the business of iron founding. The court held this to be a general restraint and void.[8] A further example is found in the case of *Whitney v. Slayton* (1855), in which the defendant upon selling his iron foundry agreed not to engage in the business of iron casting within sixty miles of the plant for a period of ten years. The court held that this partial restraint was reasonable and valid.[9] So it was that the courts in the United States, as well as in England, developed the doctrine (1) that all *general* restraints are illegal, and (2) that *partial* restraints—as to time or place—are valid if made for a valuable consideration in the sale of one's business or property.

THE EXTENSION OF THE DOCTRINE OF RESTRAINT OF TRADE TO AGREEMENTS ON PRICE

With the growth of industry and commerce in the United States, private individuals increasingly began to make agreements among themselves for the purpose of restraining price competition. To meet this situation, various state courts designated such acts as contracts in "restraint of trade." In the

[5] *Charles River Bridge Co. v. Warren Bridge Co.*, 11 Peters 402, 607 (1837).
[6] *Camblos v. Philadelphia and Reading R.R.*, 9 Phila. (Pa.) 411 (1875).
[7] *Pierce v. Fuller*, 8 Mass. 223 (1811).
[8] *Alger v. Thacher*, 36 Pick. 51 (Mass. 1837).
[9] *Whitney v. Slayton*, 40 Maine 224 (1855). There were three elements of a valid restraint of trade at common law. First, it must be only partial—as to time or place. Second, it must be founded upon a consideration. Third, the partial restraint must be reasonably appropriate—or directly related—to the consideration for which it is exchanged.

case of *Morris Run Coal Co.* v. *Barclay Coal Co.* (1871), for example, an
agreement of five coal corporations to divide sales in certain proportions and
to fix the prices of coal in unison was held to be a "restraint on trade" so large
as to interfere with the interests of the public. The general rule, the court
declared, is that all contracts in restraint of trade are illegal unless it can be
shown that they are made upon adequate consideration and upon circumstances which are reasonable and useful. "Testing the present contracts by
these principles," the court concluded, "the restrictions laid upon the production and price of coal cannot be sanctioned as reasonable, in view of their
intimate relation to the public interests."[10]

In thus broadening the term "restraint of trade" to cover agreements
among competitors to fix prices, the American state courts introduced an
unfortunate ambiguity into the law. An agreement made by a person in selling his business not to compete with the buyer does not, in itself, raise prices,
reduce the supply, or otherwise injure the public, whereas an agreement
among existing competitors on supply or prices invariably has these consequences. The court in the *Morris Run Coal* case reached the correct decision.
However, it made the validity of the restraint turn on the "reasonableness"
of an agreement not to compete which amounted to a general restraint. At
common law, all general restraints of trade were held to be invalid.

THE ADOPTION OF THE ECONOMIC DEFINITION OF
MONOPOLY INTO THE LAW

The development of "trusts" and combinations of producers in many lines
of business soon after 1880 brought much popular condemnation of the monopolies which private individuals were creating *by their own acts* (see Fig.
21). Monopoly, it was seen, could be attained by private agreements, as well
as by public grants of special privilege. This idea found its way into American law in the *North River Sugar* case decided in 1889. The *Sugar* case involved the legality of a "trust" formed for the purpose of controlling the
prices and sales policies of all the sugar refineries in the United States. The
New York Court of Appeals held that the arrangement was against public
policy and subject to dissolution. In its words, "The board, under this executed deed, can close every refinery at will; close some and open others;
limit the purchase of raw materials; artificially limit the production of refined
sugar; enhance the price to enrich themselves and their associates at public
expense; and depress the price when necessary to crush out and impoverish
a foolhardy rival; *in brief, can come as near to creating an absolute monopoly as is possible under the social, political, and economic conditions of today.*"[11]

In 1889 a case decided by the Supreme Court of Michigan likewise held

[10] *Morris Run Coal Co.* v. *Barclay Coal Co.*, 68 Pa. 173, 185–186 (1871).

[11] Reported with an affirming decision by the Supreme Court of the State of New York
in *People* v. *North River Sugar Refining Co.*, 54 Hun (N.Y.) 354, 376 (1889). Italics
supplied.

that a business combination organized for the purpose of controlling the production and prices of matches was a monopoly and against public policy. According to the Court, "All combinations among persons or corporations for the purpose of raising or controlling the prices of merchandise . . . are monopolies, and intolerable, and ought to receive the condemnation of all courts." Further, the Court observed, "Indeed, it is doubtful if free government can long exist in a country where such enormous amounts of money are allowed to be accumulated in the vaults of corporations, to be used at

FIG. 21. An illustration of the use of the term "monopoly" in popular discussion in 1881 to describe "trusts" and combinations among competitors affecting prices. This idea of monopoly was adopted by the higher state courts in the United States in 1889. (Bettmann Archive.)

discretion in controlling the property and business of the country against the interest of the public and that of the people, for the personal gain and aggrandizement of a few individuals."[12]

[12] *Richardson* v. *Buhl*, 77 Mich. 632, 658 (1889).

THE ENACTMENT OF THE SHERMAN ACT BY CONGRESS IN 1890

Increasingly the "trusts" and combinations being formed in the United States were coming to be national in their scope and field of operations. The various state governments seeking to prosecute monopoly, moreover, found themselves unable to reach the controlling units chartered by and located in other states. The prevention of monopoly and the maintenance of competition, it was widely recognized, had become a national problem calling for federal intervention. In the presidential election of 1888, this view was expressed in the campaigns of both the Democratic and the Republican parties. The platforms of both parties also promised federal intervention to control trusts and monopolistic combinations. "All who recall the condition of the country in 1890," wrote Justice Harlan some years later, "will remember that there was everywhere, among the people generally, a deep feeling of unrest. The nation had been rid of human slavery—fortunately, as all now feel—but the conviction was universal that the country was in real danger from another kind of slavery sought to be fastened on the American people, namely, the slavery that would result from aggregations of capital in the hands of a few individuals and corporations controlling, for their own profit and advantage exclusively, the entire business of the country, including the production and sale of the necessaries of life."[13]

A survey of the forces leading to the actual adoption of the Sherman Act indicates that the Republican leaders took the initiative in securing its enactment because they wanted something at that time to offset the opposition of the agricultural interests in the West to the high tariffs which the Republican Congress was then enacting. The Democrats were contending that the "tariff is the mother of trusts," and the Republicans replied with the idea that the nation could have "protection" and a policy of competition, too. Both the Republicans and the Democrats in Congress were in agreement that the principle of competition should be maintained by the federal government, and the act "to protect trade and commerce against unlawful restraints and monopolies" accordingly became law on July 2, 1890, with unanimous approval in the House and with only one dissenting vote in the Senate.

It is frequently said that the Sherman Act made contracts and conspiracies in restraint of trade or commerce explicitly illegal, whereas they were only void or unenforceable at common law. This view is correct with respect to contracts in general or unreasonable restraint of trade. Contracts or conspiracies to fix the price of necessaries, however, from earliest times were held at common law to be criminal offenses, punishable by fines and imprisonment.[14] The records of Congress indicate that the really important feature of the Sherman Act is the fact that it dedicated the federal government to the

[13] *Standard Oil Co. of New Jersey v. U.S.*, 221 U.S. 1, 83 (1911).
[14] See *King v. Norris*, King's Bench, 1758. 2 Kenyon 300; 96 Eng. Rep. 1189.

policy of maintaining the principles of market price and fair competition with reference to interstate commerce. In the words of Senator Hoar, "the great thing that this bill does" is to establish the common-law principles "which protected fair competition in trade in old times in England." Standards for fair competition were not specified in the law. Rather it was left to the federal courts to develop and apply such standards and rules as were found to be necessary to preserve price competition and to prevent monopoly.[15]

From 1890 to the present time, the Republican and Democratic parties have both supported the Sherman Act and the principles which it embodies.[16] The major parties have differed in the effectiveness of their enforcement activities, but neither one has proposed a different economic policy for the nation. In this regard, the United States, along with Canada, stands largely alone in the world in seeking to maintain a system of economic freedom.[17]

THE ESSENTIAL PROVISIONS OF THE SHERMAN ACT

There is general agreement that the purpose of the Sherman Act is to prevent monopoly and preserve and maintain the institutions of free enterprise and price competition. The principal factor in 1890 restricting and limiting competition was the action of large business interests in forming "trusts" agreements and also in organizing corporations to acquire the stock or assets of independent competing plants (see also pp. 110–111). The two main prohibitions of the law, accordingly, were aimed particularly at these evils. They declare,

Sec. 1. "Every contract, combination in the form of trust or otherwise, or conspiracy, in restraint of trade or commerce among the several states, or with foreign nations is hereby declared to be illegal. . . ."

Sec. 2. "Every person who shall monopolize, or attempt to monopolize,

[15] The terms "fair competition," "price competition," and "monopoly" are economic concepts, and a successful administration of the antitrust laws depends basically upon a clear and sound understanding of the economic principles underlying the laws. It has been said that antitrust cases are typically 95 percent economic and 5 percent legal in their nature.

[16] The Republican platform in 1952 pledged: "We shall relentlessly protect our free enterprise system against monopolistic and unfair trade practices." The Democratic platform pledged: "We reaffirm our belief in the necessity of vigorous enforcement of the laws against trusts, combinations, and restraints of trade, which laws are vital to the safeguarding of the public interest and of small competitive businessmen against predatory monopolies."

[17] England and the continental countries all formerly had laws—common law and statute law—providing for the maintenance of competition, the creation of markets, and the prevention of monopoly. See W. A. Bewes, *The Romance of the Law Merchant* (London, 1923), pp. 124–125, and Josef Kohler, *Der unlautere Wettebewerb* (Berlin, 1914), p. 3. The growth of monopolistic guilds and companies during the sixteenth century, promoted by the fiscal needs of the rulers, however, served as focal points for breaking down these market rules and customs. See also Vernon A. Mund, *Open Markets* (New York, 1948), pp. 24–28, 74–94.

or combine or conspire with any other person or persons, to monopolize any part of the trade or commerce among the several states, or with foreign nations, shall be deemed guilty of a misdemeanor. . . ."[18]

The third section of the act makes its provisions specifically applicable to commerce in any territory of the United States—Alaska, Hawaii, Puerto Rico—and in the District of Columbia, as well as to the commerce of these areas with the states or with foreign nations. In *People of Puerto Rico v. Shell Co.*, 302 U.S. 253 (1937), the Supreme Court held that the word "territory" should be construed in its most comprehensive sense to include a dependency such as Puerto Rico. "When the Sherman Act was passed (1890)," the Court stated, "we had no insular dependencies; and, necessarily, the application of section 3 did not extend beyond our continental domain." The Court reasoned that Congress meant to give the Sherman Act a broad application, and that it was logical to infer that Congress intended to include all areas to which its powers might extend.

PUBLIC REMEDIES UNDER THE SHERMAN ACT

All violations of the first three sections are subject to criminal penalties, and provision is made for punishment by fine not to exceed $5000 for each violation, or by imprisonment not to exceed one year, or both.[19] Criminal cases are essentially punitive in their nature. They seek to penalize past illegal conduct and to prevent a repetition of such conduct. In criminal cases, it is possible for a defendant to plead *nolo contendere* ("I will not contest it") with the consent of the court. This plea means that the accused party makes no contention as to whether or not he is guilty and agrees to accept the decision of the court. Actually, a plea of *nolo contendere* is tantamount to a plea of guilty. If the court accepts the plea, it is in a position to impose criminal penalties according to the provisions of the law.

The fourth section gives the Attorney General the power to enforce the act by civil proceedings to restrain, enjoin, and prohibit violations of the act. Civil actions do not involve penalties, but they do make it possible for the federal government to secure corrective and constructive changes in business conduct by requiring modifications in business organization and practice.

The government may bring either a criminal or civil action against a

[18] *United States Code,* 1946 ed., Title 15, Sections 1–8. Hereafter cited as 15 U.S.C. 1–8. The full text of all the antitrust laws may be secured in pamphlet form from the Superintendent of Documents, U.S. Government Printing Office, Washington 25, D.C., for 25¢.

[19] Upon conviction, the fine of $5000 may be levied against each party indicted and for each count (charge) in the complaint. In given cases, fines have been levied against (1) a trade association, (2) every member of the trade association, (3) the officials of the trade association, (4) the top officers in the corporations involved, and (5) the boards of directors of the corporations. Fines have also been levied on the several counts of (1) monopolization, (2) attempts to monopolize, (3) conspiracy, and (4) restraint of trade. By such means, the fine of $5000 for each violation can be pyramided into total fines of $100,000 or more.

defendant or group of defendants, and the two actions may also be pursued concurrently or successively. In civil cases a company charged with violating the Sherman Act may decide that it is quite certain that it will lose the case. In this event, the company frequently arranges with the court and the Department of Justice to sign a *consent decree* without a presentation of its case to the court. The defendant, in other words, consents to accept a court order without having been found guilty of violating the law. Consent decrees are usually worked out by negotiation between the Department of Justice and the defendant and are enforceable by means of contempt proceedings. If the defendant is not satisfied with the proposed modifications for his business behavior, he can always ask to have the case brought to trial.

It is in civil suits that the Department of Justice can make provision for a dissolution, divestiture, or divorcement of corporate mergers in order to create numerous, independent competitors (see Chap. 11, pp. 234–235). Affirmative relief may also include the compulsory licensing of patents, either royalty free or at a reasonable royalty. The civil remedy further includes the use of injunctions to forbid various business practices—such as interlocking directorships, exclusive dealing contracts, and restrictive patent agreements. Injunctions may likewise contain mandatory provisions which are positive in their nature, even though such measures are not specifically required by law.

Section 6 provides that any property owned by an illegal combination or a group of conspirators which is in the course of interstate or foreign commerce may be seized by the federal government.

PRIVATE REMEDIES UNDER THE SHERMAN ACT

The seventh section provides that any person "injured in his business or property" by anything forbidden in the act, may sue to recover threefold the damages sustained, including the costs of the suit. This is the important "treble damages" section of the law. Its purpose is to encourage private individuals injured by monopoly to take action, themselves, in enforcing the statute. A second private remedy against the monopolistic practices prohibited by the Sherman Act is provided in Section 16 of the Clayton Act (1914). This section enables a private plaintiff to sue for an injunction—a restraining order—whenever he is threatened by loss or damage by a violation of the antitrust laws.

JURISDICTION UNDER THE SHERMAN ACT

The fourth section of the law provides that the several district courts of the United States (originally designated as circuit courts) shall be invested with jurisdiction to prevent and restrain violations of the act. Such courts also have jurisdiction of the criminal and seizure sanctions, as well as both of the private remedies created by the Sherman and Clayton Acts. The higher federal courts—courts of appeal and the Supreme Court—affirm antitrust decisions upon appeal or reverse and remand them to the district courts for final disposition.

The fifth section of the act gives a federal court hearing an antitrust case authority to require all persons connected with the alleged violation to come before it even though they do not reside in the judicial district in which the court is sitting. Civil actions may be brought in any district where the defendant resides or is found. The eighth and last section of the act defines "person" or "persons" to include corporations and associations.

THE SOCIAL PHILOSOPHY OF FEDERAL JUDGES AND THE INTERPRETATION OF THE SHERMAN ACT

It has frequently been observed by distinguished lawyers that the Sherman Act, like the Constitution, is what the judges say it is. Though we all want a government of law, the fact is that there is no way to attain that end except through men. The background, training, associations, and social philosophy of the judges interpreting the law are thus of exceedingly great importance in determining the use and application of the legislation passed by Congress. A "pro-competition" statute will be of small effectiveness if the judges are not pro-competition in their point of view.

The prevailing economic philosophy of politically important people in the United States, from the adoption of the Constitution to the "New Deal" policies of President Roosevelt, was that government should largely pursue a policy of "let alone" with respect to the conduct of business activity. In accordance with a policy of economic freedom, it was thought, businessmen should be permitted to create their own methods of competition and their own "rules of the game." This view, in large measure, arose as a reaction to the restrictive policies of English "mercantilism" and from a desire not to be hampered in the pursuit of profit.

THE EARLY APPLICATION AND INTERPRETATION OF THE SHERMAN ACT

The *Sugar Trust* case of 1895 was the first important case to arise under the Sherman law. In its decision on this case, the Supreme Court through Chief Justice Fuller conceded that the American Sugar Refining Company had "acquired nearly complete control of the manufacture of refined sugar in the United States." Nevertheless, the Court held that the Sherman Act could not be applied to a combination of *manufacturing* enterprises, on the ground that manufacturing is not commerce. Even though in disposing of its product the combination had to resort to interstate commerce, the Court held that a combination of manufacturing plants, in itself, "bore no direct relation to commerce between the states."[20] As a result of this decision the control of industrial monopolies was left entirely to the states. Since the state legislatures were then largely under the domination of the large corporations, the effect of the decision was to allow industrial monopoly in the United States to grow without abatement. Indeed, it was during the years immediately following the *Sugar Trust* decision that many of the formerly com-

[20] *U.S. v. E. C. Knight Co.*, 156 U.S. 1, 9 (1895).

peting and independent enterprises of the country were united together to form the giant corporations of today.

After some years, the Court began to modify its extreme view that *manufacture* and *commerce* are separate and distinct. In the *Addyston Pipe* case (1899), it applied the Sherman Act to six pipe manufacturers who had agreed to fix prices. Again, in the *Beef Trust* case (1905), the Court condemned a collusive combination of meat packers which had virtually eliminated price competition in the purchase of livestock and the sale of fresh meat in the Middle West. In a unanimous decision Justice Holmes declared, "The very point of the combination is to restrain and monopolize commerce among the states in respect to such sales."[21]

THE SHERMAN ACT AND CONSPIRACIES TO RESTRAIN COMPETITION

In the common law, all agreements among competitors with respect to the prices of necessaries were held to be illegal "conspiracies." This rule against price fixing was made applicable in American law to all products. In developing the common-law rule on price fixing, the judges were not concerned with whether the prices were high or low. The mere fact that two or more sellers had agreed on prices were sufficient to make the action illegal. The purpose of the law was to maintain and preserve price competition in order to insure fair and equitable prices and incomes. Since an agreement on price eliminates price competition, there was no ground for modifying the prohibition in any degree. The common-law doctrine on conspiracy was incorporated into the Sherman Act, and Section 1 specifically states that "every . . . conspiracy in restraint of trade or commerce . . . is illegal."

Today, cases involving concerted action among nominally independent firms are called "conspiracy cases." According to the Supreme Court, a conspiracy is "a combination of two or more persons, by concerted action, to accomplish a criminal or unlawful purpose."[22] More briefly, Justice Holmes has stated that "A conspiracy is a partnership in criminal purposes."[23]

CONSPIRACIES SUPPRESSING COMPETITION VIOLATIVE OF THE SHERMAN ACT

The rule on conspiracies suppressing price competition was early applied by the Supreme Court in the *Addyston Pipe* case (1899).[24] In this case, six pipe manufacturers, controlling some 30 percent of the national production of cast-iron pipe, divided sales territories and fixed selling prices. The Court condemned the agreement, stating that the direct and immediate effect of price-fixing conspiracies is to destroy competition, so that the parties may

[21] *Swift and Company* v. *U.S.*, 196 U.S. 375, 397 (1905).

[22] *Pettibone* v. *U.S.*, 148 U.S. 197, 203 (1893).

[23] *U.S.* v. *Kissel*, 218 U.S. 601 (1910).

[24] *Addyston Pipe and Steel Co.* v. *U.S.*, 175 U.S. 211 (1899). The *Addyston Pipe* case made it clear and unmistakable that the type of competition required by the Sherman Act is *price competition.*

secure increased prices for themselves. All such conspiracies, the Court declared, are an illegal restraint of commerce. (See Landmark Cases, p. 672.) The law thus stated has been consistently followed by the courts, and today it may be said that concerted action to fix prices, divide sales areas, or limit production is illegal *per se* (by itself) under the Sherman Act.

The common testimony of businessmen who have endeavored to arrange collusive price-fixing plans is the difficulty which they frequently encounter in bringing and keeping others in line on price or on other restrictive arrangements. Some sellers are short of cash and cannot afford to accumulate "surplus" inventories or finance unused capacity. Others are able to make a satisfactory profit by selling at lower prices or by conducting their business independently. In view of this fact, conspirators frequently resort to the use of "peaceful persuasion," coercion, black lists, and boycotts in order to secure conformity with the purposes of the group. Such measures, the courts have held, are likewise violative of the antitrust laws and may be enjoined.

THE TRENTON POTTERIES CASE

Two additional cases which serve as landmarks in the law on collusive restraints are the *Trenton Potteries* case (1927) and the *Madison Oil* case (1940).[25] A brief review of these cases will serve to indicate the unqualified manner in which the Supreme Court condemns conspiracies restricting competition.

The *Trenton Potteries* case involved the legality of a price-fixing agreement entered into by a group of manufacturers who produced some 82 percent of the vitreous pottery fixtures made in the United States for use in bathrooms and lavatories. The evidence clearly showed the existence of an agreement to fix prices and restrict sales to jobbers, and the defendants did not contest the facts of the case. They did, however, seek to show that their motives were worthy and that their conduct was reasonable. In particular, they claimed that concerted action was necessary in order to eliminate ruinous and chaotic competition. They further maintained that the prices which they had fixed were reasonable, and that no injury to the public could be shown.

In its decision, the Supreme Court stated clearly that it was unwilling to apply the doctrine of reasonableness to price-fixing agreements. The test of illegality, the Court declared, must be judged by the effect of the restraint on competition, for the purpose of the law is to maintain competition in order to protect the public against the evils of monopoly. Since the aim of every price-fixing agreement is an elimination of price competition, the Court concluded that all agreements on price are illegal. In the words of the Court,

> The aim and result of every price-fixing agreement, if effective, is the elimination of one form of competition. The power to fix prices, whether

[25] *U.S. v. Trenton Potteries Co.*, 273 U.S. 392 (1927); and *U.S. v. Socony-Vacuum Oil Company*, 310 U.S. 150 (1940). The latter case is called the *Madison Oil* case because the trial was held in Madison, Wisconsin.

reasonably exercised or not, involves power to control the market and to fix arbitrary and unreasonable prices. The reasonable price fixed today may through economic and business changes become the unreasonable price of tomorrow. Once established, it may be maintained unchanged because of the absence of competition secured by the agreement for a price reasonable when fixed. Agreements which create such potential power may well be held to be in themselves unreasonable or unlawful restraints, without the necessity of minute inquiry whether a particular price is reasonable or unreasonable as fixed. . . .[26]

The *Trenton Potteries* case is significant not only because of the rule of law announced but also because it brings into sharp focus the divergent policy which the Supreme Court came to adopt with respect to mergers and price-fixing agreements. In the *Steel* case, it will be seen, the Court held that a control of competing enterprises *by merger* is not illegal under the Sherman Act in the absence of unworthy motives and conduct. In the *Trenton Potteries* case, on the other hand, the Court held that a restriction of price competition among competitors *by agreement* is illegal in any and all cases, because the restraint imposed is directly productive of "evil consequences."

THE MADISON OIL CASE

In the *Madison Oil* case the Court again emphasized that the factor of reasonableness has no application in price-fixing cases. This case involved the legality of a price-stabilization plan devised and managed by the major oil refiners in the Midwestern area who produced some 85 percent of the gasoline sold in that area. During the period of the National Recovery Administration (1933–1935), the defendants worked out a plan for stabilizing prices, and the arrangement was approved by the Administration. After the NIRA was held to be unconstitutional, the defendants continued to engage in price-stabilization activity; and the government thereupon filed a charge of collusive price fixing. The plan of control consisted mainly of concerted action to buy "surplus" or "homeless" gasoline, freely offered by independent refiners, which was not readily salable by them at the prices maintained by the major companies.

The major refiners sought to defend their activity on the ground that concerted action to eliminate an evil—"distress" gasoline—should not be condemned, even though it "would necessarily tend to produce fairer or higher price levels." Justice Douglas, speaking for the Court, replied that the determination of "fairer" prices cannot be left to private control. "The reasonableness of prices," he declared, "has no constancy due to the dynamic quality of business facts underlying price structures. Those who fixed reasonable prices today would perpetuate unreasonable prices tomorrow, since those prices would not be subject to continuous administrative supervision and readjustment in the light of changed conditions."[27] See Note No. 7, Landmark Cases, p. 674.

[26] *U.S. v. Trenton Potteries Co.*, 273 U.S. 392, 397 (1927).

[27] *U.S. v. Socony-Vacuum Oil Company*, 310 U.S. 150, 221–222, 225–226 (1940).

THE USE OF THE SHERMAN ACT TO DISSOLVE
CORPORATE COMBINATIONS

In 1911 the Supreme Court handed down two of the most important decisions which it had ever decided with reference to the Sherman Act. The Sherman Act, we have seen, was intended to prohibit and make illegal "every contract, combination in the form of trust or otherwise, or conspiracy in restraint of trade or commerce"; and in an effort to undertake a dissolution of the giant corporate mergers, the Department of Justice brought suit against two of the most aggressive and notorious of the combinations—the Standard Oil Company of New Jersey and the American Tobacco Company. The Standard Oil Company was organized in New Jersey in 1899 to hold the stock of some seventy different corporations engaged in operating oil refineries, oil wells, pipe lines, storage plants, and distribution facilities. It is reported that the various plants of the company produced over 200 by-products. Most of the facilities had formerly been united under a central control by means of the trust device. As early as 1882 the trust had secured a control of about 90 percent of the oil-refining business, and this percentage control was maintained in the new organization.

The American Tobacco Company was likewise a New Jersey corporation, originally incorporated in 1890. By pursuing a relentless policy of cutthroat competition, the company was able to induce independents to sell out their stock or assets, and an ownership control was rapidly secured over a large part of the tobacco industry. At the time of the suit, it was estimated that the corporation had acquired a control over some 95 percent of the cigarette business, 85 percent of plug tobacco production, 75 percent of smoking tobacco manufacture, and 80 percent of the snuff production. In both the *Standard Oil* and the *American Tobacco* cases the government asked for a dissolution of the monopolistic mergers.

The records in the *Standard Oil* and *American Tobacco* cases were replete with examples of predatory practices employed by the combinations to injure, eliminate, or buy up competitors in order to secure monopoly control. Specifically, it was found that the Standard Oil Company had (1) secured rebates and other discriminatory favors from the railroads, (2) pursued a policy of cutting prices in particular areas while maintaining or increasing them in localities in which it had no competition, (3) bribed railway and other employees for information on competitors, (4) established bogus companies to sell petroleum products at "cut" prices, (5) controlled pipe lines to the disadvantage of competitors, and (6) allocated sales areas for its subsidiaries so as to eliminate competition among them.

Similarly, in the *American Tobacco* case, it was found by the Court that the large financial power of the company was used (1) to cut prices in one area while maintaining them elsewhere in order to drive out competitors or compel them to join the combination, (2) to buy up a control over all the elements necessary for manufacturing tobacco products, so as to exclude others from the trade, (3) to spend "millions upon millions of dollars in buying out plants . . . to close them up and render them useless for the purposes of trade," (4) to require vendors, stockholders, and employees "to bind themselves, generally for long periods, not to compete in the future."

After surveying the "undisputed" evidence in the *Standard Oil* and *American Tobacco* cases, the Court held that the "acts," "purposes," and "motives" of the giant combinations showed conclusively that it was the plain duty of the Court to apply the Sherman Act and order a dissolution of the combinations. With special reference to the Standard Oil Company, the Court stated that the lower court was correct in finding that "the *acts* and *dealings* established by the proof operated . . . to cause the transfers of stock which were made to the New Jersey Corporation . . . to be a combination or conspiracy in restraint of trade."[28] Similarly, in the *American Tobacco* case, the Court declared that "the history of the combination is so . . . demonstrative of the existence from the beginning of a *purpose* to acquire dominion and control of the tobacco trade, not by the mere exertion of the ordinary right to contract and to trade, but by methods devised in order to monopolize the trade by driving competitors out of business, which were ruthlessly carried out upon the assumption that to work upon the fears or play upon the cupidity of competitors would make success possible."[29]

In the *Standard Oil* decision, the decree "commanded the dissolution of the combination, and . . . directed the transfer by the New Jersey corporation back to the stockholders . . . of the stock which had been turned over to the New Jersey company in exchange for its stock." Since a few closely associated capitalists owned most of the stock in the holding company, this decree resulted in giving the same persons a controlling interest in the subsidiary corporations. Instead of owning a controlling interest in a single company, they now owned a controlling interest in many companies. No attempt was made to require these men to divest themselves of their controlling interest in one or more of the various subsidiary corporations by requiring a public sale of the stock.

In 1915 the U.S. Commissioner of Corporations reported, "The general opinion is that this dissolution is effective neither in theory nor in fact. There is much ground for believing that it did not result in independent action or active competition between the various subsidiary companies. . . . That the dissolution of the Standard Oil Company was not more satisfactory in form and results appears to be due, however, to the manner of its accomplishment rather than to any inherent difficulty in re-establishing competitive conditions among the component parts of the combination."[30] A special study of the petroleum industry made in 1948 points out that the effect of the dissolution "was to divide the Standard Oil Company into a series of companies, each of which was supreme in a particular geographical area." Nothing was done by

---

[28] *Standard Oil Company of New Jersey v. U.S.*, 221 U.S. 1, 74 (1911). Italics supplied.
[29] *U.S. v. American Tobacco Co.*, 221 U.S. 106, 181–182 (1911).
[30] Joseph E. Davies, *Trust Laws and Unfair Competition* (Washington, 1915), p. 18.

the Court to create competition *within* a geographical sales area. Instead, within each sales territory, the study continues, each Standard Oil Company has "provided the necessary strength and machinery for price leadership and policy leadership of all kinds."[31]

The American Tobacco Company had secured its position of domination by the acquisition of assets as well as stock; and in providing for its dissolution, the Court approved a plan by which the factories, warehouses, brands, and other assets owned by the company were assigned to three large "full line" companies and some eleven small ones. Since the group of persons who controlled the American Tobacco Company secured large blocks of stock in these corporations, this decree of dissolution, it is generally agreed, was likewise one of form rather than of substance.

THE DEVELOPMENT OF THE "RULE OF REASON" IN THE STANDARD OIL AND AMERICAN TOBACCO CASES

Although the Sherman Act prohibits "every contract, combination in the form of trust or otherwise, or conspiracy," the Court shifted from an application of this prohibition to a consideration of whether or not there was an "intent" or "purpose" to monopolize an industry. In the *Standard Oil* and *American Tobacco* cases, the Court happened to find an illegal intent, but it gave no clean-cut guide in its decisions for future public policy. How about the legal status of mergers, as such? How about discriminatory prices made by a combination to enhance its profits in certain areas and to match or undercut prices in other areas? The Court gave no legal or economic analysis of these aspects of business behavior. Its view, in effect, appeared to be that anything is fair as long as it does not manifest an *intent* or *purpose* to monopolize an industry.

Indeed, in the absence of predatory acts, the Court appeared to be willing to accept mergers and such price policies as the giant corporations might pursue. In the *American Tobacco* case, in particular, it stated that the combination was illegal "not because of the vast amount of property aggregated by the combination, not because, alone, of the many corporations which the proof shows were united by resort to one device or another. Again, not alone because of the dominion and control over the tobacco trade which actually exists." This sympathetic analysis and point of view of the Court toward mergers laid the groundwork for the development of the so-called "abuse theory" of mergers (or of monopoly). In the *United States Steel* and *International Harvester* cases, which we shall next consider, the Court gave full expression to the "abuse theory." In essence, this theory means that mergers will be dissolved by the Supreme Court only when there is proof (1) of "alarming" and "ungentlemanly" conduct and (2) of an overwhelming percentage control of a given industry.

In an explanation of its action in not condemning the giant mergers in the

[31] Eugene V. Rostow, *A National Policy for the Oil Industry* (New Haven, 1948), pp. 6–7.

oil and tobacco industries, as such, the Court developed the so-called "rule of reason." According to Chief Justice White, speaking for the Court, since the Sherman Act does not specifically define acts which are in restraint of trade, the Court itself must in every case decide whether or not the particular acts have this effect. In exercising this judgment, he stated in the *Standard Oil* case, the Court must be guided by a "rule of reason." (See Landmark Cases, p. 676.) An analysis of the meaning of the term "rule of reason" is presented on pp. 676–678.

The historical meaning of "restraint of trade" in the common law, we have seen, was that of a restraint on the right of a person to carry on his trade or calling. Gradually, the courts came to accept partial (limited) restraints made on the exercise of *a trade*, if they were shown to be reasonable and based upon a proper consideration. Soon after 1850, various American state courts also began to apply the term to agreements *on prices* made by a group of competitors. Such agreements were held to be general restraints of trade and void.

In the *Standard Oil* and *American Tobacco* cases, Chief Justice White developed the view that the doctrine of reasonableness which had long been applied to contracts in *partial* restraint of trade *in the sale of a business* should also be applied to *a merger* of former competitors which completely restrained their independent action on price. In other words, the rule of reason was now to be applied to an important type of *general* restraint on trade. This line of thought involved a revolutionary break with the common-law rules against monopolistic practices. There is no standard for judging the reasonableness of a general restraint on prices, for the relationship is between the sellers *and the public*.

The rule of reason announced by Chief Justice White in the *Oil* and *Tobacco* cases had been urged by defendants in two earlier cases, but was rejected by the Court, with Justice White dissenting. *U.S. v. Trans-Missouri Freight Assn.*, 166 U.S. 290 (1897), and *U.S. v. Joint Traffic Assn.*, 171 U.S. 505 (1898). In these cases, the Court declared that the Sherman Act condemns "*every* contract, combination . . . or conspiracy in restraint of trade or commerce." To prohibit only "unreasonable" restraints of trade, it stated, would be to engage in "judicial legislation." Subsequently, in 1911, with changes in the personnel of the Court, Justice White found support for his view and wrote the majority opinion.

RULE OF REASON MAKES FOR INDEFINITENESS IN THE REGULATION OF COMMERCE

Following the decisions of 1897 and 1898 rejecting the proposal to add a rule of reason to the Sherman Act, various business leaders appealed to Congress to modify the law on the ground that the decisions were hurting the "business interests" of the country. Bills were introduced in Congress to change the Act, but they were not adopted. The general view of Congress was expressed in 1909 in a report by the Senate Judiciary Committee which declared:

The antitrust act makes it a criminal offense to violate the law, and provides a punishment both by fine and imprisonment. To inject into the act the question of whether an agreement or combination is *reasonable* or *unreasonable* would render the act as a criminal or penal statute indefinite and uncertain, and hence, to that extent, utterly nugatory and void, and would practically amount to a repeal of that part of the act. Justice Brewer, in the case of *Tozer* v. *U.S.* (52 Fed., 917), makes this perfectly clear and plain. . . . "But, in order to constitute a crime, the act must be one which the party is able to know in advance whether it is criminal or not. The criminality of an act can not depend upon whether a jury may think it reasonable or unreasonable. There must be some definiteness and certainty." . . . Defendant was found guilty in the lower court. The decision was reversed. . . .

And while the same technical objection does not apply to civil prosecutions, the injection of the rule of reasonableness or unreasonableness would lead to the greatest variableness and uncertainty in the enforcement of the law. The defense of reasonable restraint would be made in every case and there would be as many different rules of reasonableness as cases, courts, and juries. What one court or jury might deem unreasonable another court or jury might deem reasonable. . . .

To amend the antitrust act, as suggested by this bill, would be to entirely emasculate it, and for all practical purposes render it nugatory as a remedial statute. Criminal prosecutions would not lie and civil remedies would labor under the greatest doubt and uncertainty. The act as it exists is clear, comprehensive, certain, and highly remedial. It practically covers the field of federal jurisdiction, and is in every respect a model law. To destroy or undermine it at the present juncture, when combinations are on the increase, and appear to be as oblivious as ever of the rights of the public, would be a calamity.

In view of the foregoing, your committee recommend the indefinite postponement of the bill.[32]

The insight which Congress had in 1909, it is believed by many, has been fully vindicated by time. The Sherman Act, *as interpreted by the Supreme Court*, has not checked the growth of economic concentration. Its application, moreover, has given rise to great uncertainty on what the law means and what it condemns. Businessmen today seek, but do not find, a clear-cut answer to questions on which trade restraints are illegal.

THE UNITED STATES STEEL CORPORATION AND THE RESTRICTION OF COMPETITION IN THE STEEL INDUSTRY

In 1920 the Supreme Court was given a significant opportunity to use its "rule of reason" in a case involving the largest industrial combination ever formed. The United States Steel Corporation, organized in New Jersey in the early months of 1901, was a "combination of combinations." It brought

[32] Committee on the Judiciary, U.S. Senate, 60th Congress, second session, Senate Report 848, 1909, pp. 10–11.

together in one financial unit a control over a series of corporations which had already secured control over the principal plants in their respective lines of business in the steel industry. The underlying mergers had largely been formed not only to secure a combination of like plants in a given field—such as tin-plate mills, wire mills, or pipe and tube mills—but also to secure a control over raw materials and production facilities from the ore to the finished products. Mergers of like plants—such as the American Tin Plate Company, which secured a control of 95 percent of the tin-plate production in the country—were admittedly formed to restrict and control competition among the constituent units, and in adding iron ore mines, pig iron mills, and fabricating facilities the horizontal mergers sought to make certain that they would have ready supplies or ready outlets without price dictation by other monopoly groups. The principal combinations which the United States Steel Corporation acquired with its formation in 1901 were the following:

Carnegie Steel Company, 1900 (20 plants).
Federal Steel Company, 1898 (20 plants).
American Steel and Wire Company, 1899 (39 plants).
National Tube Company, 1899 (15 plants).
American Bridge Company, 1900 (26 plants).
National Steel Company, 1899 (10 plants).
American Tin Plate Company, 1898 (265 plants).
American Sheet Steel Company, 1900 (26 plants).
American Steel Hoop Company, 1899 (14 plants).

The acquisition of the foregoing combinations, together with additional iron ore and coal property, transportation lines, and other facilities gave the corporation a control over 65 to 75 percent of all lines of steel manufacturing and some 80 percent of the best iron ore reserves in the country.[33] Vertical integration had largely been accomplished by the constituent companies during the period 1880 to 1900. The corporation itself brought together major companies which were themselves engaged in competition with one another.

THE ACCEPTANCE OF BUSINESS COMBINATIONS BY THE COURTS

The Department of Justice brought action against the United States Steel Corporation in 1912. The decision of the lower court was rendered in 1915 and that of the Supreme Court in 1920. The Supreme Court upheld the lower court in a four-to-three decision and refused to order a dissolution of the corporation. According to the Supreme Court, the corporation, which at the time of the suit produced about 50 percent of all steel products, was not a monopoly. The testimony in the case, the Court stated, did "not show that

[33] Report of the Industrial Commission, *Trusts and Industrial Combinations* (Washington, 1901), Vol. 13, pp. 450, 455.

the corporation, in and of itself, ever possessed or exerted sufficient power when acting alone to control prices of the products of the industry."[34]

For many years, the record indicated, the corporation had used its economic power in trade meetings—the so-called "Gary dinners"—to unite competitors in a policy of unified action on price. Its prices at Pittsburgh became the "official" prices for all iron and steel products, and any changes announced by the corporation were (with rare exceptions) promptly adopted by other steel companies. Some nine months before the government announced its suit the dinner meetings were discontinued. The fact that the corporation had secured the coöperation of its competitors in its plan of controlling price led the majority of the Court to believe that the corporation, in itself, was not a monopoly. Moreover, since the corporation apparently was no longer meeting with its competitors, the Court held that there was an absence of "unworthy motives." In the view of the majority, "whatever there was of evil effect was discontinued before this suit was brought, and this, we think, determines the decree." See Landmark Cases: "Rule of Reason," p. 676; and "The Steel Corporation Case," p. 680.

The government's presentation of evidence in the Steel case failed to develop the fact that the concerted action among the steel mills centered on the use and maintenance of the basing-point plan of delivered prices under the leadership of the United States Steel Corporation. At the very time the case was being tried this pricing plan was being effectively maintained by the corporation even though the Gary dinners were discontinued. It remained for the Federal Trade Commission to find and condemn (in 1924) the basing-point formula for quoting identical delivered prices. (See also chap. 17.)

THE ABUSE THEORY OF MERGERS

The majority of the Court in the Steel case formally adopted the abuse theory of mergers. In the absence (1) of "unworthy motives" and "predatory acts," and (2) an overwhelming percentage control of an industry, the Court indicated that it was not willing to dissolve the giant corporations. This rule, or principle, is also known as the "Sherman Act test" for determining the legality of a merger. In support of this construction, Justice McKenna, speaking for the majority, declared, "The law does not make mere size [in the form of combinations] an offense. It, we repeat, requires overt acts, and trusts to its prohibition of them and its power to repress or punish them."

The view toward mergers adopted by the Court in the Steel case was reaffirmed in 1927 in the International Harvester case.[35] The International Harvester Company controlled some 64 percent of the output of harvesting machinery and was generally recognized in the industry as being the "price leader" which others followed. The Court, however, refused to order a dissolution of this industrial giant on the ground that "The law . . . does not make the mere size of a corporation, however impressive, or the existence

[34] U.S. v. U.S. Steel Corporation, 251 U.S. 417 (1920).
[35] U.S. v. International Harvester Company, 274 U.S. 693 (1927).

of unexerted power on its part, an offense, when unaccompanied by unlawful conduct in the exercise of its power." As in the *Steel* case, the Court in declaring this rule of law saw no restraint whatever to legitimate price competition in the combination of scores of former independents into a single financial and price-controlling unit.

In its case against the International Harvester Company, the government presented evidence showing that the company established or made the prices which were regularly followed by others in the industry. It also tried to use this evidence to prove the existence of monopoly in accordance with the economic conception of monopoly. The Supreme Court, however, refused to draw the inference of monopoly. "The fact," the Court stated, "that competitors may see proper, in the exercise of their own judgment, to follow the prices of another manufacturer, does not establish any suppression of competition or show any sinister domination."

Since the Court had accepted the idea of financial bigness—in the absence of a showing of predatory practices—it followed logically that it also had to accept the control of price by a dominating seller as a necessary consequence. The only way to eliminate price leadership in such cases would be to dissolve the dominating combination which controls such a large part of the supply that it can exercise a considerable degree of monopoly power. This the Court was unwilling to do.

In most cases, the evidence indicates, large combinations secure compliance with their "official" price policies by using coercive pressures in the form of discriminatory prices or by offering rewards in the form of higher prices. The principal fear of "retaliation" which makes for unity of action is a fear of *discriminatory* pricing. As Professor Edward H. Levi has observed, "The truth is, of course, that in most monopoly cases, *if the court has a mind to do so, it can find abuses.*"[36]

SOME ECONOMIC ERRORS IN THE VIEW THAT "MERE SIZE" IS NO OFFENSE

Many economists and legal authorities believe that in developing and applying the rule that "mere size" is no offense the Supreme Court has failed to give sufficient attention to the economic and social aspects of financial bigness. In their opinion, there are four significant errors in the position taken by the Court. First, it is pointed out that large financial size is an offense against the public if it means the restraint of competition among many formerly independent and competing firms. The acquisition of the stock or assets of former competitors gives a single price-controlling unit a more complete control over their prices than the most elaborate forms of conspiracy. Since conspiracy on price has long been held to be illegal, it follows *in principle* that an elimination of competition by an acquisition of stock or assets is likewise repugnant to the tenets of the Sherman Act.

[36] Edward H. Levi, "The Antitrust Laws and Monopoly," *University of Chicago Law Review*, February 1947, p. 158.

Secondly, the view that "mere size" is no offense is based upon the erroneous belief that large combinations are justified because they bring the "economies of mass production." In the *Steel* case in particular, the majority of the Court was greatly impressed with the idea that there are significant economies of production in large combinations. Actually, the economies of mass production apply to a single plant; and all that a combination of scores of geographically separate plants can do is to seek to maintain technical economy in the individual plants acquired. In the hearings of the Industrial Commission in 1900 on the "advantages" of mergers, Mr. William E. Reis, president of the National Steel Company, a combination of ten large steel plants and extensive coal and ore properties, was asked the following question: "Is there any saving that comes in the manufacture itself, the process of manufacture, that you get through consolidation?" Mr. Reis replied, "I think not."[37] There obviously are advantages in horizontal combinations, for otherwise they would not be formed. These advantages, however, are largely to be found in the control over the price policies of formerly competing plants which a merger gives, rather than in the economies of mass production which apply to the individual plants.

Thirdly, experience has shown that an attack on abuses alone—rather than financial size—frequently does not remedy the problem of monopoly or create the essential conditions for competition. If a given monopolistic device is curbed, it is likely that a dominant firm will be able to develop new ones. The decrees against basing-point pricing in steel and cement, for example, have not stopped the use of delivered pricing systems. Similarly, when firms have attained dominant positions in their fields—as in steel and in the nonferrous metals—they are usually able to exercise "price leadership" without resorting to the crude practices of the early trust period. Their counsel to smaller competitors is "Be Good and You'll Be Happy." As Professor Walter Adams has said, "Once a firm has attained a dominant position in the market place, it no longer has to engage in predatory practices to achieve its monopolistic ends. Its mere existence will be sufficient warning to smaller rivals that noncoöperation may be equivalent to suicide."[38]

Finally, the view that mere bigness is no offense, it is said, fails to recognize that concentrated economic power leads to the undue political influence of big business in the operation of democratic government. This problem, it will be remembered, we discussed in Chapter 3.

THE NEED FOR A STANDARD ON CORPORATE SIZE

The great amount of oligopoly which has been allowed to develop under the Sherman Act indicates clearly that the nation needs to give special attention to the problem of corporate size. Large corporate mergers may be legal

---

[37] Report of the Industrial Commission, *Testimony* (Washington, 1900), Vol. 1, Part 2, p. 947.

[38] Walter Adams, "The Rule of Reason": Workable Competition or Workable Monopoly," *Yale Law Journal*, January 1954, pp. 366–367.

under the Sherman Act, as interpreted by the courts. In the eyes of many economists, however, their existence makes effective price competition manifestly impossible.

At the present time, it appears that neither the Department of Justice nor the courts will proceed in a positive way to remedy economic concentration. The problem is complex, and it is possible that new legislation will be required to provide a clear-cut standard for use in dissolution proceedings. (See also Chap. 19.)

In the opinion of many economists and legal authorities, the government must either (1) create and maintain numerous, independent business units and effective *price* competition or (2) undertake directly to fix the prices controlled and managed by the large financial mergers.[39] As we shall see in subsequent chapters, the alternative of extending regulation of the commission type to monopolistic mergers in industry does not promise to be practical or feasible. The fact is that thus far we have not developed satisfactory techniques for effective commission control on a large-scale basis. A substantial body of opinion and evidence points to the conclusion that if we are to avoid succumbing to monopoly power we must proceed to reduce the size of that power through an unraveling of the larger financial units created by merger.

THE DOCTRINE OF CONSCIOUS PARALLEL ACTION

Historically, proof of conspiracy has been found in evidence of actual "agreement," i.e., in proof of a meeting of the minds of two or more persons to do an illegal act. Today, however, "conscious parallel action"—without overt agreement—has been accepted by the courts as proof of conspiracy. *Conscious* parallel action means uniformity of action which is "consciously done," "purposeful" or "volitional." In so far as proof can be offered showing that uniformity of action—in pricing, in denying supplies, etc.—results from some deliberate plan of action, it is likely that the courts will find conspiracy.

The leading case holding that a common course of action—without explicit proof of agreement—justifies a finding of conspiracy is the *Interstate Circuit* case (1939). (See Landmark Cases, p. 689.) This case was brought by the federal government against eight major film distributors, distributing about 75 percent of the "first-run" features produced in the United States, and two large chains of exhibitors. The exhibitors, the facts showed, sent identical letters to each distributor (naming all as addressees) threatening to withdraw their patronage unless the distributors agreed not to lease pictures to subsequent-run theaters which showed "double features" or charged an admission fee of less than twenty-five cents. The district court found that the distributors had adopted the course of action demanded by the exhibitors

[39] See, for example, "Economists' Committee on Antitrust Law Policy," *American Economic Review*, September, 1932, p. 467; and Wendell Berge, "Problems of Enforcement and Interpretation of the Sherman Act," *American Economic Review, Papers and Proceedings*, May, 1948, pp. 172–181.

218 Government and Business

and that this action constituted conspiracy. It also held that each agreement between a distributor and an exhibitor was an illegal agreement.

Upon appeal, the Supreme Court affirmed the judgment in a six to three decision. The distributors in the *Interstate* case, the Court stated, engaged in a common course of action as a result of the form letter sent by the exhibitors. Adherence to this scheme of concerted action, without any agreement, the Court declared, justifies a finding of conspiracy. In the words of the Court,

> It was enough that, knowing that concerted action was contemplated and invited, the distributors gave their adherence to the scheme and participated in it. Each distributor was advised that the others were asked to participate; each knew that coöperation was essential to successful operation of the plan. They knew that the plan, if carried out, would result in a restraint of commerce which . . . was unreasonable within the meaning of the Sherman Act.[40]

A second leading case in which parallel action led to the finding of conspiracy is *Milgram* v. *Loew's* (1950). In this case, a drive-in theater operator brought action against eight motion picture distributors, charging concerted refusal to license first-run features for use in his theater. The district court found that each distributor in refusing to license pictures to the plaintiff was aware that the others were also refusing. Said the court:

> In practical effect, consciously parallel business practices have taken the place of the concept of meeting of the minds which some of the earlier cases emphasized. Present concert of action, further proof of actual agreement among the defendants is unnecessary, and it then becomes the duty of the Court to evaluate all the evidence in the setting of the case at hand and to determine whether a finding of a conspiracy to violate the Act is warranted.[41]

Upon the basis of the *Interstate Circuit* case, the Federal Trade Commission developed the doctrine of "conscious parallel action" under Section 5 of the Federal Trade Commission Act. (*Triangle Conduit* case, 168 F. (2d) 175, 1948; affirmed by the Supreme Court, 336 U.S. 956, April 25, 1949). In its brief before the Supreme Court, the Commission declared,

> Petitioners have at all times determined their prices by the use of a highly artificial (multiple-basing point) formula . . . and the systematic use of this formula, which has involved conscious parallelism of conduct by petitioners, necessarily produces identity in their delivered prices and eliminates price competition among them.[42]

The expanded doctrine of conspiracy developed in the *Interstate* case is of far-reaching importance. In the first place, it has considerably lightened the burden of proving conspiracy in antitrust cases. "From the *Interstate*

[40] *Interstate Circuit, Inc.,* v. *U.S.,* 306 U.S. 208, 226 (1939).
[41] *Milgram* v. *Loew's, Inc.,* 94 F. Supp. 416, 419 (1950).
[42] *Clayton Mark, et al.,* v. *F.T.C., Brief for the Federal Trade Commission,* No. 464, U.S. Supreme Court, October Term, 1948, pp. 20–21,

case to date," says Professor Milton Handler, "the Court has eliminated the element of agreement from its concept of conspiracy."[43] In the second place, the new doctrine has served to weaken the presumed validity of "price leadership" based upon the *International Harvester* case. Today the whole problem of price leadership has become encompassed in the larger problem of conscious parallel action. The language of *International Harvester* does not have the importance which it used to have, and some legal experts believe that it is now virtually obsolete.

The extent, however, to which the new "circumstantial evidence" doctrine of conspiracy will be employed in bringing cases will depend upon the *attitudes* of the men in the antitrust agencies.

SUGGESTIONS FOR FURTHER READING

Arnold, Thurman W., *The Bottlenecks of Business* (New York, 1940).

Carlston, Kenneth S., "Antitrust Policy: A Problem in Statecraft," *Yale Law Journal*, November, 1951, pp. 1073–1090.

Davies, Joseph E., *Trust Laws and Unfair Competition*, Bureau of Corporations, Department of Commerce (Washington, 1915).

Dirlam, J. B. and Kahn, A. E., *Antitrust in a Free Economy* (Ithaca, 1954).

Edwards, C. D., *Maintaining Competition* (New York, 1949).

Handler, Milton, *A Study of the Construction and Enforcement of the Federal Antitrust Laws*, Monograph No. 38, Temporary National Economic Committee, 76th Congress, third session, 1941.

Harbury, C. D., and Raskind, Leo J., "The British Approach to Monopoly Control," *Quarterly Journal of Economics*, August, 1953, pp. 380–406.

Loevinger, Lee, *The Law of Free Enterprise* (New York, 1949).

Rahl, James A., "Conspiracy and the Antitrust Laws," *Illinois Law Review*, January–February, 1950, pp. 743–768.

Stevens, William H. S., *Industrial Combinations and Trusts* (New York, 1913).

Stocking, G. W. and Watkins, M. W., *Monopoly and Free Enterprise* (New York, 1951).

[43] Hearings Before the Subcommittee on Study of Monopoly Power, Committee on the Judiciary, House of Representatives, 81st Congress, first session, Part 1, Serial No. 14, 1949, p. 536.

CHAPTER 11

The Sherman Act of 1890 and Its Judicial Interpretation (Continued)

TRADE ASSOCIATIONS AND THE SHERMAN ACT

A trade association may be defined as a voluntary association of business competitors, usually in one line of business activity, for the purpose of promoting their line of business by coöperative activities of one sort or another. Legitimate kinds of trade association activity consist of sales promotion work, public relations, standardization of products, technical research, collection of statistics, formulation of just and equitable trade practices, and reporting of prices at which goods in the past have actually been sold. Illegal activity, on the other hand, consists of collusive price fixing; the use of price-reporting systems which serve to restrict price competition; the use of boycotts, black lists, "peaceful persuasion," or other forms of coercion to injure suppliers, competitors, or customers; and collective activity to keep newcomers from the field.

Since the common interest of all trade members centers on the prices received for their products, most trade associations engage in collecting and disseminating statistics and price information. The adoption of this activity by trade associations was actively sponsored during the period 1912–1920 by Mr. Arthur Jerome Eddy, a successful lawyer and author of a book entitled *The New Competition* (1912). In accordance with the "Eddy plan," trade association members report price data to an association which, in turn, makes the information available to all members. Such associations are known as "open-price associations."[1] In practice, open-price associations may be "open" only in a partial sense, for frequently they are unwilling to furnish price data and trade statistics to buyers or to the general public.

---

[1] The Federal Trade Commission defines an open-price association as one "distributing or exchanging price information." In the view of the Commission, "The distinctive activity in question is the circulation of price information as a part of the association work. The prices referred to are sales prices of commodities dealt in by association members. The word 'exchanging' is interpreted to mean that members systematically furnish information with respect to prices for the use of other members." *Open-Price Trade Associations*, letter from the Chairman of the Federal Trade Commission, 70th Congress, second session, Senate Document 226, February 11, 1929, p. 36.

MAIN REASON FOR TRADE ASSOCIATION MOVEMENT

The ideas of Mr. Eddy went further than that of creating associations to provide for price publicity; and in the full utilization of his "plan," Mr. Eddy believed that businessmen should engage in "coöperation" rather than in competition. This proposal proved to be very attractive to many business-men, and trade associations have been formed in virtually every line of business activity—from local associations of retail merchants to national associations of manufacturers of the basic commodities.[2] Mr. Eddy's book *The New Competition*, moreover, continues to be widely read. Many businessmen and lawyers look upon it as being the best available exposition of the value of trade associations to "stabilize" business and to produce "fairer" price levels.

In each industry which has been studied by the British Monopolies Commission, it has been found that the principal instrument for restrictive practices was a trade association. Likewise, in the United States, studies of collusion, price leadership, basing-point systems, and the like, have revealed the important role played by trade associations in promoting unity of action. In their analysis of trade associations, Professors Stocking and Watkins conclude that "the trade association movement represents an organized effort to moderate the rigors of competition. It reflects a lack of confidence in genuinely free enterprise, a fear of the destructive consequences of uninhibited price warfare. . . . Trade associations promulgate a gospel of live and let live."[3]

OPEN-PRICE ASSOCIATIONS CONDEMNED

The legality of open-price associations was first considered by the Supreme Court in the *Hardwood Lumber Association* case (1921). There was general agreement on the facts in this case, the Court stated, and the legal issue was essentially whether or not the open-price plan is likely to result in an elimination of price competition. A majority of the Court found that the "close coöperation" provided for in the "plan" in filing actual prices and asking prices was plainly inconsistent with the Sherman Act. In the words of the Court:

> Genuine competitors do not make daily, weekly, and monthly reports of the minutest details of their business to their rivals, as the defendants did . . . and they do not submit the details of their business to the analysis of an expert, jointly employed, and obtain from him a "harmonized" estimate of the market as it is and as, in his specially and confidentially informed judgment, it promises to be. This is not the conduct of competitors but . . . clearly that of men united in an agreement, express or implied, to

[2] The U.S. Department of Commerce reported in 1954 that there were some 12,000 active trade associations in the United States. These associations consisted of some 1600 national trade associations; 2000 state-wide associations; 800 regional associations; and 7600 local associations, mostly in the retail and service fields.

[3] George W. Stocking and Myron W. Watkins, *Monopoly and Free Enterprise* (New York, 1951), p. 234.

act together and pursue a common purpose under a common guide. . . .
The "Plan" is, essentially, simply an expansion of the gentlemen's agreement of former days, skillfully devised to evade the law. . . . The fundamental purpose of the "Plan" was to procure "harmonious" individual action . . . concerted action . . . tacit understanding that all were to act
together. . . .[4]

The general condemnation of open-price plans was again confirmed by the
Supreme Court in the *Linseed Oil Association* case (1923).[5] The price plan
in this case provided for the filing of actual prices and quoted prices, and
members agreed not to deviate from the filed prices without prior notice.
The prices collected by the association, moreover, were not available to
purchasers or to the public. In a unanimous decision the Court found that the
manifest purpose of the plan was to defeat the Sherman Act.

THE FINAL ACCEPTANCE OF OPEN-PRICE ASSOCIATIONS
BY THE SUPREME COURT

Subsequently, in the *Maple Flooring* and *Cement Association* cases (1925),
a majority of the Court held that the open-price plan in principle is a desirable and beneficial form of trade activity.[6] How is this change in the attitude
of the Court to be explained? In retrospect, it appears that the vacillating
policy of the Court with respect to open-price associations may be explained
(1) by the belief of a minority of the Court, and then a majority, that price
reporting activities in principle have merit in providing market information,
(2) by the fact that in the *Maple Flooring* and *Cement* cases the government
failed to prove that the price-reporting programs had objectionable effects,
and (3) by the fact that in each of the four cases under consideration the
Court did not have all the relevant material presented to it.

Price publicity is an essential condition of market activity; and in the
absence of governmental intervention to perform this service, it is under-
standable that private groups will undertake to meet the need. The majority
of the Supreme Court in the *Maple Flooring* and *Cement* cases, probably
with this thought in mind, appears to have been willing to sanction open-
price associations in the absence of a showing of restrictive effects upon price
competition. Thus, Justice Stone in the *Maple Flooring* decision carefully
stated, "We decide only that trade associations . . . which openly and
fairly gather and disseminate information . . . as did these defendants . . .
without, however, reaching or attempting to reach any agreement or any
concerted action with respect to prices or production or restraining competition, do not thereby engage in unlawful restraint of commerce."[7]

---

[4] *American Column and Lbr. Co.* v. *U.S.*, 257 U.S. 377, 410–411 (1921).
[5] *U.S.* v. *American Linseed Oil Co.*, 262 U.S. 371 (1923).
[6] *Maple Flooring Manufacturers' Association* v. *U.S.*, 268 U.S. 563 (1925); and *Cement
Manufacturers' Protective Association* v. *U.S.*, 268 U.S. 606 (1925). See also C. D. Edwards, *Maintaining Competition* (New York, 1949), pp. 43–45.
[7] 268 U.S. 563, 586 (1925).

SOME CONCLUSIONS ON THE LEGALITY
OF OPEN-PRICE PLANS

What conclusions can be drawn with respect to the legitimate activity of open-price associations? First, it may be said that open-price plans are consistent with the Sherman Act as long as they are confined to the collection, compilation, and dissemination of *market information* on prices and production. Thus, in the *Sugar Institute* case (1936), the Court declared, "Further, the dissemination of information is normally an aid to commerce. As free competition means a free and open market among both buyers and sellers, competition does not become less free merely because of the distribution of knowledge of the essential factors entering into commercial transactions."[8] At no time, however, the law is careful to hold, may an association be used as a device for concerted price fixing or for other trade-restraining activity.

Secondly, the generally accepted legal opinion is that the prices reported must be made available to buyers and sellers alike. In the injunction issued by the Court in the *Sugar Institute* case, for example, it was provided that the members are restrained from collecting prices if said information is not "fully and fairly" made available to the buyers and distributors of sugar. While this rule is good law, there is little evidence to indicate that many trade associations comply with it. Buyers, moreover, frequently report that they can never be certain that the price and statistical data furnished by a trade association are correct, for important members in the association may have an interest in modifying the data which are publicly reported in order to influence the attitude of buyers toward market trends.

Thirdly, there is general agreement that in so far as a trade association collects *impersonal* statistics with respect to actual prices on closed transactions, production, inventories, and sales, the service is a desirable one which is promotive of competition. It is this kind of "market information" which is made available by the security and commodity exchanges. The problem which arises in the collection of "market information" by trade groups is the desire of many business firms to collect *intimate* information on the transactions of industry members, such as list or asking prices, invoice terms, and the names of sellers and buyers.

Experience has shown that in so far as trade members report and collect *personal* data, such as *list* or *asking* prices, *off-list* prices, and the sales or purchases of *particular* companies, the practice is likely to result in coercion and trade restraints. Dominant trade members are in a position to exert pressure on weaker sellers to bring list prices *up* to a common level. Large sellers, in securing information on the sales or purchases of particular companies, moreover, are able to watch their percentage of the business in a plan of "sharing the market."

An important decision which veers toward permitting a trade group to collect and disseminate intimate market information is the *Tag Institute* case

---

[8] *Sugar Institute* v. *U.S.*, 297 U.S. 553, 598 (1936).

(1949). (See Landmark Cases, p. 692.) The decision is significant (1) because it shows the kind of activities which many trade associations are now performing and (2) because it reflects the current policy of the courts to look for substantial evils before condemning business practices.

The Tag Institute, a trade association for the tag industry, was organized in 1933 to collect and disseminate prices received by industry members on sales of tags, pin tickets, and related devices used in marking, shipping, and pricing merchandise. Each member was required to report prices, terms, and conditions of each sale or contract. Each member was also required to file list prices and to report all changes in list prices. Duplicate copies of every invoice had to be sent to the association. Members failing to report promptly and fully were fined "liquidated damages" up to 10 percent of the value of the transactions in question.

The Tag Institute disseminated to its membership the price lists of each participant. It also sent all members special daily "pink sheets" on all "off-list" transactions, giving the name of the seller, description of product, quantity, list price, actual off-list price, and the state in which the buyer resided. Any interested person was able to secure the releases upon payment of a reasonable fee.

In 1941 the Federal Trade Commission issued a complaint against the Institute and its members, charging conspiracy to restrain price competition. The Commission maintained that the "open-price plan" had resulted in the suppression of price competition and the establishment of a substantial identity of prices for tags and tag products. A cease-and-desist order was issued in 1947. Upon appeal by the Institute, the Court of Appeals in 1949 ruled against the Commission on the ground that the open-price filing had not, in fact, been used to restrain competition. In the view of the court, "Nor is there evidence of 'retaliatory action' by any subscribers to coerce other subscribers into adherence to list prices. They all engaged in off-list pricing to such an extent that it would be wholly irrational to infer that the essence of their agreement was that they would all adhere to their current price lists. . . ."[9]

THE PROVISION OF PRICE PUBLICITY AS A PUBLIC FUNCTION

The principle that trade members in open competition need and should have price publicity is sound, for they cannot compete effectively without a knowledge of *past* prices and statistics on demand and supply. Buyers want to know whether or not they are paying a price which is currently in line, and sellers wonder if they are being deceived by unverified reports of price reductions. Price publicity, experience has shown, is essential to effective competition in open markets.

In order to supply buyers and sellers of the principal agricultural products with reliable price information, the U.S. Department of Agriculture main-

---

[9] *Tag Mfrs. Institute* v. *F.T.C.*, 174 F. 2d 452, 459 (1949).

tains an extensive price-reporting service. The daily reports issued by the government on shipments, supplies, and prices on actual transactions, moreover, have proved to be very useful to farmers and trade members alike.

By way of contrast, the record of trade associations in providing price publicity is not a good one. In many cases, price data are issued only to members; and when they are made available to buyers, there is always a question about their reliability, for it is the *sellers* who are doing the reporting. In industries with few sellers (oligopoly), moreover, price publicity is likely to promote unified selling. When sellers are few, they tend to act rationally in avoiding competition, and the provision of intimate details on prices, costs, and sales greatly facilitates concerted action.

In order (1) to provide reliable market information to all interested parties and (2) to discourage and minimize the use of trade data for price-fixing purposes, it has frequently been suggested that the reporting of industrial prices and trade statistics should be handled either by some quasi-public organization, such as a commodity exchange, or by the government itself. The Federal Trade Commission Act empowers the Commission "to gather and compile information concerning . . . the . . . business, conduct, practices, and management of any corporation engaged in commerce" (Section 6), and it is possible that the Commission might legally undertake the collection and dissemination of basic market information. If government is to fulfill its function of creating and preserving effective competition, it should adopt positive measures in this area of public regulation.

THE DIVERGENCE BETWEEN THE ECONOMIC AND LEGAL CONCEPTS OF MONOPOLY

In developing and applying the law against monopoly, we have seen, the Supreme Court has directed its attention largely (1) to a condemnation of the ungentlemanly conduct and unworthy motives of mergers, and (2) to a prohibition of direct agreements among competitors fixing prices, restricting production, and dividing sales areas. The abuse theory of monopoly as applied to mergers, it is generally recognized, has had two important shortcomings. In the first place, in handling important cases—like the *Standard Oil* and *American Tobacco* cases—the Court has not been willing to provide a clear legal judgment on *business practices which are unfair*, without reference to the "motives" which govern their use. This view of the Court overlooks the fact that the purpose of business is profit making; and the motive which governs the use of *all* business practices is commercial advantage. The *means* employed to win business may be "unworthy," but the motive is not. In regulating business, government and the courts should single out business practices which are not favorable to the public interest and declare them to be illegal, *per se*.

In the second place, in its consideration of mergers—notably in the *Steel* and *International Harvester* cases—the Court has not seen any restriction whatever to legitimate price competition in the combination of scores of former independents into a single price-controlling unit. As long as a merger does not acquire an overwhelming percentage of the separate plants in the nation, and does not engage in predatory practices, it has been permitted to manage the price policies of its constituent parts with impunity.

The Supreme Court has clearly recognized the existence of monopoly in the collective action (conspiracy) of numerous independent firms on price. In the *National Cotton Oil* case, for example, the Court defined monopoly as "unified tactics with regard to prices."[10] When the same result is secured by the *acquisition* of scores of competitors, however, the Court has failed to see the presence of monopoly. This legal "blind spot" has possibly been due in part to the judicial practice of thinking of monopoly in an absolute sense—as applying to an entire nation. The legal view that a control of 50 or 64 percent of the *national* production of a particular product does not give a seller monopoly power fails to consider the economic fact that in the sale of most industrial commodities—such as steel, cement, petroleum, foundry products, and heavy machinery—there is always an area of practical shipment based upon a firm's mill price and the actual delivery charges. A merger in a contiguous area—such as one or several adjoining states—controlling only 5 percent of the sales in a given industry *in the nation* may, in fact, control up to 100 percent of the production in its own area of practical shipment. Private monopoly is always a limited and relative power, and the control over supply which enables a monopoly group to raise prices above the competitive norm is usually limited as to place.

The favorable attitude taken by the Supreme Court with respect to mergers—in contrast with its policy towards price-fixing conspiracies—it is generally agreed, has served to place a premium on the formation of mergers. The anomalous fact is that an agreement between two competitors to fix prices in a given sales area is illegal, *per se;* whereas, a *merger* of these same two concerns, in the eyes of the Court, is legal!

As a result of the failure of the courts to identify the monopoly power which grows out of a merger of competitors *in the economic areas of practical shipment,* monopoly and economic concentration in the United States have grown without abatement. It is a growth of monopoly, moreover, which promises to be highly enduring and abiding, for unified ownership gives a complete and absolute power of control over formerly independent plants. Monopoly by agreement is temporary and transitory, and the use of fines and imprisonment provides an effective means of control. In making mergers a legally permissible method of price control, however, the courts in effect have granted an immunity to an important area of private monopoly.

PROGRESS TOWARD AN ADOPTION OF THE ECONOMIC CONCEPTION OF MONOPOLY

In an economic sense monopoly exists whenever a firm, or group of firms acting in concert, in a particular sales area has such a degree of control over the output of a commodity for which there is no close substitute that it—

[10] *National Cotton Oil Co. v. Texas,* 197 U.S. 115, 129 (1905).

or they—can make the going price, or prices, which as an actual fact will be largely observed in the sales area. The presence or absence of monopoly in this sense does not turn upon the exercise of predatory practices against competitors. Such practices may or may not exist. Although monopoly may be secured by concerted action—conspiracy—among numerous sellers, it may also be secured by a merger of competitors in a given sales area. Further, it is also possible for monopoly to arise, especially when the number of sellers is few, by sellers acting jointly in pursuing a common price plan, without formal agreement.

In the antitrust cases decided by the federal courts up until 1945, the concept of monopoly which was developed and utilized in the law was largely based upon whether or not a large company used its power to exclude or injure competitors. The decisions rendered in the *Alcoa* (1945) and new *Tobacco* cases (1946), however, broke sharply with the past, and for the first time a significant step was taken toward the adoption of the economic conception of monopoly.

THE ALCOA CASE AND THE VIEW THAT PRICE FIXING IS ILLEGAL WHETHER ACCOMPLISHED BY COLLUSION OR BY SIZE

The suit against the Aluminum Company of America was a civil suit in which the government charged violation of Section 2 of the Sherman Act. The District Court dismissed the complaint, and upon direct appeal the Supreme Court was unable to secure a quorum of justices who would qualify themselves to hear the case. Thereupon, the case was referred to the Court of Appeals, which became the court of last resort. The decision in the *Alcoa* case was handed down on March 12, 1945, by Judge Learned Hand.

At the time of the suit, Alcoa controlled over 90 percent of the primary ingot production of aluminum and made a large volume of fabricated products. The Department of Justice charged the company with having a monopolistic control of the aluminum industry and with the maintenance of this control by illegal practices. It also asked for the dissolution of Alcoa and for the creation of effective competition in the production and sale of aluminum. The District Court stated that there had been some abuse of power in the past but found that presently there was none. In view of this finding, and upon the basis of the *Steel* and *International Harvester* cases, the District Court decided against the government. In the Court of Appeals, however, Judge Hand looked to the economics of the problem and held that Alcoa, in fact, possessed a monopoly of the aluminum industry in the United States in violation of Section 2 of the Sherman Act, despite the fact that it was not currently guilty of predatory practices.

Judge Hand sharply criticized the view that, although price-fixing agreements are considered to be illegal *per se*, monopolistic control over supply is not. The doctrine that "the existence of unexerted power" is no offense was also found to be unacceptable on the ground that the possession of monopoly power—the power to manage prices—necessarily means that it will be exercised in the making of prices.[11] (See Landmark Cases, p. 695.)

There is general agreement among legal commentators that the *Alcoa* case marks a clear-cut shift in the view that abuses alone are bad to the view that monopoly itself is illegal *per se*. Judge Hand, in fact, quite intentionally sought to change the divergent policy which the courts had been following in their condemnation of collusive price fixing and their acceptance of monopolistic mergers. In the eyes of the Court of Appeals price fixing is illegal whether it is effected by collusion among competitors (multiple-seller monopoly) or by the acquisition of a control over supply (single-seller monopoly).

The Court of Appeals did not specify a remedy for the monopoly which it found in the aluminum industry, for the federal government was then in process of disposing of its war-built aluminum plants. With the transfer of government-owned plants to Reynolds Metals and Kaiser Aluminum, it was estimated that Alcoa controlled 45 to 50 percent of the domestic production, Reynolds Metals about 30 to 35 percent, and Kaiser Aluminum about 20 percent.

Following the creation of the two new integrated producers, Alcoa asked the Court (1947) for a declaration that it was no longer a monopoly. Thereupon, the Antitrust Division petitioned for a divestiture of various plants and properties of Alcoa, to create a fourth domestic producer, on the ground that competitive conditions in aluminum had not been effectively created. On June 2, 1950, Judge Knox denied the government's request, but ordered persons holding stock in Alcoa and Aluminum, Ltd. (Alcoa's Canadian subsidiary) to sell their holdings in either of the two concerns. In the view of the Court, competition in the industry could be enhanced by creating an independent Canadian producer. The Court also retained jurisdiction of the case for five additional years (to 1955), during which time either the government or Alcoa may petition for a modification of the judicial action. (See Landmark Cases, p. 699.)

THE TOBACCO CASE AND THE RULE THAT THE POWER TO MANAGE PRICE IS THE TEST OF MONOPOLY

In the *Tobacco* case, decided in 1946, the federal courts took a further step toward adoption of the economic concept of monopoly. The Department of Justice filed the *Tobacco* case in 1940, charging that the "Big Three"—the American Tobacco Company, Liggett and Myers Tobacco Company, and R. J. Reynolds Tobacco Company—dominated and controlled the purchase of leaf tobacco and the sale of cigarettes in violation of Sections 1 and 2 of the Sherman Act. At the time the suit was brought the three defendants controlled some 68 percent of the cigarette business and more than 80 percent of the business in their price line. The *Tobacco* case was a criminal action, and the government sought only to punish the defendants for their past illegal conduct. No affirmative relief was asked.

[11] *U.S. v. Aluminum Co. of America*, 148 F. (2d) 416, 427–428 (1945).

In the District Court the jury found that the defendants had conspired to restrain commerce in the buying and selling of tobacco in violation of Section 1 of the Sherman Act. Upon the basis of the Court's instruction that monopoly does not require the actual exclusion of competitors from a trade, but only the "power to control and dominate interstate trade," the jury also found that the defendants were guilty of violating Section 2 of the Sherman Act. The Court of Appeals upheld the convictions. Upon appeal the Supreme Court limited its consideration of the case to the issue of whether actual exclusion of competitors is necessary to the crime of monopoly under Section 2 of the Sherman Act. The Supreme Court affirmed the position taken by the District Court, and fines totaling $255,000 were levied against the defendants. The *Tobacco* case, it may be noted, involved a "loose-knit" combination and not a merger.

In appealing their case to the Supreme Court, the tobacco companies sought to defend their behavior by declaring (1) that they had not excluded competitors, as was declared to be illegal in the old *American Tobacco* and *Standard Oil* cases (1911); (2) that they could not be guilty of the crime of monopoly, because there were three separate companies actively competing for business; and (3) that there was no direct evidence of an agreement among the three companies on price. They also urged that the present case was controlled by the *Steel* and *International Harvester* decisions, in which the Supreme Court held that the mere possession of the power to exclude—"the existence of unexerted power"—is not an offense under the monopoly section of the Sherman Act.

The facts in the *Tobacco* case, as reported in the decision of the Supreme Court, indicated that the "Big Three" had maintained a "friendly relationship" and "a community of interest" which enabled them to follow a common course of action on prices, even though there was no actual agreement. In the purchase of leaf tobacco, it was found that the defendants eliminated competition by buying predetermined percentages of the supplies offered and by scrupulously following a plan of paying the same prices for the same grades of tobacco. Likewise, in the sale of cigarettes the evidence indicated that the three defendants had consistently sold at identical prices and discounts since 1927. The Supreme Court also found that the "Big Three" tobacco companies had raised their prices in 1931—one of the worst years of the depression—in an effort to make more profit and that, although sales fell off greatly during 1932, profits rose and the companies enjoyed one of the three most profitable years in their history.

The Court commented especially on the large advertising expenditures of the three defendants—over $40,000,000 a year—and the close relationship which existed between these expenditures and the volume of sales. The Court observed that the use of large-scale advertising serves as an effective device for stifling competition. "Such tremendous advertising," the Court declared, "is . . . a widely published warning that these companies possess and know how to use a powerful offensive and defensive weapon against new competition. New competition dare not enter such a field, unless it be well supported by comparable national advertising. . . . Prevention of all potential competition is the natural program for maintaining a monopoly here, rather than any program of actual exclusion."[12]

Upon the basis of the concerted action of the defendant tobacco companies in managing prices and in maintaining a power of control over the activity of independents, the Court found that the "Big Three" were guilty of the crime of monopoly. A correct interpretation of Section 2 of the Sherman Act, the Court declared, makes the existence of *the power to exclude competitors*, as well as actual exclusion, an illegal act. The Court ignored the *United States Steel* case and indicated clearly that *the power to manage price or exclude competitors* is the controlling test of monopoly. In the words of the Court,

> The question squarely presented here . . . is whether actual exclusion of competitors is necessary to the crime of monopolization in these cases under Section 2 of the Sherman Act. We agree with the lower courts that such actual exclusion of competitors is not necessary to that crime in these cases. . . . Neither proof of exertion of the power to exclude nor proof of actual exclusion of existing or potential competitors is essential to sustain a charge of monopolization under the Sherman Act. . . . *The authorities support the view that the material consideration in determining whether a monopoly exists is not that prices are raised and that competition actually is excluded but that power exists to raise prices or to exclude competition when it is desired to do so.*[13]

There was no direct evidence of formal agreement in the *Tobacco* case. The jury, however, made a finding of conspiracy upon the basis of circumstantial evidence, and the Court accepted this conclusion. In the view of the Court, direct evidence of a formal agreement among two or more firms is not necessary in proving a conspiracy to monopolize. The illegal act, it was said, may be inferred or deduced from the various activities of the parties themselves. "The essential combination or conspiracy in violation of the Sherman Act," the Court declared, "may be found in a course of dealings or other circumstances as well as in an exchange of words. . . . Where the circumstances are such as to warrant a jury in finding that the conspirators had a unity of purpose or a common design and understanding, or a meeting of minds in an unlawful arrangement, the conclusion that a conspiracy is established is justified."[14]

THE COURT AT THE CROSSROADS
ON THE ISSUE OF MERGERS

The rapid progress made by the Supreme Court in adopting an economic conception of monopoly was temporarily halted in the *Columbia Steel* case,

[12] *American Tobacco Co.* v. *U.S.*, 328 U.S. 781, 797 (1946).
[13] *Ibid.*, pp. 781, 808–811. Italics supplied.
[14] *Ibid.*, pp. 809–810.

decided in 1948.[15] In a five-to-four decision a bare majority of the Court took a step backward toward the judicial thinking expressed in the *Steel* and *International Harvester* cases. Once again the Court indicated that it still adheres to the "rule of reason" on mergers.

In the *Columbia Steel* case, the government sought to enjoin the U.S. Steel Corporation and its subsidiaries from acquiring the assets of the Consolidated Steel Corporation, the largest independent steel fabricator on the west coast, with plants in California, Texas, and Arizona, on the ground that such an acquisition would violate Sections 1 and 2 of the Sherman Act. The government charged in particular that the acquisition of this important fabricator by the U.S. Steel Corporation would exclude other suppliers from placing orders with Consolidated Steel, since this fabricator would subsequently be supplied by the Geneva, Utah, plant of U.S. Steel, and also that the acquisition would eliminate competition between Consolidated Steel and the subsidiaries of U.S. Steel in the manufacture and sale of structural steel, pipe, and other fabricated steel products.

In a decision sharply criticized by four dissenting justices, the majority of the Supreme Court gave approval to the acquisition planned by the U.S. Steel Corporation on the ground that the restraint on competition resulting from such a merger would not be "unreasonable." Justice Reed, speaking for the majority, stated that the test of legality for vertical and horizontal mergers is the same—namely, whether or not they involve "unreasonable restraint." Although recognizing that a restriction on competition was involved in the instant case, the majority held that in its judgment the restraint was not an unreasonable one. How much of a restraint there must be to constitute illegality, the Court did not say. "We do not undertake to prescribe," the majority declared, "any set of percentage figures by which to measure the reasonableness of a corporation's enlargement of its activities by the purchase of the assets of a competitor." (See Landmark Cases, p. 685.)

REFUSAL TO SELL AND RESALE PRICE CONTROL

It is common practice for manufacturers to suggest resale prices and to refuse to sell to any distributor who does not comply. The right of a manufacturer to refuse to sell to dealers acting independently on price was given limited approval in the *Colgate* case (1919). In this case, the Court stated, "In the absence of any purpose to create or maintain a monopoly, the [Sherman] Act does not restrict the long-recognized right of trader or manufacturer engaged in an entirely private business, freely to exercise his own independent discretion as to parties with whom he will deal. And, of course, he may announce in advance the circumstances under which he will refuse to sell."[16]

One year after the *Colgate* decision the Court took steps to restrict the implications of its language on refusal to sell. In the *Schrader* case (1920),

---

[15] *U.S. v. Columbia Steel Co.*, 334 U.S. 495 (1948).

[16] *U.S. v. Colgate and Company*, 250 U.S. 300, 307 (1919).

the Court emphasized "the obvious difference between the situation presented when a manufacturer merely indicates his wishes concerning prices
and declines further dealings with all who fail to observe them, *and one
where he enters into agreements*—whether express or implied from a course
of dealing or other circumstances—with all customers throughout the different states which undertake to bind them to observe fixed resale prices. In
the first, the manufacturer but exercises his independent discretion concerning his customers and there is no contract or combination which imposes any
limitation on the purchaser."[17]

If a manufacturer suggests resale prices and refuses to deal with distributors
who do not comply, is he not actually getting an *implied* agreement from
those who buy and do business under such conditions? In buying, is not a
a person agreeing to the punitive conditions? Does not the plan involve entering into an agreement, express or implied, to maintain resale prices? In the
Bausch and Lomb case (1942), Judge Rifkind, in the District Court, held that
action by the Soft-Lite Lens Company announcing resale prices and refusing
to deal with those who do not comply, in fact, involved agreement between
the company and the wholesalers and retailers acquiring the products. Said
Judge Rifkind, "The agreement is implicit in the operation of the system.
The living reality of uniform prices . . . compels the conclusion that between the wholesalers and the distributor there was agreement or at least
acquiescence in a program of concerted action."[18]

Upon appeal, the Supreme Court sustained the District Court in its finding of agreement in a plan of price maintenance enforced by refusal to sell.
"The wholesalers," said the Supreme Court, "accepted Soft-Lite's proffer of
a plan of distribution by coöperating in prices, limitation of sales to and approval of retail licensees. . . . Whether this conspiracy and combination was
achieved by agreement or by acquiescence of the wholesalers coupled with
assistance in effectuating its purpose is immaterial."[19] Thus it is that refusal to
sell when used with a plan to maintain resale prices may carry with it the
inference of illegal agreement. The task of the court is to infer or not to
infer an agreement from the facts.

Upon being cut off from essential supplies, an injured person may attack
refusal to sell (1) on grounds that the supplier has a monopolistic position
and that alternative sources of supply do not exist; (2) that all suppliers are
joining in the refusal to sell (horizontal conspiracy); and (3) that the supplier is illegally maintaining a plan of resale prices with other customers
(vertical conspiracy). What relief can an injured party secure? At most, it
is treble damages. The desire of a plaintiff, however, is usually to get goods
and stay in business. As a matter of expediency, therefore, fabricators, wholesalers, and retailers generally see the light and comply with the punitive

[17] *U.S.* v. *A. Schrader's Son,* 252 U.S. 85, 99 (1920). Italics supplied.
[18] *U.S.* v. *Bausch and Lomb Optical Co.,* 45 F. Supp. 387, 396 (1942).
[19] *U.S.* v. *Bausch and Lomb Optical Co.,* 321 U.S. 707, 723 (1944).

terms exacted. There is no other way to get the goods desired. Real relief, it appears, must await the repeal and complete reversal by Congress of the policy embodied in Section 2 of the Clayton Act which authorizes "persons" to select their own customers in interstate commerce. (See also Chap. 18, and Landmark Cases, p. 703.)

THE SHERMAN ACT AND OLIGOPOLY

The application of the Sherman Act to several large companies which dominate an industry and act as one on price is the weakest aspect of our antitrust law program. Three forms of this type of unified selling may be distinguished. First, there is the situation in which *conspiracy* can be proved by direct or circumstantial evidence. Such a form of concerted action is clearly illegal under the Sherman Act (and also under Section 5 of the Federal Trade Commission Act). The *Tobacco* decision (1946) is a case in point.

Secondly, there is the situation in which one company is the recognized and accepted price leader, and the other companies regularly adopt and observe the prices set by the leader. In order to discipline recalcitrant followers, a price leader often resorts to sporadic price cutting, geographic discrimination, and threats of reprisal. If it can be shown that monopolistic devices have been used to effectuate price leadership, the leader can be readily prosecuted for monopoly. In the absence of abuses, however, the government has the task of proving "conscious parallel action."

Thirdly, there is the category in which several companies, of similar size and power, act as one on price, *allegedly without agreement*, because of like-mindedness, a doctrine of "live and let live," business ethics which make price cutting taboo, or a realistic fear of chaotic price cutting. Competitive rivalries may exist in advertising, quality, and service, *but not on price*. Delivered prices are usually quoted according to some formula, and the delivered prices at any destination point are usually identical.

The belief of many economists and legal experts is that the Sherman Act (as well as the Federal Trade Commission Act) *can* and *should* be applied to unified selling by a few dominant concerns who allegedly are acting "innocently and independently." The situation of oligopoly *can* be attacked (a) on the principle of conscious parallel action (implied conspiracy) or (b) under Section 2 of the Sherman Act as a condition of monopoly.

Thus far, the antitrust agencies have established no landmark cases to remedy the problem of a concentration of power in the hands of several large companies. This problem is the crucial one in the entire antitrust program, and the Antitrust Division is fully aware of its importance. The principal problems deterring vigorous action are (1) inadequate funds for initiating and prosecuting cases and (2) the difficulties involved in preparing effective forms of relief. The problem of oligopoly is far greater than that of proving guilt. Before a case is filed and prosecuted, it is most important that the government have a clear idea of the relief which *can* and *should* be secured. How should the "Big Threes" and the "Big Fours" be reorganized? Can the courts alone provide adequate relief? Should there be a reëxamination of the tariff protection granted to the industry? Should closely held primary raw materials, such as iron ore, bauxite, and molybdenum, be publicly owned? This is an area of economic analysis and study which now calls for vastly increased consideration and attention.

DISSOLUTION PROCEEDINGS UNDER THE SHERMAN ACT

The Sherman Act, we have noted, provides for criminal *and* civil remedies. Violations of Sections 1, 2 and 3 are defined as criminal acts punishable by fine or imprisonment. Increasingly, however, it is coming to be seen that punishment itself is not an adequate remedy for preserving competition, especially in the case of large business combinations. The only practical remedy, many believe, is the use of dissolution, divestiture, and divorcement proceedings under Section 4 of the Sherman Act.

The inadequacy of criminal proceedings may be illustrated by the *Tobacco* case decided in 1946. The Supreme Court upheld the conviction of the three leading tobacco companies and found that they were guilty of monopoly in controlling the buying prices for leaf tobacco and the selling prices for cigarettes. The defendants were fined but nothing was done to create the essential conditions which give rise to effective price competition. In 1948 the House Small Business Committee reported that the "Big Three" were continuing to maintain identical prices and that there was a complete lack of price competition among the companies. The Committee also stated that independent tobacco manufacturers testified that the "Big Three" were using the large profits on their tremendous cigarette business to subsidize and promote the sale of their brands of smoking and chewing tobacco, so that independent producers were rapidly being eliminated. In the opinion of the House Small Business Committee, the government's antitrust victory in 1946 was singularly ineffective.[20]

The main purpose of dissolution proceedings under Section 4 is to break up monopolistic conditions which cannot be terminated by a mere correction of current abuses. In taking this action against large monopolistic enterprises, government seeks to create effective competition by providing an increased number of independent competitors. How many independent firms are necessary to insure effective competition? To this question Professors Stocking and Watkins answer, "Just how many producers are necessary . . . no one can say precisely. But if society relies on effective competition to protect—and promote—its interests, policy should aim at as many firms as is consistent with the economies of scale."[21]

[20] Select Committee on Small Business, *Monopolistic and Unfair Trade Practices*, 80th Congress, second session, House Report 2465, December, 1948, p. 11.

[21] George W. Stocking and Myron W. Watkins, *Monopoly and Free Enterprise* (New York, 1951), p. 112.

DISSOLUTION, DIVESTITURE, AND DIVORCEMENT

The remedies of dissolution, divestiture, and divorcement are popularly called "DDD" actions. An equity suit requesting dissolution means that the government seeks to dissolve—to put out of business—an illegal combination or trade association. The term "divestiture," on the other hand, means that a defendant is required to divest—or dispossess—itself of particular plants, securities, or other assets. Divestiture is used by the government in order to set up competing firms, and ordinarily the dominant company itself is not dissolved. The term "divorcement" is used primarily to indicate the *effect* or *result* of divestiture wherein certain companies have been "chopped off" from the control of a dominant merger. In many cases, the foregoing terms are used interchangeably without regard to their technical meanings.

All the available evidence indicates that the possibility of securing effective competition is greatly enhanced by the presence of numerous independent producers. With numerous independent sellers, there is a greater diversity of interests and a wider range of judgments. A reduction in financial size, moreover, greatly reduces the power of a concern to engage in discriminatory and cutthroat pricing.

Centralized markets in the American economy declined and disappeared with the rise of mergers. In exploiting their monopoly power, dominant concerns adopted policies, such as sales to consumers alone, sales at delivered prices only, and output curtailment, which have had the effect of restricting or completely preventing market activity. The experience of the antitrust agencies has been that orders against particular abuses cannot be made effective as long as a preponderant power over supplies and prices exists, for dominant sellers are usually able to devise new patterns of control when current ones are forbidden. The only effective way to curb abuses in many sectors of the economy without resorting to direct control or ownership, it is reasoned, is to change the structure and basic policy of the dominant concerns.

THE RELUCTANCE OF THE COURTS TO INTERFERE WITH PROPERTY RIGHTS

From 1890 to 1955, nearly 100 judgments have been entered containing provisions for dissolution, divestiture, and divorcement. The business groups affected have ranged from a retail grocery association in Nome, Alaska (1906), to the Standard Oil Company and the American Tobacco Company (1911), to the "Big Five" motion picture producers (1952). Most of the judgments relate to the dissolution of trade associations or provide for *partial* divestiture by dominant companies. In the *National Lead* case (332 U.S. 319 [1945]), for example, the Supreme Court required the company to divest itself of stockholdings in various foreign concerns but refused to order divestiture of interests held in rival domestic companies, even though

National Lead and Du Pont control about 90 percent of the domestic production of titanium compounds.

In surveying the action taken by the courts in dissolution, divestiture, and
divorcement decrees, one is led to conclude that the courts have been quite
reluctant to use their authority to create the essential conditions for competition. At all times they have had the power and authority to create such
conditions, and the decrees in principle have provided for that end. The
decree in the first *International Harvester* case (1914), for example, provided for the division of the combination "in such manner and into such
number of parts . . . as may be necessary to restore competitive conditions
and bring about a situation in harmony with law." In working out plans
under the decrees, however, the courts have largely proceeded upon the
mistaken view that monopoly means single-firm, nation-wide control, and
that as long as there are several firms in a national industry effective price
competition will prevail. This view overlooks the fact that private monopoly
is a relative and limited power—relative to a particular sales territory and
limited by distance, as well as by the availability of substitute products. It
also fails to recognize that concerted action on price—with actual or tacit
collusion—is quite likely to result when the number of sellers is few (as in
the *Tobacco* case, 1946).

In framing the decree in the first *International Harvester* case, the Court
allowed the International Harvester Company to remain intact but required
it to sell three of its five "lines" of harvesting machines to an independent
manufacturer. The company, however, continued to control some two-
thirds of the national output of harvesters; and five years later, when the
Department of Justice asked for further relief, the Supreme Court refused
the request on the ground that "competitive conditions in the trade" had
been established.[22] The fact was, however, that the farm machinery industry
was then, and had long been, characterized by price leadership, concentration of output, and rigid prices. These price and output conditions have been
continued to date, and it is generally recognized that they reflect a considerable degree of private monopoly power.

Similarly, in the *American Tobacco* case (1911), the Court indicated that
it was unwilling to create any considerable number of competitors. It is
reported that before the formation of the American Tobacco combination
there were some 276 cigarette manufacturers in the United States.[23] Subsequently, the American Tobacco Company acquired a control of more
than 95 percent of the cigarette production. In formulating the dissolution
decree for the American Tobacco Company, the Court was urged to divide
the combination into *sixty* different companies. The Court declined to do so,
however, and created instead *three* "full line" companies. These companies
were given a large part of the production facilities for making smoking and

[22] *U.S.* v. *International Harvester Co.*, 274 U.S. 693, 704 (1927). See also George E.
Hale, "Trust Dissolution," *Columbia Law Review*, April, 1940, pp. 621–622.
[23] Select Committee on Small Business, *op. cit.*, p. 10.

chewing tobacco and all of the facilities for making cigarettes owned by the combination.[24]

A significant victory was won by the Antitrust Division against the "Big Five" motion picture producers. In a series of cases extending over a period of fourteen years (1938–1952) the government secured consent decrees forcing the major producers to sell their affiliated exhibition outlets. The decrees also provided for a considerable measure of dissolution in the established exhibition companies. Under the five decrees, the court ordered that more than 1200 theaters be sold to independent exhibitors and that some 1300 theaters be operated by newly formed theater companies. The results secured in the motion picture cases, however, are not typical of other dissolution decrees. The motion picture dissolutions were secured *in consent decrees*, in which the defendants consented to accept a court order.

When a defendant vigorously resists remedial action, the records show that the courts proceed with much consideration for private property. In a concurring opinion in the *Timken Roller Bearing* case (1951), Justices Reed and Vinson, for example, declared that dissolution "is not to be used indiscriminately, without regard to the type of violation or whether other effective methods, less harsh, are available."[25] In the *National Lead* case (1947) the Supreme Court refused to create two additional titanium pigment plants from the facilities of National Lead and Du Pont. In the view of the Court, "There is no showing that four major competing units would be preferable to two, or . . . that six would be better than four."[26] Likewise, in the *Alcoa* decision (1950), the court refused to create a new producer from the Alcoa empire on the ground that there was competition in the presence of the Reynolds and Kaiser companies. As long as there is more than one seller, the courts appear to believe that there is the "competition" called for by the antitrust laws.

How can one explain the reluctance of the courts to dissolve monopolistic mergers? Is it because economic or technological factors have made it clear to the justices that any substantial degree of decentralization would be undesirable? A careful reading of the dissolution judgments does not indicate that this has been the case. The factors controlling the actions of the courts appear rather to have been (1) the use of inadequate and incomplete concepts of monopoly and competition and (2) an unwillingness to disturb property relationships, except in cases characterized by flagrant abuses. "Constitutional law," Professor E. S. Corwin declares, "has always a central interest to guard."[27] In the past this "central interest" has been business property and, in particular, business corporations. Whether or not the personnel of the federal courts, and especially the Supreme Court, will become increasingly

[24] Albert C. Muhse, "Disintegration of the Tobacco Combination," *Political Science Quarterly*, June, 1913, pp. 249–278.
[25] *Timken Roller Bearing Co.* v. *United States*, 341 U.S. 593, 603 (1951).
[26] *United States* v. *National Lead Co.*, 332 U.S. 319, 352 (1947).
[27] E. S. Corwin, *The Constitution and What It Means Today* (Princeton, 1947), p. viii.

pro-competition and pro-consumer rather than pro-monopoly and pro-corporation only the future will tell.

SOME CONCLUSIONS ON DISSOLUTION PROCEDURES

If the economic problem of monopoly is to be solved within the framework of the Sherman Act, it is certain that increasing attention will need to be given to the problem of the large business combinations which now characterize American industry. No critic of mergers proposes to limit the physical size of any plant or to deny a company the right to own more than one plant. The basic question is whether or not acquisitions—past or prospective—restrain price competition. Price-fixing agreements among competing plants are illegal *per se*, and many economists and lawyers believe that the same rule should be applied to all mergers which may possibly affect price competition. The application of such a rule will not eradicate all monopoly from the fields of general business, but it will mean the taking of a long step in that direction.

Mr. George E. Hale, in a special study of dissolution decrees, concludes that our experience with the mechanics of separating monopolistic combinations proves that dissolution proceedings have not presented insuperable problems.[28] It is frequently said that "you cannot unscramble an egg." This is true for scrambled eggs, but it is not true for business mergers. If we have the will to dissolve monopolistic mergers, our experience shows that we can find a way to do it.

The effectiveness of dissolution proceedings in the past has been greatly impaired by the willingness of the courts to place the stock of the newly created entities in the hands of the same body of stockholders which controlled the combination. As an alternative procedure, Mr. Hale proposes that the courts "give all the shareholders of the combination proportionate share interests in all the successor units but require them, within a reasonable time, to elect in which one company they will retain shares, the others to be sold." This plan, it is believed, would promote a much larger degree of decentralization in the ownership of corporation securities in particular industries.

Mr. Hale also suggests that in handling new dissolution cases the government should deal with an entire industry at one time. A suit to dissolve the U.S. Steel Corporation, for example, would be unfair and unwise unless it were made to include all monopolistic mergers in the steel industry. In view of the duration and complexity of dissolution proceedings, Mr. Hale further suggests that the working out of plans for dissolution should be handled by an administrative body. The decrees of the district courts, subject to appeal to the higher federal courts, ultimately determine the effectiveness of the Sherman Act. It is, therefore, highly important that the district judges be given expert economic assistance in formulating dissolution, divest-

[28] George E. Hale, "Trust Dissolution," *Columbia Law Review*, April, 1940, p. 631.

iture, and divorcement decrees, as well as injunctions requiring the observance of certain business practices.

Section 7 of the Federal Trade Commission Act (1914) provides that in civil suits the court may refer the case to the Commission, as a master in chancery, to ascertain and report on an appropriate form of decree. Thus far the courts, in general, have not made use of this service. It is possible that legislation should be adopted to require them to utilize the services of the Commission in formulating antitrust decrees. The courts, however, at all times should be permitted to have the final determination of the case, in order to preserve the matter as a case or controversy in the courts of the United States.

SUMMARY ON THE INTERPRETATION
OF THE SHERMAN ACT

With the development of business restraints in the United States, the American courts began to apply the common-law doctrine of restraint of trade. All general restraints were held to be void, and partial restraints were held to be reasonable if based upon a proper consideration. Subsequently, the doctrine of restraint of trade was extended to price-fixing agreements made by competitors, all of whom continued in business. Such price-fixing agreements were held to be unreasonable and void. Strictly speaking, they were general restraints and void regardless of their reasonableness.

In 1911 the Supreme Court applied the idea of reasonableness *to mergers* which completely restrained independent price competition among former competitors. Thereupon, the "rule of reason" came to be made the sole test of the validity of all restraints—partial and general—except that direct price-fixing agreements were held to be *per se* unreasonable. Restraints on price competition imposed by a merger were accepted as long as the merger (1) did not acquire an overwhelming percentage of the separate plants in the nation and (2) did not engage in predatory practices. This rule of judge-made law is known variously as the abuse theory of mergers, the abuse theory of monopoly, and the "Sherman-Act test" for mergers.

Although the Supreme Court has interpreted the Sherman Act so that little, if any, restraint is placed upon price unity secured by means of corporate mergers, it has consistently condemned such unity whenever it is secured by agreement among legally separate firms. All conspiracies suppressing price competition are held to be contrary to public policy and violative of the Sherman Act. A finding of conspiracy, the courts have held, may be based (a) upon circumstantial evidence and inference or (b) upon evidence of direct agreement. The rule of implied or constructive agreement is also known as the doctrine of "conscious parallel action."

In the *Alcoa* case the federal courts made distinct progress toward correcting the divergent policy (1) of condemning price agreements and (2) of accepting mergers of competing plants. For the first time, they indicated that they were prepared to condemn monopoly, as such, whether secured by collusion or by financial size, and without reference to the existence of predatory practices. In the *Alcoa* case, Judge Hand reasoned that the possession of power to control prices necessarily means that it will be exercised in the making of prices. Monopoly power, as the power to manage prices, therefore, was condemned as such, without reference to specific abuses.

The decision in the *Alcoa* case turned on the presence of monopoly control rather than on bigness, as such. The rule that size, *per se* (by itself), is not prohibited by the Sherman Act still stands. The antitrust laws are concerned not with size, but rather with monopoly power. In the view of the Court, *monopoly*, as applied to one single company, *is the power to exclude competitors or to fix or control prices.* The existence of monopoly provides the basis for dissolution, divorcement, or divestiture proceedings.

A succinct and summary statement of the opinion of the Court toward the legality of a merger, horizontal or vertical, is found in the *Swift* case (1932). Said the Court, "Mere size, according to the holding of this Court, is not an offense against the Sherman Act unless magnified to the point at which it amounts to a monopoly . . . but size carries with it an opportunity for abuse that is not to be ignored when the opportunity has been utilized in the past" (286 U.S. 106, 116).

The weakest aspect of our antitrust law program centers on the application of the Sherman Act to price leadership and oligopoly. There is a growing economic and legal opinion that the antitrust laws *can* and *should* be applied (1) to price leadership and (2) to unified selling by a few dominant concerns which act as one on price, allegedly without agreement. The antitrust laws, various authorities believe, can be applied against price leadership on the principle that monopoly is the power to fix or control prices (*Alcoa* case). The situation of oligopoly, moreover, might be attacked (a) on the principle of implied conspiracy or (b) as a condition of monopoly—under Section 2 of the Sherman Act—on the theory that the larger companies jointly or collectively possess the power to control prices.

The large monopolistic mergers and the economic concentration which have been permitted to develop under the Sherman Act show clearly that we have gotten off on the wrong road in our interpretation of the concepts of monopoly and competition. Vast corporate mergers, which completely eliminate the price competition of formerly independent plants, may be legal under the Sherman Act as interpreted by the courts in the past, but they make it impossible for our nation to maintain a policy of effective price competition. There is a substantial body of opinion among economists and legal experts that the only alternative to succumbing to monopoly power is to reduce the size of that power through a dissolution or divestiture of the larger mergers. We have never really tried this policy, except in a very limited way.

SUGGESTIONS FOR FURTHER READING

Adelman, M. A., "Integration and Antitrust Policy," *Harvard Law Review*, November, 1949, pp. 27–77.

Adams, Walter, "Dissolution, Divorcement, Divestiture: The Pyrrhic Victories of Antitrust," *Indiana Law Journal*, Fall, 1951, pp. 1–37; and "The Aluminum Case: Legal Victory, Economic Defeat," *American Economic Review*, December, 1951, pp. 915–922.

Carlston, Kenneth S., "Vertical Integration and the Law," *Vertical Integration in Marketing*, Bureau of Economic and Business Research, University of Illinois, Bulletin 74, 1952, pp. 148–169.

Edwards, C. D., *Maintaining Competition* (New York, 1949).

Kronstein, H. and Miller, Jr., J. T., *Regulation of Trade* (Albany, 1954).

Loevinger, Lee, *The Law of Free Enterprise* (New York, 1949).

Mason, Edward S., "Monopoly in Law and Economics," *Yale Law Journal*, November, 1937, pp. 34–49.

Nicholls, W. H., *Pricing Policies in the Cigarette Industry* (Nashville, 1951).

Stocking, G. W. and Watkins, M. W., *Cartels in Action* (New York, 1946); and *Cartels or Competition* (New York, 1948).

Wilcox, Clair, *Competition and Monopoly in American Industry*, Monograph 21, Temporary National Economic Committee, 76th Congress, third session, 1940.

CHAPTER 1 2

The Administration of the Sherman Act

THE PURPOSE AND SCOPE OF THE SHERMAN ACT

Although uncertainty frequently exists with respect to the interpretations placed upon the Sherman Act, there is general agreement that the sincere and consistent purpose of this statute is (1) to prevent the exercise and growth of monopoly and (2) to retain as far as possible, and to restore, the business practices of free enterpise and price competition. The processes of the Sherman Act are legal in nature, but its substance and purpose are essentially economic. Monopoly, mergers, price discrimination, pricing formulas, freight absorption, phantom freight, mill net prices, free enterprise, price competition, markets, and market price are basically economic concepts; and those in charge of enforcing and applying the antitrust laws have before them the opportunity and responsibility of shaping and directing business conduct along lines which give effect to the principles of competition. The Sherman Act is not merely an "antimonopoly" statute designed to punish past illegal conduct. It is also a "pro-competition" statute; and the Attorney General, as well as a private individual, is authorized to initiate civil suits to restrain violations and to create the conditions which are necessary for the operation of fair and orderly competition.

In principle, the Sherman Act is applicable to all business activity (including banking) carried on among the states, with foreign nations, and in and with territories subject to the jurisdiction of Congress, unless specific exemptions have been made or provided by judicial interpretation of general language. In practice, however, it is applied mainly to the fields of general business, particularly manufacturing and merchandising. Since 1935, when antitrust enforcement began to be somewhat more active, suits have been brought against firms and individuals in the various lines of general business, as well as in the fields of insurance; medical services; the small-loan business; automobile financing; labor organization; motion picture production and distribution; the railroad and motor transport industries; the distribution of milk, poultry, and other agricultural products; the production of coal, natural gas, and other extractive commodities; retail food distribution; news reporting; newspaper publishing; music publishing; the making of loans secured by mortgages; the broadcasting and telecasting of professional games; and commercial fishing.

THE ENFORCEMENT OF THE SHERMAN ACT

In 1903 a special Antitrust Division was created in the Department of Justice to enforce the Sherman Act. This agency is headed by an "Assistant Attorney General, Antitrust Division," and includes attorneys, economists, and special investigators. The Antitrust Division administers the Sherman Act and related antitrust statutes and joins with the Federal Trade Commission in exercising concurrent jurisdiction under the Clayton Act.[1] In addition to its duty of enforcing the antitrust laws, the Division has the responsibility of enforcing the administrative orders of the Federal Trade Commission, Interstate Commerce Commission, Civil Aeronautics Board, Federal Communications Commission, Securities and Exchange Commission, Commodities Exchange Commission, and the Secretary of Agriculture. The Solicitor General handles all litigation before the Supreme Court which arises over the orders issued by the administrative agencies which are listed above.

An additional activity of the Antitrust Division consists of consulting with businessmen on the legality of proposed trade association activity, business mergers, and prospective commercial policies. In reviewing the proposals which are presented to it, the Division asks for a full disclosure of all relevant facts. If the parties concerned agree to eliminate features of doubtful legality, the Division will thereupon stipulate that it will not bring criminal action on the basis of the facts presented. However, it reserves the right to bring a civil action at a subsequent time, if competition appears to be restrained.

Antitrust cases originate (1) in the complaints of businessmen who are being injured by monopolistic practices, (2) in the suggestions made by other government agencies, and (3) in the research activity of the Division itself. About 90 percent of the cases, it is estimated, arise in the complaints of independent businessmen who report that they are being injured or threatened by monopolistic practices. A far greater number of violations are reported and found than can be prosecuted by the Division with its available staff; and the final selection of cases for prosecution turns on the availability of evidence, the legal issues involved, the impending injury to small competitors, and the particular business practices which currently appear to be important ways of effecting monopoly control. The Antitrust Division develops its cases both upon the basis of investigations conducted by the Federal Bureau of Investigation and upon the evidence obtained in a grand jury proceeding called by a district court. At the present time, most of the investigations are made by the FBI, which is a unit of the Department of Justice.

[1] A summary of the essential provisions of the minor antitrust statutes is presented at the end of this chapter. The Federal Trade Commission and Clayton Acts will be treated in subsequent chapters.

THE USE OF CRIMINAL PENALTIES TO DETER MONOPOLY ACTION

Monopoly has long been considered to be a crime against society; and if the Division believes that a group of businessmen should be punished for their past illegal conduct, it initiates a criminal case. A criminal conviction provides for the imposition of fines or imprisonment or both. The historical purposes of such penalties are (1) to make monopoly unprofitable and (2) to subject the monopolists to public ignominy.

Corporation officials accused of violating the Sherman Act typically have been persons of high social standing in their communities, and the Antitrust Division has found that juries and the courts have been unwilling to impose prison sentences on such persons. During the life of the Sherman Act, some 110 individuals have served prison sentences. These individuals have been trade union officials or racketeers, not businessmen. An example of the unwillingness of the courts to impose prison sentences on respectable businessmen is found in a case involving the General Motors Corporation. In this instance, all of the officers were found to be innocent, but the corporation itself, an impersonal entity, was convicted of monopolistic action!

The fines which have been imposed in criminal cases have also reflected extreme consideration for the business interests, and it is generally agreed that they likewise have not been a deterrent to monopoly action. Since 1890, for example, the average fine imposed under the Sherman Act has been only about $2000 per defendant. This is a small penalty in comparison with the monopoly profits which have been—and which can be—secured by monopoly action.

CIVIL SUITS AS AN INSTRUMENT OF BUSINESS REGULATION

From an economic point of view, criminal actions to punish past illegal conduct are an incomplete and negative form of regulation. They do not resolve economic issues or make provision for the essential conditions of free enterprise and price competition. Their chief value lies in cases—such as conspiracy cases—in which all the government wants is conformity with an applicable rule of law—e.g., independent action on price.

Experience has shown that in most situations, if competition is to be maintained, government must act positively to create and maintain in the basic industries *the conditions* which are essential for the effective operation of competition (see Chapter 6, pp. 90-91). It is here that civil suits become important. Their usefulness and proper role lie primarily in dealing with problems of size and market organization as distinguished from conspiracy. The undisputed purpose of the Sherman Act is to retain and restore price competition, and the principal purpose of civil suits under the act accordingly is—or should be—to provide the conditions which are essential for the operation of effective competition.

The Antitrust Division has made a commendable beginning in getting the courts to require corrective action and remedial measures to make competition work more effectively. Decrees have been entered, for example, requiring an industry or a concern (1) to sell at f.o.b. mill prices at the buyer's request, in addition to any other method of price quotation; (2) to inform the Department of Justice of proposals to acquire stock or assets in other companies; (3) to refrain from opening any new branch offices for a period of five years; (4) to dispose of various plants and companies, with an injunction against a sale to officers, directors, or agents of the parent company, as well as against interlocking directorates and joint stock ownership in the separate businesses; (5) to license patents or dedicate certain patents to the public, royalty free; (6) to sell not more than 35 percent of the total production of a basic commodity; and (7) to liquidate or abandon designated trade associations. No one of these requirements imposed by judicial decree is specified in the Sherman Act. Fashions in monopoly, however, change from period to period, and it is sound policy to provide a general legislative mandate against monopoly and for competition, with the particular details to be worked out by administrative agencies and the courts.

A criticism frequently made of the Sherman Act is that it lacks certainty. In large measure this fact, to the extent that it is true, arises from the fewness of antitrust cases which have been decided. What is needed is more decisions applying the Sherman Act which will provide "rules of the game" to make competition fair, aboveboard, and effective.

Over the years our failure to regulate and implement competition has led to the widespread growth of monopoly. At the present time, government has the triple task (1) of *eradicating* monopoly, (2) of taking steps to prevent the adoption of new monopolistic practices, and (3) of providing positive rules for the regulation of competition.[2] Civil decrees, which provide affirmative relief, have an important role to play in the fulfillment of this task, for they make it possible for government to require by court order the observance of rules and conditions making for effective price competition.

SETTLEMENT OF CASES WITHOUT PRESENTATION OF EVIDENCE

The Department of Justice is frequently willing to permit defendants to plead *nolo contendere* or to sign a consent decree, without bringing a case to trial. Defendants, moreover, are often eager to settle cases in this manner. Several reasons account for these respective points of view. First, government attorneys may believe that they can secure more effective relief if they

---

[2] Examples of positive rules which various economists have suggested for governmental adoption are (1) the requirement of f.o.b. mill prices, uniform to all buyers at the mill; (2) the requirement that corporations sell at posted prices to all customers offering cash or approved credit; and (3) the provision of publicity on the prices of actual transactions, sales, and supplies available. See also chap. 5.

participate with the court in formulating a consent decree. Having developed the case, they feel that they know what should be done to remedy the evils. Secondly, the settlement of cases without the taking of evidence saves time and money. Government attorneys desire to save money in order to prosecute additional cases. Private defendants, on the other hand, are quite prepared to settle a case quickly when they are convinced that they are going to lose it.

Thirdly, private defendants are often eager to settle their cases by a plea of *nolo contendere* or by a consent decree *in order to avoid treble damage suits under Section 7 of the Sherman Act and Section 4 of the Clayton Act.* The Clayton Act provides that "a final judgment or decree" in any antitrust case, "to the effect that a defendant has violated said laws," shall be *prima facie* evidence of illegal action in a private suit for treble damages. Any person injured by the monopolistic practice can introduce the judgment or decree, and thereupon he needs only to prove the damages sustained. Consent decrees and judgments on pleas of *nolo contendre*, however, have been held *not* to constitute "a final judgment or decree," and thus they do not provide a basis for treble damage suits. Violators of the antitrust laws frequently worry more about treble damage suits than about public penalities, and they accordingly are quite willing to accept court settlements which preclude private liability.

TREBLE DAMAGE SUITS AS AN INSTRUMENT OF ENFORCEMENT

The Sherman and Clayton Acts provide that "any person who shall be injured in his business or property" by monopolistic practices may sue for threefold the damages sustained, regardless of the amount of the injury. The term "any person," it would seem, includes consumers, and it appears that a consumer, or group of consumers, could bring action against price-fixing conspiracies for overpayments on the products they buy.

Business enterprises have made, and are now making, extensive use of the "treble damage" provisions. Instead of complaining to the government about an injurious practice or about exclusion from the business field, an enterpriser may initiate a private damage suit.

In recent years, there have been at least five times as many private treble damage suits as government prosecutions (see Table 18). Most of the pri-

TABLE 18.   Government and Private Antitrust Cases Commenced During the Years 1942–1954.

	1942	1943	1944	1945	1946	1947	1948	1949	1950	1951	1952	1953	1954
Government cases:													
Civil	35	24	12	20	18	33	19	39	42	37	20	16	21
Criminal	....	40	13	9	15	11	18	27	34	16	12	16	10
Private civil cases	70	40	50	27	68	64	78	162	157	209	261	212	163

(Source: Annual Reports of the Director of the Administrative Office of the United States Courts, Washington, D.C.)

vate suits are settled out of court, for the defendants are anxious to suppress publicity on their illegal acts. Little information is available on the actual damages secured, but it is believed that the cash settlements are frequently substantial.

Treble damage suits provide a useful and desirable *supplement* to public prosecution. The *main* burden of enforcement, however, should be carried by the government, itself, as the agency of the nation as a whole. It is only the government which can conduct a consistent and coördinated program of creating the *essential conditions* for competition. Public prosecution should be a major—not a minor—instrument for maintaining competition.

SECURING COMPLIANCE WITH COURT DECREES

When court decrees have been entered prohibiting certain business practices and requiring the observance of others, the Antitrust Division has the further task of inspecting and policing the past defendants to see whether or not they are complying with the court orders. The unfortunate fact is that the Division has had neither the staff nor the money to make continuing checks on industry compliance. In most cases, information on decree violations has been presented to the Division by individuals who have a grievance against the past defendants. During the entire history of the Sherman Act, fines have been imposed in contempt of court cases in only three instances, and in all other cases the violators of court decrees have been given only a reprimand and a further court order.

CAUSES OF THE WEAK ENFORCEMENT OF THE ANTITRUST LAWS

It is often said that the Sherman Act has been a failure because it has not prevented the enormous growth of economic concentration and monopoly which presently exist in the United States. There is no doubt that economic concentration and monopoly have grown enormously—and are still growing. A basic factor which has contributed to this condition, economic and legal experts agree, has been the weak enforcement of the antitrust laws.[3] For many decades the Sherman Act was virtually unused. Scarcely a finger was lifted against monopoly. A summary of the cases instituted under the Sherman Act each year since 1890 shows that vigorous enforcement activity really did not get underway until about 1940. The truth is that the policy of the Sherman Act has hardly been tried.

1. *Half-hearted Interest by the Executive, Judicial, and Legislative Branches of Government.* It is generally agreed that the major reason for the weak enforcement of the Sherman Act has been the fact that over the years our public authorities—executive, judicial, and legislative—frequently have

[3] Other important factors which have contributed to the rise of economic concentration have been (1) the legalization of the holding company device (see Chaps. 7 and 19) and (2) the failure of the efforts of Congress in the Clayton Act to prevent corporate mergers which substantially lessen competition (see Chap. 16).

not had the will or desire to enforce the law. At no time, moreover, has the Department of Justice had adequate funds for enforcement activity. During the administration of President Cleveland, the Attorney General, Richard Olney, a former corporation lawyer, actually worked with various business groups to get the Sherman Act repealed! From March 6, 1893, to June 7, 1895, Mr. Olney instituted only six proceedings under the Sherman Act, and all of these cases were brought against labor unions and labor leaders![4] Even President Theodore Roosevelt, it is said, "at first roared like a lion against monopoly" but "at last cooed as gently as any sucking dove about letting business coöperate, and about the need to distinguish between good trusts and bad ones, with the disturbing implication that he would do the choosing."[5]

The federal courts, likewise, have contributed to the relative ineffectiveness of the Sherman Act. Important actions on their part which have served to weaken it have been (1) the spurious distinction which the Supreme Court made in the *Sugar Trust* case (1895) between manufacturing and commerce; (2) the addition of the so-called "rule of reason" to the Sherman Act in the *Standard Oil* and *American Tobacco* cases (1911); (3) the use of the rule of reason in the *Steel* case (1920) to justify a merger which restrained the competition of scores of formerly independent plants; (4) the consideration of "motives" and "abuses" in applying the Sherman Act (the abuse theory of mergers) rather than the existence of monopoly as an actual economic condition. All these instances of "judge-made" law point to the fact that the federal courts have not had an active interest in applying the Sherman Act.

Finally, Congress itself over the years has not been willing to enact supplementary legislation to prevent the whittling away of the Sherman Act by adverse court decisions. Indeed, as we shall see in the next chapter, Congress has, in fact, contributed substantially to the whittling away process by granting numerous exemptions from the Sherman Act. At all times, moreover, Congress has been unwilling to appropriate adequate funds to provide for comprehensive enforcement activity.

Why, it may be asked, have the executive and judicial branches of government often been unwilling to give whole-hearted support to the Sherman Act? Why has Congress long been unwilling to provide adequate funds for its enforcement? There is general agreement that the main reason is to be found in the pressure of organized special interests and in the seductive influence of substantial campaign contributions. As Dr. William McCracken has said, "If one were to ask me why our antitrust laws and enforcement had been of almost no avail, I would say that it is due primarily to the 'Fourth Division of Government,' namely, lobbies and pressure groups."[6]

[4] Thomas K. Fisher, "Antitrust During National Emergencies," *Michigan Law Review,* May, 1942, p. 975.

[5] Frank A. Fetter, *Democracy and Monopoly* (Princeton, 1939), p. 16.

[6] Dexter M. Keezer (ed.), "The Antitrust Laws: A Symposium," *American Economic Review,* June, 1949, p. 716.

The expenses of political parties must be paid by someone, and no President, it appears, has been able to resist completely the influence of the chief financial supporters of his political party.

The influence of pressure groups may express itself in the appointment of the Attorney General and in the nomination of judges for appointment to the federal courts. Until about 1910 a majority of the appointees to the Supreme Court were men who had made distinguished records as corporation lawyers. These men had long been trained in serving the interests of large corporations and they brought to the Court a background and habit of thinking which made them unwilling to do much more than frown upon the predatory practices of monopoly.

The apathy of the executive and legislative branches of government toward the antitrust laws has also expressed itself in the small appropriations which have been requested and granted for the Antitrust Division of the Department of Justice. Prior to 1935 the annual appropriation was never in excess of $300,000, and frequently it was only $100,000. At no time did the Division employ more than twenty-five attorneys. During the administration of President Theodore Roosevelt, when "trust-busting" activity was put forward as a major economic function of government, the Antitrust Division consisted of five attorneys and four stenographers.

Soon after our unfortunate experience with legalized monopoly in the National Recovery Administration (1933–1935), President Franklin D. Roosevelt recommended an expanded program of antitrust enforcement. The Division's appropriation was thereupon increased from $475,000 in 1938 to $2,325,000 in 1942. Even so, according to Thurman Arnold, who was in charge of the Antitrust Division from March 7, 1938, to March 16, 1943, the appropriations secured for antitrust enforcement were sufficient only to permit the Division to be concerned with "the dramatization of an ideal." Continuous practical regulation, he stated, was out of the question. Since World War II, competent authorities report that the Antitrust Division, as well as the Federal Trade Commission, have been securing only about one-half of the funds which they need to operate effectively.[7]

2. Ineffectiveness of the Prosecution as Compared With the Defense Counsel. In part, the difficulty which has been encountered in enforcing the antitrust laws is explained by the lavish expenditures which have been made by private corporations in comparison with the amounts available to the federal government. The total appropriation of the Antitrust Division for *all* antitrust work has only been around $3,000,000 per year in recent years. Since one major antitrust suit costs the government between $350,000 and $750,000, it is obvious that there are not sufficient funds for conducting many cases. A business combination, on the other hand, not infrequently spends as much as the entire antitrust budget in defending a single case in the federal courts. According to the Antitrust Division, one of the defendants in the *Hartford-Empire* case (1945) spent approximately $900,000

[7] See also Walter Adams, "The Sherman Act and Its Enforcement," *University of Pittsburgh Law Review*, Spring, 1953, pp. 335–336.

in the trial of the case in the District Court, and an estimated $500,000 to $800,000 in appealing the case to the Supreme Court. The expenditures of the other seven corporate defendants in the case were not known but were estimated to be in excess of $1,000,000.[8] The legal expense of the defendants in the *Madison Oil* case (1940) is reported to have been somewhere between $2,000,000 and $2,500,000.[9] In the *Cement* case (1948), it is estimated that the defendant companies spent over $11,000,000.

3. *Inadequate Use of Economic Analysis by the Regulatory Agencies and the Courts in Applying the Laws on Competition.* In many instances, attorneys for the government have failed to make adequate or, in fact, any use of economic experts in important antitrust suits. Private corporations, on the other hand, have spared no expense in the employment of economists to assist in defending monopolistic business practices. Such men have been employed (1) to assist in collecting data and in framing issues and (2) to testify as expert witnesses.

It is believed that the public advantage would be greatly served by requiring the courts to employ economic experts of their own to aid them in evaluating the opinions of the partisan experts. On the average, a federal judge in a district court hears only one or two antitrust cases in his entire career, and there is little opportunity for him to build up a fund of experience on antitrust litigation. The typical federal judge, moreover, has had little training in economics. In 1945 the Federal Rules of Criminal Procedure were modified to provide federal judges with authority to appoint expert witnesses upon their own motion. This legislation will make it possible for the federal courts to secure the services of impartial economic experts, if they so desire.

PROPOSALS MADE FOR THE MORE EFFECTIVE ENFORCEMENT OF THE SHERMAN ACT

It is frequently said that the Sherman Act should be rewritten to bring it up to date with modern conditions. There is little evidence, however, that any change in the basic law is needed. Its purpose, we have said, is to prevent monopoly and to maintain and preserve competition in the principal lines of business activity. If the free competitive system is to be maintained, it is evident that the substantive law of the Sherman Act itself must be retained.

A study of the literature available on the antitrust laws shows that there are some eight main proposals currently advanced for making the Sherman Act more effective. A brief analysis of these remedial suggestions follows.

1. *All-Needed Executive and Legislative Support of Present Statutes.*

[8]*United States Versus Economic Concentration and Monopoly*, Staff Report to the Monopoly Subcommittee of the Committee on Small Business, House of Representatives, 79th Congress, second session, 1946, pp. 248–255.

[9]*Antitrust in Action*, Monograph No. 16, Temporary National Economic Committee, 76th Congress, third session, 1941, p. 80.

The proposal most frequently urged by authorities on the Sherman Act to make its application more effective is that of providing larger appropriations for enforcement activity. The Temporary National Economic Committee, especially, emphasized in its final report that the Department of Justice and the Federal Trade Commission "are admittedly undermanned and meagerly budgeted. No law, and particularly no law of the type here discussed, can be stronger than the zeal and resources of the agencies of enforcement into whose care it is entrusted. We strongly urge the absolute necessity of providing funds for these agencies adequate to the task which confronts them."[10]

A comparison of the appropriations made for antitrust law enforcement with those made for the direct control of prices by public commissions shows at once the meagerness of the appropriations to maintain competition in general industry and also the relatively heavy cost required to maintain a policy of direct control in particular segments of the economy. The appropriations for administrative expense, and number of employees of the major federal regulatory agencies in 1954 are shown in Table 19.

TABLE 19. A Comparison of the Appropriations and Number of Employees
of the Major Federal Regulatory Agencies.

Agency	1954 Appropriation	Total Personnel
1. Antitrust Division, Department of Justice	$ 3,150,000	479
2. Federal Trade Commission	4,053,800	611
Total	$ 7,203,800	1090
1. Civil Aeronautics Board	$ 3,777,000	561
2. Federal Communications Commission	7,400,000	1200
3. Federal Power Commission	4,300,000	659
4. Interstate Commerce Commission	11,284,000	1881
5. Federal Maritime Board	350,000	50
6. Packers and Stockyards Administration	655,700	110
7. Securities and Exchange Commission	5,000,000	744
Total	$32,766,700	5196

(Source: Executive Office of the President, Bureau of the Budget. Fiscal years of the federal government are from July 1 to July 1. The period to July 1, 1954, is the fiscal year of 1954.)

2. *Increased Penalties.* Many authorities recommend that the courts be authorized to impose more stringent maximum fines in criminal suits for violation of the Sherman Act. The purpose of a fine is to serve as a deterrent as well as a punishment. The present maximum of $5000 for each count, however, does not cause most potential offenders to fear the law. Indeed, the Department of Justice has stated that "In some respects the penalties are so

[10] *Final Report and Recommendations of the Temporary National Economic Committee,* 77th Congress, first session, Senate Document 35, March 31, 1941, p. 35.

low that violation is regarded by businessmen as a good business risk."[11]

During a thirteen-year period, a Congressional Committee reported in 1953, the courts levied fines against General Motors on five occasions for violating the antitrust laws. The total of the fines was $11,000. Du Pont was fined a total of seven times and paid a sum of $42,500.[12] The inadequacy of the present penalties was vividly stated by Judge Rifkind in the *National Lead* case (1949). Said Judge Rifkind: "A violation of the antitrust laws which persisted from some time in the early twenties to the 1940's, with respect to which the criminal liability is discharged by the payment of $5000 a count, hardly seems to me to be the nature of penalty which is likely to discourage violations of the antitrust laws as far as the criminal laws are concerned, but that is a problem for Congress."

As early as 1900, ten years after the passage of the Sherman Act, a House Committee urged the adaption of more stringent penalties. In its words, "These penalties are deemed insufficient. The illegal combinations in the law mentioned are not deterred a moment by fear of a fine not exceeding the amount named. . . . Your committee therefore recommends that the penalties be made more severe by fixing a minimum fine and by adding imprisonment in every case."[13]

The Temporary National Economic Committee, after making a three-year study of economic concentration, concluded unanimously in 1941 that a fine of $5000, "is clearly inadequate as a deterrent to businessmen or to groups of businessmen whose incomes are in the millions, and the committee therefore recommends that the maximum limit for fines be raised to at least $50,000, leaving discretion with the court to assess the penalty according to the means and circumstances of the defendant and according to the extent to which it has profited by the violation of the act."[14]

Numerous antitrust authorities suggest that additional forms of penalties be imposed for antitrust violations. Dr. Walton Hamilton, for example, proposes that a corporation violating the act be required to forfeit "to the United States a sum equal to twice the total of the net income accruing during the period of wrongdoing. An offending officer is likewise to forfeit to the government double the compensation he has received during the period of violation. In addition, an executive may for an appropriate period be separated from his corporate office for such malfeasance in the discharge of his duties."[15]

[11] *United States Versus Economic Concentration and Monopoly*, 79th Congress, 1946, p. 250.

[12] *Increasing Criminal Penalties Under the Sherman Antitrust Act*, House Report 271, 83rd Congress, first session, 1953, p. 2.

[13] *Protection of Trade and Commerce Against Unlawful Restraints and Monopolies*, House Report 1506, 56th Congress, first session, 1900, p. 2.

[14] *Final Report and Recommendations of the Temporary National Economic Committee*, 77th Congress, first session, Senate Document 35, March 31, 1941, p. 40.

[15] *Antitrust in Action*, Monograph No. 16, Temporary National Economic Committee, 76th Congress, third session, 1941, p. 104.

3. *Registration of Trade Associations.* A third suggestion for strengthening the Sherman Act calls for the registration of trade associations. Thus, the Temporary National Economic Committee proposed that "All trade associations whose participating members are engaged in interstate commerce be required to register with an appropriate federal agency and to file periodical reports of their activities. All such associations should also be required to give adequate publicity to all of their activities." According to the Committee, "The frequency with which such associations are found engaged in practices which prevent the operations of a freely competitive economy, urges the necessity of more adequate regulation of their activities in the public interest."[16]

4. *Legislation to Give the Antitrust Division the Power of Subpoena.* As a means of expediting antitrust enforcement, numerous authorities propose that the Antitrust Division be given free access to the books and files of all companies operating in interstate commerce whenever the occasion demands. The Federal Trade Commission is authorized to require by *subpoena* all records relating to a particular investigation, but the Antitrust Division does not have this power. The word "subpoena" is a legal term (Latin: under penalty) which means a command to appear under penalty.

Most of the investigation work for the Antitrust Division is done by the F.B.I. This method of securing information has distinct limitations. Persons contacted by the F.B.I. are not under oath in giving information, and frequently they do not tell the truth. Industry leaders, moreover, are becoming increasingly sophisticated. In many instances, they will neither talk to the F.B.I. nor open their files for inspection. The only recourse which the Antitrust Division has in securing business records is to request them in grand jury proceedings. This is a time-consuming process, and frequently it is thwarted by legal technicalities.

5. *Patent Reform.* It is generally agreed by antitrust authorities that the patent laws of our country must be substantially changed if the principle of competition is to be made effective. Patents, said the Temporary National Economic Committee, have been used "as a device to control whole industries, to suppress competition, to restrict output, to enhance prices, to suppress inventions, and to discourage inventiveness."[17] A special examination of patents and the antitrust laws will be made in a subsequent chapter.

6. *Supplemental Legislation on Size and Price Leadership.* In important sectors of the economy, we have seen, competition has been eliminated by the formation of mergers. At the present time, central financial units (holding companies) control the stock or assets of scores of formerly competing plants. It is paradoxical that the courts have seen no restraint whatever to legitimate price competition in such combinations, whereas they have held,

---

[16] *Final Report and Recommendations of the Temporary National Economic Committee,* 77th Congress, first session, Senate Document 35, March 31, 1941, p. 38.

[17] *Final Report and Recommendations,* 77th Congress, first session, Senate Document 35, 1941, p. 36.

at the same time, that direct price agreements among competitors are illegal, *per se*. An intelligent scheme of statutory construction, it is suggested, should proceed on the principle that the merger of two large corporations, or a large corporation and a small one, which are in direct competition, is illegal whenever the resulting restraint in a given sales area is substantial (not trivial).

If industrial monopoly and economic concentration are to be remedied in the near future, it seems likely that it will be necessary for Congress (1) to indicate clearly, by legislation or otherwise, that the antitrust laws condemn oligopoly and price leadership and (2) to provide some form of assistance to the courts in speeding up the dissolution of *existing* combinations of formerly independent (or potentially competing) plants. See also Chapter 19.

7. *Freedom of All to Buy or Sell.* When plans for decentralizing industry are discussed, it is frequently declared that in numerous industries the government will be able to do little more than to change unitary monopoly or duopoly into a condition of oligopoly—that is, a condition of several but not many sellers. This observation, however, fails to recognize the historical fact that the number of *independent sellers* in central markets for the basic commodities—such as steel, the nonferrous metals, and sugar—has invariably been considerably *greater* than the number of *first-hand producers*.

Until the latter part of the nineteenth century, independent dealers (merchants) in the United States largely performed the task of distributing the basic industrial products. They got in touch with the various first-hand producers and concentrated supplies at central points for sale to fabricators and other users. When the industrial mergers were formed (beginning about 1897), however, the managers of the large companies found that their power to control prices was limited by the presence of supplies held by the independent merchants. Merchants had long performed the function of accumulating heavy inventories during periods of low prices for sale as demand increased. This practice served to stabilize production and employment. To the monopolistic mergers, however, it meant that "free" supplies came into direct competition with their own output during a period of rising demand when they sought to profit by their monopoly control. In order to eliminate the troublesome competition of independent merchants, the large combinations in the basic industries quite generally adopted a concerted policy of "fencing in" the demand for their products by refusing to sell to merchants and other nonconsuming interests.

Independent merchants are an important and essential group in market trading. Their participation in the marketing process means that a basic commodity is placed in many hands, and this fact promotes effective competition. Merchants, buying for inventory and storage in local or central warehouses, moreover, help to provide first-hand producers with a ready selling outlet, and a quick and sustained demand promotes full production and steady employment.

A basic rule of market law is that every person has "of common right" the liberty to buy and sell in open markets. If this freedom is to be enjoyed today, the law should require corporations controlling supplies of basic commodities to sell at prevailing prices to all dealers and fabricators who offer cash "on the counter." With the sale of essential supplies freely to all persons, it is probable that independent dealers will again come into existence, and central markets can again be established at the principal points of supply concentration.

8. *F.o.b. Mill Pricing.* A final constructive measure which various authorities believe should be adopted (by the courts or by Congress) in a program of strengthening the Sherman Act is a rule of law requiring all plants to sell at f.o.b. mill prices, uniform to all buyers at the mill, with delivered costs differing by the actual freight from the shipping mill.[18] With f.o.b. mill pricing, it is said, each locally separate mill can independently determine its own base price in accordance with its changing conditions of demand and supply.

F.o.b. mill prices, uniform to all buyers at the mill, develop naturally and automatically in a system of competitive markets. The need to require f.o.b. mill prices *by law*, various economists state, arises in the fact that in many industries (such as cement and beet sugar) the various mills are few in number and geographically separated from one another. The result is that each mill frequently has degrees of *local monopoly power* which it can exploit by charging nearby customers higher mill net prices than those located at distant points. If there is only one seller at a given place *and if he is allowed to discriminate*, it is practically certain that he will do so, for he can thereby make more profit. Section 2 of the Sherman Act declares monopoly to be illegal; and in the application of this section it is reasoned that government has the duty and obligation to prohibit discrimination at the point of production which grows out of the presence of local monopoly power.

The foregoing proposals, which bear directly upon the Sherman Act and its enforcement, it should be noted, do not cover all the remedies which need to be applied to implement a policy of competition. There is considerable agreement among economists in the antitrust field that if we really want a competitive economy we must also make provision for (1) the adoption of a national charter system for corporations engaged in interstate and foreign commerce; (2) the reëxamination of the exemptions from the Sherman Act which have been granted to various industries and activities; (3) the reduction of tariff rates, especially in the case of those industries which are presently monopolistic (as evidenced by the existence of large mergers, the

[18] See, for example, Frank A. Fetter, "Exit Basing Point Pricing," *American Economic Review*, December, 1948, pp. 815–827; and the statement of Walter B. Wooden, associate general counsel, Federal Trade Commission, in Hearings Before a Subcommittee of the Committee on Interstate and Foreign Commerce on S.R. 241, *Study of Pricing Methods*, U.S. Senate, 80th Congress, second session, 1948, pp. 699–701. For a formal definition of the phrase "f.o.b. mill pricing," see the "Glossary of Terms" in chap. 17, p. 398.

use of pricing formulas, and the practice of export dumping); (4) the condemnation of large-scale advertising when the effect is substantially to lessen
competition; and (5) the adoption of monetary and fiscal policies to aid in
stabilizing income and employment levels.

ANTITRUST ENFORCEMENT AND ASSISTANCE FOR SMALL BUSINESS

The measures presented in the preceding paragraphs for strengthening
competition bear directly upon the welfare of small business, for small business suffers, in particular, from three commercial practices widely used by
big business. These practices are (1) the refusal of large producers controlling major sources of supply to sell freely to all dealers and fabricators
who offer cash payment, (2) the exercise of geographic price discrimination
by which a large concern maintains prices in one sales area while reducing
them in the locality of a small business to prevent it from growing bigger,
and (3) the buying out of small and medium-sized competitors who seek to
get established and extend their sales area by being competitive on price and
quality.

In the great majority of cases, small business must buy basic commodities
—such as steel and copper—from large companies which own their own
fabricating facilities. Since the large companies have little interest in building up competitors, they sell to independent fabricators if they desire, when
they desire, in quantities which they desire, and at prices which they desire.
At the present time, there are no free and open markts in the United States
for most of the basic industrial commodities in which *anyone* can buy at
prices that are the resultant of *bids and offers*.

If a small business is able to get established, it soon finds its existence
plagued by the discriminatory price policies of large rivals. In order to
attract customers, small business usually prices its goods—such as bread,
vegetable oil, or paper bags—somewhat lower than those of a large rival.
This is not unfair competition, for the prices of a local business are usually
reduced uniformly to all buyers. A large rival, operating in several sales areas,
however, is in a position to "retaliate" by "meeting" the prices of the local
competitor, *in a discriminatory way*, either to offset any price advantage
which small business may have or to cut below the prices charged by small
business. Thereupon, small business loses its independence, and the alternatives open to it are (1) to go along with the local prices made by the large
rival, (2) to sell out to the large combination, or (3) to liquidate its business.

Since price wars are costly and injured parties may sue for damages, big
business in the United States has increasingly turned to the purchase of
competitors as the most practical way of eliminating competition. The purchase of a competitor, even at an inflated price, is advantageous to a large
rival, for it can thereby entirely eliminate the low prices in a particular sales
area and substantially increase its income.

WHAT IS A SMALL BUSINESS?

In the Small Business Act of 1953, Congress defined a small business concern as "one which is independently owned and operated and which is not dominant in its field of operation." The Small Business Administration, itself, has supplemented this definition with the refinement that the term

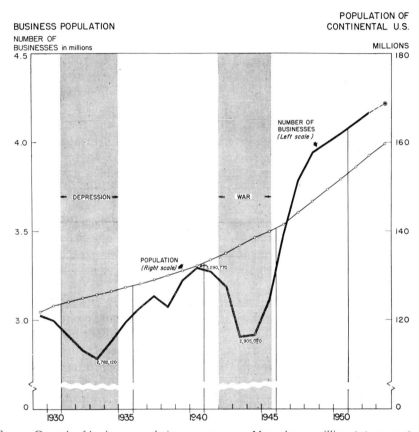

FIG. 23. Growth of business population, 1929 to 1953. More than 4 million (96 percent) of the estimated 4,212,400 operating business enterprises in the U.S. are classified as "small business." (Source: *First Semi-Annual Report of the Small Business Administration*, Washington, D.C., 1954.)

shall be applied generally for government procurement purposes to "any concern which employs 500 or fewer persons, including affiliates." This concept is also used by the Department of Commerce. Some authorities believe that there can be no single definition of small business and that the term should be defined on an industry-by-industry basis. Many companies, for example, are small in comparison with multimillion-dollar companies, but they are big in their own industry. Various representatives of small business, it may be added, have suggested that the term be applied to any concern which does not have enough money to support its own lobbyists in Washington, D.C.!

It is estimated that there are some 4,212,400 business enterprises in the United States—both incorporated and unincorporated—in mining, manufacturing, wholesaling, retailing, and the service trades. See Fig. 23. More than 4 million—4,045,000—of these business firms are classified as "small" upon the basis of criteria used by the Small Business Administration.

SMALL BUSINESS NEEDS "A FAIR FIELD AND NO FAVOR"

In recent years Congress has shown an increasing desire to preserve and encourage small business. The main purpose of the Robinson-Patman Act (1936) was to protect small business buyers from discriminatory prices in favor of big business buyers. Various government agencies—such as the Department of Justice, the Federal Trade Commission, and the Department of Commerce—have also been given, or have assumed, general responsibilities for helping small business to survive on its merits. In 1953 Congress established the Small Business Administration and provided it with capital for making loans to small business firms which cannot obtain funds from private lenders. The concern of government for the survival of small business is fully in accord with its function to maintain the essential conditions of free enterprise. At the present time, moreover, it is especially important for government to encourage and protect small business, for the burden of providing competition largely rests on small business units which act independently on price.

Experience has shown that small business does not need subsidies or special favors in order to prosper. It does, however, need an equal chance to obtain the agents of production and to continue in business without being crippled by the discriminatory prices of large rivals "to meet competition." It also needs a chance to stay in business without being acquired by financial combinations. In large measure, remedies for the problems of small business are to be found in a general program for strengthening the antitrust laws.

POSITIVE RESULTS OF THE ANTITRUST PROGRAM

The frustrations and defeats of the prosecution in antitrust suits frequently cause students to overlook the beneficial effects of our antitrust program. Results are not what they might have been, but a considerable measure of competition has been preserved.

Since 1939, the Antitrust Division has initiated proceedings against scores of business enterprises, large and small. In cases against the following companies, selected to show the importance of many of the concerns involved, the government has secured a *favorable* court decision, providing for a penalty or for a modification of business organization or behavior. Companies in this category include the A. B. Dick Co., Allied Chemical and Dye Corp., Aluminum Co. of America, American Brass Co., American Can

Co., American Tobacco Co., American Optical Co., Bausch and Lomb Optical Co., Borden Co., Columbia Gas and Electric Corp., Continental Can Co., Corning Glass Works, Crown Zellerbach Corp., Diamond Match Co., Eli Lilly and Co., Ethyl Gasoline Corp., General Electric Co., General

Swift & Company

UNION STOCK YARDS · CHICAGO 9, ILLINOIS

John Holmes
President

July 14, 1953.

Directors and Officers
Chicago Department Heads
Meat Packing Plant Managers
Branch House District Managers
Branch House Managers, including Panama and Puerto Rico
Dairy and Poultry Territory Managers
Dairy and Poultry Plant Managers
Ice Cream Plant Managers
Refinery Managers
Oil Mill Managers
Plant Food Managers
Technical Products Plant Manager
All District and Traveling Auditors
All Salesmen:

ANTI-TRUST LAWS

I desire to stress again that every employe is required to handle our business strictly in accordance with the law and that Swift & Company and its associated companies insist on careful and full compliance with all federal and state anti-trust laws. This is the responsibility and obligation of each employe.

VIOLATIONS NOT ONLY SUBJECT SWIFT & COMPANY TO SEVERE PENALTIES AND HEAVY EXPENSE OF LITIGATION BUT ALSO SERIOUSLY DAMAGE ITS REPUTATION.

EMPLOYES ARE ALSO INDIVIDUALLY AND PERSONALLY LIABLE AND ARE SUBJECT TO FINE OR IMPRISONMENT FOR VIOLATIONS TO WHICH THEY ARE A PARTY.

You must carefully observe federal and state anti-trust laws, and you are absolutely forbidden to enter into any agreement, combination, conspiracy, plan or scheme, or exchange of information, relating to or verging on price fixing, resale price maintenance (except under Fair Trade Acts on advice of General Counsel), limitation of production, division of territory, allotment of tonnage, or in any way in restraint of trade or designed to create a monopoly.

You are never to enter into any arrangement or combination, either personally or for Swift & Company, or any of its associated companies, either written or verbal, which would in any manner violate the foregoing.

Please acknowledge receipt.

John Holmes

FIG. 24. Letter from the president of Swift & Company admonishing management to observe the antitrust laws. (Permission of Swift & Company.)

Motors Corp., Great Atlantic and Pacific Tea Co., Johnson and Johnson, Kraft Cheese Co., International Salt Co., Libbey-Owens-Ford Glass Co., Masonite Corp., National Lead Co., Owens-Illinois Glass Co., Paramount Pictures, Inc., Proctor and Gamble Co., Pullman Co., Safeway Stores, Inc., Sherwin-Williams Co., Socony-Vacuum Oil Company, Standard Oil Co., (Indiana), Standard Oil Co. of California, Standard Oil Co. of New Jersey, Timken Roller Bearing Co., United Shoe Machinery Corp., United States

THE CHASE

Fig. 25. A cartoon of 1928 which appeared during the crest of the "new era" of business prosperity. Public attitudes toward "big business" shift with variations in prosperity and depression. When times are good, it is reasoned that high-level output and steady employment are the direct result of large corporations and their business practices. When depressions come, however, the public is disillusioned; and the more radical political groups demand overall economic planning and public ownership, as well as various demagogic ideas for reorganizing society. Periods of economic stress are almost certain to be encountered now and then. Many economists urge the prompt adoption of remedial measures to correct the chief evils of capitalism, for our system of free enterprise may not survive another period of mass unemployment and business depression. (Orr in the *Chicago Tribune*.)

Gypsum Co., U.S. Pipe and Foundry Corp., Univis Lens Co., Warner Bros. Picture, Inc., Westinghouse Air Brake Co., and W. P. Fuller and Co.[19]

As a result of antitrust prosecutions, American capitalism is very different from the capitalism which exists in western Europe. The Sherman Act has definitely served to eradicate and prevent open conspiracy and cartel arrangements. It has prevented and restrained flagrant competitive abuses. It stands also as a statue of liberty promising enterprisers the legal right to open business operations in fields of their own choice. Many American corporations make a sincere effort to comply fully with the policy of competition (see Fig. 24). This is in sharp contrast to business policy in western Europe.

When price-fixing arrangements do exist in the United States, they are usually unstable, for the participants know that unity of action is illegal and nonenforceable. Price-fixing "rings" are continually being upset by certain sellers who break away. The common testimony of American business leaders is the difficulty of bringing and keeping rivals in line on price.

The Sherman Act also provides business firms with a means for protecting themselves against monopolistic abuses. As we have seen, any person injured by monopolistic activity may sue for threefold the damages sustained. Further, the Clayton Act (Section 16) enables a person to sue for a restraining order whenever he is threatened by a violation of the antitrust laws. These provisions provide a large measure of protection against coercion and predatory activity. The freedom which American business firms enjoy in introducing new technology, new processes, and new products—in comparison with those in western Europe—is undoubtedly to be explained in large part by the freedom of enterprise which the antitrust laws support.

The Sherman Act makes available a sound and practical remedy for the problem of economic concentration. It is true that dissolution proceedings have hardly been tried and that efforts to unravel centralized control have been inadequate. However, precedents for dissolution activity have been established, and greater efforts in this area await only the support of influential groups.

THE BASIC FACTORS WHICH SHAPE PUBLIC POLICY

In the final analysis, whether the Sherman Act is retained in full force and made more effective depends upon whether or not independent businessmen, and the people generally, want this sort of economic regulation. As Thurman Arnold has said, "Unfortunately, all antitrust law enforcement under any plan depends on the public attitude. It does not make much difference what your instrument for carrying out antitrust policy is, it will not be effective unless there is a strong demand."[20]

[19] Commerce Clearing House, Inc., *The Federal Antitrust Laws With Summary of Cases* (Chicago, 1952). This book presents in chronological order summaries of all antitrust cases instituted by the Dept. of Justice since 1890.

[20] "The Antitrust Laws: A Symposium," *American Economic Review*, June, 1949, p. 690.

It is not likely that persons—in large or small enterprises—enjoying monopolistic arrangements (such as mergers, holding company privileges, trade association controls, resale price-maintenance legislation, laws prohibiting sales below cost, and pricing systems involving freight absorption) will make a demand for antitrust law enforcement. Rather, the demand, if it is to grow, will have to come from independent businessmen, from farm and labor groups, and from the general public. The economic interest of the very large majority of the adult population—the voting electorate—lies in a policy of competition. Competition makes for innovation, progress, cheapness, and plenty, whereas monopoly leads to greater scarcity, high prices, and economic stagnation.

In the past, our economic organization has largely been formed and dictated by the interests of important economic groups. The problem of the present is whether these groups will continue to shape public policy or whether it will be shaped by the majority of the people. If it is to be the latter, there is the further question of whether the majority will demand (1) a policy of competition as embodied in the Sherman Act or (2) a policy of authoritarian control as expressed in overall economic planning or social ownership. It is unlikely that the great majority of people will ever reason out an economic philosophy by their own efforts. Their thinking will rather be determined largely by their leaders. The policy of competition has an advantage in the political arena, for it is an integral part of our political, legal, and economic institutions. The American people, moreover, have a deep-seated suspicion of monopoly and economic concentration. In view of these facts, it is possible that political leaders will increasingly turn their attention to a policy of making competition more effective.

Economic conditions are an important factor influencing public attitudes (see Fig. 25). If a prolonged business depression should develop before a policy of competition can be made more effective, it is possible that a majority of the people will demand a greater amount of direct government control and government ownership. The plan of having the government directly organize the use of resources has the advantage of being readily understood by the masses. A major problem faced by those desiring to make the policy of competition effective is that of devising ways to give the measures which must be adopted to implement the Sherman Act a high degree of political interest and popular appeal.

SUPPLEMENTARY ANTITRUST LEGISLATION OTHER THAN THE FEDERAL TRADE COMMISSION AND CLAYTON ACTS

1. The *Wilson Tariff Act* (1894), as amended by the act of February 12, 1913, 15 U.S.C. 8, is applicable to price fixing in the import trade. It declares that every combination, conspiracy, trust, agreement, or contract is illegal when it is intended to operate in restraint of trade or competition in the importation of goods from any foreign country into the United States. The penalties are similar to those of the Sherman Act.

2. The *Panama Canal Act* (1913), 15 U.S.C. 31, contains a provision stating that any vessel owned or operated by a concern which is doing business in violation of the antitrust laws shall not be permitted to pass through the Panama Canal. It does not appear that this provision has ever been enforced.

3. The *antidumping provisions of the Revenue Act of 1916*, 15 U.S.C. 72, contained in Title VIII ("Unfair Competition"), prohibit importing or selling imported articles at a price substantially less than the market price of the articles in the country of their production plus freight, duty, and other expenses incident to their importation into the United States, provided that such acts are done with an intent to injure an industry or the establishment of an industry in the United States. Penalties are similar to those of the Sherman Act.

4. The *unfair practices provisions* (section 303) *of the Tariff Act of 1930*, 19 U.S.C. 1337, stipulate that an import duty shall be placed on goods entering the United States equal to the net amount of any bounty or subsidy which is granted in the country of production or export by government or by any person, partnership, association, cartel, or corporation.

SUGGESTIONS FOR FURTHER READING

Clark, John Bates, *The Control of Trusts* (New York, 1901).
Congress and the Monopoly Problem—Fifty Years of Antitrust Development 1900–1950, Select Committee on Small Business, House of Representatives, Document 599, 81st Congress, second session, 1950; and *Supplement*, 82nd Congress, 1951.
Edwards, C. D., *Maintaining Competition* (New York, 1949).
Final Report and Recommendations of the Temporary National Economic Committee, 77th Congress, first session, Senate Document 35, March 31, 1941.
Foreign Legislation Concerning Monopoly and Cartel Practices, Report of the Dept. of State to the Select Committee on Small Business, U.S. Senate, 82nd Congress, second session, 1952.
Kaplan, A. D. H., *Small Business: Its Place and Problems* (New York, 1948).
Keezer, Dexter M., "The Antitrust Laws: A Symposium," *American Economic Review*, June, 1949, pp. 689–724.
Monopoly and Cartels, Hearings, Select Committee on Small Business, U.S. Senate, 82nd Congress, second session, 1952.
Review of Small Business, Final Report, Select Committee on Small Business, House of Representatives, 82nd Congress, second session, 1952.
A Study of the Construction and Enforcement of the Federal Antitrust Laws, Monograph 38, Temporary National Economic Committee, 76th Congress, third session, 1941.
A Study of the Development of the Antitrust Laws and Current Problems of Antitrust Enforcement, Report of the Dept. of Justice to the Select Committee on Small Business, 82nd Congress, second session, 1952.

CHAPTER 1 3

The Exemption of Particular Industries and Activities
from the Antitrust Laws

The Sherman Act, as well as supplementary antitrust legislation, we have noted, is applicable in principle to all forms of private business carried on in interstate and foreign commerce. The Sherman Act itself makes no exception and declares that *every* restraint of trade and commerce is unlawful. In giving effect to the antitrust statutes as a system of economic regulation, the Department of Justice has sought to preserve and maintain the insitutions of free enterprise and price competition in all lines of business not given over to public price control by commissions.

THE GRANTING OF EXEMPTIONS FROM THE
ANTITRUST LAWS

Various business groups, from earliest times, have found an economic advantage in acting in unison in the sale of goods by fixing prices and reducing output or sales. In some cases, the desire for collective action stems from the anarchic and chaotic conditions of price making which develop when business rivalry is carried on without public rules or regulations. In other cases, the desire arises in the belief that a group is being disadvantaged by monopolistic action on the part of another industry group. On all occasions, however, experience shows that there is also a strong and continuing desire on the part of the members of such groups to avoid price competition with each other, even competition which is fair and aboveboard.

Since concerted action on price is unlawful under the Sherman Act, politically important or economically powerful groups, bent on pursuing their commercial advantage, find that they must either openly violate the law or take steps to have Congress change the law in its application to them. The first alternative is not a satisfactory one, for there is always the possibility of criminal suits and the disgrace of criminal convictions. Moreover, since the members of such business groups are typically well established in the community and active in social and civic affairs, there is usually a strong desire to be law-abiding and law-observing. The practical alternative, therefore, from their point of view is to have the law changed.

The attitude of big business with respect to getting what it wants in matters of public policy is clearly revealed in a statement made by Mr. Irving

264

S. Olds, chairman of the United States Steel Corporation, in connection with the decision of the Supreme Court in the *Cement case* (1948) outlawing the use of the basing-point plan of delivered prices. Instead of indicating a willingness to comply with the law, Mr. Olds frankly stated that industry is "faced with two alternatives—either to seek remedial legislation or to educate the Supreme Court."[1]

Economic policy is a matter of alternatives, and competitive action on price making, subject to public rules and regulations, could be maintained in most areas of business, if people had the will and courage to do it. For a variety of reasons, however, Congress has been repeatedly induced and persuaded to narrow the field covered by the antitrust laws and to take long steps toward the acceptance of a system of private monopoly. The policy of monopoly was accepted some decades ago by various European countries, and it is striking to consider how far the United States has already gone in the same direction.

In the following sections, consideration will be given to the principal industries or activities which have been exempted from the federal antitrust laws. The areas now excluded, in whole or in part, consist of (1) labor unions (1914 and subsequently by judicial decision); (2) agricultural coöperative marketing associations (1914 and 1922); (3) water carriers in foreign and domestic commerce (1916); (4) business associations in export trade (1918); (5) companies coöperating in defense production (1950); (6) handlers of agricultural products who make marketing agreements with the Secretary of Agriculture (1933 and 1937); (7) associations of aquatic producers (1934); (8) manufacturers and handlers of hog-cholera serum and hog-cholera virus (1935); (9) sellers of trademarked products using resale price-maintenance contracts (1937); (10) air carriers (1938); (11) telegraph companies (1943); (12) associations of insurance companies (1920 and 1945); and (13) railroads and other surface carriers (1948).

I

LABOR AND AGRICULTURAL ORGANIZATIONS

Section 6 of the Clayton Act (1914) provides, "Nothing contained in the anti-trust laws shall be construed to forbid the existence and operation of *labor, agricultural, or horticultural organizations, instituted for the purposes of mutual help, and not having capital stock or conducted for profits,* or to forbid or restrain individual members of such organizations, from carrying out *the legitimate objects thereof;* nor shall such organizations, or the members thereof, be held or construed to be illegal combinations or conspiracies in restraint of trade under the anti-trust laws." (15 U.S.C. 17. Italics supplied.)

In addition, Section 20 states,

[1] *Journal of Commerce,* April 28, 1948.

"No restraining order or injunction shall be granted by any court of the United States . . . in any case between an employer and employees, or between employers and employees . . . involving, or growing out of, a dispute concerning terms or conditions of employment, unless necessary to prevent irreparable injury to property . . ." (29 U.S.C. 52.)

BACKGROUND FOR SECTION 6 OF THE CLAYTON ACT

There is general agreement that the object of Section 6 of the Clayton Act was to clarify the law with respect to the *legal status* of labor, agricultural, and horticultural associations. Samuel Gompers, president of the American Federation of Labor, in particular, contended before the House Committee considering new antitrust legislation that "under the interpretation placed upon the Sherman Antitrust Law by the courts, it is within the province and within the power of any administration at any time to begin proceedings to dissolve any organization of labor in the United States. We do not want to exist as a matter of sufferance, subject to the whims or to the chances or to the vindictiveness of any administration or of an administration officer."[2]

The policy of concerted action by labor groups—as well as by groups of farmers—was coming to be accepted by the general public, and sufficient support was found in Congress to provide that unions and agricultural coöperatives are not in themselves violative of the antitrust laws. Many years of experience in the field of labor relations had convinced various public leaders that collective action by labor is necessary to offset the superior bargaining power of large industrial corporations. Individual workers are urgent sellers, invariably in need of ready cash. They have little knowledge of market forces, and their skill at bargaining is usually inferior to that of an employer. There are also few workers who are indispensable to an employer, whereas the loss of a job is usually of great importance to a worker. Not infrequently, moreover, employers themselves act in unison in wage negotiations and in deciding upon the maximum rates which they will pay within a given community. For these reasons, in particular, it has been found socially desirable to strengthen the bargaining position of labor in order to make it more certain that wages will reflect the value contribution made by labor.

SECTION 20 OF THE CLAYTON ACT AND THE ECONOMIC WEAPONS OF TRADE UNIONS

The desire of the unions as expressed in Section 20 was to curb the unrestricted use of injunctions by the federal courts to restrain picketing, persuasion, boycotting, and "conspiring to quit," as well as the activity of union officials in calling strikes. On its face, Section 20 purported to im-

[2] Committee on the Judiciary, *Anti-Trust Legislation*, 63rd Congress, second session, House Report No. 627, May 6, 1914, p. 15.

munize strikes, picketing, and boycotting from injunctions or restraining orders issued by a federal court. It was also generally believed that Section 20 went further and actually legalized the traditional trade union weapons of economic force.

The interpretation and application of Section 20 by the courts, however, soon revealed that they were unwilling to restrict in any greatly significant way the granting of labor injunctions. In *Duplex* v. *Deering*, 254 U.S. 443 (1921), the Supreme Court considered business activity to be a "property right," and held that an employer's business could not be hindered by pressures exerted by union members who were not employees of the plant directly involved in the strike. Section 20, the Court held, restricted the use of the injunction only in favor of those concerned as parties in the dispute. In subsequent cases, the Supreme Court further emasculated Section 20, and the grievances of labor against the use of labor injunctions became almost as great as they were before the enactment of the Clayton Act.

It is generally agreed by labor economists that the "hostility" of the judges toward the plain intention of Congress to accept labor unions and their traditional devices for exerting economic force finally led to the adoption of the Norris-LaGuardia Act in 1932. This act took away from the federal courts the power to issue injunctions in labor disputes, except in cases of fraud or violence. The Wagner Act of 1935 was a further product of the judicial hostility toward labor. In this legislation Congress not only gave workers the legal right to organize and bargain collectively but also required employers to bargain with unions duly established by majority vote.

THE ACCEPTANCE OF AGRICULTURAL COÖPERATIVES

The conditions which exist in the sale of labor services are also frequently found in the sale of farm products. Local dealers are few in number, and processors of farm products are usually organized in large corporate units. As a result, farmers in many cases have little or no active buying competition for their products. In order to strengthen their bargaining position, Congress likewise found it to be sound public policy to permit the formation of associations of farmers organized as coöperatives. Under this legislation farmers may legally join hands in the coöperative marketing of their own commodities.

A coöperative *marketing* association may be defined as a group of producers working together to sell their products without competing against one another. (See also Glossary of Terms at the end of Chap. 7.) The arrangement usually provides for equal voting power for each member and for a sharing of the revenue in accordance with the amount and quality of products sold by each member through the association. In order to provide for a centralized economic control, it is usual for the association to make a "marketing contract" which provides that the members will sell their products only through the association.

THE HUTCHESON CASE AND THE FURTHER EXEMPTION OF UNIONS FROM THE
SHERMAN ACT

Most legal authorities agree that the purpose of Section 6 of the Clayton
Act was to give labor and farm associations only a *limited* immunity from
the Sherman law. The exercise of private monopoly power has never been
recognized by the courts as being "legitimate" in the absence of explicit legislative sanction, and the activity of unions and associations of farmers was
specifically restricted in the Clayton Act to "legitimate objects."[3]

In the *Hutcheson* case (1941), Professor Edward S. Corwin observes, the
Court "largely released labor combinations from the control of the Sherman
Act, a result which was attained by a singularly bold exercise of the power
of statutory construction."[4] Briefly, the majority of the Court in the *Hutcheson* case held that if a labor union does not combine or conspire with an
employer group it may engage largely in any sort of activity which promotes
its interest. Justice Frankfurter, speaking for the Court, declared: "So long
as a union acts in its self-interest and does not combine with non-labor
groups, the licit and the illicit . . . are not to be distinguished by any judgment regarding the wisdom or unwisdom, the rightness or wrongness, the
selfishness or unselfishness of the end of which the particular union activities
are the means."[5] In no case, however, the Court emphasized, is a union
privileged to join with a business group to injure the trade of other business
firms or to fix product prices.

Subsequently, in the *Allen Bradley* case, 325 U.S. 797 (1945), the Court
again held that a labor union could not combine with employers to restrain
competition in the sale of merchandise. This rule, the Court observed, follows logically, for otherwise the prohibition on price fixing and restraint of
trade by business groups would be emasculated. In the words of Justice
Black, "The primary objective of all the anti-trust legislation has been to
preserve business competition and to proscribe business monopoly. . . . If
business groups, by combining with labor unions, can fix prices and divide
up markets, it was little more than a futile gesture for Congress to prohibit
price-fixing by business groups themselves."

The effect of the *Hutcheson* case was to place back in the hands of Congress the question of the degree of monopoly power which labor unions
should be permitted to exercise. Congress, we have seen, has complete and
absolute authority to regulate commerce among the states; and the regulation of labor combinations to prevent monopolistic practices is clearly a
problem for Congress to solve. (See also Chap. 26.)

[3] In *U.S.* v. *King*, 250 F. 908 (1915), it was held that the Aroostook Potato Shippers'
Association, a coöperative marketing association, could not engage in business practices
which were illegal under the Sherman law. Section 6 of the Clayton Act, the Court declared, is no defense against monopolistic action.
[4] E. S. Corwin, *The Constitution and What It Means Today* (Princeton, 1941),
pp. vii–viii.
[5] *U.S.* v. *Hutcheson*, 312 U.S. 219, 231–232 (1941).

II

COMMON CARRIERS BY WATER IN FOREIGN COMMERCE, IN INTERSTATE COMMERCE ON THE HIGH SEAS, OR ON THE GREAT LAKES

The Shipping Act of 1916, as amended, provides that every common carrier by water in foreign commerce, in interstate commerce on the high seas, or on the Great Lakes, as well as any persons engaged in forwarding or furnishing wharfage, dock, warehouse, or other terminal facilities in connection with a common carrier by water, shall immediately file a copy of all *agreements* with another carrier or person subject to the act with respect to rates, fares, charges, and other coöperative arrangements. All such agreements, if approved by the Maritime Board, it is provided, shall be exempt from the federal antitrust laws, including suits for threefold damages by persons injured by monopolistic practices. (46 U.S.C. 801, 814.)

The reasons which Congress had for granting shipping lines an exemption from the antitrust laws were explained by the House committee as follows:

> It is the almost universal practice for steamship lines engaging in the American foreign trade to operate, both on the inbound and outbound voyages, under the terms of written agreements, conference arrangements or gentlemen's understandings, which have for their principal purpose the regulation of competition through either (1) the fixing or regulation of rates; (2) the apportionment of traffic . . . ; (3) the pooling of earnings from all or a portion of the traffic; or (4) meeting the competition of nonconference lines . . .
>
> Moreover, steamship agreements and conferences are not confined to the lines engaging in the foreign trade of the United States. They are as universally used in the foreign trade of other countries as in our own. The merchants of these countries now enjoy the foregoing advantages of coöperative arrangements, and to restore open and cutthroat competition among the lines serving the United States would place American exporters at a disadvantage in many markets as compared with their foreign competitors.[6]

Various groups of American exporters and consignees also supported the proposal to legalize the making of rate agreements by the conference method on the ground that formal rate schedules would make for stability in their operations. Cutthroat and discriminatory competition, they reported, served to disrupt their business negotiations. The actual consummation of a business transaction in foreign trade may take weeks or months; and during this period exporters like to have stable freight rates, if possible, so that foreign buyers can know what their delivered costs will be.

FUNCTIONS OF THE FEDERAL MARITIME BOARD

The Shipping Act of 1916, in granting exemptions, also made provision

[6] Committee on the Merchant Marine and Fisheries, *Report on Creating a Shipping Board*, 64th Congress, first session, House Report 659, May 9, 1916, pp. 27–28.

for a regulatory commission to supervise common carriers by water operating in foreign commerce, in interstate commerce, or on the Great Lakes. This commission is now designated the Federal Maritime Board (see Tables 9 and 10, p. 80).

The Federal Maritime Board (1) regulates rates and services of American and foreign flag carriers engaged in the foreign commerce of the United States; (2) regulates charges of persons engaged in forwarding or furnishing wharfage, dock, warehouse, or other terminal facilities used in connection with common carriers by water; (3) passes upon agreements made by water carriers with respect to rates and trade practices; (4) protects shippers against unfair and discriminatory practices; and (5) determines and awards subsidies to place United States shipbuilding and ship operation on a parity with foreign construction and operation.

The Federal Maritime Board also regulates offshore common carriers which serve our territories and possessions. The authority it exercises over such carriers is considerably more rigid than the authority it has over carriers in foreign commerce. Regulation of carriers by water engaged in interstate (domestic) commerce on the high seas and on the Great Lakes was transferred to the Interstate Commerce Commission in 1940, and this latter agency now exercises jurisdiction over water carriers operating coastwise, intercoastal, and upon inland waters of the United States.

In the actual making of foreign shipping rates, practically all the American flag carriers operating in a certain area—such as the Pacific coast and the Orient—join with the foreign flag carriers also operating in that area, to bind themselves into a rate-making conference. Each company agrees to abide by the rates which are established by a majority or some other percentage vote. Foreign shipping rate conferences are thus international cartels. All the rates agreed upon by a conference of carriers touching United States ports must be submitted to the Martime Board and also kept open for public inspection at the offices of the conference and the carriers. The Maritime Board does not specifically approve rates, but all rates are subject to disapproval by the Board.

III

EXPORT TRADE

The Export Trade Act—the "Webb-Pomerene Law" (1918)—provides in Section 2 that nothing contained in the Sherman Act "shall be construed as declaring to be illegal an association entered into for the sole purpose of engaging in export trade and actually engaged solely in such export trade, or an agreement made or act done in the course of export trade by such association, *provided* such association, agreement, or act is not in restraint of trade within the United States, and is not in restraint of the export trade of any domestic competitor of such association." (15 U.S.C. 62.)

At the present time, some fifty export associations are in active operation under the terms of the Webb-Pomerene Act. "Webb associations," as they are called, typically concern themselves with price fixing and sales allocation. Actual business transactions are usually carried on by members in their own sales organization. Each association is required to file copies of its organizational papers with the Federal Trade Commission and make periodic reports of its activities. The Commission, in turn, has the function of seeing that the agreements are on file and of studying the reports and activities of the associations to determine whether or not they are in accordance with the law. If the Commission believes that violations exist, it makes an investigation and issues a recommendation for modification, if such is warranted by the facts. The Export Trade Act, however, has no "teeth" in it, and the Commission has no authority to require compliance. It can, however, refer its findings and recommendations to the Department of Justice for appropriate action. The Department of Justice, itself, without specific direction by the Commission, may also initiate prosecutions.

FORCES LEADING TO THE ENACTMENT OF THE WEBB-POMERENE ACT

The moving force, or interest group, which initiated the demand for a relaxation of the Sherman Act as applied to domestic exporters appears to have been the large copper producers. Thus, in 1940 Mr. Cornelius Kelley, president of the Anaconda Copper Mining Company, testified before the T.N.E.C. that as early as the Taft administration (1908–1912) he had sought to secure Congressional approval of "the proposition that the restrictions of our antitrust Act should be so modified as to enable exporters, not only of copper, but of all products, to combine in order to match the combined buying power that they were up against on the other side"—namely, the cartels and monopolistic buying groups in Europe. "The result," Mr. Kelley stated, "was an agitation that finally resulted in the passage of the so-called Webb-Pomerene Act."[7]

WEBB ASSOCIATIONS AND FOREIGN CARTELS

During the debates on the Webb-Pomerene Act, fears were expressed by various members of Congress that domestic exporters would use the law to form cartel agreements with foreign combinations. Senator Pomerene resolutely stated, however, that American firms would not be privileged to join hands with foreign cartels. The Sherman Act, he declared, is still the basic law of the land.

Soon after the act of 1918 was passed, however, various export associations began to make alliances with foreign cartels; and in 1946 it was reported that some fifteen associations had actually made agreements with foreign producers at one time or another.[8] Many of these agreements con-

---

[7] Hearings Before the Temporary National Economic Committee, 76th Congress, third session, Part 25, Cartels, 1940, p. 13113.

[8] Small Business and the Webb-Pomerene Act, 79th Congress, second session, Senate Subcommittee Print 11, 1946, pp. 14–15.

tained provisions which restricted price competition in international markets, divided sales areas, and placed restraints on potential competitors.

The position of the Federal Trade Commission is now, and has been, that
agreements between Webb associations and foreign competitors are not
objectionable if they do not affect the import trade or the domestic commerce of the United States. In a letter to domestic silver producers, July 31,
1924, the Commission stated:

> The purpose of the act seems to have been to provide a method for
> eliminating competition in foreign markets among domestic producers.
> . . . There seems to be no reason why a Webb-Pomerene association com-
> posed of nationals or residents of the United States and actually exporting
> from the United States, might not adopt a trade arrangement with non-
> nationals reaching the same market, providing this market was not the
> domestic market of the United States and the action of this organization
> did not reflect unlawfully upon domestic conditions.[9]

The position taken by the Commission in 1924 has been consistently ad-
hered to throughout the operation of the Webb-Pomerene law. In the view
of the Commission, every agreement or act of a Webb association must
meet certain tests. They are as follows:

1. The act or agreement of a Webb association, whether it be with
Americans or foreigners, must be "in the course of export trade" from this
country. In other words, it must not be an agreement *as to production* in
this country or abroad nor may it be related primarily to business outside
the scope of export.

2. Such an act or agreement must not restrain the trade of a domestic
competitor. Outside exporters are not to be coerced or forced into a Webb
law group, nor can an association deliberately injure the business of a
competitor in this country.

3. Such an act or agreement must not "artificially or intentionally" enhance or depress prices *in this country*. It is recognized that any shipment
in export may have some effect upon domestic business but a plan or policy
pursued by the association "intentionally" to fix prices in this country is
prohibited.

4. Such an act or agreement must not "substantially lessen competition
or otherwise restrain trade" in the United States. This includes restraint of
domestic trade *or* of the import trade.

The Department of Justice, in contrast with the Federal Trade Commission, has taken the position that Webb associations formed under the act
of 1918 are not privileged to join hands with foreign producers or associations of producers. Upon the basis of this view, the Department has brought
action under the Sherman Act against a number of Webb associations which
had entered into agreements with foreign competitors. In the *Alkali* case,
for example, the Department of Justice contended that an agreement be-

[9] Temporary National Economic Committee, *Export Prices and Export Cartels*,
Monograph 6, 1940, p. 127.

tween a Webb law association and a foreign competitor was unlawful *per se*, on the ground that it was not the intent of Congress to permit such an agreement. That issue, however, was not decided in the case because the Court held as a fact that there was restraint of trade *in this country* and *restraint of the import trade.*[10]

As we have indicated, under the rules of interpretation followed by the Federal Trade Commission, it is possible for a Webb association to enter into an agreement with foreign competitors *with reference to trade in a foreign country*. The agreement, however, must be in the course of export trade of the association and not in restraint of trade in this country, the import trade of the United States, or in restraint of domestic competitors.

THE VIEW THAT THE WEBB-POMERENE ACT IS INCOMPATIBLE WITH AMERICAN POLICY AND SHOULD BE REPEALED

Successful Webb associations, the records show, are typically found in industries controlled by three or four companies (oligopoly). According to the Department of Justice, such associations usually have had a long history of antitrust litigation and have engaged in patent-control programs, market sharing, and basing-point pricing. The Webb-Pomerene privilege, it thus appears, is mainly desired and used as an additional device for strengthening monopolistic control.

Many eminent economists and statesmen believe that the Webb-Pomerene Act should be repealed. The main reasons advanced for this belief are the following: (1) the legislation provides a mechanism for fixing domestic prices; (2) the act is chiefly used by large corporations to strengthen their dominant bargaining power; and (3) the law stands as a damaging deviation to our domestic policy of competition and our declared international position of eliminating all cartels and cartel-like structures. In international discussions on cartels our official policy is weakened by the very existence of the Webb-Pomerene Act, and we are thereby prevented from prevailing upon other countries to move a little closer to our traditional position.

The growing view is that if we are to advocate an anticartel policy we must be prepared to practice it at home. This means that the Webb-Pomerene Act should be repealed or modified to prohibit restraints on price competition in the export trade. It also means that vigorous action should be adopted to eradicate all forms of monopoly control in our domestic trade. A number of congressmen agree that repeal is the proper policy to adopt towards the Webb-Pomerene Act. They emphasize, however, that political support for repeal would be difficult to obtain because of the opposing strength of big business. In the words of Congressman Multer (New York), "I do not think we could repeal it. I do not think you could get enough of the Congress to vote for repeal of it with all of the pressures of the large companies that are now getting these advantages under the Webb-Pomerene Act."[11]

[10] *U.S. v. U.S. Alkali Export Association*, 86 F. Supp. 59 (1949).

[11] Hearings Before the Subcommittee on Study of Monopoly Power, Committee on

IV

ASSOCIATIONS OF PRODUCERS OF AGRICULTURAL PRODUCTS

The Capper-Volstead Act (1922), "an act to authorize association of producers of agricultural products," provides that

Persons engaged in the production of agricultural products *as farmers, planters, ranchmen, dairymen, nut, or fruit growers,* may act together in associations, *corporate or otherwise, with or without capital stock,* in collectively processing, preparing for market, handling, and marketing *in interstate and foreign commerce,* such products of persons so engaged. *Such associations may have marketing agencies in common;* and such associations and their members may make the necessary contracts and agreements to effect such purposes. . . . If the Secretary of Agriculture shall have reason to believe that any such association monopolizes or restrains trade in interstate or foreign commerce *to such an extent* that the price of any agricultural product is unduly enhanced by reason thereof, he shall serve upon such association a complaint. (7 U.S.C. 291, 292. Italics supplied.)

REASONS FOR THE ENACTMENT OF THE CAPPER-VOLSTEAD ACT

The Clayton Act (1914), we have seen, gave farmers the assurance that agricultural coöperative associations are not in themselves violative of the antitrust laws, provided that they are operated for mutual help, have no capital stock, and are not conducted for profit. Following the enactment of this legislation, there developed much uncertainty with regard to the action which a coöperative might take to influence prices. The Clayton Act legalized the *existence* of agricultural coöperative associations, and presumably the antitrust laws still applied to their *activities.* The Clayton Act, moreover, gave legal status only to associations "not having capital stock," and increasingly agricultural marketing associations were coming to find advantages in the corporate form of organization.

Interested farm groups, accordingly, sought legislation in Congress (1) declaring that the formation of an *incorporated* coöperative association having capital stock is not in itself in violation of the antitrust laws and (2) legalizing *concerted action* by the members of a coöperative marketing association *to enhance the prices of their products.*

The Capper-Volstead Act does not create or authorize the creation of coöperative marketing associations. All such associations are formed under the laws of the various states; and in general it may be said that a group of persons cannot act as a marketing association *under the name of a coöperative* unless they are duly organized under the coöperative law of a state. The basic purpose of the Capper-Volstead Act is to provide that "farmers" acting

the Judiciary, House of Representatives, Serial 14, Part 3, 81st Congress, second session, 1950, p. 97.

together in associations—"corporate or otherwise"—for processing and marketing products in *interstate* commerce, may act in unison to affect the prices of their commodities.

The important favors now granted to the coöperative marketing associations are (1) an authorization to organize and (2) the privilege of acting in concert with respect to prices, so long as the price of any agricultural product is not *unduly enhanced by reason thereof*. The authority to scrutinize prices is placed in the hands of the Department of Agriculture rather than in the Department of Justice. If the Secretary of Agriculture believes that monopoly power is being exercised to such a degree that the price of an agricultural product is unduly enhanced, he is empowered to issue a complaint. If, after a hearing, the Secretary finds that the complaint is justified, he is directed to issue a cease-and-desist order. No penalties are provided; but if the association does not comply, provision is made for the Attorney General to take appropriate steps in a federal district court to secure compliance.

At the present time, agricultural coöperatives are an important factor in the marketing of farm products. It is reported that there are almost 10,000 agricultural coöperatives in the United States (see Table 20). The membership consists of more than 7,000,000 farmers. In 1950–1951, the total gross volume of business handled by these associations was $10.5 billion.[12] Marketing coöperatives, generally, also purchase supplies for their members. In a number of cases, however, separate coöperative associations exist for purchasing and for conducting service operations, i.e., trucking, cotton ginning, warehousing, and the operation of locker plants.

THE EXERCISE OF MONOPOLY POWER BY AGRICULTURAL MARKETING ASSOCIATIONS

The Capper-Volstead Act, it may be said, provides agricultural producers with a substantial exemption from the antitrust laws. A single coöperative association may enter into contracts with scores of farmers which require them to market their products only through the association. Two or more associations, complying with the act, it is also provided, "may have marketing agencies in common." Thereupon, the price of a particular agricultural product, the law recognizes, may be influenced by an association so long as it is not "unduly enhanced." What limitation on the making of price increases is imposed by this provision? The law establishes no standard except the "opinion" of the Secretary of Agriculture, and it can hardly be expected that he will discourage farm groups in their activity to secure better prices.

It should be noted that the Capper-Volstead Act does not completely exempt the marketing activity of farmers' coöperatives from the operation of the antitrust laws. In the *Borden* case (1939), the Supreme Court held that an agricultural coöperative cannot join with "other persons"—such as dealers, distributors, or labor unions—to fix prices or restrain trade. The *Borden* case

[12] A. L. Gessner, *Statistics of Farmers' Marketing, Purchasing, and Service Cooperatives, 1950–1951*, U.S. Department of Agriculture, March 1953.

involved the legality of the price-fixing activities of a milk marketing cooperative. This association, it was found, had entered into a conspiracy "with
major distributors and their allied groups, with labor officials, municipal
officials, and others, in order to maintain artificial and non-competitive prices
to be paid to all producers for all fluid milk produced in Illinois and neighboring states and marketed in the Chicago area." In declaring this agreement
of a coöperative with "other persons" to be an illegal restraint of trade, the
Court declared, "The right of these agricultural producers thus to unite in
preparing for market and in marketing their products, and to make the
contracts which are necessary for that collaboration, *cannot be deemed to
authorize any combination or conspiracy with other persons* in restraint of
trade that these producers may see fit to devise."[13]

TABLE 20.   Number of Farmers' Marketing, Purchasing, and Service Coöperatives,
1950–1951.

Commodity group	Local associations Number	Large-scale associations Number	Total
Cotton and products	503	23	526
Dairy products	1688	240	1928
Fruits and vegetables	751	121	872
Grain	2172	26	2198
Livestock and products	496	40	536
Nuts	34	6	40
Poultry and products	109	17	126
Tobacco	....	24	24
Wool and mohair	83	27	110
Miscellaneous	144	3	147
Total marketing	5980	527	6507
Purchasing	3092	116	3208
Service	255	7	262
Total marketing, purchasing, and service	9327	650	9977

(Source: A. L. Gessner, *Statistics of Farmers' Marketing, Purchasing, and Service Cooperatives*, U.S.
Department of Agriculture, Washington, D.C. March, 1953.)

It also appears that members of an agricultural coöperative are not privileged to undertake by agreement any action *to limit the production of crops
or to destroy crops*. In 1951, for example, the Antitrust Division brought
action against an association of lettuce growers in California, charging an
agreement to reduce the amount of lettuce produced by destroying supplies
during the peak of the harvest season. The government was granted an
injunction restraining the defendants from destroying the lettuce crop in
accordance with any agreement, and the decision was subsequently affirmed
by the Supreme Court.[14]

[13] *U.S.* v. *Borden Co.*, 308 U.S. 188, 205–206 (1939). Italics supplied.
[14] *U.S.* v. *Grower-Shipper Vegetable Assn. of California*, 344 U.S. 901 (1952).

Exemption of Particular Industries from Antitrust Laws 277

Coöperatives commonly raise prices by withholding supplies and by excluding from sale certain portions of the whole supply. Such "surpluses" are sometimes sold abroad at low prices (export dumping), converted into specialty products (such as the use of almonds for almond butter and oil), diverted into lower-order uses (such as the use of dried prunes and raisins for livestock feed), or destroyed. Members of a coöperative association, we have seen, cannot legally take private action by agreement to limit crop production by destroying supplies. Under the various state and federal marketing agreement programs, however, handlers (dealers), including coöperatives, appear to be privileged to dispose of "surpluses" as they desire (see below, pp. 281–285). The federal government itself, moreover, may engage in crop limitation activity under the parity-price legislation (see Chap. 23, pp. 510–511).

v

ANTITRUST EXEMPTIONS GRANTED DURING NATIONAL
EMERGENCIES

A. Suspension of the Federal Antitrust Laws with Respect to All
Business During the Great Depression (1933–1935)

Section 5 of the National Industrial Recovery Act (N.I.R.A.), 48 Stat. L. 195 (1933), provided that "while this title is in effect and for 60 days thereafter, any code, agreement, or license approved, prescribed, or issued and in effect under this title . . . shall be exempt from the provisions of the antitrust laws of the United States."

The impact of the great depression which began in 1929 brought many demands from business leaders for a modification or suspension of the federal antitrust laws. A business depression stimulates the operation of price competition, for individual sellers seek to find a selling outlet for supplies which do not move at the established prices. During the course of the depression, big business—which had grown very much bigger as a result of the mergers of 1920–1929—accordingly found that the remaining independent sellers were reducing their asking prices in order to be able to deal. That was real competition. Big business, however, being burdened with heavy fixed costs, did not want price competition. In its eyes, a competitor on price was a "chiseler."

The complaint of big business against the antitrust laws was not that they were being too vigorously enforced. Enforcement activity, in fact, was largely nonexistent. Rather, the complaint arose because big business could not openly and legally take steps to fix prices and curb production. Many plans were presented by the leaders of big business for the "self-government" of industry. In an effort to make such plans tempting to the public, it was also proposed that government and business coöperate in providing minimum wages, shorter hours, an abolition of child labor, and various kinds of social insurance.

The theory sponsored by the advocates of N.I.R.A.—who were not college professors, as popularly believed, but leaders of big business and organized labor—was that the Sherman Act imposed and made necessary the "ruthless competition" which was giving consumers bargains at the expense of labor and capital. If prices could be raised by legalized monopoly action, it was claimed, wages could be raised, and the larger purchasing power would hasten prosperity. This view, however, as many economists then indicated, is illusory. If higher wages and profits are secured by *some* industries—such as coal—consumers generally are required to turn over more of their income to the favored producers for the same or fewer goods. The process is simply one of transferring income from one group to another. Moreover, if the costs and prices of *all* products were simultaneously increased by the same percentage, the gains in total purchasing power would be offset by the loss in total purchasing power occasioned by the high prices. There is no magic in price-cost raising experiments to bring back prosperity.

In accordance with the procedure established in the act, trade associations were invited to draw up "codes of fair competition" and present them to the National Recovery Administration (N.R.A.) for approval. After being approved by the N.R.A. and signed by the President, the codes became law. Although the act contained a provision that the codes should not permit monopoly or monopolistic practices, this proviso was openly violated and ignored. Nearly fifty of the codes filed by the major industries and given public approval contained price-fixing provisions which were managed by the industries themselves. Such codes, it has been said, were actually codes of "no-competition" or of "monopolistic limitation of competition."[15]

Price increases under the N.R.A. program were universal, and consumer protests became widespread and vehement. President Roosevelt who sponsored N.I.R.A. "as the most important and far-reaching legislation ever enacted by Congress," subsequently came to regard the relaxation of the antitrust laws as a most serious error which should be speedily remedied. Finally, on May 27, 1935, the Supreme Court held the act to be unconstitutional in the *Schechter Poultry* case, largely on the ground that the violations charged under the Poultry Code were concerned with local business which had only an "indirect" effect upon interstate commerce and which consequently were beyond the scope of national power.[16] The decision of the Court was widely acclaimed by the people; and many shared the feeling of Senator King of Utah who declared, "Thank God for the Supreme Court."

The Antitrust Laws and Economic Recovery. What policy should the United States pursue with respect to the antitrust laws during a period of business depression? There is widespread agreement among economists that

[15] Edward S. Mason, "The Report of the President's Committee on the NRA," *Quarterly Journal of Economics*, May, 1937, p. 548.

[16] *Schechter Bros.* v. *U.S.*, 295 U.S. 495 (1935). See also Edward S. Corwin, "The Schechter Case—Landmark or What," *New York University Law Quarterly Review*, January, 1936, pp. 151–190.

what is needed to bring high-level employment and production is *rising consumers' demand*. How can a greater consumers' demand be called forth? At this point, differences of opinion develop, but a considerable number of economists emphasize that a policy of artificially raising prices and wages operates to check demand and restrict employment. The best and surest way to end a recession, they point out, is to decrease prices by effecting economies and increasing efficiency. Many urge, therefore, that the antitrust laws be vigorously enforced during a period of depression. Thus, in 1932, in the midst of the great depression, 127 leading economists, affiliated with 43 universities in 24 states, sent a memorandum to the resolutions committee of each political party urging a vigorous enforcement of the antitrust laws. In particular, these economists advocated a

> Rejection of the assertion made by those seeking to break down the Sherman Act, that it makes necessary the development of excessive capacity and wasteful over-production, and the equally false assertion that this was one of the causes of the present industrial depression. On the contrary, the most competent economic opinion, as well in Europe as in this country, can be cited in support of the view that a strong contributing cause of the unparalleled severity of the present depression was the greatly increased extent of monopolistic control of commodity prices which stimulated financial speculation in the security markets. There is growing doubt whether the capitalistic system, whose basic assumption is free markets and a free price system, can continue to work with an ever widening range of prices fixed or manipulated by monopolies.[17]

Economists rarely urge direct wage reductions, but they do recommend cost reductions through increased efficiency. The economic error involved in a plan of making artificial wage increases to stimulate recovery is well expressed by Dr. Jacob Viner as follows:

> Wages, as we have seen, are both costs and incomes. As costs, they certainly are obstacles to employment; as income, they certainly are a stimulus to employment. They have that ambivalent role, and we must always remain aware of it. It seems to me, however, that discussion sometimes overlooks the distinction between wage rates per person per hour or per day and the size of the payroll. Any measure which guarantees an increase in the payroll at a time of unemployment is sure to promote either fuller employment or inflation or a mixture of both. But it doesn't necessarily follow (and I think many economists have taken that step without further argument) that any increase of wage rates will have the same consequences. An increase of wage rates may quite conceivably reduce the payroll. . . .[18]

If and when a severe depression again occurs, it is likely that organized business and large corporations will make new efforts to gain a general

[17] "Economists' Committee on Antitrust Law Policy," *American Economic Review*, September, 1932, pp. 465–469.
[18] Jacob Viner, "The Role of Costs in a System of Economic Liberalism," *Wage Determination and the Economics of Liberalism* (Washington, 1947), p. 32.

suspension of the antitrust laws. Our experience with the N.R.A., however, shows clearly that this policy retards recovery and creates problems more acute than the evils of the depression.

B. Certificates of Immunity Against Antitrust Prosecution Granted to Business Enterprisers in Wartime Production

Section 12 of the Small Business Mobilization Act (1942), 56 Stat. 357, provided that "whenever the Chairman of the War Production Board shall, after consultation with the Attorney General, find, and so certify to the Attorney General in writing, *that the doing of any act or thing, or the omission to do any act or thing, by one or more persons* . . . is requisite to the prosecution of the war, such act, thing, or omission shall be deemed in the public interest and no prosecution or civil action shall be commenced with reference thereto under the antitrust laws of the United States or the Federal Trade Commission Act. . . . This section shall remain in force until six months after the termination of the present war." (Italics supplied.)

During the course of the war, more than 200 certificates of immunity were granted to various groups of business enterprisers—in big business firms as well as in small ones. The certificates granted stated simply a recommendation for joint action—such as joint action for "transporting petroleum," "the production of certain naval equipment," "penicillin production," "the marketing of petroleum," "General Electric and Westinghouse Co."— and provided that the doing of any act with reference thereto was requisite to the prosecution of the war.

It is important to note that the activity immunized was "any act or thing" done by one or more persons engaged in wartime production which would be considered to be illegal under the antitrust laws. Such acts could include price fixing, a division of sales territory, a restriction of production, or the elimination of competitors. In effect, the grant of immunity was in the nature of a grant of pardon for any illegal act—civil or criminal—which a person or persons might do in connection with joint action in the war effort. In no way was the immunity restricted to the doing of a specific directive issued by the W.P.B.

Antitrust Exemption in the Korean Mobilization Program

Section 708 of the Defense Production Act (1950-1955), as amended, authorizes the President to consult with representatives of industry, business, finance, agriculture, and labor on the making of voluntary agreements to further defense mobilization. No act requested by the President, the law provides, in pursuance to such a voluntary agreement, shall be construed as being within the prohibitions of the antitrust laws or the Federal Trade Commission Act. Provision is made for the Department of Justice and the Federal Trade Commission to scrutinize the requests and agreements. Approval by the Attorney General is also required before the exemptions can become effective. Since world tensions are likely to continue beyond 1955, it is possible that Congress will renew the exemption for companies coöperating in defense production.

From the standpoint of public policy, there do not appear to be real and compelling reasons for making *general* grants of immunity from the antitrust laws in time of war. A grant of immunity is a tremendous favor, and since the granting of such a favor is discretionary, it is possible for all sorts of abuses to develop in the administration of the law.

The immunity provided in the Defense Production Act of 1950, restricting exemptions to acts specifically requested by the government and found to be in the public interest, appears to reduce the dangers of abuse. If the defense officials believe that a *particular* arrangement is necessary for the defense program, it is appropriate for the government to grant an immunity for *that arrangement*. To grant an immunity without limitation, however, would seem to be too big a favor to pay for getting the coöperation of certain industries in time of war.

VI

AGRICULTURAL MARKETING AGREEMENTS

The Agricultural Marketing Agreement Act of 1937, as amended, authorizes the Secretary of Agriculture "to enter into marketing agreements with processors, producers, associations of producers, and others *engaged in the handling* of any agricultural commodity or product thereof." Further, the Act provides that "the making of any such agreement shall not be held to be in violation of any of the antitrust laws of the United States, and any such agreement shall be deemed to be lawful: *Provided*, That no such agreement shall remain in force after the termination of said sections." (7 U.S.C. 601–608b. Italics supplied.)

The plan to use marketing agreements as a method for enhancing farm income was originally adopted in 1933 as a part of the "New Deal" for farmers. The view was that agricultural commodities should have a current purchasing power with respect to the things which farmers buy approximately equivalent to their purchasing power in the base period (generally 1909–1914). In order to enhance farm prices, the federal government made provision (1) for "production control" in the case of numerous basic commodities and the payment of "benefit payments" to coöperators and (2) for the establishment of marketing agreements, especially in lines of production not covered by the benefit payment program. Provisions for the use of marketing agreements were reënacted in 1937, and this legislation has been continued to date.

A "marketing agreement" is a voluntary contract entered into by the Secretary of Agriculture and *handlers* of a particular agricultural commodity which is in the current of interstate commerce or which burdens, obstructs, or affects interstate commerce in the commodity. Such an agreement, in the first instance, affects only those who sign it. However, provision is made in the law for making the terms of the marketing agreement applicable to all handlers of the commodity, whether or not they sign the agreement. This is done by the issuance of a "marketing order" by the Secretary of Agriculture, declaring that the terms of the marketing agreement shall be effective upon all handlers of the crop in a given area. A "handler" is a wholesale dealer or distributor who buys from producers and resells in a controlled market area.

A marketing order can be issued by the Secretary of Agriculture to strengthen a marketing agreement only when (1) the *handlers* of not less than 50 percent—by volume—of the commodity covered by the agreement sign the agreement and (2) at least two-thirds of the *growers*—by number or by volume—approve the issuance of the order. The two-thirds majority means two-thirds of those voting in the referendum. If handlers fail or refuse to sign a marketing agreement, the Secretary may issue a marketing order on his own volition if he finds that such a procedure is the only practical way of enhancing the prices paid to first-hand producers. Most marketing agreements have been strengthened by marketing orders, and in some cases marketing orders have been issued without marketing agreements. Marketing agreements may cover *any* agricultural commodity. Marketing orders, however, may be issued only for certain designated products—mainly fresh fruits, vegetables, nuts, and milk.

In 1954 the Department of Agriculture reported that there were some 24 federal marketing agreements and 25 marketing orders in effect for fruits, vegetables, and nuts (see Table 21). There were also marketing agreements and orders for the handling of shade-grown cigar leaf tobacco and for anti-hog-cholera serum and hog-cholera virus.

Some 49 federal marketing orders were also in operation during 1954 applicable to the handling of milk in various areas. The Agricultural Marketing Agreement Act of 1937 provides (Section 8c, Par. 5) for the issuance of an order classifying milk in accordance with the form or purpose for which it is used. It also provides for the establishment of a price for each use classification which *all handlers* are required *to pay* to producers or coöperative associations of producers. As is the case with all orders issued under the Agricultural Marketing Agreement Act of 1937, a public hearing must precede the issuance of a marketing order for milk, and no order can be issued unless it is approved by at least two-thirds of the producers, by number or volume, who deliver milk for sale in the marketing area to be covered by the regulation.

The minimum prices fixed in milk orders are established on a formula basis which takes into consideration the supply and demand for milk, general economic conditions, and the value of milk for manufacturing purposes. These formula prices can be changed only after a public hearing at which suggested changes must be justified. The order establishes minimum prices for each use classification, and "surplus" prices are those which are paid for milk in excess of fluid requirements. "Surplus" milk is utilized in making cheese, ice cream, powdered milk, and other manufactured products. Federal milk orders do not permit the destruction of any milk which is delivered to a handler (milk dealer) by a producer unless the producer is paid for such destroyed milk.

TABLE 21.   Marketing Agreements and Orders in Effect for Fruits, Vegetables, and Nuts, 1954.

Commodity	Area by States
Grapefruit	California and Arizona
Lemons	California and Arizona
Oranges (navel)	California and Arizona
Oranges, grapefruit and tangerines	Florida
Tokay grapes	California
Peaches	Colorado
Peaches	Georgia
Peaches	Utah
Bartlett pears, plums, and Elberta peaches	California
Beurré hardy pears	California
Winter pears	Oregon, Washington, California
Dried prunes	California
Raisins	California
Fresh peas and cauliflower	California
Potatoes	Idaho and Oregon
Potatoes	Colorado
Potatoes	Oregon and California
Potatoes	North Carolina and Virginia
Potatoes	Eastern South Dakota
Potatoes[a]	Massachusetts, Rhode Island, Connecticut, New Hampshire, and Vermont
Potatoes	Washington
Almonds	California
Filberts	Oregon and Washington
Pecans	Georgia, Alabama, South Carolina, Florida, and Mississippi
Walnuts	California, Oregon, and Washington

[a] Marketing order issued without an accompanying marketing agreement.

The purpose of a marketing agreement or a marketing order is to control the marketing of a particular commodity so as to raise prices to farmers *to the parity level.* In influencing prices, it is provided as a basic rule that no action may be taken under an agreement or order which establishes or maintains prices *above the parity* level.

Under the federal law, agreements may be made and orders may be issued fixing the *minimum* prices which handlers shall *pay* producers *for milk.* Resale prices for milk may not be fixed. For all other commodities, however, agreements and orders may not contain provisions fixing specific prices, and control over prices is exercised *indirectly* by controlling the supplies which are shipped to consuming centers.

Supply control under a marketing agreement program rests upon the handlers and is exercised by a "control board" selected by the Secretary of Agriculture from members of the trade. This board regulates the quantities which may be shipped to particular central markets during a specified

FIG. 26. Crates of illegal oranges. Under the marketing agreement for navel oranges, it is illegal for handlers to resell small-sized navel oranges, i.e., oranges 2¼ inches in diameter or smaller, in the United States or Canada. All such oranges can be sold only for conversion into by-products such as juice, or for export to countries other than Canada. This makes it possible to secure higher prices for the large-sized oranges, for it removes lower-priced substitutes. (Photograph: *Daily News*, Los Angeles.)

period. Products set aside to decrease *market* supplies are diverted to other uses—such as livestock feed—or are sold abroad at low prices (see Fig. 26). In order to assist in improving the prices of products *sold in regular market channels*, Congress has provided funds for purchasing quantities of those products which show a price "weakness." The supplies so purchased are thereupon sold abroad or used for domestic relief purposes.

The control board also investigates and makes reports on violations to the Secretary of Agriculture. The Secretary, in turn, reports violations to the Department of Justice for prosecution. Three types of legal action may be taken against a violator. They consist of (1) civil action to secure an injunction preventing the person from further violation, (2) criminal action to impose a fine of not less than $50 and not more than $500 for each violation, and (3) civil action to assess damages equal to three times the value of the product shipped in violation of the order.

A number of states have adopted legislation to provide for the making of state-wide marketing agreements and orders in accordance with procedures similar to those specified in the federal law. Growers and processors in California, in particular, have turned to the use of such legislation to enhance their incomes. In 1954 some 30 commodities were covered by marketing agreements and orders under the laws of that state. Products under marketing programs include apples, bedding plants, dates, dried figs, grapefruit, honey, lemons, lettuce, lima beans, olives, peaches, pears, plums, prunes, raisins, walnuts, and wine. Supplies in excess of "reasonable market requirements" for the season, salable at the prices a trade group would like to get, are set aside and diverted to other uses or outlets. The California legislation has been held to be constitutional as a valid exercise of the police power of the state (see also Chap. 28, p. 641).

AGRICULTURAL MARKETING AGREEMENTS AND OUR TRADITIONAL POLICY OF COMPETITION

Federal and state legislation providing for the establishment of marketing agreements, it may be observed, gives handlers of agricultural products the privilege to form legalized monopolies or cartels, if approval for concerted action is secured from the respective federal or state secretary of agriculture.

The use of marketing agreements as a means for enhancing farm prices was introduced during the period of the great depression. At that time the plight of farmers was a serious one, and Congress and various state legislatures were willing to approve a measure which made for artificial scarcity and higher prices. At the present time, however, with widespread needs—at home and abroad—for more and better food at lower prices, a policy of legalized monopoly in the pricing of essential foodstuffs, many economists believe, cannot be socially justified.

Persons stating the case *for* marketing agreements emphasize that prices for numerous farm products, such as milk, are not determined in open market trading at central assembly points. Rather, in many situations, such prices are determined by the unilateral decisions of *organized dealers* or by the joint action of dealers and producers. In such cases, the public has no voice in price determination and no remedy against extortion. A policy of giving the government supervisory power over prices, it is reasoned, provides greater assurance that the prices fixed will be equitable as among all groups.

VII

ASSOCIATIONS OF PRODUCERS OF AQUATIC PRODUCTS

The Fishery Coöperative Marketing Act of 1934 provides that

persons engaged in the fishery industry, *as fishermen*, catching, collecting, or cultivating aquatic products, or *as planters* of aquatic products on public or private beds, may act together in associations, corporate or otherwise, with or without capital stock, in collectively catching, producing, preparing for market, processing, handling, and marketing in interstate and foreign commerce, such products of said persons so engaged. . . . If the Secretary of Commerce shall have reason to believe that any such association monopolizes or restrains trade in interstate or foreign commerce to such an extent that the price of any aquatic product is unduly enhanced by reason thereof, he shall serve upon such association a complaint. (15 U.S.C. 521. Italics supplied.)

Under the Reorganization Plan of 1939, the authority to supervise prices, serve complaints, and issue cease-and-desist orders was given to the Secretary of the Interior.

In the report of the House committee on the proposed Fishery Coöperative Marketing Act, it was stated that "The purpose of this bill is to provide for the fishery industry coöperative associations such as are provided for farmers by the Capper-Volstead Act. This bill applies to producers of aquatic products and not to farmers."[19] The only essential difference in the two acts, it may be noted, is that scrutiny over the prices charged by associations of fishermen or planters of aquatic products is exercised by the Secretary of the Interior whereas the Secretary of Agriculture fulfills this function in the case of agricultural marketing associations.

MARKETING PROBLEMS CONFRONTING FISHERMEN

One of several economic difficulties faced by fishermen is the fact that they usually have meager resources, poor bargaining power, and little or no information on market conditions. Fishing boats are generally owned by individual fishermen, and the owner usually serves as captain and as a fisherman along with a crew. When ownership does exist, the fishing boats are usually heavily mortgaged, and the mortgages are often held by the fish dealers or fish canneries. In some cases, fishing boats are owned outright by

---

[19] Committee on Merchant Marine, Radio, and Fisheries, *Authorizing Associations of Producers of Aquatic Products*, 73rd Congress, second session, House Report 1504, May 7, 1934, p. 1.

fish dealers and processors. Historically, fishermen have usually been paid in "shares"; and in many cases they continue to work with the captain on a share basis, with a specified deduction being made for the boat. The typical income for most fishermen is thus an income on their labor.

A further economic problem of fishermen arises in the fact that fishing is conducted over wide areas, and frequent deliveries must be made to local buyers to prevent spoilage. As a result, there are few large concentration points for the delivery of fresh fish, and fishermen typically find that there is little or no buying competition in the purchase of their products. Fishermen, moreover, have to sell their products as soon as they are caught, and they are thus urgent sellers. Dealers and processors, on the other hand, are in a position to refrigerate, freeze, salt, or can the fish and sell it when supplies are less plentiful.

The economic problems of fishermen have long been recognized by public officials, and the enactment of the act of 1934 was largely sponsored by persons in government in an attempt to aid the fishermen. In March 1954, the Fish and Wildlife Service reported there were 77 fishermen's coöperative associations in operation. The number of fishery coöperatives in the various states is shown in Table 22.

TABLE 22.   Number of Fishery Coöperatives in the United States and Alaska, 1954.

Alaska	6	Michigan	1
California	16	Minnesota	3
Florida	9	Oregon	2
Idaho	1	New Jersey	3
Louisiana	4	Rhode Island	1
Maine	10	Washington	13
Maryland	1	Wisconsin	1
Massachusetts	4	Texas	2

(Source: Fish and Wildlife Service, U.S. Dept. of the Interior.)

Coöperative associations are utilized largely for bargaining purposes, and only a few fishermen's associations maintain established places of business or endeavor to serve as dealers or processors of the fish caught by their members. In most cases, fishermen do not have the necessary financial resources for establishing a coöperative association to process or market fish.

VIII

MANUFACTURING AND HANDLING OF HOG-CHOLERA SERUM AND HOG-CHOLERA VIRUS

Section 57, 49 Stat. 750, approved August 24, 1935, as an amendment to the Agricultural Adjustment Act, provides that "the Secretary of Agriculture shall have the power, after due notice and opportunity for hearing, to enter into marketing agreements with manufacturers and others engaged in the handling of anti-hog-cholera serum and hog-cholera virus . . . as is in the current of interstate or foreign commerce. . . . Such persons are hereafter in this Act referred to as 'handlers.' The making of any such agreement shall not be held to be in violation of any of the antitrust laws of the United States, and any such agreement shall be deemed to be lawful." (7 U.S.C. 852.)

Congress undertook to exercise a control over the manufacturing and handling of hog-cholera serum and hog-cholera virus primarily to insure an adequate supply of uniform, high-quality, fresh products, sufficient to meet ordinary demands as well as those which might arise from an epidemic. Other factors leading to the adoption of the law were a need to stamp out unfair methods of competition and unfair trade practices in the marketing of serum and virus products.

About 80 percent of the annual production of hogs, it is estimated, is treated with hog-cholera serum and hog-cholera virus. In the use of the virus and serum, hogs are artificially infected with a mild case of cholera, and the serum is used to cure the disease and to immunize the hogs against future infection.

When the officials of the Department of Agriculture began to work with manufacturers of anti-hog-cholera products to secure uniform standards and adequate reserve supplies, the manufacturers, it is reported, insisted that they be permitted to set a price which would cover the higher costs involved. The *quid pro quo* for their coöperation, therefore, was the granting of their request that the antitrust laws be relaxed so that producers could assure themselves of adequate prices.

At the present time, there are some thirty-five firms producing hog-cholera serum and hog-cholera virus; and in accordance with the marketing agreement which has been made, all firms sell at the same base price, with transportation allowed and prepaid to wholesalers or retailers anywhere in the United States. This price is established and managed by a "control agency" of twelve members, representing manufacturers and distributors.

IX

RESALE PRICE-MAINTENANCE CONTRACTS

The Miller-Tydings Fair Trade Act (1937), amending the Sherman Act, provides

That nothing herein contained shall render illegal, contracts or agreements prescribing minimum prices for the resale of a commodity which bears . . . the trade-mark, brand, or name of the producer or distributor of such commodity and which is in free and open competition with commodities of the same general class produced or distributed by others, when contracts or agreements of that description are lawful as applied to intrastate transactions . . . (15 U.S.C. 1.)

The purpose of the Miller-Tydings Act is to legalize the making of resale price-maintenance contracts in *interstate* commerce when such contracts are legal under state laws. By its terms, such contracts are removed from the prohibitions of the Sherman Act (1890) and are declared not to be an unfair method of competition under the Federal Trade Commission Act (1914). A resale price-maintenance contract, as we shall explain in a subsequent chapter, is a contract made by a manufacturer of trademarked products which fixes the minimum wholesale and retail prices of such products as they move on to the final consumers (see Chap. 21).

X

AIR CARRIERS

The Civil Aeronautics Act (1938) provides that consolidations, mergers, interlocking directorships, and agreements between or among carriers with respect to rates and a pooling of earnings are prohibited unless they are approved by the Civil Aeronautics Board. Any person affected by such *approved* orders, the act provides, "shall be, and is, relieved from the operations of the 'antitrust laws' . . . in so far as may be necessary to enable such person to do anything authorized, approved, or required by such order." (49 U.S.C. 488, 489, 492, 494.)

The air transportation industry in the United States developed with practically no economic regulation. Rate wars and cutthroat competition were frequent, and by 1938 a number of the carriers were facing serious financial trouble. During the hearings in 1938 on the bill to create the Civil Aeronautics Authority, an industry spokesman testified that chaotic conditions in the air transportation industry made it impossible to secure adequate investment funds. More than one-half of the private capital which had been invested in the air transportation system, it was stated, had already been lost.[20]

The difficult financial position of the industry, at the time the Civil Aeronautics Act was being written, appears to have been the principal reason which Congress had for permitting concerted action by the carriers on rates, provided that such agreements are approved by the Authority. It may be noted that the exemption granted to air carriers is essentially the same as that extended to the water carriers, as discussed in the section on the Shipping Act of 1916.

XI

TELEGRAPH COMPANY MERGERS

Section 221, 48 Stat. 1080, approved March 8, 1943, provides that telegraph company mergers approved by the Federal Communications Commission are not within the purview of the antitrust laws which would otherwise make the transactions unlawful. (47 U.S.C. 221, 222[b], 222[c].)

This legislation was requested of Congress by the Federal Communications Commission in order to end the wasteful duplication of telegraph facil-

[20] Committee on Interstate and Foreign Commerce, *Civil Aeronautics Bill*, 75th Congress, third session, House Report 2254, April 28, 1938, pp. 1-2.

ities. The Western Union Telegraph Company and the Postal Telegraph Company controlled the domestic public message service, and the opinion of the Federal Communications Commission was that substantial economies could be effected by the merger.

In reporting on its study of the proposed legislation, the House Committee on Interstate and Foreign Commerce also emphasized the costly waste of maintaining duplicate facilities. According to the Committee,

> Already the government, through the Reconstruction Finance Corporation, has advanced around $9,000,000 to Postal to keep it going. Postal's current monthly loss is around $400,000. The Nation cannot afford to lose the telegraph service capacity represented by the facilities of that system. The existence of strong competitive modes of communication outside the telegraph industry means, moreover, that merger of the domestic telegraph carriers will not result in a monopoly in the domestic communications field. If such a merger occurs, there will still remain severe and effective competition between the merged telegraph company and the telephone and the air-mail.[21]

On May 13, 1943, the Western Union Company announced the completion of an agreement by which it would purchase the Postal system outright, and the proposed agreement was subsequently approved by the Federal Communications Commission. From an economic point of view, a merger of the only two telegraph companies in the nation does, in fact, create a monopoly in the telegraph business. The competition of air-mail and telephone services can only be classed as *substitute* competition.

XII

INSURANCE COMPANIES

The McCarran Act (1945) partially exempts insurance companies from the federal antitrust laws. After June 30, 1948, it is provided that the federal antitrust laws shall be made applicable to the business of insurance "to the extent that such business is not regulated by the state law." (15 U.S.C. 1011–1013.)

At the time of their establishment in the United States, insurance companies—like banks—considered themselves to be a local business, subject to control by the states. An early group of Supreme Court decisions supported this view and held that insurance was not "commerce" and therefore not subject to federal regulation.[22] As a result, most of the states adopted various systems of regulation. Many abuses, however, developed under state regulation. In particular, important groups of insurance companies adopted the practice of meeting together to make their rates by agreement.

---

[21] Committee on Interstate and Foreign Commerce, *Consolidations and Mergers of Domestic Telegraph Carriers*, 78th Congress, first session, House Report 69, February 1, 1943, p. 3.

[22] *Paul* v. *Virginia*, 8 Wall. 168 (1868). The other cases are reviewed by Justice Black in *U.S.* v. *South-Eastern Underwriters Assn.*, 322 U.S. 533 (1944).

In 1944 the Supreme Court rendered its decision in the *South-Eastern Underwriters Association* case, which the Department of Justice had brought to test the validity of monopolistic action in rate making in the fire insurance field.[23] In brief, the Court held that the "business of insurance" is commerce and that the federal antitrust laws are applicable to insurance companies which conduct their activities across state lines. This decision meant (1) that every insurance company engaging in interstate commerce—and most companies are—shall henceforth act independently in making its rates and (2) that there shall be no private agreements or coercion on rates among insurance companies.

The state antitrust laws have never been effectively enforced, and many insurance company executives believed that they were effectively insulated from the principles of free enterprise and price competition. The *South-Eastern* decision, placing insurance companies under the Sherman Act, accordingly, proved to be very unsettling, for it threatened to upset collective action in rate making. Thereupon, insurance companies turned their attention to Congress. At first an attempt was made to secure general legislative exemption from the Sherman Act for the insurance business. This approach failed, however, and a compromise measure was finally worked out in the McCarran Act of March 9, 1945.

The McCarran Act affirms the principle of state regulation, which the insurance companies desire to preserve, and provides that no act of Congress shall be construed to invalidate or supersede laws enacted by the states to regulate insurance companies. However, after June 30, 1948, the act declares, the Sherman, Clayton, and Federal Trade Commission Acts "shall be applicable to the business of insurance to the extent that such business is not regulated by State law." The meaning of this legislation is that in so far as the states provide "regulation," over rates, the Department of Justice is kept out. In effect, therefore, the McCarran Act grants the insurance companies a *partial exemption* from the federal antitrust laws.[24]

In a special statement on the McCarran Act, President Roosevelt declared on March 10, 1945, "Congress did not intend to permit *private* rate-fixing, which the Antitrust Act forbids, but was willing to permit actual regulation of rates by affirmative action of the states." The burden of direct control has thus been placed squarely on the shoulders of the states.

Are the forty-eight individual states now providing a satisfactory level of regulation and direct control over the insurance industry? This is a controversial question. In most states, rates for fire, casualty, and inland marine insurance are *initially* fixed by private "rating bureaus" whose services (formulation of rates) are subscribed to by the companies. Life insurance rates are usually free of control, and public supervision is primarily con-

---

[23] *U.S. v. South-Eastern Underwriters Assn*, 322 U.S. 533 (1944).

[24] The McCarran Act provides further that the Sherman Act shall continue to be applicable "to any agreement to boycott, coerce, or intimidate, or act of boycott, coercion, or intimidation."

cerned with the financial soundness of life insurance companies. Rates for ocean marine insurance are not controlled.

The case for state regulation of insurance finds support in the fact that the state commissions are typically maintaining high standards for the investments made by insurance companies and for the adequacy of their reserves to meet policy commitments. The state commissions, moreover, perform an essential service (a) in regulating the types and coverage of policies sold within their respective jurisdictions and (b) in assisting policy holders to secure a prompt and fair settlement of their claims. State commissions are aware of local problems, and their activities are responsive to the needs of local people. The main issue in state regulation is whether the forty-eight states, acting individually, can and do provide adequate control over rates to keep them down to competitive levels.

The McCarran Act contemplates that state control will protect the public from excessive rates, in lieu of competition under the federal antitrust laws. What form does state control take? State insurance legislation typically provides that "premium rates for insurance shall not be excessive, inadequate, or unfairly discriminatory." What is an excessive rate? No standards are given, and each of the state commissions proceeds to approve or disapprove rates in accordance with its own views and opinions. The effectiveness of rate control is further limited by the fact that most states do not have adequate facilities for supervising rates. In many instances, the state insurance commission consists of one commissioner and only a few staff members. Inadequate personnel and funds appear to be the rule. The office of insurance commissioner, moreover, is a political position, either appointive or elective, and frequent changes in personnel make it difficult to pursue a firm and consistent policy.

At present, it appears that buyers of insurance secure a considerable measure of protection against excessive rates from (1) the considerable number of companies operating in each field, (2) the pressure of various companies to offer moderate rates in order to secure business, and (3) the operation of mutual companies which refund a portion of the premium income to policyholders. If a plan of competition on rates were *promoted* by the government, instead of being curtailed, it is probable that it would provide a very much greater protection against excessive rates. At the same time, state control could be utilized to supervise sales and the adequacy of rates at local levels.

SPECIAL EXEMPTION ENJOYED BY MARINE INSURANCE COMPANIES

A special exemption from the antitrust laws was granted to associations of marine insurance companies in the Merchant Marine Act of 1920 (Act of June 5, 1920, c. 250, 41 Stat. 988, 46 U.S.C. 885). According to this statute, "Nothing contained in the 'antitrust laws' . . . shall be construed as declaring illegal an association entered into by marine insurance companies . . . to transact a marine insurance business and reinsurance business in the United States."

The exemption granted to associations of marine insurance companies appears to have been made on the ground that it would serve to encourage their development. Thus, the Senate Committee on Commerce in its report on the legislation declared, "If we can develop marine insurance as it should be developed in this country, we can do nothing better for an American (merchant) marine. Only about 10 percent of our hull insurance and only about 25 or 30 percent of all kinds of our marine insurance are done today by American companies."[25]

XIII

RAILROADS AND OTHER SURFACE CARRIERS SUBJECT TO CONTROL BY THE INTERSTATE COMMERCE COMMISSION

The Reed-Bulwinkle Act (1948), Public Law 662, 80th Congress, second session, amending the Interstate Commerce Act, provides that

(2) Any carrier party to an agreement between or among two or more carriers relating to rates, fares, classifications, divisions, allowances, or charges . . . may, under such rules and regulations as the Commission may prescribe, apply to the Commission for approval of the agreement, and the Commission shall by order approve any such agreement . . . if it finds that, by reason of furtherance of the national transportation policy declared in this Act, the relief provided in paragraph (9) should apply. . . .

(9) Parties to any agreement approved by the Commission . . . are . . . hereby relieved from the operation of the antitrust laws with respect to the making of such agreement, and with respect to the carrying out of such agreement in conformity with its provisions and in conformity with the terms and conditions prescribed by the Commission.

The essence of the Reed-Bulwinkle Act is that agreements on rates made by railroads, truck lines, and inland waterway carriers subject to the jurisdiction of the Interstate Commerce Commission, if approved by and filed with the Commission, shall be relieved from the operation of the antitrust laws. The Commission, moreover, is instructed to approve rate agreements if it finds that they further the national transportation policy (see Chap. 24). In addition to the exemption provided in the Reed-Bulwinkle Act, the Transportation Act of 1940 (49 U.S.C. 5) provides that agreements made with respect to a division of traffic and joint rates, as well as mergers, leases, and acquisitions, if approved by the Interstate Commerce Commission, shall be exempted from the operation of the antitrust laws. The act of 1940 amended and codified a series of earlier acts providing for such types of joint action by the railroads. The provisions in the Reed-Bulwinkle Act, legalizing monopolistic activity on rate making, it may be noted, are essentially the same as those contained in the Shipping Act of 1916 and the Civil Aeronautics Act of 1938.

[25] Committee on Commerce, *Promotion and Maintenance of the American Merchant Marine*, 66th Congress, second session, Senate Report 573, May 4, 1920, p. 9.

The Supreme Court in the *Trans-Missouri Freight Association* (1897) and *Joint Traffic Association* (1898) cases held that the Sherman Act applies to agreements on rates in the railroad field, as well as in industry, and declared that combinations of railroads for fixing rates are illegal.[26] Subsequently, however, the Sherman Act was not again applied to collective action on rates until 1942, when the Department of Justice initiated a grand jury investigation in Chicago against the price-fixing activities of rate bureaus and carrier-shipper rate conferences. The point of view taken by the Department of Justice was that joint action by the railroads in the form of rate bureaus, conferences, or otherwise, to agree upon and fix the rates that are filed with the Interstate Commerce Commission, is illegal *per se*. A "rate bureau," it may be noted, is an association of carriers operating in a certain area, formed for the purpose of fixing the rates to be submitted to the Interstate Commerce Commission. A "carrier-shipper conference," on the other hand, is a meeting of carriers and shippers in a given region or area to consider proposed changes in rates. Rate conferences are arranged by the organized railroads, and their purpose is to give shippers an opportunity to express their views on rate proposals and also to provide the carriers with an opportunity to estimate more precisely the rates which the traffic will bear.

The position of the Department of Justice was subsequently strengthened by the decision of the Supreme Court in 1945 in *Georgia v. Pennsylvania R.R. Company*.[27] The state of Georgia had charged a group of carriers with collusive action to maintain rates which were discriminatory to Georgia, and in a preliminary decision the Court held by a five-to-four vote that the state could bring action against the alleged conspiracy. In the view of the Court, the Sherman Act was still fully applicable to the railroads.[28]

The determined effort of the Antitrust Division to prosecute railroad rate agreements, as well as the decision in the *Georgia* case, stimulated efforts by the Association of American Railroads to seek exemption from the antitrust laws by legislative action. In the view of the railroads, rate bureaus and rate conferences had been continuously and openly used for over fifty years. They had been used, moreover, with the full knowledge of the Interstate Commerce Commission and the Department of Justice. Collective action on rates, it was stated, provides a practical procedure whereby any shipper or any carrier may propose rate changes, secure advance notice of any proposed changes, and present evidence against rate changes which would affect his business adversely. The legislative battle over the Reed-Bulwinkle bills was bitter and prolonged, but finally in June, 1948, the organized railroads were able to secure the passage of the desired legislation over a presidential veto.

---

[26] 166 U.S. 290 (1897) and 171 U.S. 505 (1898).
[27] 324 U.S. 439 (1945).
[28] 324 U.S. 439, 456–457 (1945).

THE NEED TO RECONSIDER THE EXEMPTIONS WHICH HAVE BEEN GRANTED TO THE ANTITRUST LAWS

It is fully recognized that in certain segments of the economy (notably in the case of railroads, air lines, telegraph lines, shipping lines, labor unions, and coöperative associations) it is not possible or practical to have two-sided price competition of the open-market type. It is possible, however, in such cases, to preserve and maintain *competitive pressures* to moderate the extreme demands made by certain sellers. A particular railroad company, for example, having considerable degrees of local monopoly power along its line, is usually competitive with other railroads at certain points. It is also frequently competitive with other forms of transportation—such as water, motor, and air. It is possible for government to utilize these competitive pressures to moderate the demands of a given railroad company for higher rates by requiring each business unit to make its rates independently. The resulting competition is not perfect or pure, or even the type normally called for by the antitrust laws. It is, however, a form of *competitive pressure*—or substitute competition—which the antitrust laws contemplate and which Congress can effectively maintain, if it has the will and courage to do so.

In the case of labor unions, the principle of collective bargaining is now firmly established and accepted. The acceptance of collective bargaining, however, does not mean that there must be a complete organization of all *employers* in a national industry or of all *employees* in that industry for bargaining purposes. That would mean complete, two-sided monopoly, without competitive pressures to moderate the demands of either party. In the case of coöperative associations, it is possible that a large measure of competitive action can be preserved if a coöperative is not permitted to control a large part—or all—of the national production of a particular commodity. It is recognized that the bargaining power of individual members can be strengthened by collective action; and as long as no restriction of output or membership is attempted, such bargaining gains do not injure the general public. If a given coöperative association were restricted in its activities to a limited locality which did not cover the entire area of production, it would rarely be in a position to gain by reducing its output, for other groups would expand *their* production with any increase in price.

In all cases, it may be observed, the exemptions granted to particular industries and activities were secured by the political pressure and influence of special interest groups. Private, commercial advantage is thus the basic reason for the existence of the special exemptions. In each instance, there is substantial reason to believe that the public interest would be served either (1) by maintaining as much independent action as is possible among the various utility or coöperative units in a given industry or (2) by maintaining real price competition among the numerous independent sellers, especially in wholesale, retail, and export trade.

A long step has been taken in the direction of a universal system of legalized private monopoly. The further acceptance of such a system, it is generally believed, can only lead to a greater amount of government intervention in business, for consumers, generally, will increasingly demand the imposition of direct controls over the privately managed prices and business incomes. The alternative is the maintenance of a policy of competition and economic freedom. If the latter is to be done, it will be necessary to reconsider and reëxamine all of the exemptions which have thus far been made to the antitrust laws.

Suggestions for Further Reading

Abrams, S. K., "Antitrust Laws in National Emergency," *Minnesota Law Review*, April, 1952, pp. 490–505.

Casselman, P. H., *The Coöperative Movement and Some of Its Problems* (New York, 1952).

Edwards, C. D., *Maintaining Competition* (New York, 1949).

Evans, Frank, and Stokdyk, E. A., *The Law of Agricultural Coöperative Marketing* (Rochester, 1937).

Fournier, Leslie T., "Webb-Pomerene Law," *American Economic Review*, March, 1932, pp. 18–33.

Hawkins, Wallace, and Wallace, Charles B., "Antitrust During National Emergencies," *Texas Law Review*, December, 1945, pp. 51–72.

Lester, Richard A., "Reflections on the 'Labor Monopoly' Issue," *Journal of Political Economy*, December, 1947, pp. 513–536.

Machlup, Fritz, "Monopolistic Wage Determination as a Part of the General Problem of Monopoly," *Wage Determination and the Economics of Liberalism*, Chamber of Commerce of the United States (Washington, 1947).

Rohrer, Margaret, *State Regulation of Insurance* (Berkeley, 1951).

Stelzer, Irwin M., "Economic Consequences of a Successful Antitrust Prosecution," *Insurance Law Journal*, February, 1954, pp. 86–90.

CHAPTER 14

Patents and the Activity of Government
in Advancing Technology

A basic economic function of government, we have seen, is to create and establish institutions which will increase the real income—the level of living —of consumers generally. As a means of effectuating this function, governments in Europe early undertook to encourage technology and the useful arts by granting inventors and authors property rights in their inventions or writings for limited periods of time. In the present chapter, we shall consider the activity of the United States in promoting the progress of science by granting property rights in the form of patents as a reward for invention. Consideration will be given to the nature of patents, to the monopolistic abuses which have arisen in their use, and to various proposals which have been made for improving the work of government in stimulating industrial research and invention.

Patent grants are a part but not the whole of the means employed by government to stimulate research. In this chapter we shall also give attention to the growing activity of the federal government in sponsoring research by the direct expenditure of funds. At the present time, the United States government is the largest sponsor of industrial research in the world, and the view of many national leaders is that its present research activities should be further expanded in the years which lie ahead. The steady march of science and technology, it is emphasized, is an essential condition for the production of more and better goods, as well as for military security.

How, it may be asked, is the rate of advance of technology to be maintained? How are the gains of technology to be made available to the people —to the nation as a whole? (See Fig. 27.) It is here that the social sciences come into use to supplement the work of the technological sciences. One of the purposes of competition is to provide a means by which improvements in technology will be passed on to consumers in the form of more and better goods at lower prices. In so far as there is active price competition and independent enterprise, control over market supplies cannot be exercised, and growing quantities of economic goods made possible by improved technology become available to all at lower prices. Government in the economic sphere, therefore, has the twofold duty (1) of stimulating invention and the useful arts and (2) of adopting measures which will insure that the fruits of

material progress will be passed on to the masses in the form of a constantly
rising level of living.

It is frequently said that advances in technology have far outstripped advances in the social sciences, and that the great need of today is the development of means to control technology. A study of our antitrust laws
and their enforcement indicates, however, that the basic problem in social

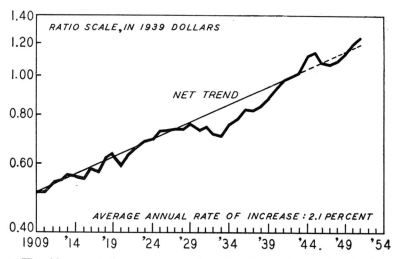

Fig. 27. The rising trend of output per man-hour in private industry. Growing improvements in *technology* are an important factor accounting for the rising trend in produc-
tivity. The gain in output per man-hour is the joint product of labor *and* material agents.
Labor's claim on its share of the rising output is an important factor in wage negotiations.
(Source: John W. Kendrick, "National Productivity and Its Long-Term Projection," a
paper before the Conference on Research in Income and Wealth, National Bureau of
Economic Research, May, 1951; and data from the National Industrial Conference Board,
New York City.)

control today is not so much one of new techniques of control as it is one
of making our present techniques effective. In the last analysis, social control
means political control, and we are faced with a fundamental problem of
adopting and applying the economic knowledge which experience has shown
to be sound and workable.

THE USE OF PATENTS TO INDUCE DISCLOSURE
OF NEW IDEAS

With the rise of strong national states in Europe at the close of the Middle
Ages, sovereigns began to exercise their power in ways which they believed
would increase the general good. In England in 1331, for example, John
Kempe, a weaver from Flanders, was given a grant of the king's protection
in return for his promise to teach the weaving art to workers in England.
Gradually the kings began the practice of making patent grants as a reward
to enterprisers for introducing new arts and processes. Although the pre-

rogative of the kings was frequently abused by the practice of granting patent rights for contributions to the royal treasury, the growing power of Parliament in England largely curbed such abuses by the enactment of the Statute of Monopolies in 1624. This famous statute condemned private monopoly in the regularly established trades but recognized limited grants of exclusive privilege for "new manufactures."

In holding out a property right to inventors, the sovereigns sought to induce inventors to bring "trade secrets" *out into the open* so that they could be made a part of the common knowledge of society. As an inducement and reward for doing so, *litterae patentes* were granted to inventors giving them the right to exclude others from making, using, or vending their invention for a limited number of years, after which the invention was to become free to all to use without restriction. The word "patent," it may be noted, comes from the Latin *patens*, present participle of *patere*, "to be open," and the "open letters" granted by a sovereign to inventors were addressed to all citizens in the realm.

Legal authorities have long considered the granting of patent rights to inventors to be a fair method of compensating them for the expense and arduous work which are usually involved in research and scientific invention. Inventions, it is often said, are a product of genius, but it has also been observed that genius is about 2 percent inspiration and 98 percent perspiration. The right of limited monopoly offered to inventors is thus a sort of *quid pro quo* for the time, effort, and money which ordinarily must be spent in developing a new formula, machine, or process.

In formulating the relations of government to business in the United States, the framers of the Federal Constitution provided in 1787 that "The Congress shall have power . . . to promote the progress of science and useful arts, by securing for limited times to authors and inventors the exclusive right to their respective writings and discoveries" (Art. 1, Sec. 8). The constitutional provision on the making of grants of "exclusive right" to authors and inventors was implemented by statute law in 1790, 1793, 1836, 1870, and 1952. The Patent Act of 1952 was adopted to codify existing patent statutes and also to make actual changes in the statutes, particularly with reference to the conditions for patentability.[1]

THE MONOPOLY ASPECT OF PATENTS

A patent in American law may be defined as a grant from the government to an inventor of "the right to exclude others from making, using, or selling" the invention claimed in the patent grant. The right to exclude others exists for a period of 17 years and extends throughout the United States and its territories. When the government actually issues a patent to an inventor, it sends him a certificate, with a blue ribbon and red seal, in which it is stated

[1] The complete text of the Patent Act of 1952, together with the explanatory notes of the Congressional Committee, is available in the *Journal of the Patent Office Society*, August, 1952.

that the government has granted the inventor the right to exclude others from making, using or selling the invention. In principle, a patent is the grant as recorded on the certificate; but in the vernacular, the word "patent" means the printed copy of the specifications and claims. A printed copy of any invention on which a United States patent has been issued may be secured from the Patent Office for 25¢.

A patent grant gives an inventor the right to exclude others for a limited period of time from making, using, or selling a product—such as glass bottles —*according to the formula, machine, or method developed by the inventor.* What the patent does for an inventor is merely to give him a right—in effect, a sword—by which he can exclude others from practicing *his* invention. The phrase "exclusive right," when used in the field of patents, means the right to employ legal processes to exclude others. The phrase "patent monopoly," in turn, refers to the property right vested in an inventor and created by statute, to exclude others from the practice of the invention set forth in the claims of the patent.

It is sometimes said that the patent system of exclusive rights is incompatible with our antitrust law policy of preventing monopoly and maintaining competition. Both arrangements, however, have as their purpose the encouragement of production and economic abundance. The basic purpose of patents is to encourage inventors by giving them exclusive rights over their inventions. Although others cannot use a patent without permission of the owner, they are free to invent something of their own, toward the same end. This stimulates rivalry to make improvements. The public advantage in getting new products, or more economical processes of production, it is believed, outweighs the evils of exclusive control which, presumably, will continue for only a limited period of time. The "main object" of a patent grant, as Justice Storey declared in 1830, is "to promote the progress of science and useful arts," and the reward held out to inventors is merely a means to that end.[2] Likewise, in the *Mercoid Corporation* case (1944), decided more than one hundred years later, the Court declared that "It is the public interest which is dominant in the patent system," and every claim of a patent owner is to be tested by this principle.[3]

THE ADMINISTRATION OF THE PATENT SYSTEM

Any person, except an employee of the Patent Office, may apply for a patent by submitting an application to the Patent Office in Washington, D.C. In filing an application, inventors usually find it advantageous to employ the services of counsel skilled in patent matters to make sure that the patent specifications and claims properly describe and claim the invention. Patent counsel can also aid an applicant in many of the problems which arise during the development and exploitation of his invention. An inventor must pay an initial filing fee of $30 and another $30 upon the issuance of the

[2] *Pennock* v. *Dialogue*, 2 Peters 1, 19 (1830).
[3] *Mercoid Corp.* v. *Mid-Continent Investment Co.*, 320 U.S. 661, 665 (1944).

patent. Counsel fees, of course, are extra. About 60 percent of the patent applications filed with the Patent Office result in patents.

When a patent application is received by the Patent Office, it is referred to the appropriate division for study and investigation by the examiners of that division. There are sixty-seven divisions in the Patent Office, and each one specializes in the innovations which arise in a given category of products —such as optics and photographic apparatus. The period from the filing of the application to its issue as a patent or its abandonment is known as the "prosecution before the Patent Office"—sometimes called the period of patent pending, although this term has no legal significance. During the "prosecution," the patent examiners make a search of the prior art (earlier patents and other publications) to ascertain the newness of the disclosed and claimed invention. If the facts warrant, certain or all of the claims of the application are rejected as unpatentable. The claims of the application may, thereupon, be amended or modified in accordance with the original disclosure of the application. New subject matter relating to the invention, however, may not be added to the disclosure in the application as originally filed.

The average period from the date of filing a patent application to the date of issuance or abandonment is over three years. In some cases, patents remain pending for five years or more. Such long periods of delay are largely to be explained by the shortage of staff in the Patent Office, by the large backlog of applications, by interference proceedings, and by appeals from the examiners and the Patent Office.

If a patent application satisfies the appropriate division, the application is allowed and a patent is granted upon payment of the final fee. Patent applications which are finally rejected by the examiner, on the other hand, may be carried to the Board of Appeals in the Patent Office. It is reported that the Board of Appeals reverses the decisions of examiners in part or in whole in nearly one-half of the appeal cases. A patent is only *prima facie* valid, and its validity may always be questioned in an appropriate court action.

Under the Constitution and patent laws of the United States, patents are granted only to individual "inventors." Individual patent owners, however, are permitted to license or assign their patents to other persons, to corporations, or to the government. The usual practice of corporations and governmental departments is to require employees to assign to the employer all inventions developed in the course of their employment. Some companies pay extra compensation for new inventions; but ordinarily extra payment is not provided on the ground that technical employees and those engaged in research are only doing that which they are hired to do.

THE RIGHT TO EXCLUDE OTHERS DEPENDS UPON THE SCOPE OF THE PATENT AND PROOF OF INVENTION

A patent right, we have said, is the right to exclude others from making, using, and selling a product, formula, process, or method conceived by the inventor. In applying for a patent it is necessary for an inventor (1) to describe the invention and (2) to state precisely and distinctly the invention which is claimed—such as a process for making tungsten filaments for use in electric lamps, the use of gas in electric lamp bulbs to increase the intensity of the light, a way to make a synthetic vitamin, a method for creating high-vacuum tubes, or a process for bronzing iron by the application of heat and oil. The "claim" or "claims" of the invention mark out the four corners of the process, mechanism, method, or formula which an inventor claims as his new invention and from which he seeks to exclude others. A patent right, when granted, excludes others only from that which is delineated by the claims of the patent. Everything else is free from exclusion. It follows that a person infringes the patent of another only when he comes within the scope of another's patent. At all times, a person is free to "invent around" a patented invention, if he is capable of doing so.

THE CHARACTERISTICS OF PATENTABLE INVENTIONS

The Patent Act of 1952 provides that patents will be granted to "whoever invents or discovers any new and useful process, machine, manufacture, or composition of matter, or any new and useful improvement thereof." A formula, method, or device, in order to be patentable, must be (1) "new" and (2) "useful." The term "new" means that the claimed innovation was not known to the public prior to the date of the patent application. In addition, (3) a particular contribution must have "some mysterious ingredient connoted in the term 'invented.' "[4] In general, it may be said that the courts have sought to make patentable "invention" turn either (a) upon the existence of a substantial degree of individual ingenuity in developing the new process or (b) upon the presence of a substantial degree of technical advance in the object invented or in the process of producing something. The first rule, which is called the *subjective* test, emphasizes the degree of inventive genius shown by the inventor. Its existence in a given situation is indicated, apparently, by whether or not the new process would surprise a person skilled in the regular method of manufacture. The invention must reveal "inventive genius" or "a flash of creative genius" and be really startling. The second rule is called the *objective* test. This test makes patentability turn on the objective element of technical advance in the process, method, or device.

The doctrine that a new device or process must involve "the flash of genius" to be patentable has been frequently used by the Supreme Court in its efforts to develop and apply a standard for patentable invention. In the *Cuno Engineering* case (1941), in particular, Justice Douglas, speaking for the Court, declared:

> We may concede that the functions performed by Mead's combination were new and useful. But that does not necessarily make the device patentable. Under the statute the device must not only be "new and use-

[4] *The American Patent System*, Report of the National Patent Planning Commission (Washington, 1943), p. 14.

ful," it must also be an "invention" or "discovery." Since *Hotchkiss v,
Greenwood*, decided in 1851, it has been recognized that if an improvement is to obtain the privileged position of a patent more ingenuity must
be involved than the work of a mechanic skilled in the art. "Perfection of
workmanship, however much it may increase the convenience, extend the
use, or diminish expense, is not patentable." The principle of the Hotchkiss
case applied to the adaptation or combination of old or well-known devices for new uses. *That is to say the new device, however useful it may
be, must reveal the flash of creative genius, not merely the skill of the
calling.* If it fails, it has not established its right to a private grant on the
public domain.

Tested by that principle Mead's device was not patentable. We cannot
conclude that his skill in making this contribution reached the level of
inventive genius which the Constitution authorized Congress to reward.[5]

The "flash of genius" doctrine or test has been actively opposed by spokesmen for large corporations, for their desire is to secure patents on inventions
which are the product of teams of men working in a routine way. In the
laboratories of large corporations, research projects are conducted over
periods of several years by paid employees, and the results are achieved by
the step-by-step progress of all the workers rather than by the genius of any
one individual. As Judge Arnold said in the *Potts* case (1944), "Each man is
given a section of the hay to search. The man who finds the needle shows
no more 'genius' and no more ability than the others who are searching
different portions of the haystack." In a corporate research organization,
Judge Arnold added, "The 'inventor' is paid only a salary, he gets no royalties, he has no property rights in the improvements which he helps to create.
To give patents for such routine experimentation on a vast scale is to use the
patent law to reward capital investment, and create monopolies for corporate
organizers instead of men of inventive genius."[6]

The strict use of the "flash of genius" doctrine, it is generally recognized,
would greatly reduce the number of valid patents, for only in a small number
of cases can the inventions of large-scale laboratories be identified as the
results of creative genius. Many large corporations depend upon patents to
perpetuate their position and power; and for this reason they urge that consideration be given to the technical advance in the innovation itself rather
than to individual achievement.

CONGRESS REJECTS THE "FLASH OF GENIUS" TEST

In an effort to resolve the controversy over the "flash of genius" doctrine,
Congress in the Patent Act of 1952 adopted a standard for patentability
which rejects the "flash of genius" test. The new statute provides that patentability shall turn on "the differences between the subject matter sought
to be patented and the prior art" (Section 103). *If the differences are sub-*

[5] *Cuno Engineering Corp.* v. *Automatic Devices Corp.*, 314 U.S. 84, 90–91 (1941).
Italics supplied.
[6] *Potts v. Coe*, 140 F. (2d) 470, 474–475 (1944).

stantial, a patent will be issued. If, however, the differences would have been obvious at the time of the claimed innovation to a person having ordinary skill in the art, a patent will not be granted.

Section 103 explicitly states that "Patentability shall not be negatived by the manner in which the invention was made." This means that it is immaterial whether the invention was developed by a "flash of genius" or by long toil and experimentation in well-financed laboratories. The proviso in Section 103, the records show, was specifically directed to decisions based upon the *Cuno Engineering* case which set forth the "flash of genius" approach, and also to those based upon the *Potts* case which took a dim view of inventions resulting from planned research in the laboratories of large corporations. It is believed that this provision of the Patent Act of 1952 is so specific in indicating the intention of Congress to set aside the *Cuno* and *Potts* cases that the courts will be unable to avoid recognizing the new rule.[7]

The Patent Act of 1952, it may be noted, does not provide detailed standards or rules for determining "invention." It is possible, therefore, for a court which is unsympathetic to patents to disclaim the *Cuno* and *Potts* cases and at the same time hold a particular patent invalid on the ground that the changes do not rise to the status of invention. In the *United Mattress Machinery* case (1953), a Court of Appeals stated that Congress had made no detailed attempt in the Patent Act of 1952 to define the term "invention" and that it was for the courts, themselves, aided only by case law, to determine what constitutes invention and what does not.[8]

The problem of providing a uniform standard for testing inventions still remains. Whether or not an innovation constitutes "invention" depends in large measure upon the personal, political, and economic attitudes of a particular court. Patent attorneys generally regard certain Courts of Appeal as being more favorable to patents than others. The Supreme Court, itself, has varied in the support which it has given to patentees. Following 1937 and the emergence of the "New Deal" economic and political climate, there developed a trend in decisions which progressively weakened the patentee's position. It is possible that a climate more favorable to patent owners will again develop.

INFRINGEMENT SUITS AND THE INVALIDATION OF PATENTS

In manufacturing activity, business firms are almost constantly faced with the problem of making something whose production is covered in some way by patents held by others, or of having someone else turn out a product on which they have a patented method of production. Since each firm having

---

[7] In *Gagnier Fibre Products Co.* v. *Fourslides, Inc.*, 98 USPQ 9, 12 (1953), District Judge Picard acknowledged that Sec. 103 of the Patent Act of 1952 rejects the "flash of genius" test used in the *Cuno* case.

[8] *United Mattress Machinery Co.* v. *Handy Button Machine Co.*, 98 USPQ 296, 299 (1953).

a patent proposes to keep anyone else from making the product according to its invention without its permission, a large number of infringement suits necessarily arise in business. An infringement suit is one brought by a patent owner against a person allegedly encroaching upon his patent right.

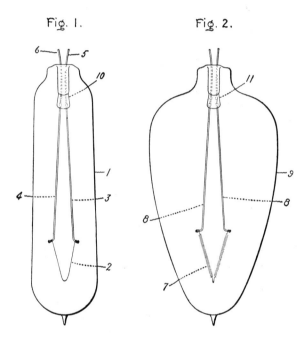

I. LANGMUIR.

INCANDESCENT ELECTRIC LAMP.

APPLICATION FILED APR. 19, 1913.

1,180,159.

Patented Apr. 18, 1916.

2 SHEETS—SHEET I.

Fig. I.   Fig. 2.

Witnesses:
George W. Filden
J. Ellis Glen

Inventor:
Irving Langmuir,
by
His Attorney.

FIG. 28. A drawing of the Langmuir patent issued in 1916 for an incandescent lamp (a) filled with compressed gas and (b) having a tungsten filament of large diameter. This patent was held to be valid in an infringement suit in *General Electric Co.* v. *Nitro-Tungsten Lamp Co.*, 261 F. 606 (1919) and 266 F. 994 (1920). In the view of the courts, the idea of a "gas-filled" lamp with a large filament was a "meritorious" invention, for the arrangement made possible more and better light with the same amount of electric energy.

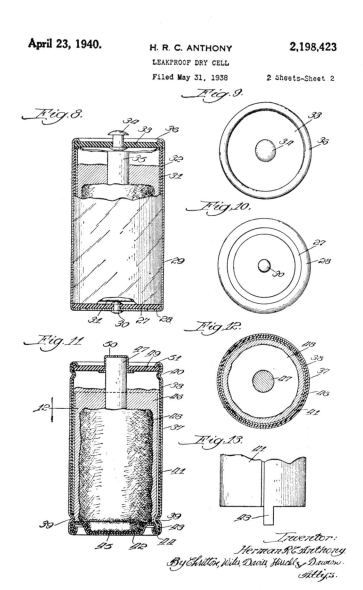

April 23, 1940.　　H. R. C. ANTHONY　　2,198,423

LEAKPROOF DRY CELL

Filed May 31, 1938　　2 Sheets-Sheet 2

FIG. 29. A drawing of the patent for a leakproof dry cell. This sketch illustrates the method of producing a leakproof dry cell on which a patent was issued by the U.S. Patent Office in 1940. Although flashlight batteries had been made for some fifty years, no manufacturer had succeeded in producing a leakproof dry cell prior to the invention patented by Mr. Anthony. The U.S. Supreme Court upheld the validity of the patent in an infringement suit in *Goodyear Tire and Rubber Co.* v. *Ray-O-Vac Co.*, 321 U.S. 275 (1944), by majority vote, on the ground that the device prevented both leakage and swelling in a dry cell and was an advance in the prior art. Justices Black, Douglas, Murphy, and Jackson dissented, with Justice Black declaring that the use of solid containers to hold substances "pre-dated the dawn of written history." This patent is one of the very few which has been held valid by the Supreme Court in recent years.

The striking thing about infringement suits is the fact that a substantial part of the patents litigated have been held by the courts to be unenforceable in the particular cases, either (1) because the activity of the accused is held to be outside the scope of the plaintiff's patent or (2) because the plaintiff's patent really represents no "invention." One well-known patent attorney declares that his experience with a large number of patents over a period of nearly two decades has led him to conclude that "out of one hundred patents, ninety can be discarded with little more than a cursory examination. Of the remaining, nine will not withstand a strict examination. This leaves, at the most, one patent that has more than a fighting chance of being declared enforceable."[9] Illustrations of patents which have been held to be valid in infringement suits are shown in Figs. 28 and 29.

The fact that a great many patents are held to be invalid and unenforceable is to be explained largely (1) by the inadequate search made by the Patent Office of the records of prior use to determine whether or not the public had prior knowledge of the invention claimed, and (2) by the lower standards for invention followed by the Patent Office in comparison with those adopted by the courts. Even among the courts, there is variation in the standards used for determining invention, depending upon the personal, political, social, and economic attitudes of the various judges.

The Patent Act of 1952, we have seen, established tests for patentability more favorable to patentees than existed under the old legislation. No part of the new law, however, made provision for harmonizing the standard for invention used by the Patent Office and the standard used by the courts. Experienced patent attorneys believe that the Patent Office will continue to be very liberal in granting patents and that the courts will continue to follow their own course in holding patents invalid. It seems likely, therefore, that any substantial reduction in the percentage of patents declared invalid in the future will depend mainly upon changes in the economic and political climate which surrounds the courts.

The persons most severely injured by the action of the federal courts in declaring so many of the patents litigated to be unenforceable are small business firms and independent inventors. A supercorporation, having large financial resources, can threaten a small concern with infringement suits and force it to pay costly royalties for the use of patents of doubtful validity. It can also use its financial power to force a small business to sell or forgo the use of patents whose validity can be proved only by expensive litigation. All too often, it is said, patent controversies are determined not by the merits of the case but rather by the financial power of a company to "sweat it out."

There is general agreement among patent authorities that if our patent system is to fulfill its essential functions, steps will need to be taken (1) to provide a greater degree of uniformity in the standard of invention followed

[9] Daniel G. Cullen, "The General Lawyer and Patent Problems," *Lawyers Guild Review*, September, 1946, pp. 585–589.

by the Patent Office and the standard followed by the courts and (2) to reduce in some way the great expense involved in testing the validity of patents.

THE USE OF PATENT RIGHTS TO CONTROL AN INDUSTRY

A patent right, we have seen, gives an enterpriser the right *to exclude others* from making, using, and selling a product according to the formula or process claimed in the invention. This does not give an inventor the positive right to make, use, or sell the invention as he pleases. Persons holding patents are still subject to all state and national laws which apply to the making, using, or selling of goods—such as the antitrust laws, the food and drug laws, and laws prohibiting false advertising.

Very often there are several alternative ways of producing a product— such as gypsum wallboard, which is a core of gypsum between two paper liners. Frequently, moreover, patents cover only one aspect of the total productive process—the alternative ways of folding the paper over the edges of gypsum wallboard, for example. Since rival processes exist, dominant enterprises in their drive for profits are led to bring rival patents or rival enterprises under their control *so as to monopolize an industry*.

The chief abuses in the use of patents in the American patent system, it is generally agreed, arise in the activities of a patent owner or owners to monopolize the sale of a given class of goods. Such efforts usually take form (1) in the restrictive conditions imposed by a patent owner upon a licensee who arranges to use a patent, (2) in the restrictive agreements made by competitors in pooling or interchanging their several patent rights, and (3) in the practice of a dominant producer to buy up and acquire a control over all or a large part of the patents in a given field of production. We shall now consider these various business arrangements and the attitude of the law toward them.

1. THE IMPOSITION OF RESTRICTIVE CONDITIONS ON A LICENSEE

A patent owner may sell his invention, use it himself, or license others to share its privileges. Very often a patent owner finds it advantageous to permit one or more competitors to use a patent, with or without payment of a royalty fee. Such action is usually dictated by considerations of reciprocal favor and private advantage. It may be that a patent owner would like to secure the use of certain patents from a rival firm. In some cases, a patent owner may grant a license to a competitor in order to avoid the possible problem of patent infringement and the need to test the validity of his patent in the courts. This procedure also is often practiced reciprocally. A patent owner may likewise grant a competitor a license with the thought of keeping him from developing an alternative process.

In making a license contract, a patent owner typically includes terms and conditions which restrain competition between himself and the licensee in the sale of the patented products. The restrictions imposed may take many forms. A patentee may require a licensee to confine his sales to a certain area or to a certain type of product. Tying clauses requiring a licensee to buy unpatented materials from the patentee are frequently used. The most common restrictive provisions apply to the prices which a licensee may charge for the products made and sold according to the patented formula. Other restrictions include those placed on the quantity and quality of the goods produced. The Department of Justice is constantly at work in searching out factual data on restrictive licensing agreements, and notable progress has been made in outlawing some of the most flagrant abuses.

THE GENERAL ELECTRIC CASE

A leading case involving the restriction of competition between a patentee and a licensee was the *General Electric* case decided in 1926. The facts of the *General Electric* case were that the defendant General Electric Company owned patents covering the manufacture of certain types of electric lamps. General Electric, the patentee, licensed the Westinghouse Company to make lamps under this patent on condition that it sold only at prices fixed by the patentee. The government brought suit against the two companies, charging that the agreement violated the Sherman Act.

In considering the case, the Supreme Court summarized the main issue as follows: "If the patentee . . . licenses the selling of the articles, may he limit the selling by limiting the method of selling and the price?" The Court answered in the affirmative, stating, "We think he may do so *provided the conditions of sale are normally and reasonably adapted to secure pecuniary reward for the patentee's monopoly. . . .* When the patentee licenses another to make and vend and retains the right to continue to make and vend on his own account, the price at which his licensee will sell will necessarily affect the price at which he can sell his own patented goods. It would seem entirely reasonable that he should say to the licensee, 'Yes, you may make and sell articles under my patent but not so as to destroy the profit that I wish to obtain by making them and selling them myself.' "[10]

The decision in the *General Electric* case, most legal authorities agree, looked at a patent-licensing arrangement entirely from the point of view of the patent owner and the licensee. Private advantage rather than public welfare was made the test for the legality of a license agreement. From an economic standpoint, it may be said that a patent owner is entitled to receive a reasonable royalty for the use of his patent by another. However, the licensee should ever be free to manufacture and sell his products at prices which reflect *his* efficiency and *his* estimate of market forces.

Efforts to Limit the Scope of the General Electric Decision. Upon the basis of the *General Electric* decision, the view developed that one who uses patents as a basis for price-fixing arrangements is by that fact exempted from

[10] *U.S. v. General Electric Co.*, 272 U.S. 476, 490 (1926).

the laws against restraint of competition. Patents and licensing agreements, it was believed, insured a blanket exemption from the Sherman Act for price-fixing purposes. The use of patents for making price agreements thereupon spread rapidly in many lines of business. The *General Electric* case, it may be noted, involved a *single* license from a *single* licensor to a *single* licensee on a *single* product. In adopting the principle of the decision, however, business firms holding patents came to arrange price-fixing agreements with *all* or most of their competitors in a given line of business.

A second principle involved in the *General Electric* case was the validity of a series of agency contracts between General Electric and a large number of distributors under which General Electric (1) designated the distributors as its agents and (2) controlled the prices and terms of sale at which the distributors could sell the lamps produced by General Electric. The Court found that the distributors were the bona-fide agents of General Electric, and that there was nothing unlawful in General Electric's control over the prices, terms, and conditions upon which the distributors, as its agents, could sell the lamps.

The *Masonite* case (1942) was brought primarily to limit the scope of the 1926 *General Electric* decision with respect to price fixing through so-called agency contracts, while the *Line Material* and *Gypsum* cases (1948) were brought to test the validity of a price-fixing, patent-licensing agreement between a number of competitors.

THE MASONITE CASE

The facts in the *Masonite* case were that a group of competitors making hardboard and insulation board became involved in a dispute over the validity of certain patents used in manufacturing these building materials. As a method of settling the dispute, the competitors entered into agreements with one another which provided (1) that Masonite would make all the hardboard in the industry, (2) that the competing manufacturers would distribute this product on an "agency" basis, giving Masonite a guarantee of payment, and (3) that each would adhere to the prices and terms fixed by Masonite. The government charged that the combination in the hardboard industry was a price-fixing conspiracy and illegal *per se* under the Sherman Act.

The basic theory underlying the *Masonite* case was that it was illegal for a group of competitors or potential competitors, through the device of agency contracts, to agree to suppress and eliminate competition among themselves. If such an agreement were lawful, there would be nothing to prevent a group of manufacturers *of any given product* from deciding that they could more profitably concentrate their production in the hands of one single company and have all the other companies designated as agents to distribute those products at prices fixed by the manufacturing company. In this way, competition in the production as well as in the distribution of the product would be effectively eliminated.

The defendants contended that since Masonite had the exclusive patent right to produce Masonite hardboard, it was permissible for Masonite to agree with its competitors that they would become agents of Masonite. The Court assumed that Masonite competitors were actually agents of Masonite but held that an agreement among virtually all competitors, or potential competitors, in an industry which effectively limited and restrained competition among them, was violative of the Sherman Act whether it was under the guise of an agency relationship or otherwise.[11]

THE LINE MATERIAL AND GYPSUM CASES

The *Line Material* and *Gypsum* cases decided by the Supreme Court in 1948 involved the issue of whether a patentee may fix the prices at which *multiple* licensees must sell a patented product. The government asked the Court in both cases to overrule the *General Electric* case on the ground (1) that price-fixing agreements are illegal *per se* under the Sherman Act and (2) that a patent right confers only the right to exclude competitors—not to join with them in price fixing. In the *Line Material* case, a majority of the Court held that it was not necessary to overrule the *General Electric* case in order to decide against the patent-licensing arrangement presented in that case. However, four of the justices sharply attacked the 1926 decision. Although the *General Electric* decision on patent-licensing agreements still stands, the majority indicated in both the *Line Material* and the *Gypsum* cases that it will look with disfavor on such agreements containing restrictive provisions when made *with more than one licensee*.

The facts in the *Line Material* case were that two principal producers of fuse cutouts, used in protecting an electric circuit from a short circuit or overload, made a cross-licensing agreement for the use of an essential, complementary patent held by each company. The agreement provided that each patentee would fix the price on the product made by the licensee. The two companies—Line and Southern—agreed further that Line could license other producers to use the patents provided the licensees maintained the prices fixed by Line. The Supreme Court held that the agreement between Line and Southern for the cross-licensing of patents and the reciprocal fixing of prices was illegal *per se*. According to Justice Reed, speaking for the Court, "The merging of the benefits of price-fixing under the patents restrains trade in violation of the Sherman Act in the same way as would the fixing of prices between producers of non-patentable goods. . . . When patentees join in an agreement as here to maintain prices on their several products, that agreement, however advantageous it may be to stimulate the broader use of patents, is unlawful *per se* under the Sherman Act. It is more than an exploitation of patents. There is the vice that patentees have combined to fix prices on patented products."[12]

[11] *U.S. v. Masonite Corp.*, 316 U.S. 265 (1942).
[12] *U.S. v. Line Material Co.*, 333 U.S. 287, 311–315 (1948).

The Gypsum Case

The *Gypsum* case, decided the same day as the *Line Material* case, involved a price-fixing arrangement among the licensed producers of gypsum wallboard, a product made in accordance with a number of patents. The facts of the case were that the dominant producer, the United States Gypsum Company, following several patent controversies with competitors, entered into a separate patent-licensing and price-fixing agreement with each of the principal producers of gypsum wallboard in the United States. Since each agreement was an individual one, the company maintained that upon the basis of the *General Electric* case its license arrangements were legal. The government, however, charged a violation of Sections 1 and 2 of the Sherman Act and pointed especially to the use by the company of a subsidiary corporation—Board Survey, Inc.—to check on the prices of the various licensees in order to insure complete compliance with the prices dictated by Gypsum.

The Supreme Court upheld the government in the *Gypsum* case and declared that a series of individual licensing arrangements did not come within the *General Electric* case. "Lawful acts," said Justice Reed, "may become unlawful when taken in concert." In particular, Justice Reed emphasized that "The *General Electric* case affords no cloak for the course of conduct revealed in the voluminous record in this case. That case gives no support for a patentee, acting in concert with all members of an industry, to issue substantially identical licenses to all members of the industry under the terms of which the industry is completely regimented, the production of competitive unpatented products suppressed, a class of distributors squeezed out, and prices on unpatented products stabilized."[13]

There is general agreement among legal authorities that the effect of the *Line Material* and *Gypsum* cases is to restrict sharply the extent to which a patent owner can now use his patent as a device for monopolizing an industry by licensing other producers. The government has not fully won its principle that *all* price-fixing agreements shall be tested by the Sherman Act, but the sharply divided Court in the *Line Material* case gives hope that it may some day win a recognition of this rule.

The New Wrinkle Case

Since the *Line Material* and *Gypsum* cases, the Antitrust Division has continued to press for the invalidation of price fixing in patent licensing plans. The *New Wrinkle* case (1952) involved two competitors who had been engaged in litigation over their respective patents covering the manufacture of wrinkle finish enamels. In settling their dispute, these firms organized a new company, jointly owned, to hold the rival patents. The new company thereupon licensed substantially all—over 200—manufacturers of wrinkle finishes in the United States. The licensing arrangements made with these

---

[13] *U.S.* v. *U.S. Gypsum Co.*, 333 U.S. 364, 400 (1948).

manufacturers contained price-fixing provisions. The Court condemned the scheme, declaring: "We see no material difference between the situation in *Line Material* and *Gypsum* and the case presented by the allegations of this complaint. An arrangement was made between patent holders to pool their patents and fix prices on the products for themselves and their licensees. The purpose and result plainly violate the Sherman Act."[14]

THE INTERNATIONAL SALT CASE

The Supreme Court has consistently held in a long line of cases that a patent owner cannot misuse his patent to control the sale of unpatented products by the use of tying clauses in patent agreements. In the *International Salt* case, decided in 1947, in fact, the Court held that the licensing of patented devices on condition that certain unpatented materials be used with the patented devices is illegal *per se*. The facts in the *Salt* case were that the International Salt Company had leased its patented machines for dispensing salt in industrial processes—such as fish canning and meat packing—only on condition that the licensees would purchase supplies of unpatented salt from the company. Some 900 of such leasing contracts were found to be operative. The government charged that the tying clauses violated Section 1 of the Sherman Act and Section 3 of the Clayton Act. The company in its reply contended that tying clauses were not illegal *per se* and further that its contracts were not unreasonable restraints upon competition.

Justice Jackson, speaking for the Court in the *International Salt* case, held that a patent confers only a limited monopoly on the invention itself, and no right at all to restrain the trade of an unpatented product. In his words, "By contracting to close this market for salt against competition, International has engaged in a restraint of trade for which its patents afford no immunity from the antitrust laws. . . . Not only is price-fixing unreasonable, *per se*, but also it is unreasonable, *per se*, to foreclose competitors from any substantial market. . . . Under the law, agreements are forbidden which 'tend to create a monopoly,' and it is immaterial that the tendency is a creeping one rather than one that proceeds at full gallop; nor does the law await arrival at the goal before condemning the direction of the movement."[15]

2. PATENT POOLS AND CROSS-LICENSING AS DEVICES FOR CONTROLLING AN INDUSTRY

A second major device used by patent owners for controlling an industry is that of restrictive agreements made by competitors for the interchange of their patents, either by the use of a "patent pool" or by a more limited cross-licensing arrangement. A patent pool is an arrangement by which two or more patent owners throw their individual patents into a pool and receive in return a license to use all the patents in the pool. In some instances, patent pools may be in the public interest. Patents frequently cover *improvements*

[14] *U.S. v. New Wrinkle, Inc.*, 324 U.S. 371, 380 (1952).
[15] *International Salt Co. v. U.S.*, 332 U.S. 392, 395 (1947).

on basic inventions; and if various producers cannot use the latest technology, the public as well as individual producers suffer. An example of a desirable patent pool is found in the automobile industry.

The automobile plan is open to any bona-fide manufacturer of cars or trucks. Each member authorizes the Automobile Manufacturers Association to grant licenses to its patents to other members taking part in the plan, without royalty payment and without any requirement that the other parties to the plan shall have patents subject to the agreement. The licenses are unrestricted in every way. In other words, there is no restriction with respect to the price of the products embodying the patented inventions, to the industrial or territorial field of use, or to the quantity of production. The minimum dues of the association are nominal and would not prevent any company from becoming a member.

The current agreement authorizes the association to grant licenses under patents owned on January 1, 1940, with certain patents being excepted, particularly those covering designs and features exclusively applicable to commercial vehicles as distinguished from passenger cars. Patents on inventions developed in parts-making divisions of members are also excluded, as are patents acquired for the use of such parts-making divisions. Parties to the agreement are authorized to make, use, and sell the inventions, or to have them made for the members by others for use and sale by the members.[16] Available evidence indicates that the automobile patent plan is working very satisfactorily and that it serves a useful purpose in enabling industry to build better and safer passenger cars and trucks without extensive patent involvement.

There is nothing in patent pools, as such, which makes them violative of the Sherman Act, for the mere pooling of patents does not mean that a producer gives up his freedom to manage his business independently. The abuses of patent pools arise (1) when the pool is closed to other responsible producers or is made available to them only upon the payment of excessive royalties and (2) when the pool uses its patents to license others—or its own members—on condition that they will maintain prices or operate only in certain territories or fields of operation. All such restrictive arrangements are contrary to the spirit of the antitrust laws, as the Court has said in numerous cases ranging from the *Bathtub* case of 1912 (226 U.S. 20) to the *Hartford-Empire* case of 1945 (323 U.S. 386).

A brief discussion of the *Hartford-Empire* case will serve to illustrate the abuses which sometimes arise in pooling arrangements, and also the corrective relief which the courts are now imposing on abused patents. The facts presented an appalling story in which the Hartford-Empire Company, in coöperation with other leading manufacturers of glassware, pursued a ruthless plan of litigation against patent owners in the glassware industry, "expensive beyond the dreams of the average man," to corral a control over

---

[16] Based upon data from the Automobile Manufacturers Association, Detroit 2, Michigan, the organization which is in charge of the patent plan.

a large part of the patents for making glassware. Thereupon Hartford-Empire and some eight other leading glassware manufacturers entered into an elaborate patent pool and cross-licensing system which gave the group an effective control over the entire industry. In 1938 the defendants had over 800 patents in the glass container industry centralized in their pool, and some 94 percent of the glass containers manufactured in the United States were produced on machines licensed under the pooled patents.

The license agreements made by the Hartford group with smaller manufacturers were highly monopolistic and restricted the quantity of containers they could manufacture, the prices they could charge, as well as the type, color, size, and weight of the glassware they could produce. The District Court found that as a result of the patent policies of the defendants—their acquisition and pooling activities, restrictive licensing plans, tying contracts, and continuous efforts to control product prices and royalty payments—price competition in the glassware industry had been suppressed, monopoly control attained, and further invention and technological progress discouraged. Upon the basis of these findings, the District Court held that the defendants were in violation of Sections 1 and 2 of the Sherman Act and Section 3 of the Clayton Act.

The case against the Hartford defendants was conclusive, and the main problem for the District Court was that of determining the appropriate relief. The most important provision of the decree dealing with patents was the stipulation that all the abused patents involved in the case be licensed royalty-free to any applicant, and that all future patents be licensed at reasonable royalties.

The defendants appealed the decree in the *Hartford* case to the Supreme Court, claiming that their patent rights had been improperly abrogated. In a comprehensive review of the decree, the Supreme Court in a four-to-three decision remanded the case with numerous significant changes. The provision of the decree requiring that the abused patents be licensed royalty-free was reversed on the ground that such harsh treatment was unnecessary in the dissolution of the combination. In place of this requirement, the Supreme Court held that all existing and future patents should be licensed to all applicants at reasonable royalties. The majority of the Court also reversed the portion of the decree enjoining the defendants from suppressing patents. In the view of the majority, a patent owner has the legal right to use or not to use his invention as he may desire.[17]

The government was quite disappointed in the modifications of the decree made by the Supreme Court. A careful study of the problems of creating competition in patent-controlled fields had convinced the government that abused patents must be made available to all, royalty-free. The extra cost placed upon a new competitor in having to pay royalties to the established firms on many patents—some, perhaps, of doubtful validity—it was believed, would impose a serious barrier to competition. The very problem of

[17] *Hartford-Empire Co. v. U.S.*, 323 U.S. 386, 415 (1945).

determining reasonable royalties, moreover, was looked upon as presenting many new difficulties which the government and the courts were not prepared to handle.

BILATERAL OR MULTILATERAL CROSS-LICENSE AGREEMENTS

The essential idea of a patent pool is that each member puts *all* his own patents into a pool and gets in return a license to use *all* the other patents in the pool. A second type of cross-licensing arrangement is that of an agreement between competitors in which each grants the other an exclusive license to use *designated* patents, usually with specified territorial limitations. This sort of plan is commonly adopted in the international field, in which dominant firms in different countries having patents on similar formulas or methods granted by their respective governments agree (1) to interchange patents in a given field, as well as all future improvements and technical knowledge, and (2) to divide sales territories in designated portions of the world.

An example of a typical international cartel involving a multilateral cross-licensing patent agreement is found in the *National Lead* case, decided by the Supreme Court in 1947. The facts of the case were that around 1920 two Americans, a Frenchman, and a Norwegian each invented and secured patents on processes for converting titanium, the ninth most abundant element in the earth, into a white pigment for use in making paints, vitreous enamels, rubber goods, paper, glass, and many other products. The National Lead Company secured the American patents, a Norwegian company bought the Norwegian patents, and Du Pont subsequently acquired the French patents. Thereupon, the three companies entered into an elaborate conspiracy to interchange present patents, to fix prices and divide sales areas, and to provide one another with future patents and a knowledge of improvements in technology.

As a result of the monopolistic arrangements sponsored by National Lead, Du Pont, and their foreign associates, the combination was able to exercise complete world-wide control over the manufacture of titanium and over its sales and prices in designated trade areas. The United States government charged the American defendants with a violation of Sections 1 and 2 of the Sherman Act and asked for the creation of competition in the American industry.

Judge Rifkind, in the District Court, found the American defendants guilty of the violations charged, declaring that "when the story is seen as a whole, there is no blinking the fact that there is no free commerce in titanium. Every pound of it is trammelled by privately imposed regulation. The channels of this commerce have not been formed by the winds and currents of competition. They are, in large measure, artificial canals privately constructed."[18] In the decree awarded to the government, the District Court directed that there should be compulsory licensing of all present

[18] *U.S. v. National Lead Co.*, 63 F. Supp. 513, 521 (1945).

patents, as well as of all patents acquired within five years, at "reasonable" royalties. The decree also provided that technical information, along with the patents, be disclosed at reasonable prices. The government had asked that the abused patents be made available royalty-free, but this relief was not granted. The District Court stated that it would have liked to have granted this request but felt that it was controlled by the views of the Supreme Court —as expressed in the *Hartford-Empire* case.

Upon appeal to the Supreme Court, the government requested that the *Hartford-Empire* case be overruled on the grounds (1) that abused patents should be made unenforceable and (2) that the requirement of reasonable royalty licensing arrangements is inadequate and unworkable. In the view of the government, the provision that a newcomer must pay "reasonable" royalties would place him at a distinct competitive disadvantage and enable National Lead and Du Pont to maintain their dominance in the field.

The Supreme Court in a four-to-three decision, however, refused to grant the request of the government. In the words of Justice Burton, speaking for the majority, "We feel that, without reaching the question whether royalty-free licensing or a perpetual injunction against the enforcement of a patent is permissible as a matter of law in any case, the present decree represents an exercise of sound judicial discretion."[19] The majority thus reaffirmed its view in the *Hartford-Empire* case that abused patents should be licensed to all, but at "reasonable" royalties. Justice Burton indicated further in the majority opinion that a cross-licensing arrangement between large corporations in principle is illegal unless the patents are made available to others on a "reasonable" basis.[20]

3. THE CONCENTRATION OF PATENTS IN THE HANDS OF A SINGLE OWNER TO CONTROL AN INDUSTRY

The third—and final—way in which patents are sometimes used to control an industry is based upon the concentration of patents in the hands of a single owner. When a firm secures dominant financial size—usually by means of merger—it also secures large financial power. This power makes it possible for the firm (1) to acquire large numbers of patents by purchase and research and (2) to discourage others by instituting continuous and financially embarrassing patent suits. Independent inventors soon find that the dominant company is the most likely buyer for their inventions, and the company becomes able to buy new patents largely on its own terms. The process of patent acquisition, once begun, grows like a rolling snowball, and

[19] *U.S. v. National Lead Co.,* 332 U.S. 319, 338 (1947).
[20] Patents have been made available royalty-free or dedicated to the public in a number of *consent* decrees. Thus, in the *A. B. Dick Mimeograph* case, the decree provided that the company forthwith "take such steps as may be necessary to dedicate, transfer, and assign to the public all United States Letters Patent . . . reading on or claiming stencil duplicating machines, stencils, or stencil duplicating supplies or raw materials." *U.S. v. A. B. Dick Co., Final Judgment,* Civil Action No. 24188, District Court of the United States for the Northern District of Ohio (1947).

the dominant company finds that it is able to control an industry by controlling access to the most efficient and most improved methods of production.

Thus far, the government has made only a small beginning in the task of investigating and destroying the monopoly power which is secured by a concentration of patents in the hands of a single owner. Section 2 of the Sherman Act provides ample authority for the government to use in proceeding against large-scale patent owners and hoarders. If the Department of Justice had sufficient funds for enforcing the antitrust laws, it is possible that a considerable part of the abuses of patent concentration, as found in the *Hartford-Empire* case, could be eliminated without having to make a change in the patent laws.

REMEDIAL MEASURES PROPOSED FOR CORRECTING ABUSES IN THE AMERICAN PATENT SYSTEM

In view of the many abuses which characterize the American patent system, and also the fact that government has become the principal sponsor of research, it is sometimes suggested that the use of patents to improve technology is an "outworn" and "outmoded" institution. Research at the present time, it is observed, is increasingly coming to be a coöperative undertaking; and the exclusive rights of the patent system are serving chiefly to make possible a concentration of technical knowledge in the hands of a few large corporations, for use if they please, when they please, and to the extent that they please.

The growing doubt in the minds of many Americans about the efficacy of our present patent system is reflected in the defensive tone of the report of the National Patent Planning Commission made in 1943. This Commission, appointed by President Roosevelt, it may be noted, included such leading industrialists as Owen D. Young of General Electric and Charles F. Kettering of General Motors. According to the Commission, "The American people and their government *should* recognize the fundamental rightness and fairness of protecting the creations of its inventors by the patent grant. The basic principles of the present system *should* be preserved."[21] Most people, it is believed would be willing to support this view, provided that positive action is taken by government to remedy the abuses presently existing.

The literature on proposals for improving the operation of our patent system is extensive. Here, again, the problem is not the fact that technology has outrun our knowledge for controlling it, but rather the fact that society seems to be impotent to utilize even a reasonable amount of the knowledge which it possesses.

Proposals for correcting the abuses and and other shortcomings currently found in the American patent system involve (1) a more vigorous enforcement of the antitrust laws, (2) a procedural change in the administration of

[21] *The American Patent System*, Report of the National Patent Planning Commission (Washington, 1943), p. 7. Italics supplied.

patent law, and (3) basic changes in the substantive law on patents. Since we have already discussed the need for a more vigorous enforcement of the antitrust laws, we shall turn to a consideration of the other two categories. Patent law reform, it may be noted, has been an urgent public need for decades, and there is little disagreement among independent patent authorities on basic remedial measures which should be adopted.

A PROPOSED PROCEDURAL CHANGE

PUBLIC HEARINGS ON THE ISSUANCE OF PATENTS

At present, patent applications are kept secret until the patent is actually granted. This arrangement places the final burden of checking novelty and prior use upon the Patent Office. Some patent authorities believe that if the public were given an opportunity to supply pertinent information, the Patent Office could do a much better job of evaluation—on the principle that "all of us know more than some of us." The National Patent Planning Commission, for example, declares that "There should be some provision whereby information and facts bearing upon the validity of a patent can be brought to the Patent Office thereby giving it an opportunity to re-examine its decision to grant a patent and also to afford the public a full opportunity to challenge the validity and to bring about a revocation of an improperly granted patent."[22] It is possible that such a proposal would check the issue of invalid patents to the "independent" to a much greater extent than to large corporations. If a field is dominated by a few financial giants which "get along together," it is likely that objections would be offered only to the applications filed by a newcomer or an independent.

PROPOSED CHANGES IN THE SUBSTANTIVE
LAW ON PATENTS

I. THE ADOPTION OF A UNIFORM STANDARD FOR INVENTION

A basic problem in the American patent system which needs correction is the fact that the Patent Office and the courts do not use the same standards for testing inventions. It is widely recognized that the Patent Office grants far more patents than the courts will accept as representing invention. The result is continuous patent litigation. It is recognized that many practical difficulties are involved in working out a standard for invention which will be in the public interest. The problems, however, appear to be ones which can be solved by experts if they put their minds to it. Since the public interest is at stake, it is suggested that Congress should secure technical assistance on this matter from independent patent experts and from professors of law and engineering in our universities, for these men are in the best position to give objective advice and guidance.

[22] *Ibid.*, p. 12.

2. COMPULSORY LICENSING

The really controversial remedial measures suggested for the American patent system are those which call for a compulsory licensing of patents. Some authorities and investigating committees recommend a plan for the general compulsory licensing of all future patents; others propose the compulsory licensing only of patents which have been abused or suppressed. Large business corporations and their legal spokesmen are vigorously opposed to any and all forms of compulsory licensing.

In an objective appraisal of general compulsory licensing, Dr. Floyd L. Vaughan concludes that "Compulsory licensing would be an effective means for dealing with industrial monopoly and restraint of trade, and for preventing conflict in the use of the latest technology."[23] Likewise, Dr. Victor Abramson states, "If it could be successfully administered, the public benefits which might be derived from the general compulsory licensing of patented inventions would indeed be many. Inventions would be unlikely to lie idle because of inertia, and even less so because of design. The owners of dependent inventions would have ready access to essential auxiliary technology. Since all could use the most advanced technology, production generally would be on a higher level and prices would reflect this fact."[24]

The principle of compulsory licensing of patents was adopted by Congress in the Atomic Energy Act of 1946 with respect to patents granted for the *nonmilitary* use of atomic energy. It is possible for inventors to secure patents on the nonmilitary utilization of atomic energy, but the Commission is authorized to declare any such patent "affected with a public interest" and provide for its licensing on a reasonable royalty basis. If the patent owner and licensee cannot agree on a royalty fee, the Commission is authorized to determine it.[25] Congress adopted the principle of compulsory licensing for patents covering the nonmilitary use of atomic energy in order to make the peacetime benefits of this discovery widely available to all. Thus far, the compulsory licensing provision has not been used, and the Patent Advisory Panel to the Commission, apparently reflecting the desires of important industry groups, has recommended that this provision should be exercised sparingly.

THE DIRECT SPONSORING OF RESEARCH BY GOVERNMENT

In most cases today, governments do not rely upon patents alone for getting the inventions and discoveries which a nation needs for its economic and military welfare. A patent stimulates private invention, and private invention today is largely conducted by business corporations for business

[23] Floyd L. Vaughan, "Patent Policy," *American Economic Review, Papers and Proceedings*, May, 1948, p. 227.

[24] Victor Abramson, "The Economic Bases of Patent Reform," *Law and Contemporary Problems*, Spring, 1948, pp. 350–351.

[25] 42 U.S.C. 1811.

profit. Profit is a legitimate motive, but profit making does not always lead to undertakings which are in the greatest public need. It is for this reason that governments themselves are now becoming important sponsors of industrial research and important holders of patents. (See also Chap. 8, pp. 154–155.)

An anomalous aspect of the industrial research sponsored by various federal agencies in the United States is the absence of a uniform system among the agencies for acquiring the patents which grow out of the expenditure of federal funds. A large part of the research sponsored by the federal government is carried out by private industry under the direction of some governmental agency. The Department of Agriculture, the Tennessee Valley Authority, and the Atomic Energy Commission generally retain a control over the patents which are developed by private contractors, whereas the Army, Navy, and many other departments permit private corporations to secure the patent rights, but usually with a proviso that the patents will be royalty-free to the government. When the government owns patents, its general policy is either to dedicate them to the public or to issue royalty-free licenses to all applicants.

THE CONTROL OF TECHNOLOGY SECURED BY THE USE OF FEDERAL FUNDS

The question of the policy which the government should follow with respect to the ownership of patents developed with federal funds is a highly important one. Private corporations, of course, are eager to secure a control over all inventions they develop in research activity financed by the government. Moreover, as long as they own the large laboratories which are necessary for use in conducting government research, they are in a strong position to insist upon contracts giving them the commercial rights to the resulting patents. During World War II, in particular, it is reported that the large corporations were unwilling to accept government research contracts which did not give them commercial rights to all patents developed in the course of such research.[26]

In 1946 a special Senate committee reported that "over 90 percent of the contracts made between government agencies and private industrial laboratories for scientific research and development placed the ownership of patents with the contractor, the government receiving a royalty-free license for its own use. The research contracts of the War Department, Navy Department, Reconstruction Finance Corporation, and Office of Scientific Research and Development—which accounted for 98 percent of the federal funds spent for research in private industrial laboratories—were generally of this nature." The Senate report emphasized further, "This means, in effect, that the large corporations which carried on the great bulk of the

[26] U.S. Department of Justice, *Investigation of Government Patent Practices and Policies* (Washington, 1947), Vol. 2, pp. 299, 302, 463.

federally financed wartime industrial research will have control, through patents, of the commercial applications of that research."[27]

The best economic and legal opinion is that the government itself should secure all patents developed in the course of the research which it finances. Such patents can then be licensed royalty-free to all applicants, and the benefits of modern science can be made available to all enterprisers for competitive development.

Upon the basis of an exhaustive three-year study of patents and patent regulation, the Attorney General in May, 1947, submitted a comprehensive report to President Truman recommending that all technological developments financed by federal funds should be owned or controlled by the government.

By terms of Executive Order No. 10096, issued January 23, 1950, federal employees assigned to research functions are now required to convey the patent rights in resulting inventions to the government. Only rare cases (such as where a specialist who has already made considerable progress on a particular device, is brought into the government to complete his research) are exceptions made to this general rule. The new policy established for federal employees, it may be noted, seems to be working quite effectively. Apparently, it has not dried up the flow of inventive ideas, as opponents of the Attorney General's recommendations prophesied.

Thus far no action has ever been taken in regard to inventions made in the course of government contracts with private industry, research or otherwise. Each federal agency is free to prescribe its own policy. By and large, the agencies have continued to follow the practices described in the Attorney General's report. This means that with few exceptions the federal agencies leave ownership of inventions to private corporations, subject to a license to the government.

SUGGESTIONS FOR FURTHER READING

Bennett, W. B., *The American Patent System—An Economic Interpretation* (Baton Rouge, La., 1943).

Federico, P. J., "Compulsory Licensing in Other Countries," *Law and Contemporary Problems*, Spring, 1948, pp. 295–309.

Fox, Harold G., *Monopolies and Patents* (Toronto, 1947).

Kaempffert, W. B., *A Popular History of American Invention* (New York, 1924); and *Invention and Society* (Chicago, 1930).

Kreeger, David Lloyd, "The Control of Patent Rights Resulting from Federal Research," *Law and Contemporary Problems*, Autumn, 1947, pp. 714–745.

Temporary National Economic Committee, *Final Report and Recommendations*, 77th Congress, first session, Senate Document 35, 1941.

Toulmin, Jr., Harry A., *Handbook of Patents* (Charlottesville, 1954).

U.S. Department of State, "Governments as Sponsors of Industrial Research

---

[27] Report of the Smaller War Plants Corporation, *Economic Concentration and World War II*, 79th Congress, second session, Senate Committee Print 6, 1946, p. 53.

and as Owners of Patents," *Documents and State Papers*, May, 1948, pp. 67–91. Contains a valuable survey of the work of leading nations in sponsoring research by direct expenditure. An interesting account of Soviet patent law is also included.

Vaughan, F. L., *Economics of Our Patent System* (New York, 1925); "Patent Policy," *American Economic Review, Papers and Proceedings*, May, 1948, pp. 213–234.

Wood, Laurence I., *Patents and Antitrust Law* (Chicago, 1942); and "Patent Combinations and the Antitrust Laws," *George Washington Law Review*, December, 1948, pp. 59–96.

Woodling, George V., *Inventions and Their Protection* (Albany, 1954).

CHAPTER 15

The Federal Trade Commission

We have seen that the purposes of the antitrust laws are (1) to prevent monopoly and (2) to preserve *fair* competition. The economic principle of competition, in turn, consists of (a) freedom of entry and (b) two-sided price competition in the determination of prices.

The purpose of the present chapter is to analyze the work of the Federal Trade Commission, a special administrative agency charged with the duty of preventing "unfair methods of competition" or "unfair or deceptive acts or practices" in interstate commerce. Consideration will also be given to business practices which various economists and legal authorities regard as being "unfair," but which are not as yet condemned by the law.

UNFAIR COMPETITION FROM AN ECONOMIC POINT OF VIEW

In a pioneer study of "unfair competition," Dr. W. H. S. Stevens states that the concept "is a term difficult either to define or explain. To different individuals it connotes different things. The lawyer's view of unfair competition, for example, is based upon the statutes and the decisions of the courts; that of the economists upon economic consequences and results. To the lawyer, a method which is legal is not unfair. To the economist, on the other hand, legality *per se* is no criterion of fairness."[1]

A task of the economist is thus to study business practices and methods from the standpoint of whether or not they promote the process of competition. If certain forms are found (1) to injure, restrict, or limit competition or (2) to cause it to have undesirable results, they are identified as "unfair" methods of competition from an economic point of view. Eventually such methods of competition may find their way to the *legal* list of unfair practices. In the work of studying and identifying unfair methods of competition, economists have the influential aid of competitors who are injured by the particular business practices. It is the political influence of this group, moreover, which plays an important part in shaping the law on unfair competition.

Broadly speaking, "fair" competition may be considered to be any competitive business practice or method which promotes the social purpose of

[1] W. H. S. Stevens, "Unfair Competition," *Political Science Quarterly*, June, 1914, p. 282.

competition—namely, the provision of more and better goods at lower prices. Recognized in economics as well as in the law is the fact that in the conduct of competitive business anyone is free to engage in an occupation of his own choice, without restriction by those already in the field. Established firms do not like to see newcomers appear, but freedom of entry is an essential part of the institution of competition. Likewise, the action of a rival seller in offering goods of better quality or at lower prices is accepted as a part of the basic social purposes of competition. A further aspect of the competitive process is the principle that no one is entitled to have a profit or income as a matter of right. Profits must be won by the efficient satisfaction of consumer desires; and the elimination of weak and inefficient enterprisers by the more efficient ones is not regarded as unfair competition, so long as all sellers have an equal and fair chance to survive.

Unfair competition begins to creep into the business process when particular practices or methods are employed *by some sellers* to hamper, restrict, or hinder *others* and to deny them the opportunity of surviving *or expanding* on the basis of their productive efficiency. From earliest times, for example, certain business firms have injured others by such practices as using false weights, disparaging a rival's merchandise, copying a rival's trade symbols, and passing off a given product for that of a competitor. These practices were condemned in the common law and continue today to be universally regarded as unfair methods of competition. With the rise of the railroads and monopolistic mergers, various forms of price discrimination came to be regarded as the principal forms of unfair competition. Today, in large measure, the problem of unfair competition continues to center on the practice of discriminatory pricing—(1) as to places, (2) as to kinds and uses of goods, and (3) as to persons. (See also Chap. 9, pp. 181–185.)

From an economic point of view, advertising has been identified as an unfair method of competition (1) when it is false and (2) when it is used excessively. Deceptive and misleading advertising fits into the category of misrepresentation, and its use may be either a fraud upon the public or an injury to a competitor or both.

Excessive advertising has been frequently condemned by economists, antitrust lawyers, and certain businessmen as an unfair method of competition. The use of large-scale, mass advertising, it is said, enables a financially dominant firm "to blanket the market" and win consumer preference, even though a small producer stands ready to offer better service, superior quality, and lower prices. The very fact of being able to employ large-scale advertising gives an advantage to a few producers which is not equally available to smaller but perhaps just as efficient firms. In the Tobacco decision (1946), the Supreme Court, itself, described the very large advertising expenditures of the major cigarette companies as "a powerful offensive and defensive weapon against new competition" (see also Chap. 11, p. 229).

Professor F. W. Taussig of Harvard University was one of the first economists to condemn the excessive use of advertising. Although recognizing that advertising may serve a good purpose in stimulating desires and introducing new products, Professor Taussig emphasized that it may also serve as a weapon of destructive competition. In his words,

Among articles equally good, that which is systematically paraded is likely to be most readily sold. People are led to buy Jones's wares rather than Smith's. One might suppose that if Smith's wares were equally good, and were sold at a lower price (made possible by eliminating the advertising expense), he would hold his own in spite of Jones's preposterous puffing. But, in fact, Jones's wares are preferred; some vague impression of superiority is produced by the incessant boasting. Plentiful cash is the *sine qua non* of an effective advertising campaign. The large producer, or would-be monopolist, has here again a tactical advantage.

The same is true of other means for popularizing your goods—prizes, premiums, gifts, pictures, what not. These delude the purchaser into the belief that he is getting something for nothing. Like mendacious advertising, they rest on the gullibility of mankind, and are effective in proportion as they are carried out on a large scale.[2]

Some economists recommend that positive steps be taken to curb the large-scale advertising expenditures of oligopolistic industries. Professor W. H. Nicholls, for example, suggests the enactment of a progressive tax on the total advertising outlays of any given company.[3] No action as yet, however, has been taken by government to limit or restrict the advertising expenditures of large combinations. Since the newspapers, magazine publishers, and radio companies would vigorously and effectively oppose any such action, it is unlikely that a limitation on advertising expenditures will be imposed in the near future.

Another business practice which economists early came to regard as being "unfair" is the sale of goods on condition that the buyer will lease, sell, purchase, or use other products of the supplier. Such arrangements are called exclusive dealing or tying agreements. Sometimes a company leases or sells a patented machine only on condition that users will buy related supplies from the particular supplier. Frequently a dominant seller requires a buyer to take his full line of goods as a condition of buying some particular brand or special item. This is called "full-line forcing." Still another practice is that of requiring a dealer to handle only the products of a given supplier as a condition of getting any supplies at all. These various practices, it may be noted, are still frequently used at the present time. The Department of Justice and the Federal Trade Commission, however, as we shall see in the next chapter, are constantly endeavoring to stamp them out.

Many additional forms of questionable business practices were, and still are, used by dominant firms to advance their monopoly control. They include the maintenance of black lists of distributors who engage in price

[2] F. W. Taussig, *Principles of Economics* (New York, 1924), Vol. 2, p. 450.
[3] W. H. Nicholls, *Price Policies in the Cigarette Industry* (Nashville, 1951), pp. 412–415.

competition; the boycotting of firms refusing to join in a price-control plan; a refusal to sell to independent merchants, dealers, or competing processors; espionage by bribing an employee of a competitor; the payment of secret commissions; and the use of vexatious patent suits, threats, and other forms of intimidation. Most of these practices, as we shall see later in the present chapter, are now condemned by the law.

BACKGROUND FOR THE FEDERAL TRADE COMMISSION AND CLAYTON ACTS (1914)

The evidence presented in the *Standard Oil* and *American Tobacco* cases showed clearly that *cutthroat competition* was a principal tool used by mergers to eliminate independents and to extend their area of control. Although the Supreme Court condemned the "intent and purpose" of these mergers to secure monopoly control, it failed to declare that their methods of competition, as such, were unfair. A considerable part of the business community became greatly disturbed over this fact; and demands were made upon political leaders to provide legislation identifying and prohibiting the means of unfair competition, *without regard to intention or motive*. In the political campaign of 1912, both the Republicans and the Democrats promised new legislation to prohibit unfair competitive practices. The general view of leaders in both parties was that if the tools of incipient monopoly could be outlawed, the further and nation-wide development of monopoly could be prevented.

In the work of the House and Senate committees on proposals for prohibiting unfair competitive practices, general agreement was reached (1) that the principle of fair competition should stand as the basic economic policy of the nation and (2) that unfair competition should be prohibited in order to cut off monopoly in its incipiency. "The most certain way to stop monopoly at the threshold," said the House committee, "is to prevent unfair competition."[4] Several attempts were made to define the term "unfair competition" and to enumerate the practices which were deemed to be unfair. The prevailing view, however, was that there should be a blanket prohibition of unfair competition, and that the determination of acts falling within this category should be left to a special trade commission. According to the House committee, "It is impossible to frame definitions which embrace all unfair practices. There is no limit to human inventiveness in this field. Even if all known unfair practices were specifically defined and prohibited, it would be at once necessary to begin over again. If Congress were to adopt the method of definition, it would undertake an endless task."

THE FEDERAL TRADE COMMISSION ACT

The general views of Congress on the prohibition of unfair methods of competition were embodied in the Federal Trade Commission Act, which

[4] *Conference Report, Federal Trade Commission*, 63rd Congress, second session, House Report 1142, September 4, 1914, p. 19.

was signed by President Woodrow Wilson on September 26, 1914. The principal provisions of this legislation may be summarized as follows:

1. Provision is made for the creation of a Federal Trade Commission of five members to be appointed by the President, with the advice and consent of the Senate, for terms of seven years. No more than three of the commissioners shall be members of the same political party.

2. The heart of the Federal Trade Commission Act is Section 5, which prohibits "unfair methods of competition" in interstate commerce. In summary form, Section 5 states that *"Unfair methods of competition in commerce are hereby declared unlawful. . . .* Whenever the commission shall have reason to believe that any such person, partnership, or corporation has been or is using any unfair methods of competition in commerce, and *if it shall appear to the commission that a proceeding by it in respect thereof would be to the interest of the public,* it shall issue and serve . . . a complaint."

Section 5 was early interpreted by the courts to mean that a questionable business practice may be attacked by the Commission only when there is a "specific and substantial" *public* interest in the prevention of the particular practice involved. Thus, the *Klesner* case (1929) involved a controversy between two sellers of lamp shades over the use of the firm name "The Shade Shop." Klesner adopted the name although it was used by a competitor only a short distance away, and the Commission ordered him to cease and desist its use. The Supreme Court dismissed the case on the ground that the interest concerned was primarily a private one. In the view of the Court, there must be a public concern in the controversy between competitors, as would be true if a case involved "flagrant oppression of the weak by the strong."[5] Controversies which are private in nature, without a substantial public interest, are matters of private rights and remedies to be handled by the civil law in private suits.

A further important interpretation of Section 5 was made in the *Raladam* case, decided in 1931. The facts of this case were that the Raladam company manufactured and sold "an obesity cure," which it advertised as being safe, effective, and convenient to use. The Commission found that the product contained a dangerous drug which could not be safely used except under medical direction and advice. A cease-and-desist order was issued, and the company appealed the case, claiming that unfair competition was not involved. The Supreme Court agreed with the Commission that the advertisements were "dangerously misleading," and that the public had an interest in preventing the use of such methods. Nevertheless, the Court ruled against the Commission for the reason that the injurious methods *had not injured a competitor.* Unfair competition, the Court stated, implies injury to a competitor.[6]

3. The need for providing *consumers* with protection against unfair and

---

[5] *F.T.C. v. Klesner,* 280 U.S. 19, 28 (1929)
[6] *F.T.C. v. Raladam Co.,* 283 U.S. 643, 652 (1931).

injurious practices led to the enactment in 1938 of the Wheeler-Lea amendment to the Federal Trade Commission Act. By the terms of this legislation, Section 5 was amended to prohibit "unfair or deceptive acts or practices" in interstate commerce. In the House report on the proposed amendment to Section 5, it was stated, "By the proposed amendment to Section 5, the Commission can prevent such acts or practices which injuriously affect the general public as well as those which are unfair to competitors. In other words, this amendment makes the consumer, who may be injured by an unfair trade practice, of equal concern, before the law, with the merchant or manufacturer injured by the unfair methods of a dishonest competitor."[7] The Wheeler-Lea amendment also fixes the date when cease-and-desist orders issued by the Commission are to become final and binding. A further addition (Section 15) provides for the definition of the term "false advertising" as "an advertisement other than labeling which is misleading in a material respect," and makes the definition applicable to the advertising of foods, drugs, curative devices, and cosmetics.

4. Section 6 of the Federal Trade Commission Act empowers the Commission to collect and make available to the President, Congress, and the public factual data with respect to "the organization, business, conduct, practices and management of any corporation engaged in commerce, excepting banks and common carriers." This section of the act has served a very useful purpose; and since its inception, the Commission has prepared and published some 150 general investigations and 370 cost studies. The investigations of the Commission have covered the gas and electrical utilities, the telephone industry, meat packing, tobacco processing, the oil industry, chain stores, farm implements, the basing-point system, resale price maintenance, mergers, and international cartels. Many of these reports have proved to be highly significant and have provided the basis for new remedial legislation—for example, the Packers and Stockyards Act, the Securities Act of 1933, the Securities Exchange Act of 1934, and the Public Utility Holding Company Act of 1935.

In 1949 the Hoover Commission reported that the Commission's "economic work—instead of being the backbone of its activities—has been allowed to dwindle almost to none." Since 1949, limitations of funds have caused the economic work of the Commission to decline still further.

5. Sections 12 to 15 of the Federal Trade Commission Act, as amended by the Wheeler-Lea Act, authorize the Commission to safeguard the public by preventing the dissemination of *false advertisements* with respect to foods, drugs, cosmetics, and therapeutic devices used in the diagnosis, prevention, or treatment of disease. An amendment of 1950 adds that advertisements for oleomargarine or margarine cannot describe such oleomargarine or margarine as a dairy product. Persons who falsely advertise under Sections

[7] Committee on Interstate and Foreign Commerce, *Extension of Federal Trade Commission's Authority over Unfair Acts and Practices and False Advertising*, 75th Congress, first session, House Report 1613, August 19, 1937, p. 3.

12 to 15, with an intent to mislead and where the product is injurious to health, upon conviction by a district court may be fined up to $5000 and given a prison sentence of not more than six months, or both, for the first offense. Second and succeeding convictions carry a penalty of not more than $10,000 and not more than one year in prison or both.

The basic federal law with respect to food, drugs, and cosmetics is the federal Food, Drug, and Cosmetic Act of 1938, entitled "An Act to prohibit the movement in interstate commerce of *adulterated* and *misbranded* food, drugs, devices, and cosmetics, and for other purposes." This regulatory legislation, which replaced the original Food and Drug Act of 1906, is administered by the Food and Drug Administration of the Federal Security Agency. The federal Food, Drug, and Cosmetic Act prohibits *adulteration* and *misbranding*, whereas the Federal Trade Commission Act prohibits *false advertisement*. Strictly speaking, the sale of untruthfully labeled food and drugs, in many situations, is a form of unfair competition, and the Federal Trade Commission on occasion in the past has exercised a concurrent jurisdiction with the Food and Drug Administration. On December 5, 1946, however, the Federal Trade Commission announced that henceforth it would not institute proceedings against false labeling or branding in cases falling within the direct responsibility of the Food and Drug Administration. This action was taken to avoid conflict and duplication of effort.

OTHER ACTS ADMINISTERED BY THE FEDERAL TRADE COMMISSION

In addition to the Federal Trade Commission Act, the Commission administers the following measures of economic regulation:

1. Sections 2, 3, 7, and 8 of the Clayton Act (1914), as amended by the Robinson-Patman Act (1936). The Clayton Act provides that the Federal Trade Commission and the Department of Justice shall have concurrent jurisdiction over the enforcement of the provisions of the Clayton Act. Either agency may proceed against violators, and action is taken by the one which gets to it first. The pertinent sections of the Clayton Act, as amended by the Robinson-Patman Act, are those dealing (a) with various forms of price discrimination (Section 2); (b) with exclusive dealing arrangements and tying contracts (Section 3); (c) with the acquisition by a corporation of stock in competing enterprises (Section 7); and (d) with certain kinds of competitive interlocking directorates (Section 8). These sections will be discussed in detail in the following chapter.

2. The Export Trade Act of 1918, popularly known as the Webb-Pomerene Act. This legislation was discussed in Chapter 14.

3. The Wool Products Labeling Act of 1939, known as the "Truth in Fabrics" law. The purpose of the Wool Products Act is to protect manufacturers, merchants, and consumers against deception and unfair competition in articles which are made in whole or in part of wool. Before the enactment of this legislation, there were a great many abuses in the sale of woolen articles. Reused wool was sold as new wool; products sold as "all

wool" often contained less than 5 percent wool; and "part wool" garments frequently meant only that woolen thread was used for stitching the button-holes. The Wool Labeling Act was adopted as a result of the efforts of wool growers, consumers, and legitimate woolen manufacturers.

The act of 1939 provides that all products containing wool, except carpets, rugs, mats, and upholsteries, must disclose on a label attached to the mer-chandise the kind and percentage of each fiber contained in the product, including the respective percentages of "wool," "reprocessed wool," and "reused wool." The name of the manufacturer or distributor must also ap-pear on the label, and the label must remain on the merchandise when it is delivered to the consumer. The Commission maintains a staff of inspectors to check on compliance by manufacturers, distributors, and retailers; and enforcement is conducted by means of conferences, stipulations, trade prac-tice conferences, and use of cease-and-desist orders.

4. Certain provisions of the Lanham Trade-Mark Act of 1946. The Lan-ham Act provides that the Federal Trade Commission may apply to the Commissioner of Patents, whose office administers trademark legislation, for a cancellation of registered trademarks which are deceptive, immoral, or scandalous; which have been obtained fraudulently; or which are in violation of other provisions of the Lanham Act.

5. The McCarran Insurance Act of 1948 gives the Commission certain jurisdiction over the insurance business. This activity of the Commission is highly complex because it varies from state to state with variations in state law.

6. The Fur Products Labeling Act of 1951. This legislation is modeled after the Wool Products Labeling Act of 1939. Its purpose is to protect consumers and industry members against the misbranding, false advertising, and false invoicing of furs and fur products moving in interstate commerce. The widespread use of deception and false advertising in the sale of furs, such as use of the term "mink blended coney" for rabbit fur, gave rise to demands within the industry for corrective legislation. Manufacturers and distributors are now required to attach labels on garments showing the name of the animal which produced the fur; country of origin; and whether the fur is bleached or dyed, or composed of paws, tails, bellies, or waste furs. Retailers may substitute their own labels, but must retain the informa-tion from the original labels for a period of three years.

7. The Flammable Fabrics Act of 1953. By the terms of this legislation, prohibitions are placed on the manufacture for sale, the sale, the importa-tion, or the transportation for sale of any wearing apparel which "is so highly flammable as to be dangerous when worn by individuals."

ENFORCEMENT PROCEDURE UTILIZED BY THE FEDERAL TRADE COMMISSION

The Federal Trade Commission, we have seen, is empowered to prevent, in the public interest, (a) unfair methods of competition and deceptive acts and practices as forbidden in Section 5 of the Federal Trade Commission

Act; (b) the prohibited practices in the Clayton Act (Sections 2, 3, 7, and 8), as amended by the Robinson-Patman Act; and (c) practices which are prohibited in the Export Trade Act, the Wool Products Labeling Act of 1939, the Fur Products Labeling Act of 1951, and the Flammable Fabrics Act of 1953. In enforcing these regulations, the Commission utilizes three different procedures, namely, (1) individual and industry-wide conferences to secure voluntary compliance with rules of fair competition; (2) negotiation of stipulations with accused parties to abandon objectionable practices; and (3) legal action based upon the issuance of formal complaints. These three procedures are respectively called the coöperative method (or "administrative treatment"), the consent method, and the compulsory method for preventing the use of unfair trade practices.

Evidence for making complaints against business firms is secured by the Commission from its own investigations, from consumers, and often from the reports of one competitor against another. Approximately 10 percent of the cases selected are generated by the Commission's own investigations, and about 90 percent arise in the complaints of consumers, competitors, customers, and other governmental agencies.

1. ADMINISTRATIVE TREATMENT

Letters of Discontinuance. The staff of the Commission handles many problems of false and misleading acts and practices by contacting accused parties and discussing the issues with them. In so far as possible, the Commission seeks to settle such problems on a friendly basis. If the accused party will agree to discontinue the practice, and will sign a letter to that effect, the matter is often dropped at once. The policy is to give business a "break" if it is willing to coöperate. The "administrative treatment" differs from the "stipulation procedure" discussed below in that the letter of discontinuance need not be submitted to the Commission for approval. In the main, administrative treatment is used (a) if the accused is not a chronic violator and (b) if the public interest can be protected by a statement that the practice will be stopped.

Trade Practice Conferences. If deceptive acts and practices are being rather widely used within a given industry, the Commission may invite trade members to attend a "trade-practice conference." The use of trade practice conferences was first instituted in 1919 by Commission members who sought to secure an acceptance of rules of fair competition by industry on a voluntary and coöperative basis rather than by legal prosecution. At the present time, the Commission is currently spending a substantial part of its budget on this type of work. The view of the Commission is that trade conferences afford a useful means for solving many problems of unfair competition on an industry-wide basis with a minimum of time and money.

Trade practice conferences may be called by the Commission upon its own motion or upon application by an industry group. In sponsoring a trade conference, the Commission invites industry members to meet with staff members from the Commission to discuss and develop rules for the conduct of business in the particular industry concerned. Public hearings are held on the proposed rules, and thereupon the rules adopted are submitted to the Commission for approval. Once they are approved, industry members, in effect, are put on notice that if they subscribe to and comply with the approved rules of business etiquette, they will to that extent be in harmony with the law. Trade practice conferences are handled within the Commission by the Bureau of Consultation (see Fig. 52).

It may be noted that only those rules are adopted which an industry group is willing to accept. Legal action, moreover, is never taken for the violation of a rule, as such, for the rules are advisory only. If complaints and an investigation indicate that a continuing violation exists, the Commission charges a violation of the basic statutes and not of a trade practice rule.

Classes of Rules. The rules formulated by a trade conference apply (a) to recognized methods of unfair competition which trade members and the Commission agree should be specifically prohibited in the particular industry and (b) to certain practices which trade members themselves believe would be promotive of fair competition. Rules in the first category are called *Group I Rules.* They cover trade practices which the Commission considers to be illegal. Thus, in the Trade Practice Rules for the Wholesale Confectionery Industry, it is specified that business practices such as commercial bribery, defamation of competitors or disparagement of their products, and coercion to fix prices are unfair trade practices. *Group II Rules,* on the other hand, embrace industry practices which trade members would like to encourage. They consist of rules to be observed with respect to such matters as the return of merchandise, the issuance of information to consumers on how to care for products made by the industry, and the handling of business disputes by arbitration.

Commission Policy on Administrative Treatment. The Federal Trade Commission has stated that its policy is not to dismiss cases by administrative treatment or to settle them by stipulation if the violations "involve intent to defraud or mislead; false advertisements of foods, drugs, devices or cosmetics which are inherently dangerous or where injury is probable; suppression or restraint of competition through conspiracy or monopolistic practices . . . violations of the Clayton Act . . . (or) where the Commission is of the opinion that such procedure will not be effective in preventing continued use of the unlawful methods, acts, or practices." The records indicate, however, that the Commission has used, and continues to use, the trade practice rule-making procedure for dismissing or suspending a variety of cases involving deception and discrimination.[8] How is this deviation to be explained? In part, the Commission's practice appears to reflect an effort to secure *industry-wide* correction of certain trade abuses. In part, however, the practice also reflects an apathy of various commissioners to an enforcement

[8] Select Committee on Small Business, *Antitrust Law Enforcement*, 81st Congress, second session, House Report 3236, January 1, 1951, pp. 30–32, 91.

of the Clayton Act, as amended, in any sort of a thoroughgoing way. Following the adoption of a set of trade practice conference rules, the Commission makes almost no investigation of industry compliance. "All the available evidence," declared the House Committee on Small Business in 1952, "points to extensive noncompliance with rules and to leniency in dealing with offenders."[9] Upon occasion, however, staff members of the Commission do contact trade members and seek to get them to abide by a trade practice rule. If a firm persists in violating the rule, the Commission may thereupon attempt to secure a stipulation on discontinuance or it may issue a formal complaint. A policy of counseling an industry group to "go and sin no more" provides little reason or compulsion for obeying the anti-trust laws. Monopolistic and deceptive practices are highly profitable arrangements. If they are to be stopped, government, in most cases, must "step on someone's toes." This the trade practice conference procedure does not do.

Experience has shown that trade practice conference rules, at their best, are those which apply to problems of misrepresentation. In the formulation of definitions for such terms as "taffeta," "satin," "shrinkproof," "waterproof," "rainproof," and "gold-filled," Commission and industry coöperation has proved to be genuinely useful. It is a good plan to expose tentative definitions and standards to the cross fire of criticism in order to develop unexpected meanings and interpretations. Since the definitions and standards are to be applied to a particular industry group, it is proper for this criticism to come from those who are most intimately acquainted with the industry.

2. STIPULATION PROCEDURE

The Commission settles many cases of unfair competition by means of stipulations. This procedure gives a proposed defendant an opportunity to agree with staff members of the Commission that the objectionable practice should be abandoned. If an agreement can be reached, the business firm signs a stipulation, an admission of the material facts and *an agreement* to discontinue the unlawful practice, and no formal complaint is issued. The agreement, however, must be approved by the Commissioners. It is also made a matter of public record, and the respondent is required to submit a report within sixty days on the manner in which he is complying with the agreement. If the stipulation is subsequently violated, the Commission proceeds by complaint and order; and, if necessary, the order is carried to a Court of Appeals for enforcement. The Bureau of Consultation in the Commission includes the division which handles stipulations (see Fig. 30).

The stipulation procedure adopted by the Commission has proved to be an effective method for correcting a large number of violations with a minimum expenditure of time and money. See also Table 23. In general, up to the present time, the stipulation procedure has been largely confined to the

[9] Final Report of the Select Committee on Small Business, House of Representatives, 82nd Congress, second session, House Report 2513, 1952, p. 293.

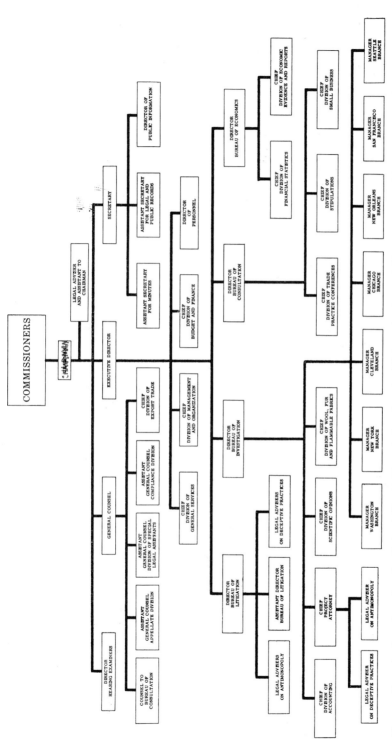

Fig. 30. Organization chart for the Federal Trade Commission (1954). All investigative activities are centered in the Bureau of Investigation; all trial work is in Bureau of Litigation; and voluntary compliance procedures are handled by the Bureau of Consultation.

TABLE 23. Federal Trade Commission:
Stipulations Negotiated.

Fiscal Year	Number of Stipulations Accepted
1949	139
1950	164
1951	157
1952	131
1953	121
1954	70

(Source: Federal Trade Commission. The period of July 1, 1948 to July 1, 1949, is the fiscal year of 1949.)

settlement of cases of false and misleading advertising which grow out of the Commission's continuous scrutiny of radio and periodical advertising.

3. THE SETTLING OF CASES BY LEGAL PROCEDURE

Section 5 (b) of the F.T.C. Act and Section 11 of the Clayton Act, as amended, provide that the Commission "shall issue and serve . . . a complaint" whenever it shall have reason to believe that an unfair method of competition, a deceptive act, or a monopolistic practice is being used in interstate commerce. The settlement of cases by securing letters of a discontinuance, by the dismissal of cases upon acceptance of trade practice rules, and by the stipulation procedure, is thus an innovation not contemplated by the law.

In using the complaint procedure, the accused party (the respondent) is made a defendant in a formal legal proceeding conducted by the Bureau of Litigation within the Commission. A *complaint* is issued against the defendant, and provision is made for a public hearing before a trial examiner (also called "hearing examiner"), who is a staff member of the Commission. Trial examiners are, in effect, judges. Under the Administrative Procedure Act they are independent of the Commission and its staff.

Proceedings before a trial examiner are conducted much like a court trial. The Commission and the defendants are both represented by their own attorneys. At the conclusion of the hearings, the trial examiner issues a report containing (1) his findings and (2) an "initial decision," i.e., a dismissal or a cease-and-desist order. Under certain circumstances, to save time and expense, the Commission may authorize the disposition of a formal proceeding by the acceptance of a stipulation (see Table 26).

The decision of the trial examiner becomes the decision of the Commission 30 days after service upon the respondent unless (1) the respondent appeals the decision to the Commission, (2) the Commission postpones the effective date, or (3) the Commission, itself, decides to review the case. If the Commission reviews the case, its attorneys and those of the respondent file briefs with the Commission. Subsequently, a public hearing is held and each side argues the case orally before the commissioners. The commissioners thereupon either (a) dismiss the complaint or (b) issue their findings of fact with an order to cease and desist from the unlawful practice.

Cease-and-desist orders, it may be noted, are negative instruments of control. They tell a respondent what he may not do; not what he must do. The Federal Trade Commission Act, *as interpreted by the Commission*, does not clothe the Commission with authority to direct and require "fair competition" or to prescribe a positive course of conduct.

A defendant may appeal a cease-and-desist order to the appropriate Court of Appeals. The Federal Trade Commission Act provides that "the findings of the commission as to the facts, if supported by testimony, shall be conclusive." The function of the Court, therefore, is one of making a final determination of the rules of law. The Court of Appeals may affirm, set aside, or modify the order of the Commission, and it may also require the Commission to secure further factual evidence. If a defendant secures an adverse judgment in the Court of Appeals, he has the possibility of a final appeal to the Supreme Court.

The Wheeler-Lea amendment provides that if a defendant under the Federal Trade Commission Act or the Wool Labeling Act plans to appeal an order of the Commission, he must do so within sixty days or the order becomes final and binding. Final orders of the Commission are enforced by contempt proceedings initiated in a District Court by the Attorney General. If a continuing offense is proven, each day will carry a penalty *up to* $5000 per day, at the discretion of the judge.

Cease-and-desist orders issued under the Clayton Act do not become final by the lapse of time. This means that if the Commission desires to enforce an order to cease and desist under the Clayton Act, it must petition a Court of Appeals for enforcement or await the completion of an appeal for review filed with the Court by the respondent. If and when the Court of Appeals affirms the order, contempt proceedings may be brought against the respondent. The penalty for contempt of court is whatever amount the court believes is appropriate.

CONSENT SETTLEMENTS—DEFAULT ORDERS

In an effort to save time and expense in settling formal cases, the Commission in 1951 adopted a modified cease-and-desist order procedure. If there appears to be a reasonable probability of reaching an agreement on a remedy, the parties may seek to negotiate a settlement. Thereupon, if agreement is reached, a regular cease-and-desist order is prepared which represents a settlement acceptable to the staff and the Commission, as well as to the respondent. This is called a "consent order." See also Table 26.

There is little doubt that the new settlement procedure provides a speedy way for disposing of formal cases. It is possible, however, that in working out a consent settlement, the Commission may agree to *minimum* forms of relief in an effort to secure acceptance by respondents. Thus far, the number of consent orders has not been sufficiently large to determine whether or not they provide adequate relief in the public interest.

A further procedure to expedite the handling of formal complaints was adopted by the Commission in 1951. It is the practice of issuing "default orders." If a respondent fails to answer a formal complaint, or if he admits all the material allegations, the trial examiner and the Commission, it is provided, shall enter a "default order." Prior to the adoption of this rule, the Commission's practice was to hold hearings on complaints even when respondents failed to file an answer or to appear at the hearings.

THE MEANING OF THE TERM "UNFAIR COMPETITION" UNDER SECTION 5

Section 5 of the Federal Trade Commission Act, as amended, we have seen, prohibits (1) unfair competition in relation to the activities of competitors and (2) unfair and deceptive acts and practices employed against consumers. In applying and interpreting Section 5, what meaning have the courts and the Commission placed upon the term "unfair competition"?

The decision of the Supreme Court in the *Gratz* case (1920) was a highly important one in marking out the meaning of the term "unfair competition." In this case, a majority of the Supreme Court developed the view that unfair competition includes (1) practices involving deception, misrepresentation, and fraud, which have long been condemned in the common law, and (2) practices "against public policy because of their dangerous tendency unduly to hinder competition or create a monopoly."[10] The *Gratz* case is significant because it indicated that the Court would include in the category of unfair competition concerted action *by competitors* to create a monopoly. In most instances, the idea of unfair competition had been applied to any act or method which injures or *excludes* a competitor. Now the concept was coming to embrace the *inclusive* acts of competitors to suppress competition or to create a monopoly. This point of view was carried further by the Supreme Court in the *Beech-Nut Packing* case, decided in 1922. Here the Court held that a price-fixing scheme which had the effect of destroying competition was a form of unfair competition because it restrained "the natural flow of commerce and the freedom of competition in the channels of interstate commerce which it has been the purpose of all the antitrust acts to maintain."[11]

A further significant case developing the scope of the Commission's jurisdiction under Section 5 was the *Pacific States Paper* case, decided in 1926. This case was an action brought against a group of local trade associations, their members, and a regional association in the paper industry on the Pacific Coast. Each association, the record showed, prepared price lists which were circulated among association members and regularly observed by them in making sales to customers. The Supreme Court condemned the practice and

[10] *F.T.C.* v. *Gratz*, 253 U.S. 421, 427 (1920).
[11] *F.T.C.* v. *Beech-Nut Packing Co.*, 257 U.S. 441, 454 (1922).

held that any business procedure which has a tendency to lessen competition and to fix uniform prices is an unfair trade practice under the Federal Trade Commission Act. In its words, "An understanding express or tacit that the agreed prices will be followed is enough to constitute a transgression of the law.[12] Upon the basis of the *Pacific States Paper* case, in particular, the Federal Trade Commission has established its jurisdiction to proceed against any form of concerted action by competitors which hinders, restricts, or suppresses competition. Thus at the present time, cases against concerted action on price, express or implied, as well as individual acts in restraint of trade, may be brought by the Department of Justice under the Sherman Act or by the Federal Trade Commission under the F.T.C. Act. See also Table 24.

TABLE 24. Federal Trade Commission: Summary of Antimonopoly Activities Under Section 5 (F.T.C. Act) and Sections 2, 3, 7, 8 (Clayton Act, as amended).

Fiscal Year	Complaints Issued	Cease-and-Desist Orders
1949	55	9
1950	27	16
1951	29	23
1952	29	26
1953	29	24
1954	30	25[a]

a Includes one consent order.
(Source: Federal Trade Commission.)

ACTION BY THE FEDERAL TRADE COMMISSION AGAINST MISREPRESENTATION, DECEIT, AND RELATED PRACTICES

A second broad category of business practices which the Federal Trade Commission and the courts have held to be "unfair competition" includes misrepresentation, oppression, deceit, and fraud. The cases arising in this category are by far the most numerous, for they typically stem from the everyday activity of *individual* competitors. Business is a profit-making activity; and if there is profit in certain practices, some unscrupulous businessmen are led to employ them on the ground that "business is business." Fair competition is not a natural process which can be left alone to develop of its own accord. It is rather the end result of a large amount of government intervention to provide (1) private remedies in civil courts to adjust the private disputes and injuries of individuals in their commercial activities and (2) "rules of the game" formulated by government to insure that competitive activity is in the public interest.

The list of unfair competitive practices shown in Table 25 is based upon

[12] *F.T.C. v. Pacific States Paper Trade Association*, 273 U.S. 53, 62 (1926).

Table 25. Digest of Federal Trade Commission Cease-and-Desist Orders with Respect to Unfair Methods of Competition.[a]

Acquiring confidential information unfairly.
Acquiring stock of competitor.
Advertising falsely or misleadingly.
Appropriating tradename or mark wrongfully.
Appropriating values created by a competitor's ingenuity, labor, or expense.
Bribing customers' employees.
Claiming indorsements or testimonials falsely.
Claiming trade-name rights wrongfully.
Coercing and intimidating.
Combinations of dealers (1) to prevent others from procuring goods or (2) to influence the trade policy of competitors or suppliers.
Combinations or agreements to fix, enhance or depress prices.
Cutting off competitors' access to customers, or market.
Cutting prices arbitrarily to discipline a competitor acting independently on price.
Dealing on exclusive and tying basis.
Delivering short measure.
Disparaging competitors and their products.
Enforcing payments wrongfully.
Enticing away competitors' employees.

Inducing breach of competitors' contracts.
Interfering with competitors or their goods.
Maintaining resale prices (except as legalized under state legislation and the Miller-Tidings Act).
Misbranding or mislabeling.
Misrepresenting oneself and goods.
Offering deceptive inducements to purchase.
Operating secret subsidiary.
Passing off a product as and for that of a competitor.
Securing signatures wrongfully.
Selling below cost with intent to injure competition.
Simulating competitor or his product.
Spying on competitors.
Subsidizing business of one or more customers.
Threatening infringement suits, not in good faith, to stifle competition.
Using misleading names with respect to the identity of a seller or his goods.
Using or selling lottery devices—such as punchboards and pushcards—in merchandising a product.

[a] *Digest of Decisions of the Federal Trade Commission* (Washington, 1940) and *Annual Reports of the Federal Trade Commission*. A weekly summary of Federal Trade Commission complaints, decisions, and orders may be secured by writing to the Publications Division, Federal Trade Commission, Washington, D.C.

the cease-and-desist orders which have been issued by the Federal Trade Commission from time to time since its establishment. Each category represents situations in which individual business firms have sought by a particular means to hinder, limit, or injure one or more competitors.

An example of the type of work done by the Commission in condemning unfair competition based upon misrepresentation and deceit is found in orders of the Commission against the General Motors Corporation and the Ford Motor Company. Each of these orders was upheld in the Courts of Appeal.[13] The business practice challenged by the Commission in these cases was one of advertising a so-called "6% Plan" for financing the sale of automobiles. The advertisements stated that the rate of interest was only 6 percent on "your unpaid balance." In fact, however, the customer was charged 6 percent on the original amount of the account—the original unpaid balance—from the date of the obligation until the date that the account was closed. The Commission demonstrated that when interest is calculated in this manner, the effective rate is approximately $11\frac{1}{2}$ percent. A cease-and-desist order was accordingly issued. The companies carried the order to the

[13] *General Motors Corp.* v. *F.T.C.*, 114 F. (2d) 33 (1940); *Ford Motor Co.* v. *F.T.C.*, 120 F. (2d) 175 (1941).

Courts of Appeal, claiming that they had always included in their statements the notation "It is not 6% interest, but simply a convenient multiplier anyone can use and understand." The Courts of Appeal held, however, that the advertising was misleading on the ground that in a good many cases buyers would believe that they were paying 6 percent interest only on the current unpaid balance.

PREDATORY PRICE CUTTING UNFAIR UNDER SECTION 5

A prevalent fear of independents is that a dominant enterprise will use its financial power to cut prices below its actual accounting costs, with resulting injury to independent sellers. Section 5 of the Federal Trade Commission Act has been applied to prohibit sales below cost *with the intent to injure competition*. In *E. B. Muller* v. *F.T.C.*, two dominant and allied sellers of chicory decided to eliminate their only competitor, R. E. Schanzer, of New Orleans.[14] Granulated chicory was deliberately sold at cost, or slightly below cost, for several years. The predatory intent of the dominant sellers was revealed in their business correspondence. One letter, for example, stated "I certainly hope that we can . . . eliminate him entirely, by making prices that he cannot meet without losing money."

The Court of Appeals sustained the Commission's cease-and-desist order prohibiting the predatory price cutting. According to the court, "The fact that the sales were not greatly below cost does not aid the petitioners. It was not necessary that the evidence show that Schanzer [the independent] suffered loss. The purpose of the Federal Trade Commission Act is to prevent potential injury by stopping unfair methods of competition in their incipiency."

UNFAIR PRACTICES FROM THE STANDPOINT OF CONSUMERS

The essential purpose of the Wheeler-Lea amendment to the Federal Trade Commission Act, we have seen, is to safeguard consumers (1) by empowering the Commission to prohibit "unfair or deceptive acts or practices" (Section 5), and (2) by formulating a definition of the term "false advertisement" applicable to the advertising of food, drugs, curative devices, and cosmetics (Section 15). Section 15 of the Federal Trade Commission Act, as amended, defines a false advertisement as follows (italics supplied):

> The term "false advertisement" means an advertisement, *other than labeling*, which is *misleading in a material respect;* and in determining whether any advertisement is misleading, there shall be taken into account (among other things) not only *representations made* or *suggested* by statement, word, design, device, sound, or any combination thereof, but also the extent to which the advertisement *fails to reveal facts material* in the light of such representations or material with respect to consequences

[14] 142 F. (2d) 511 (1944).

which may result from the use of the commodity to which the advertisement relates under the conditions prescribed in said advertisement, or under such conditions as are customary or usual.

Whether or not an advertisement will be construed as being "false" or as making representations which are "deceptive" depends upon whether the advertisement is "misleading in a material respect." The word "material" means *not trivial*, and its application in any given case involves questions of degree and judgment. The fundamental questions to be considered in judging an advertisement are: (1) What are the representations? and (2) Are they true or not? False claims, misleading impressions, and false comparisons are all contrary to the Federal Trade Commission Act. The Commission is continually dealing with representations made by inference, innuendo, or suggestion. Advertising statements do not have to be categorical or unqualified to be condemned by the law.

Sections 12 to 15 of the F.T.C. Act, as amended by the Wheeler-Lea Act, authorize the Commission (1) to prevent the dissemination of *false advertisements* for food, drugs, cosmetics, and therapeutic devices; (2) to require advertisers to reveal that such products are dangerous or that their use may cause injury to bodily health when such is the case; and (3) to bring suits to enjoin the use of false and misleading advertisements in the food, drug, cosmetic and device field when it is believed that such "would be to the interest of the public."

In the adjudication of Section 13, giving the Commission power to bring suits to enjoin alleged false advertisements, the courts have held that injunctions will be issued upon a showing of "potential pecuniary injury to the public."[15] This means that it is not necessary for the Commission to show that a product is intrinsically detrimental or that it is inherently dangerous. If the item is falsely advertised, and if it appears that the public is likely to spend money for it in a substantial way, an injunction may be granted.

The use of injunctive suits to restrain false advertisements, pending final disposition by administrative proceedings, saves the public many millions of dollars each year. In 1951, for example, the Commission secured an injunction against the sale of Imdrin, a drug preparation composed principally of aspirin, thiamine chloride, calcium succinate, and caffeine. In nationwide advertising, Imdrin was presented as an adequate, effective, and reliable treatment for arthritis, rheumatism, neuritis, sciatica, gout, neuralgia, fibrositis, and bursitis. The Commission alleged that the representations were false, and the Court of Appeals granted a restraining order. Subsequently, a cease-and-desist order was issued. With the issuance of the injunction against the advertisements, sales of Imdrin fell sharply. It is estimated that resulting savings to the public in a year amounted to several million dollars.

During the course of a year, the Commission accepts stipulations and issues orders against a great variety of unfair and deceptive acts and prac-

[15] *F.T.C. v. National Health Aids, Inc.*, 108 F. Supp. 340, 348 (1952).

tices. The matters include (1) medicinal remedies which promise relief for cancer, general debility, pyorrhea, arthritis, leprosy, pneumonia, heart disease, tuberculosis, asthma, and a host of other diseases; (2) cigarette advertising and its spurious claims; (3) correspondence schools and diploma mills; (4) encyclopedias and books; (5) orthopedic shoes; (6) inflammable sweaters; (7) sales of merchandise without disclosure of foreign origin or with false and misleading labels; and (8) the use of fictitious prices in the sale of merchandise. See Table 26.

TABLE 26. Federal Trade Commission: Summary of Antideceptive Practices Work under Section 5 (F.T.C. Act), the Wool Products Labeling Act, and the Fur Products Labeling Act.

Fiscal Year	Cases Disposed of Administratively	Complaints Issued	Stipulations Accepted After Formal Complaint Issued	Cease-and-Desist Orders
1949	a	45	a	39
1950	53	97	a	63
1951	281	80	9	98
1952	269	75	4	108
1953	362	72	1	82 (includes 18 consent orders)

a Data not available.
(Source: Federal Trade Commission.)

COMMISSION HANDICAPPED BY INADEQUATE FUNDS

Each year the newspapers, magazines, radio, and television programs contain considerable amounts of advertising which is characterized by false claims, misleading impressions, and false comparisons. How is this to be explained? In large measure, the use and existence of such forms of advertising is to be explained by the fact that the Commission does not have sufficient funds to enforce the law in a thoroughgoing and vigorous way. Applications for complaints received from businessmen and consumers total about 2800 per year. The Commission, however, is able to initiate only a small fraction of the cases which should be prosecuted in the public interest.

Expenditures for advertising have increased enormously since 1914. It is estimated that some 225 million dollars were spent on advertising in 1914, and that today the sums spent run from 6½ to 7 billion dollars each year. The number of persons working on deceptive practices, however, remains about the same as it was in 1914. At the same time, the staff has had to add to its work load the Wheeler-Lea Act (1938), the Wool Products Labeling Act (1939), the Fur Products Labeling Act (1951), and the Flammable Fabrics Act (1953).

The Commission recognizes that its staff cannot render adequate service in policing false and misleading advertising. As an alternative procedure, it has turned to members of the advertising industry, themselves, to enlist their coöperation and assistance in curbing abuses in advertising by means of voluntary action.[16]

[16] See also Printers' Ink, May 29, 1953, p. 10.

"PUFFING" STILL PERMITTED UNDER THE WHEELER-LEA AMENDMENT

The Wheeler-Lea amendment does not restrict the traditional practice of a seller to engage in "puffing" in the sale of his wares. The courts themselves, moreover, have accepted the use of such words as "perfect," "amazing," "prime," "wonderful," "extra fancy," and "excellent" as legitimate "puffing" in the sale of products, even though the evidence indicates that the words are not appropriate. In the *Kidder Oil* case (1941), for example, a company sold a lubricating oil containing graphite. The advertisements for the product claimed that it was a "perfect" lubricant which would actually enable one to operate a motorcar an "amazing distance" after the oil was finally used up. The Commission charged that the advertisements were extravagant, deceptive, misleading, and false, and issued a cease-and-desist order.

Upon appeal, the Court of Appeals set aside the significant part of the Commission's order on the ground that the extravagant language was only "innocent puffing." In the words of the Court, "What might be an 'amazing distance' to one person might cause no surprise to another. So far as we know, there is nothing 'perfect' in this world, but still it is a common term, which undoubtedly means nothing more than that the product is good or of high quality. We can conceive of situations where the use of such words might be deceptive and even fraudulent. As used by petitioner, however, we are of the opinion that they are nothing more than a form of 'puffing' not calculated to deceive."[17] Again, in the *Carlay* case (1946), the Court of Appeals held that the use of the words "easy," "simple," and "safe" in connection with the sale of a product for removing excess weight was merely puffing or dealer's talk upon which a charge of misrepresentation could not be made.[18]

OFFENSIVE ADVERTISING AS A PROFIT-MAKING ACTIVITY

The action of the courts and Congress in accepting and permitting a large measure of exaggeration and flamboyant statements in present-day advertising, it is generally recognized, costs consumers a substantial sum of money. Each year, for example, consumers are induced to spend an estimated $100,-000,000 for cold remedies, although competent medical opinion advises that rest and a liquid diet are in most cases the best means of treatment. The advertisements of the large tobacco companies, in particular, frequently seek to create impressions which cannot find support in competent medical opinion.

The great body of offensive, deceptive, and misleading advertising is generally agreed to have its basis in the profit-making activities of large-scale advertisers whose actions are dictated by a regard for their profit and loss

[17] *Kidder Oil Co. v. F.T.C.*, 117 F. (2d) 892, 901 (1941).
[18] *Carlay Co. v. F.T.C.*, 153 F. (2d) 493, 496 (1946).

statements. If their advertising agencies can show results in developing sales
and profits, the advertisers typically approve the programs without regard
to moral or ethical considerations. The agencies are thus "under the gun"
to get results—to sell the goods which they are paid to promote.

In selling products to the American public—"to the great American mass
market"—the typical advertising agency appears to be ready to scuttle precise truth, good morals, and ethical principles in order to promote the business of their clients. Thus, Howard G. Sawyer, vice-president of a leading
advertising agency in New York City, declares, "Who . . . can be expected
to be so quixotic as to stand upon principles at the risk of losing business?"
The successful advertiser, he states, works on the principle that "the consumer is a jerk." To make money for your client, he counsels, approach the
public "at a low mental level, pander to its cheaper nature, hammer away
hard enough at what you want it to do and you'll get results."[19]

MEASURES FOR STRENGTHENING THE EFFECTIVENESS OF THE FEDERAL TRADE COMMISSION

Persons who have followed closely the work of the F.T.C. conclude that
the Commission has barely "scratched the surface" of the problem of unfair
competition and monopolistic pricing. At the same time they believe that the
need today for public intervention to create and maintain competition is far
greater than it was in 1914. Why has the Commission failed to operate more
effectively? What can be done to strengthen its activities?

1. THE NEED FOR GREATER EXECUTIVE AND LEGISLATIVE SUPPORT FOR THE
COMMISSION

In the past the President and the Senate all too frequently have used appointments to the Commission for the purpose of rewarding faithful party
members, without regard to their economic beliefs or training. Such appointments have been a principal cause for much of the ineffectiveness of the
Commission's work. The Commission has also been continuously handicapped by inadequate appropriations. Individual cases are brought and won,
but there is not sufficient money to go out into the field to investigate compliance or possible violations by other business firms.

Basically, the effectiveness of the Commission depends upon (1) the competence and "public mindedness" of the men appointed to serve as commissioners, (2) the ability, training, and experience of staff members appointed to investigate and prosecute cases, and (3) the amount of money
which the Commission has to use in its work. If the public really desires an
effective Commission, it will be necessary for the President to appoint able
men who have an interest in maintaining effective competition and for Congress to give these men all needed financial support.

[19] Howard G. Sawyer, "The Consumer Is a Jerk," *Printers' Ink*, March 1, 1946, pp.
23–25.

2. The Adoption of a Rule-Making Power

A weakness of the Federal Trade Commission Act, as interpreted by the Commission, is the absence of power to make imperative rules. Section 6(g) of the Act provides that the Commission may make "rules and regulations for the purpose of carrying out the provisions of the Act." The Commission, however, has construed this provision narrowly to mean rules for the internal administration of the Commission. At no time has it claimed or used the power to make imperative rules for business conduct.

A "rule" is a prescribed guide for conduct or action. It is a specific guide— one which leaves little or no room for interpretation. Thus, a rule might provide that "It shall be illegal to sell or offer to sell products at prices which are purported to be reduced from what are in fact fictitious prices." With a criterion of unfair competition established, the Commission would have only to get the facts to determine lawful or unlawful behavior. Businessmen would also know the exact limits beyond which they should not go. The establishment of imperative rules, moreover, would permit the Commission to apply the law to an entire industry group—"Here is the rule; everyone must comply."

In the absence of rule-making power, the Commission must proceed on a case-by-case basis. This means that it must (1) get the facts and (2) apply them to the general policy of the law, subject to review by a Court of Appeals and the Supreme Court. No one knows how the changing and varied personnel on the Commission and the courts will interpret and apply the general provisions of the law in disposing of cases until a case is brought and decided. After a case has been decided, moreover, the rule of law in the decision is usually construed as applying only to the particular set of facts. It is a rule worked out to solve a case at hand. Anyone attempting to express an opinion on what the court meant by anything it has said is likely to find himself in an argument. This is true, moreover, whether the problem discussed is one of basing-point pricing, misrepresentation, or criminal law. With a rule-making power, business regulation can be made more specific, more consistent, more stable, and more universal in its application.

The formulation and use of "trade practice" rules indicates that industry, as well as the Commission, finds it useful to have specific "guide posts" and "warning flags." Trade practice rules, however, are *advisory* rules, not imperative rules, and business firms are free to observe them or not as they desire. Each violation must be prosecuted as a violation of the Federal Trade Commission Act and not as a violation of a rule. Advisory rules merely express and embody the commission's understanding of the law.

3. An Expeditious and Timely Settlement of Cases

A major criticism of the Federal Trade Commission's activities is the time-consuming nature of its operations. The significance of delay arises in the fact (1) that business practices, such as local price cutting, change with changes in competitive conditions, and (2) that delay in prosecution frequently gives a business concern adequate time to enjoy the full advantage of an illegal act. An independent producer, moreover, is likely to get discouraged in waiting for public relief and yield to the will of the dominant firms.

Investigation shows that it has taken the Commission ten years or more to issue a cease-and-desist order or a dismissal in certain important antimonopoly and false and misleading advertising cases (see Table 27). Many

TABLE 27. Federal Trade Commission: Age of Formal Antimonopoly Cases Pending on July 1, 1952.

Period of Pendency	Number of Cases	Period of Pendency	Number of Cases
Less than 1 year	2	From 10 to 15 years	25
From 1 to 2 years	6	More than 15 years	6
From 2 to 3 years	13		—
From 3 to 5 years	21	Total	85
From 5 to 10 years	12		

(Source: *Final Report of the Select Committee on Small Business*, House of Representatives, 82nd Congress, second session, House Report 2513, 1952.)

cases require periods of three to five years for their completion. If a person files charges with the Commission, he should not, upon the basis of past experience, expect to secure relief for several years. Even then the complainant faces the prospect of further delay because of appeals to, and prolonged litigation in, the federal courts.

There are a number of factors which account for the delay in processing cases through the Commission. Trial attorneys frequently complain about the inadequacy of initial investigations and the need to make supplementary investigations. In a great many cases, moreover, the Commission has been unwilling to permit its attorneys to use the power of subpoena in securing evidence. During the course of a trial much time is lost because of the Commission's policy to be bound by judicial technicalities and rules of procedure.

A principal factor making for delay has been the weak and vacillating attitudes of the Commissioners, themselves, toward the issues in dispute. After investigational work has been completed, it frequently has taken the Commission six months to a year to decide whether or not a formal complaint should be issued. In some cases, the Commission has taken from three to nine years to decide whether to issue a complaint or close the case. If and when an "initial decision" has been appealed to the Commission, the Commission has taken from one to three years or even longer to decide upon the appropriate disposition of the case.

The vacillating attitude of the Commission in deciding what to do about a case reflects, in part, the fact that respondents, their counsel, and other persons having an interest in a case, commonly meet with Commissioners and staff members participating in the deciding function to discuss cases which are in process of being decided. The Administrative Procedure Act prevents a government attorney handling one of the Commission's cases of adjudication (a case to be heard or tried) from discussing it with any one of the Commissioners, the trial examiner, or others employed by the Commission who have the responsibility for making the decision.[20] At the same time, however, the Act does not condemn, or provide penalties for, action by respondents and their counsel in approaching Commissioners and such staff members charged with the responsibility of deciding a case. All too often, it appears, Commissioners are induced to believe that various cases can be settled or dismissed by the elapse of time or by the acceptance of trade practice conference rules. The Administrative Procedure Act protects a respondent from having his case of adjudication discussed *ex parte* (without his being present). It does not, however, protect the public from *ex parte* discussions and considerations initiated by the private interests directly concerned. This criticism of the harm to the public flowing from delays in handling cases because of private conferences with Commissioners is not peculiar to the Federal Trade Commission. It applies with equal force to all administrative agencies subject to the Administrative Procedure Act.

4. The Provision of Penalties for Monopolistic Price Fixing and Unfair Competitive Practices

It is important to remember that the Commission is powerless to punish individuals and corporations who engage in monopolistic practices and destructive methods of competition. A cease-and-desist order merely directs a defendant not to repeat his offense in the future. This approach was taken by Congress because it was believed that the Commission could stop unfair practices *before* they could inflict much damage on the economy.

At the present time, the Commission finds itself concerned with monopolistic practices which have been long established. The basing-point formulas, which were condemned by court decisions during 1945–1948, for example, had been in use for periods up to fifty years. The final adjudication of a case may require five or ten years, and during this period the public and competitors may suffer considerable damage. In all such cases, the penalty of a cease-and-desist order is too mild. If monopoly is to be effectively deterred, the law should provide for the levying of penalties against proven monopolistic action. The Commission, itself, moreover, should be empow·ed to request an injunction against monopolistic and unfair practices, whenever it appears that substantial (not trivial) damage *may* result to the public or competitors. If the Commission's injunctive power as applied to food, drugs, and cosmetics, were so extended, it would greatly deter many business firms from engaging in such activity.

[20] U.S.C. Sec. 1001 (1946). The Administrative Procedure Act defines the procedures to be followed by federal administrative agencies in conducting their activities.

SUGGESTIONS FOR FURTHER READING

Antitrust Law Enforcement by the Federal Trade Commission and the Antitrust Division, Department of Justice, Select Committee on Small Business, 81st Congress, second session, House Report 3236, 1951.

Derenberg, Walter J., *Trade-Mark Protection and Unfair Trading* (Albany, 1936). Edwards, C. D., *Maintaining Competition* (New York, 1949).

Functional Operation of the Federal Trade Commission, Hearings, Select Committee on Small Business, House of Representatives, 81st Congress, second session, 1950.

Geller, Max, *Advertising at the Crossroads* (New York, 1952).

Henderson, Gerard C., *The Federal Trade Commission* (New Haven, 1924).

Holt, W. Stull, *The Federal Trade Commission* (New York, 1922).

Miller, John P., *Unfair Competition* (Cambridge, 1941).

Monopolistic Practices and Small Business, Staff Report to the F.T.C. for the Select Committee on Small Business, U.S. Senate, 82nd Congress, second session, 1952.

Stevens, W. H. S., "The Trade Commission Act," *American Economic Review,* December, 1914, pp. 840–855; "Unfair Competition," *Political Science Quarterly,* June and September, 1914, pp. 282–306, 460–490.

Wallace, Robert A., and Douglas, Paul H., "Antitrust Policies and the New Attack on the Federal Trade Commission," *University of Chicago Law Review,* Vol. 19 (Summer, 1952), pp. 1–40.

CHAPTER 16

The Clayton Act and Its Judicial Interpretation

During the debates on the Clayton Act, Senator Walsh of Montana declared: "The purpose of the legislation of which the pending bill forms a part is to preserve competition where it exists, to restore it where it is destroyed, and to permit it to spring up in new fields."[1] With this chief purpose in mind, Congress enacted the Clayton Act which was signed by President Woodrow Wilson on October 15, 1914.

The heart of the Clayton Act is Section 2, which prohibits price discrimination in the sale of "commodities of like grade and quality" when the effect is to injure or prevent competition. Price discrimination is identified by considering variations in the prices currently received by a seller at his mill (after deducting freight allowed or defrayed by the seller), in the sale of the same class of goods to various buyers in the same trade classification under substantially similar conditions.

A further provision of the Clayton Act affirms the right of sellers to select their own customers. Additional measures place prohibitions, under specified conditions, on (1) the use of exclusive sales or tying contracts, (2) the corporate ownership of stock in competing corporations, and (3) interlocking directorates in large banks and competing corporations.

Following the passage of the Clayton Act, it was found that certain sellers frequently made prices to very large buyers lower than those charged other buyers, under the guise of quantity discounts. In order to strengthen the prohibition on this type of discrimination, Congress passed the Robinson-Patman Act (1936), which amended Section 2 of the Clayton Act.

The Clayton Act, as amended, also provides that "any person" injured by practices condemned in the legislation may sue in any district court and recover threefold the damages sustained, including costs of the suit. The Federal Trade Commission Act, in contrast, does not provide right of private suit for treble damages.

THE PROBLEM OF GEOGRAPHIC PRICE DISCRIMINATION AND THE FORMULATION OF SECTION 2 OF THE CLAYTON ACT

The principal objective which Congress had in mind in drafting Section 2 of the Clayton Act was clearly stated by the House committee as follows,

[1] *Congressional Record*, October 5, 1914, Vol. 51, p. 16145.

Section 2 of the bill is intended to prevent unfair discriminations. It is expressly designed with the view of correcting and forbidding a common and widespread unfair trade practice whereby certain great corporations and also certain smaller concerns which seek to secure a monopoly in trade and commerce by aping the methods of the great corporations, have heretofore endeavored to destroy competition and render unprofitable the business of competitors by selling their goods, wares, and merchandise at a less price in the particular communities where their rivals are engaged in business than at other places throughout the country.[2]

In attempting to get at the problem of cutthroat competition, proposals were made to prohibit discrimination outright—in all of its various forms. The Senate committee, however, insisted upon a proviso to permit discrimination "in good faith to meet competition" on the ground that some discrimination will tend to promote competition. The idea presented, in effect, was that some discrimination (sporadic and anarchic in type) enables a manufacturer to reach out into other sales areas and compete with distant sellers. Apparently as a compromise measure, Congress therefore accepted the idea of permitting discrimination practiced "to meet competition."

ESSENTIAL FEATURES OF SECTION 2

In its final form Section 2 of the Clayton Act provided, "That it shall be unlawful for any person engaged in commerce . . . to discriminate in price between different purchasers of commodities . . . *where the effect of such discrimination may be to substantially lessen competition or tend to create a monopoly* in any line of commerce, provided, that *nothing herein contained shall prevent discrimination in price . . . in the same or different communities made in good faith to meet competition.*" (Italics supplied.) A further proviso in Section 2 stated that a difference in prices "on account of differences in the grade, quality, or quantity of the commodity sold, or that makes only due allowance for difference in the cost of selling or transportation," shall not be considered to be discrimination. The Commission, itself, has taken the position that differences in price based upon trade status (functional discounts) are not forbidden by the Act.

The basic idea of discrimination is that of charging some person or persons a higher price than that charged others for the same class of commodities without a good and valid reason. Price differences on account of grade, quality, quantity, cost of selling, or cost of shipping are specified in Section 2 as being valid reasons for price differences. By the terms of the act, price discrimination is not illegal *per se*, but rather "where the effect . . . may be substantially to lessen competition." The phrase "where the effect . . . may be" has been interpreted by the Court to mean where a future effect (injury to competition) is reasonably probable, rather than certain or remotely possi-

[2] Committee on the Judiciary, *Antitrust Legislation*, 63rd Congress, second session, House Report 627, May 6, 1914, pp. 8–9.

ble. It appears that the term "substantially" was inserted to indicate that the law is not concerned with trifles.

When a discriminator "cuts" prices to injure a competitor engaged in the same line of business, it is the "lower price" which is considered to be illegal, if the result is substantially to lessen competition. Discrimination may also be practiced by a seller for the purpose of getting a difference in prices as between his customers. In this case, attention is shifted to the "higher price." If one customer has a higher cost-price than another, without a valid reason, the effect may be substantially to lessen his ability to compete. Discrimination always involves a "higher price" and a "lower price," and the rule against discrimination in Section 2 has been held by the courts to be applicable to discriminatory higher prices as well as to discriminatory lower prices.[3]

The term "price" is not defined in the Clayton Act, as amended. Most of the discussion, by economists and lawyers, on the definition of price which should be used in applying the Act has been based upon winning a lawsuit. Defendants have urged that price be defined as the amount paid by a buyer at his destination, including freight. A basing-point seller usually quotes the same delivered price to customers at a given destination point, and it is argued that delivered-price selling is not discriminatory. The government, however, has taken the position that price is the amount received by the seller *at his mill* after deducting actual freight cost, allowed or defrayed by the seller. Price discrimination, it is said, is measured by differences in a seller's "mill-net returns."

The problem is to look at the definition of price on a level above that of winning a law suit. Historically, economists have typically qualified the word price in some way. That is, they have used the word with an adjective, such as "market price," "f.o.b. mill price," or "delivered price." Some adjective, it appears, is necessary if we are to be precise. Historically, too, "market prices," as developed in *central* markets, have usually been taken as the kind of prices which public policy should seek to promote. Market price, in this sense, is the price of the commodity, as such, at the point of centralization. It does not include the cost of shipping the products from the central market to scattered destination points. Market price, so considered, is an f.o.b. shipping-point price.

THE PROVISO "IN GOOD FAITH TO MEET COMPETITION"

Section 2 of the original Clayton Act, we have seen, included a proviso stating that the prohibition on discrimination does not apply to "discrimination in price in the same or different communities made in good faith to meet competition." The difficulty of trying to draw a line between (1) discriminatory price cutting to suppress competition and (2) discriminatory price cutting "to meet competition" was recognized by several members of Congress, but the problem was not resolved. Senator Cummins, for example, declared, "Made in good faith to meet competition—Imagine the government en-

[3] *George Van Camp and Sons v. American Can Co.*, 278 U.S. 245, 254 (1929); and *American Can Co. v. Ladoga Canning Co.*, 44 F. (2d) 763 (1930).

deavoring to prove that a particular instance of price cutting was not made in good faith to meet competition!"[4]

The fact is that discrimination is usually practiced "to meet competition" —either by matching a competitor's price or by undercutting it—for a seller would not cut his price *to some customers* unless there was a competitive reason to do so. Businessmen do not practice discrimination merely for the sake of discriminating. Under Section 2 of the original Clayton Act the "meeting competition" proviso came to be regarded as a complete defense to the charge of illegal price discrimination.[5] Thus the prohibition on price discrimination in Section 2 was virtually nullified by the proviso permitting discrimination "made in good faith to meet competition."

THE DUAL MEANING OF THE PHRASE "MEETING COMPETITION"

The term "meeting competition" had its origin in competitive markets in which various sellers lower their asking prices to be in line with a new equilibrium of the forces of demand and supply. A seller meets the lower offers of other sellers(made when there is a preponderance of supply over demand) in order to be able to deal at all; and the new price so established *yields him the same net amount* on all transactions made at the same moment of time. In a central or primary market, sellers do not "meet competition" by engaging in price discrimination.

As applied to price discrimination, on the other hand, the term "meeting competition" means the cutting of net prices to buyers *in a certain area, or only in a limited number of situations*, without lowering them to all other customers. Meeting competition, in this sense, is the very act of discrimination.

The phrase "in good faith" has no precise or generally accepted economic or legal meaning. It refers to a state of mind on the part of the accused. Presumably, it means that a seller discriminates "with a pure heart and a pure mind" only for the purpose of meeting the equally low price of a competitor. Discriminators invariably affirm "good faith," and it is doubtful that "bad faith" can ever be proved in the absence of written evidence or a public statement indicating an "intent" to injure a competitor. The opinion of numerous economic and legal authorities is that in regulating competition, government should outlaw practices whose *effects* are undesirable, in terms of service to society, without regard to the intent or motive with which they are pursued.

SECTION 2 AND THE RIGHT TO SELECT ONE'S OWN CUSTOMERS

The final proviso in Section 2 provides that "*nothing herein contained shall prevent persons* engaged in selling goods, wares, or merchandise in commerce *from selecting their own customers in bona fide transactions* and not

---

[4] *Congressional Record*, August 25, 1914, p. 14228.
[5] See, for example, *F.T.C. v. Staley Mfg. Co.*, 324 U.S. 746, 752–753 (1945).

in restraint of trade." (Italics supplied.) The intent of Congress in adopting
the Federal Trade Commission and Clayton Acts was to declare illegal all
business practices which are likely to promote monopoly. In considering
various types of unfair conduct, much attention was given to the practice of
large mergers, controlling the output of basic commodities, particularly of
iron and steel, coal, and the nonferrous metals, to refuse to sell to dealers and
small fabricators who were dependent upon the mergers for supplies. Prior
to the time of the mergers, industrial firms ordinarily sold freely to all dealers
and fabricators. The great mergers, however, adopted the policy of selling
only to fabricating users of their own choice, in order to eliminate independents who might otherwise compete with them in selling the basic commodities or fabricated products.

A provision (Section 3) was accordingly included in the first draft of the
Clayton Act making it "unlawful for the owner or operator of any mine or
for any person controlling the product of any mine engaged in selling its
product in commerce to refuse arbitrarily to sell such product to a responsible person, firm, or corporation, who applies to purchase such product."[6]
This provision, in particular, the House report indicated, was designed to
eradicate the most extreme form of discrimination found in the practice of
the large mergers in coal, iron, copper, and other minerals to refuse to sell to
dealers and small manufacturers.

In the final enactment of the Clayton Act, the original Section 3 was entirely eliminated, and in its place there was adopted the opposite policy of
legalizing the right of "persons" to select their own customers. A corporate
merger is considered by the courts to be a "person," and thus the Clayton
Act openly legalizes the highly effective monopolistic practice of large corporations arbitrarily to refuse to sell to certain buyers at the same time that
they are selling freely to others.

THE COURTS AND THE POLICY OF REFUSING TO SELL

In an exchange society a person is legally free to enter into business contracts or not as he may desire, and it is upon this general principle that the
courts have accepted the asserted right of a corporate seller to select his own
customers. Thus, in the *Cream of Wheat* case (1915), the Court of Appeals,
in affirming the right of the company to select its own customers, declared:
"We had supposed that it was elementary law that a trader could buy from
whom he pleased and sell to whom he pleased, and that his selection of a
buyer or seller was wholly his own concern."[7] As authority for this view, the
Court cited "*Cooley on Torts*, p. 278." At the reference given, Professor
Cooley states, "It is a part of every man's civil rights that he be left at liberty
to refuse business relations with any person whomsoever, whether the refusal

---

[6] Committee on the Judiciary, *Antitrust Legislation*, 63rd Congress, second session,
House Report 627, May 6, 1914, p. 10.
[7] *Great Atlantic & Pacific Tea Co.* v. *Cream of Wheat Co.*, 227 Fed. Rep. 46, 48–49
(1915).

rests upon reason, or is the result of whim, caprice, prejudice, or malice."[8]

The courts have recognized that a public utility enterprise—such as a railroad—is bound to serve all persons who come to it, at prices which are reasonable and nondiscriminatory. The "public character" of such enterprises, the courts have held, makes them different from the business of a trader or manufacturer, which is considered to be "entirely private." There is valid reason for the law to recognize the right of a seller to sell to whom he pleases in an economy of many buyers and sellers, for any buyer can easily supply his needs by turning to another seller. In the present-day economy of large corporate mergers, however, a refusal to sell in many situations means that an independent dealer or fabricator must cease his business operations.

A conspiracy of two or more sellers, or one or more sellers and one or more competing buyers, to prevent another buyer from obtaining merchandise is an illegal restraint of trade under either Section 5 of the Federal Trade Commission Act or under the Sherman Act. In numerous situations, however, given buyers simply find that no one of the large corporations will sell them the desired products. The very real difficulty of proving conspiracy in such cases means that an independent buyer must often accept his fate and go out of business.

The affirmation in Section 2 of the right of a private business to select its customers, it may be noted, is qualified by the phrase "and not in restraint of trade." Today, the courts appear to be somewhat more willing to construe the "right" of a seller to refuse to sell with a concern for monopolistic and trade-restraining effects. (See Landmark Cases, p. 703.) A person denied supplies, however, still has the burden and expense of proving unreasonable restraint, and it is always possible that he will not get a favorable decision.

REFUSAL TO SELL A CONTINUING ABUSE

There is abundant evidence indicating that legislation making it unlawful to refuse to sell is as urgently needed today as it was in 1914. The antitrust agencies, for example, report that "refusal to sell" is one of the most frequent complaints which they receive. When sellers have various degrees of control over the whole supply of certain goods in a market, they tend to exercise this power by selling only in small quantities, by selling only to actual users, or by stipulating conditions on purchase or resale. In selecting certain customers and in refusing others, such sellers seek to accomplish one or more objectives:

1. To eliminate *dealers* who acquire inventories of primary commodities and compete with the primary producers in reselling such commodities.
2. To enforce a program of resale price maintenance.
3. To curb and limit the development of unintegrated fabricators who compete with the integrated producers in the sale of fabricated products.

[8] Thomas M. Cooley, *Law of Torts* (Chicago, 1880), p. 278.

4. To comply with demands of large, high-profit retailers that other retailers using low markups be denied supplies.
5. To conform to the demand of an employers' association that members settling privately with a labor union be denied supplies.

TYING RESTRICTIONS UNDER THE CLAYTON ACT

Tying contracts and exclusive dealing arrangements have long been condemned by economists as unfair methods of competition. The courts, however, have proceeded slowly in outlawing such contracts. The sale or lease of patented products with tying restrictions, in particular, was accepted by the Supreme Court as a valid form of contract. Thus, in the *Mimeograph* case (1912), the Court upheld the right of the A. B. Dick Company to sell its mimeograph machines on condition that they be used only with stencils, paper, ink, and other supplies made by the A. B. Dick Company. In the view of a majority of the Court, such a restriction was valid on the ground that a patent owner can use or suppress a patent as his interests may dictate.[9]

The decision of the Supreme Court in the *Mimeograph* case, as well as the growing use of tying arrangements to exclude competitors from the field, led Congress specifically to include in the Clayton Act a provision forbidding the use of tying restrictions *which substantially lessen competition*. Section 3, in substance, condemns the following arrangements whenever there is substantial injury to competition:

1. "Tie-in" sales: the sale of a machine on condition that the buyer will also buy materials to be used with the machine.[10]
2. Exclusive dealerships: the sale of goods on condition that the customer (dealer) will not buy the goods of a competitor.
3. "Full-line forcing": the sale of one line of goods on condition that the customer (dealer) will also buy the other lines produced by the seller.[11]
4. Requirements contracts: the sale of a product on condition that a customer will buy his subsequent needs of that product from the seller.

The *Standard Oil of California* decision (1948) on exclusive dealing arrangements brought life and vitality to Section 3. The Standard Oil Company was the largest seller of gasoline in the "western area," Arizona, California, Idaho, Nevada, Oregon, Utah, and Washington. Dealers under contract with the company were required to purchase and sell only those petroleum products, tires, tubes, batteries, and accessories handled by the company. The District Court found that competition was substantially lessened by these contracts. In reaching this decision, Judge Yankwich reasoned that there was *a substantial lessening of competition* because the contracts covered "a substantial number of outlets and a substantial amount of products." The relevant factor in determining legality or illegality, he declared, *is whether or not a*

[9] *Henry v. A. B. Dick Co.*, 224 U.S. 1 (1912).
[10] See also *United Shoe Machinery Corp. v. U.S.*, 258 U.S. 451 (1922).
[11] See also *Pick Mfgr. Co. v. General Motors Corp.*, 299 U.S. 3 (1936).

substantial amount of trade is covered by the contracts. If it is, the exclusive dealing contracts are illegal. Questions of injury to competitors, size of seller, reasonableness of the restraint, protection of good will, and benefits to the customers, the court concluded, are not standards to be considered in applying Section 3.[12]

The Standard Oil Company appealed the ruling of the District Court to the Supreme Court. In a five-to-four decision, the Supreme Court upheld the principle that the validity of contracts under Section 3 is to be tested by whether a "substantial portion of commerce is affected"—rather than by an actual demonstration that competitive activity is diminished. Justice Frankfurter, speaking for the majority, found support for this rule of law by reference to the Congressional discussions on the Clayton Act. In these discussions the view was developed that even the elimination of competition in a single town would "substantially lessen competition."[13] See Landmark Cases, p. 706.

SECTION 7 AND THE PROHIBITION OF MERGERS BY STOCK ACQUISITION

Prior to 1914, mergers in the United States were largely formed by the corporate acquisition of stock in separate and competing enterprises. A large corporation could exchange a portion of its stock for the stock of a competing plant, or it could use its cash to acquire a controlling interest in the outstanding stock. In an effort to stop this widely used method of restricting independent enterprise, and thus to nip monopoly in the bud, Congress included in the Clayton Act a provision prohibiting monopolistic mergers. Section 7 provides that "no corporation engaged in commerce shall acquire . . . the whole or any part of the stock . . . of another corporation . . . *where the effect of such acquisition may be to substantially lessen competition between the corporation whose stock is so acquired and the corporation making the acquisition,* or to restrain such commerce in any section or community, or tend to create a monopoly in any line of commerce." (Italics supplied.)[14]

Soon after the Clayton Act was adopted, clever corporation lawyers observed that Section 7 did not say anything about corporate action to acquire

[12] *U.S. v. Standard Oil Co. of California,* 78 F. Supp. 850, 857 (1948).
[13] *Standard Oil of California v. U.S.,* 337 U.S. 293 (1949). In subsequent cases the Court has indicated that it regards the *Standard* decision as a sound interpretation. See *Richfield Oil Corp. v. U.S.,* 343 U.S. 922 (1952).
[14] Under Section 11 of the Clayton Act, as amended, the enforcement of Section 7, as well as of Sections 2, 3, and 8, is assigned to the *Federal Reserve Board* for the field of banking; to the *Interstate Commerce Commission* for common carriers subject to its jurisdiction; to the *Federal Communications Commission* where applicable to common carriers engaged in wire or radio communication or radio transmission of energy; to the *Civil Aeronautics Authority* for air carriers and foreign air carriers subject to the Civil Aeronautics Act of 1938; and to the *Federal Trade Commission* for all other types of interstate commerce.

the *assets* of competitors. Instead of acquiring the stock of a competing firm, it was evident that a corporation could buy the firm's assets outright—just as a person would buy an automobile or a house. Thereupon, corporations seeking to build up their control over other concerns turned their attention to an acquisition of the assets of rival corporations. The decision of the Supreme Court in the *Steel* case (1920) indicated that the Court was willing to accept mergers in the absence of ungentlemanly conduct, and business leaders proceeded forthwith to form mergers on a broad scale by an acquisition of assets.

In acquiring the assets of a corporation, corporation executives sometimes found that it was *first* necessary to acquire the stock of a rival firm. By controlling a part or a majority of a rival's stock, a corporation could readily compel, induce, or direct a rival to sell its assets. Many large corporations, therefore, adopted the practice of first acquiring the stock of a rival and then of using the stock to acquire the assets.

Since corporation mergers were openly and widely formed by the dual procedure of acquiring first the stock and then the assets, the Federal Trade Commission decided to test the validity of this subterfuge in the federal courts. The Supreme Court in 1926, however, by a five-to-four decision, held that the Federal Trade Commission had no power to curb mergers if the acquiring corporation had used its stock purchases to acquire the assets before the Commission had issued its complaint. In the opinion of the Court, the plain language of Section 7 does not prevent the acquisition of physical assets of competing concerns.[15] Later, in 1934, also by a bare majority, the Court held that the Commission was powerless to act if a corporation used its stock purchases to acquire assets before the Commission had issued its final order banning the acquisition of the stock.[16] As a result of these decisions, the action taken by Congress in 1914 to prevent monopolistic mergers was completely nullified.

THE ANTIMERGER ACT OF 1950

The Federal Trade Commission repeatedly urged Congress to plug the loophole in Section 7 by amending the Clayton Act to prohibit the acquisition of assets, as well as stock. Finally on December 29, 1950, the essential legislation was enacted. The amendment prohibits the acquisition of stock *or assets* "where in any line of commerce in any section of the country, the effect of such acquisition may be substantially to lessen competition, or to tend to create a monopoly." All types of mergers are banned—vertical, horizontal, and conglomerate—provided the Commission can show that the effects *may be* a substantial lessening of competition or a tendency to create monopoly.

The original Section 7 prohibited any acquisition where the effect may be

[15] *F.T.C.* v. *Western Meat Co.*, *Thatcher Mfg. Co.* v. *F.T.C.*, and *Swift and Co.* v. *F.T.C.*, 272 U.S. 554 (1926).
[16] *Arrow-Hart and Hegeman Electric Co.* v. *F.T.C.*, 291 U.S. 587 (1934).

substantially to lessen competition *between the corporation whose stock is acquired and the corporation making the acquisition.* A literal application of this rule would prohibit the merger of two *small* companies. Since a merger of two small companies might be desirable in building up a stronger competitor, Congress revised Section 7 to condemn acquisitions which *substantially* lessen competition in any section of the country. By using the term "substantially," Congress sought to avoid a concern over trifles.

Congressional committee reports indicate that the main idea of the revision was to bar the merger of two large firms or of a large firm with a small one, and not that of two *small* companies.[17] The Senate Judiciary Committee, in particular, emphasized, "The committee wish to make it clear that the bill is not intended to revert to the Sherman Act test. The intent here, as in other parts of the Clayton Act, is to cope with monopolistic tendencies in their incipiency and well before they have attained such effects as would justify a Sherman Act proceeding."[18]

It is possible that the owner of a small concern may earnestly desire to sell to a major company in order to retire from business or to settle an estate. The view of Congress, however, was that the public interest in maintaining competition warrants the restriction on private advantage. Business enterprises seek to buy as cheaply as possible and to sell dear. When there are no independents to moderate these extremes, the public suffers.

THE PILLSBURY CASE

The Commission initiated its first formal proceeding under the new Antimerger Act on June 16, 1952. A complaint (Docket 6000) was issued against the Pillsbury Mills, Inc., the second largest flour milling company in the nation. The complaint charged that Pillsbury acquired the assets of two important competitors in the southeast area of the United States—the "hot biscuit" territory. The two competitors were (a) Ballard and Ballard, producers of flour, flour base mixes, and animal feeds, and (b) the Duff Baking Mix Division of American Home Foods, Inc., a producer of flour base mixes. As a result of these acquisitions, it was charged, Pillsbury gained a position in the southeastern area as the second largest seller of family flour; became the largest seller of bakery flour and mixes; and secured an almost complete monopoly on flour mixes.

In the *Pillsbury* complaint the Commission charged that both Pillsbury and the acquired concerns were substantial factors in the flour field and that the effect of the acquisitions was substantially to lessen competition. The Commission attorneys emphasized in the hearings that a distinction should be made between the "Sherman Act test" for the illegality of mergers and the new "Section 7, Clayton Act test." Congress had declared, they stated, that

[17] Hearings before a Subcommittee of the Committee on the Judiciary, U.S. Senate, *Corporate Mergers and Acquisitions*, 1949–1950, pp. 131, 135–138.
[18] Committee on the Judiciary, U.S. Senate, Report 1775, 81st Congress, second session, 1950, pp. 4–5.

the revised Section 7 was to bar piecemeal acquisitions which are not forbidden by the Sherman Act (as interpreted by the courts).

The Sherman Act test, we have seen, is essentially whether or not the acquisition gives the dominant acquiring firm an overwhelming percentage control of the total market. When one large concern acquires another, does it result practically in single-seller monopoly control? Where a large concern extends its power by successively acquiring small competitors, the individual acquisitions are considered to fall short of Sherman Act violations (under existing decisions). The result, however, is the disappearance of significant competitors and the creation of oligopoly. Only very small, local companies remain as independents.

Small, successive acquisitions are often not impressive, but the cumulative effect of the purchases is to convert an industry of numerous independents into one of oligopoly. This process of gaining economic control is sometimes called the "salami theory." By taking small slices, one can eventually secure a large part of the supply. Sherman Act complaints may thereupon be issued, but the record on dissolution and divestiture suits does not hold much promise (see Chap. 11).

INCLUSION OF "RULE OF REASON" IN SECTION 7 CASES

The hearing examiner in the *Pillsbury* case gave an initial decision April 22, 1953, dismissing the complaint. In his opinion, the evidence presented by the Commission's attorneys did not prove a substantial lessening of competition in the total market for flour. The hearing examiner construed the language of Section 7, "substantially to lessen competition," to mean the acquisition of an overwhelming control of the total market. By this construction, Section 7 was interpreted, like the Sherman Act, to prohibit only unreasonable restraints of trade.

The Commission attorneys appealed the initial decision to the Commission, itself. They urged that the "substantiality test" should be used in Section 7 cases, that is, "where a leading factor in the relevant market having a substantial share of that market, acquires another factor in that market also having a substantial share of that market."

On December 28, 1953, the Commission issued an order holding that the evidence in the *Pillsbury* case established a *prima facie* case of illegality. The case accordingly was remanded to the hearing examiner. In the Commission's view, the proper test for Section 7 cases lies somewhere between the standard proposed by its own attorneys and the Sherman Act test used by the hearing examiner. The Commission refused to accept the "substantiality doctrine" urged by its attorneys (whether or not a substantial share of the market was affected by the acquisition), on the ground that the Commission, itself, should examine all relevant factors ("rule of reason"). At the same time it rejected the Sherman Act test (overwhelming control), stating that "the Clayton Act requires a lower standard of proof" than the Sherman Act. As an indication of its thinking, the Commission stated that "More specifically, the merger in *U.S. v. Columbia Steel Co.* (1948), which was examined under the Sherman Act, would probably not have been approved had the new Section 7 been in existence and invoked against it."[19] (See Landmark Cases, p. 709.)

The opinion of the Commission in the *Pillsbury* case, it may be noted, added the "rule of reason" to Section 7. This means that there is no clear-cut rule on mergers which are violative of the law. As the Commission, itself, stated: "There must be a case-by-case examination of all relevant factors in order to ascertain the probable economic consequences." The attorneys for the Commission urged an objective test (whether a substantial portion of commerce is affected) as an indispensable condition for developing proof and deciding cases. Without such a test, many believe, no one can really know what Section 7 currently means.

PROHIBITIONS ON INTERLOCKING DIRECTORATES IN COMPETING CORPORATIONS

As a further means of preventing restraints on competition in their incipiency, Congress provided in Section 8 of the Clayton Act that interlocking directorships in competing corporations of certain size shall be illegal. When a person is on the board of directors of two or more corporations, he is in a position to help shape the activities of the several concerns so as to avoid price competition. It was this possibility which Congress sought to prevent. Section 8 accordingly provides that no person shall be a director in two or more corporations (other than banks and common carriers) if any one has capital, surplus, and undivided profits in excess of $1,000,000 and if such corporations are competitors. The law does not require the government to find that the interlocking arrangement reduces competition. The fact of the interlock, itself, makes for illegality. With respect to banks, the law provides that no director, officer, or employee of a bank "operating under the laws of the United States," under certain conditions, shall be connected with another bank in the federal system; and no director, officer, or employee in a private or state bank, under certain conditions, may be a director in a bank operating under the laws of the United States.

The provision in the Clayton Act prohibiting interlocking directorates among industrial and commercial corporations has not been an effective measure for two principal reasons. First, the antitrust agencies have not had adequate funds for enforcing the law. From 1914 to date, almost nothing has been done to secure compliance either by complaint or by formal prosecution. Available time and money have rather been used for prosecuting abuses which were more immediate and flagrant than those arising under Section 8.

Secondly, the legal prohibitions on interlocking directorates can be, and are, easily evaded. The president or treasurer (not a director) of one com-

---

[19] In the Matter of Pillsbury Mills, Inc., Docket No. 6000, *Opinion of the Commission,* December 28, 1953.

pany, for example, may serve as a director in a competing company. This is an interlocking relationship but not an interlocking directorate. A director of one corporation, moreover, may be represented on the board of a competing corporation by one of his relatives or by his lawyer or accountant. The law may also be evaded if each of two competing concerns has a director on the board of a third corporation—an "indirect" interlock (see Fig. 14). The Clayton Act further omits any reference to the interlocking relationships among industrial concerns and banks, among two or more potentially competing concerns (concerns which might become competitors if it were not for an existing interlock), or among industrial and commercial concerns related as buyer and seller. In each of these situations, interlocking directorates serve to restrict competition or to prevent arm's length bargaining.

QUANTITY DISCOUNTS AS A DEVICE FOR DISCRIMINATION

Congress stated in the Clayton Act that price differences "on account of differences in the grade, quality, or quantity of the commodity sold" are not, by definition, to be considered discrimination. At the same time, however, Congress did not provide any rules to govern the making of such price differences. To what extent, for example, could a lower price made to a large buyer be defended on the ground that it was actually a quantity discount? Gradually, evidence began to accumulate which showed that large sellers were making substantial price differences between their customers upon the pretense of differences in the quantity purchased. This fact led the Federal Trade Commission to endeavor to relate price differences on account of quantity directly to differences in the cost of selling.

Along with the striking expansion of chain stores during the period following World War I, there developed growing complaints from independent distributors on the unfair practices used by the chains. Upon the basis of these complaints, Congress requested the Federal Trade Commission in 1928 to make a comprehensive study of the chain store problem. In the course of this study, which was conducted over a period of six and one-half years, the Commission secured much additional data on the use of quantity discounts and special allowances as a device for discrimination. The Commission concluded that "the ability of the chain store to obtain its goods at lower cost than independents, and of large chains to obtain goods at lower cost than small chains, is an outstanding feature of the growth and development of chain-store merchandising. These lower costs have frequently found expression in the form of special discounts, concessions, or collateral privileges which were not available to smaller purchasers."[20]

THE MAIN PURPOSE OF THE ROBINSON-PATMAN ACT

The comprehensive study on chain stores prepared by the Federal Trade Commission gave rise to numerous proposals in Congress for amending the

[20] Federal Trade Commission, *Final Report on the Chain Store Investigation*, 74th Congress, first session, Senate Document 4, 1934, p. 24.

Clayton Act to curb the abuse of injurious quantity price discriminations (as to persons). Two bills of identical wording (H.R. 8442 and S. 3154) were introduced in June, 1935; and after extensive debate, long public hearings, and numerous amendments, the two bills were merged and adopted as the Robinson-Patman Act. President Roosevelt signed the new legislation on June 19, 1936. The Robinson-Patman Act amended Section 2 of the Clayton Act and included an additional provision of its own (Section 3) making it a criminal offense to engage in certain discriminatory practices.

The proposed legislation became known as the "Chain Store Bill," and its main purpose was generally recognized to be that of protecting smaller retail merchants—grocers, druggists, and others—against injury from discriminatory lower prices secured by their large competitors "because of their tremendous purchasing power." A large amount of evidence had shown that many of the "economies" and much of the "efficiency" of financially large corporations arose in their superior bargaining power—in their ability "to throw their weight around" in determining buying prices, as well as selling prices. Such economies, Congress believed, did not, and do not, reflect genuine producing and selling efficiencies. Senator Robinson declared in the Senate shortly before the final passage of the bill, "The sole purpose of the proposed legislation is to prevent unfair discriminations by a seller in favor of certain purchasers who have enormous purchasing power."[21]

ROBINSON-PATMAN ACT CONDEMNS DISCRIMINATION IN FAVOR OF LARGE BUYERS

Section 2 of the original Clayton Act was designed primarily to prevent injurious discriminations, especially those arising in the exercise of *geographic* discrimination. The Robinson-Patman amendment sought (a) to strengthen the prohibition against price discrimination and (b) to make it applicable to discriminations between or among persons competitively engaged in the *same* area (*personal* discrimination). The main problem of personal discrimination, it was found, is that of large-scale buyers receiving, and a seller secretly conceding to such buyers, price concessions which cannot be justified on the basis of cost savings.

Price discrimination, in favor of large buyers, takes several forms. The quoted price is the starting point from which a seller makes concessions for special deals; discounts for volume purchases; cash discounts; allowances for advertising and promotional services; and variations in guarantees and replacement arrangements. Such concessions, variations, and allowances may be justified on the basis of cost savings. However, they may also *serve as a cloak for substantial reductions in the price of the product, itself*. Large buyers are frequently able to secure products of like grade and quality at prices substantially less than those paid by small buyers, after making due allowance for the cost reductions of large-scale purchases.

The price discriminations enjoyed by large buyers, and against which the

[21] *Congressional Record*, June 1, 1936, p. 8419.

Robinson-Patman amendment was designed, are generally accomplished by three methods:

1. The making of discounts for volume purchases which cannot be justified by the lower cost of selling and delivering the large quantities.
2. The purchase of products such as canned foods and tires under private labels at prices which are substantially lower than those at which similar products of like grade and quality are sold to competing buyers under seller's labels.
3. The granting of advertising and promotional allowances on purchases made by large-scale buyers which are not granted on proportionally equal terms to other competing buyers.

Price differences, made by a seller, which make only due allowance for differences in his costs, resulting from the differing methods or quantities in which his goods are sold or delivered, are not considered to be discriminatory. In answering the charge of illegal price discrimination, a seller may use the defense that the lower prices charged for goods of "like grade and quality" reflect the cost savings in handling large-scale purchases. The purpose of the Robinson-Patman Act is to prohibit the making of price differences between purchasers which are greater than the cost reductions from large-scale buying, when the effect is to injure competition.

THE MORTON SALT CASE—AN INTERPRETATION
OF THE QUANTITY DISCOUNT RULE

Section 2(a) of the Robinson-Patman Act, we have seen, makes it unlawful to discriminate in price, but permits a respondent to show that his price differences, based upon differences in quantities sold, make only due allowance for differences in cost of manufacture, sale, or delivery. The leading court case which has been decided on discriminatory lower prices based upon quantity buying is the *Morton Salt* case. This case involved the use of cumulative quantity discounts given on the basis of a purchaser's actual or prospective purchases during a period of one year. The Commission found that the price differential granted to the chain stores constituted a discrimination in price, and that its effect was to injure competition between the small retailers and the chains. It also found that the respondent had failed to show that the differences in price were justified by differences in cost or made in good faith to meet an equally low price of a competitor. The contention of the company, on the other hand, was that its quantity discounts were open and available to all on equal terms, without special favor or secret rebate, and therefore not discriminatory within the meaning of the Robinson-Patman Act.

In a carefully prepared opinion, Justice Black, speaking for the Court, found that the quantity discounts were discriminatory and illegal under Section 2(a). With respect to the company's argument that its discount schedule had not, in fact, caused injury to competition, Justice Black replied that "The statute requires no more than that the effect of the prohibited price discriminations 'may be substantially to lessen competition . . . or to injure, destroy, or prevent competition.' "[22] (See Landmark Cases, p. 711.)

Upon the basis of the *Morton Salt* case, the rule appears to be firmly established that henceforth a seller, charged with illegal discrimination, must be prepared to justify his quantity discounts by showing actual cost savings. Cost accounting systems will need to be maintained to secure a reasonable estimate of the savings which accrue in quantity sales—in packing and shipping, in clerical expense, in manufacturing, and in selling.

THE "QUANTITY LIMIT PROVISO" OF THE ROBINSON-PATMAN AMENDMENT

One of the proposed drafts of the new legislation on quantity discounts prohibited the granting of discounts on quantities purchased in excess of a carlot. The idea was that there should be some limit beyond which quantity differentials should not be permitted. This principle, it was observed, has long been followed by the Interstate Commerce Commission, in regulating railroad rates, and it was believed that it would be sound public policy to make a similar requirement for industrial prices.[23] The proposal brought forth considerable opposition from organized industry groups, and a modified version of the carlot quantity limit proviso was drafted.

The new draft, which was subsequently adopted by Congress and made a part of Section 2 (a) of the Clayton Act, reads as follows: "*Provided, however*, that the Federal Trade Commission may, after due investigation and hearing to all interested parties, fix and establish quantity limits, and revise the same as it finds necessary, as to particular commodities or classes of commodities, *where it finds that available purchasers in greater quantities are so few as to render differentials on account thereof unjustly discriminatory or promotive of monopoly in any line of commerce.*" Thus it is that the Federal Trade Commission now has the authority to fix and establish *quantity limits* under the conditions so prescribed.

In commenting on the addition of the revised quantity limit proviso to Section 2 (a) of the Clayton Act, the Senate Committee on the Judiciary stated,

This proviso is added by recommendation of your committee. It is designed to enable, when necessary, the determination of quantity limits as to various commodities, beyond which quantity price differentials shall not be permitted even though supported by differences in cost.

It rests upon the principle that where even an admitted economy is of a character that is possible only to a very few units of over-shadowing size in a particular trade or industry, it may become in their hands nonetheless the food upon which monopoly feeds, a proboscis through which it saps

---

[22] *F.T.C.* v. *Morton Salt Co.*, 334 U.S. 37, 42–43 (1948). As a result of the decision of the Supreme Court in 1948, all quantity discounts were withdrawn by the Morton Salt Company, and no discounts for quantity buying have since been applicable.

[23] Hearing Before the Committee on the Judiciary, *To Amend the Clayton Act*, House of Representatives, 74th Congress, first session, 1935, pp. 27, 222.

the lifeblood of its competitors; and that in forbidding its use and fore-going its benefits the public is but paying a willing price for its freedom from monopoly control. A similar limitation has been applied without challenge for nearly half a century in the field of transportation, in refus-ing to extend freight rate differentials beyond the carlot quantity.[24]

APPLICATION OF THE QUANTITY LIMIT PROVISO

The Commission has had numerous requests to establish quantity limits for various products. As an initial effort, the Commission adopted a resolution on July 7, 1947, calling for an investigation of the rubber tire industry in order to secure information for use in determining whether or not it should fix quantity limits in that industry. This resolution was adopted, it was said, because of the vast number of complaints received from independent tire dealers, who claimed that the policy of the manufacturers to charge inde-pendent dealers substantially higher prices than those charged large buyers was driving the independents out of business. The "large buyers" were the mail-order concerns and oil companies who bought "private brand" tires which were of "like grade and quality" as those sold to independents.

The Commission issued a quantity-limit rule for replacement tires and tubes on January 4, 1952. Briefly stated, the rule provides that a quantity of 20,000 pounds, approximately one carload, ordered at one time for delivery at one time, is the maximum quantity which may be used to justify price differentials based upon quantity. This means that a tire distributor who orders several carloads must pay the same price per carload as a distributor who orders one carload at a time. The rule does not apply to tires sold to automobile manufacturers for use on new cars.[25]

The Commission found that the largest buyers of replacement tires paid from 26 to 30.5 percent less for passenger tires and from 32 to 40 percent less for truck tires than the prices paid by the smaller buyers. Large volume discounts enabled the "mass merchandisers" to sell tires and tubes at retail prices about equal to the cost of the smallest distributors. From 1926 (when the substantial differentials first appeared) to 1947, the share of the replace-ment business done by the smaller dealers declined from about 90 percent to 52 percent. Further, the Commission found that the fewness of big buyers and the price advantages which they secured in large volume buying were having the effect of concentrating tire production in the hands of the largest tire manufacturers. In its decision, the Commission observed that the Inter-state Commerce Commission has long refused to grant transportation rate differentials justified by cost savings when they are not within the scope of

[24] Committee on the Judiciary, *To Amend the Clayton Act*, 74th Congress, second session, Senate Report 1502, January 16, 1936, p. 6.
[25] The rule, itself, reads as follows: "The quantity limit as to replacement tires and tubes made of natural or synthetic rubber for use on motor vehicles as a class of com-modity is twenty thousand (20,000) pounds ordered at one time for delivery at one time."

small-scale business concerns. The lowest rate in railroad transportation is typically a carload rate.

The action of the Commission in fixing a limit beyond which additional quantity discounts for replacement tires and tubes cannot be given brought forth strong protests from the large tire manufacturers and mass distributors. Court action contesting the validity of the rule was immediately initiated, and it is possible that there will be prolonged litigation over the Commission's rule.[26]

ADDITIONAL PROVISIONS OF THE ROBINSON-PATMAN ACT

The chain store investigations conducted by the Federal Trade Commission showed that large corporate buyers secured discriminatory low prices not only on the pretense of quantity discounts but also by getting rebates for brokerage services when no actual brokerage services were rendered.[27] In marketing, many manufacturers use brokers in selling to wholesalers and large retailers. The broker represents the manufacturer and is paid a commission (for instance, 2 percent) on the manufacturer's price (for example, $10). The practice of some chains was to buy direct and demand the brokerage fee as a deduction (which would mean 20¢ off) from the manufacturer's price which all other buyers, using brokers, paid. Section 2 (c), which was enacted to remedy this situation, provides that "It shall be unlawful for any person engaged in commerce . . . to pay or grant, or to receive or accept, anything of value as a commission, brokerage, or other compensation, or any allowance or discount in lieu thereof, *except for services rendered in connection with the sale or purchase of goods, wares, or merchandise.*" (Italics supplied.) All such allowances are prohibited, as such, except for services actually rendered, regardless of their effect upon competition.

An example of the type of problem arising under Section 2 (c) is found in the *Great Atlantic & Pacific Tea Company* case (1939). After the enactment of the Robinson-Patman amendment, the company directed its field buyers to reduce their buying prices by the amount of the brokerage which it had formerly received. The company maintained that in buying direct from first-hand producers it saved the expense of a broker. The Commission and subsequently the Court of Appeals, however, rejected this view on the ground that an employee of the buyer cannot render services to a seller. In the words of the Court, "The agent cannot serve two masters, simultaneously rendering services in an arm's length transaction to both. While the phrase, 'for services rendered,' does not prohibit payment by the seller to his broker for *bona fide* brokerage services, it requires that such service be

[26] A summary of the main arguments *for* and *against* the Commission's ruling is presented in the Final Report of the Select Committee on Small Business, House of Representatives, 82nd Congress, second session, House Report 2513, 1952, pp. 296–297.

[27] Federal Trade Commission, *Final Report on the Chain Store Investigation*, 74th Congress, first session, Senate Document 4, 1935, p. 62.

rendered by the broker to the person who has engaged him. In short, a buying and selling service cannot be combined in one person."[28]

Sections 2 (d) and 2 (e) of the Robinson-Patman amendment are concerned with the granting of allowances, discounts, services, or facilities to buyers for promotional and advertising purposes—including newspaper, magazine, and radio advertising; window displays; handbills; and the furnishing of demonstrators. All such allowances, it is provided, must be granted on "proportionately equal terms" to large as well as small purchasers. The purpose of this requirement, the Senate report stated, was to prohibit discriminatory low prices granted to the chain stores under the pretense of advertising allowances. The prohibition in these instances requires no proof of injury and permits no defense by cost.

Senator Logan, who had charge of the legislation on the Senate floor, explained the application of Sections 2 (d) and 2 (e) as follows: "But if the seller grants an advertising allowance to one customer there is no reason why he should not grant, under identical circumstances, the same allowance to another customer based upon the quantity of the purchases. If one man buys $100,000 in goods and should be allowed $1,000 for advertising purposes, and another buys $10,000 in goods, he ought to be allowed $100 for advertising. That is not prohibited by the bill. So long as the same advertising allowances are made proportionately on the amount of purchases there is no prohibition in the bill against them."[29]

Section 2 (f) of the Robinson-Patman Act provides that it shall be unlawful for a *buyer* of commodities "knowingly to induce or receive a discrimination in price prohibited" by the act. This provision supplements Sections 2 (a), (d), and (e), which extend the prohibition to *sellers*. In construing this section, the Supreme Court has held that a buyer, to be guilty of "knowingly" inducing or receiving injurious discriminations, (1) must know that he is getting a lower price than competitors are paying and (2) must know that the lower price cannot be justified by cost savings.[30] In substance this means that if a buyer asks no questions on cost savings in relation to the lower prices, he can keep himself clear of the law. Upon the basis of the present interpretation of Sections 2 (f), it appears that large buyers are virtually unrestrained in using their financial power to gain lower cost prices than smaller competitors are able to secure.

[28] *Great Atlantic & Pacific Tea Co.* v. *F.T.C.*, 106 F. (2d) 667, 674–675 (1939). See also *Southgate Brokerage Co.* v. *F.T.C.*, 150 F. (2d) 607 (1945).

[29] *Congressional Record*, March 3, 1936, p. 3116.

[30] *Automatic Canteen Co. of America* v. *F.T.C.*, 346 U.S. 61 (1953). In this decision, the court ruled against the Commission in its charge that *Automatic Canteen* had induced suppliers of candy, gum, and nuts to grant it lower prices than competitors paid. Some items, the Commission had found, were sold to small firms at prices 33 percent higher than to *Automatic Canteen*. The court held that the Commission must prove (1) that the lower prices were not justified by cost savings and (2) that the buyer knew that they were not justified by cost savings. In most cases, it is generally believed, this places an impossible burden of proof upon the Commission.

Section 3 of the Robinson-Patman Act provides that certain types of price discrimination shall be criminal offenses, punishable by a fine of not more than $5000 for each violation, and imprisonment for not more than a year, or both. The enforcement of this section is under the jurisdiction of the Department of Justice. The business practices specifically prohibited by Section 3 are (1) participation by any person in any transaction "which discriminates to his knowledge against competitors of the purchaser," (2) the sale of goods in *one sales area* at prices lower than in *another area* for the purpose of eliminating a competitor, and (3) the sale of goods at *unreasonably low* prices for the purpose of eliminating a competitor.

Section 3 of the Robinson-Patman Act lay unused from 1936 until 1948. On July 30, 1948, however, the Department of Justice filed two criminal cases against a group of dairies in the Chicago area, charging them with becoming a party to a continuing contract with the Great Atlantic & Pacific Tea Company, in which the company was granted a secret percentage rebate, discount, and allowance. Subsequently, in 1952, the government dropped the cases because of inadequate evidence.

THE EXEMPTION OF DISCRIMINATION "TO MEET COMPETITION"

Under the original form of Section 2, a qualification was made permitting "discrimination in price in the same or different communities made in good faith to meet competition." Presumably, under this proviso, a dominant seller quoting a discriminatory low price in a distant area would be able to match the price of the rival *or undercut it.* Section 2 (b) of the Robinson-Patman amendment, however, placed a new limitation on the exemption of discrimination "in good faith to meet competition." The amended section reads as follows: "Upon proof being made . . . that there has been discrimination in price . . . the burden of rebutting the *prima facie* case thus made . . . shall be upon the person charged. . . . Provided, however, that nothing herein contained shall prevent a seller rebutting the *prima facie* case thus made *by showing that his lower price* . . . was made in good faith *to meet an equally low price of a competitor.*" (Italics supplied.) This means that a discriminating seller may show that he cut prices on some sales to meet the price of another seller, but he is not permitted to show that he undercut that price. Discrimination to undercut is forbidden.[31]

Many congressmen expressed the view that the exemption of discrimination "to meet an equally low price of a competitor" should be eliminated *entirely* on the ground that the proviso seriously weakened the main prohibition. Such action was not taken. The sponsors of the Robinson-Patman bill, however, indicated that the reply of "meeting competition" was not to be a complete defense. According to Congressman Utterback, "It is to be noted . . . that this does not set up the meeting of competition as an absolute bar

---

[31] Committee on the Judiciary, *Prohibition of Price Discriminations*, 74th Congress, second session, House Report 2287, March 31, 1936, p. 16.

to a charge of discrimination under the bill. It merely permits it to be shown in evidence. This provision is entirely procedural."[32]

JUDICIAL INTERPRETATION OF THE PROVISO "MEETING COMPETITION"

The issue of whether "meeting a competitor's price" is a complete defense to the charge of price discrimination or only a "procedural aid" was presented to the courts in the *Standard Oil of Indiana* case (1949). The Federal Trade Commission charged the Standard Oil Company with illegal discrimination in selling gasoline in Detroit to distributors, including a large retailer, at a price 1½ cents under the price to some 358 other retailers. The Commission alleged that this discrimination resulted in injury to competition at the retail level. Standard offered certain cost data to establish the lower cost of selling to quantity buyers, but the Commission found that the data did not bear upon conditions in the Detroit area. Thereupon, Standard declared that it was simply meeting the lower price quoted by a competitor, and that "meeting competition" is a complete and valid defense. The Commission refused to accept this point of view and maintained that price discrimination *which injures competition is illegal.*

The Court of Appeals in 1949 upheld the Commission's view that "meeting competition" is not a valid justification for discrimination if injury has, in fact, resulted. The Court reasoned that Congress, in amending the Clayton Act in 1936, sharply restricted the right to discriminate. In the Robinson-Patman amendment, said the Court, the good-faith proviso is not a complete defense but only a "procedural aid." This means that when the Commission alleges illegal discrimination, the accused can answer that it was done in good faith. However, if the Commission shows that injury to competition not only was probable but actually occurred, the good-faith proviso ceases to be a defense.[33] The Standard Oil Company promptly appealed this decision to the Supreme Court.

It is significant to note that during the period in which the *Standard Oil of Indiana* case was pending, there occurred a change in the attitude of the commission on price discrimination. The point of view developed that discrimination in good faith *should be* permitted, particularly in industries in which economic power has become concentrated in the hands of a few sellers (oligopoly). In such industries, it was reasoned, price competition among sellers is often weakened or nonexistent. In so far as it operates, it takes the form of discriminatory price concessions. If the Robinson-Patman Act is applied, it may stifle this *limited* competition. By permitting some discrimination, however, it is possible for some degree of price competition to develop among oligopolistic sellers. Upon the basis of this line of reasoning, the Commission publicly announced in June 1949, that ". . . all of the Commissioners believe that *on balance* it would be preferable to make the good

[32] *Congressional Record*, Vol. 80, June 15, 1936, p. 9418.
[33] *Standard Oil Co. v. F.T.C.*, 173 F. (2d) 210 (1949).

faith meeting of competition a complete defense."[34] Beyond doubt, the new attitude of the Commission that good faith should be a complete defense considerably weakened the position of the government attorneys in appealing the *Standard* case to the Supreme Court.

In a five-to-three decision, the Supreme Court reversed the *Standard Oil of Indiana* decision and ruled that even though competition is injured, a seller may justify price discrimination by showing that the lower price was made in good faith to meet the lower price of a competitor.[35] (See Landmark Cases, p. 719.) The majority conceded that Congress had made certain changes in the original Clayton Act to restrict the practice of discrimination. However, none of the changes in the amendment, it was stated, changed the "actual core of the defense." In the view of the majority, "wherever a lawful lower price of a competitor threatens to deprive a seller of a customer, the seller, to retain that customer, may in good faith meet that lower price" [by discrimination].

The majority, no doubt, believed that its decision preserved the right of a seller "to compete." This, however, is only one side of the coin. On the other side, is the fact that the use of price discrimination by a dominant seller is a club which serves *to discourage* price competition by independent sellers. If an independent seller knows that his price is going to be matched, *by the use of price discrimination*, he will be reluctant to make price reductions, because the lower discriminatory price may not be raised when market conditions improve. Favored retailers—those getting the discriminatory *lower* price—also have an advantage over retailers paying the discriminatory *higher* price.

Justice Reed, in the minority opinion on the *Standard* case, spoke sharply against the "erroneous" conclusion that "meeting competition" is a complete defense. In his view, Congress in 1936 clearly intended to narrow the avenue of escape for price discriminators. The decision of the majority, he declared, means that "no real change has been brought about by the amendment," and leaves "what the seller can do almost as wide open as before." In effect, he concluded, the law on discrimination has been taken back in substance to the law of 1914 which permitted discrimination made in good faith to meet competition.

THE NATURE OF COMPETITION

The *Standard Oil of Indiana* case crystalizes the conflict of thinking on the meaning of the word "competition." There is general agreement that the policy of competition is a desirable one for government to maintain. The Supreme Court, itself, in the *Standard* case declared that "The heart of our national economic policy has long been faith in the value of competition." But what does "competition" mean?

[34] Hearings Before Subcommittee No. 1 of the House Committee on the Judiciary on S. 1008, 81st Congress, 1st session, June 8 and 14, 1949, p. 61. Italics supplied.
[35] *Standard Oil Co.* v. *F.T.C.*, 340 U.S. 231 (1951).

There are two main schools of thought on the meaning of the term competition. The one originated (a) in circles using monopoly practices and (b) with attorneys and economists defending private corporations against charges of monopoly and unfair competition. Its essential aspects are to be found in legal briefs; in the writings of various legal and economic experts; and finally, in the *Standard Oil of Indiana* decision (1951). In defining the term, its architects have "defined it down to fit an actual industry," such as oil or steel, as presently organized. Further, in securing its adoption, they have applied their efforts to the administrative agencies and the courts to get the statutes construed in a way which will fit their suggested pattern.

The other concept of competition was developed in the early law on open markets; in the legislation of Congress against discrimination adopted in 1887 (I.C.C. Act), 1914 (Clayton Act), and 1936 (Robinson-Patman Act); and in the writings of many American economists, beginning with J. B. Clark's pioneer work, *The Control of Trusts* (1901). In developing this concept of competition, economic and legal experts defined the term with reference to central markets in which (1) transactions are made openly and publicly, (2) all persons have the right to buy and sell, and (3) each seller treats all of his buyers essentially alike. Competition of this type, it is believed, is the kind called for by the antitrust laws.

In brief, the essence of the two concepts may be summarized as follows:

1. THE CONCEPT OF UNLIMITED, UNREGULATED COMPETITION

Competition is an unlimited, unfettered activity, waged without rules or penalties, and legitimate as long as it is pursued in good faith to make profits. Price cutting, price raiding, and price discrimination are all legal methods of competition. There are no fixed rules of fairness or reasonableness which regulate competition. A seller must ever be free to protect himself against competitive price attacks. One cannot complain about the injuries which discrimination brings, if a policy of competition is to be maintained.

Discrimination in price to "meet" or "beat" the "delivered prices" of distant competitors, it is said, is fundamental to the competitive system. A discriminatory reduction in mill-net prices to secure customers *is* competition, even when a seller regularly "matches" the prices of distant competitors. Any restriction on price discrimination is a restriction on competition.

The kind of competition desired by large business, it may be added, includes a substantial amount of coöperation with respect to prices, output, and excess capacity. Formal collusion is condemned, but private restraints to curb excessive competition are believed to be appropriate. The facts on restraint, it is said, must be weighed in the public interest and judged by a "rule of reason."

2. THE CONCEPT OF COMPETITION AS A REGULATED PROCEDURE

Competition in business, experience has shown, should be a regulated procedure, carried on within rules and limits. Without rules and penalties, competition becomes a contest of financial power; and big firms win over smaller competitors, regardless of productive efficiency.

In central markets, with price publicity, freedom of entry, and rules of fair dealing, competitive forces develop prices which are free from discrimination. A reduction *to one buyer* brings a reduction in price *to all buyers* from the same seller. If a buyer sees that he is being charged more than the "going price," he will change his patronage. A seller in a central market cannot get away with price discrimination. The purpose of the Clayton Act, as amended, is to maintain competition of a nondiscriminatory type analogous to that found in open, competitive markets.

Persons "injured" by the lower prices resulting from sellers' competition are the less efficient. No advocate of competition proposes that legislative protection be extended to them.

Price discrimination, on the other hand, is a *limited* kind of competition which works in two ways to create monopoly. First, in cutting prices in one locality, a discriminating seller is able to make up the "lower" prices on other sales. This an independent, single-plant competitor cannot ordinarily do. Local, *small-sized competitors* are injured, irrespective of their efficiency.

Secondly, in discriminating among *its customers*, a discriminating firm places some—those paying the "higher" price—at a disadvantage in relation to others—those paying the "lower" price. Nondiscriminatory treatment of customers at the mill, however, affords small and big buyers a comparable purchasing price. All such persons buying for resale are thus given an equal start, *as in a real market*. This is the essential purpose of the Robinson-Patman Act—to require *a seller* to treat all of his buyers on more or less equal terms.

DISCRIMINATION AS A TOOL OF MONOPOLY

In the Clayton and Robinson-Patman Acts, Congress declared that price discrimination is not a competitive practice but, on the contrary, is a monopolistic practice. Discrimination was recognized as a device by which monopoly grows and advances itself. The purpose of the legislation of 1914 and 1936 was to condemn discrimination and thus to strike at monopoly in its incipiency.

Modern-day advocates of discrimination urge that discrimination be permitted, even if competition is destroyed, so long as it is done in "good faith." They ridicule the idea that monopolistic practices should be attacked in their incipiency. In their view, government should take action against business only when *dominant* monopoly is achieved. Since the Sherman Act has been interpreted to condemn the creation of national monopolies (the *Oil* and *Tobacco* cases, 1890), they contend that the only legislation we need is the Sherman Act. The laws against discrimination, they say, should either be repealed or substantially modified.

In support of their position, advocates of discrimination state that the Sherman Act stands for "hard" competition (discriminatory pricing); whereas the Clayton Act, as amended, calls for "soft" competition (non-

discriminatory pricing). Those defending the Clayton and Robinson-Patman Acts, on the other hand, maintain that, in truth, price discrimination is
a "soft" kind of competition (for a monopolistic seller), because it relieves a
seller of the need to reduce his prices uniformly to all customers. See also
Glossary of Terms at the end of this Chapter.

The Clayton and Robinson-Patman Acts, their supporters maintain, are
fully compatible with the Sherman Act. The Clayton Act, as amended, applies to the prices of *one* seller. It strikes primarily at the *effects* of local
and limited monopoly (incipient and attained), particularly price discrimination. Section 1 of the Sherman Act, on the other hand, applies to the prices
of *a group* of sellers. It condemns conspiracy and unified selling which give
rise to monopoly power, including the power to discriminate. Each law has
for its purpose the creation and maintenance of fair and open price competition. Each stands for the principle that business survival should be based upon
economic efficiency. A dominant firm, with the power to discriminate, can
reduce its prices on some sales not because of efficiency, but because it can
recoup its losses elsewhere. It is only when discrimination is restrained that
business rivalry can operate as a "contest of efficiency" in which the more
efficient have a chance to succeed.

THE NEED TO RESTUDY THE PRACTICE OF PRICE DISCRIMINATION

Vast amounts of public testimony, commission investigation, and legal
analysis with respect to discrimination have led to the declarations of national policy in 1887, 1914, and 1936, condemning price discrimination as
a monopolistic measure. Historically, the view of Congress has been that
the law should protect competition—that it should not condone anything
which would injure competition. The *Standard Oil* decision vitiates this
principle. Someday Congress must decide anew (a) if the law should permit
discrimination "in good faith" to meet competition, regardless of injurious
effects upon competition or (b) if discrimination should be condemned
whenever it injures competition.

Various business groups—especially large multiplant companies—vigorously press for the privilege of discriminating in price, regardless of injury
to competition. The cutting of prices (mill-net returns) to a few customers
and not to others is more profitable than that of making a general reduction
to all customers. It also gives a dominant seller a power to limit or restrict
the growth of local competitive forces. Furthermore, it permits the use of
systematic freight absorption in a plan of delivered pricing.

Small business firms, on the other hand, declare that price discrimination
is an unfair method of competition which violates the principle of equal opportunity for all. In their view, competition should be regulated by requiring
a seller to treat his customers on more or less equal terms (Robinson-Patman
Act). At the same time, the Sherman Act should be applied to dissolve concentrated economic power (a chief source of the ability to discriminate). The

Robinson-Patman and Sherman Acts, it is said, should *both* be applied to a given industry. Failure of government to do so, they emphasize, means the abandonment of our declared policy of fair competition.

The basic problem which must be grasped by the courts and the people is the significance of the practice of price discrimination. Is price discrimination a competitive or a monopolistic practice? The law, as presently construed, permits or tolerates a substantial amount of discrimination. In large measure, the nation is back to the conditions of 1900 when discrimination flourished unchecked. Today, we must again relive and restudy the business practices of discrimination and decide anew the prohibitions to be made.

PROPOSALS FOR STRENGTHENING THE CLAYTON ACT

The principal proposals which have been suggested for strengthening the Clayton Act include amendments:

1. To provide that cease-and-desist orders under the Clayton Act, like orders under the Federal Trade Commission Act, shall become final, if not appealed within sixty days.
2. To outlaw unequivocally geographic price discrimination by requiring f.o.b. mill pricing.
3. To provide that "good faith" shall *not* be a complete defense for price discrimination which, in fact, injures competition.
4. To condemn loss-leader selling by prohibiting discrimination between or among different commodities or similar commodities of different grade and quality in reselling at retail any commodity at less than net cost of such commodity delivered to the retailer's place of business, where the effect may be to injure competition.
5. To reverse the policy embodied in Section 2, as applied to corporate sellers of basic commodities, which authorizes "persons" to select their own customers in interstate commerce.
6. To prohibit interlocking arrangements between corporations which experience has shown restrict price competition, prevent arm's length relationships in buying and selling, or otherwise work to the disadvantage of the general public.
7. To provide that tying restrictions are illegal, *per se.*

Some persons and groups urge that presently existing evils in business create a pressing need for the adoption of each of the foregoing remedial measures. Others resist and oppose any increase in government regulation or any change in the *status quo.* Large producers, in particular, are apathetic or opposed for they are able to compete and survive without a change in the "rules of the game."

The main task ahead is to learn more about current business practices. Upon the basis of such studies, Congress and the people will gain a better understanding of the remedial legislation, if any, which should be enacted. Business competition is a form of human behavior, and the problem of government is to provide rules which will insure that this behavior will be conducted in accordance with good manners and good morals.

GLOSSARY OF TERMS

"Hard Competition": Price discrimination which is not restrained or restricted by legal rules. A discriminator can bear down "hard" in his price cutting, in the absence of a legal prohibition on discrimination, because he is able to charge more elsewhere. This term describes a *limited* kind of competition, limited to certain customers or places. It is not the kind of competition found in central markets.

"Soft Competition": Rivalry in selling, advocates of price discrimination declare, in which the right to make "price cuts" is curbed by the Robinson-Patman Act.

The terms hard and soft competition were developed by persons in favor of price discrimination. Supporters of the Robinson-Patman Act condemn hard competition as defined above. In their view, it is competition of the jungle type, waged without fair rules of the game.

The notion of soft competition, they add, is fallacious. Section 2 of the Robinson-Patman Act in no way restricts a seller in making price reductions which are uniform to all buyers at the mill, with reasonable differentials for differences in services, quality, or costs involved. Such price reductions are, in fact, the very essence of real competition. No supporter of the antitrust laws would propose to curb them.

SUGGESTIONS FOR FURTHER READING

Austin, Cyrus, *Price Discrimination and Related Problems Under the Robinson-Patman Act,* American Law Institute (Philadelphia, 1950).

Austin, Robert W., "The Robinson-Patman Act—Is It in the Public Interest?" *Section of Antitrust Law,* American Bar Association, 1952, pp. 92–106.

Barnes, Irston R., "Economic Issues in the Regulation of Acquisitions and Mergers," *Ohio State Law Journal,* Summer 1953, pp. 279–306.

Edwards, C. D., *Maintaining Competition* (New York, 1949); and Federal Trade Commission, *The Bearing of the Robinson-Patman Act upon the Policy of the Sherman Act.* (Washington), 1952.

MacIntyre, Everette, "Section 2 (a)—Its Application to the Quantity Price," *Robinson-Patman Act Symposium* (New York, 1948).

Miller, John P., *Unfair Competition* (Cambridge, 1941).

Patman, Wright, *The Robinson-Patman Act* (New York, 1938).

Sheehy, Joseph E., "The Robinson-Patman Act—Is It in the Public Interest?" *Section of Antitrust Law,* American Bar Association, 1952, pp. 107–119.

Stevens, W. H. S., "The Clayton Act," *American Economic Review,* March, 1915, pp. 38–54; "An Interpretation of the Robinson-Patman Act," *Journal of Marketing,* July, 1937, pp. 38–45.

Thorp, Willard L., "Price Discrimination and Cost," *Journal of Accountancy,* March, 1937, pp. 183–186.

Trade Practice Bulletin, William J. Warmack, Publisher, Washington 21, D.C. A monthly service covering matters before the Federal Trade Commission.

CHAPTER 17

Basing-Point and Zone-Delivered Pricing Systems— Case Studies of Industrial Pricing Methods

---

One of the most important applications of the Federal Trade Commission and Clayton Acts, as amended, to business practices is found in the basing-point cases. These cases have created a tremendous amount of controversy on the nature and meaning of competition. Today, basing-point and zone systems are described by their critics as "the chief instrument by which American cartels exercise a control over prices" and by their advocates as "a business practice which promotes competition and benefits buyers."

The use of delivered-pricing systems in the American economy continues to be widespread. Arguments for and against such pricing methods, moreover, are continually being made in the press, trade journals, corporation reports, the *Congressional Record*, as well as in complaints filed with the antitrust agencies.

The Supreme Court, in a series of decisions culminating in the *Cement* decision (1948), declared that the basing-point practice is a monopolistic method of pricing. Basing-point industries thereupon appealed to Congress for legislation to legalize the practice. At present, Congress and the American people face the problem of deciding what to do about pricing systems. Should our antitrust laws be changed to accomodate them to an important business practice? Or should the business practice be changed to comply with the law?

THE DEVELOPMENT OF BASING-POINT SYSTEMS

Although the basing-point plan was first used as early as 1880, its systematic and continuous use appears to have come with the creation of the United States Steel Corporation in 1901. The formation of the Corporation, "a combination of combinations," placed in the hands of one management a control over the major combinations then existing in the steel industry. If the Corporation had continued to quote uniform f.o.b. mill prices at its separate mills, freight costs would have given certain mills advantages over others in selling at various centers of consumption. In order, therefore, to maintain unity of action on price and at the same time to avoid giving mills located near a consuming center an advantage in getting business, the Corporation in 1901 adopted the practice of selling all iron and steel products, except rails, at its various mills at delivered prices only.

The delivered prices quoted by the Corporation were the sum of a base price at Pittsburgh plus rail freight from Pittsburgh to the destination, regardless of the actual origin of shipments or the actual freight cost incurred. All steel mills—those controlled by the Corporation as well as independents—followed the lead of the Corporation in quoting delivered prices on the basis of "Pittsburgh-plus," even though they made and sold steel locally (as in Chicago) or shipped it from a distance into the neighborhood of Pittsburgh.

The problem which a central financial unit has in unifying the local and distant sales policies of its constituent companies has been noted by a number of economic and legal authorities. Walter B. Wooden, a long-time student of basing-point pricing, explains the situation as follows: "The full advantages of chain production are dependent upon the chain's maintenance of a system of pricing that reduces undue conflict between its own plants variously located. Such conflict would arise if the buyers were permitted to get their goods at a lower cost from one plant of the chain than from another. To permit that creates a tendency toward price competition among members of the family group that was established to avoid it."[1]

DELIVERED-PRICING SYSTEMS BECOME WIDELY USED

Soon after the adoption of the basing-point plan in the steel industry in 1901, the practice was extended to the cement industry. Outside of steel and cement the practice was little used until around 1912, after which time its use spread rapidly. Some examples of commodities in addition to iron and steel which came to be sold on a *single* basing-point plan include cast-iron soil pipe, glucose, malt, maple flooring, welded chain, zinc, lead (St. Louis plus freight differentials), and copper ("Connecticut Valley" plus freight differentials). In certain industries two or more bases were established by the price leaders. Some of the products which came to be sold on a *multiple* basing-point system include iron and steel after 1924, cement, hardwood lumber, gasoline, sugar, chemical fertilizers, milk and ice-cream cans, asphalt roofing material, small arms ammunition, corn products, gypsum products, hard-surface floor coverings, linseed oil, rigid steel conduit, firebrick, lubricating oil, and plate glass.

THE NATURE OF THE BASING-POINT FORMULA

The basing-point plan is a method of price quotation by which a number of sellers regularly and systematically arrive at identical delivered prices. The delivered price for any destination is determined by adding to a base price at a given point, called the basing point, the freight charge—usually rail freight—from such point to the point of delivery, regardless of the actual origin of the shipments or the actual freight cost incurred. All buyers at a given destination, accordingly, are given the same quotation. Rail freight is used in figuring delivered prices in order to insure identical delivered prices. If some mills used motor freight rates, some water freight rates, and

[1] Walter B. Wooden, "The Defense of Delivered Price Systems," *George Washington Law Review*, December, 1946, p. 31.

others rail freight rates, the delivered prices would not all be the same, and competition would not be completely avoided. In the event that a mill charges a customer the rail freight and uses a cheaper form of transportation to make delivery, it makes a profit on the freight charge. (See also the definitions given in the "Glossary of Terms" at the end of the present chapter.)

Producers in a given industry may employ a *single* basing point for the entire country, or they may use *two or more* bases for the country. In some cases, every mill may be the governing base mill for its contiguous area. The base prices at the various base mills may be either equal or unequal. Under the multiple basing-point system each seller quotes a delivered price which is the lowest combination of a base price at any mill plus the rail freight from that mill to a particular destination.

At present, it is a common practice for *each* geographically separate mill to quote a local f.o.b. mill price for nearby sales and then to reduce its mill-net price on distant sales (by absorbing freight) to meet the delivered prices of distant sellers. This practice is variously called "competitive freight absorption" and "f.o.b. selling with freight equalization." A seller in shrinking his mill net to match the delivered price of another mill, however, is actually quoting a "combination price" which is the sum of (a) the base price of *another mill* plus (b) the freight from *that* mill to the buyer's destination. This is the essence of basing-point pricing. Basing-point pricing continues to be an important commercial practice.

THE PRACTICE OF FREIGHT ABSORPTION

The price relationships of the multiple basing-point system are illustrated in Fig. 31. A, B, and C are mills selling in their own localities, at other points, and in town E. A and B are basing points. The base prices are equal, and the rail delivery costs are as shown on the diagram. The base at B is the governing base for sales in town E, a principal consumption center, and each mill will accordingly quote the base price at B plus the rail freight from B on sales in E and in adjoining territory. In selling at E, mill A will have its mill net reduced 5¢ by "freight absorption." *Freight absorption is the excess of the actual freight paid in making delivery over the amount of the freight item used in calculating the delivered price.*

Strictly speaking, the term "freight absorption" is a misnomer. In "absorbing" or "allowing" freight a mill must pay the railroad for making delivery; and the amount received by a mill after deducting actual freight *is the mill net price which it realizes on the particular sale.* Variable amounts of freight absorption result in variable mill net prices. The case is thus one of price discrimination or "dumping"—that is, one of making a difference in prices without a corresponding difference in quality, service, or conditions in the terms of sale.

On sales at town B, for example, mill A will quote the base price at B, pay a delivery cost of 15¢ per unit, and receive a mill net price of $1.45. On sales at town C, mill A will quote the base price at B plus 20¢ freight, pay a delivery cost of 35¢ per unit, and likewise receive a mill net price of $1.45.

When mill A sells in town A, on the other hand, it receives a mill net price of $1.60. *The mill net price is the amount received by a seller at the mill after deducting actual freight cost, allowed or defrayed by the seller.*[2]

THE PRACTICE OF CHARGING PHANTOM FREIGHT

When mill C (Fig. 31) sells at its point of production, it will quote the base price at B ($1.60) plus the rail freight from B to C (20¢), which gives a delivered price at C of $1.80. Since mill C charges its local customers a freight item of 20¢ per unit which it does not pay in making delivery, it collects a tribute in the form of "phantom freight." *Phantom freight is defined as the excess of the freight item charged over the freight actually paid in*

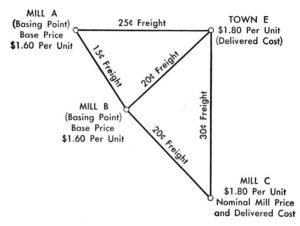

Fɪɢ. 31. The multiple basing-point system is one in which base prices are established at two or more locations for use in selling goods at identical delivered prices. In using the basing-point system, each seller quotes a delivered price which is the lowest combination of a base price plus rail freight from that base to a particular destination. On sales in the territory contiguous to B, all mills quote the base price at B plus freight from that base to destination, whereas on sales in the neighborhood of A, all mills quote the base price at A plus freight from that base to a destination point.

making delivery. In collecting phantom freight a mill receives a price higher than the base price by the amount of the so-called phantom freight. It may be noted that mill C continues to collect phantom or fictitious freight on all sales made up to a point halfway freightwise toward B, since it adds more freight on such sales than it actually pays out in making delivery. The price of $1.80 quoted by mill C on sales in C is sometimes called a "nominal" mill

[2] In studies made for the cement industry, Professors J. M. Clark and Arthur R. Burns found that more than one-half (69 to 86 percent) of the base mill shipments of cement of the five largest producers were made at prices which netted them less than their base prices. In some instances, the shrinkage of mill nets ranged as much as 75¢ per barrel below the base price. *The Cement Institute et al. v. Federal Trade Commission, Respondent, Brief for Respondent,* in the United States Court of Appeals for the Seventh Circuit (1946), pp. 69–70.

price for the reason that it is not the actual net price received on sales in distant areas—such as at A, B, or E.

In using the basing-point system, the various mills (with rare exceptions) never compete on price (see Table 28). No seller ever quotes lower prices

TABLE 28. Identical Delivered Prices Resulting from the Use of the Basing-Point Formula in the Cement Industry.[a]

No. of Bid	Name and Address of Bidder	Total Price	Discount (days)
1	Monarch Cement Company, Humbolt, Kans.	$3.286854	10¢ per bbl. 15 days
2	Ash Grove Lime & Portland Cement Co., Kansas City, Mo.	3.286854	10¢ per bbl. 15 days
3	Lehigh Portland Cement Company, Kansas City, Mo.	3.286854	10¢ per bbl. 15 days
4	Southwestern Portland Cement Co., El Paso, Texas	3.286854	10¢ per bbl. 15 days
5	Oklahoma Portland Cement Co. Oklahoma City, Okla.	3.286854	10¢ per bbl. 15 days
6	United States Portland Cement Co. Denver, Colo.	3.286854	10¢ per bbl. 15 days
7	Consolidated Cement Corp., Fredonia, Kans.	3.286854	10¢ per bbl. 15 days
8	Trinity Portland Cement Company, Dallas, Texas	3.286854	10¢ per bbl. 15 days
9	Lone Star Cement Company, Dallas, Texas	3.286854	10¢ per bbl. 15 days
10	Universal Atlas Cement Company, Waco, Texas	3.286854	10¢ per bbl. 15 days
11	Colorado Portland Cement Co., Denver, Colo.	3.286854	10¢ per bbl. 15 days

[a] This table is an abstract of bids for furnishing and delivering 6000 barrels of cement received by the office of the U.S. Engineer, Tucumcari, New Mexico, April 23, 1936. The award was made to bidder No. 3, Lehigh Portland Cement Company, by a drawing of lots. Source of data: Federal Trade Commission, *In the Matter of the Cement Institute et al.* Docket No. 3167, Commission's Exhibit No. 175-A, November 6, 1938.

than another seller in an effort to secure additional sales. Although a non-base mill absorbs freight in shipping into a distant sales area, the customer never pays a lesser amount for the goods delivered. If sales decline, mills following the formula refrain from making price reductions to stimulate buying and jointly accept unused capacity and unemployment for a part of their labor force. Any initiative as to price reduction lies with the base mill. The essence of the basing-point plan is the use of the base price and freight of *some other mill* for pricing purposes.

THE SELECTION OF BASE MILLS

In studying the operation of basing-point pricing systems it is important to remember that such systems were developed by large corporate mergers as a means of securing unity of action among their own plants, as well as with single-plant competitors. Mergers make it possible for one or a few companies to exercise price leadership, and pricing systems are the device which price leaders use to make their control effective over an entire sales area.

As a general rule, it may be said that the selection of a base mill or mills is made by a price leader, and the base price or prices announced are accepted and adopted by all other mills. In 1924, for example, the Federal Trade Commission found that the U.S. Steel Corporation established the base prices in the steel industry and that its prices were generally followed by its competitors. Also, in 1936, Mr. W. A. Irvin, president of the U.S. Steel Corporation, testified before a Senate committee that it was his company which set the prevailing prices for steel. The chairman of the Senate committee had stated, "All the witnesses thus far give the impression that their prices were set only to meet competition. . . . It seems to be extremely difficult to find out who the bell wether [i.e. price leader] is, and who fixes the prices originally that they follow to meet that competition." To this statement Mr. Irvin replied, "I would say we generally make the prices."[3]

In selecting a base mill or mills, a price leader considers a variety of factors including (1) the maximization of its own profit, (2) the maintenance of its price leadership, and (3) the area of economical shipment for the commodity. When freight costs are high in relation to the price of the product and production facilities are scattered throughout the nation, sales are usually confined to certain designated zones or regions; and it is usual for a base and base price to be established for each zone. When freight costs constitute a lower percentage of the product price, on the other hand, as they do in the case of steel and sugar, it is usual for the price leader or leaders to establish a fewer number of basing points for the entire country.

Basing-point pricing systems have been adopted not only through the exercise of price leadership by a dominant seller, but also through the coöperative endeavors of individual enterprisers. In competing on price, a locally separate mill may reduce its mill-net prices in selling at the fringe of its sales area. Distant rivals selling at the same destination points may do likewise. In order to avoid this price competition at the geographic margin of their respective sales areas, geographically separate sellers may find a common interest in adopting some sort of a coöperative pricing system.

Basing-point systems have also been adopted in patent license arrangements. The practice is for a patent owner (the "licensor") to provide in the license agreement with individual manufacturers (the "licensees") that a basing-point system shall be adopted and collectively used by each licensee. The concerted use of a basing-point plan eliminates price competition among multiple sellers and permits the fullest possible exploitation of the patent monopoly rights.

[3] Federal Trade Commission, *Report to the President on Steel Sheet Piling* (Washington, 1936), pp. 6–7.

THE DETERMINATION OF THE BASE PRICE

Since the essence of the basing-point formula (in contrast with f.o.b. mill pricing) is the sale of goods at the price of *some other mill* plus freight from *that mill*, it is evident that the way in which the "some other mill" calculates its base price is a highly important matter. The base price is the price which others follow to "meet competition," it is said.

A statement of the way in which a price leader in the cement industry determines a base price was reported in detail in a pamphlet published by the Lone Star Cement Corporation, one of the "Big Five" producers which owns some ten mills in various parts of the United States. According to the company's pamphlet, entitled *Trade Ethics and Marketing Policies,*

The price of *Lone Star* Cement is made up of the following:
1. Manufacturing Cost, the major parts of which are labor, fuel, and supplies; over all of which we have no control;
2. Selling Cost;
3. Packing and Loading Costs;
4. Taxes and Depreciation Costs; and
5. Reasonable Profits on our Investments.

The total of these items, equals what we term our "Base Price." This "Base Price," plus transportation charges, would constitute the delivered price in every market if we had no competition.

The price we actually quote any cement buyer is influenced by two factors:

First—Our "Base Price," plus the freight charge from our mill to the customer's town;

or

Second—Our competitor's "Base Price," plus the freight charge from his mill to the customer's town.

In the first instance, our "Base Price" is the *maximum* return which we receive even in those towns which, due to their location, enjoy a lower freight rate from our mill than from our competitor's mill.

In the second instance, as we cannot get more than our competitor's price, we quote a price which we expect will be identical with that asked by the competitor whose lower freight rate gives his product the advantage at that point.

As good will and continued patronage are the only premiums the trade will pay for *Lone Star* Cement, it is obvious that in order to make a sale, we must meet the lowest *bona fide* price quoted the buyer by any other reputable manufacturer. This is exactly what we do in the second instance![4]

It is significant to note that the Lone Star company states that its "base price" plus transportation charges determine its delivered prices in its con-

---

[4] The pamphlet issued by the Lone Star Cement Corp. is reproduced in *Federal Trade Commission* v. *The Cement Institute, et al., Brief of Respondents,* in the Supreme Court of the United States, October Term, 1947, Vol. 1, Appendix A, pp. 474-476.

tiguous territory. Such prices are essentially monopolistic, based upon what the traffic will bear *without the rivalry* of other competitors.

At the same time that a given leader determines a governing "base price" by estimating the price he believes is warranted, other geographically separate companies which are financially dominant in their areas establish base prices which are controlling for their sales territories. In shipping into another sales territory, a basing-point mill and its followers in one geographic area, thereupon use (and match) the established base price (plus freight) which governs in the distant area. No seller reduces the delivered price to any customer below that required by the formula. Although the absorption of freight made in shipping into another sales area looks like a generous gift, the customer never pays a lesser amount than the applicable base price plus freight from that basing point to his destination.

THE USE OF THE MULTIPLE BASING-POINT SYSTEM IN THE SUGAR INDUSTRY

The actual use of a multiple basing-point system may be observed in the sugar industry. All sugar—cane and beet—is sold at basing-point delivered prices. Each seaboard city having one or more sugar refineries is regarded as a basing point (see Fig. 32), and the base prices at the several basing-point mills tend to be identical. In quoting delivered prices, each locally separate mill (see Fig. 32) quotes the base price plus the freight from the base to the customer's location which gives the lowest combination of base price and freight rate. Thus, if a buyer in Pittsburgh wants to buy a carload of sugar, all refiners interested in selling will quote the base price plus the freight rate from Baltimore, since Baltimore is the nearest basing point freightwise to Pittsburgh. If a buyer in Chicago, Illinois, wants to buy a carload of sugar, all mills will use the base price at New Orleans plus the freight rate from New Orleans to Chicago, for New Orleans is the nearest basing point freightwise to the customer's location. If, however, a buyer in New Orleans wants to buy a carload of sugar, all mills will quote the New Orleans price without an addition of freight, for the customer is located at a basing point. The sugar refiner making the sale always pays the actual freight charges, and the buyer is billed for the sugar at the seaboard base price plus the cost of transporting sugar from the nearest seaboard refining point to his location.

If a buyer in Dallas, Texas, wants to buy a carload of sugar, all mills will quote the seaboard base price plus the freight rate from Sugarland (Houston), Texas, for Sugarland is the nearest cane refining point freightwise to Dallas. Further, if a buyer in Chinook, Montana, wants to buy a carload of sugar, all mills (including the local mill in Chinook) will quote the San Francisco base price plus the rail freight from San Francisco to Chinook.

A study of the map (Fig. 32), showing the location of cane and beet sugar refineries, will indicate that inland beet sugar factories collect a large amount of phantom freight on local sales and absorb a substantial amount of freight on sales in areas along the east and west coasts and in the South. The cane

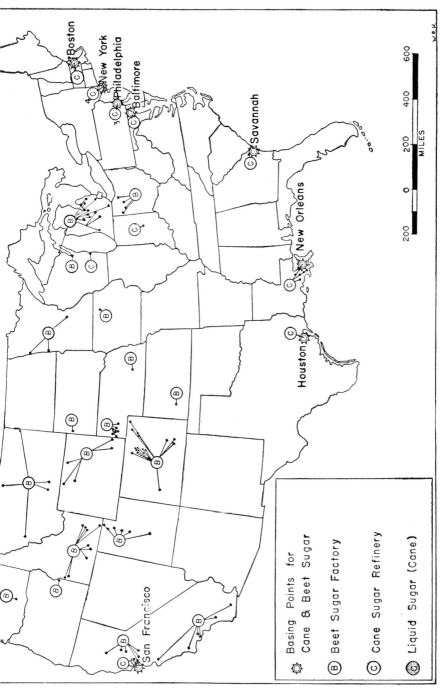

Fig. 32. The basing-point system as used in the sale of beet and cane sugar. Each locally separate mill quotes the base price plus the freight from the base to the customer's location which gives the lowest combination. (Source of data: Trade reports and *Weekly Statistical Sugar Trade Journal*.)

Basing Points for

- ☼ Cane & Beet Sugar
- Ⓑ Beet Sugar Factory
- Ⓒ Cane Sugar Refinery
- ◉ Liquid Sugar (Cane)

Boston
New York
Philadelphia
Baltimore
Savannah
New Orleans
Houston
San Francisco

MILES

200   0   200   400   600

W.R.H.

sugar refiners charge a local price which is sufficiently high so that they can absorb freight when they sell their sugars in the sales area adjacent to another seaboard base. The sugar industry is characterized by a considerable amount of crosshauling—that is, cane sugar is shipped from California to Denver, and beet sugar is shipped from Denver to the west coast. Sugar buyers in Montana, Idaho, Utah, and Colorado—the heart of the beet sugar production area—frequently complain about the fact that they must pay the highest prices in the United States for sugar which is produced and consumed locally. Only about 20 percent of the beet sugar produced in the Rocky Mountain area is sold in the eleven western states.

THE FREIGHT-ALLOWED OR ZONE-DELIVERED PRICING SYSTEM

A second type of delivered pricing formula is the "freight-allowed" or "zone-delivered" method of price quotation. When used jointly by two or more sellers, this system also results in identical delivered prices and an avoidance of price competition. The freight-allowed method of pricing appears to have been first used in the sale of tobacco products. Its use in this field came with the formation of the American Tobacco Company in 1890. During the period 1890–1900 such products as water meters, wire rope, retail scales, meat slicers and choppers were sold in this way. From 1900 to 1904 more products were added to the list, including pipe tools, vises, pipe cutters, auger bits, wood-boring tools, screw drivers, and machine knives. From 1908 to 1910 the practice spread to automobile tires, brake lining, and chemical products. In 1912 manufacturers of tire chains and electric lamps began to sell their products with an allowance of freight. With the legalization of price fixing during the National Recovery Administration (1933–1935), many more products were quoted on this basis; and today new applications are continuing to be made from time to time.

Under the freight-allowed system, each seller quotes an identical base or zone price *containing an average freight item* and then "allows" the freight from his mill to destination. The delivered price so established may prevail for destinations anywhere in the entire country or within a specified zone. Sellers convert from f.o.b. pricing to delivered pricing by adding an "average freight item" to their f.o.b. prices. This is done by estimating what it has cost a seller, or a group of sellers, to ship the product to destinations in the particular zone or area for which a uniform price is being established.

In allowing freight, the goods may be sent prepaid or the buyer may be directed to pay the freight and deduct it from the invoice before remitting payment. Products sold freight allowed include some costing several thousand dollars and weighing many tons, as well as some of trifling cost and weight.

With a zone-delivered pricing system, customers living near a mill are required to pay a "loading" (essentially "phantom freight"), which the seller may use in part in absorbing freight and retain in part as a monopoly profit (see Fig. 33). In the instance of a candy bar or a package of cigarettes, the phantom freight involved is of no practical significance. However, in the great majority of cases the delivery cost is a significant percentage of the product price, and the arbitrary collection of phantom freight forces many buyers to pay prices bearing no relation to actual costs of delivery. A further criticism of all zone-delivered pricing systems is that they provide locally separate sellers with a formula for quoting identical delivered prices which effectively eliminates any price competition.

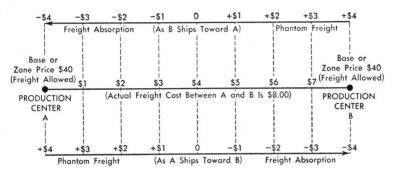

Fig. 33. The freight-allowed or zone-delivered pricing system. The base or zone prices include a sum to cover the "average freight" from the mill to the points in the zone, and a uniform price is made to all customers within that zone. In this example the average freight is assumed to be $4 per unit. The upper line shows the fictitious freight differentials of sellers at B as they ship toward A. Up to a point midway between the two production centers, sellers at B charge *more* for freight than the freight actually costs (phantom freight). In shipping beyond the midpoint, they charge *less* for freight than it actually costs (freight absorption). The lower line represents the fictitious freight differentials of sellers at A as they ship toward B.

In using the freight-allowed or zone-delivered pricing system, locally separate mills quote a base or zone price in one of four principal ways: (1) with freight allowed to destination, (2) with freight allowed and prepaid, (3) with freight allowed within zones, or (4) with freight allowed to distribution points. A discussion of these various classes of zone-delivered prices follows.

1. Full Freight Allowed to Destination

One group of the products sold freight allowed consists of manufactured goods sold to industrial users and dealers on the basis of one list or mill-base price (f.o.b. factory) for the entire country with full freight allowed to destination (any established freight station). With this pricing system, the buyer pays the actual freight, deducts it from the quoted price, and remits the remainder to the seller. A representative list of such goods is shown in Table 29.

TABLE 29. Representative Goods Sold F.O.B. Factory Full Freight Allowed to Destination (minimum order required is shown in parentheses).

Arc welding machines	High-grade zinc
Tire chains (24 pairs)	Mechanical rubber goods (100 lbs.)
Brake lining (100 lbs.)	Leather transmission belting (100 lbs.)
Multiblade fans, blowers, and air washers	Steam condensers (traps)
Household electrical appliances	Sheet-metal fittings ($200)
Files and rasps (150 lbs.)	Asbestos products
Machine knives	Water meters (150 lbs.)
Rubber-soled canvas footwear (100 lbs.)	V-drive pulleys and belts (100 lbs.)
Lubricated plug valves (500 lbs.)	Pneumatic tools and hoists
Steel split pulleys	Stillson pipe wrenches (200 lbs.)
Copper wire (insulated or plain), cable, sheets, and tubing (200 lbs.)	Air compressor hose (500 ft.)
Brass and bronze wire or cable (200 lbs.)	Rubber and fabric transmission belting (100 lbs.)
Mechanics' hand tools	Chain hoists (hand operated), trolleys, and winches (100 lbs.)
Flexible steel and aluminum conduit (100 lbs.)	Marine specialties and ship fixtures (100 lbs.)
Flexible metal hose (100 lbs.)	Soft drinks
Bakelite	Rubber fuel tanks
Aluminum, primary	Rubber cement
Aluminum, rolling and drawing	Small arms

2. FREIGHT ALLOWED AND PREPAID

A second category of products sold on a zone basis includes those sold "f.o.b. factory, freight allowed *and* prepaid" to any freight station in the United States. In this method of pricing, the seller pays the actual freight and the buyer pays the quoted price. Table 30 presents a typical list of goods sold to industrial users or dealers at one list price for the entire United States, with freight allowed and prepaid. In some cases the practice is to sell with freight allowed, or allowed and prepaid, at the seller's option.

TABLE 30. Representative Goods Sold F.O.B. Factory Freight Allowed and Prepaid to Destination.

Cadmium	Groceries, trademarked items—such as canned soup, shortening, cereals, cake flour, and canned dog food (1 carload)
Industrial motors and controllers	
Electric lamps (standard packages)	
Biologicals, arsenicals, insulin, and other drug specialties	Automobile tires and tubes (200 lbs.)
Coated abrasives (200 lbs.)	Cash registers, accounting machines, adding machines, and check-writing machines
Rubber-covered building wire	
Cable accessories and magnet wire (100 lbs.)	Notions—such as zippers, buttons, pins (variable minimums)
Dictating machines and accessories	
Typewriters	Cotton thread (100 lbs.)
Glazier tools (100 lbs.)	Cigarettes and tobacco products
Matches, stick	Candy bars (100 lbs.)
Copper, wire bars, cathodes, ingots, and ingot bars (carload lots)	Kraft paper

3. FREIGHT ALLOWED WITHIN ZONES

Many products are sold to dealers and industrial users with freight allowed or prepaid within given zones. Usually the number of zones ranges from two to five, and manufacturers variously located in the United States usually follow the leader on the zones and base prices which are established. Table 31 gives a representative list of goods sold by this method.

TABLE 31. Representative Products Sold to Industrial Users and Dealers with Full Freight Allowed to Destination Within Given Zones.

Arc-welding electrodes (100 lbs.)	Lubricating oil, grease, and kerosene dispensing equipment
Hard-fiber twine	
Insulating board products	Hydraulic lifts (gasoline station)
Waterworks valves	Sash pulleys (100 lbs.)
Scales, meat choppers, slicers, and coffee mills	Folding chairs and school chairs
Power cable	Chain, sprockets, gears, and power transmission machinery (100 lbs.)
Street-lighting equipment, reactors, feeder regulators (100 lbs.)	Wire rope (200 lbs.)
Distribution transformers	Liquid chlorine
Portable air compressors	Feed water heaters
Portable elevators	Crosscut saws and handles, hacksaw blades and frames, handsaws, and saw tools (100 lbs.)
Glass containers	
Brass and copper strip (100 lbs.)	
Paint	Lye
Screws, nuts, bolts	Hand-lift trucks
Electric grinders	Paper bags
Gasoline service station pumps	Water softeners
Blotting paper	Matches, book
Soap and glycerine products	Hard-surface floor coverings

4. FREIGHT ALLOWED TO DISTRIBUTING POINTS

A pricing policy which approximates the practice of allowing freight to any freight station in the United States is found in the practice of manufacturers to quote prices f.o.b. factory, or in some cases by zones, with freight allowed to jobbers and distributors. Under this arrangement, dealers and industrial users (as buyers) usually pay the transportation charges from the distributing point to destination. Table 32 presents a list of some typical

TABLE 32. Representative Products Sold Freight Allowed or Prepaid to Distributors.

Portable electric tools (100 lbs.)	Firearms (100 lbs.)
Various chemical products	Dry-cell batteries and flashlights (200 lbs.)
Air rifle shot (200 lbs.)	Pliers, wrenches, and small tools (100 lbs.)
Oil cans, oilers, fillers, and torches	Rock drills (100 lbs.)
Electric fans (100 lbs.)	Auger bits, wood-boring tools, and screw drivers ($100)
Plumbing fixtures (carload lots)	
Ladders	Manila rope (200 lbs.)
Brass and copper products	Road machinery
Kraft paper and kraft container board	

products which are sold freight allowed (or prepaid) to wholesalers, jobbers, or distributors.

REASONS GIVEN BY SELLERS FOR THE USE OF THE FREIGHT-ALLOWED POLICY

Numerous reasons for the origin of the pricing policy of freight allowed are suggested by producers, among which are the following:

1. The practice of quoting f.o.b. factory, freight allowed (or allowed and prepaid) is said to have arisen as a form of occasional, exceptional, secret price concession. In the water meter business, for example, it is reported that salesmen are given a series of discounts which they may grant, if necessary, to get the business, and as a final concession they are permitted "to allow the freight."

2. The freight-allowed method of price quotation is said by certain producers to be used as an encouragement to the placing of a fair-sized order. It is evident, however, that the great bulk of the freight-allowed sales is not to be explained in this way. Quantity discounts may be made without any freight allowance and certainly without *full* freight allowance.

3. A policy of quoting f.o.b. factory with a full or partial freight allowance, it is said, is sometimes adopted by a locally separate mill in an effort to expand its volume of business. Local business is readily secured anyway because other sellers are not nearby; and by including an average freight item in the price it is possible to hold down the delivered price in more distant areas. Thus, a business consulting firm reported that "in an effort to keep the average ultimate prices as low as possible to the consuming public . . . *and thus increase the market area,* our client last year adopted a zone-pricing system as the first step toward a uniform freight-allowed price throughout the entire area." In selling into another territory, a mill usually seeks to match the delivered price of its distant rival; and the profitable way to do this is to "allow the freight" (that is, by discriminating, not lowering the uniform base price).

4. A policy of quoting prices freight allowed is sometimes used by manufacturers who seek to maintain a uniform *retail* price for their products everywhere in the United States. One manufacturer, for example, stated that its policy is to "carry the freight burden"—by including an average freight item in the price—so that retail prices will be the same in the East and West. A manufacturer may wish to have a uniform retail price in order to advertise the price nationally or to expand its area of sales by the use of an average freight item.

It may be noted that some products—such as shoes and men's clothing—are often sold at an open f.o.b. factory price, with actual freight to be paid by the retailer, for retail sale at a uniform price everywhere in the United States. This practice means that distant dealers have a lower profit margin than those living nearer to the point of production.

5. The policy of quoting prices freight allowed is sometimes used by

manufacturers in order to place their distributors in adjoining territories on "an equal competitive basis." Thus, a manufacturer of kraft paper bags and wrapping paper reported: "Since our distributors compete with each other as well as with the distributors of paper products manufactured by other companies, they obviously must start with competitive costs in order to have competitive resale prices."

THE MAIN REASON FOR THE PRESENT FULL-FREIGHT-ALLOWED POLICY

The various reasons given by manufacturers for the origin of the freight-allowed policy have, no doubt, a certain degree of validity. However, they all refer to times and situations in which the discriminatory allowance of freight is done independently, without a uniform rule followed by an entire industry. But if this unsystematic practice is replaced (however it comes about) by the systematic practice of *full* freight allowance and identical (nominal) factory prices, all competitive variation in delivered prices disappears and the practice becomes in essentials a system or formula for quoting identical delivered prices. The main and continuing reason for the policy of selling merchandise freight allowed thereupon is to provide locally separate producers in an industry with a convenient formula for securing "unity of action with respect to price."

In the words of a rubber-tire manufacturer, "The principal reason why shipments in our industry are made f.o.b. factory with freight allowed to destination is to eliminate one factor of competition and place all units of the industry on an equal basis regardless of geographical location in so far as the cost factor of transportation is concerned." A manufacturer of pulleys said, "The natural function of freight allowance is to enable the different concerns in an industry to compete on an equal basis." A manufacturer of plumbing fixtures said, "The policy of freight allowed has come about in our opinion in order that manufacturers might favorably compete with each other in all parts of the United States."

SUBSTITUTE FORMS OF COMPETITION

The coöperative use of delivered pricing systems, we have seen, results in the quotation of identical delivered prices. With the elimination of price competition, major producers have turned increasingly to nonprice forms of competition. Competition in advertising, premium giving, and entertainment, in particular, have become important substitutes for price competition. The modern sales technique is that of "blasting the market." Today most persons know the leading brand names nearly as well as their own!

The major soap and cigarette producers quote identical delivered prices to distributors *and* spend many millions in radio, television, newspaper, and magazine advertising to influence buying. In the soap industry, it is estimated in the trade, advertising accounts for about 30 percent of the total costs of leading producers.

Other forms of competitive sales effort include (1) gifts, presents, and various forms of entertainment to secure the favor and good will of buyers; (2) competitive trade-in allowances; (3) essay, jingle, and box-top contests; (4) arrangements for the purchase of silverware and other merchandise; (5) coupons usable as part payment for purchases; (6) "two for the price of one" and similar types of offers; (7) assistance to retailers in displaying merchandise; and (8) provision of demonstrators and samples.

METHODS USED TO MAINTAIN DELIVERED-PRICING SYSTEMS

If demand declines and sales fall off, or if a desired volume of business cannot be done at the controlling base prices, some mills (usually single-plant competitors) are tempted to deviate from the delivered-price system by quoting lower prices *in certain areas or to selected customers* in order to increase their business.[5] As soon as knowledge of the price reductions becomes known to other sellers, the evidence shows, the price leader takes immediate steps to discipline the mill showing a price independence. One method used by price leaders in basing-point industries is to impose a "punitive base price" on the mill competing on price equal to the lowest mill net secured by the price reductions. Thus, the vice-president of the Lehigh Portland Cement Company, a price leader, testified as follows with respect to the action of his company in imposing bases on non-basing-point mills.

> Question: "And where you found competitors making such deals and transactions secretly, you say you put in a price that made them take as low as that on all their business; isn't that right?"
> Answer: "That was one of the effects of our action."[6]

The method of disciplining those showing a price independence is illustrated in Fig. 34. If mill B, for example, should make a secret price quotation at X of $1.80 and if the price leader (mill A) should learn about it, A might very quickly impose on B a punitive base price of $1.70—the resulting mill net of B on sales at X. This action would force B to take a maximum net price of $1.70 on *all* sales in its contiguous area.

In the hearings of the Federal Trade Commission on the cement industry, the evidence presented showed that the imposition of a punitive base price quickly makes a recalcitrant ask for terms. Thus, the president of a cement mill in Nebraska, which had been competing on price, found that a low base

[5] In explaining the development of actual competition in price in the cement industry during the business depression of 1930–1931, the vice-president of a large cement company testified before the Federal Trade Commission that "we found that they [our competitors] did not make the same price to all customers, but *in some cases* gave customers lower prices than the published quotations, while in other cases they did not give similar concessions." *Federal Trade Commission* v. *The Cement Institute et al., Brief of Respondents*, Vol. 1, Appendix A, In the Supreme Court of the United States (October Term, 1947), p. 495. This is the typical way in which price competition develops in other basing-point and zone-delivered pricing systems.

[6] *Ibid.*, p. 499.

price had been imposed on his mill and wrote to the price leader: "While in Omaha yesterday, I found that you had placed a base on our Nebraska mill, and you may imagine my surprise to find you had done a thing like that. . . . If you had hired a man to stab me in the back, or burned our plant, I wouldn't be more surprised than I am at what you have done. . . . I cannot take such action on your part as other than a deliberate attempt to ruin our business."[7] The price leader replied that he would be "glad to confer . . . in person," and in due time arrangements were made to have the punitive base price removed.

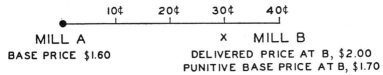

FIG. 34. Imposition of a punitive base price. Mill A is the basing point and mill B is a non-base mill. In sales at X the delivered price is $1.90. If mill B should make a price quotation at X of $1.80 to get the business—and flout the leadership of the base mill—mill A may impose a punitive base price at B of $1.70, simply by quoting a base price of $1.70 on sales made in B's area.

In justification of its action of imposing a punitive base, a price leader commonly claims that the offender cut prices in the first instance, and that the naming of a new base price is simply an act of "meeting competition." In quoting the new price, however, the leader makes it applicable only in the area of the independent seller, and only when its leadership is flouted. The act is really one of discriminatory monopoly pricing rather than of normal competitive behavior.

A second disciplinary measure employed by a price leader against a mill which tries to compete on price is "price raiding." Price raiding means that delivered prices are "cut" in particular local areas, or to particular customers, in a *discriminatory way*, expressly to injure the concern showing a price independence. In cutting prices to discipline an independent, the price leader may, and frequently does, instruct its salesmen to "get the business" by quoting any price which is necessary to do it. Such prices are variously called "special" or "arbitrary" prices. The resulting price chaos is usually known as a "price war." The ability of a price leader to cut price to extremely low levels in certain areas is based either upon financial strength or upon monopoly control in other areas in which the losses may be recouped.

CAN BASING-POINT AND ZONE-DELIVERED PRICING SYSTEMS EXIST OR BE MAINTAINED WITHOUT SOME FORM OF COÖPERATION AMONG COMPETITORS?

A significant question bearing on delivered-price systems is whether a policy of identical delivered prices according to formula can be followed by a group of sellers without collusion, agreement, or understanding. In-

[7] *Ibid.*, pp. 504–505.

dustry members stoutly and vigorously maintain that identical delivered prices reflect the uniform prices in a normal market, free from collusion and coercion. Critics of basing-point pricing, on the other hand, declare that this is a bogus claim, based upon the erroneous idea that every destination point is a normal market in which the delivered price is determined by the free play of demand and supply.

In the Federal Trade Commission hearings on delivered prices in the cement industry, consideration was given to the probability of getting identical bids from sellers acting independently.[8] An expert in mathematics called by the Commission was asked the following question: "Suppose that sixteen competitors in sealed bids name identical delivered prices at a given destination, so that their delivered price bids match exactly; that is, quote identical delivered prices at that one destination. Now, if we assume that their bids are made without any prearrangement, collaboration, or understanding or agreement, what is the probability that the sixteen bids will be identical at that one destination in terms of dollars and cents?"[9] It was assumed further that the various sellers would either bid $1.78 or $1.79 per unit. There have been many actual cases, it may be added, in which sixteen or more bidders have bid identical prices at many destinations rather than at only one destination. The question was under these conditions what is the probability that all sixteen sellers acting independently will bid an identical price at one destination point? According to the witness, the probability would be $\dfrac{1}{32,768}$! This is equivalent to three chances in 100,000 calls for bids that prices would be identical. On the probability of the sixteen independent sellers' making identical bids at three destinations instead of one, the witness declared that the chance would be equivalent to that of picking out a particular half-dollar from a row of half-dollars laid side by side extending from the earth to the sun.[10]

When sellers act independently on price, there are many factors leading them to reduce or raise their *asking* prices. Some sellers have unused capacity and urgently want additional business. Others have lower costs. Some have better raw materials, more efficient managements, and relative freight advantages. The judgment of different individuals on trends in prices and costs is also highly variable. Some are "bulls" and others are "bears" in their attitude toward prices.

[8] The theory of probability deals with the possibility that a given chance event will occur. Thus, what is the possibility of drawing an ace from a full pack of fifty-two cards? The answer is that there are four ways of success and fifty-two ways of success and failure—that is, four divided by fifty-two, or one-thirteenth. This means that if one draws 130 cards, he can expect to get ten aces. If he drew all aces or no aces, he would know that something was wrong.

[9] *The Cement Institute, et al.* v. *F.T.C., Transcript of Record,* in the United States Court of Appeals for the Seventh Circuit, Vol. 8, p. 18597 (filed September 1, 1943).

[10] From the testimony of Professor C. O. Oakley, Haverford College, in *ibid.,* pp. 18585–18630.

In spite of all the reasons which ordinarily make for a diversity of judg- ment among individual sellers on price, basing-point and zone-delivered prices are regularly and systematically identical. The mathematics of proba- bility indicate that when such a chance event as price identity occurs regu- larly—like the regular drawing of aces from a pack of cards—some plan or human arrangement is responsible for the result.

Various economists take the view that when sellers are only few in num- ber, concerted action on price can occur without explicit collusion, agree- ment, or understanding. Under conditions of *duopoly* and *oligopoly*, it is said, the fear of "retaliation" restricts a seller in reducing his price. Since a price change by one seller is likely to cause a similar reduction—or a greater one—by his rivals, it is reasoned that sellers (when they are few) are likely to act as one without agreement.

The crux of the problem of pricing when sellers are few *and locally sepa- rate* is the fact competition between mills having degrees of local monopoly power *may become chaotic if they are allowed to discriminate.* Local mo- nopoly power gives a seller the ability to exploit nearby customers and "cut" prices elsewhere to injure a rival showing independence in his pricing policy. Once price cutting begins *in certain areas,* it can quickly become chaotic *in those areas,* because one or more of the sellers can make up losses *in other areas.* Since some mills do not enjoy local monopoly power they are obvi- ously going to be exceedingly careful about competing in price with a large merger. Large companies themselves, owning mills in several localities, also see the advantage of systematically restraining competition to avoid local price cutting which might be carried to ruinous levels.

All available historical studies indicate that delivered-price plans were established and maintained in iron and steel, cement, the nonferrous metals, and other principal commodities by means of formal meetings and agree- ments.[11] In many industries delivered-price plans were also established dur- ing the period of the National Recovery Administration (1933–1935) when the antitrust laws were suspended.

When once established, delivered-pricing systems tend to become regarded as a business "custom" which each succeeding generation of business execu- tives accepts as the normal way of doing business. New mills coming into production, moreover, may adopt the pricing system which they find with-

[11] The *Statement of the Case, Brief and Argument by Attorneys for the Federal Trade Commission,* and *Trial Examiner's Report on the Facts in Federal Trade Commission v. U.S. Steel Corporation,* Docket 760 (Washington, 1924), present a detailed record showing that the basing-point system in the iron and steel industry was established and maintained by meetings, discussions, agreements, and monopolistic coercion. Also, in 1944 the Federal Trade Commission reported after long study and extensive public hear- ings that basing-point practices in the cement industry "originated in agreements entered into as long as 20 to 30 years ago and have persisted, with the support of collective action, in substantially their original form." *The Cement Institute, et al. v. Federal Trade Com- mission, Findings as to Facts and Conclusions* (September, 1943), Vol. 24, pp. 15983– 15984. For further historical data bearing on the introduction of pricing systems, see Frank A. Fetter, *The Masquerade of Monopoly* (New York, 1931).

out formal meeting or agreement with their competitors. Every follower, however, acts in a restrained manner or as if he were forbidden to reduce the delivered price required by the formula. In view of this consistent mutuality of behavior on the part of sellers, various economists, as well as the Federal Trade Commission and the courts, have held that the collective use of basing-point and zone-delivered formulas typically involves agreement or a mutual restraint on individual action which is tantamount to agreement.

ARGUMENTS USED TO JUSTIFY BASING-POINT PRICING AND THE ANSWERS OF THOSE OPPOSING THE PRACTICE

Many industries are currently employing delivered pricing systems which involve systematic freight absorption and divergent mill net prices. Forceful arguments to justify such pricing methods are made by basing-point industries and their spokesmen. At the same time, critics of discriminatory pricing methods, including numerous economists, many independent businessmen, and various farm and labor groups, declare that such arguments are distorted, fallacious, and unsound. The question of what to do about basing-point pricing promises to be a continuing economic problem for many years to come.

Public and legal opposition to long-established basing-point systems has led some businessmen and writers to suggest that there is a difference between (a) basing-point pricing and (b) competitive freight absorption, i.e., the practice of reducing one's net price on some sales to meet the delivered price of a distant seller. A seller in shrinking his mill net on some sales to meet the delivered price of another mill, however, is actually quoting a "combination price" which is the sum of (a) the base price of *another mill* plus (b) the freight from *that* mill to the buyer's destination. This is the essence of basing-point pricing.

The principal arguments advanced *for* and *against* the use of delivered pricing methods which involve systematic freight absorption are as follows:

Arguments in Favor of Basing-Point Pricing and Freight Absorption	Arguments Against Basing-Point Pricing and Freight Absorption
1. The identity of delivered prices resulting from systematic freight absorption demonstrates the existence of effective competition. Agreement may not be presumed from identity of delivered prices, for the price of a homogeneous commodity in a competitive market is uniform.	1. Systematic freight absorption results in price matching, not price competition. The mill-net prices of a freight-absorbing seller are divergent, whereas the mill-net prices of a seller in a central market are uniform. Market prices are f.o.b. shipping point prices, and buyers pay the actual freight.
2. Systematic freight absorption and crosshauling give buyers a wider	2. With freight absorption, buyers have no choice on prices. There

choice of sellers. Buyers who cannot purchase all their requirements from nearby plants can buy from distant suppliers at the same delivered cost. The elimination of crosshauling would be a serious blow to the railroads.

3. The price rigidity in basing-point systems makes for stability in the economy. The profits of basing-point industries are not excessive during periods of depression. Taxes, railroad rates, and other costs must be met. If prices were forced down, wages would have to be cut.

4. Delivered prices are quoted because buyers prefer to buy at delivered prices. Figuring freight rates is frequently complicated, and buyers usually request that delivered prices be quoted. Freight absorption also benefits consumers, for many do not have to pay the full shipping charges. Consumers get a "break."

5. The use of pricing formulas prevents chaotic price cutting. Geographically separate producers must systematically restrain price cutting in each other's area or be ruined. With unrestrained price competition, overhead costs can be ignored, and prices can be cut to injure competitors. The better solution is the price leadership plan as a *modus vivendi*.

6. Systematic freight absorption makes it possible for a seller to secure a larger volume of business by selling in distant sales areas. Fixed costs per unit are reduced. *Local prices do not need to be cut to get orders at distant points.*

is no price competition to moderate excessive local prices, i.e., "all the traffic will bear." Crosshauling of identical products from one sales area into another is wasteful. F.o.b. mill pricing would eliminate this uneconomic practice.

3. Basing-point and zone prices are rigid over long periods of time. Rigid prices increase the intensity of a depression and retard recovery. Sellers in industries with declining prices face losses and maladjustments in buying at high, rigid basing-point prices. Unemployment is aggravated.

4. No critic opposes the quotation of f.o.b. mill prices plus actual freight. Freight absorption, however, means discriminatory mill prices. Local buyers are forced to pay phantom freight; distant customers do not pay the full freight. Distant sales are subsidized by higher returns obtained on sales to nearby customers.

5. Delivered pricing systems do not eliminate all local price cutting. Price leaders still use it on occasion to discipline recalcitrants. The effective solution is to require f.o.b. mill prices, uniform to all buyers at the mill. Thereupon, a large seller in cutting prices in one locality must cut prices in all areas. This would be very costly. Local price cutting would be discouraged.

6. Dumping into another's sales territory does not increase a seller's business if the other reciprocates. Sellers just "swap" business. If a seller "out-dumps" his rival, he reduces the rival's sales and increases the rival's costs. *A reduction of local prices to get orders at distant points would be real competition.*

7. A geographically separate mill is justified in charging local buyers phantom freight and high local prices, for they would have to pay this freight if the local mill had not been built.

7. Phantom freight places an unfair cost burden on local customers. Consumers are denied the advantages of their location at a production point.

8. Any drastic change in pricing methods will upset and disrupt long-established economic relationships to which business has now become adjusted. If regular and systematic freight absorption is abolished, numerous concerns located at a distance from consuming centers are likely to be put out of business.

8. High local prices and systematic freight absorption provide an umbrella for badly located, high-cost plants. A restoration of price competition may cause certain inefficient and poorly located mills to be abandoned. This is an inevitable and desirable aspect of a progressive economy.

GLOSSARY OF TERMS FREQUENTLY USED
IN DISCUSSIONS OF BASING-POINT
AND ZONE-DELIVERED PRICES

Base Mill: A mill whose location is used as a basing point in determining transportation costs. The price charged by a base mill is matched by other mills desiring to sell in the territory served by the base mill; and in such cases, the various sellers quote the "base price" plus freight from the "base mill" to the customer's location.

Base Price: The price at a given point, called the basing point, which sellers regularly use in quoting delivered prices for a given area. There may be one or several basing points, and each mill of a seller and his locally separate rivals may serve as the basing point for its adjacent area in the particular seller's distribution system. In quoting delivered prices, sellers quote the particular "base price" plus freight from the basing point to the customer's location which gives the lowest combination of price and freight cost. The essence of the basing-point plan is the use of the base price and freight of *some other mill* for pricing purposes.

Basing-Point Formula: A system of pricing in which one or more basing points are used. The delivered price is determined by adding to an established price at a given point, called the basing point, the freight charge—usually rail freight—from such a point to the point of delivery, regardless of the actual origin of shipments or the actual freight cost incurred in the shipment.

Delivered Price: This is the buyer's cost of the goods delivered at the buyer's place of business. It is a collective term for two prices: (1) the net realized price received by the seller at the point of shipment plus (2) the price of transportation—actual, averaged, or fictitious—included in the quotation.

F.O.B. Mill Pricing: The quotation of prices f.o.b. a seller's mill, which are uniform for goods of the same quality, to all buyers in the same trade classification, purchasing at the mill in similar quantities, with delivered costs to various destinations differing by the actual freight, payable by the buyer, from the shipping mill. (See also Chap. 6, p. 98, footnote 14.)

Freight Absorption: The excess of the actual freight paid out by the seller in making delivery over the amount of the freight item used in calculating the delivered price to the buyer.

Freight Equalization: The practice of charging a customer the freight cost which he would pay in getting delivery from a nearer supplier, rather than the seller's actual transportation cost. In a plan of freight equalization, every mill is usually regarded as a base; and sellers regularly quote the freight rate *and* the base price of another mill in selling at destinations within the freight territory of that mill.

Mill Net Price (or Return): The amount received by the seller at his mill after deducting actual freight cost, allowed or defrayed by the seller.

National Uniform Delivered Price: The quotation of the same delivered price anywhere in the United States, based upon the inclusion of an average freight item.

Phantom Freight: The excess of the freight item charged the buyer over the freight actually paid out by the seller in making delivery.

Zone-Delivered Price: The quotation of a single delivered price in a given zone, based upon the inclusion of an average freight item. The country is divided into two or more geographical areas or zones, and a uniform delivered price (which usually includes a transportation increment averaged for the zone) is applicable in each zone.

Suggestions for Further Reading

Backman, Jules, *Price Practices and Price Policies* (New York, 1953).

The Basing-Point Problem, Monograph 42, Temporary National Economic Committee, 76th Congress, third session (Washington, 1941).

Burns, A. R., *The Decline of Competition* (New York, 1936).

Fetter, Frank A., *The Masquerade of Monopoly* (New York, 1931).

Hearings Before the Committee on Interstate Commerce, *S. 4055, To Prevent Uniform Delivered Prices*, U.S. Senate, 74th Congress, second session, 1936.

Machlup, Fritz, *The Basing-Point System* (Philadelphia, 1949).

Mund, Vernon A., *Open Markets* (New York, 1948); "The 'Freight Allowed' Method of Price Quotation," *Quarterly Journal of Economics*, February, 1940, pp. 232–245.

Oxenfeldt, Alfred R., *Industrial Pricing and Market Practices* (New York, 1951).

Simon, William, *Geographic Pricing Practices* (Chicago, 1950).

Small Business Objections on Basing Point Legislation, Hearings, Select Committee on Small Business, House of Representatives, 81st Congress, first session, 1949.

Study of Federal Trade Commission Pricing Policies, Interim Report, Committee on Interstate and Foreign Commerce, U.S. Senate, Document 27, 81st Congress, first session, 1949.

United States Steel Corporation, *T.N.E.C. Papers*, 3 Vols. (New York, 1940).

CHAPTER 18

The Legality of Basing-Point and Zone-Delivered Pricing Systems

BACKGROUND OF THE BASING-POINT CASES

It was not until 1921 that the government began to prosecute pricing systems as a special device of monopoly. This delay is to be explained by the fact that government authorities did not immediately comprehend the nature or meaning of the pricing systems and their use in restricting price competition. The practice of cutthroat competition (local price cutting) was well understood, and Congress took action to prohibit its use in the Clayton Act (1914). The more subtle forms of systematic discrimination, however, which had largely come to displace cutthroat competition, remained unnoticed or were not understood.

When the Federal Trade Commission finally issued a complaint against the United States Steel Corporation in 1921, for using the Pittsburgh-plus system of pricing, it did so not because of its own investigations and convictions but rather because of the complaints of certain midwestern fabricators who were being injured by the practice of charging phantom freight in the sale of steel products. The evidence presented at the hearings on the *Pittsburgh-Plus* case gave government officials, economists, and the public their first real understanding of the nature of basing-point pricing. Upon the basis of this understanding, the Commission in 1924 rendered its decision ordering the Corporation and its subsidiaries to cease and desist the sale of steel products "upon any other basing point than where the products are manufactured or from which they are shipped."

Since 1924 the Federal Trade Commission has collected a mountain of evidence with respect to the use of various pricing systems, and orders have been issued against many firms in various industry groups to cease and desist the use of such pricing formulas. In the *Corn Products* case, decided in 1945, the Supreme Court rendered its first decision in a case directly involving the use of basing-point pricing. It completely upheld the order of the Commission prohibiting the use of a single basing-point plan in the sale of glucose (corn syrup).

In other decisions—the *Staley* case (1945), the *Cement* case (1948), and the *Rigid Steel Conduit* case (1949)—the Supreme Court further upheld the Commission in its efforts to eradicate discriminatory pricing and unfair methods of competition. Several important cases upholding the Commission have also been decided in Courts of Appeal without being carried to the Supreme Court. These have included the *Malt* case (1945), the *Milk Can* case (1946), the *Crepe Paper* case (1946), and the *Pittsburgh-Plus* case (1948).

Today a primary economic problem facing Congress and the American people is that of taking action either (1) to enforce a general compliance with the rulings of the courts on the illegality of basing-point and zone-delivered pricing systems or (2) to proceed openly to legalize the use of such pricing methods. The task of securing compliance with the decisions of the courts is not an easy one, for vested interests of great magnitude are at stake. It is possible that a clue to the action which Congress will take toward the general problem of monopoly in the American economy may be had by observing the action which it takes toward the use of pricing systems.

In studying the rulings of the courts which outlaw the use of basing-point and zone-delivered pricing systems, it should be noted that in most cases such pricing systems *are only a special device* of a group of sellers acting in unison. Back of their use there are usually the continuing problems of mergers, giant holding companies, conspiracy, interlocking directorates, and other forms of monopoly control. Pricing systems are a part but not the whole of the economic problem of monopoly, and an elimination of discriminatory pricing methods, in themselves, is not alone sufficient to insure the establishment of genuinely competitive pricing.

The purpose of the present chapter is to analyze the application which has been made of the antitrust laws to the use of basing-point and zone-delivered pricing methods. The Sherman Act and Section 5 of the Federal Trade Commission Act, it will be remembered, condemn price fixing and concerted action to avoid competition (conspiracy). Further, Section 2 (a) of the Clayton Act outlaws discrimination in price when the effect is substantially to lessen competition—either (1) *with other sellers* or (2) *between the customers* of a discriminating seller. Basing-point and zone-delivered pricing systems may be attacked in the courts under any one or all of these laws. Under the Sherman and Clayton Acts, as amended, moreover, any person injured in his business or property by the use of such pricing systems may sue for treble damages.

THE PITTSBURGH-PLUS CASE (1924–1948)

The complaint issued by the Federal Trade Commission in the *Pittsburgh-Plus* case charged the U.S. Steel Corporation and its subsidiaries with a violation of Section 5 of the Federal Trade Commission Act and Section 2 of the Clayton Act. In the main, the case centered on the presence of discriminations in price which injured competition among the buyers of steel products, as well as among the sellers. Buyers in the area of Chicago, for example, were required to pay $7.60 a ton phantom freight—the freight "plus" from Pittsburgh—on steel produced by the local subsidiaries of the Corporation. Independent steel mills likewise observed the Pittsburgh-plus formula in a plan of following the leader on price. With this extra cost burden, fabricators of steel in Chicago could not ship eastward to any extent, for their prices were substantially higher than those of the Pittsburgh fabricators who did not have to pay the phantom freight. A number of steel users in the Middle West, it was found, had been forced to discontinue the manufacture of a variety of steel products because of higher costs. The Commission estimated that imaginary freight charges included in the prices of farm implements made in the Chicago area cost farmers in eleven western states around $30,000,000 annually.[1]

In attempting to defend its practice of selling steel products at a Pittsburgh base price plus the rail freight from Pittsburgh, regardless of their origin, the Corporation developed the so-called "surplus-deficit" argument. The area around Pittsburgh, it was said, was a surplus area for steel, and all other areas were deficit areas. Upon the basis of this premise, the Corporation reasoned that the delivered cost in other regions—such as around Chicago or Pueblo—must necessarily be the Pittsburgh price plus the full freight from Pittsburgh, in order to attract a flow of steel products from Pittsburgh.

The economic experts employed by the Commission answered the Corporation by pointing out that in accordance with this hypothesis, steel products produced in the Middle West would not flow eastward into an area of surplus. Actually, however, the records showed that steel products produced by various mills in the Chicago area were regularly shipped eastward to Pittsburgh and beyond. The facts were that the Corporation was maintaining a high monopolistic price level for steel products (which other mills faithfully followed) and that its subsidiaries and other western mills thereupon "dumped" surplus supplies at lower *net realized* prices on sales eastward into the "surplus" area.

Upon the basis of its findings, the Commission ordered the United States Steel Corporation to cease and desist the use of the Pittsburgh-plus method of pricing. The Corporation accepted the order without appeal to the courts and promised to comply "in so far as it is practicable to do so." In fact, the Corporation made only a gesture to comply with the Commission's order. A few new basing points were established—such as Buffalo and Bethlehem—for certain products, but the new base prices were related to the Pittsburgh base plus the rail freight. In substance, the new plan of pricing became a formal multiple basing-point system with the various base prices equal to the Pittsburgh base plus all or part of the freight from Pittsburgh.

Although its cease-and-desist order was openly violated, the Commission refrained from making application to a Court of Appeals for an enforcement order. Finally, in 1938, with the enactment of the Wheeler-Lea amendment to the Federal Trade Commission Act, it was provided that all orders of the Commission would automatically become final and enforceable, unless carried to a Court of Appeals within sixty days. On May 18, 1938, the Corpora-

[1] *In the Matter of United States Steel Corporation et al., Findings,* 8 F.T.C. 34–35 (1924).

tion filed a petition with the Court of Appeals in Philadelphia, asking the Court to set aside the Commission's order of 1924.

The *Pittsburgh-Plus* case remained pending in the Court from May 18, 1938, until October 5, 1948, when the Corporation consented to sign a "decree of affirmance and enforcement" of the order issued by the Commission in 1924. The long delay in bringing the case to a close is to be explained largely by the fact that neither the Corporation nor the Commission was eager to have the case come up for trial. The Corporation, of course, was pleased to postpone action, for delay meant that it could continue to use the basing-point system with impunity. The Commission, on the other hand, it has been suggested, was willing to grant delay in expectation of securing favorable court decisions in cases which it had pending against the glucose, cement, and conduit industries. It was possible that the very size and magnitude of the steel industry might make the courts unwilling to "upset the applecart"; but with favorable decisions and precedents in other industries, the case against steel would be impregnable.

The Commission, in fact, was successful in winning its cases in other industries, and the Corporation in October, 1948, saw no alternative but to sign a consent decree. The order of the Commission, which the Corporation has agreed to observe, provides in substance that the corporation will refrain (1) "from quoting . . . rolled steel products upon any other basing point than that where the products are manufactured or from which they are shipped" and (2) "from selling . . . such steel products . . . without clearly and distinctly indicating . . . how much is charged for such steel products f.o.b. the producing or shipping point, and how much is charged for the actual transportation of said products."[2] (See also below, pp. 415–416.)

THE CORN PRODUCTS CASE (1945)

The Corn Products Refining Company is the largest manufacturer of corn product derivatives in the United States, with plants in Chicago and Kansas City. The company established a base price for glucose at Chicago ($2.09 per unit of 100 lbs.) and sold its output at both plants at the Chicago base price plus rail freight from Chicago. Customers in Kansas City bought glucose from the local plant and were charged a delivered price of $2.49 per unit, of which 40¢ was phantom freight (see Fig. 35). In selling in Lincoln, Nebraska, the company charged customers a freight item of 45¢ per unit although the actual freight from Kansas City was only 13¢. On such sales the company collected phantom freight of 32¢ per unit. Whenever the freight from Kansas City was higher than from Chicago, the Kansas City plant engaged in freight absorption.

In its decision in the *Corn Products* case, the Supreme Court found that the company's use of the basing-point formula in the sale of glucose "*results inevitably in systematic price discriminations,*" since the prices they receive

---

[2] *U.S. Steel Corp.* v. *F.T.C., Decree of Affirmance and Enforcement*, United States Court of Appeals for the Third Circuit, October 5, 1948.

upon deliveries from Kansas City bear relation to factors other than actual costs of production or delivery." On some shipments the plant at Kansas City collected phantom freight, and in other cases it engaged in freight absorption. "This difference," the Court observed, "results in varying *net* prices to petitioners at their factory at Kansas City, according to the destination of the glucose. The *factory net* varies according as petitioners collect phantom freight or absorb freight, and in each case in the amount of this freight differential."[3]

In the view of the Court, the divergent mill net prices received by the Kansas City plant were "systematic" discriminations (1) because the Kansas City plant regularly quoted the base price at Chicago plus rail freight from that point to destination and (2) because it absorbed just enough freight (no more and no less) to match the base price plus the rail freight from the base to the customer's location. The resulting discriminations were thus regular and systematic in nature rather than sporadic.

Fig. 35. The basing-point system condemned by the Supreme Court in the *Corn Products* case. The Corn Products Refining Company has plants in Chicago and Kansas City. Its pricing policy was to sell glucose at a Chicago base price plus rail freight from Chicago to the customer's location, even though the product was made in Kansas City and sold in adjoining territory.

Whether or not discrimination in price stands condemned by Section 2 (a) of the Clayton Act, the Court observed, depends upon whether the effect of such discrimination is substantially to lessen competition. Upon the basis of the record, the Court found injury to competition in that buyers of glucose in Kansas City and numerous other cities were forced to pay substantial amounts of phantom freight which their competitors in Chicago did not have to pay. Some of the buyers of glucose were candy manufacturers who sold their products nation-wide, and the Court found that a fictitious freight charge ranging up to 40¢ per unit of glucose substantially lessened their ability to compete.

THE STALEY CASE (1945)

The *Staley* case likewise involved the sale of glucose at a Chicago base price plus rail freight from Chicago. The Staley Manufacturing Company, a producer of corn products located at Decatur, Illinois, adopted the pricing system of the Corn Products Refining Company and sold its products as if they had been produced in Chicago. Customers in St. Louis (see Fig. 36), for example, were charged 16¢ per unit for freight, although it cost the company

[3] *Corn Products Refining Co. v. F.T.C.*, 324 U.S. 726, 732–733 (1945). Italics supplied.

only 10¢ per unit to ship glucose from Decatur to St. Louis. On sales in Chicago, the company charged no freight and absorbed a freight item of 14¢ per unit in making delivery. As in the *Corn Products* case, the Commission charged that the company was engaging in price discrimination—as measured by variations in the mill net price—which substantially lessened the ability of certain customers to compete in the sale of products made with glucose. Such discriminations, the Commission maintained, were prohibited by Section 2 (a) of the Clayton Act.

The company answered by stating that the discriminations involved in its pricing policy were made "in good faith to meet an equally low price of a competitor"—the Corn Products Company— and that they accordingly were permitted by Section 2 (b) of the Clayton Act. The Supreme Court found that this defense was not factually true and again condemned the individual use of a single basing-point plan under Section 2 (a) of the Clayton Act.[4] (See Landmark Cases, p. 715.)

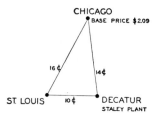

Fig. 36. The basing-point system condemned by the Supreme Court in the *Staley* case. The Staley Manufacturing Company is a producer of glucose located at Decatur, Illinois. Its pricing policy was to quote the Chicago base price plus freight from Chicago to the customer's location. A customer in St. Louis was charged 16¢ freight, while a customer in Chicago was charged no freight at all.

BASING-POINT PRICING AND SECTION 5 OF THE FEDERAL TRADE COMMISSION ACT

Section 5 of the Federal Trade Commission Act has been interpreted by the courts to prohibit concerted action in price making, and the Commission has also utilized this provision of the law in its efforts to prohibit the use of pricing systems. In the *Malt* case, decided in 1945, the Court of Appeals upheld the Commission in an order issued under Section 5 against some eighteen manufacturers of malt. The various defendants located at different production points sold malt at identical delivered prices. Each producer quoted the base price at Chicago plus rail freight from Chicago to the customer's location, regardless of the point of origin or the actual freight cost incurred. The Commission found that the action of the respondents in quoting identical delivered prices in accordance with the basing-point formula was based upon agreement and prohibited by Section 5 of the Federal Trade Commission Act, and the Court of Appeals upheld the Commission.

Although there was little, if any, direct evidence of an express agreement in the *Malt* case, the Court of Appeals held that such proof was not necessary. "The agreement," said the Court, "may be inferred or implied from the acts and conduct of the parties as well as circumstances pertinent thereto." Upon

[4] *F.T.C.* v. *A. E. Staley Mfg. Co.*, 324 U.S. 746, 750–751 (1945).

reviewing the use of the basing-point system by the respondents to quote identical delivered prices, the Court concluded that "it is difficult to discern how the various steps necessary to produce the result could have been taken with such meticulous care and regularity in the absence of an agreement."[5]

The *Milk Can* case, decided in 1946, involved the use of a multiple basing-point plan in the sale of milk and ice-cream cans, with every mill serving as a basing point. The Commission found that the respondents maintained a plan of freight equalization in order "to match competitor's prices," with the result that "the delivered cost of their products was the same, regardless of from whom purchase was made or from which producing point the goods purchased were shipped." Industry members maintained that their pricing system did not result from any combination or agreement, and that its use promoted competition. The Commission, however, found considerable evidence to indicate the existence of a "planned common course of action" and issued an order condemning the pricing system.

The Court of Appeals upheld the Commission's finding of agreement to fix prices in violation of Section 5. In the words of the Court,

> It is argued, perhaps correctly, that such a freight system had long been employed by industry so that members thereof might deliver their product at the same price. In fact, the Commission recognizes that this freight equalization plan was used by petitioners prior to the organization of the Institute. . . . The fact still remains that it was employed by petitioners for the purpose of fixing the delivered price of their product and by such use price competition was eliminated or at any rate seriously impaired. On the face of the situation, it taxes our credulity to believe, as argued, that petitioners employed this system without any agreement or plan among themselves.[6]

The *Crepe Paper* case (1946) involved the use of a zone-delivered pricing system by the principal producers of crepe-paper products. The country was divided into three zones for pricing purposes, and uniform prices were established in each zone. Industry members sought to defend their pricing system by declaring that identity in price was the result of keen competition—not agreement. The Commission and subsequently the Court of Appeals, however, rejected this defense on the ground that the industry's use of a zone-delivered pricing system was based upon agreement, actual or implied.

Much evidence was presented by the Commission to prove that the zone-delivered pricing plan had been established by agreement during the period of the N.R.A., when the enforcement of the antitrust laws was suspended. Since that time, it was found, industry members continued to act in unison in maintaining the system. Upon the basis of this and other circumstantial evidence, the Commission concluded that the crepe-paper producers were engaged in maintaining prices by means of tacit agreement or understanding. The Court of Appeals upheld the Commission, declaring, "We think the

[5] *U.S. Maltsters Assn.* v. *F.T.C.*, 152 F. (2d) 161, 162, 165 (1945).
[6] *Milk and Ice Cream Can Institute* v. *F.T.C.*, 152 F. (2d) 478, 482 (1946).

artificiality and arbitrariness of the zone structure is so apparent it cannot withstand the inference of agreement."[7]

THE RIGID STEEL CONDUIT CASE

The *Rigid Steel Conduit* case involved the use of a multiple basing-point plan by fourteen corporate manufacturers of rigid steel conduit, representing over 93 percent of the producing capacity of the industry. Rigid steel conduit is a steel pipe which has been cleaned and enameled or galvanized, particularly on the interior. It is used as a container for electric wiring installed in buildings and other construction projects. The Commission charged that the respondent manufacturers had formed a conspiracy to fix prices by the adoption and use of a multiple basing-point plan, with bases at Pittsburgh and Chicago.

Although the Commission secured no direct evidence of a contract signed by the respondents to eliminate price competition, it was able to present a large amount of circumstantial evidence—such as letters and office memoranda—indicating that various industry members had actively coöperated in securing the adoption and use of the basing-point plan by means of industry meetings, the preparation of "freight adder books," and the formation of a trade association to supervise the use of the pricing system. Following a hearing conducted in 1942, and the presentation of almost 7000 pages of testimony by the Commission and the respondents, the Commission issued a cease-and-desist order, which the respondents promptly carried to the Court of Appeals.

Count I of the Commission's complaint charged that the respondents had formed a price-fixing *conspiracy* in the sale of rigid steel conduit by adopting and using a multiple basing-point plan of delivered prices, in violation of Section 5 of the Federal Trade Commission Act. This was the same charge which the Commission had made in the *Malt*, *Milk Can*, and *Crepe Paper* cases. In Count II, the Commission added the further charge that the petitioners had individually violated Section 5 "through their concurrent use of a formula method of making delivered price quotations with the knowledge that each did likewise, with the result that price competition between and among them was unreasonably restrained." Count II, it may be noted, did not rest upon questions of agreement or conspiracy, but rather upon the *concurrent use* of a basing-point system, *with the result that customers were denied the benefit of price competition* and the advantage of their proximity to points of production.

In its brief before the Court of Appeals, the Commission made it clear that Count II was directed against the use of the basing-point system *per se* in that case, and not against an agreement to use the basing-point system, because in that case it had been found as a fact that its use had *resulted* in restraint of trade. The respondent manufacturers admitted in their reply that they used

[7] *Fort Howard Paper Co. v. F.T.C.*, 156 F. (2d) 899, 907 (1946).

the basing-point system but contended that such method of pricing is competitive and that its use is required by the laws of economics.

THE DECISION OF THE COURT OF APPEALS IN THE CONDUIT CASE (1948)

With respect to Count I in the *Conduit* case, the Court of Appeals found the existence of a price-fixing conspiracy involving the use of a multiple basing-point system. "Our study of this record and of the applicable law," said the Court, "has convinced us that the Commission was justified in drawing the inference that the petitioners acted in concert in a price-fixing conspiracy." The Court held that a conspiracy can be proved by circumstantial evidence, and that "the existence of a plan or method which equalizes the delivered costs or prices of competitors having widely different freight costs to given destinations constitutes strong evidence in itself on an agreement to use such a plan or system." Further, the Court stated that "price uniformity especially if accompanied by an artificial price level not related to the supply and demand of a given commodity may be evidence from which an agreement or understanding, or some concerted action of sellers operating to restrain commerce, may be inferred."[8]

Count II of the *Conduit* case brought forth the most vigorous opposition of the respondent producers of conduit pipe. Upon the basis of all the evidence, however, the Court concluded that the Commission had made no error in finding that the concurrent use of basing-point pricing is an unfair method of competition. In the words of the Court,

> As already noted, each conduit seller knows that each of the other sellers is using the basing-point formula; each knows that by using it he will be able to quote identical delivered prices and thus present a condition of matched prices under which purchasers are isolated and deprived of choice among sellers so far as price advantage is concerned. Each seller must systematically increase or decrease his mill net price for customers at numerous destinations in order to match the delivered prices of his competitors. Each seller consciously intends not to attempt the exclusion of any competition from his natural freight advantage territory by reducing the price, and in effect invites the others to share the available business at matched prices in his natural market in return for a reciprocal invitation.

The decision in the *Conduit* case with respect to Count II stands for the principle that the basing-point system as used in the conduit industry was used in violation of Section 5 of the Federal Trade Commission Act because it was shown as a matter of fact to have been used with trade-restraining results.

THE APPEAL OF THE CONDUIT CASE TO THE SUPREME COURT

Industry members vigorously protested the ruling on Count II and forthwith appealed it to the Supreme Court, claiming that their method of pricing represented active and normal competition. On April 25, 1949, the Supreme

[8] *Triangle Conduit and Cable Co.* v. *F.T.C.*, 168 F. (2d) 175, 179 (1948).

Court upheld the Federal Trade Commission's order under Count II by a four-to-four tie vote. The Court announced its decision in a twenty-three-word order and stated that Justice Jackson had taken no part in the case.[9]

THE CEMENT CASE (1948) AND THE ISSUE OF SYSTEMATIC FREIGHT ABSORPTION

Following the decisions in the *Corn Products* and *Staley* cases, an extensive controversy developed over whether the decisions outlawed freight absorption as well as phantom freight. The Supreme Court in the glucose cases appeared to condemn both freight absorption and phantom freight on the ground that each causes variations in the mill net prices received from customers which are not related to "any proper element of actual cost." Chief Justice Stone, however, in writing the decisions in the glucose cases, emphasized the injury to competition which results from the charging of phantom freight. Moreover, the glucose cases involved the use of a single basing-point system, and many industrialists and their lawyers hoped that another ruling could be made with respect to the use of multiple basing-point plans in which high base prices are maintained and freight is absorbed. Chief Justice Stone also stated in the *Corn Products* case that "it does not follow that respondents may never absorb freight when their factory price plus actual freight is higher than their competitor's price."[10]

Upon the basis of the several straws of hope, counsel for the cement industry sought to develop the view before the Court of Appeals and then before the Supreme Court that freight absorption to match the delivered price of another mill is wholesome competition, while the requirement of f.o.b. mill pricing would promote areas of local monopoly around each mill.

THE CEMENT DECISION (1948)

The *Cement* case was started by the Federal Trade Commission in 1937, and hearings were conducted before the trial examiner during a period of three years. The record of the case, as presented to the Supreme Court, consisted of some 49,000 pages of testimony and 50,000 pages of exhibits. The findings of the Federal Trade Commission itself covered over 175 pages. Never before had the Federal Trade Commission made such a complete and thorough investigation of a basing-point industry.

The facts in the *Cement* case showed that about one-half of the cement mills in the United States were located at basing points. The non-basing-point mills sold their products at the base price and the freight rate of some other mill. Delivered prices at any destination point were found to be identical, regardless of the location of the seller or the actual freight cost incurred.

The Federal Trade Commission charged in Count I of its complaint that the cement producers had restrained price competition in violation of Section 5 of the Federal Trade Commission Act by the concerted use and mainte-

[9] *Clayton Mark et al.,* v. *F.T.C.,* 336 U.S. 956 (1949).
[10] 324 U.S. 746, 757.

nance of the multiple basing-point system of pricing. In support of this charge, the Commission presented a substantial amount of evidence showing that the industry members had acted collectively to maintain the system by means of trade meetings, the use of special freight rate books, joint action in refusing to sell cement to purchasers who furnished their own trucks, the boycotting of dealers who handled foreign cement, and the use of price wars to discipline industry members who failed to follow the leaders on price. Count II of the Commission's complaint, as a counterpart to Count I, charged that the respondents were engaged in systematic price discrimination which substantially lessened competition between and among said respondents, in violation of Section 2 (a) of the Clayton Act.

The Court of Appeals held that the basing-point delivered prices charged by respondents were illegal in so far as they involved the collection of phantom freight, but declared that discrimination arising in freight absorption was justified by Section 2 (b). The Commission thereupon appealed the case to the Supreme Court.

Count I in the Cement Decision. Justice Black, speaking for the Court in a six-to-one decision, held that the use of the multiple basing-point plan in the cement industry was an illegal method of pricing on both of the counts made by the Commission. With respect to Count I, Justice Black declared, "We sustain the Commission's holding that concerted maintenance of the basing point delivered price system is an unfair method of competition prohibited by the Federal Trade Commission Act."[11] Justice Black characterized the basing-point delivered-price system as "a handy instrument to bring about elimination of any kind of price competition" and stated that there was abundant evidence to show that its use in the cement industry was an unlawful price-fixing conspiracy. In the view of the Court, the Commission was fully justified in finding "understanding, expressed or implied, from evidence (1) that the industry's Institute actively worked, in coöperation with various of its members, to maintain the multiple basing-point delivered price system; (2) that this pricing system is calculated to produce, and has produced, uniform prices and terms of sale throughout the country; and (3) that all of the respondents have sold their cement substantially in accord with the pattern required by the multiple basing-point system."

The Court also sustained the Commission in its finding that historically the basing-point system used in the cement industry originated in the collusive agreements of many of the present respondents; and further that its use was perfected and extended from time to time by deliberate action until about 1929, when the system was declared to be a "custom" and "usage" of the trade. This finding was vigorously contested by the industry, which sought to establish the view (1) that the basing-point system originated and developed "spontaneously" without the concerted aid of industry members and (2) that the system is a competitive method of determining prices.

In developing its case before the Commission, the industry presented a

[11] *F.T.C. v. Cement Institute,* 333 U.S. 683, 720 (1948).

number of distinguished economists from our leading universities to support its economic views. The Supreme Court considered this testimony but found it unacceptable. Justice Black stated that "It may possibly be true, as respondents' economists testified, that cement producers will, without agreement express or implied and without understanding explicit or tacit, always and at all times . . . charge for their cement precisely, to the fractional part of a penny, the price their competitors charged." However, he concluded that this view certainly "runs counter to what many people have believed, namely, that without agreement, prices will vary—that the desire to sell will sometimes be so strong that a seller will be willing to lower his prices and take his chances."

Count II in the Cement Decision. Turning to Count II in the Commission's complaint, Justice Black reaffirmed the decisions of the Court in the *Corn Products* and *Staley* cases. In explaining and interpreting these cases, he stated that both the *higher* and the *lower* mill net prices resulting from phantom freight and freight absorption are discriminatory. Repeating a statement from the *Staley* case, he emphasized, "Since such freight differentials bear no relation to the actual cost of delivery, they are [or result in] systematic discriminations prohibited by section 2 (a) whenever they have the defined effect upon competition." The Court found that the resulting discriminations in the sale of cement did have the defined effect on competition, for their systematic use by multiple sellers in the basing-point plan had the effect of *eliminating price competition between the sellers.* Thus, the Court in the *Cement* case established the point that systematic freight absorption by multiple sellers is illegal under Section 2 (a) because it was used to match delivered prices and avoid price competition.

Section 2 (b), the Court concluded, does not permit a seller "to use a sales system which constantly results in his getting more money for like goods from some customers than he does from others. We held to the contrary in the *Staley* case." The very adoption and use of such a discriminatory pricing system, the Court stated, "in itself was evidence of the employment of the multiple basing-point system by the respondents *as a practice* rather than as a good faith effort to meet 'individually competitive situations.' "[12]

FINAL DECREE IN THE CEMENT CASE

The final decree issued by the Court of Appeals in the *Cement* case—"commanding obedience" to the Federal Trade Commission's order—prohibits the *concerted* sale of cement at prices determined in accordance with the multiple basing-point delivered-price system or any other plan or system which results in identical price quotations at a customer's location. The decree also specifies a long list of acts and practices used in connection with a basing-point system which are likewise prohibited when *concertedly* used. Such prohibited acts include (1) "Quoting or selling cement at delivered prices calculated as or systematically equivalent to the sum of the base price

[12] *Ibid.,* p. 725. Italics supplied.

in effect at, plus common-carrier transportation charges from, any point other than the actual shipping point; and (2) Quoting or selling cement at delivered prices which systematically include a common-carrier transportation factor greater or less than the actual cost of such common-carrier transportation from the point of shipment to destination."[13]

F.O.B. MILL PRICING AND THE LAW

Upon the basis of the *Corn Products, Staley, Cement*, and related decisions, what methods of pricing are now legal? On what basis can a businessman sell his products and be certain that he is complying with the law? These questions were asked of Mr. Walter B. Wooden, associate general counsel of the Federal Trade Commission, at the hearings of the Senate Committee on Trade Policies in November, 1948. Mr. Wooden replied that the only way for businessmen to avoid all possibility of discrimination—and thus possible illegality under the law—is to charge f.o.b. mill prices uniform to all customers at the mill, with delivered prices determined by adding the actual freight from the shipping mill to the customer's location.[14]

F.o.b. mill prices, uniform to all customers, come about automatically under conditions of effective competition in local, central, or primary markets; and the purpose of the antitrust laws is to preserve and maintain fair competition analogous to that found in open, competitive markets. The antitrust laws and court decisions do not require businessmen to sell at uniform f.o.b. mill prices. However, in outlawing methods of pricing which *avoid* or *injure* price competition, the Federal Trade Commission and the courts have done much to make illegal any alternative method of selling.

THE METHODS OF PRICING WHICH VARIOUS INDUSTRY GROUPS DESIRE

The ruling of the Supreme Court in the *Cement* case that *systematic* price discrimination by multiple sellers is illegal gave rise to vigorous efforts on the part of numerous industry groups to induce Congress to legalize the use of basing-point and zone-delivered pricing systems. Such business groups want to be able to continue to sell their products at delivered prices which *regularly* and *systematically* yield varying mill net prices—as a result of phantom freight or freight absorption.[15] Some sellers still openly defend phantom freight. In their view, a local mill is justified in charging local buyers phantom

[13] *The Cement Institute et al.*, v. *F.T.C.*, *Final Decree*, United States Court of Appeals for the Seventh Circuit, July 27, 1948, p. 4.

[14] Hearings Before a Subcommittee of the Committee on Interstate and Foreign Commerce, *Study of Pricing Methods*, U.S. Senate, 80th Congress, second session, 1948, pp. 244–245.

[15] See, in particular, the testimony of business leaders in *Delivered Pricing and the Future of American Business*, Chamber of Commerce of the United States (Washington, 1948); and Hearings Before a Subcommittee of the Committee on Interstate and Foreign Commerce, *Study of Pricing Methods*, 80th Congress, second session, 1948, especially pp. 1374–1375.

freight calculated from a distant shipping point, for they would have had to pay this freight if someone had not chosen to build a mill in their town. The acceptance of this view, of course, would mean that consumers would secure few benefits from local economic development, except the advantage of having additional employment opportunities in the community. In most cases, however, business groups are willing to forgo the *outright* charging of phantom freight, provided that they are permitted to charge *high local prices* (containing an average freight item) and then engage in regular and systematic freight absorption to match prices in other sales areas.

The fact is that both phantom freight and freight absorption require customers living near a mill to pay high net prices in order to subsidize sales to distant customers. Both phantom freight and freight absorption place an unjustifiable overcharge on local customers. On this point, the manager of a trade association of the principal canneries in the middle Atlantic states reported to a Senate committee in 1948 that "the pricing of products f.o.b. factory is the most economic way to do business," because "it only stands to reason that if freight to some distant point is absorbed, it must necessarily be paid by some customer close by."[16]

THE CLAIM THAT THE LAW ON DELIVERED-PRICING SYSTEMS IS UNCERTAIN

It is possible that most, if not all, basing-point and zone-delivered pricing plans used in American industry in 1948 were—and still are—illegal under the Federal Trade Commission and Clayton Acts, as interpreted by the courts in the basing-point cases. Few, if any, industries, however, made any substantial change in their pricing methods. Instead of taking steps to comply with the law, organized industries turned their efforts toward securing a legalization of basing-point and zone-delivered pricing systems on the ground that the basing-point decisions were uncertain and needed clarification.[17] Actually, the problem in the great majority of cases was not that the law was uncertain, but rather that it required a revolutionary change to be made in present-day pricing methods! As one authority has expressed it, "The trouble with the existing law was not that it was unclear, but that it was becoming painfully clear, and the hope of practitioners of the basing-point system was not to clarify the trend but to reverse it."[18]

BASING-POINT DECISIONS GO BENEATH THE SURFACE OF THE MONOPOLY PROBLEM

The existence and understanding of effective, two-sided price competition in many segments of the economy has become "a lost art." A considerable number of business leaders, in fact, have never practiced such a form of com-

[16] Senate Trade Policies Committee, Release 15, November 7, 1948, p. 2.

[17] See, for example, Committee on Interstate and Foreign Commerce, *Study of Federal Trade Commission Pricing Policies*, 81st Congress, first session, Senate Document 27, 1949, pp. 45–63.

[18] Earl Latham, *The Group Basis of Politics* (Ithaca, 1951), pp. 97–98.

petition. When the cement industry was told by an official in the Federal Trade Commission in 1948 that it must cease and desist the use of basing-point pricing because this method of pricing was not genuinely competitive, the industry attorney replied, "My clients just do not know what you are talking about."

The record on exemptions from the antitrust laws, as we have seen, indicates that if important antitrust cases are won—that if anything more than the surface is scratched—the business concerns affected go at once to Congress to secure legislative modification. Politically important elements do not wish to have any change in the *status quo*, and tremendous pressure is put upon Congress to set aside the judicial ruling. The point of view taken by the interests concerned is that "established business practices have been going on for a long time, and that they therefore should not be disturbed."

PRESSURE ON CONGRESS TO CHANGE THE LAW

A vast campaign of pressure on Congress was instituted by the basing-point lobby during the years 1948, 1949, and 1950, to legalize the basing-point practice. In the words of Senator Wayne Morse (Oregon), "This lobbying effort was one of the best organized, one of the most heavily financed, and one of the most adroitly deceptive that has ever been addressed to the Congress of the United States."[19]

The goal of the proposed legislation was to legalize the use of discriminatory delivered pricing systems *in the absence of direct evidence of agreement* (*conspiracy*). Actual conspiracies, as we have seen, are exceedingly difficult to prove; and the basing-point industries want to stop the condemnation of their pricing systems (a) on the grounds of inferred conspiracy or (b) upon proof of a substantial lessening of price competition.

In particular, the industries concerned desire to legalize the following:

1. The charging of uniform delivered (freight-allowed) prices to all buyers of a given product regardless of the point of delivery;
2. The charging of uniform delivered prices for a given product to all buyers within any geographical zone (freight allowed within zones); or
3. The absorption, allowance, or averaging of freight charges by a seller (multiple basing-point pricing), even when such freight absorption results in delivered prices "identical" with those charged by another seller of like goods.

THE PROPOSED DEFINITION OF PRICE

In their efforts to legalize systematic price discrimination, basing-point industries also proposed that "price" be defined as "the consideration paid or agreed to be paid by a purchaser for any commodity" (H.R., 2820, 82nd Congress, first session, 1951). They desire such a concept of price in order to prevent the use of the *Staley* decision in identifying price discrimination (see Chap. 16). In this case, the Court looked upon price discrimination as

[19] *Congressional Record*, May 31, 1949, Vol. 95, p. 7028.

the making of a difference in the *net amount* charged to different buyers by a given seller. "Price," in other words, was regarded as the amount received by the seller *at his mill* after deducting actual freight cost, allowed or defrayed by the seller. All basing-point and zone-delivered pricing systems involve divergent mill-net prices. Basing-point advocates, therefore, wish to shift attention to *the amount paid by a purchaser*, for under delivered pricing systems, the amounts paid by all buyers *at a given destination point* are identical.

THE PASSAGE AND VETO OF BASING-POINT LEGISLATION

Numerous bills have been introduced in Congress to legalize basing-point pricing. In 1949, Senator O'Mahoney of Wyoming, in particular, took the lead in sponsoring such legislation. During the course of the debates, he openly declared that "one of the purposes which I entertained in offering this provision was to make sure that the system which has been used, without criticism, by the sugar-beet industry, of selling at delivered prices by absorbing freight, should not now be disturbed."[20] (See also Chap. 17.) Many other Congressional leaders supported the legislation in behalf of the steel, cement, gasoline, and other basing-point industries which were located in their particular geographic areas. Upon the basis of widespread geographic support, Congressional approval of a bill to legalize basing-point pricing (S. 1008) was secured in June 1950.

The basing-point bill was enacted over the vigorous opposition of a minority who sought to maintain the effectiveness of the antitrust laws. Senators Douglas, Long, Morse, Magnuson, Kefauver, and Langer, and Representatives Patman and Jackson, in particular, resisted all efforts to injure or weaken the antitrust laws. These men carried the case to President Truman and actively pressed for a veto of the new legislation.

On June 16, 1950, President Truman issued a veto message, condemning the basing-point legislation. In his view, the legislation contained confusing and uncertain provisions which might be interpreted as permitting the basing-point practices recently found to be illegal. He declared: "When further amendments of the antitrust laws are needed to meet new problems, they should be enacted in a form which clearly preserves the basic purpose of these laws—the protection of fair competition and the prevention of monopoly."[21]

THE IMPACT OF CONGRESSIONAL PRESSURE ON COMMISSION POLICY

During the year of 1948 the Federal Trade Commission reached the high-water mark in its drive to deal with basing-point monopoly. In April of that year, the Commission *called upon industry generally to abandon the use of*

---

[20] *Congressional Record*, June 1, 1949, Vol. 95, p. 7071.
[21] The veto message appears in Hearings, Committee on the Judiciary, House of Representatives, *Study of Monopoly Power*, 82nd Congress, first session, Serial 1, Part 5, 1951, pp. 253–255.

basing-point delivered pricing systems.[22] In its view, most of the industry-wide pricing systems used to arrive at identical delivered price quotations were probably illegal.

The position taken by the Commission in 1948 on basing-point pricing was soon thereafter modified as a result of Congressional opposition. Congress did not succeed in its efforts to legalize basing-point pricing, but it did succeed in weakening Commission policy. In settling the case (August 10, 1951) against the American Iron and Steel Institute and 90 steel producers, charged with using the basing-point practice, the Commission ordered the Institute and its members to discontinue "any planned common course of action, understanding or agreement" in basing-point pricing. The prohibition applied to *planned* common action rather than to the use of basing-point pricing, as such. In particular, the Commission qualified its order by stating,

1. The Federal Trade Commission is not considering evidence of uniformity of prices or any element thereof of two or more sellers at any destination or destinations alone and without more as showing a violation of law.
2. The Federal Trade Commission is not acting to prohibit or interfere with delivered pricing or freight absorption as such when innocently and independently pursued, regularly or otherwise, with the result of promoting competition.[23]

The foregoing qualifications reflect an almost complete change in the attitude of the Commission toward basing-point pricing. Now the crucial factor is not what one does, but the spirit in which one does it. As long as basing-point pricing is done "innocently and independently," it appears to be within the law.

Since the efforts made by Congress to legalized basing-point pricing, the Commission has indicated that it will not initiate proceedings against the use of delivered pricing systems *except on clear-cut grounds of conspiracy.* The *Pittsburgh Plus, Corn Products, Staley* and *Conduit* (Count II) cases, it will be remembered, were not based upon conspiracy charges. In these cases, the Supreme Court found the basing-point practice itself to be a form and method of monopoly. To the extent that the Commission now accepts the practice, despite the decisions of the Supreme Court, it is widening further the area of exemptions from our antitrust law policy.

Although the basing-point industries have not as yet succeeded in changing *the law* on delivered pricing, they have succeeded in changing *the administration* of the law. Governmental action to eliminate the coöperative use of basing-point and zone systems of pricing, it appears, has been set back fifteen to twenty years. Someday the Commission and Congress will have to appraise again this significant business practice.

[22] "F.T.C. Warns All Lines to Drop Basing Points," *Journal of Commerce*, April 29, 1948, p. 1.
[23] *Federal Trade Commission* v. *American Iron and Steel Institute, et al., Order to Cease and Desist*, Docket 5508, 1951, p. 6. This case was a follow-up to the initial proceeding against the U.S. Steel Corporation in the *Pittsburgh-Plus* case. It included substantially all steel producers in the United States.

THE DILEMMA OF PERMITTING DISCRIMINATION "IN GOOD FAITH"

In so far as a seller discriminates regularly in using another's basing point, we have seen, the Court has held that he is not discriminating in good faith to meet the equally low price of a competitor (*Staley* case). (See also Appendix, p. 715.) However, in so far as this seller (a) quotes his own f.o.b. mill price for local and nearby sales, and then (b) *discriminates regularly to meet the lower delivered price of distant competitors*, the Commission does not expressly prohibit the discrimination (*Steel Institute* order).

Upon the basis of the foregoing constructions, the Commission has fallen into a great dilemma. If *two or more* geographically separate mills quote f.o.b. mill prices and regularly discriminate (by absorbing freight) to meet delivered prices in each other's "back yard," are they not getting *the same result* as the concerted use of a multiple-basing point system (Count II in the *Cement* case)? Is not the practice one of conscious parallel action (Count II in the *Conduit* case)? Is not the buyer again faced with the stone wall of identical price quotations?

Similarly, if two or more geographically separate firms regularly use a zone system of delivered prices, with resulting identity of delivered prices, how can the practice withstand the inference of conspiracy (*Crepe Paper, Malt,* and *Milk Can* cases)?

Basically, the choice which the Commission, the courts, and Congress must make is (1) to legalize or accept the use of regular and systematic freight absorption or (2) to condemn its coöperative use by two or more sellers. Mr. Charles L. Hogan, President, Lone Star Cement Co., testified in the *Cement* hearings that the only workable alternative to f.o.b. mill pricing is "f.o.b. *destination* pricing," i.e., some form of basing-point or zone pricing.[24] Which system of pricing is best for the economy, for the nation as a whole?

MAIN REASONS SOME BUSINESSMEN OPPOSE F.O.B. MILL PRICING

Freight absorption is primarily a technique employed by large, multiplant companies. The desire of a large firm to shift away from f.o.b. mill pricing arises (1) when it seeks to sell in distant markets by shrinking its mill net prices on distant sales and (2) when it seeks to act coöperatively with a number of geographically separate sellers in basing-point and zone-delivered pricing.

In particular, the basic reasons why certain business interests wish to discriminate are as follows:

1. To Limit the Development of New Capacity in Outlying Areas

Small business, selling locally, has no motive or opportunity to discriminate. A large producer, however, may be in a position to ship into a distant

[24] *The Cement Institute et al.,* v. *F.T.C., Transcript of Record,* Vol. 14, U.S. Court of Appeals, 1943, p. 10200.

area, to limit or restrict new competition, *without reducing prices in his own sales area.* F.o.b. pricing, however, prevents a seller from going outside the territory in which he has a freight advantage unless he reduces his local prices.

2. To Engage in Coöperative, Unified Selling

Geographically separate sellers, seeking to act as one on price, must equalize freight costs in some way in order to avoid giving mills near a consuming point an advantage in getting business. Basing-point and zone systems, we have seen, were developed for this purpose. Both involve geographic discrimination. Various business groups desire these systems and accept discrimination as a necessary consequence.

3. To Force Compliance in Unified Selling

Geographic discrimination makes it possible for a dominant firm to cut its delivered prices in particular local areas, while maintaining them elsewhere, to injure, weaken, or discipline a concern which shows price independence.

4. To Avoid Lowering Prices on Local Business

The practice of freight absorption, we have seen, typically means the charging of high local prices (phantom freight) and the cutting of net prices on distant deliveries. With f.o.b. mill pricing, a local seller would have to reduce prices on his "most favorable business" in order to ship outwards. This would wipe out his local monopoly profits.

THE LOCAL-MONOPOLY ARGUMENT AGAINST REQUIRED F.O.B. MILL PRICING

A contention of basing-point industries in opposing f.o.b. mill pricing is that an abolition of freight absorption will create local monopolies. This argument, it may be noted, assumes that a locally separate mill will not reduce its base price in order to reach out and sell in a principal consuming area.

There is abundant historical and empirical evidence to indicate that locally separate producers do, in fact, reduce their mill prices on local sales, when competitive conditions force them to do it, in order to reach the great consuming centers. Prior to the formation of the large mergers and their concerted refusal to sell to independent merchants (beginning about 1897), industrial products were typically sold f.o.b. the market centers or f.o.b. the shipping point. The very fact that a basic commodity (such as steel or copper) was in numerous hands—primary producers, merchants, jobbers, speculators, and fabricators—helped to provide effective competition, and situations of "local monopoly" were rare and exceptional. At the present time, the prices of wheat, lettuce, apples, beans, potatoes, and many other agricultural products are sold at f.o.b. shipping point prices. Such prices, moreover, are *less* in the producing areas than in the markets of Chicago and New York by the actual cost of freight and handling charges.

In the case of agricultural products, competition in *local* markets serves to prevent price discrimination at the point of production. In the case of many manufacturing industries, however, the number of mills at a production point is frequently not sufficient to insure effective price competition. *As a result, locally separate producers are in a position to charge high local prices while cutting net prices on distant sales.* The requirement of f.o.b. mill prices, uniform to all buyers at the mill, would operate to reduce high local prices, for most enterprises desire to reach out and sell in other areas. A possible condition of local monopoly might therefore be largely reduced to one of form.

REASONS FOR GOING FURTHER IN THE DIRECTION OF F.O.B. MILL PRICING

F.o.b. mill prices continue to be used by many business enterprises, particularly in industries in which price competition operates effectively. In such instances, f.o.b. mill pricing is accepted as being eminently fair, just, and equitable. A seller secures a uniform profit margin on all shipments, regardless of their destination. Buyers, on the other hand, pay the exact freight costs and are free to choose their own methods and types of transportation.

Numerous legal experts believe that the legal requirement of f.o.b. mill pricing would provide a rule which would be administratively simple to enforce. Violations could be tried in a few hours. The present rule of permitting discrimination "in good faith" leads to cases which require years to investigate and prosecute. *The task of enforcement is beyond the means of the antitrust agencies.*

Various economists have also advocated the unequivocal outlawing of geographic price discrimination by requiring publicly posted f.o.b. mill prices, uniform to all buyers at the mill. These economists recognize that f.o.b. mill pricing alone is not sufficient to create effective competition. Full remedial action, they point out, will require a vigorous prosecution of all conspiracies, interlocking arrangements, monopolistic mergers, and other ties making for unity of action on price.

The economic ends sought by the proposed requirement of f.o.b. mill pricing are essentially four:

1. To Give Buyers and Fabricating Industries (a) the Advantage of Their Location (by Eliminating an Overcharge for Freight) and (b) the Privilege of Arranging for the Purchase of Their Own Transportation

Basing-point and zone-delivered pricing systems force buyers to purchase two commodities—the manufactured goods and freight—on terms and conditions determined solely by the producers. In charging phantom or fictitious freight, a mill forces a buyer to purchase transportation service which he does not want and which he does not get. This gives a particular mill net prices *higher* than the base price by the amount of the fictitious freight. On the other hand, in the case of absorbed freight, the railroad is paid the actual freight cost, and the mill secures net prices which are *lower* than the base price by the amount of the absorbed freight.

Buyers (fabricators) located at or near a non-base mill do not want to pay phantom freight, for such a charge places them at a competitive disadvantage with fabricators located at or near a base mill. Likewise, buyers located near a base mill which is engaging in freight absorption find that they are denied the advantage of their location and are forced to pay high local prices which help to defray the delivery costs to other buyers.

2. To Outlaw the Device of Local Price Cutting (Sporadic and Cut-throat)

This aspect of price discrimination was discussed in Chapter 9, pp. 183–184, and in Chapter 16, pp. 350–351.

3. To Promote a Decentralization of Industry

Industrial pricing systems which employ eastern base prices (such as Pittsburgh or East St. Louis) plus rail freight make for high cost prices in the West and South and discourage the development of local fabricating industries. Local fabricators which do develop, moreover, are unable to ship their products eastward to any appreciable extent in competition with fabricators situated near an eastern basing point, for the delivered costs of their basic supplies are higher.

In so far as basic commodities (such as aluminum) are produced in the West and South and sold "freight allowed," local prices are high—as high as elsewhere in the country—and fabricators find no cost advantage in building plants near the sources of supply. The sale of fabricated products (such as copper wire, sheets, and tubing) by eastern mills at zone-delivered prices (by including an average freight item) also serves to discourage the development of distant fabricators, for the established mills, in effect, are able to "dump" into the distant areas by absorbing some or all of the freight—at the expense of their nearby customers.

4. To Provide Locally Separate Mills with a Genuine Motive to Compete on Price

The requirement of f.o.b. mill pricing will undoubtedly result in a reduction in prices *at* locally separate mills, for a given seller cannot get distant business by quoting a high base price plus freight. Locally separate mills will thus be given a genuine motive to reduce their mill prices, even though local competition is lacking. Consumers living adjacent to a producer will also get the advantage of their location, as they do under conditions of effective price competition. With the collective use of basing-point and zone-delivered pricing systems, sellers do not have a motive—a competitive pressure or compulsion—to reduce prices *to all buyers* in order to provide a selling outlet for their capacity.

In Figure 37, mill A, located at Denver, Colorado, desires to sell in the great consuming center of San Francisco. If it is not permitted to absorb 50¢ in freight to do so, it must reduce its base price to $3.50 *on all of its sales.* The effect of a prohibition of discrimination thus is to give mill A a competitive motive to reduce its base price. If mill A can absorb freight on distant sales, it does not have this motive. Rather its motive is one of charging a high base price, to the injury of nearby customers. A prohibition of freight absorption, however, will provide locally separate mills with a compelling motive to reduce their mill prices *to all buyers*—in order to expand their sales areas—and it is this fact which causes basing-point industries to oppose an outlawing of price discrimination.

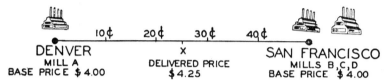

FIG. 37. F.o.b. mill pricing provides a strong incentive to compete on price. If freight absorption is permitted, mill A can sell into the large consuming center of San Francisco without reducing its base price. A requirement of uniform f.o.b. mill prices, however, would provide mill A with a strong motive to reduce its base price in order to continue selling into the San Francisco area. This action would greatly benefit customers in and near Denver.

THE BUSINESS INTEREST VERSUS THE NATIONAL INTEREST IN MAINTAINING PRICE COMPETITION

An acceptance of monopoly, experience shows, leads increasingly to demands for government to engage in public price control in order to safeguard the public from the abuses of excessive prices and restricted output. In securing an exemption from the inhibitions of the antitrust laws, therefore, businessmen are actually building a system in which their freedom will be largely, if not entirely, restricted. Why is it, then, that business leaders are frequently willing to adopt restrictions on price competition? Basically, the answer to this question is to be found in the fact that the purpose of business is profit making, and businessmen typically look at things in the way in which they affect their business. If a certain policy is good for a person's business, it tends to be favored, regardless of its long-run consequences.

So many leaders of industry [says General William J. Donovan, one of the nation's leading corporation lawyers] look to the immediate rather than to the ultimate. They fail to see that business pays a price to government for every bit of security that it demands *and that price is closer government control.* And we as lawyers have contributed to that short view. Too often the lawyer has yielded to the demand of the business man who says, "I do not want a lawyer to tell me what I cannot do. I want a lawyer who will tell me how I can do what I want to do." Too often what he wants to do is that which should not be done in the public interest. But the lawyer gives him a loophole. It so often happens that the loophole of the present is only a noose around his neck in the future.[25]

Persons sponsoring changes in the antitrust laws typically declare that they stand for "competition." The National Industrial Recovery Act (1933–1935), for example, legalized price fixing *and made any violation an unfair method of competition!* Many businessmen have never known any other method of competition than that which is found in the use of basing-point and zone-delivered pricing systems. Any other method of competition to them is "visionary." They advertise extensively; their salesmen compete for business; and their delivered prices are "identical" with other sellers at every destination point. From their point of view, this is fair competition.

Some economists describe the *sales* and *service* competition found in oligopolistic industries as "workable competition." If the several firms in the given industry appear to be progressive in research and capital investment, and if they are actively seeking business and new outlets, these economists look upon the situation as being an acceptable one of "workable" competition (or "workable" monopoly).

The concept of competition embodied in our antitrust laws, however, calls for *price* competition analogous to that found in central and primary markets. Price competition and freedom of entry have had a long period of development in the history of the world. They began slowly to arise in the ancient world and reached a high state of development in the open markets of the Middle Ages. In 1890 Congress formally adopted the principles of "fair competition" as they were developed in the early English common law on open markets.

Today, a basic economic question for our nation to decide is whether it desires to maintain (1) the price competition contemplated by the antitrust laws or (2) the sales competition and price identity found in the use of delivered-pricing systems. It is widely recognized that the decisions of the Supreme Court in the basing-point cases got to the heart of the economic problem of monopoly. The action which Congress and the antitrust agencies take with respect to these decisions may well determine whether the United States moves toward larger amounts of public control and ownership or toward the maintenance of free institutions.

SUGGESTIONS FOR FURTHER READING

Clark, J. M., "The Law and Economics of Basing Points," *American Economic Review*, March, 1949, pp. 430–447.

Delivered Pricing and the Law, Chamber of Commerce of the United States (Washington, 1948).

Edwards, C. D., "The Effect of Recent Basing Point Decisions upon Business Practices," *American Economic Review*, December, 1948, pp. 828–842; "Geographic Price Formulas and the Concentration of Economic Power," *Georgetown Law Journal*, January, 1949, pp. 135–148.

[25] William J. Donovan, address before the Commerce Committee of the American Bar Association, Boston, August 26, 1936, pp. 24–25. Italics supplied.

Fetter, Frank A., "Exit Basing Point Pricing," *American Economic Review*, December, 1948, pp. 815–827.

Final Report and Recommendations of the Temporary National Economic Committee, 77th Congress, first session, Senate Document 35, 1941.

Hearings Before a Subcommittee of the Committee on Interstate and Foreign Commerce, *Study of Pricing Methods*, U.S. Senate, 80th Congress, second session, 1948.

Johnson, William S., "The Restrictive Incidence of Basing Point Pricing on Regional Development," *Georgetown Law Journal*, January, 1949, pp. 149–165.

Sage, George H., *Basing-Point Pricing Systems Under the Federal Antitrust Laws* (St. Louis, 1951).

Stocking, George W., "The Law on Basing Point Pricing: Confusion or Competition," *Journal of Public Law*, Spring, 1953, pp. 1–28.

Wooden, Walter B., "The Delivered Price, Generally," *Robinson-Patman Act Symposium*, Commerce Clearing House (New York, 1947); "The Concept of Unlawful Discrimination as It Applies to Geographic Price Differences," *Georgetown Law Journal*, January, 1949, pp. 166–182; "Section 2 (a)—Its Application to a Basing Point Delivered Price," *Robinson-Patman Act Symposium*, Commerce Clearing House (New York, 1948).

CHAPTER 19

Federal Regulation of Business Corporations

Thus far in the study of public regulation we have directed our attention primarily to the rules established by the federal government to preserve and maintain competition and to prevent monopoly. Competition, we have seen, is an economic process which is—or should be—(1) waged in accordance with rules and penalties and (2) kept within the bounds of social welfare by public administration. We have also observed that fair and orderly price competition and independent enterprise—as contemplated by the antitrust laws—are not self-creating and self-maintaining institutions. Unless the essential conditions for economic competition, as discussed in Chap. 6, are maintained by government, effective competition with respect to price and quality will not fully develop.

A principal factor which has operated to frustrate and destroy the essential conditions for price competition has been the revolutionary change in the size of our business units. In place of a system of (1) private property, widely diffused, (2) *independent* business enterprise (corporate or individual), and (3) active price competition, there exists over wide areas a condition of large corporate mergers, centralized financial control, and unified action with respect to price. The management of the financial giants, moreover, is typically in the hands of small minority groups of stockholders or self-elected, self-perpetuating officials, having little or no responsibility either to the investors or to consumers.

In the view of many economists, the condition of large corporate mergers is not truly a system of private enterprise (or capitalism)—in which individuals have a substantial ownership stake in the enterprises they control. Rather it is a system of corporationism—that is, a system in which the control of private wealth is centralized and pyramided into the hands of a few persons who do not have a substantial ownership interest in the businesses they personally direct. In a regime of supercorporations, the ownership and control of private wealth are sharply separated; and the long-recognized virtues of private property become seriously weakened or nonexistent.

Increasingly, public leaders in the economic field are directing their attention to the problem of business organization and to the size of the business unit. A growing number of such persons declare that if private property, individual enterprise, and competition are to survive, government must intervene to control the formation, size, and responsibilities of business corporations. In so far as possible, it is emphasized, corporate organization must be simplified; standards must be established for the creation and operation of corporations; and action must be taken to dissolve financial mergers of formerly competing plants which do not enhance productive efficiency.

The purpose of this chapter is to present the principal measures thus far adopted (1) to regulate business corporations and (2) to provide for a decentralization of supercorporations. Consideration will also be given to proposals for implementing our antitrust law policy by requiring federal charters and standards for all corporations engaging in interstate commerce.

THE NEED FOR FEDERAL REGULATION

The stock-market crash of 1929 and the failure of such large corporations as Kreuger and Toll, the International Match Company, and the Insull utility combination, causing a loss of millions to thousands of stockholders, brought to light many serious abuses and excesses in corporate activity. The broad powers conferred on directors by corporate charters gave them almost unlimited and absolute power over the issuance of securities, the exchange of securities, the payment of dividends, the making of reports to stockholders, the conduct of reorganizations, and the acquisition and control of other corporations. As a result of these powers of control and the separation of management from ownership, it was found that in many cases officers and directors were operating corporations for speculative and manipulative gains and for their own personal benefit, without taking a "long view" toward the welfare of the business or the public.

The corporate abuses and excesses revealed themselves most vividly in the utility field. The period of 1920–1929, we have seen, was one in which the formation of public utility mergers was especially extensive. Centralized financial control in the principal branches of industry—such as steel, the nonferrous metals, oil, and sugar—had already taken place. The dynamic, currently active field for speculative and monopolistic merger activity was the utilities.

Investigations by the Federal Trade Commission and Congressional committees, in particular, revealed the existence of a large variety and number of unsound corporate practices, especially in the management of public utility *holding* companies.[1] The evidence secured in various investigations showed (1) that securities were often issued in excess of the value of the assets held by a corporation; (2) that many corporations engaged in stock financing far beyond any legitimate foreseeable business need and plowed their extra cash back into the stock market through loans to brokers; (3) that dividends were

[1] Important investigations were: Hearings Before the Committee on Interstate and Foreign Commerce on H.R. 4314, *Federal Securities Act*, 73rd Congress, first session, 1933; Hearings Before the Committee on Banking and Currency on S.R. 84, *Stock Exchange Practices*, 72nd Congress, 1932, six parts, and 73rd Congress, 1933, twenty parts; and Report of the Federal Trade Commission to the Senate of the U.S., pursuant to Senate Res. No. 83, *Utility Corporations*, 70th Congress, first session, 1928. In Serial Set vols. 8855, 8856, 8857, 8858.

sometimes paid out of capital when earnings were insufficient; (4) that securities were issued and sold to the public without revealing significant information and with an actual misrepresentation of earnings and the uses to which the funds were to be applied; (5) that prices of securities on the stock exchanges were frequently manipulated in order to induce public buying or selling; (6) that deceptive and unsound methods of accounting were often used in recording assets, liabilities, and earnings; (7) that holding companies frequently charged their affiliates excessive fees for services rendered; and (8) that capital accounts were sometimes "loaded" in order to establish a base for excessive rates.

THE SECURITIES ACT OF 1933

The problem of regulating the sale of corporate securities had been under review by Congress for many years prior to 1929. Following the collapse of the stock market, public opinion speeded the adoption of pending legislation in the Securities Act of 1933. The Securities Act was originally administered by the Federal Trade Commission. With the enactment of the Securities Exchange Act in 1934, however, the administration of both of these laws was placed in the hands of the Securities and Exchange Commission. This agency was created in 1934 and is composed of five members appointed for terms of five years.

The Securities Act of 1933 is sometimes called "The Truth in Securities Act." Its purpose is to require a full disclosure of all material facts with respect to the issuance of *new* securities before they are publicly offered for sale, so that an investor will have sufficient information to make an intelligent judgment of a security before he buys it. The Act places a burden *on the seller* to disclose pertinent information on the securities to be sold. Its viewpoint is "let the seller beware." Certain securities and transactions are exempted, namely, securities of governmental bodies, banks, charitable organizations, railroads, and building and loan associations, and also any transactions by a person other than an issuer, underwriter, or dealer, or not involving a public offering.

The Securities Act applies to securities sold to the public in interstate commerce or through the mails. Before securities subject to the act can be sold, the issuing company must file a registration statement with the Securities and Exchange Commission giving all the material facts with respect to the corporation, its organization, the nature of its business, the purposes for which the money is to be used, the compensation of officers, the profit and loss and balance sheet records, and other relevant data. It is also required that a digest of the registration statement be given to all persons to whom the securities are offered for sale by means of any prospectus, written or by radio. The law is not concerned with the merits of the offering. The only requirement is that a full disclosure be made of all pertinent details. In a broad way, the Act of 1933 seeks to expedite the flow of capital into legitimate business enterprises.

The Securities Act contains three sanctions: first, the authority given the S.E.C. to prevent by stop order or injunction the sale of securities because of false material statements or failure to furnish material information; second, the civil liability of those responsible for the flotation of the issue for false, untrue, or inadequate material representations; and third, the criminal liability for the willful use of a fraudulent scheme or device or the willful mistatement or omission of a material fact. Persons convicted of fraudulent acts are thus subject to private suits for damages, as well as to governmental suits for fines and prison sentences.[2]

THE SECURITIES EXCHANGE ACT OF 1934

The purposes of the Securities Exchange Act of 1934 are (1) to eliminate fraud, manipulation, and other abuses in the trading of securities, both on the organized exchanges and in the over-the-counter markets; (2) to make available to the public information regarding the condition of corporations whose securities are listed on any national securities exchange; and (3) to regulate the use of the nation's credit in securities trading. Each securities exchange in the United States is required to register with the Securities and Exchange Commission, as are all brokers and dealers using the mails or other instrumentalities of interstate commerce in the sale of securities. The records of the exchanges, brokers, and dealers are also inspected periodically in order to determine whether or not the registrants are complying with the law. If violations are found to exist, the Commission is empowered to revoke a firm's registration.[3]

Main Objective of the Act of 1934

In regulating the trading of securities, the law seeks to maintain free and open markets, on the exchanges as well as in over-the-counter dealing. Prices of securities, the law affirms, should be determined by the free operation of the forces of demand and supply, without fraud, manipulation, or private control. In so far as dealers sell privately, the law requires them to sell at a price which is reasonably related to the going price in the open market.

In order to provide investors with *current* information on corporate securities, the act of 1934 requires all corporations whose securities are traded on any of the national exchanges to register their securities with the Commis-

[2] For a comprehensive analysis of the Securities Act of 1933, see Edward T. McCormick, *Understanding the Securities Act and the S.E.C.* (New York, 1948).

[3] The national securities exchanges registered with the S.E.C. consist of the following: (1) Boston Stock Exchange; (2) Chicago Board of Trade; (3) Cincinnati Stock Exchange; (4) Detroit Stock Exchange; (5) Los Angeles Stock Exchange; (6) Midwest Stock Exchange; (7) New Orleans Stock Exchange; (8) American Stock Exchange; (9) New York Stock Exchange; (10) Philadelphia-Baltimore Stock Exchange; (11) Pittsburgh Stock Exchange; (12) Salt Lake Stock Exchange; (13) San Francisco Mining Exchange; (14) San Francisco Stock Exchange; (15) Spokane Stock Exchange; and (16) Washington Stock Exchange. An "exchange" is an auction-floor market. Over-the-counter markets, by contrast, consist of dealers and brokers conducting transactions in their places of business.

sion and file periodic reports of their business activity. All corporation reports secured by the Commission under the law are available for public inspection.

TRADING BY INSIDERS

A further provision of the Act (Section 16) requires influential stockholders (persons owning more than 10% of any class of a security), directors, and officers of corporations with securities registered on a national exchange to file reports of transactions in the securities of their companies. A similar provision is contained in the Public Utility Holding Company Act of 1935 and the Investment Act of 1940. The reports must be filed with the Commission once a month. If persons covered by the section ("insiders") make a profit by buying or selling the securities of their own companies within a six-months period, they may be required by the corporation or by a stockholder to turn the profits back to the corporation. Upon the basis of the fraud provisions of the Act, insiders buying stock from a person who is not an insider, and possessing information that the stock is worth more than the current price, are under obligation to disclose this information to the seller. If they do not, the seller may subsequently sue and collect damages (Rule X-10-B-5).

The primary purpose of Section 16 was to destroy "vicious practices unearthed at the hearings" which revealed "the flagrant betrayal of their fiduciary duties by directors and officers." Many millions of dollars, it was found, were frequently made by insiders who had advance information of significant corporate activity—such as the increase or passing of dividends.[4] In order to assist investors in learning whether insiders are buying or selling, the Commission publishes a monthly summary of transactions by such persons. Interested students may secure this publication by writing to the Commission.

As a means of regulating speculation in securities, the Federal Reserve Board is given authority to prescribe rules and regulations on the amount of credit which can be extended by brokers or banks to those buying securities which are registered on a national exchange. The Securities and Exchange Commission itself is empowered to regulate the borrowing of brokers, dealers, and members of the security exchanges.

The national exchanges provide an auction market for some 3000 corporate stocks. By way of contrast, the over-the-counter markets (private dealers and brokers) are an informal market for some 5400 actively traded corporate stocks. Corporations whose securities are traded in the over-the-counter markets are not subject to the rules (1) requiring that significant financial information be made available to the S.E.C. and the public or (2) curbing the abuses of speculative dealing by corporate insiders.

[4] Cook, Donald C. and Feldman, Meyer, "Insider Trading Under the Securities Exchange Act," *Harvard Law Review*, January, 1953, pp. 385–422.

REGULATION OF THE PROXY SYSTEM

Under Section 14 (a) of the Securities Exchange Act of 1934 the Commission is given authority to regulate proxy solicitation with respect to securities listed on national securities exchanges.[5] Authority over proxy solicitation is likewise granted to the Commission by Section 12 (a) of the Public Utility Holding Company Act of 1935 and Section 20 (a) of the Investment Company Act of 1940 in connection with the securities of companies subject to those acts. The basic idea of Congress in giving these powers to the Commission was that corporate management is a stewardship which should be directed by the informed judgment of the stockholders. In principle, the stockholders have the right to prescribe the rules by which the management shall operate the business. They also have the power to change the management. In fact, however, with the formation of large financial corporations and with the diffusion of ownership among many scattered investors, stockholder control has largely come to be replaced by management control. Stockholder meetings are usually a mere formality at which the management votes the proxies sent in by absentee owners.

In exercising its powers over proxy solicitation, the Commission has sought to give stockholders an effective opportunity to participate in the control of their corporations (see Fig. 38). Management is required to include in the proxy statement *all* of the proposals which it intends to present at the annual meeting and to give the stockholders an opportunity to vote on these proposals. Information submitted to the stockholders must be adequate and truthful, and a disclosure must be made of the remuneration of officers and directors. Stockholders themselves are privileged to submit proposals in the proxy material and to prepare a 100-word statement on such proposals for inclusion in the proxy material submitted by management.

The belief of the Securities and Exchange Commission is that the proxy system can be modified to provide an annual meeting substantially equivalent to a meeting of the stockholders in person. In the words of Commissioner Robert H. O'Brien,

I know that the old-fashioned meeting cannot be revived. Admittedly, that is impossible. It is not impossible, however, to utilize the proxy machine to approximate the conditions of the old-fashioned meeting. The proxy machine can be used to afford to the stockholders a means of communicating with each other, to give them the opportunity to submit proposals to their fellow stockholders, and to secure the collective judgment of those stockholders on their proposals. . . . Our experience shows that stockholders are eager to avail themselves of this privilege. They are beginning to feel that they have a part to play and they are willing to undertake it.[6]

[5] The authority of the Commission to prescribe rules and regulations with respect to the solicitation of proxies does not extend to unlisted securities, i.e., to those traded over the counter. A proxy, it may be noted, is a document giving authority to act for another.

[6] Robert H. O'Brien, "Stockholders and Corporate Management," an address made

AMERICAN TELEPHONE AND TELEGRAPH COMPANY

This Proxy Solicited by Management for Annual Meeting April 21, 1954

The undersigned hereby appoints Cleo F. Craig, John W. Davis, Arthur W. Page, Elihu Root, Jr. and Samuel A. Welldon, and each or any of them, attorneys, with the powers the undersigned would possess if personally present, to vote all stock of the undersigned in American Telephone and Telegraph Company at the annual meeting of its stockholders to be held on April 21, 1954, and at any adjournment thereof, upon the election of Directors and upon other matters properly coming before the meeting. Without otherwise limiting the generality hereof, said attorneys are directed to vote on the proposals set forth in the accompanying proxy statement as follows:

On proposals by certain stockholders.
The Directors favor votes AGAINST these proposals.

	FOR	AGAINST
1. Restricting officers' pensions	☐	☐
2. Regional meetings	☐	☐

On proposal by the Directors.
The Directors favor votes FOR this proposal.

	FOR	AGAINST
3. Lybrand, Ross Bros. & Montgomery as Auditors	☐	☐

Unless a contrary direction is indicated this proxy when returned properly signed will be voted AGAINST proposals 1 and 2 and FOR proposal 3.

Dated ...., 19

(Signature of Stockholder)

P R O X Y

Fig. 38. A typical proxy card giving management (1) authority to elect a board of directors consisting of the particular nominees described in a statement sent with the proxy and (2) discretionary authority to vote a stockholder's stock in accordance with the management's own judgment on matters presented at the meeting concerning which the management is not aware at the time the solicitation is made. The S.E.C. is seeking to provide stockholders with a more active participation in corporate control on the principle that management is a stewardship which should be directed by the informed judgment of the stockholders. Under S.E.C. rules, owners of listed securities may now submit proposals in the proxy material sent to all stockholders by the management and request a yes or no vote. If the management opposes the proposal, a 100-word statement in favor of the proposal may also be presented for inclusion in the proxy material. The right to have proposals included in the management's proxy

The promulgation of proxy rules by the Commission has helped in some degree to revitalize stockholder participation in corporate affairs. Much additional work along this line, however, needs to be done. Many believe, for example, that it would be desirable to require all corporations with listed securities to solicit proxies. Almost one-fourth of the registered corporations do not solicit proxies. In many cases, this reflects a desire of directors to perpetuate themselves in office by avoiding action to secure a quorum at scheduled annual meetings. Companies with securities traded over the counter, moreover, are not subject at all to the proxy rules of the Commission. It has been proposed, further, that the Commission formulate standards for corporations to use in preparing their annual reports. At the present time, the reports of corporations to their stockholders vary greatly in the information they give, in the clarity of their expression, and in the accuracy of the disclosures they make.

A problem arises also in the election of the management. Each year the stockholders are presented with a single slate of nominees prepared by the management itself. If the stockholders vote, the management wins; and if they do not bother to vote, the same management holds over for another year. It has been suggested that stockholders should be permitted to make their own nominations, and that these nominations should be included in the soliciting material sent out to the security holders by the management. The Commission has considered this proposal but has not adopted it. In the Commission's opinion, the proposal is one which should be adopted and made effective by the corporate managements themselves.[7]

ADDITIONAL REGULATIONS TO PROTECT INVESTORS

As a result of the many abuses which were found to exist in the organization and operation of investment trusts and in the conduct of investment counseling firms, Congress enacted the Investment Company Act of 1940 and the Investment Advisers Act of 1940. This legislation requires all investment trust companies to register with the Securities and Exchange Commission and prescribes rules for their conduct. Investment advisers are also required to register with the Commission, and prohibitions are placed on the use of any scheme, device, or practice to defraud or mislead a client. The Commission is empowered to enforce the provisions of the laws and to make

---

before the Conference Board, New York City, January 21, 1943, p. 2. Securities and Exchange Commission (Washington, 1943). Several agencies have come into being to represent stockholders at annual meetings. They include the Gilbert Brothers, 1165 Park Avenue, New York City, who attend numerous meetings and press for greater corporate democracy. The Gilberts are willing to vote the proxies of other stockholders issued by companies in which they are stockholders. The Federation of Women Shareholders in American Business, Inc., New York City, likewise represents stockholders' interests and seeks to place qualified women on boards of directors.

[7] *Ibid.*, p. 4. Rules with respect to stockholder nominations could be included in the corporate charters and required as a condition for the issuance of a charter. See also, below, p. 441.

such rules and regulations as are necessary to carry out the purposes of the legislation.[8]

FEDERAL REGULATION OF PUBLIC UTILITY CORPORATIONS TO PROTECT INVESTORS AND CONSUMERS

The many abuses which were found to exist in the operation of public utility holding companies led to a demand for special regulatory legislation in the electric and natural gas utility fields. This demand came not only from investors who had lost millions of dollars in the failure of utility enterprises during the early part of the depression, but also from consumers who were being forced to pay unreasonable rates as a result of the controls exercised by holding companies over operating subsidiaries. Since a large part of the utility operations was carried on across state lines, it was impossible for the state commissions to exercise any sort of effective control. The speculative collapse of the Insull group of utility holding companies in 1932, in particular, emphasized the great need for federal control, and the question of public utility regulation became a major issue in the presidential election of that year. Finally, in 1935, after a vigorous struggle in both houses of Congress, the sponsors of federal control secured the enactment of the Public Utility Holding Company Act.

In making a request for the enactment of the Public Utility Bill, President Roosevelt declared that it was hoped that in five years arrangements could be made to dissolve all utility holding companies which could not justify themselves as being necessary for the effective functioning of the operating companies which they controlled. Holding companies, he continued, ought not to be permitted to profit from dealings with subsidiary companies when these companies have no chance to bargain with others to secure a better price. "If we could remake our financial history in the light of experience," he stated, "certainly we would have none of this holding company business. It is a device which does not belong to our American traditions of law and business. . . . It is a corporate invention which can give a few corporate insiders unwarranted and intolerable powers over other people's money. In its destruction of local control and its substitution of absentee management, it has built up in the public utility field what has justly been called a system of private socialism which is inimical to the welfare of a free people."[9]

The vast holding company system, President Roosevelt and his advisers believed, not only failed to perform a demonstrably useful purpose but also served to make effective regulation impossible. In the words of President Roosevelt, "it is idle to talk of the continuation of holding companies on the assumption that regulation can protect the public against them. Regulation has small chance of ultimate success against the kind of concentrated wealth and economic power which holding companies have shown the ability to

[8] 15 U.S.C. 80(a-1)-80(a-52); and 15 U.S.C. 80(b-1)-80(b-21).
[9] *The Public Papers and Addresses of Franklin D. Roosevelt,* Vol. 4 (1935), (New York, 1938), pp. 100–101.

acquire in the utility field. No Government effort can be expected to carry out effective, continuous, and intricate regulation of the kind of private empires within the Nation which the holding company device has proved capable of creating."[10]

THE PUBLIC UTILITY HOLDING COMPANY ACT OF 1935

The Holding Company Act was approved by Congress on August 26, 1935, after passing the Senate with a margin of only one vote. Utility company executives spent thousands of dollars in an effort to defeat the bill, and many of the proposals for control had to be compromised in order to secure adoption. Even so, the act stands as one of the most significant forms of control which has ever been passed by Congress. Its principal provisions are as follows:

1. All interstate public utility *holding company* systems engaged in the electric utility business or in the retail distribution of natural or manufactured gas must register with the Securities and Exchange Commission. They must also file certain basic data and submit annually such information as the Commission deems necessary to effectuate the purposes of the act. A holding company is defined by the act as a corporation which holds 10 percent or more of the voting stock of a public utility company or another holding company.

2. In general, all gas and electric holding companies must be limited "to a single integrated public-utility system, and to such other businesses as are reasonably incidental, or economically necessary . . . to the operation of such integrated public-utility system." Under certain conditions, it is possible for the Commission to permit a holding company to control more than one integrated system. A single integrated public utility system is considered to be one or more units of generating plants, transmission lines, and distributing facilities which may be economically operated as a single interconnected system in a single area or region, in one or more states, and not so large as to impair efficiency in management or effectiveness in regulation.

3. The act provides that all holding companies above the "second degree" must be dissolved, unless an exception is made by the Commission. A corporation which controls an operating company (by owning and voting some or all of its stock) is known as a "first degree" holding company; and a corporation controlling the first holding company, in turn, is called a "second degree" holding company. The purpose of prohibiting more than two tiers of holding companies is to simplify the holding company system and to redistribute voting power among security holders on a fair and equitable basis.

4. The approval of the Commission is required for the issuance of new securities and for the acquisition of additional utility assets or securities. The Commission has authority to fix the "fair purchase price" for any securities or assets which are acquired, and to deny any acquisition which

[10] *Ibid.*, p. 100.

does not "serve the public interest by tending towards the economical and efficient development of an integrated public-utility system."

5. The financial and commercial relations of holding companies and their subsidiaries are brought within the control of the Commission. All registered holding companies must report their service, sales, and construction contracts for Commission approval.

6. Interlocking directorates with banking companies are prohibited, and intercompany borrowing is made illegal.

7. The Commission is empowered to require holding companies to use uniform accounting systems and to file periodic reports. It is also authorized to formulate such rules and regulations for the control of utility holding companies as it may deem necessary to carry out the purposes of the act.

8. Finally, it is provided that it shall be unlawful for any holding company or its subsidiaries to make contributions to any political party or candidate in federal, state, or local campaigns, or to engage in lobbying activities without specific approval by the Commission.[11]

The Securities and Exchange Commission has made noteworthy progress in carrying out the purposes of the Holding Company Act. During the fiscal year 1947, holding companies were required to divest themselves of thirty-one subsidiaries with assets of $1,978,000,000. From December 1, 1935, to June 30, 1951, 753 utility companies with assets of $10,311,000,000 were divested from holding company systems. Most of these companies are now independent operating utilities. Most of them, moreover, are now fully subject to state control. In general, divestments are carried out by the sale of securities in the open markets, by outright distributions, or by the issuance of purchase warrants to stockholders of the parent company. Notable progress has also been made in simplifying corporate structures and in redistributing voting power among the various security holders. The Commission estimated in 1952 that about 85 percent of its overall work of integration and simplification had been completed.[12]

In regulating the sale of new securities, the Commission has adopted the rule (with certain exceptions) that securities issued by companies under the Holding Company Act shall be sold by competitive bidding. Competitive bidding means a public offering of securities with sealed bids opened in the presence of bidders and with sale to the highest bidder. This wholesome rule was introduced to provide "arm's length bargaining" in the sale of securities—that is, to insure that an issuing company will be free to receive bids from various buyers as well as from its regular investment banker.

The provisions of the Holding Company Act do not call for the complete elimination of all holding companies in the public utility field. Any

[11] 15 U.S.C. 79–79(z–6).

[12] For a detailed account of the procedures followed by the Securities and Exchange Commission in administering the Holding Company Act, see Report of the Securities and Exchange Commission, *The Public Utility Holding Company Act of 1935*, Select Committee on Small Business, U.S. Senate, 82nd Congress, second session, June 3, 1952.

holding company which can qualify as a "single integrated system" is permitted to continue as a regional enterprise. All such systems remain subject to regulation by the Securities and Exchange Commission with respect to financing, intercompany transactions, service charges, and other activities, as noted above. The Commission estimates that about 20 regional holding company systems, with assets of some $7 billion will be permanently subject to its jurisdiction.

THE PROVISION OF ADDITIONAL PROTECTION FOR INVESTORS AND CONSUMERS IN THE PUBLIC UTILITY FIELD

The Public Utility Act of 1935 sought primarily to control the abuses which were found to exist in the electric and gas utilities as a consequence of the holding company form of organization. Title II of the Utility Act of 1935 is the Federal Power Act of 1935. This act gave the Federal Power Commission authority to regulate mergers, the issuance and acquisition of securities, and interstate rates and service, in the electric utility field. The jurisdiction of the Federal Power Commission over those matters is limited to the *operating* company level. Supervision over the *holding company* systems, as we have seen, is vested in the Securities and Exchange Commission.

Further protection to consumers in the utility field was provided by Congress in 1938 with the enactment of the Natural Gas Act. This act gives the Federal Power Commission authority over the rates and service of companies transporting natural gas in interstate commerce and selling it at wholesale in interstate commerce. The Natural Gas Act does not provide authority to regulate security issues, but it does require that certificates of public convenience and necessity be secured before the construction of new interstate natural gas facilities is undertaken.

THE PRESENT AREA OF CONFLICT IN PUBLIC POLICY

We have seen that thus far Congress has provided a considerable measure of regulation over corporations in the public utility field for the protection of investors and consumers. At the present time, major issues in public policy are proposals (1) to make corporate managers responsible to the corporate owners and (2) to extend public regulation over supercorporations *in industry and commerce* to protect the interests of small business and consumers, generally.

The lack of responsibility of many corporate officials to their stockholders is still a problem which remains unsolved. Professor William Z. Ripley, a long-time student of business corporations, has declared, "There is nothing yet in the Securities, Securities Exchange, or Utility Holding Acts covering the relationship between the *owners* and the *management* which holds the latter to an accountability for its administration of its trust, except as provided by the charters under which those managements exercise those powers. And those charters are not derived from the federal government but from the different states. So that these responsibilities as between the owners and the tier of management are in a condition resembling nothing but chaos."[13] The principal charter-granting states, as we have seen, have done little to provide public regulation, and as a consequence all sorts of charter provisions have been established which give directors and officials many powers of control without specific responsibility to the corporate owners.

In a summary of the T.N.E.C. findings with respect to the relations between corporate managers and their stockholders, Dr. David Lynch states that "Apparently there has developed a code which permits the exploitation of corporate stewardship for personal gain. The ordinary requirements of integrity and trust usually demanded of lesser men, and in little things, too frequently have been set aside when dealing with big things involving large sums."[14] It is primarily when corporate officials go too far in abusing their trust that stockholders bring legal action against the improper conduct. Even then the expense involved in bringing a lawsuit usually discourages intervention by most of the stockholders.

A further aspect of the present-day corporation problem is the impact of large corporations on small business and consumers. In Chap. 12, we discussed the business practices of large companies which operate to the detriment of small business. At the present time, consumers also express complaint in the continuing high cost of living in relation to wages and salaries. In the fields of general business, there is much *sales* competition, but in large areas there is little or no *price* competition.

The problem of public regulation in industry centers on the financially large, multiplant corporations, that is, corporations controlling many geographically separate plants in the same and in widely diverse lines of business. Large financial size has recognized *private* advantages. At the same time, however, it may result in a number of economic evils. First, large size in American industry has typically come about as a result of mergers; and mergers in many fields have meant the destruction of price competition among formerly independent and competing plants. With the disappearance of competition, prices have become "administered" and "stabilized." Such forced stability of particular prices tends to prevent full employment and aggravates depression. When demand declines, large business takes little or no action to stimulate consumption by reducing prices. Instead, output is curtailed in order to prevent a break in prices.

Secondly, large financial size has fostered certain types of business behavior which are not in the public interest. Such behavior includes concerted action on prices; discriminatory pricing to limit and injure competitors; blacklisting and boycotting of competitors; tacit agreements to restrict the production, sale, and distribution of particular commodities; price leadership and price following; price rigidity; restrictions on newcomers; coercion of independents; the use of financial power to secure discriminatory purchase

[13] Hearings Before a Subcommittee of the Committee on the Judiciary on S. 10, *Federal Licensing of Corporations,* 75th Congress, first session, 1937, Part 3, pp. 270–271. Italics supplied.
[14] David Lynch, *The Concentration of Economic Power* (New York, 1946), p. 282.

prices; undue influence in the legislatures and the courts; suppression of patents; wasteful advertising; spurious product differentiation; technological progress without cost savings being passed on to consumers; inefficiency in the coördination of diverse activities; and backwardness in the introduction of new processes.[15]

Critics of large business units declare that regulatory efforts to curb abuses have been largely ineffective. When one abuse is condemned, business behavior is commonly changed, and the unlawful end is pursued in a modified way. A policy of attacking abuses, it is said, is essentially one of treating symptoms rather than basic causes. If monopolistic behavior is to be remedied, it is believed, government must act *positively* to create the essential conditions for competition, namely, (1) numerous, independent buyers and sellers and (2) market rules for conducting business openly and aboveboard.

FEDERAL CHARTERS OR LICENSES AS A REMEDY FOR CORPORATE ABUSES

Government reports and court cases are filled with factual information demonstrating that a large part of our present economic ills are traceable (1) to the gaps, vagaries, and laxity of corporation law and (2) to the concentration of economic power in the hands of a few corporations in each industry. As a result of the charter-issuing policies of the forty-eight states, there is a deplorable absence of rules and standards for the organization and internal government of business corporations.

Today, we are faced with the alternatives (a) of being contented with the abuses of concentrated economic power as we know them or (b) of taking consistent action to remedy these evils. There is general agreement among students of public policy that the conservative, practical approach to take in regulating corporate enterprise is one of establishing *uniform standards* in the public interest for all corporations engaged in interstate commerce. In some cases, such standards can be applied effectively by existing federal commissions. In other cases, and as a supplementary mechanism, various experts believe that standards for corporate activity should be enforced through a system of federal charters or licenses.[16]

The proposal of requiring federal charters or licenses for corporations

[15] Evidence on the abuses of economic concentration may be found in the reports of the Temporary National Economic Committee (summarized by David Lynch in *The Concentration of Economic Power*, New York, 1946); in court cases involving monopolistic activity and discriminatory pricing; in Congressional reports on monopoly and economic concentration, such as *Hearings Before the Subcommittee on Study of Monopoly Power*, Committee on the Judiciary, House of Representatives, 81st Congress, second session, 1950, Serial 14, Part 4 A, esp. pp. 966–991; and in the reports of the Federal Trade Commission and the Department of Justice.

[16] Since state governments receive filing fees and annual license or franchise taxes from business corporations chartered in their states, some authorities believe that the states should be allowed to continue their control over the granting of corporate charters. The attainment of unifom standards in corporate regulation, they suggest, can be secured under state laws by requiring *federal licenses* as a condition for engaging in interstate commerce.

engaging in interstate commerce is one which many economists regard as being of paramount importance. By establishing standards and "rules of the game" which must be observed by corporations as a condition (a) for coming into existence and (b) for engaging in interstate commerce, public regulation can do much to prevent the development of abuses and the exercise of private monopoly power.

A system of federal charters or licenses would greatly simplify the problem of business regulation. Business enterprisers seeking to enjoy (a) the valuable privileges of a corporate charter and (b) the right to engage in interstate commerce would be granted charters provided that they would agree to fulfill designated responsibilities in the public interest. The securing of valuable corporate privileges would be made to turn on the assumption of far

SAMPLE COPY

Certificate of Incorporation

OF THE

𝕿𝖍𝖎𝖘 𝖎𝖘 𝖙𝖔 𝕮𝖊𝖗𝖙𝖎𝖋𝖞   That we . . . . .

do hereby associate ourselves into a corporation, under and by virtue of the provisions of Title 14, Corporations, General, Revised Statutes, and the several supplements thereto and acts amendatory thereof, and do severally agree to take the number of shares of capital stock set opposite our respective names.

𝕱𝖎𝖗𝖘𝖙: The name of the corporation is . . . . .

𝕾𝖊𝖈𝖔𝖓𝖉: The location of the principal office is . . . .   Street,

in the   of   , County of

The name of the agent therein and in charge thereof, upon whom process against this corporation may be served, is

𝕿𝖍𝖎𝖗𝖉: The objects for which this corporation is formed are . . .

[The objects for which a corporation is formed are determined and placed in the certificate of incorporation by the persons who apply for the charter.

Most certificates of incorporation provide for the buying and selling of real estate and for the transaction of any business which will enhance the value of the stock of a corporation. The right to buy, own, vote, and sell the stock of other corporations is also usually included.]

The corporation shall also have power to conduct its business in all its branches, have one or more offices, and unlimitedly to hold, purchase, mortgage and convey real and personal property in any State, Territory or Colony of the United States and in any foreign country or place.

𝕱𝖔𝖚𝖗𝖙𝖍: The total authorized capital stock of this corporation is . . . . .

𝕱iftly: ′The names and post-office address of the incorporators and the number of shares sub-

scribed for by each, the aggregate of which ($) is the amount of capital stock with which

this company will commence business, are as follows:

Name.	Post-Office Address.	Number of Shares.

𝕾ixth: The period of existence of this corporation is unlimited.

𝕴n 𝖂itness 𝖂hereof, we have hereunto set our hands and seals the

day of   , A. D. nineteen hundred

Signed, sealed and delivered in the presence of . . . . .

Fig. 39. The form of corporate charter used by the state of New Jersey. Note the space (under "Third") in which persons seeking a corporate charter may designate the objects and purposes of the corporation. Some authorities believe that the granting of valuable corporate privileges should be made to involve the assumption of specific obligations in the public interest. Suggested terms and conditions for inclusion in the charter grant are presented in the text.

greater obligations to the public than the payment of filing fees and annual franchise taxes, as is largely true today (see Fig. 39). In setting forth desirable courses of conduct, government would act to minimize the development of abuses. "An ounce of prevention," it has been said, "is worth a pound of cure"; and this maxim applies fully to the regulation of business.

A plan of federal charters or licenses also would provide for a system of regulation which is largely self-enforcing. The inclusion of strict terms in corporation charters would give management, directors, stockholders, and the public a knowledge of their respective rights and duties. Stockholders would be informed of their rights against management, and management would know the standards which they should observe in relation to stock-holders and the public. The self-interest of stockholders and the public would thereupon be enlisted to see that corporations observe the rules which were agreed upon as a condition for doing an interstate business.

SUGGESTED TERMS AND CONDITIONS FOR CORPORATIONS ENGAGING IN INTERSTATE COMMERCE

Various standards have been proposed for inclusion by the federal government in charters or licenses to corporations seeking to engage in interstate commerce. In summary form, they include the following:

1. Prohibition of interlocking relationships between nominally independent corporations either engaged in the same line of industry or buying and selling from each other in interstate commerce.
2. The issuance of adequate official publicity by corporate managements in reliable, useful, and complete reports. Corporations with securities listed

on a national exchange must provide such information in reports to the S.E.C. Similar requirements apply to companies subject to the Public Utility Holding Company Act of 1935 and the Investment Company Act of 1940. However, there are no laws, state or federal, which require corporations with unlisted securities, traded over the counter, to provide reliable reports, even to their own stockholders. Some well-known corporations which do not report to the S.E.C. are Anheuser-Busch, Bausch and Lomb, Botany Mills, Dictaphone Corp., Pabst Brewing, Permanente Cement, and the Weyerhaeuser Timber Co.

As early as 1900 the Industrial Commission recommended that the larger corporations be required to publish annually properly audited reports, showing in reasonable detail their assets and liabilities and profits and losses. "The purpose of such publicity," it was said, "is to encourage competition when profits become excessive, thus protecting consumers against too high prices, and to guard the interests of employees by a knowledge of the financial condition of the business in which they are employed."

In 1946, and again in 1949, the S.E.C. made a study of the financial reports of a representative group of corporations which do not file their statements with the Commission. *Most* of these reports, it was found, were misleading or inadequate in some degree. The S.E.C. has repeatedly urged Congress to enact legislation requiring all corporations having at least $3,000,000 in assets and at least 300 security holders to make public reports to the Commission. Such a requirement, the Commission believes, will make it possible to curb false and misleading statements, so that security holders will have a basis for exercising an informed judgment.[17]

3. Full disclosure of transactions by officers and directors with the companies and affiliates of the controlling corporation.

4. Mandatory proxy solicitation at least once a year and the provision of adequate information for use by security holders in exercising their corporate franchise.

5. The restriction of corporate powers to those essential to a single main purpose and kind of business.

6. Stocks of corporations to be owned and voted only by natural persons. This was the law on corporations for many centuries prior to 1888, when New Jersey legalized the holding company privilege. The adoption of this proposal would have the consequence of outlawing completely the holding company device.

7. The establishment by law of a high standard of responsibility for corporate officers and directors in relation to the owners of a corporation. Corporate officials, it is said, should be vested in fact as well as in law with the fiduciary obligation of trustees. Stockholders must have the expectation of fair dealing on the part of their officers and directors, for experience has shown that stockholders' rights cannot be protected by private suits against improper conduct. In most cases, the great majority of stockholders have neither the time nor the money to investigate and prosecute irresponsible corporate officials.

[17] Securities and Exchange Commission, *A Proposal to Safeguard Investors in Unregistered Securities* (Washington, 1950), pp. 1–3.

8. A provision that each member of the board of directors must own a certain minimum percentage of the stock of the corporation. Such a provision, it is said, would (a) correct in some degree the present separation of ownership and control and (b) prevent or discourage the election of directors who acquire only a few qualifying shares in order to represent a banking firm or a competing company.

9. A requirement that corporations which control two or more plants making salable products, or which engage in more than one kind or line of business, shall prepare and publish profit and loss statements *for each separate plant and for each distinct kind of business*. Large corporations typically publish only "consolidated" accounting reports which reveal nothing about the profitability of various operations. Some units of a large concern may be deliberately operated at a loss to injure a competitor, and the use of consolidated reports makes it easy to conceal such activity.

10. A provision requiring each publicly held corporation to have a clearly stated dividend policy. When profits are earned, stockholders are entitled to receive a reasonably large share. Some authorities believe that corporate managements should be required to pay out a substantial part of the profits to their stockholders. The percentage of profits required for dividends, it is proposed, should be arranged on a graduated basis, with the percentage low for small corporations and rising to 100 percent for the largest companies. Advocates of this provision declare that it would (a) protect small stockholders against having their just share of profits used to satisfy the whims of irresponsible corporate management and (b) aid in preserving the capitalist system by retarding the growth of giant corporations. The federal government, itself, has a very real interest in preventing the unwarranted retention of liquid earnings by corporations. Not infrequently, controlling stockholders promote the accumulation of excessive liquid earnings by a corporation, by refusing to declare dividends, in order to reduce their personal incomes and avoid heavy personal surtax payments.[18]

11. A provision that a stockholder may cumulate or concentrate his votes on one or more candidates for the board of directors (cumulative voting). By this arrangement a stockholder owning 10 shares and voting on 9 directors may cast 90 votes for one nominee instead of 10 votes for each of nine persons. Cumulative voting gives minority stockholders a greater opportunity of securing an independent director (not closely identified with the operating management). The corporation laws of some twenty-one states now specifically provide for cumulative voting.

12. The legal requirement that the officers and directors of a corporation (not the corporation itself) shall be personally liable for fines growing out of specified violations of the antitrust laws which they conceive and direct.

13. A provision that stockholders shall be permitted to make their own nominations in the election of the management, and that nominations so made shall be included in the soliciting material sent out to the security holders by the management.

[18] See James K. Hall, *The Taxation of Corporate Surplus Accumulations*, Joint Committee on the Economic Report, Washington, 1952.

14. The development and application of an appropriate standard for size. Congress has made repeated efforts to halt the concentration of economic power. In 1950, we have seen, the Clayton Act was amended to prohibit the acquisition of stock *or assets* which substantially lessens competition. The attention of various economists and statesmen is now turning to the determination of an appropriate standard on size for corporations which have already attained a dominant position.

Professor Walter Adams proposes that corporations controlling 10 percent or more of the supply (tons, pounds, or barrels) of a product moving in interstate commerce, or having assets in excess of $25,000,000 shall come under federal scrutiny. If a federal commission finds that the activity of such a corporate giant is characterized by ineffective price competition, unused capacity, and price rigidity, it can provide for an unraveling ("unwinding," "unmerging") of the corporation and for the creation of numerous independent concerns. If, however, the commission finds that the large corporation fully meets standards of performance in the public interest, it can permit the concern to continue.[19]

Other economic experts propose that the Sherman Act be amended to establish a "rebuttable presumption" that concentration in excess of a specified percentage is illegal. Corporations which desire to attain or retain a size in excess of the prescribed limit would be required to justify the large financial size in terms of service to society.[20]

Dr. C. D. Edwards suggests that the "competitive standard" should be taken as our guide for the degree of bigness which is permissible.[21] In his opinion, a large corporation should be open to challenge whenever it appears that its size has "adverse effects" upon competition. The effect of bigness upon competition may be tested by considering (1) whether the *behavior* of the concern is monopolistic or (2) whether its *structure* in relation to others gives it the power to control the market, regardless of the way in which this power is exercised.

Dr. Edwards believes that an attack on size is justifiable if the objectionable effects of large size outweigh possible beneficial aspects, and further, if the objectionable effects cannot be destroyed by selective means (such as cease-and-desist orders or injunctions). He states that no concern should be so large as to control the "market," that is, its competitors, its customers, or its suppliers.

It is possible that in a particular situation the evidence may indicate (1) that the large size of a concern is the result of modern technology rather

[19] *Hearings Before the Subcommittee on Study of Monopoly Power*, Committee on the Judiciary, House of Representatives, 81st Congress, first session, Serial 14, Part 2-B, 1950, pp. 1313–1314; and "Is Bigness a Crime," *Land Economics*, November, 1951, p. 293.

[20] Report of the Committee on Cartels and Monopoly in George W. Stocking and Myron W. Watkins, *Monopoly and Free Enterprise* (New York, 1951), p. 553. See also Fred I. Raymond, *The Limitist* (New York, 1947), pp. 108–133.

[21] C. D. Edwards, "Public Policy and Business Size," *The Journal of Business of the University of Chicago*, October, 1951, p. 286.

than the acquisition of competitors, the control of raw materials, or the ownership of fabricating units; and (2) that technology itself impairs the operation of effective price competition. In such a situation, Dr. Edwards declares that government should adopt some form of commission control to promote business efficiency and to safeguard the public against the abuses of concentrated economic power.

SUMMARY

Substantial progress has been made toward providing investors with reliable information on corporate activity and with regulated markets for the purchase and sale of securities. Procedures have also been established to provide for the decentralization of financial control in the organization of electric and gas utilities. The important tasks of the future with respect to supercorporations are mainly two: (1) to establish the responsibility of management to the actual owners, so that stockholders will have some measure of control over their property; and (2) to formulate a public policy with respect to corporate size, mergers, and centralized financial control in the principal fields of industry. There is no logical reason for applying holding company legislation only to the electric and gas utility fields. Centralized financial control and monopolistic price policies similarly exist in the various branches of industry, commerce, banking, and transportation.

Our declared public policy is one of maintaining effective price competition in all lines of business which are not given over to public price control by commissions. In the preceding chapters on the antitrust laws we considered the legislation which the federal government has adopted to eliminate monopolistic practices. This machinery provides a basic means for bringing about a decentralization or dissolution of supercorporations. The proposal of requiring (1) federal charters for all corporations engaging in interstate commerce and (2) an observance of standards with respect to corporate size and activity is a practical and necessary means for implementing our traditional antitrust policy.

SUGGESTIONS FOR FURTHER READING

Drucker, P. F., *Concept of the Corporation* (New York, 1946).
Bonbright, James C., and Means, Gardiner C., *The Holding Company* (New York, 1932).
Graham, Benjamin, and Dodd, David L., *Security Analysis* (New York, 1951).
Brandeis, Louis D., *Other People's Money* (New York, 1914).
Buchanan, N. S., *The Economics of Corporate Enterprise* (New York, 1940).
McCormick, Edward T., *Understanding the Securities Act and the S.E.C.* (New York, 1948).
Owens, Richard N., *Business Organization and Combination* (New York, 1951).
Purdy, Harry L., Lindahl, Martin L., and Carter, William A., *Corporate Concentration and Public Policy* (New York, 1950).

Raymond, Fred I., *The Limitist* (New York, 1947).
Ripley, William Z., *Main Street and Wall Street* (Boston, 1927).
The Public Utility Holding Company Act of 1935, Report of the S.E.C. to the Select Committee on Small Business, U.S. Senate, 82nd Congress, second session, 1952.

CHAPTER 20

The State Antitrust Laws as an Instrument of Regulation

In the federal system, the regulation of intrastate or local commerce is re-served to the states. Intrastate commerce, in general, is any commercial activity which begins and ends within a state. Although the Supreme Court has broadened the concept of interstate commerce to cover local business which seriously affects commercial activity among the states, there is still an important area of economic activity which is commonly considered to be intrastate and subject only to regulation by the individual states.

The area of intrastate commerce is significant. It typically includes, or may include, the production and sale of bread, beer, local wines, gasoline, ice, coal, fuel oil, lumber, milk, ice cream, local produce, used cars, insurance, cleaning and dyeing, laundry, hospital services, undertaking services, cemetery services (including gravestone installation), garage services, parking facilities, hotel and housing facilities, building and road construction, photoengraving, printing, theater and recreational facilities, local transportation, and banking services. A large number of personal service enterprises are local in nature. They include the activities of architects, barbers, optometrists, physicians, surgeons, dentists, pharmacists, accountants, photographers, surveyors, and veterinarians. Numerous heavy and bulky products, such as cement, sand, gravel, bricks, concrete building blocks, and drain tile, are also produced and consumed locally because of high transportation costs.[1]

Within the area of local commerce, the state governments have the task of performing the same economic functions of regulation which the federal government performs at the national level. Such functions include the prohibition of false advertising, the prevention of monopoly and unfair competition, the control of local utilities, and the adoption of labor legislation for local trades. The incorporation of business enterprises and the regulation of insurance companies, as we have seen, continue to be exercised by the states, even though the enterprises actually engage in interstate commerce.

The purpose of the present chapter is to consider the regulation of business at the state level to maintain competition and prevent monopoly. Students desiring additional information on the activities of their own state in main-

[1] See also Jesse W. Markham, "The Effectiveness of the Federal Antitrust Laws: Comment," *American Economic Review*, March, 1950, pp. 167–169.

taining freedom of entry and price competition and in preventing unfair competition may secure it by writing to the Attorney General for that state.

STATE PROVISIONS RELATING TO MONOPOLY AND RESTRAINT OF COMPETITION

The constitutional and statutory provisions against monopoly which have been adopted by the state governments are a reflection of the general belief of consumers, farmers, labor, and independent businessmen that a policy of competition is essential to their economic welfare. Some twenty-seven states have adopted constitutional provisions which condemn monopoly, restraint of trade, restraint of competition, price fixing, and, in some cases, concerted action to limit output (see Table 33, pp. 457–458). Some forty-one states, moreover, have enacted statutory provisions against such offenses.

A few examples of the constitutional prohibitions will serve to indicate the strong feeling of the state founders against monopoly.[2] According to the constitution of Arizona, "Monopolies and trusts shall never be allowed in this State, and no incorporated company, copartnership, or association of persons in this State shall directly or indirectly combine or make any contract . . . to fix the prices, limit the production, or regulate the transportation of any product or commodity. The legislature shall enact laws for the enforcement of this section by adequate penalties, and in the case of incorporated companies, if necessary for that purpose, may, as a penalty, declare a forfeiture of their franchises." The principle that monopolies "shall never be allowed" is also expressed in the constitutions of Arkansas, Tennessee, Texas, Washington, and Wyoming.

The constitution of New Hampshire provides that "free and fair competition in the trades and industries is an inherent and essential right of the people and should be protected against all monopolies and conspiracies which tend to hinder or destroy it."

In South Carolina the constitution provides that "the general assembly shall enact laws to prevent all trusts, combinations, contracts, and agreements against the public welfare."

The constitution of Louisiana declares that "all combinations, trusts, or conspiracies in restraint of trade or commerce, and all monopolies or combinations to monopolize trade or commerce, are hereby prohibited in the State of Louisiana."

The constitution of North Carolina provides that "perpetuities and monopolies are contrary to the genius of a free state and ought not to be allowed"; and the constitution of Maryland declares that monopolies "are odious, contrary to the spirit of a free government and the principles of commerce, and ought not to be suffered."

[2] A compilation of state antitrust law provisions is presented in *State Antitrust Laws and State Price Control Legislation,* prepared by the Marketing Laws Survey, Works Progress Administration (Washington, 1940); and *Final Report on the Chain Store Investigation,* 74th Congress, first session, Senate Document 4, 1935.

STATUTE PROVISIONS WITH RESPECT TO MONOPOLISTIC RESTRAINTS

The state legislatures in Idaho, Louisiana, Maine, New Mexico, New York, and Wisconsin have adopted antitrust statutes which are essentially the same as the Sherman Act of 1890. Thirteen states (Arizona, California, Florida, Kansas, Mississippi, Montana, Nebraska, New Hampshire, North Dakota, Ohio, South Dakota, Texas, and Virginia) have enacted antitrust statutes similar to the following (which is the wording of the Ohio statute):

> A trust is a combination of capital, skill, or acts by two or more persons, firms, partnerships, corporations, or associations . . . for either, any, or all of the following purposes:
> [1] To create or carry out restrictions in trade or commerce.
> [2] To limit or reduce the production, or increase or reduce the price, of any commodity or merchandise.
> [3] To prevent competition in manufacturing, making, transportation, sale, or purchase of merchandise, produce, or commodity.
> [4] To fix at any . . . standard . . . figure . . . its price to the public or consumer. . . .
> [5] To make or enter into . . . any contracts, obligations, or agreements . . . not to sell, dispose of, or transport any article . . . below a common standard figure or fixed value . . . or settle the price of any article . . . between themselves and others, so as to directly or indirectly preclude a free and unrestricted competition among themselves. . . . Every such trust as is defined herein is declared to be unlawful, against public policy, and void.

In general, it may be said that all the state antitrust statutes seek to prevent collective action which is designed to restrain price competition or to prevent others from exercising a trade of their own choice.

Many states having antitrust statutes, as well as those not having such legislation, have provided that agricultural coöperatives and labor unions shall not be deemed to be illegal combinations. States which have resale price-maintenance legislation also have provided that resale price-maintenance contracts shall be exempted from the antitrust laws. The various state antitrust laws provide for the levying of fines up to $5000 for each violation and for imprisonment for periods ranging from six months to ten years. Enforcement of the state antitrust laws is normally a duty of the state attorney general, and in some cases the county and district attorneys are also given the responsibility of enforcement.

SPECIAL ANTITRUST LAWS FOR LOCAL COMMERCE

All the forty-eight states have adopted one or more special antitrust statutes applicable to certain designated industries. These statutes, in most cases, reflect the existence of some particular commercial abuse which the legislatures have sought to correct by specific legislation. Many of the special statutes provide that railroad corporations shall not own parallel or competing lines. Special regulations are also commonly provided for the prevention of restraints in the wholesale and retail liquor business. Some states—such as Arkansas, Arizona, Iowa, Kansas, Louisiana, Michigan, New Hampshire, Nebraska, Oregon, South Carolina, South Dakota, and Washington—provide that fire insurance companies shall not be permitted to make agreements or understandings to fix or maintain insurance rates or premiums. Wisconsin has a special statute providing that Swiss cheese dealers shall have their licenses revoked if they are found to be engaged in any practice in restraint of competition. Other states have special antitrust statutes applicable to pipe lines, banks, stockyards, cold storage enterprises, grain dealers, bridge owners, cotton gin operators, motor carriers, advertising companies, electrical utilities, the purchase of tobacco and grain, and the sale of news service, coal, various foodstuffs, and commercial fertilizers.

From an economic and legal standpoint, special antitrust laws applicable to general business are an incomplete instrument of control. The protection of consumers requires that price competition be effectively maintained in *all* lines of business which are not turned over to public price fixing by commissions. It follows that what is needed is a broad, general, and comprehensive statute, applicable to the sale of all commodities (physical products and services—such as the services of dry cleaners, architects, garages, and barbershops). Thereupon, if additional legislation is found to be necessary to cope with restrictive agreements in special situations—such as agreements between agricultural coöperatives, labor unions, railroads, electrical utilities, or other industries or activities in which various degrees of monopoly control are accepted—it could be adopted to supplement the general antitrust statutes.

STATE STATUTES PROHIBITING PRICE DISCRIMINATION

By the time the Clayton Act was passed by Congress in 1914, nineteen states had already adopted legislation against geographic price discrimination which works an injury to competition. The purpose of these statutes was to prevent the common practices of large sellers (1) in cutting selling prices in one area to destroy a local competitor, while raising or maintaining the prices on like products in other areas; or (2) in raising buying prices in a certain community in which a competitor was located, while making up losses by paying low prices in areas in which competition was not active.

At the present time, some twenty-seven states have comprehensive statutes which prohibit, with various qualifications, any person or corporation, engaged in the production, manufacture, or sale of a commodity, from engaging in geographic price discrimination (see Table 33, pp. 457–458). Some of the statutes specify that the prohibition extends to *"selling* such commodity at a lower rate in one section, community, or city . . . than such person . . . charges for such commodity in another section, community, or city . . . after making due allowance for the difference, if any, in the grade or quality and in the cost of transportation" (Delaware). Other statutes (such as the Iowa law) provide that the prohibition shall cover *"purchasing* said commodity at a higher rate or price in one section, locality, community, city, or town than is paid for such commodity by such party in another section . . . after making due allowance for the difference, if any, in the grade or quality and in the actual cost of transportation." This difference in the two types of statutes reflects the fact that in certain states the problem has been one of preserving selling competition (between manufacturers, wholesalers, and retailers), whereas in agricultural communities the principal problem has been one of maintaining buying competition in the purchase of farm products. Practically all the statutes qualify the prohibition on discrimination by adding the phrase "for the purpose of creating a monopoly or destroying the business of a competitor."

In some states (such as Mississippi) the law against geographic price discrimination extends to buying as well as to selling activities. The Wisconsin statute covers discrimination between persons *within* the same locality (personal discrimination) and also discrimination between two or more areas. The various antidiscrimination laws are criminal statutes and provide for the levying of fines or imprisonment, or both. Their enforcement is typically a duty of the state attorney general.

Although state statutes prohibiting geographic price discrimination greatly restrict individual freedom of contract, the state and federal courts have uniformly upheld such laws if "intent" to destroy competition is included as a part of the offense. The Supreme Court of Iowa, in upholding the validity of an antidiscrimination statute in that state, for example, declared,

> One of the great legislative problems of the day is to protect fair competition in the business world without unduly interfering with the freedom of contract. . . . It is quite manifest that a company sufficiently large in its capital and in the scope of its business could obtain a monopoly for itself in whatever territory it chose, by adopting the methods which are enumerated and prohibited in the statute. The temporary maintenance of artificial prices for the sole purpose of destroying a weaker competitor and creating a monopoly is one of the modern evil inventions. All that is required for its sure success is that there be great inequality of financial resources in favor of the offending party.[3]

In 1912 the United States Supreme Court upheld the antidiscrimination statute of South Dakota. This code reads, in part, as follows: *"Any person doing business in this State . . . who intentionally, for the purpose of destroying the competition* of any regular established dealer . . . or . . . the competition of any person . . . *shall discriminate between different sections, communities, or cities of this State by selling* such commodity at a lower rate in one section . . . than such person . . . charges for such commodity in another section . . . after equalizing the distance from the point of production . . . shall be deemed guilty of unfair discrimination." (Italics supplied.)

[3] *State v. Fairmont Creamery of Nebraska,* 133 N.W. 895, 898 (1911).

The company charged with discrimination contended that the law was illegal because it unreasonably limited individual freedom of contract. Justice Holmes, however, speaking for a unanimous Court, upheld the statute on the ground that if an instrument of trade war is found to be against public policy, its use may be prohibited.[4]

SPECIAL STATUTES PROHIBITING DISCRIMINATION IN DESIGNATED INDUSTRIES

In addition to the comprehensive statutes prohibiting geographic price discrimination, many states (see Table 33, pp. 457–458) have adopted special laws against geographic price discrimination. A number of states (Arizona, Indiana, Mississippi, Missouri, Nebraska, North Dakota, Ohio, Oregon, South Dakota, Tennessee, Utah, Vermont, and Wisconsin) have laws which prohibit discrimination in the buying of milk, cream, or butterfat—with the intention or for the purpose of destroying or injuring the business of a competitor. Some states extend the prohibition to the buying of agricultural products typically produced within their borders (Arkansas, Idaho, Michigan, Minnesota). Florida has a special law with respect to price discrimination in the sale of commercial fertilizer, and Kansas has a special law prohibiting price discrimination in the sale of news and news reports.

In general, it may be said that the special statutes and many of the general statutes against price discrimination have been drafted with reference to a particular problem rather than to a broad prohibition on discrimination injurious to competition, whether it occurs in buying or selling. If the state governments are to attack the problems of price discrimination as they generally exist in business, it is probable that most states will need to reëxamine their present statutes.

THE ATTEMPT OF MINNESOTA TO PROHIBIT PRICE DISCRIMINATION WITHOUT REGARD TO INTENT OR PURPOSE

A Minnesota statute of 1909 prohibited local price discrimination whenever it was done "with the intention of creating a monopoly or destroying the business of a competitor." The difficulty of proving "intent" or "purpose" led the legislature in 1923 to amend the law by making geographic price discrimination illegal, *without regard to intent or motive*. A *given* buyer of farm products, for example, was required to pay *his customers* the same price for like commodities at all points of purchase, after making proper allowance for transportation costs. The paying of "higher" prices in one local area "to meet competition" while paying "lower" prices elsewhere was not permitted.

In 1924 the state of Minnesota brought action under the new antidiscrimination statute against the Fairmont Creamery Company, a large centralized

[4] *Central Lumber Co. v. South Dakota,* 226 U.S. 157 (1912).

creamery located in Sioux City, Iowa. This creamery maintained buying stations for butterfat at various points in Minnesota and was engaged in paying higher prices at certain points than at others, after making due allowance for transportation costs. In attempting to justify this action, the company contended that freedom of contract, guaranteed by the Constitution, gave it the right to pay higher prices in one locality as compared with another, in order to "meet" the buying competition of local creameries. The state of Minnesota, on the other hand, replied that freedom of contract is not absolute, and that the statute was enacted to prevent the very practice employed by the company.

The Supreme Court of Minnesota in 1925 upheld the validity of the anti-discrimination statute on the ground that the act was designed to prevent the use of price discrimination by large centralized creameries to injure locally owned coöperative and independent creameries.

A centralized creamery [said the Court], supplied with ample capital and facilities, has the ability and meets the temptation to destroy competition at a buying station by overbidding, absorbing the resultant losses, if any, through the profits of its general business, and, when competition is ended, to buy on a noncompetitive basis. If it does all this successfully, it has a monopoly, and may or may not treat producers justly. The statute seeks to prevent the destruction of competition by forbidding overbidding unless the dealer makes prices at other buying points correspond after proper allowances for the cost of transportation. If the statute is obeyed, destroying competition is expensive.[5]

Upon losing the decision in the state supreme court, the Fairmont Company appealed its case to the United States Supreme Court. A divided Court, with Holmes, Brandeis, and Stone dissenting, held that the state could not so restrict the "freedom of contract." Since the statute prohibited discrimination "irrespective of motive," the Court declared that it was "an obvious attempt to destroy plaintiff in error's liberty to enter into normal contracts, long regarded, not only as essential to the freedom of trade and commerce, but also as beneficial to the public."[6]

A study of price determination in open markets indicates that the Court was in error in taking the view that business done at *discriminatory prices* is the "usual way heretofore regarded as both moral and beneficial to the public." The "usual way" of doing business which has moral, legal, and economic sanction is in open markets, with *each* trader treating *his* customers essentially alike at any given time. In the *Fairmont Creamery* case there were no competitive markets for cream at the various collecting stations along the same rail line, as the Court assumed. At some points the company had the advantage of a monopoly condition, and at others the presence of an independent creamery made necessary the payment of a higher price.

[5] *State* v. *Fairmont Creamery Co.*, 202 N.W. 714, 716 (1925).
[6] *Fairmont Creamery Co.* v. *Minnesota*, 274 U.S. 1, 9 (1927).

The method of competition accepted by a divided Court in the *Fairmont Creamery* case has long been condemned by many economists as unfair. With the advantage of local monopoly power in one area, a large buyer is in a position to pay unduly low prices at certain points and artificially high prices at others. Under such conditions, a small plant operating in one area only does not have a chance to survive on its merits. Freedom of contract is an essential institution of capitalism, and buying and selling *in a central market* should be given the utmost freedom of expression. Whenever a locally separate buyer or seller, however, enjoys degrees of local monopoly power, it may be necessary for government to restrict the exercise of this power in the interest of preserving competition.

ANTITRUST LAW ENFORCEMENT AT THE STATE LEVEL

A survey made by the author indicates that only four states are actively engaged in enforcing their antitrust laws. These states are Texas, Missouri, Wisconsin, and New York. The Office of the Attorney General of Texas gave the following summary of its antitrust activity as of 1954.

You are advised that there have been numerous antitrust cases filed by the Attorney General during the past ten years, but unfortunately very few of these cases ever reach the appellate courts. This is due to the desire of companies prosecuted for antitrust violations to avoid any unfavorable publicity that might result from the public trial of such suits. As a result, most antitrust prosecutions in this state are ordinarily settled and penalties paid and a permanent injunction issued at the trial court level.

One of the leading cases which has reached our appellate courts in recent years and which has established the basic standard of pleading and proof under the Texas antitrust laws is *State v. Ford Motor Company*, 169 S.W. 2d 504, affirmed 142 Tex. 5, 175 S.W. 2d 230. In this case the State was successful. . . .

Perhaps the most significant antitrust prosecution now pending in our appellate courts is *State v. Arkansas Fuel Oil Company*. This action was instituted against the ten major oil companies doing business in Texas for a combination to fix and maintain uniform and non-competitive prices on tank wagon gasoline sales. . . .

You are further advised that during the past ten years almost every type of good and commodity manufactured, distributed or sold in this state has come under the scrutiny of this office. Among these are included, for example, the milk and ice cream distributors, clothing, drugs, automotive accessories, musical instruments, soft drinks, sewing machines, office supplies, luggage, liquor, radios, washing machines, air conditioning units, vacuum cleaners, and electrical appliances of every kind. At the present time we have numerous other businesses under investigation which will doubtless result in antitrust suits. . . .

There is continued local support in this state for a vigorous enforcement of the antitrust laws. This office, as it has in past administrations, is continuing to make investigations of all antitrust complaints which come to our attention.

The Attorney General of Missouri wrote in 1954 as follows:

The Office of the Attorney General has instituted a number of antitrust cases within the past several years. The cases fell into two principal categories: (1) vertical price fixing by manufacturers and (2) horizontal price fixing primarily engaged in by retailers.

The business groups affected by the cases involved manufacturers and bottlers of soft drinks, distillers of liquors, drug supply houses, automotive accessories manufacturers and distributors, fertilizer manufacturers, and retailers of liquified petroleum gas.

ANTITRUST ACTIVITY IN WISCONSIN

In 1947 the Wisconsin legislature appropriated funds to create an antitrust division for the enforcement of the state antitrust laws. These laws, for the most part, had not been enforced since their enactment in 1893. The newly created Antitrust Division commenced its activity in November 1947. During the period from November 1947 to February 1951, the Division received 68 complaints on alleged monopolistic practices in the sale of some 31 different commodities, as well as 15 complaints on monopolistic activity in the service trades.

An example of antitrust work in Wisconsin is found in the action taken against the Retail Gasoline Dealers Association of Milwaukee, Inc. The complaint alleged that the defendants had agreed to fix and increase the retail sale price of gasoline. This case was successfully prosecuted, and a favorable decision was won by the state on May 11, 1949.[7] (See also Fig. 40.)

In 1954, Mr. George F. Sieker, attorney in charge of the Antitrust Division, reported on antitrust activities as follows:

The state antitrust program in Wisconsin is continuing without abatement. We have at the present time about 30 matters under active investigation and 10 other matters in various stages of court and administrative proceedings. Since we have only two attorneys, neither one devoting full time to antitrust, that is a little more than we can comfortably handle.

While our cases are characteristically not as large as the better-known federal antitrust cases, neither are they so small as to be insignificant. For example, we are currently prosecuting four grocery chains (A & P, Kroger, National Tea and Piggly-Wiggly) and six dairies for unfair trade practices in the granting and inducing of secret rebates in the Madison area. We have just successfully completed a price fixing case against six dairies in Racine and recently obtained an injunction (and forfeitures) against five dairies and a labor union in Manitowoc.

At the present time, we have investigations pending in about twenty different industries including construction, building supplies, chemicals, sporting goods, beverages, wood products and many others. That we have been conservative in filing complaints is shown by the fact that since the division and program were initiated by Mr. Bessman in 1947, we have won

---

[7] *Wisconsin* v. *Retail Gasoline Dealers Association of Milwaukee,* Case No. 213-601, Circuit Court, Milwaukee County, State of Wisconsin, May 11, 1949.

every case which we have commenced. Most of them have been by consent judgments, but several have gone up to the Supreme Court of Wisconsin.

A new development has been that private damage suits and claims are beginning to arise from state antitrust prosecutions, following the federal pattern.

Sock Him Again if You Find an Opening!

FIG. 40. A cartoon from the *Milwaukee Journal* (1949) illustrating the enthusiastic popular support of the action taken by the state attorney general of Wisconsin against the retail gasoline dealers of Milwaukee. (By permission.)

We have so far escaped any major jurisdictional problems and any jurisdictional conflicts. We take the position that even though a conspiracy or combination in restraint of trade may be interstate in its operation, if part of it is executed in Wisconsin and affects or restrains local commerce, it is a violation of our state antitrust law. So far no one has successfully challenged our jurisdiction, although we call upon out-of-state corporations which do business in Wisconsin within the meaning of the antitrust law, to furnish us with information and stand trial where called upon.

The great majority of the complaints we receive are disposed of informally. Letters, conferences, industry-wide conferences, investigations, and explanations result in most of the violations found being corrected before they have gone very far.

ANTITRUST ENFORCEMENT IN CALIFORNIA

The state of California has a comprehensive antitrust statute, called the Cartwright Act, which was adopted in 1907. It covers local commerce, and its declared purpose is "to promote free competition in commerce, and all classes of business." In 1909 an amendment to the act was adopted which permitted price-fixing agreements and associations which were designed to secure a "reasonable profit." Although this amendment was generally believed to be unconstitutional, it served to discourage state prosecution, and local monopolistic agreements appear to have flourished with impunity. Finally, in 1946, the Supreme Court of California, in the *Speegle* case, held that the amendment was invalid.[8] This decision restored the full force and validity of the act and made it possible for the attorney general of California to attack any and all monopolistic restraints in local commerce.

Soon after the Cartwright Act was restored to full force and effect, numerous complaints were filed with the state attorney general, alleging the existence of monopolistic abuses. Nothing was done to provide relief, and appeals were thereupon made to the federal Department of Justice. On January 12, 1948, Mr. John F. Sonnett, assistant attorney general, Department of Justice, went to California and openly called upon Mr. Fred N. Howser, attorney general for California, to enforce the state antitrust law.[9] Mr. Sonnett pointed out that antitrust violations in California were widespread. During the past ten years, he declared, the federal government itself had prosecuted some 132 cases in California—an average of one major *interstate* case per month. During this same period, he alleged, the state authorities had taken no action whatsoever.

Subsequently, the attorney general and the district attorney for San Francisco County of California brought action against an association of janitorial contractors. The proceeding, entitled, *People v. Building Maintenance Contractors' Association*, was a civil action. The prosecution was successful, and judgment for the state was affirmed by the Supreme Court of California, December 11, 1953 (41 A.C. 737).

GENERAL INDIFFERENCE TO ANTITRUST
ENFORCEMENT AT THE STATE LEVEL

Antitrust enforcement activity in states other than Texas, Missouri, Wisconsin, and New York appears to be largely or entirely in a moribund condition. The attorneys general in virtually all of the other states reported as follows: "Antitrust activity in our state is dormant."

"Little public interest has been shown in this state, as is demonstrated by the fact that the legislature has never enacted an antitrust law."

[8] *Speegle* v. *Board of Fire Underwriters*, 29 Cal. (2d) 34 (1946).
[9] *Congressional Record*, April 6, 1948, p. 4242.

"Legislature has refused to appropriate funds requested for enforcement of antitrust laws."

"We have no antitrust litigation at all at this time. You may classify it as you like."

"No cases have ever been brought under the antitrust laws of this state."

"With great displeasure I have to report that state antitrust activities do not exist."

"Only one action has been brought under the state antitrust act in the last ten years."

"We do not have any state antitrust laws, and hence we cannot supply you with information on enforcement activity."

"We do not have antitrust legislation in our state, and no antitrust prosecutions are conducted."

"We would characterize the antitrust activity in this state as being watchful but neither vigorous nor very active."

"To the best of my knowledge, no suits have been brought within the last ten years involving the act."

"Antitrust law enforcement is inactive." This, by far, was the answer most frequently given.

"Antitrust enforcement in our state is non-existent."

"We have brought no antitrust cases in the last ten years."

"Inasmuch as there exist no antitrust laws in our state, we have made no prosecutions." Actually, this particular state has a statutory provision against "any combination or agreement . . . for the purpose of fixing or maintaining a higher price . . . for ice, coal, or any other necessity of life."

"To our knowledge no antitrust cases have been brought in this state during the past ten years."

"We have no antitrust law in West Virginia."

"Our office is not set up to obtain information on antitrust law violations."

"Our enforcement activity is lackadaisical."

"There have been no antitrust cases brought in the state of Tennessee within the past ten years, and I would say that there exists no present sentiment favoring antitrust litigation."

"I suppose that antitrust activity in this state could be characterized as passive."

"No antitrust cases have been brought during the past ten years."

"Our last case was brought in 1924—the *Fairmont Creamery* case."

PRIVATE DAMAGE SUITS AT THE STATE LEVEL

Few persons seem to know that the treble damage provision is a common feature of the state antitrust laws. If, and when, this information becomes more widely known, it is possible that private suits will become an important factor in state antitrust law enforcement. Private damage suits are a useful device in securing antitrust law enforcement; however, primary reliance should be placed on action by a state enforcement agency.

The Idaho antitrust law contains a typical treble-damage provision. It provides that "Any person who shall be injured in his business or property . . . by reason of anything forbidden or declared unlawful . . . may sue therefor . . . and shall recover threefold the damages by him sustained and the costs of suit, including a reasonable attorney's fee." The sales-below-cost statues of nine states also permit the recovery of treble damages. Any person, it is usually provided, who is injured by a violation of the act may sue for three times the actual damages sustained. State statutes having this provision are those of Arkansas, Colorado, Kentucky, Maine, Michigan, Montana, Oregon, Utah, and West Virginia.

The Indiana antitrust statute has an unusual provision which may have possibilities of relief for industrial buyers and consumers who are faced with monopolistic pricing in local trades—as in milk, cement, bricks, gasoline, caskets, funeral services, cleaning and pressing, and the laundering of clothes. The statute provides that "any person or persons or corporations that may be injured or damaged . . . may sue and recover . . . the full consideration or sum paid by him or them for any good, wares, merchandise or articles the sale of which is controlled by such combination or trust." This provision is also found in the antitrust laws of several other states.

TABLE 33.   State Antitrust Statutes.

State	Antitrust Laws Prohibiting Monopoly, Restraint of Trade, Restraint of Competition, Price Fixing, and/or Limitation of Output		Special Antitrust Laws Applicable to Designated Industries	Anti-Discrimination Statutes	
	Constitutional Provision	Statutory Provision		General	Special
1. Alabama	x	x	x	none	none
2. Arizona	x	x	x	none	x
3. Arkansas	x	x	x	x	x
4. California	none	x	x	x	x
5. Colorado	none	none[a]	x	x	none
6. Connecticut	x	x	x	none	none
7. Delaware	none	none	x	x	none
8. Florida	none	x	x	x	x
9. Georgia	x	x	x	none	none
10. Idaho	x	x	x	x	x
11. Illinois	x	x	x	none	none
12. Indiana	none	x	x	none	x
13. Iowa	x	x	x	x	x
14. Kansas	none	x	x	x	x
15. Kentucky	x	none	x	x	x
16. Louisiana	x	x	x	x	none
17. Maine	none	x	x	none	none
18. Maryland	x	none	x	none	none
19. Massachusetts	none	x	x	x	none
20. Michigan	none	x	x	none	x
21. Minnesota	none	x	x	x	x

TABLE 33.   State Antitrust Statutes.   (*Continued*)

State	Antitrust Laws Prohibiting Monopoly, Restraint of Trade, Restraint of Competition, Price Fixing, and/or Limitation of Output		Special Antitrust Laws Applicable to Designated Industries	Anti-Discrimination Statutes	
	Constitutional Provision	Statutory Provision		General	Special
22. Mississippi	x	x	x	x	x
23. Missouri	none	x	x	x	x
24. Montana	x	x	x	x	x
25. Nebraska	x	x	x	x	x
26. Nevada	none	x[b]	x	none	none
27. New Hampshire	x	x	x	none	none
28. New Jersey	none	x[c]	x	none	none
29. New Mexico	x	x	x	none	x
30. New York	none	x	x	none	x
31. North Carolina	x	x	x	x	none
32. North Dakota	x	x	x	x	x
33. Ohio	none	x	x	none	x
34. Oklahoma	x	x	x	x	none
35. Oregon	none	none	x	x	x
36. Pennsylvania	none	none[b]	x	none	x
37. Rhode Island	none	x[d]	x	none	none
38. South Carolina	x	x	x	x	x
39. South Dakota	x	x	x	x	x
40. Tennessee	x	x	x	none	x
41. Texas	x	x	x	none	x
42. Utah	x	x	x	x	x
43. Vermont	none	x	x	none	x
44. Virginia	x	x	x	x	none
45. Washington	x	x	x	x	none
46. West Virginia	none	none	x	none	none
47. Wisconsin	none	x	x	x	x
48. Wyoming	x	x	x	x	x
Total	27	41	48	27	28

[a] The Colorado antitrust law was declared to be unconstitutional in *Cline* v. *Frink Dairy Co.*, 274 U.S. 445 (1927), as not providing for due process of law. It has not been reënacted to meet the constitutional objection.
[b] Nevada and Pennsylvania have general statutes prohibiting conspiracies to cheat or defraud any person or corporation.
[c] The New Jersey statute applies only to the corporate acquisition of stock in other corporations where the effect may be to substantially lessen competition.
[d] The Rhode Island statute provides for the prosecution of offenses which are illegal at common law. Source of data: *State Antitrust Laws* and *State Price Control Legislation*, prepared by the Marketing Laws Survey, Works Progress Administration (Washington, 1940).

REASONS FOR THE NONENFORCEMENT OF STATE ANTITRUST STATUTES

It is sometimes said that state antitrust law enforcement is largely or entirely nonexistent because there are no problems of monopolistic restraints, as there were when the statutes were adopted. The available evidence on monopolistic practices, as well as antitrust activity in Texas, Wisconsin, Missouri, and New York, however, points to the contrary. At the present time, most of the state antitrust laws are "sleeping beauties" (1) because the state legislatures have failed to provide funds for enforcement and (2) because they have failed to create effective machinery for enforcement.

The condition of antitrust-law enforcement at the state level is hurtful evidence for those who advocate and believe in states' rights as against federal intervention. Today, for the most part, there is little or no protection for consumers against excessive, monopolistic prices in important areas of *intrastate* commerce (see Fig. 41).

FIG. 41. A cartoon from a labor bulletin urging the state attorney general to enforce the antitrust law in Washington state. (By permission.)

A basic reason for the failure of state legislatures to provide funds for enforcement is the fact that often many state politicians secure the support of local industries in winning their elections. Thereupon, such officials are not in a position to attack the people and business firms who aided them. In many states persons pulling the strings in state politics do not want the state antitrust laws enforced. How can this situation be corrected? At the present time, an opportunity exists for young, ambitious lawyers to take the case of state antitrust law enforcement to the people by running for the office of attorney general. Young men and women having a broad interest in politics also have an opportunity to seek election to the state legislatures on the issue of preserving and enforcing the basic principles of the American economic system.

If the state governments, generally, do not take steps to provide for a vigorous enforcement of their antitrust laws, it would appear that consumers will face a continuing problem of high costs of living in fields where monopolistic practices exist. Some groups of consumers may be able to maintain their relative position by union activity in pressing for higher wage demands. A great many consumers, however, have no alternative but to pay the noncompetitive prices. Such prices inevitably mean a lower level of living, for production under conditions of monopoly is restricted to amounts which can be sold at the prices which sellers would *like* to get.

SUGGESTIONS FOR FURTHER READING

"Cartwright Act—California's Sleeping Beauty," *Stanford Law Review*, December, 1949, pp. 200–210

Cassady, Ralph, Jr., "Legal Aspects of Price Discrimination: State Law," *Journal of Marketing*, April, 1947, pp. 377–389.

Davies, Joseph E., *Trust Laws and Unfair Competition*, Bureau of Corporations, U.S. Department of Commerce (Washington, 1915).

Geffen, Ralph J., "Antitrust Law in Wisconsin," *Wisconsin Law Review*, July, 1951, pp. 657–684.

Hall, Ford P., *Government and Business* (New York, 1949).

Markham, J. W., "The Effectiveness of the Antitrust Laws: Comment," *American Economic Review*, March, 1950, pp. 167–169.

Owens, Richard N., *Business Organization and Combination* (New York, 1951).

Seager, Henry R., and Gulick, Charles A., *Trust and Corporation Problems* (New York, 1929).

State Antitrust Laws, prepared by the Marketing Laws Survey. Supt. of Documents (Washington, 1940).

State Price Control Legislation, prepared by the Marketing Laws Survey. Supt. of Documents (Washington, 1940).

CHAPTER 21

Resale Price-Maintenance Legislation

Many state governments have enacted laws for the declared purposes of preventing loss-leader selling and sales below cost. These laws are variously known as (1) "fair-trade" or resale price maintenance acts and (2) "unfair-practices" acts. In the present chapter we shall consider the nature and purposes of resale price-control legislation, as well as the principal arguments for and against its application.

FEATURES OF RESALE PRICE MAINTENANCE

A "fair-trade" law makes it possible for a manufacturer or distributor of products bearing the "trade-mark, brand, or name of the producer" to fix by contract the minimum or actual wholesale and retail prices of such products as they move on to the final consumers. Such a control of prices is called *resale* price maintenance. In the fair-trade laws of 24 states the *owner* of the trademark (a manufacturer) *or* his duly authorized distributor may initiate a fair-trade contract. Under the fair-trade laws of the remaining 21 states, only the trademark owner may initiate a fair-trade contract.

Although New Jersey enacted a permissive resale price-maintenance law as early as 1914, it was not until the adoption of the California Fair Trade Act of 1931 and its significant amendment of 1933 that states generally adopted laws legalizing resale price control. At the present time, all states except three—Missouri, Texas, and Vermont—and the District of Columbia have statutes permitting the control of resale prices.

A fair-trade act is said to provide for "vertical" price control. This means that a price agreement may be made between two sellers at different levels, that is, between a manufacturer and a wholesaler, a manufacturer and a retailer, or a wholesaler and a retailer.

Resale price-control laws do not provide for enforcement by the public authorities. Any legal action must be taken by individuals or corporations who believe that they have been injured. In some instances, manufacturers, such as the General Electric Co., establish special departments to enforce their fair-trade programs. In other instances, trade associations assess dealers for funds to police the programs and prosecute violations. The enforcement of resale-price arrangements is based primarily *on persuasion*. Every effort is

461

made to convince low-profit sellers that fair trade is necessary and beneficial. When persuasion fails, resort is made to litigation.[1]

Experts on fair trade advise their clients that a fair-trade merchandising system requires rigid enforcement. If established prices are not systematically enforced, "discount houses" will thrive and consumers will feel that they are being gouged by other retailers.

BACKGROUND FOR THE ENACTMENT OF RESALE PRICE-MAINTENANCE LAWS

The growing sale of specialty products with distinctive brands and trademarks, particularly after 1900, gave rise to efforts on the part of certain manufacturers to control the resale prices of their products. Since such products were often unique and distinctive, their manufacturers frequently had power to manage prices; and attempts were made in certain cases to enhance profits by fixing prices at the wholesale and retail levels. Government agencies charged with enforcing the antitrust laws, however, took the position that vertical agreements to maintain resale prices were an illegal restraint of trade.

The leading case declaring resale price contracts illegal was one involving the Dr. Miles Medical Company. This company had made contracts with over 400 wholesale dealers and some 25,000 retailers to maintain stipulated prices at wholesale and at retail. Each violation of the contract carried a penalty of $25 and the prospect of a cessation of business relations. The defendant was accused of securing supplies for sale at less than the stipulated prices; and action was brought to test the validity of the restrictive agreements.

The Court in the *Miles* case held that resale price contracts were in violation of the Sherman Act in that they substantially lessened or eliminated competition among the wholesalers and the retailers of the Miles products. In the words of the Court, "The complainant having sold its product at prices satisfactory to itself, the public is entitled to whatever advantage may be derived from competition in the subsequent traffic."[2] The Federal Trade Commission Act, passed in 1914 to outlaw "unfair methods of competition," was also interpreted to prohibit resale price contracts, and it further supported the rule of law announced in the *Miles* case.[3]

Following the *Miles* decision, manufacturers interested in establishing re-

[1] Penalties for selling below fair-trade prices can be severe. In 1953, Sunbeam Corporation sued Masters, Inc., New York, a leading "discount house," for selling certain appliances below fair-trade prices. The court ordered Masters to pay Sunbeam $8284.89 as follows: $330 for net profits on cut-price sales; $3404.56 for auditor's fees paid in examining defendant's books; $3900.33 for the legal services of Sunbeam's attorneys; $650 for Sunbeam's investigating costs. It also ordered Masters to pay $1316 for stenographic services and $6930 as a fee for the Special Master in Equity who heard the case. The total cost, not including Masters' own legal fees, was $16,530.89.

[2] *Dr. Miles Medical Company* v. *John D. Park and Sons*, 220 U.S. 273, 409 (1911).

[3] *F.T.C.* v. *Beech-Nut Packing Co.*, 257 U.S. 441 (1922).

sale price control in interstate commerce usually sought to attain it in one of the following ways:

1. By refusing to sell to dealers who act independently on prices.
2. By selling through sales agencies owned by the manufacturer. Inasmuch as the products are sold in its own branches, a manufacturer is able to exercise complete control over resale prices.
3. By shipping goods to dealers on consignment. In consignment selling, an owner transfers goods to an agent with power to sell but retains title until the goods are sold. A consignor has the legal right to control resale prices if the consignee is in truth an agent. *U.S. vs. Masonite Corp.*, 316 U.S. 265 (1942).
4. By distributing products through exclusive dealerships. Exclusive sales arrangements are legal, but the courts have held that they cannot be used as a means for resale price control. *U.S. v. Bausch and Lomb Optical Co.*, 321 U.S. 707 (1944).

The control of resale prices by refusing to sell to dealers who do not follow suggested prices was given qualified support by the Supreme Court in the *Colgate* case (1919). In this case, the Court declared, "In the absence of any purpose to create or maintain a monopoly, the [Sherman] act does not restrict the long-recognized right of trader or manufacturer engaged in an entirely private business, freely to exercise his own independent discretion as to parties with whom he will deal. And, of course, he may announce in advance the circumstances under which he will refuse to sell."[4] Although the *Colgate* decision has not be overruled, it has been substantially whittled away. In a number of cases, the courts have held that *in selling* and *in acquiring* goods to be sold at specified prices, the parties enter into an illegal agreement to fix prices. Manufacturers, however, continue to suggest resale prices, and they continue to announce their refusal to sell to those who do not comply. Buyers, moreover, do not have the right to compel manufacturers to sell for cash. As a practical matter, therefore, distributors have little incentive to protest a plan of suggested prices if they want to get the products of a particular seller. (See also Chap. 11, pp. 231–233.)

THE LEGALIZATION OF RESALE PRICE MAINTENANCE

Refusal to sell enables a manufacturer to exercise a considerable degree of control over the resale prices of *their distributors* (wholesalers). In the case of retail trade, however, the number of retailers makes it difficult for most manufacturers to deal *directly* with them. Competition at the retail level has always been difficult to control because of the large number of independent sellers involved. Experience with resale price control, however, had shown that identical retail prices for trademarked products could be secured by means of resale price contracts. Increasingly, therefore, manufacturers of branded merchandise and trade association leaders in the retail field—particularly in drugs—turned their efforts toward securing a legalization of re-

[4] *U.S. v. Colgate and Co.*, 250 U.S. 300, 307 (1919).

sale price maintenance. Since the economic position of wholesalers is closely related to the profit returns of retailers, they too, joined in advocating resale price legislation.

The impact of the depression in 1930 and the growth of chain and cut-rate stores offering limited services and lower prices crystallized the efforts of independent retailers and wholesalers into a broad and powerful movement. From 1929 to 1933, the Department of Commerce reports, chain stores and mail order houses increased their share of total retail sales from 21 percent to 27 percent.

The approach taken by independent retailers and wholesalers in their effort to restrict the competition of chain stores and mail-order houses was that of using price-maintenance contracts drawn by the manufacturers of trade-marked articles. A large number of the items sold at retail are trademarked; and increasingly it was realized that if resale price maintenance could be legalized, a considerable amount of price competition could be restricted at the retail level. This idea was particularly sponsored by the retail and wholesale trade associations in California, as well as by the California Retail Drug Alliance. Similar organizations in other states also became the principal groups which actively and aggressively sought the enactment of resale price-maintenance legislation in their respective areas.

The first of the new fair-trade acts was passed by the California legislature in 1931 and amended in 1933. This statute legalized the use of resale price contracts in intrastate commerce on any commodity (1) "which bears the trade-mark, brand, or name of the producer or owner" and (2) "which is in fair and open competition with commodities of the same general class produced by others." The agreed-upon prices were to prevail at all times, except for (1) closing-out sales, (2) the sale of damaged and deteriorated goods, and (3) the sale of goods by order of a court.

The 1933 amendment to the California statute added the highly significant provision that a single agreement to fix the resale price of a trademarked product is applicable to all other like sellers even though they do not sign a price-maintenance contract.[5] This amendment, which came to be known as the "nonsigners' clause," makes it possible for a manufacturer to make a resale price agreement with a *single* wholesaler or retailer and thereupon require *all* other wholesalers or retailers in the state to charge the same resale price for the given product. Any distributor having notice of the contractual arrangement and not conforming to the prices so fixed is at once subject to legal suit on the charge of unfair competition and price cutting (see Fig. 42). The nonsigners' clause made the resale price-control laws a potent and most

---

[5] The 1933 California amendment reads as follows: "Wilfully and knowingly advertising, offering for sale or selling any commodity at less than the price stipulated in any contract entered into pursuant to the provision of Section 1 of the Act, whether the person so advertising, offering for sale or selling is or is not a party to such contract, is unfair competition and is actionable at the suit of any person damaged thereby." *California Statutes*, 1933, chap. 260. This clause is included in almost identical form in nearly all the various state acts.

effective method for bringing about *horizontal* price fixing at the retail level. In view of this fact, the California statute and amendment of 1933 were rapidly adopted by other states at the request and importunity of organized trade groups.

Since the resale price-control laws applied only to intrastate transactions, a powerful organized pressure was put upon Congress to legalize the making of resale price-maintenance contracts in *interstate* commerce. This was an indispensable step in providing for the control of prices at the local level, for most trademarked products are manufactured in one locality and sold

AIREX FAIR TRADE NOTICE

Notice is hereby given that effective immediately the complete line of AIREX SPINNING EQUIPMENT, manufactured by Airex Corporation, New York City, is fair traded at current catalog list prices for the State of Washington. Dealers and jobbers will be governed accordingly.

AIREX CORPORATION
McCune-Merifield Co.
Sales Representatives
Seattle

Fɪɢ. 42. Copy of a fair-trade notice under the nonsigners' clause published in a metropolitan newspaper. Some manufacturers give "notice" by means of a letter sent to each wholesaler (jobber) and to each retailer. The Airex Corporation manufactures fishing reels and equipment.

throughout the nation. In response to the demands of state and local trade associations, Congress in 1937 enacted the Miller-Tydings Act, amending the Sherman Act to exempt resale price agreements in interstate commerce when commodities are shipped into states in which such contracts are legal. The amendment further declared that the making of resale price contracts shall not be regarded as unfair competition under Section 5 of the Federal Trade Commission Act.

THE SUPREME COURT SUSTAINS RESALE PRICE MAINTENANCE

The first and leading decision of the Supreme Court on the validity of the state fair-trade acts came in the case of *Old Dearborn Distributing Company* v. *Seagram Distillers Corporation*, decided on December 7, 1936.[6] In the *Dearborn* and related cases, the Court upheld the validity of the Illinois and

[6] 299 U.S. 183 (1936). Other cases on appeal at the same time were *McNeil* v. *Joseph Triner Corp.*, 299 U.S. 183 (1936) (Illinois); and *Pep Boys, Manny, Moe, and Jack* v. *Pyroil Sales Co.*, and *C. G. Kunsman* v. *Max Factor and Co.*, 299 U.S. 198 (1936) (California).

California fair-trade laws in their entirety. The effect of the decisions was to bring about an enactment of fair-trade laws in most of the remaining states; and at the present time only Missouri, Texas, Vermont, and the District of Columbia have no laws providing for resale price maintenance.

The *Dearborn* case involved the retail sale of bottled whiskey at prices below those stipulated in a resale price-maintenance contract made under the fair-trade law of Illinois. An important issue was the validity of the "non-signers' clause," which makes a retailer subject to resale price control even though he does not sign a contract. Justice Sutherland, speaking for the Court, found no fault with this provision in the case of a dealer "who has had definite information respecting such contractual restriction and who, with such knowledge, nevertheless proceeds wilfully to resell in disregard of it." Said Justice Sutherland, "Appellants were not obliged to buy." Moreover, the Court stated, the restriction on price applied specifically to the sale of products which were identified by the trademark, brand, or name of the manufacturer, and the aim of the law is to protect this property of the producer.[7]

In the further development of its decision, the Court emphasized that a manufacturer of branded products still retains possession of the trademark and good will even though the commodity has been sold. This fact, the Court stated, gives the trademark owner a continuing interest in the commodity. In the words of the Court, "Appellants own the commodity; they do not own the mark or the good will that the mark symbolizes. And good will is property in a very real sense, injury to which, like injury to any other species of property, is a proper subject for legislation."

AN APPRAISAL OF THE DEARBORN DECISION

From a public point of view the decision in the *Dearborn* case has many shortcomings. Although it may be true, in the first place, that a retailer is not obliged to buy a trademarked product, the fact is that most or all of the leading products handled in a given line of business (i.e., those providing most of the sales) may be subject to resale price maintenance. Also, the public demand may be such that particular brands must be handled if a retailer is to conduct his business.

Secondly, the Court in its decision emphasized the need *of manufacturers* for legislation to protect the good will embodied in their trademarked products. Actually, the organized drive for resale price legislation came largely from independent retailers and wholesalers who were interested in restricting price competition at the retail level. Available evidence indicates, moreover, that in some cases it is the organized retailers who take the lead and bring pressure on manufacturers to adopt resale price control. Indeed, in some cases organized wholesalers, or wholesalers and retailers, employ fair-trade legislation to fix resale prices without the consent or desire of manufacturers who make the trademarked products. A well-known druggist,

[7] 299 U.S. 193–194.

operating retail stores in Virginia and the District of Columbia, testified in 1952 that "Virtually every retail druggist within any of the 45 states having fair-trade laws belongs to a retail drug association, and each of these associations has a committee known as a fair-trade committee. This committee is used for the purpose of coercing manufacturers into fixing the price on his product."[8] Since the *Dearborn* decision, the Department of Justice has initiated and won a number of cases against organized retailers who have coerced, forced, and intimidated manufacturers into using price maintenance agreements.[9]

THE COMPLAINTS OF INDEPENDENT RETAILERS

In defending their pleas for resale price-control legislation, retail trade associations raised a cry against the use of leaders and loss leaders by chain stores seeking to increase their sales volume. A *leader* is defined as a product offered for sale at less than its usual or customary price for the purpose of inducing customers to buy it as well as other articles in the seller's shop. In most cases, products used as leaders are advertised, trademarked items, for the quality of such goods is fairly well standardized and consumers are quick to respond to slight variations in price. A *loss leader*, on the other hand, is variously defined as a product which is sold (1) below the net invoice or replacement cost *plus* the average or usual cost of doing business or (2) below the net invoice or replacement cost (also called "laid-down" cost).

Sometimes retail sellers complain that loss leaders are being used when the prices quoted by another seller are below *their* net purchase cost plus *their* average cost of doing business. This is clearly a fallacious view, for the average cost of any given firm may differ substantially from that of other firms. Frequently, the term "loss leader" is also applied to products sold below the particular seller's usual markup. This is likewise fallacious, for the idea of price competition means that a seller will reduce his markup, when necessary, to attract customers. It is also unsound to insist that a given seller apply his average cost of selling all goods to the cost of selling a given line. This view disregards differences in the rate of turnover of the various lines, as well as differences in the cost of selling the various individual lines. *Products sold at less than net invoice or replacement cost are clearly loss leaders.*

1. THE PROBLEM OF SALES AT REDUCED PRICES

There is considerable evidence to indicate that a principal problem faced by independent retailers seeking resale price controls was not the problem of loss leaders, as such, but rather that of genuine price competition with chain and limited-service stores. The Federal Trade Commission's investigation of

[8] Testimony of Samuel Rosenthal, Hearings before the Committee on the Judiciary, House of Representatives, *Resale Price Maintenance*, 82nd Congress, second session, Serial 12, 1952, p. 432.

[9] Report of the Committee on the Judiciary, *Amending the Sherman Act with Respect to Resale Price Maintenance*, 82nd Congress, second session, House Report 1516, 1952, pp. 20–21, 31–39.

chain stores, for example, revealed that most chain store officials were opposed to the use of loss leaders.[10] A real problem faced by independents, however, was the fact that chain stores were able to sell products at generally lower prices because of the economies of large-scale buying and selling and the offering of limited services.

It is truly disconcerting to find that other sellers are trying to attract customers by quoting prices below those usually or customarily secured. This, however, is the essence of price competition. Sellers must recover their total costs from their total sales; and if costs are not fully allocated to some items, they must be secured from higher prices on other products. This fact tends to keep competitive sellers from reducing certain prices more than is necessary to secure the desired volume.

In regard to the problem of leader and loss-leader selling, the Federal Trade Commission concluded its survey with the statement, "The subject of 'loss-leader selling' seems to be surrounded by considerably more emotionalism and wishful thinking than actual information based on scientific study."[11] The fact of the matter was that in a great many instances independent retailers were confronted with the competition of other sellers having lower costs and offering limited services. These sellers were willing to reduce prices to secure increased volume and provide a selling outlet for their goods and services. When such rivalry is conducted in a open and nondiscriminatory manner, it is fully consistent with a policy of competition. If a free-enterprise system is to be maintained, it must always be possible for newcomers to enter a field and compete with established firms by offering merchandise at lower markups.

2. The Real Problem—Injurious Price Discriminations

Although chain and other limited-service stores brought new and socially desirable economies to the merchandising field, their behavior was not, and is not, always fair and socially desirable. Three evils, in particular, exist. First, large retail chains frequently secure discriminatory lower purchase prices. In its special study on chain stores (1934), the Federal Trade Commission reported that the chains had followed a persistent policy of seeking out and demanding special and unwarranted price concessions.[12] The Robinson-Patman Act was enacted in 1936 in an effort to curb the abuse of injurious quantity price discriminations (see Chap. 16).

A second evil is that of commodity or use discrimination. A well-diversified retailer (selling a wide variety of products) may be in a position to engage in commodity discrimination to injure a seller specializing in one or a few items. (See Chap. 9, pp. 184–185.) The diversified seller may cut prices

[10] Report of the Federal Trade Commission, *Chain Store Leaders and Loss Leaders*, 72nd Congress, first session, Senate Document 51, 1932, pp. 4–6.

[11] Federal Trade Commission, *Resale Price Maintenance* (Washington, 1945), p. 258.

[12] Federal Trade Commission, *Final Report on the Chain Store Investigation*, 74th Congress, first session, Senate Document 4, 1935, pp. 24–28, 57.

in a discriminatory way on certain products while making larger profits on other lines in which competition is not effective. At the present time, the antitrust laws place no effective restraint on the various forms of loss-leader selling.

A third unfair practice employed on occasion by the large retail chains was, and still is, that of geographic price discrimination. Instead of reducing prices uniformly in all its locally separate stores, a large chain sometimes cuts prices only in certain regions or communities in which the competition of independents is especially active. It was this evil which Congress sought to curb in the Clayton Act of 1914. The "good faith" proviso, however, has virtually rendered the restraint ineffective.

The Federal Trade Commission stated in its final report on chain stores,

Chains frequently sell the same quality goods at the same time at different prices in their various stores. This manifests itself in the form of leaders and so-called "loss leaders" at some stores, in the pricing of private brands, and in differences between the headquarters' price and the branch-store price on many articles. *The ability of chain stores to vary prices among their different branches and thus to average their profit results is one of their chief advantages over independents.* In other words, it is one of the chief elements in the growth of chain-store systems to their present dimensions and there is no ground for expecting a different effect upon their future growth. This means that chain-store systems will probably continue to increase in size and tend more and more toward a monopolistic position.[13]

In 1946 the New York Great Atlantic & Pacific Tea Company was convicted of monopolistic action under the Sherman Act.[14] One of the practices of the company was that of selling at discriminatory lower prices in various localities. Although the Court did not rule upon this aspect of the complaint, it presented in its decision many concrete examples showing that it was not uncommon for the A & P Company to raise prices in areas where there was little competition and to reduce them below the levels in any of their other stores in areas where competition was very active. The differences in the prices between the A & P stores in various localities, the Court found, "At times had nothing to do with differentials in transportation." In one typical instance listed by the Court the manager of an A & P store told his competitor, "I am going to turn all my guns on you." Thereupon, the A & P Company "cut" prices in its stores near those of the competitor below its prices in any of the other regular A & P supermarket stores.

THE APPLICATION OF RESALE PRICE MAINTENANCE

In general, there are three important categories of products which do not lend themselves to resale-price control. One category includes highly styl-

---

[13] Federal Trade Commission, *Final Report on the Chain Store Investigation*, 74th Congress, first session, Senate Document 4, 1935, pp. 50–51. Italics supplied.

[14] *U.S.* v. *New York Great A & P Tea Co.*, 67 F. Supp. 626 (1946).

ized, seasonal merchandise, such as women's dresses. In most cases, manufacturers and retailers alike believe that the pricing of such merchandise should be free in order to insure clearance of seasonal items which are likely to become obsolete during the off-season. A second category consists of high-ticket merchandise which is commonly sold on a trade-in basis. Such products include automobiles, refrigerators, gas and electric ranges, television and radio sets. Experience has shown that resale-price control on these items can be evaded by the granting of "excessive" trade-in allowances. A third large category of products which does not lend itself to fair trading includes perishable commodities—such as dairy products, vegetables, and fresh meats. Here, again, flexible pricing is essential in order to insure clearance before spoilage or quality deterioration. In the fresh meat industry, for example, a ruling maxim is "Sell it or smell it."

The principal fields in which fair trade is important are the following:

Automotive parts and accessories	Housewares, hardware, and paint
Alcoholic beverages	Jewelry, watches, and silverware
Books, music, and publishing	Photographic supplies
Clothing and wearing apparel	Stationery and office supplies
Cosmetics	Textiles
Drugs	Tobacco and smoking accessories
Electrical appliances	Toys and sporting goods
Home furnishings	

In the main, resale price maintenance is successfully applied in the sale of brand-name products which are highly advertised, nonperishable, and widely distributed. A further condition for the fair-trading of a particular product is that most, or nearly all, manufacturers of widely-used branded products which are close substitutes join in making fair-trade contracts with their distributors. If one large-scale drug manufacturer, for example, sets a fair-trade price on his nationally advertised ammoniated toothpaste and another large-scale manufacturer does not, he is clearly at a disadvantage. The maintained price can easily be undermined by lower prices on close substitutes. Professor J. P. Miller summarizes the problem as follows: "Where there is a high degree of substitution between branded products, successful price maintenance will be achieved only where rivals follow similar policies."[15]

THE INTEREST OF MANUFACTURERS AND DISTRIBUTORS IN RESALE PRICE CONTROL

A manufacturer finds an interest in maintaining price identity and generous margins for his wholesalers and retailers in order to secure many outlets for his products. Also, when two or more manufacturers of the same class of goods fair trade their products, each is protected against loss of sales to the

[15] J. P. Miller, *Unfair Competition* (Cambridge, 1941), p. 260. Large local retailers, such as Macy's, frequently develop private brands which are sold at prices below the fair-traded national brands. The private brands, however, do not account for a substantial part of the sales in most trade areas.

other because of price competition at the local level. By maintaining local prices, moreover, manufacturers ease the pressure which distributors may exert on them to reduce the mill or factory prices. Higher final prices provide a larger source of profit for each link in the distribution chain.

Organized distributors, usually retailers, frequently press for the establishment of resale-price maintenance when manufacturers do not take the lead. Their interest is higher retail markups and price identity. In some instances, the antitrust agencies report, the request of organized retailers for resale-price maintenance has been supported by concerted action in pushing brands which are price maintained and by boycotting brands which are not. Such organized efforts, it may be noted, stand condemned by the antitrust laws.

Resale price arrangements, it appears, are most effectively maintained (a) when the manufacturers of brands which are close substitutes collectively desire to maintain resale prices *and* (b) when organized retailers of the few leading brands, which account for most of the business, coöperate in establishing and policing resale price arrangements. In a penetrating study of resale price control, Ward S. Bowman, Jr. concludes, "Favorable conditions for resale price maintenance entail some substantial departure from competitive conditions among both sellers and resellers."[16]

FAIR TRADE CONTRACTS IN INTERSTATE COMMERCE DECLARED UNENFORCEABLE AGAINST NONSIGNERS.

The effectiveness of resale price contracts was substantially restricted by the Supreme Court in *Schwegmann Bros. v. Calvert Distillers Corp.* (1951).[17] Calvert and Seagram, whiskey manufacturers, maintained fair-trade pricing on products which they sold in interstate commerce to dealers in Louisiana. The fair-trade price for "Calvert Reserve" whiskey was $4.37 per fifth, including tax; but Schwegmann Bros., a nonsigner in New Orleans, sold it for $3.25. The Louisiana Fair Trade Act contained the "nonsigner" clause, and Calvert and Seagram brought suit to enjoin Schwegmann Bros. from selling at the lower price.

In defending their low-price policies, Schwegmann contended that the use of the nonsigner clause in interstate commerce violated the Sherman Act. The lower courts rejected this defense, but Schwegmann appealed to the Supreme Court. In a 6-to-3 decision the Supreme Court upheld Schwegmann and declared that the Miller-Tydings law does not give immunity to nonsigner arrangements. The nonsigner provision does not appear in the legislation of 1937, and the Court stated that it would not read the provision into the amendment. Only voluntary, *signed* resale price contracts, it held, are exempted from the Sherman Act. Speaking of the Miller-Tydings amendment, Justice Douglas stated for the Court,

[16] Ward S. Bowman, Jr., "Resale Price Maintenance—A Monopoly Problem," *The Journal of Business of the University of Chicago*, July, 1952, p. 150.

[17] 341 U.S. 384 (1951).

The Act sanctions only "contracts or agreements." If a distributor and one or more retailers want to agree, combine, or conspire to fix a minimum price, they can do so if state law permits. Their contract, combination, or conspiracy—hitherto illegal—is made lawful. . . . When they seek, however, to impose price fixing on persons who have not contracted or agreed to the scheme, the situation is vastly different. That is not price fixing by contract or agreement; that is price fixing by compulsion. That is not following the path of consensual agreement; that is resort to coercion.

The Miller-Tydings amendment was thus construed to apply only to parties *who sign* resale price contracts and not to "nonsigners" who had notice of the fixed prices. Since most branded articles are shipped in interstate commerce, and since most resale price arrangements are based on state nonsigner provisions, the decision struck a serious blow to resale price programs.

A weakening of resale price maintenance also occurred in *Sunbeam Corp. v. Wentling* (1950). This action was brought by Sunbeam against Wentling, a mail-order dealer in Pennsylvania, and a nonsigner, for making sales, intrastate *and interstate,* of Sunbeam electric shavers at less than the price Sunbeam had fixed for Pennsylvania. In its first decision, the Court of Appeals denied Sunbeam protection against Wentling in making *interstate sales* at less than the price for Pennsylvania. The Pennsylvania statute, the court said, cannot govern or burden interstate commerce, that is, "sales by Pennsylvania retailers to consumers in other states."[18]

Following the *Schwegmann* decision, the court concluded in a second decision in the *Wentling* case that a person who does not sign a price maintenance contract cannot be subjected to the nonsigner provision of a state law, on sales made within a state, where interstate commerce is involved.[19]

The main effect of the *Wentling* decision, it appears, was to give a mail-order house in one state, as a nonsigner, the legal right to sell and ship into another state at prices below the locally maintained prices. The Wentling decision gave rise to demands for a "home-town" amendment to make mail-order operators observe a *fixed* retail price in interstate shipments.

McGUIRE ACT ADDS NONSIGNER CLAUSE TO FEDERAL LAW

Practitioners of resale price maintenance found that the *Schwegmann* and *Wentling* decisions were very unsettling. A manufacturer seeking to maintain resale prices thereafter had the task of making and policing individual contracts with the thousands of his retailers in each state. This was much too troublesome in most situations. Local retailers acting in unison also faced the price competition of mail-order houses selling in interstate commerce. Much pressure was accordingly placed upon Congress to amend the Miller-Tydings Act (1) by adding the nonsigner clause and (2) making the resale-

[18] *Sunbeam Corp. v. Wentling,* 185 F. (2d) 903, 908 (1950).
[19] *Sunbeam Corp. v. Wentling,* 192 F. (2d) 7 (1951).

price agreement established in one state applicable to sales into other states. As finally adopted by Congress in 1952, the McGuire Act (Public Law 542) reverses the *Schwegmann* and *Wentling* decisions and makes permissible the use of the nonsigner clause within a given state, in accordance with the legislation of the state, by manufacturers selling in interstate commerce. The Act also authorizes the fixing of minimum or *stipulated* (actual) resale prices. Enforcement action, however, is authorized only for sales *below* the prescribed prices. Upon the basis of the McGuire Act, a manufacturer is able to require *all* retailers in a "fair-trading" state to observe the minimum or actual prices which are fixed in a written contract made with *one* retailer in that state.

The McGuire Act also contains a clause designed to remedy the "mail-order loophole" made by the *Wentling* decision. The Act declares that neither the authorized agreements nor the nonsigner arrangements "shall constitute an unlawful burden or restraint upon, or interference with, [interstate] commerce." Fair-trade sponsors hope that this provision will restrain mail-order houses and other retailers from quoting prices to out-of-state buyers which are lower than the fair-trade prices in the state in which the mail-order house is located. Whether or not the courts will permit local fair-trade arrangements to control interstate sales can only be determined by court decisions.[20]

The fight for the McGuire bill was led by the *Bureau of Education on Fair Trade*, New York City, an organization backed chiefly by such large drug concerns as Bristol-Meyers, Coty, McKesson and Robbins, and Eli Lilly and Co.; the *American Fair Trade Council*, Gary, Indiana, an association of diversified manufacturers; and such trade associations as the National Association of Retail Druggists, the National Association of Chain Drug Stores, and the National Wholesale Druggists Association. Some 1300 local, regional, and national trade associations, it is estimated, supported and fought for the McGuire bill. Vigorous protests to the bill were made by labor, farm, and consumer organizations, but the organized industry groups proved to be the more influential.

NONSIGNER CLAUSE –THE HEART OF FAIR TRADE

In many lines of business, manufacturers distribute their products through wholesalers to thousands of retailers. The great majority of retailers are small, and the only way their wants can be served by a manufacturer is through wholesalers. In the drug business, for example, there are probably a minimum of 200,000 retailers of such drug store items as toothbrushes, shav-

---

[20] In 1953 the Supreme Court refused to review a Court of Appeals decision upholding the constitutionality of the McGuire and Louisiana Fair Trade Acts. *Schwegmann Bros.* v. *Eli Lilly*, 205 F. (2d) 788 (1953); certiorari denied, 346 U.S. 856. This action, fair-trade supporters declare, indicates that the Court believes that the McGuire Act and state fair-trade laws are constitutional. Legal experts, however, reply that the Court has broad discretion in refusing to hear petitions for review, so that the basic question of constitutionality remains unanswered.

ing soap, and razor blades. This is true in many other lines of business. In all such cases, it is much too troublesome for a manufacturer to make and maintain resale-price contracts with *every* retailer. It is for this reason that advocates stress the vital importance of the nonsigner clause.

The opponents of fair trade, on the other hand, are equally vigorous in opposing the nonsigner clause. They declare that it is unfair because it binds a person to a contract to which he is not a party. In principle, and in practice, all retailers of a given product in one state can be bound by a single fair-trade contract. This, it is alleged, is arbitrary and beyond the present constitutional powers of a state government to permit.

Some seventeen state supreme courts have held that the nonsigner's clause is a legal restriction on freedom of contract. The supreme courts of Michigan, Georgia, and Florida, however, have declared that legislation requiring compliance by nonsigners is "outside the scope of the police powers of the state." In the view of the Michigan court, the nonsigner clause is unconstitutional because it bears no reasonable relation to public morals, health, safety, or general welfare. "The process of reducing prices" by competition, observed the court, does not bring evils to the general welfare.[21]

THE CASE *FOR* AND *AGAINST* FAIR TRADE

In general, any measure will be found to have advantages and disadvantages. The task of the student is to determine which is dominant. With this point of view in mind, we shall examine the arguments *for* and *against* fair trade.

The main issues raised in the discussion of fair trade are the impact of the practice on (1) competition, (2) productive efficiency, (3) unfair practices, (4) protection of brand names, (5) the level of prices, and (6) the interest of consumers. The arguments in favor of fair trade are those advanced by manufacturers, wholesalers, and retailers, who employ resale price maintenance. The arguments against, on the other hand, are those made by persons in the antitrust agencies, by businessmen who oppose fair trade, by various specialists in marketing, and by labor and consumer groups.

I

THE MAINTENANCE OF COMPETITION

CASE FOR FAIR TRADE

Resale price control, its supporters declare, does not eliminate competition, for the price-fixed goods still have the competition (1) of other fair-traded products and (2) of nonfair-traded merchandise. Retailers, moreover, continue to vie with one another rendering service to consumers.

A manufacturer of fair-traded products is free to price his lines as he de-

[21] *Shakespeare Co. v. Lippman*, 334. Mich. 109, 54 N.W. 2d, 268 (1952).

sires. There is nothing in the law, moreover, which prevents retailers from selling private brands and unbranded merchandise at any price that they desire. Such competition compels manufacturers to establish fair-trade prices which will win customer acceptance, if they wish to sell their products. Fair-trade prices, therefore, are tested for their reasonableness every day in that most exacting laboratory, the over-the-counter market to consumers. If, by chance, two or more manufacturers in a given field "act as one" in establishing fair-trade prices, they are subject to prosecution for monopolistic behavior under the Sherman Act.

The nonsigner clause comes into play as a part of the state's system against unfair competition only if a retailer decides to carry fair-trade products. No retailer is required to carry fair-traded merchandise.

CASE AGAINST FAIR TRADE

Opponents emphasize that price maintenance is a device for preventing price competition (a) at wholesale and (b) at retail in the sale of branded merchandise. Under the cloak of this legislation, private persons are given the power to fix prices horizontally, applicable (a) to *all* wholesalers and (b) to *all* retailers of the branded merchandise in a given state. If such action were taken directly, it would be illegal. However, when it is taken under resale-price legislation, it is legal *and* enforceable by the courts!

The power to fix the resale prices of a branded product, sold by many independent retailers, is entrusted to a private seller engaged in serving his own pecuniary interests. The price so fixed is not subject to change or review for fairness by any retailer. It may be arbitrary or extortionate. In many important situations, moreover, competition does not operate to moderate extortionate pricing, for other nationally advertised products which are close substitutes are fair-traded, too! The importance of maintaining effective price competition at the wholesale and retail levels is indicated by the fact that on many items, such as electrical appliances, approximately one-half of the retail price goes to pay for the retail and wholesale markups.

Sellers not a party to fair-trade contracts are legally bound to observe the price, regardless of their own costs, methods of doing business, or business efficiency. It is easy to say that a seller does not have to handle fair-trade merchandise. In many lines, however, the leading brands provide most of the sales; and if a retailer is to enter or remain in business, he must handle the fair-traded products.

In industries dominated by three or four large manufacturing firms, there is a tendency for the various firms to "peg" their factory prices at levels comparable to those of the leader and to use zone or basing-point pricing (see Chap. 17). If and when these firms make resale price agreements with their local dealers, price competition is eliminated all the way through to the final consumers. The view that resale price maintenance transfers price competition from retailers to manufacturers is largely illusory.

II

PRODUCTIVE EFFICIENCY

CASE FOR FAIR TRADE

Fair trade contributes to an orderly marketing mechanism through which the public can enjoy the benefits of mass production. The fixing of adequate margins of profit makes it possible for many small retailers to remain in business. This provides a manufacturer with a larger number of retail outlets and assures him of the widest possible distribution for his products. No manufacturer can afford to price his product for the convenience of the inefficient distributors because he would price himself out of the market.

Resale price contracts also serve to prevent economic concentration in the retail field. Large chain stores usually have lower costs or lower cost prices; and if open price competition were permitted, many small retail stores would be eliminated.

CASE AGAINST FAIR TRADE

Resale price maintenance ignores the factor of productive efficiency. In seeking to maintain widespread distribution for his products, a manufacturer sets markups which operate to permit many high-cost and inefficient distributors to stay in business. These fixed and arbitrary markups must thereupon be used regardless of a seller's efficiency, scale of operations, method of merchandising, or type of service rendered. The "proper" *retail* margin for a specific product should be determined by the free play of competitive forces, not by the authoritarian judgment of a manufacturer far removed from the retail business.

Since a retailer cannot increase his sales by reducing costs and prices, he has little incentive to strive for lower costs. Rather, with fixed prices, he finds an incentive to increase his outlays—newspaper advertising, radio and television programs, elegant store furnishings, and expensive displays—in an effort to stimulate buying. Resale price maintenance is thus an anti-efficiency measure. It promotes cost-raising methods of selling and denies consumers the benefits of lower costs and more efficient ways of doing business.

III

UNFAIR PRACTICES

CASE FOR FAIR TRADE

Resale-price maintenance provides small retailers with protection against the price-juggling and price-cutting activities of large retailers. Large retailers commonly use leaders to build up their business and lure customers to their stores. Since low prices are quoted on the featured merchandise, the public is led to believe that prices are also low on all other items, branded as well as private and unbranded. Many small firms specialize in branded merchandise. They cannot afford to use loss leaders, for their volume of business is small.

A retailer's *gross margin* is an overall *average* which he finds he needs to pay operating costs and make a reasonable profit. Some products carry a higher markup than the *average*, and some carry a lower markup. The practice of certain chains and giant retailers is to use a low markup on popular branded merchandise and a high markup on nonfair-trade products. This gives them customer good will and much free advertising. Hard-working independent retailers cannot compete with this sort of unfair price juggling.

Large retail outlets—chain stores and department stores—on some occasions, and in certain areas, also engage in prolonged selling at below-cost prices. When a local store cannot make up its losses in other departments, or in other areas, it is forced to close. Independent businessmen have found no adequate remedy for the evils of price juggling except the practice of resale price maintenance.

CASE AGAINST FAIR TRADE

The principal competitive evils which confront independent merchants are (1) sales below net invoice cost at the buyer's place of business (true loss-leader selling); (2) geographic price discrimination; and (3) personal discrimination, with price favors and other concessions granted to large distributors. The sound way to remedy these evils is to approach them directly by strengthening the laws against price discrimination.

The widespread use of resale-price maintenance is likely to bring more evils for independent retailers than those which it seeks to remedy. With a scheme of artificial pricing, competition is often forced underground. The growth of "discount houses" providing little or no service, but offering discounts of 15 to 40 percent, undoubtedly has been promoted by the practice of fair trade. Mail-order houses, chain stores, and big department stores also have introduced their own private brands for use in underselling the fair-trade items. Macy's in New York, it is reported, has more than 1400 items branded with its own trademark. In some cases, efficient retailers who can afford to sell for less than the fair-trade markup use the high profit margins on fair-trade items to offset price reductions on other products. The fair-trade practice thus makes it possible to subsidize the sales of other merchandise to the detriment and injury of independents who do not carry private brands.

The generous margins of fair trade, experience shows, may also be offset by the growth of an excessive number of retail outlets. At the present time, for example, grocery stores, dime stores, and other retail outlets are establishing medicine counters for the sale of highly profitable, price-fixed drug items. A survey made in 1951 found that "eighty-five percent of the nation's leading supermarkets and superettes now sell selected health and beauty aids, compared with only 37 percent 10 years ago."[22] Fifty-five percent of

[22] *Progressive Grocer*, February, 1952, p. 50.

the sales of Colgate tooth paste, it was found, were being made in food store outlets. The drug stores strongly oppose the sale of a rapid-turnover drug items by other types of stores, but they have not as yet found a way to prevent it.

Fair-trade pricing brings a further problem in restricting the independence of retailers. In surrendering the right to determine his own margins and asking prices, a retailer becomes a mere outlet for a large manufacturer. A significant aspect of freedom of enterprise is gone—the freedom to manage the inner workings of one's own enterprise. Instead of being subject to planning by government, which business deplores, many thousands of small retailers are now, in fact, subject to economic planning by big business.

IV

PROTECTION OF BRAND NAMES

CASE FOR FAIR TRADE

Resale-price maintenance helps to protect the reputation of branded goods which are highly advertised. Advertising builds a halo around a product and creates an added value which manufacturers seek to maintain. This prestige value can be injured or destroyed by loss-leader selling.

Selling at reduced prices is injurious because substantial variations from the usual price cause buyers to suspect that the quality of the product has deteriorated or that the product has been cheapened. As a result, the public loses confidence and respect for the product. The public also becomes confused as to what is a fair price to pay. At the same time, many retailers find that they cannot make a reasonable profit in meeting the lower prices of other retailers, and their selling energies are thereupon devoted to products having a higher markup. Loss-leader selling thus works to the injury of manufacturers who have secured brand acceptance through years of intensive advertising.

CASE AGAINST FAIR TRADE

Branded goods are not entitled to special protection (1) against price competition at the retail level and (2) against variations in retail markups, reflecting differences in productive efficiency, methods of merchandising, and services rendered. The lawful purpose of a brand is to permit an owner to identify his product and to show ownership or origin. Our laws now provide adequate protection against the infringement, substitution, or illegal use of such trademarks. Once the legitimate purpose of trademarks has been served, the owners of trademarks should take their place with others in the competitive market.

Loss-leader selling may be an evil in the case of branded merchandise, as well as in the case of unbranded products. In formulating remedial measures, consideration should be centered on the problem of unfair competition, as such. Resale price maintenance, which restricts *all* price competition, fair and unfair, is not a desirable method for controlling loss leaders.

There is little if any evidence to indicate that low retail prices on branded merchandise injure the manufacturer-consumer relationship. The damage which a manufacturer fears is the possibility that high-profit retailers will boycott his products if competing retailers sell them at low prices. Experienced merchandisers state, however, that manufacturers can usually overcome such boycotts if they have patience and courage. The strong consumer demand for branded products, as well as the loss of business to low-price retailers, can usually be expected to change the boycotting policies of high-profit retailers.

V

THE LEVEL OF PRICES—A "BATTLE OF THE SURVEYS"

CASE FOR FAIR TRADE

Resale-price maintenance makes for prices which are fair and stable. The objective of a manufacturer in fixing resale prices is to provide dealers with a fair markup to cover expenses and leave a net profit. Both unduly low and unduly high prices are prevented. Numerous price surveys show (1) that fair-trade prices have a better record in resisting inflation than nonfair-trade merchandise and (2) that fair-trade prices on certain national brands are actually lower in fair-trade states than in nonfair-trade states.[23]

In a very real sense, the pay-off to the consumer is in the overall prices of a particular store in which he shops, rather than in the prices of a few, selected items. There is no reported instance of a single retail store-wide markup—the average overall—which is greater because of fair trade or which would be less if fair trade were repealed.

CASE AGAINST FAIR TRADE

A large and growing number of price studies are available for comparing prices in fair-trade and nonfair-trade areas. All of the surveys made *in the populous centers* of fair-trade and nonfair-trade states show that the fair-trade prices *are much higher* than the competitive prices in Texas, Missouri, Vermont, and the District of Columbia.[24] In explaining the basis for the

[23] Report of the Select Committee on Small Business, *Fair Trade: The Problem and the Issues*, House Report 1292, 1952, p. 9; and Hearings Before the Committee on Interstate and Foreign Commerce, *Resale Price Fixing*, U.S. Senate, 82nd Congress, second session, 1952, p. 65. New price surveys are constantly being made by the sponsors of fair trade. It is suggested that students interested in securing current material on the levels of fair-trade prices write to the Bureau of Education on Fair Trade, 205 East 42 St., New York City 17; and to the American Fair Trade Council, Inc., 11 East 44 St., New York 17, N.Y.

[24] See, for example, Hearings Before the Antitrust Subcommittee of the Committee on the Judiciary, House of Representatives, *Resale Price Maintenance*, 82nd Congress, second session, Serial 12, 1952, pp. 429-476, as well as the Congressional reports and hearings listed at the end of the present chapter.

higher retail prices in fair-trade states, Mr. J. E. Webb, a retailer in Florida, says that "The average fair-trade prices are set up for a retail markup of approximately 33⅓ to 50 percent. Our retail store can make a liberal net profit with an 8 percent markup in tobaccos; 13 percent markup in the supermarkets; 15 percent markup in wines and liquors; 18 percent markup in fast turnover drugs and patents."[25]

In some cases, fair-trade prices are set somewhat below the nominal prices printed on the bottles or wrappers. Some druggists in noncompetitive sales areas in nonfair-trade states sell at the printed prices on the bottle or wrapper. By comparing the fair-trade price in New York City with the nonfair-trade price in an old-line drug store in Vermont, it is possible to find examples of prices which are higher in nonfair-trade states. It may be doubted, however, that the drug trade is animated by philanthropic motives. If prices in nonfair-trade states were really higher than in fair-trade states, the fair traders should logically demand a repeal of all fair-trade laws!

Fair-trade prices are more rigid and inflexible than competitive prices. With price management, price changes depend upon the deliberate, volitional action of those exercising control. During a period of prosperity and business expansion, prices maintained under fair-trade contracts undoubtedly do show greater resistance to inflation. During a period of business recession and depression, however, this same price rigidity serves to aggravate and prolong the depressed conditions. Consumer demand is reduced at the maintained prices, and price reductions are not generally made to stimulate buying. With price competition, on the other hand, prices adjust themselves downwards to provide a new equilibrium at which a growing volume of business can be done.

VI

THE CONSUMER'S INTEREST

CASE FOR FAIR TRADE

Resale-price maintenance fixes fair prices and protects consumers from so-called "bargain" sales. Consumers know prices in advance, day in and day out, and they can plan their expenditures more effectively. The practice also saves time, for consumers can buy without haggling over prices and without shopping around.

It is in the consumer's interest to have the mass distribution of trademarked products which is made possible by the existence of many independent retailers. It is also in the consumer's interest to prevent the growth of retail monopolies to the point where they can eliminate the independent retailer through the unfair competition of price juggling. The elimination of the competition of small business is not in the interest of the consumer economically; nor is the elimination of the man who wants to run his own business desirable from a social standpoint.

[25] Letter to the *Washington Post*, Washington, D.C., March 18, 1952.

CASE AGAINST FAIR TRADE

Consumer groups, labor unions, and farm organizations have all condemned resale-price control. In their view, the practice means the fixing of high, noncompetitive prices by private parties for their own benefit. No provision is made for public hearings on the fairness of retail markups or for a government commission to intervene against excessive markups.

The practice also denies consumers the benefits of more efficient forms of retailing. The same price is charged in all stores, and consumers are not permitted to pay a price which is related to retailing costs and the services which they purchase. Retail-price maintenance stands as a stone wall against lower prices made possible by new techniques and greater efficiency in the distribution of branded merchandise.

THE NEED TO STRENGTHEN PRESENT LEGISLATION AGAINST PRICE DISCRIMINATION

Resale-price maintenance is offered by its proponents as a remedy for price cutting and loss-leader selling. A large part of these evils can be traced directly to *price discrimination*. It follows that the logical approach to take against the evils responsible for resale price maintenance is that of curbing injurious discrimination.

To what extent do existing laws against price discrimination provide an adequate remedy? Although most of the states have laws against price discrimination (see Chap. 20), it does not appear that any cases have been brought under these laws against local price cutting at the retail level. Actually, an injured person cannot expect to secure relief under the state laws, for they permit price discrimination "made in good faith to meet competition."

Likewise, the Robinson-Patman Act, which requires a seller to treat all his customers on more or less equal terms, in fact, provides inadequate protection. As interpreted by the Supreme Court, the law permits a dominant seller to discriminate in price, even when the effect is to injure competition, when it can be shown that the seller discriminates in good faith to meet competition (see Chap. 16). If state and federal laws against price discrimination are to be made effective, it is essential that amendments be adopted declaring that "good faith" is not a complete defense to the charge of discrimination whenever it can be shown that competition, in fact, is injured.

Further, the present antitrust laws place no effective restraints on discriminations in the sale of different products, i.e., the problem of loss-leader selling. In the *Sears* case, for example, the Federal Trade Commission issued an order against the loss-leader selling of sugar by Sears, Roebuck and Co., after finding that Sears was selling sugar at prices below its invoice cost. The Court of Appeals set aside the order, declaring, "We find in the statute no intent on the part of Congress, even if it has the power, to restrain an owner of property from selling it at any price that is acceptable to him or from giving it away."[26] As interpreted by the courts, Section 5 of the Federal Trade Commission Act condemns sales below cost only when they are made *with the intent to injure competition*. In practice, the task of proving "illegal intent" in antitrust cases is virtually impossible, for a seller can usually allege "good faith" to meet or beat competition. Business practices, as we have stated, should be evaluated upon the basis of their effects. If the effects are bad, the practices should be prevented, regardless of motive.

As a means of curbing the practice of loss-leader selling, it has been proposed that *some limit* or restraint be placed on this kind of discrimination, particularly at the retail level, without reference to "intent to injure competition." The proposal is that the antitrust laws be amended to make it illegal "to discriminate between or among different commodities or similar commodities of different grade and quality *by reselling at retail* in or affecting commerce *any commodity at less than net cost of such commodity delivered to the retailer's place of business* . . . where the effect . . . may be substantially to lessen competition."[27] Such a law would not specify any particular markup, but it would provide a floor below which prices could not be deliberately cut. An exception, of course, would be made for price reductions to clear seasonal or excessive inventories and distress stocks of merchandise.

PERCENTAGE MARKUPS A MATTER OF INTERNAL BUSINESS POLICY

Proponents of fair trade are unwilling to support an amendment prohibiting sales below a seller's acquisition costs. Under such a law, they declare, any large retailer could feature a well-known national brand at or just above cost, and at the same time overprice other products to make up his loss in gross margin. Small competitors, it is said, would still be faced with unfair price juggling.

In taking the foregoing position, fair-trade advocates implicitly contend that each article sold should bear a percentage markup roughly equivalent to a store's average gross margin. This contention, however, fails to recognize that the markups which a competitive seller *can take* on different items, in terms of what the traffic will bear, varies from store to store, depending upon such factors as the class of trade served, specialties handled, rate of inventory turnover, existing competition, and established reputation. It also fails to recognize that operating costs vary from seller to seller and from product to product, depending upon efficiency, services rendered, location, methods of merchandising, and so forth. In a system of free enterprise, the appropriate markup for particular goods is a problem for the individual business firm. It is a matter of internal business policy.

[26] *Sears, Roebuck and Co.* v. *F.T.C.* 258 F. 307, 312 (1919).
[27] This proposal was presented by Mr. Everette MacIntyre of the Federal Trade Commission in Hearings Before the Committee on Interstate and Foreign Commerce, *Resale Price Fixing*, U.S. Senate, 82nd Congress, second session, 1952, pp. 41–42.

Merchants must recover their total costs from total sales. If costs are not fully allocated to some items, they must be secured by higher prices on other items. A merchant commonly seeks to adjust prices and costs in accordance with "what the traffic will bear." In most cases, however, the traffic will not bear an out-of-line price, because of the active competition of other retail sellers.

RESALE PRICE-MAINTENANCE IN CANADA

The Combines Investigation Act condemns all agreements and arrangements which restrict competition or fix resale prices "to the detriment or against the interest of the public." Decisions under the law on fair-trade contracts, however, did not establish any clear-cut rules, and resale price-maintenance agreements grew with impunity in many lines of business.

In 1951 the government became concerned over the growing extent of resale price maintenance and invited the Committee Studying Combines Legislation to develop a report and recommendations on the practice. The Committee invited briefs from all interested parties, held many meetings at which interested persons were given opportunity to discuss and amplify their representations, and made an exhaustive study of the operation of resale price control. In summarizing its investigations, the Committee stated that resale price fixing "represents a real and undesirable restriction on competition by private agreement or 'law' and its general tendency is to discourage economic efficiency. . . . In our opinion, the prescription and the enforcement of minimum resale prices must be viewed as manifestations of a restrictive or monopolistic practice which does not promote general welfare." The Committee accordingly recommended that the practice be made illegal.[28]

Following the report of the Combines Committee, the Parliament of Canada, after extensive public hearings by a Joint Committee of the Senate and House of Commons, enacted legislation (December 29, 1951) (a) declaring resale price maintenance to be illegal and (b) making it an offense to refuse to sell, to withdraw a franchise, or to take any other form of action as a means of enforcing minimum resale prices.[29] This legislation stands in sharp contrast to public policy in the United States.

The Canadian government recognizes that loss-leader selling may be a problem in periods of deflation and relative abundance. It believes, however, that methods other than resale price maintenance should be employed to remedy the evil.

SUMMARY

The issue of resale price maintenance is highly controversial. Each reader is urged to study the arguments for and against this arrangement and to make up his own mind on appropriate policy.

[28] *Resale Price Maintenance*, an Interim Report of the Committee to Study Combines Legislation, Ottawa, 1951, p. 71.

[29] 15–16 George VI, Chapter 30, *An Act to Amend the Combines Investigation Act*, 1951. See also the Annual Report of the Commissioner of the Combines Investigation Act, Ottawa, 1952, pp. 4, 8.

Some economists believe that resale price control is an insignificant evil when compared to the major restraints on trade in the economy.[30] Ineffective antitrust law enforcement, in their view, makes it necessary for small business to join hands in protecting itself. If a policy of competition is to be fostered, they add, it should be inaugurated in the major areas of monopoly and oligopoly.

Other economists hold that the merits of resale price maintenance in curbing unfair competition are outweighed by numerous disadvantages, private as well as public. They agree that resale price maintenance prevents the loss-leader selling of branded products. This relief, however, they point out, is obtained at the cost of private horizontal price fixing and the elimination of price competition (a) among wholesalers and (b) among retailers. The policy of sound and fair competition is sacrificed to get rid of a small area of unfair competition.

The relief afforded by resale price maintenance, it is added, is only a partial relief. In important areas, the problems of loss-leader selling and price discrimination still continue. Even with resale price maintenance there remains the problem of loss-leader selling of products without trademarks or with the private labels of retailers. The problem of discriminatory discounts and unwarranted price concessions granted to large mass distributors and mail-order houses also still remains to cause cost handicaps for smaller business concerns. No remedy, moreover, is provided for the sale of products "of like grade and quality," such as canned goods, tires, or appliances, to large distributors under private labels at lower discriminatory prices.

Critics of resale price maintenance conclude that the primary cause of unsound competition is price discrimination and true loss-leader selling. New legislation, they believe, should be adopted to curb these evils, as such.

SUGGESTIONS FOR FURTHER READING

Amending the Sherman Act with Respect to Resale Price Maintenance, Report of the Committee on the Judiciary, 82nd Congress, second session, House Report 1516, 1952.

Fair Trade: The Problem and the Issues, Report of the Select Committee on Small Business, 82nd Congress, second session, House Report 1292, 1952.

Federal Trade Commission, *Final Report on the Chain Store Investigation*, 74th Congress, first session, Senate Document 4, 1935; *Resale Price Maintenance* (Washington, 1945).

Frankel, Marvin, "Price Maintenance, Price Wars, and the Distributor," *Current Economic Comment*, University of Illinois, November, 1953.

Grether, E. T., *Price Control Under Fair Trade Legislation* (New York, 1939); *Resale Price Maintenance in Great Britain (with an Application to the Problem in the United States)*, University of California Publications in Economics, Vol. II (Berkeley, 1935).

Minimum Resale Prices, Hearings, Subcommittee of the Committee on Inter-

[30] See, for example, Walter Adams "The Schwegmann Case," *University of Detroit Law Journal*, November, 1951, p. 17.

state and Foreign Commerce, House of Representatives, 82nd Congress, second session, 1952.

Resale Price Fixing, Hearings, Committee on Interstate and Foreign Commerce, U.S. Senate, 82nd Congress, second session, 1952.

Resale Price Maintenance, Hearings, Antitrust Subcommittee of the Committee on the Judiciary, House of Representatives, 82nd Congress, second session, Serial 12, 1952.

Resale Price Maintenance, an Interim Report of the Committee to Study Combines Legislation (Ottawa, Canada, 1951).

A Statement on Resale Price Maintenance, Board of Trade (London, 1951).

CHAPTER 22

Laws Prohibiting Sales Below Cost

CONTINUING EFFORTS TO LEGISLATE AGAINST LOSS-LEADER SELLING

Resale price-maintenance legislation, it was soon found, did not give retailers and their supplying wholesalers the complete protection which they desired. In 1939, for example, it was estimated that "probably not over 15 percent of total retail sales can be expected to come within the scope of price-maintenance legislation in the near future."[1] The fair-trade laws, it will be remembered, are only permissive, and in numerous instances retailers were not able to induce manufacturers to "fair-trade" their products. The fair-trade laws, moreover, are applicable only to branded merchandise, and in many cases price competition shifted from such products to bulk and unbranded ones. In an effort, therefore, to secure legislation covering all products sold at retail, retail and wholesale trade associations, especially in the grocery field, began about 1938 to turn their efforts to securing the enactment of so-called "unfair-practices" acts or laws prohibiting sales below cost. According to a special study of the Temporary National Economic Committee, the "general intent" of trade groups in seeking such legislation was "to apply to all commodities restrictions similar to those applied to identifiable goods by the price-maintenance laws."[2]

At the present time there are some thirty-one states with statutes prohibiting any dealer in the lines of business covered from selling below *his* cost of production with the *intent*, in most cases, of injuring competition. Several state courts have held such legislation to be unconstitutional, but the laws, in their amended or original form, continue to be operative in twenty-eight states.[3] The California Unfair Practices Act of 1935 was the first of the mini-

---

[1] Ralph Cassady, Jr., "Maintenance of Resale Prices by Manufacturers," *Quarterly Journal of Economics*, May, 1939, p. 455.

[2] *Problems of Small Business*, Monograph 17, Temporary National Economic Committee, 76th Congress, third session, 1941, p. 202.

[3] The thirty-one states are Arizona, Arkansas, California, Colorado, Connecticut, Idaho, Kansas, Kentucky, Louisiana, Maine, Maryland, Massachusetts, Michigan, Minnesota, Montana, Nebraska, New Hampshire, New Jersey, North Dakota, Ohio, Oklahoma, Oregon, Pennsylvania, Rhode Island, Tennessee, Utah, Virginia, Washington, West Virginia, Wisconsin, and Wyoming. The statutes in Michigan, New Jersey, and Ohio are inoperative because of adverse court rulings.

mum markup laws, and it has been widely adopted in some form by many other states. The California "model" legislation applies to any concern doing business within the state. Other state laws have been patterned after a second model statute which was prepared by the National Food and Grocery Conference Committee. This basic statute applies only to wholesalers and retailers.[4] The Michigan statute is limited to bakery and petroleum products; and the Louisiana law is applicable only to drugs, cosmetics, and allied products sold at retail. In most of the other cases, however, the laws cover "any article, product, commodity, thing of value, service, or output of a service trade." All of the state laws exempt (1) closing-out or liquidation sales, (2) sales of damaged or deteriorated goods, and (3) sales made upon an order of a court; and most of the laws make exceptions for sales of perishable and seasonable goods.

The California statute and some of the laws patterned after it also declare price discrimination under certain circumstances to be illegal. This section of the California law had been enacted earlier; and in many cases, as we saw in the chapter on the state antitrust laws, state legislation against price discrimination came into existence long before the unfair-practices acts. Since antidiscrimination laws were designed primarily to prevent monopolistic practices, they are treated in our present study with the federal and state laws against monopoly.

THE PROHIBITION OF SALES BELOW COST

The principal provision in the unfair-practices acts is the section making it unlawful for any person (a) to sell any article below *his* cost (b) to give away any article or product, "for the purpose of injuring competitors or destroying competition." The practice of using loss leaders is usually specifically prohibited. A loss leader in the California statute is defined as "any article . . . sold at less than cost . . . to induce, promote, or encourage, the purchase of other merchandise, or which may have the tendency . . . to mislead . . . purchasers . . . or which diverts trade from or otherwise injures competitors."

The California and related statutes specifically and carefully define the standard of cost below which any sale is presumed to be illegal. Section 3 of the California act provides, "The term 'cost' . . . as applied to *production* is hereby defined as including the cost of raw materials, labor, and all overhead expenses of the producer; and as applied to *distribution* 'cost' shall mean the invoice or replacement cost, whichever is lower, of the article or product to the distributor or vendor *plus* the cost of doing business by said distributor and vendor." The terms "overhead expenses" and "cost of doing business," the act provides, shall be "defined as all costs of doing business incurred in the conduct of such business and must include without limitation the following items of expense: labor (including salaries of executives and officers),

[4] *State Price Control Legislation*, prepared by the Marketing Laws Survey, Works Progress Administration (Washington, 1940), pp. xlviii–li.

rent, interest on borrowed capital, depreciation, selling cost, maintenance of equipment, delivery costs, credit losses, all types of licenses, taxes, insurance, and advertising." (See Table 34 for an illustration.)

TABLE 34.   University Florists, Inc.

1. Cost of merchandise or raw materials (invoice cost plus costs of acquisition and delivery to seller's place of business)	$12,500
2. "Cost of doing business"—also called "operating expenses" or "overhead expenses." This includes	$ 7,500
1. Rent paid to others	
2. Salaries and wages	
3. Depreciation	
4. Taxes	
5. Bad accounts	
6. Allowances for theft, spoilage, etc.	
7. Supplies—paper, twine, etc.	
8. Advertising	
9. Delivery costs	
10. Heat, light, power	
11. Donations	
12. Insurance	
13. Repairs on equipment	
14. Interest paid to others	
15. Telephone, telegraph, and postage expense	
3. Business or accounting costs	$20,000[a]

[a] Estimation of business or accounting costs. If estimated sales are 20,000 units, the per unit "accounting cost" is $1.00. Any sale below $1.00, is presumably "a sale below cost." Business or accounting costs, it should be noted, do not include (1) a "fair profit" to the owners on their invested capital or (2) reasonable salaries to owner-managers in the case of individual proprietorships and partnerships.

It may be noted that the statute provisions on costs merely prescribe a *minimum* scale of costs which a business firm *must* include. The only interest charge, for example, which a seller is compelled to include is interest on *borrowed* capital. Under these statutes, however, there is no question that a seller *may* include *any costs* which he chooses—such as (1) a "fair profit" to the enterpriser on his invested capital and (2) reasonable salaries for working owners and partners. Whether or not a sale is below cost must be determined in each case by taking into consideration the accounting procedures of the merchant. Any reasonable system of allocating costs may be used.

COST SURVEYS

In order to ascertain the cost of doing business, and also to meet the problem of differences in the costs of various producers, the California model statute provides that cost surveys conducted by an industry group or trade association may be used as *prima facie* evidence of cost. Other statutes require a definite percentage markup—such as 12 percent—over the invoice or replacement cost, and provide that any sale at less than such a figure is prima facie a sale below cost. Prima facie means "at first view"; and in sales-below-cost legislation it means that any person selling for less than the cost estimated by an industry survey or by the percentage markup specified in the law loses his case unless he can prove to the court that his costs are actually lower.

The Montana statute specifically empowers a state commission to establish cost surveys whenever a request is made by ten or more persons. Such cost surveys are deemed to be "competent evidence" in proving the costs of any person complained against under the act. In making a cost survey, moreover, the commission is given authority to issue subpoenas and to secure any desired books, records, correspondence, documents, or other evidence from any person being investigated. The Montana statute is generally regarded by business groups as being a particularly effective and really enforceable type of statute.

THE ENFORCEMENT OF UNFAIR-PRACTICES ACTS

The time, legal expense, and trouble involved in court cases is usually sufficient to bring about a considerable degree of compliance with the prices fixed by trade association groups or with the markups specified by law. Three methods of enforcement are provided, however, to bring possible recalcitrants into line. First, it is usually provided that any person may take action to enjoin violations of the act. The California act specifically states that any person or trade association may bring such action without even alleging or proving actual damages. If a person, or trade group, believes that he has been damaged, he can also sue to recover damages in addition. Secondly, provision is sometimes made for the bringing of criminal actions against violators. The California and related statutes, for example, provide that any person violating the act is guilty of a misdemeanor for each violation and is subject to a fine ranging from $100 to $1000 and imprisonment for not more than six months. Thirdly, the laws typically provide that action against violators can be brought by the state attorney general or by the county prosecuting attorney.

In most cases, state authorities do not have the necessary funds for initiating cases under the unfair-practices acts. The task of collecting evidence, making cost surveys, and selecting concerns to be prosecuted, therefore, is generally undertaken by interested trade groups. When a case is originated by a dealer or trade group, the state authorities, however, will usually serve as a prosecuting agency.

The California and related statutes provide that a defendant may not claim lower costs because he pays his labor less than the prevailing wage scale. In the case of concerns which employ members of the owner's family, it is required that "such services shall be charged as an expense of the business in which rendered and at the rate of the wage for the services rendered prevailing at the time of the service at the place where rendered."

In order to meet the difficulty of proving "intent" to injure competitors in selling below cost, some statutes provide that a sale below cost is evidence of unlawful intent. Others provide that a sale below cost itself is evidence of a violation. The California and Washington statutes, on the other hand, provide that in any action "proof of one or more acts of selling or giving away any article or product below cost . . . together with proof of the injurious effect of such acts, shall be presumptive evidence of the purpose or intent to injure competitors or destroy competition."

THE APPLICATION OF UNFAIR-PRACTICES ACTS BY STATE AND LOCAL TRADE ASSOCIATIONS

Although the unfair-practices laws prohibit *a person* from selling below *his* cost, their actual application is typically based upon cost surveys and markup estimates prepared by local and state retail and wholesale trade associations. Indeed, a principal function of many retail and wholesale trade associations has become (1) that of determining the legal standard for prices in an application of the unfair-practices acts and (2) that of policing local and state industry groups to insure that the "legal" prices are fully observed.

Studies which have been made of the application of minimum-price legislation all indicate a common pattern of procedure. Some sort of cost survey for a particular sales area is typically undertaken by trade association officers. A common method is simply to send a post card to trade members asking them to indicate their cost of doing business for a given year. Upon receiving the replies, an identical "legal" price is thereupon established for the use of all dealers in a particular area. A statement made by the manager of the Washington Merchants' Association describes the way in which dealers have approached the problem. According to this trade association executive, "Under the law, a store . . . selling for example, tobacco . . . must raise its price to the level of cost plus mark-up which tobacco dealers set as the standard. Similarly, grocers, druggists, clothiers, and others will set standards of cost and mark-up which must be observed by all firms selling groceries, drugs, or clothes. . . . Prices for anything cannot be lower than the established cost basis in any buying area."[5] Another trade association executive has declared, "The new law permits of industrial self-regulation with the controls set up and administered by the business men themselves. . . . The members within that industry must get together and work out their own corrective programs."[6]

Studies of the Federal Trade Commission indicate that the cost surveys conducted by trade associations usually involve a great deal of group discussion and that the final price figures adopted typically represent common understanding, agreement, and unified action.[7] In describing the application of the California act in the wholesale tobacco trade in northern California, the Commission gives the following report by the association's secretary. "Well, when we first started out as an Association under General Hugh Johnson under the N.R.A. Code Authority, the General fixed the minimum mark-up for our jobbers at 3 percent. After the N.R.A. was held to be

[5] *Northwestern Merchant*, April, 1939, p. 16.
[6] *Ibid.*, May, 1939, p. 8.
[7] Federal Trade Commission, *Resale Price Maintenance* (Washington, 1945), pp. 854–872.

unconstitutional, we still used the same minimum mark-up. Today our jobbers use a minimum mark-up of 4%. This mark-up is based on a survey of the tobacco wholesalers' cost of doing business. I conducted said survey." In western Washington the wholesale and retail tobacco dealers, it is reported, sought "to have a completed cigarette and tobacco figure uniform throughout the trading area." Their method of procedure was as follows: "First, a survey was made in the wholesale field . . . in order that a base price could be established whereby some common ground for fixing a minimum in the retail field could be worked out. This survey showed the cost of doing business in the jobbing field as approximately six (6) percent. Therefore, the price on cigarettes and tobacco was established throughout the retail field as identical by all jobbers. This provided a platform upon which to work out the retail schedule." The survey conducted in the retail field showed that the retail cost of doing business was approximately 19.5 percent.[8]

An example of the procedure used to determine "legal" prices by trade association members in the grocery field in western Washington is reported by a trade journal as follows: "There were more than one hundred in attendance and after some discussion, it was agreed to set the minimum mark-up at ten (10) percent instead of the six percent we had been working on up to that time."[9] A month later it was reported in the same trade journal, "The new ten (10) percent mark-up on all grocery items is working very fine. There have been a few errors, but no intentional violation of this agreement. Possibly if we keep our heads cool and cooperate, we may be able to make a few dollars this year."[10]

In a careful study of unfair-practices legislation, G. J. Feldman reports, "Cost surveys have been conducted in some states in a most informal manner, frequently by a mere vote of an interested group as to what the cost should be. In some states the 'cost' established by these surveys has been raised progressively year by year until it has reached decidedly uneconomic levels."[11] The studies of Saul Nelson indicate that "retail grocery associations in several states have seized the opportunity to issue periodic lists of minimum prices proclaiming that sales below these prices will be considered *prima facie* evidence of violation."[12] Professor Charles F. Phillips has urged that continuing studies be made of the operation of unfair-practices laws in the various states. "Is it not true," he asks, "that in many cases they are being enforced by horizontal combinations of retailers which are acting in violation of our antitrust laws?"[13]

It is striking to realize the amount of the additional profit which can be

[8] *Northwestern Merchant*, October, 1939, p. 10.

[9] *Ibid.*, April, 1940, p. 7.

[10] *Ibid.*, May, 1940, p. 17.

[11] George J. Feldman, "Legislative Opposition to Chain Stores and Its Minimization," *Law and Contemporary Problems*, Spring, 1941, p. 347.

[12] Saul Nelson, "Round Table on Preserving Competition Versus Regulating Monopoly," *American Economic Review*, March, 1940, p. 218.

[13] Charles F. Phillips, "Some Studies Needed in Marketing," *Journal of Marketing*, July, 1940, p. 20.

secured by concerted action to raise prices just a cent or two. In reporting on an antitrust case involving bakers in the Philadelphia area, for example, Dr. C. D. Edwards stated, "The conspiracy which raised the price of bread by a cent in the *Philadelphia area* involved a diversion of from four to eight million dollars a year into the income of bakers in that area. It necessarily meant a corresponding shrinkage of the market available for other parts of the food industry. Had this gone unchecked, nothing would have been more natural than for other groups to protect themselves by similar conspiracies."[14]

THE POLICING AND ENFORCEMENT OF UNFAIR-PRACTICES ACTS BY TRADE ASSOCIATIONS

Since the state laws prohibiting sales below cost do not usually provide for a state policing agency, the task of securing compliance has been largely assumed by state and local wholesale and retail trade associations. One principle which these associations early came to learn was that without *continual* policing activity there is little hope for securing an observance of the uniform prices established by group action. As a result, trade association executives have organized a variety of procedures and agencies for watching to see that the agreed-upon prices are observed. Assessments are levied on retailers and wholesalers to secure funds for policing activity; and special bureaus are established to scrutinize newspaper advertisements and to shop the various stores for price violations. No information is available on the amount of money which is spent on policing activity, but trade sources express the view that it has been substantial.

If a violation is found, the retailer concerned is contacted by a trade association executive and encouraged in a friendly way to observe "the law." If, however, any resistance is shown, the retailer complained against is told firmly to "get in line or else." A continued violation brings a citation from the office of the prosecuting attorney. The prospect of an expensive legal suit with the probable need to employ expert witnesses on cost usually is sufficient to bring about speedy compliance. In some instances, however, it has been necessary for a trade association to have the prosecuting attorney issue a formal complaint and bring the case to trial. The decisions of the state courts vary with the cases, but there has been a sufficient number of convictions to put fear into the hearts of retailers inclined to show a price independence.

In most instances, trade association executives seek to bring about an observance of legal prices by persuasion rather than by legal enforcement. "Coöperation, not coercion" is the rule, and an appeal to the courts is usually made only as a last resort. In the words of a trade association manager, "This law is predicated on united action, tolerance, and good will. . . . There may be some exceptional case where only the policeman can get results, but

---

[14] From a speech by C. D. Edwards before the Associated Grocery Manufacturers of America in New York City, reported in *Pacific Northwest Grocer and Meat Dealer,* January, 1942, p. 6.

we will go farther and secure more lasting results by using moral suasion, good will attitudes towards the industry, and . . . rational appeasement where differences arise, than we will if we pin our faith too generally to the letter of the law and the powers of the courts." A survey of sales-below-cost statutes conducted by the Department of Justice, Ottawa, Canada, in 1953, secured the response that the success of the law "depends largely on voluntary compliance and on the support given it by wholesalers and retailers." Another state, in common with most of the others replying, wrote that "much of the Act's effect" is achieved without prosecution.[15] In taking this point of view, association leaders in the distributive trades clearly recognize the problems which they face in legal actions. The many difficulties involved (a) in estimating depreciation and other overhead costs and (b) in securing the cost prices and direct selling expenses of an alleged violator are sufficient to make the association executives know that they will do better by not getting these problems before the courts too often.

Trade leaders also are reluctant to press for vigorous court action because they fear that the unfair-practices legislation may be tossed out of court as a price-fixing measure. Many states have constitutional provisions against monopolistic activity, and there is also the possibility that interstate commerce may be involved.

Since the county and state prosecuting attorneys are elected officials, a strongly organized pressure group can usually induce them to write firm letters of protest to anyone selling below the "legal" prices. The fear of prolonged and expensive court proceedings, the desire to avoid publicity and ill will, coupled with the friendly and cordial moral suasion of association executives, thereupon are often sufficient to bring about a considerable measure of compliance.

THE LEGALITY OF STATE LAWS PROHIBITING SALES BELOW COST

So far, the legality of the state laws prohibiting sales below cost has not been tested in the United States Supreme Court. In California, Colorado, Montana, Tennessee, Wyoming, and Washington the state courts have upheld the respective state acts as a valid exercise of the police power to protect the public welfare. An indication of the general line of reasoning adopted by the state courts in these cases may be found in a decision of the California Supreme Court. The California case was brought especially to test the validity of the California Unfair Practices Act. The Court was presented with an agreed-upon set of facts in which the defendant freely admitted that he had sold tobacco products for less than cost *to injure his competitors.* The only issue before the state Supreme Court was the constitutionality of the law. The Court upheld the statute as a legitimate exercise of the state's police power. According to the Court,

[15] *Loss-Leader Selling,* Restrictive Trade Practices Commission, Department of Justice (Ottawa, Canada, 1954), pp. 282–284.

It must be borne in mind that this statute does not regulate the selling of commodities—it is the predatory trade practice of selling below cost with intent to injure competitors which the legislature on reasonable grounds has determined is vicious and unfair that is prohibited. . . . The statute embodies the concept that sales made at a loss to the seller, when made for the purpose of injuring or destroying competition, are predatory and anti-social in character. The economic wisdom of such a concept may be debatable, but being debatable, the legislature is empowered to choose between its acceptance or rejection. The statute, so far as the facts here involved are concerned, goes no further than reasonably necessary to effectuate that choice.[16]

The unfair-practices acts are inoperative in the states of Ohio, Michigan, and New Jersey, because of adverse rulings by the state courts. The Ohio law was invalidated because it was found to have a tendency to result in identical prices, and the Michigan act was held to be invalid because of the vagueness of the statute in defining cost. In New Jersey the unfair-practices act was declared to be illegal on the ground that its provisions were too uncertain and too indefinite to enable a person to know exactly the lawful course which he should pursue. The Court also indicated that it was exceedingly reluctant to see any restriction placed on the common-law right of buyers and sellers to establish prices by free bargaining.[17]

THE UNFAIR-PRACTICES ACTS AND THE SHERMAN ANTITRUST LAW

In view of the widespread evidence that the unfair-practices acts were being applied and made operative by means of collective action, the federal Antitrust Division in 1941 under Thurman Arnold brought charges of collusive price fixing against numerous wholesale and retail groups in various parts of the country. Some nine cases were brought, and in them it was charged that the defendants had violated the Sherman Act in agreeing upon markups and prices, both at wholesale and at retail. Most of the cases were settled by the entry of pleas of *nolo contendere*—a plea which neither admits nor denies guilt, but leaves the decision to the court—and the imposition of fines. In several instances, consent judgments were also entered enjoining the practices attacked.

The first of the cases filed by the federal government charging collusive price fixing under the state unfair-practices acts was brought against the Colorado Food Distributors' Association and its individual members. This trade group had been organized in 1937 to enforce the unfair-practices act in the grocery business in Colorado. For some time, members of the association had been operating with a minimum retail markup of 9 percent. Then the president of the association called a meeting of its members and asked

[16] *Wholesale Tobacco Dealers' Assn. of Southern Calif., Inc., v. National Candy & Tobacco Co., Inc.,* Supreme Court of California, 82 Pac. (2d) 3, 17, 19 (1938).

[17] *Serrer v. Cigarette Service Co.,* 74 N.E. (2d) 853 (1947); and *State v. Packard-Bamberger and Co.,* 8 Atl. (2d) 293 (1939).

"association members to show their hands if their costs were less than 12 percent. No hands went up."[18] Upon the basis of this "cost survey," the association declared the legal retail markup to be 12 percent, with 14 percent for those doing their own warehousing. The Department of Justice charged the group with illegal price fixing under the Sherman Act, and the defendants paid fines totaling some $45,300 without contesting the action.[19]

In 1941 a federal case was instituted in Massachusetts against the Massachusetts Food Council, Inc., a trade association organized by chain stores, supermarkets, independent retailers, and wholesalers in that state. The Council was described as one of the most effective agencies ever formed for applying and policing an unfair-practices act. In settling the case, the District Court assessed fines and entered a consent judgment abolishing the Council and enjoining the collective action of the members on price. A similar case was brought in Connecticut against the Connecticut Food Council and its members. Pleas of *nolo contendere* were entered and fines of $32,500 were assessed.[20]

During 1941 charges of collusive price fixing were also brought against retail and wholesale trade associations in Los Angeles, San Francisco, and Seattle. In all instances, fines ranging up to $5000 for each violation were levied against the various trade members for price-fixing activities. The actions taken against the trade groups in southern and northern California were the only ones to be carried to a Court of Appeals. The Court of Appeals upheld both convictions and affirmed the view that the fixing of retail prices of food and groceries in these cases restrained interstate commerce, since a large part of the products were brought into the state for sale at the fixed prices.

In the case against the Food and Grocery Bureau of Southern California, an association serving several thousand retailers in southern California, the Court of Appeals found that the Bureau had issued periodic price sheets to the trade indicating the minimum prices at which food and grocery items should be sold. Its price lists were also accompanied with instructions to retailers to observe the prices carefully. The price list on butter and eggs, for example, stated, "Grocers: Adhere Strictly to These Butter and Egg Prices." The Court found that the Bureau was also active in investigating the prices charged by retailers and that it brought pressure to bear on anyone selling below the price lists which it issued. The Court condemned these various activities and held that all "agreements stabilizing . . . prices either at a maximum or a minimum or through a formula violate the Sherman Act."[21]

In a similar decision the Court of Appeals upheld the conviction against the California Retail Grocers and Merchants Association, the trade organization of food dealers in northern California. This association, the Court found,

[18] *Business Week*, December 28, 1940, p. 18.
[19] *Ibid.*, February 22, 1941, p. 46.
[20] *Ibid.*, November 8, 1941, p. 8.
[21] *Food and Grocery Bureau of Southern California* v. *U.S.*, 139 F. (2d) 973–975 (1943).

likewise used the Unfair Practices Act as a vehicle for fixing prices. The association also had a record of pursuing a vigorous program of enforcement and of bringing legal action against retailers who sold below the fixed prices, whether or not there was an intention to injure a competitor. The declared purpose of the association, the Court found, was "price stabilizing," which it effected "by preventing the sale of any such merchandise below prices fixed by the conspirators."[22]

Action by the federal government against collusive price fixing carried on under the guise of the unfair-practices acts was discontinued with the imposition of price controls during World War II. In 1942 the Office of Price Administration set price ceilings on most products sold at retail, and this control was continued until June, 1947. A principal problem of dealers during the war period and immediately thereafter was one of securing higher price ceilings from the O.P.A., and little or no use was made of the unfair-practices acts, as such. With the end of retail price control, moreover, retail prices rose sharply and dealers had little reason to be concerned with the action of competitors in selling goods at low prices.

UNFAIR-PRACTICES ACTS USED PRIMARILY DURING "BUYERS MARKETS"

In the main, retailers and wholesalers turn their attention to unfair-practices acts during a period when demand at established prices weakens. At such time, competition among sellers makes for lower prices, and various sellers find an interest in trying to prevent this competition, if possible. In so far as contemporary fiscal and monetary policies may result in a gradually rising price level, it is possible that the unfair-practices acts will remain largely unutilized. With the recurrence of deflation or business recession, however, and the adjustment of competitive prices toward lower levels, it is probable that numerous organized groups of merchants will again resort to the statutes in an effort to maintain prices.

Most loss-leader selling, experience has shown, is found in the grocery store and drug store fields. It is mainly in these areas that trade groups seek to utilize the sales-below-cost statutes. In the case of more expensive items, group efforts to restrict price competition are commonly rendered ineffective by the practice of making excessive trade-in allowances as a part of the purchase price.

In any event, unfair-practices acts continue to remain on the statute books; and groups of retailers and wholesalers, from time to time, continue to utilize the legislation. In these efforts, they usually find that the state law-enforcement authorities, as elected officials, give sympathetic assistance in the application of cost-survey pricing.

Any protection for consumers at the retail level, it appears, must come from federal intervention, for state authorities in many states seem to be

[22] *California Retail Grocers and Merchants Association* v. *U.S.*, 139 F. (2d) 978–983 (1943).

principally concerned with the interests of organized trade groups. The limited financial resources of the federal antitrust agencies, however, make it possible for them to prosecute only the most flagrant examples of monopoly action. The Department of Justice and the Federal Trade Commission both report that they do not have adequate personnel or funds to proceed effectively against monopolistic action even in the case of resale price-maintenance legislation. The problems involved in extending their antitrust prosecutions to the whole field of retail and wholesale trade can only mean that a broad area is left in which organized trade groups can act collectively in their own interests and to the detriment of consumers.

DO UNFAIR PRACTICES ACTS PROVIDE PROTECTION AGAINST TRUE LOSS-LEADER SELLING?

An independent retailer frequently finds himself faced with a competitor who is selling a particular product—such as shortening or bananas—at less than acquisition cost. Or, he may be troubled by a competitor who is giving away merchandise, by drawings, contests, or tie-in arrangements. Do the unfair practices acts provide a retailer with protection against these kinds of unfair competition? The answer is largely "no."

If a sale is found to be below cost (or if a product is being given away), that fact alone does not usually constitute a violation of the acts. Most state laws require proof that the sale or gift was made *with the intent to injure and destroy competition.* The sale or gift, in and of itself, does not constitute proof of such intent. Additional evidence must be presented to show a predatory motive. Experience has shown that the task of proving "illegal intent" in such cases is exceedingly difficult. Sellers allege "good faith" to meet or beat competition; and in the absence of letters or declarations that "I am going to eliminate you," there is no ready way to identify "bad faith."

As an alternative to the unfair practices acts, legislative bodies could enact a statute making it illegal "to discriminate between or among different commodities or similar commodities of different grade and quality by reselling at retail . . . any commodity at less than net cost of such commodity delivered to the retailer's place of business . . . where the effect . . . may be substantially to lessen competition." (See also Chap. 21, p. 482.) Such a law would prevent true loss-leader selling (sales below the laid-down cost). It would be readily enforceable. An injured party, moreover, would be spared the virtually impossible task of proving a predatory motive.

Prizes, gifts, and premiums—like loss leaders—are frequently used to expand sales and thwart the growth of competitors. As Professor F. W. Taussig has said, "These delude the purchaser into the belief that he is getting something for nothing. Like mendacious advertising, they rest on the gullibility of mankind, and are effective in proportion as they are carried out on a large scale."[23]

How far should government go in curbing the use of premium giving?

[23] F. W. Taussig, *Principles of Economics* (New York, 1930), Vol. 2, p. 450.

Certain gifts, such as calenders, are clearly a legitimate gesture for gaining good will. Other items, such as automobiles and trips to Europe, can only be financed by large companies with "long purses." Where the line should be drawn between gratuities which are reasonable and those which constitute unfair competition is a problem for special study and administrative determination.

UNFAIR-PRACTICES ACTS ENCOURAGE UNIFIED SELLING

The action of the state legislatures and state courts in permitting industry groups to fix minimum prices upon the basis of cost surveys conducted by industry members themselves tends to encourage unified selling. The laws provide that no "person" shall sell for less than *his* cost of production. The very fact that "cost surveys" or fixed percentage markups may be used as prima facie evidence of cost, however, indicates that the sponsors of the laws contemplated group action on price. Also, the manifold difficulties involved in conducting a genuine cost survey make it clear that "surveys" are really a device for setting the prices which dealers would like to secure.

An honest and careful cost survey would require large expense and much technical skill. Even then *public authorities would need to check the cost calculations* and work out acceptable formulas for evaluating the "fair value" of the productive agents and inventories owned by the business enterprises and acquired in earlier cost periods. There would also be the troublesome problem of estimating depreciation charges, selling expenses, and executive salaries. Further difficulties would be encountered in working out an acceptable plan for distributing the variable and overhead costs over the many hundreds of items sold in a retail store. All these problems go far beyond those contemplated by trade groups when they ask the association secretary to make a cost survey.

The available evidence indicates that when trade groups coöperate in determining minimum prices upon the basis of a cost survey, their action inevitably ends in setting a "legal" price by means of discussion, compromise, and joint agreement. In any actual cost survey individual costs would show a wide range from the lowest to the highest cost estimates. Out of all the chaotic and conflicting guesswork of the hundreds of retail dealers some common price or markup figure must be selected if the trade group is going to achieve its purpose of avoiding competitive action on price. If the unfair-practices acts were to describe the use which in most cases has been made of them the phrase "no sales below cost" would have to be changed to read "no sales below the price set by an industry group."

THE ERRONEOUS CONCEPTS OF COMPETITION AND MONOPOLY EMBODIED IN THE UNFAIR-PRACTICES ACTS

The California model statute and the related state laws based upon it contain a section stating, "The legislature declares that the purpose of this act is to safeguard the public against the creation or perpetuation of monopolies and to foster and encourage competition." How can this section be reconciled with the actual use which has been made of the laws prohibiting sales below cost?

In advocating the adoption of the unfair-practices acts, trade groups publicly stated that they were strongly in favor of "competition." Various trade papers, for example, contained statements of the sponsors declaring, "We desire no laws to destroy or even weaken competition. We want laws to keep competition decent and clean"; "The Unfair Sales Act . . . does not seek to . . . destroy competition"; and "We home-owned retail food merchants of Washington are not opposed to free competition."[24] What kind of competition did these advocates have in mind? A clue is found in the annual address of the president of the Washington Merchants' Association for 1939, in which it was stated, "With the passage of the Unfair Practices Act, for which credit is largely due this association . . . competition will shift from price to management."[25] Sales competition—and not price competition—is thus the type of competition which the sponsors of unfair-practices acts contemplated when they declared their faith in competition.

Sales or service competition tends to change the relative quantity of business going to each seller. It does not, however, increase the total number of units of goods going to all consumers, for the quantity of goods sold is a function of price. From the standpoint of public policy, the type of competition called for by the antitrust laws is *price competition*, which is individual, spontaneous, and independent in nature. It is with this type of competition that the benefits of increased efficiency, technological progress, high productivity, and improved methods of operation accrue to the public in the form of more and better goods at lower prices. Although sales or service competition is desirable, it is an incomplete and inadequate type of competition and does not provide a fair and equitable means for the determination of prices and incomes. It is not, moreover, the type of competition called for by the antitrust laws.

The sponsors of the unfair-practices acts also declared that their desire was to "safeguard the public against the creation . . . of monopolies." What did they mean by this statement? A study of trade journal articles written at the time the unfair-practices acts were being enacted indicates that the "monopoly" which the independent retailers wanted to curb was the competition of the chain stores. In the minds of many retailers, chain stores at that time were considered to be "Wall Street Chiselers" and "enormous vampires feeding upon our economic lifeblood." Since the independent retailers were unable to secure legislation taxing the chain stores out of existence, they turned to a policy of coöperating with them whenever that could be done. The very fact of coöperation and collective action on price, however, created a condition of monopoly which makes the operation of unfair-practices acts totally inconsistent with their stated purposes.

[24] *Northwestern Merchant*, February, 1937, p. 3; and *Pacific Northwest Grocer and Meat Dealer*, June, 1941, p. 1.
[25] *Northwestern Merchant*, November, 1939, p. 8.

PUBLIC POLICY AND THE UNFAIR-PRACTICES ACTS

In surveying the nature, purposes, and consequences of the "fair-trade" and "unfair-practices" acts, one finds that the two measures are species of the same genus. Both seek to employ government intervention to maintain and protect the profit margins which sellers would like to secure. As A. D. H. Kaplan has said, "Apparently a large segment of small business is becoming conditioned to a climate of administered prices, which small business generally opposed in the early days when monopoly control was the big issue. The main difference—and not an unimportant one—seems to be that whereas big business is usually prepared to do its own policing of such administered prices, small business lacks the strength to make prices stick without the aid of government as policeman."[26]

The criticisms of resale price-maintenance laws which were presented in the preceding chapter apply with equal force to the general use which has been made of laws prohibiting sales below cost. In restricting and eliminating price competition, the unfair-practices acts likewise result in higher prices, higher margins of profit, a shift to "cost-raising" types of competition, the maintenance of rigid prices in the face of declining demand, and the tendency to bring about an overcrowding in the distributive trades. In large measure, the road which we have chosen to follow in adopting fair-trade and unfair-practices legislation is one of monopolistic restrictions. Is this the road the American people want to take in the years which lie ahead?

In view of the facts (1) that private monopoly control is indefensible and (2) that a broad extension of direct public control over prices is not feasible, it follows that the appropriate public policy for the wholesaling and retailing trades is one of maintaining and restoring effective price competition. This means that the "unfair-practices" acts and the "fair-trade" laws should be reëxamined by the courts and the legislatures. At the same time, it is recognized that wholesale and retail merchants are entitled to have rules which in truth make for "fair trade" and an elimination of "unfair practices." In large measure, these rules are to be found in a strengthening of the laws against price discrimination and in providing legislation against true loss-leader selling, as such.

SUGGESTIONS FOR FURTHER READING

Federal Trade Commission, *Resale Price Maintenance* (Washington, 1945).
"Further Developments in the Field of Statutory Bans Against Selling Below Cost," *Virginia Law Review*, February, 1948, pp. 201–209.
Grether, E. T., *Price Control Under Fair Trade Legislation* (New York, 1939).
Loss-Leader Selling, Restrictive Trade Practices Commission, Department of Justice (Ottawa, Canada, 1954).
Lovell, Richard H., "Sales Below Cost Prohibitions," *Yale Law Journal*, January, 1948, pp. 391–425.

[26] A. D. H. Kaplan, *Small Business: Its Place and Problems* (New York, 1948), p. 205.

McAllister, Breck, "Price Control by Law in the United States," *Law and Contemporary Problems*, June, 1937, pp. 273–300.

Problems of Small Business, Monograph 17, Temporary National Economic Committee, 76th Congress, third session, 1941.

State Price Control Legislation, prepared by the Marketing Laws Survey, Works Progress Administration (Washington, 1940).

Tannenbaum, Robert, "Cost Under the Unfair Practice Acts," *Journal of Business*, January, 1939, pp. 1–65.

CHAPTER 23

The Direct Control of Business

CONTROL OVER THE INNER WORKINGS OF BUSINESS

The public control of industry fits into our category of price and income determination by *authority*. It means specific action by government to determine, approve, or modify prices, investments, and the use of resources. Government, in some degree, becomes a participant in the making of basic entrepreneurial decisions. In acting directly to control prices or outputs, government may (1) set the minimum, maximum, or actual prices; (2) restrict production or withhold or destroy portions of existing supplies; (3) restrict demand by rationing and by imposing export controls; (4) establish subsidies or bounties to create or protect the domestic production of specific commodities; and (5) grant licenses or permits for new investment or construction.

Under conditions of free enterprise and price competition, by way of contrast, government does *not* directly determine the business of production, interchange, or pricing. It does not participate in the inner workings of a business enterprise. Its duty is rather one of planning the institutional framework within which production, prices, and incomes are determined by the free play of market forces.

It is generally agreed that during times of war and rearmament for defense the exercise of direct governmental control over prices and uses is necessary in order to restrict profiteering, retard the development of inflation, and insure an adequate allocation of supplies for military use. Likewise, most persons would agree that in the case of public utilities direct control is necessary in order to protect consumers against excessive charges. The controversial aspects of authoritarian price control center on whether or not governmental authority should be used to control the prices and output of certain commodities in order (1) to *improve* the economic position of individuals who produce them or (2) to *protect* the public in the case of certain key industries, such as steel and oil, which are characterized by oligopoly and unified selling.

The purpose of the present chapter is to illustrate and discuss the growing use of public control in the American economy. Consideration will first be given to the *legal basis* for direct price control in a system based upon competition and "freedom of contract." Attention will then be directed to the adoption of public control in important areas as an alternative to, and in place of, a policy of regulation. The functional meanings of the terms "regulation" and "control," it will be recalled, were defined and distinguished in Chapter 5.

THE LEGAL BASIS FOR DIRECT PRICE CONTROL IN ANGLO-SAXON LAW

During the Middle Ages, the sparse population and the fewness of sellers in various occupations gave rise to the exercise of direct control by government over the prices and sales policies of various trades—such as those of bakers, millers, tailors, victualers, innkeepers, wharfingers, and ferry operators. In these cases, the small number of sellers—sometimes only one—in a given town or locality frequently resulted in nonservice and the charging of extortionate prices. As a supplement to the policy of competition, therefore, the law imposed the direct obligation on such sellers to serve all customers at reasonable rates.

An early legal discussion of the power of government to control directly the prices in various callings is found in a treatise written in 1676 by Lord Matthew Hale, chief justice of the King's Bench of England. Lord Hale wrote that in the regulation of commerce government has the power not only to create markets and prevent forestalling but also to control excessive prices in situations which have a monopoly character. A ferry, for example, operated for the use of all the king's subjects, was declared to be "a thing of public interest and use." The owner of such a ferry was required to serve all who would use it and to charge only reasonable tolls.

In his treatise *De Portibus Maris* (1675) Lord Hale developed the theory of direct regulation as follows: "If the king or subject have a public wharf, unto which all persons that come to that port must come and unlade or lade their goods as for the purpose, because they are the wharfs only licensed by the queen . . . or because there is no other wharf in that port, as it may fall out where a port is newly erected; in that case there cannot be taken arbitrary and excessive duties . . . neither can they be inhanced to an immoderate rate, but the duties must be reasonable and moderate. . . . For now the wharf and crane and other conveniences are affected with a public interest, and they cease to be *juris privati* only."[1] Although Lord Hale did not define the meaning of the phrase "affected with a public interest," the examples he used in relation to it indicate that he applied it to situations in which a seller possesses some degree of monopoly power.

EARLY ATTEMPTS TO CONTROL TRANSPORTATION RATES IN THE UNITED STATES

An important factor in the American Revolution was the desire of many business leaders to be free from the restrictions of British mercantilism. The pattern of control in the new nation, accordingly, became one of economic

[1] *De Portibus Maris* (1675), in Francis Hargrave, *Tracts Relative to the Law of England* (London, 1787), pp. 77–78.

freedom. Informal market centers were established in the larger towns; and the growing number of merchants, manufacturers, and importers provided an active price competition.

The principal occasion for government intervention on price arose with the development of transportation facilities—the turnpike roads, canals, and later the railroads. Conditions of local monopoly usually existed along the various routes, and state governments began to exercise control over monopoly power. The usual procedure was to include in the charters granted to companies for operating turnpike roads and canals a clause requiring the tolls charged to be reasonable. With the beginning of railroad construction in 1830, similar provisions were included in the charters and franchises granted to the railroads. These early charter provisions on rates, however, proved to be only "gestures" toward public control. In most cases, the transportation companies, especially the railroads, were active in politics, and their influence on the state legislatures served to prevent any sort of effective regulation.

The economic group which finally came to demand effective government intervention to control railroad rates was the Patrons of Husbandry. This group, popularly known as the Grange, attained a membership of some 750,000 by 1875 and became a new and important factor in American politics. As a result of its influence, "granger laws" were passed in Illinois, Minnesota, Iowa, Wisconsin, and Missouri during the period 1869–1875, subjecting railroad rates to legislative control. The legislation adopted by the state of Illinois in 1871 established maximum rates for freight and passenger service on the railroads, as well as for the storage of grain in public warehouses. The validity of the state regulatory legislation was promptly contested in the courts, and the case involving the Illinois warehouse law of 1871 was the first of the various cases to be appealed to the United States Supreme Court. This was the famous case of *Munn* v. *Illinois*, which was decided by the Supreme Court in 1877 in favor of the state of Illinois.

THE INTRODUCTION OF THE DOCTRINE "AFFECTED WITH A PUBLIC INTEREST" INTO AMERICAN LAW

In taking steps to enforce the Illinois warehouse law of 1871, the state authorities brought action against Munn and Scott, owners of grain elevators in Chicago, for failure to take out licenses as required by law. Munn and Scott appealed to the courts, claiming that the legislation deprived them of property without due process of law. The Supreme Court of Illinois, however, upheld the legislation on the grounds of public welfare. The owners of the warehouses, it declared, were an "organized combination of monopolists . . . with but one heart, and that palpitating for excessive gains."[2]

The *Munn* case was thereupon taken to the United States Supreme Court. In upholding the Illinois statute, the Court introduced into American constitutional law the doctrine that direct price control is justified in the case

[2] *Munn* v. *People*, 69 Ill. 80, 93 (1873).

of businesses "affected with a public interest." "Looking, then, to the common law," the Court declared, ". . . we find that when private property is 'affected with a public interest, it ceases to be *juris privati* only.' This was said by Lord Chief Justice Hale more than two hundred years ago." Property, the Court continued, becomes "clothed with a public interest" and subject to public regulation "when used in a manner to make it of public consequence, and affect the community at large." When does the use of property make it of public consequence? The examples cited by the Court indicate that it is primarily when property is used in business activity under conditions which involve some degree of monopoly. It is then that the law imposes on a seller the direct obligation to be reasonable in his terms and to serve all customers.

In the study of the facts of the *Munn* case, the Court found that Chicago was the center of the greatest grain market in the world. Although there were some fourteen storage warehouses for grain, these facilities were ownd by nine firms. Each year, moreover, the nine firms agreed among themselves on the rates to be charged for the storage of grain.

Thus it is apparent [the Court declared] that all the elevating facilities through which these vast productions "of some seven or eight great states of the West" must pass on the way "to four or five of the states on the seashore" may be a "virtual monopoly." . . . They stand . . . in the very "gateway of commerce," and take toll from all who pass. . . . Every bushel of grain for its passage "pays a toll, which is a common charge," and, therefore, according to Lord Hale, every such warehouseman "ought to be under public regulation, viz., that he . . . take but reasonable toll." Certainly, if any business can be clothed "with a public interest and cease to be *juris privati* only," this has been.[3]

The decision in the *Munn* case upholding the legislative determination of maximum rates for grain elevators was applied at once by the Court to the cases which it had pending on railroad rate regulation.[4] "Carriers for hire," the Court found, are likewise "clothed with a public interest" and are subject to public regulation for the common good. In 1884 the "public utility" concept was also applied to companies supplying water. "That it is within the power of the government," the Court declared, "to regulate the prices at which water shall be sold by one who enjoys a virtual monopoly of the sale, we do not doubt."[5]

In 1914 the concept "affected with a public interest" was broadened by the Court in the *German Alliance Insurance* case. This case involved the legality of an act passed by the Kansas legislature providing for the regulation of fire insurance rates. The Court held that the fire insurance business was one of "public concern." In its opinion the statute served to protect

[3] *Munn v. Illinois*, 94 U.S. 113 (1877).
[4] *Chicago, Burlington and Quincy R.R. v. Iowa*, 94 U.S. 155 (1877), and *Peik v. Chicago and Northwestern Railway*, 94 U.S. 164 (1877).
[5] *Spring Valley Water Works v. Schottler*, 110 U.S. 347, 354 (1884).

the public against "arbitrary terms" and was thus in accord with the regulation of railroads, street railways, grain elevators, and wayside inns. According to the Court, "We may venture to observe that the price of insurance is not fixed over the counters of the companies by what Adam Smith calls the higgling of the market, but formed in the councils of the underwriters, promulgated in schedules of practically controlling constancy which the applicant for insurance is powerless to oppose, and which, therefore, has led to the assertion that the business of insurance is of monopolistic character and that 'it is illusory to speak of a liberty of contract.' It is in the alternative presented of accepting the rates of the companies or refraining from insurance . . . that we may discover the inducement of the Kansas statute."[6]

RESTRICTING THE DOCTRINE OF DIRECT CONTROL TO CASES IN WHICH MONOPOLY IS "NATURAL" OR INEVITABLE

The broad interpretation placed by the Court upon the phrase "affected with a public interest" in the *German Alliance* case was subsequently narrowed and limited in its application to businesses usually regarded as "public utilities"—that is, those in which monopoly had come to be accepted as being "natural" or inevitable because of technical conditions. Thus, in the *Wolff Packing* case, decided in 1923, the Court held that an act of the Kansas legislature providing for compulsory arbitration and the fixing of wages by government was invalid as applied to the food, clothing, and fuel industries. In the case at hand, the Court found that the Wolff Packing Company, which was engaged in the preparation of meat products, was "in active competition" with other meat packers. "It has never been supposed," the Court declared, "since the adoption of the Constitution, that the business of the butcher, or the baker, the tailor, the woodchopper, the mining operator, or the miner was clothed with such a public interest that the price of his product or his wages could be fixed by state regulation." If the "public interest" doctrine could be extended by the legislature to any industry at will, said the Court, "there must be a revolution in the relation of government to general business. . . . It will be impossible to reconcile such result with the freedom of contract and of labor secured by the Fourteenth Amendment."[7]

In four subsequent cases the Court by majority opinion refused to extend the "public interest" doctrine to industries which are outside of the narrow concept of public utilities.[8] In taking this position, the view of the Court was that "freedom of contract" provided for an *indirect* control of price by means of competition. It was primarily when monopoly was found to be "natural" or inevitable that the Court recognized the need for direct control

[6] *German Alliance Insurance Co.* v. *Lewis*, 233 U.S. 389, 416–417 (1914).

[7] *Wolff Packing Co.* v. *Kansas*, 262 U.S. 523, 537, 539–540 (1923).

[8] *Tyson Bros.* v. *Banton*, 273 U.S. 418, 429 (1927); *Ribnick* v. *McBride*, 277 U.S. 350 (1928); *Williams* v. *Standard Oil Co.*, 278 U.S. 235 (1929); and *New State Ice Co.* v. *Liebmann*, 285 U.S. 262 (1932).

and read into the Constitution the common-law doctrine that the public is entitled to protection against arbitrary and unreasonable prices.

THE JUDICIAL ACCEPTANCE OF PRICE CONTROL BY AUTHORITY FOR PURPOSES OTHER THAN THE REGULATION OF MONOPOLY

The general line of reasoning established by the Supreme Court in limiting the application of the "public interest" doctrine to businesses in which monopoly was generally recognized as being inevitable was sharply and abruptly modified in 1934 in *Nebbia v. New York*.[9] This case involved the legality of a New York statute providing for the control of milk prices at retail by a state board. The purpose of the regulatory legislation was to *increase* the incomes of the dairymen; and in upholding the action of the legislature in determining prices directly, the Court gave sanction to the *general principle of price and income determination by the method of authority.* (See Landmark Cases, p. 723.)

During the great depression, the dairy producers, as well as those in other agricultural industries, suffered severe economic hardship in having to buy industrial products at rigid, inflexible prices while selling their own products at competitive prices. In many cases farmers were also burdened with heavy debts contracted during a period of high prices which had to be paid by selling farm products at the low prices of the depression period. In an attempt to help dairy farmers, nearly one-half of the states adopted milk-control laws designed to fix minimum prices for the sale of milk.

The position taken by the attorneys for Mr. Nebbia was that direct legislative fixation of prices violates the freedom of contract guaranteed by the Fourteenth Amendment except in the case of businesses "affected with a public interest"—that is, in the case of public utilities which are in their nature monopolies. The milk industry, it was contended, had none of these characteristics. Justice Roberts, speaking for the Court, agreed with these contentions, stating "We may as well say at once that the dairy industry is not, in the accepted sense of the phrase, a public utility. We think the appellant is also right in asserting that there is in this case no suggestion of any monopoly or monopolistic practice." However, Justice Roberts asked, "if, as must be conceded, the industry is subject to regulation in the public interest, what constitutional principle bars the state from *correcting existing maladjustments by legislation touching prices?* We think there is no such principle."[10] Upon the basis of this reasoning, a majority of the Court upheld the New York statute.

THE FURTHER EXTENSION OF DIRECT PRICE CONTROL

The changed attitude of the Supreme Court with respect to price fixing as announced in the *Nebbia* case was soon brought to bear on several addi-

[9] *Nebbia v. New York*, 291 U.S. 502 (1934).
[10] 291 U.S. 531-532. Italics supplied.

tional cases which involved legislative price determination. In 1937 the Court, in a five-to-four decision, upheld a statute of the state of Washington fixing minimum wages for women.[11] In reaching its decision, the Court indicated its extreme concern over "the exploitation of a class of workers who are in an unequal position with respect to bargaining power and are thus relatively defenseless against the denial of a living wage." As in the *Nebbia* case the Court declared its willingness to permit a state to use its police power to determine prices and incomes for the benefit of one group as against another.

In 1940 the Court upheld the validity of the Bituminous Coal Act enacted by Congress in 1937.[12] The act of 1937 provided for the establishment of a Bituminous Coal Commission with authority to regulate the sale and fix the minimum prices on coal moving in or directly affecting interstate commerce. A primary purpose of the legislation was to raise the average level of prices, so as to permit operators generally to pay higher wages negotiated by collective bargaining. In the opinion of the Court, the establishment of minimum prices for coal was a proper exercise of the power to regulate interstate commerce. The control of price, it stated, is an aspect of the regulation of commerce, and the power of Congress over interstate commerce is complete and unlimited.

Again, in 1941, the Court upheld the Fair Labor Standards Act of 1938, which was enacted by Congress to fix the minimum wages of all employees, except those in certain designated groups, who are engaged in interstate commerce or in producing goods for interstate commerce.[13] The authority for Congress to exercise such price control, the Court held, was to be found in the power of Congress to regulate commerce and to make all laws "necessary and proper" for carrying into effect its delegated powers. (See Landmark Cases, p. 669.)

The sharp fall in farm prices in relation to industrial prices which developed soon after 1929 focused attention on the plight of the farmers (Fig. 43); and legislation to provide farmers with higher prices and incomes was made an important part of the proposed "New Deal." The original Agricultural Adjustment Act of 1933 passed by Congress to correct the "disparity" between the prices of farm and nonfarm products was held to be unconstitutional in 1936, largely on the ground that farmers were "coerced" to sign contracts to curtail production.[14] The act of 1938, however, was reformulated to meet certain constitutional objections; and a more liberal Court held that the new legislation was a valid exercise of the power of Congress to

[11] *West Coast Hotel Co. v. Parrish*, 300 U.S. 379 (1937).
[12] *Sunshine Anthracite Coal Co. v. Adkins*, 310 U.S. 381 (1940). The National Bituminous Coal Commission (1937), which later became the Bituminous Coal Division (1939), expired on August 23, 1943. There is no government control today over the prices of coal.
[13] *U.S. v. Darby*, 312 U.S. 100 (1941).
[14] *U.S. v. Butler*, 297 U.S. 1 (1936).

regulate interstate commerce and to make all laws "necessary and proper" to that end. "Any rule," the Court declared, "which is intended to foster, protect, and conserve that commerce, or to prevent the flow of commerce from working harm to the people of the nation, is within the competence of Congress."[15]

FARMERS' PRICES

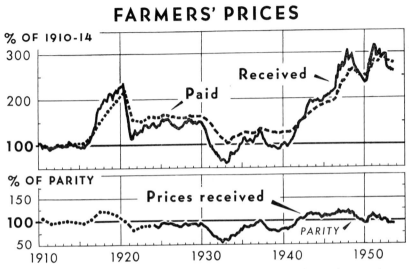

FIG. 43. Indexes of prices received and paid by farmers, United States, by months, 1910–1954. The relationship between farm and nonfarm prices existing during the period 1909–1914 was changed during World War I when farm prices rose to higher levels than industrial prices. After 1920, however, farmers not only lost their advantage but came to experience a marked disadvantage. The disparity between farm and nonfarm prices became the greatest during 1930–1933, when farm products had only about one-half of their prewar (1909–1914) purchasing power. (Source: U.S. Department of Agriculture.)

In the Agricultural Adjustment Act of 1938 Congress made provision for (1) the adoption of soil conservation measures, (2) the establishment of production and marketing quotas, and (3) the making of loans on farm products, in an effort to bring the prices of various agricultural products up to a stated percentage of "parity." A parity price in the legislation was defined as that price for a commodity which will give it the same purchasing power (with respect to the articles which farmers buy) that it had during the base period (August 1909 to July 1914). Per-unit price relationships during the five year period 1909–1914 were considered to be equitable and not subject to the distortions of World War I or the depressed period for agriculture which followed the war.

---

[15] *Mulford* v. *Smith*, 307 U.S. 48 (1939); and *Wickard* v. *Filburn*, 317 U.S. 111 (1942). The act of 1938 covered the "basic commodities of corn, wheat, cotton, rice, tobacco, and peanuts." Mandatory supports, however, were provided only for wheat, corn, cotton, and later peanuts. Additional commodities were placed under price-support programs during World War II.

PROCEDURES USED TO PROVIDE HIGHER PRICES
FOR CERTAIN PRODUCERS

In general, it may be said that *higher* prices effected by authoritarian control were secured, and are presently being secured, (1) by the establishment of minimum levels below which no product can be sold, (2) by providing for a restriction of production to insure the attainment of higher prices, (3) by using discriminatory pricing (as in the case of milk) to maximize sales revenue, (4) by making loans and purchases to support prices at or near the levels established by law, and (5) by paying subsidies to bring incomes up to a more favorable level.

In so far as "low" prices are the result of monopolistic buying practices, it is possible for government to raise them by legislative fiat without restricting supply. Minimum wage legislation, for example, can often be justified on the ground that there is a considerable degree of monopoly in the purchase of labor. Under such conditions, governmental price fixing simply serves to give an economic group a price more nearly in accord with its competitive worth.

In most cases, the objective of government in providing higher prices for agricultural products has been, and presently is, to raise such prices to an approximate parity with the prices maintained and secured by industry. Since 200 bushels of wheat would buy a mowing machine in the period of 1909–1914, it is reasoned that 200 bushels of wheat should have a price which will give it the same purchasing power today. The desired objective is not competitive worth, but rather prices in line with those in industry—and, in many cases, managed or administered by industry itself. Quantities of a commodity which cannot be sold at "parity prices," or at given percentages of parity, are considered to be surplus. A surplus is usually defined as that quantity which cannot be sold at prices which producers believe to be fair or reasonable.

In its efforts to achieve the objective of agricultural prices which bear a close parity with industrial prices, the federal government adopted the principle of creating *artificial* scarcity. Beginning in 1933 the production of basic agricultural products was curtailed by government control in amounts ranging up to 40 percent of the production of preceding years. The policy of curbing production to secure higher prices was continued in various degrees until the 1944 season, when the unprecedented demands for foodstuffs occasioned by World War II temporarily provided "parity prices" without the placing of artificial restrictions on production.

The Agricultural Act of 1948, including the amendments of 1949, 1950, and 1952, reëstablished the authority of the Secretary of Agriculture to require compliance with acreage allotments and marketing quotas. *Acreage allotments* serve as goals for the amount of production needed for consumption at designated prices. They may be announced by the Secretary of Agriculture for any commodity, and compliance by individual farmers is voluntary. Coöperation with the program, however, determines eligibility for commodity loans. *Marketing quotas* may be applied only to "basic" commodities. They put teeth into acreage allotments by restricting the amount which individual farmers may sell. Farmers exceeding their quotas forfeit price support benefits and are required to pay penalties. Marketing quotas must be approved by two-thirds of the farmers voting in a referendum.

Marketing quotas have been established principally for cotton and wheat. In 1954, for example, the marketing quota program for wheat required wheat farmers to reduce their plantings by some 4.5 million acres. Farmers planting more than their individual quotas were subject to penalties on the excess production.

The Agricultural Act of 1949 provided mandatory price-support operations for coöperating farmers (those who do not knowingly exceed their acreage allotments) producing (1) "basic" commodities—corn, cotton, wheat, rice, tobacco, and peanuts—and (2) designated nonbasic agricultural commodities—wool (including mohair), tung nuts, honey, milk, butterfat, and the products of milk and butterfat, at various levels not in excess of 90 percent of parity. Price supports for other agricultural commodities are permissive. *Present laws for all but the six designated basic crops are "permanent" (continuous until changed)*. Special legislation to support prices on the six basic commodities during the 1953 and 1954 seasons at 90 percent of parity expired at the end of 1954. New legislation adopted in 1954 provided flexible supports, ranging from 82.5 to 90 percent, for the "basic" crops of corn, cotton, wheat, rice, and peanuts. Acreage allotments and marketing quotas for crops in large surplus were continued. Tobacco is covered by a special provision which provides support at 90 percent of parity as long as farmers approve marketing quotas for their crops.

THE FARM PROBLEM

The case for government intervention in the pricing and output of agricultural products rests on the premise that there are, at present, significant differences between agriculture and industry which warrant special treatment. In brief, the major differences between agriculture and industry are seen to be the following:

1. Prices and outputs in the major industries are now subject to a considerable degree of "management" and "administration" by the large corporations ("price leadership," basing-point and zone systems of pricing, oligopoly, and conspiracy). In periods of recession, monopolistic industries tend to peg their prices and restrict production, while competitive industries reduce their prices to provide a selling outlet for normal supplies. Thus, during the period 1929 to 1932, *production in industry* was curtailed by about 50 percent. Prices of some industrial products did not decline at all. Steel prices dropped 15 percent; automobile prices, 13 percent; and industrial prices, generally, 25 percent. *Agricultural production*, on the other hand, was actually increased during the period 1929–1932, and prices fell 56 percent. (See also Fig. 54, p. 656.)

Farmers, acting by themselves, cannot manage prices and output because they are too numerous. The result is that during periods of recession, farmers are caught in a serious price-cost squeeze. Farm prices decline sharply, but farm costs do not. Agricultural output is maintained, but industrial output is sharply curtailed.

2. Agricultural products, on their way to the ultimate consumers, flow through various processing, fabricating, handling, warehousing, and transporting industries. Ineffective competition, oligopoly, or monopolistic conspiracies at any given stage of productive activity will increase the toll at that point and decrease the amounts which remain for the first-hand producers.

In 1945, the farmer received approximately 53 percent of the consumer's food dollar; in 1948, 50 percent; and in 1953, barely 44 percent. At the present time, specific studies are not available to explain the growing spread between what the housewife pays and what the farmer gets. Farm spokesmen declare that the small size of most farm units and the limited bargaining power of farmers make it necessary for farmers to secure governmental assistance in marketing.

3. Many farm groups, especially those producing wheat, cotton, rice, and beans, are particularly subject to the changing demands of foreign nations. Following the outbreak of World War II, there was a large increase in production to meet foreign needs. The Korean war further stimulated demand, and exports reached a peak of more than $4 billion during 1951–1952. Since that peak period, agricultural exports have fallen and it is possible that they will continue to decline (see Fig. 44).

A large part of the flow of goods abroad was financed by American aid. The problem today is one of making it possible for foreign nations, most of which continue to need additional foods and fibers, to earn dollars by selling their minerals, oil, and speciality items in the United States. Farmers have a big stake in the creation of a freer system of trade. Unless foreign outlets are expanded, farmers face the prospect of making substantial reductions in domestic production.

4. Agricultural production is a high-risk industry. The size of a farmer's crop depends not only upon his own efforts, but also upon weather and temperature conditions, the amount of rainfall, the timing of rainfall in relation to crop maturity, insect infestation, and plant diseases. The adjustment of production to market conditions also requires longer periods of time than in other industry. Many crops require a year for their production. The expansion of some, such as livestock, requires several years. Other crops, such as fruit and nuts, can be increased only within a period of eight to ten years. Decreases in production likewise frequently impose serious problems. Orchards continue to bear fruit regardless of market conditions; and dairy herds give milk in good times and bad. Farmers are rarely in a position to adjust output to sharp declines in market demand.

In recent years, farmers have turned increasingly from the use of draft animals and natural fertilizers to the use of tractors, commercial fertilizers, hybrid seeds, chemical pesticides, herbicides, and synthetic feed supplements. Cash outlay costs have been greatly increased. This has tended to make the farmer much more vulnerable to sharp price declines and to the occurrence of poor harvests.

5. The nation, as a whole, has a vital interest in maintaining the fertility and productiveness of the soil. Under our private-ownership system, individual farmers are the "stewards" or "custodians" of this basic natural resource. If they do not secure adequate incomes in relation to nonfarm groups, they will not be in a position to engage in soil-conserving practices.

VALUE OF U. S. FARM EXPORTS

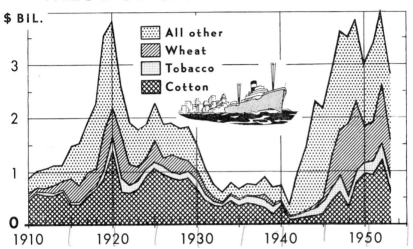

FIG. 44. The sharp decline in agricultural exports since the peak year of 1951–1952 has made for large surpluses and lowered farm prices. (Source: U.S. Department of Agriculture.)

The particular feature of the farm problem which has caused it to have critical national importance is the price-cost squeeze which develops during periods of recession. From an economic point of view, it would be sound policy to attack the causes of the rigid and inflexible prices in industry which give rise to the disparity problem. This would require vigorous enforcement of the antitrust laws, the outlawing of basing-point and zone systems of pricing, and constructive action to reduce economic concentration (oligopoly). Since it appears unlikely that government, in the near term, will adopt vigorous and far-reaching measures to reduce artificial price rigidities, the heart of the farm problem is likely to be with us for many years to come. Both political parties are committed to the practice of price assistance for agricultural commodities, and the question at issue is the form which it should take.

THE PRESENT FARM PROGRAM

Price supports have been, and continue to be, the cornerstone of the federal farm program. In addition to price assistance, the federal government provides farmers with farm credit, loans for rural electrification and rural telephone systems, scientific research and extension work, crop insurance, technical aid, and payments for engaging in soil conservation practices.

Price assistance to farmers is provided, in the main, through the following measures:

1. The promotion and encouragement of agricultural marketing coöperatives. (See Chap. 13.)
2. The Agricultural Marketing Agreement Act of 1937, as amended, which authorizes the use of marketing agreements and orders, controlling the sale of enumerated products, including fruit, vegetables, nuts, and milk, in interstate commerce. This legislation has three stated objectives: (1) to raise prices to "parity" levels; (2) to protect consumers by providing that private control shall not raise prices above parity; and (3) to maintain minimum standards of quality and maturity. (See Chap. 13.)
3. The purchase of agricultural commodities under Section 32 of the Agricultural Act of 1935, as amended. This legislation authorizes the Secretary of Agriculture to spend an amount equal to 30 percent of the gross import duties collected under the customs for the following purposes:
    (a) To encourage the export of farm products by the payment of benefits or indemnities.
    (b) To purchase farm products for use in the school-lunch program, for distribution to low-income groups, and for diversion programs (e.g., the use of raisins for livestock feed).
    (c) To reëstablish farmers' purchasing power by making payments in connection with the normal production of products for domestic use.
    During the fiscal year period of 1936–1953, more than $2 billion were collected and spent under Section 32 programs. Section 32 funds are used largely for strengthening the domestic prices of fruits, cotton, vegetables, grain, eggs, poultry, and dairy products; and for making payments to domestic exporters to enable them to sell at the lower prices prevailing in foreign markets.
4. The purchase of agricultural products under the National School Lunch Act of 1946. This legislation authorizes the Department of Agriculture to purchase food for direct distribution to schools and to provide grants-in-aid to the states for use in buying food for school lunches. Agricultural products are also made available to schools under Section 32 programs, as noted in the foregoing section.
5. The sale of wheat abroad under the International Wheat Agreement. Thus far, export sales of wheat under this agreement have involved subsidy payments to cover the difference between the domestic price of wheat and the export price. (See below, p. 519.)
6. The establishment of quotas on the importation and domestic production of sugar and the payment of subsidies to domestic producers of sugar beets and sugar cane under the Sugar Act of 1948, as amended. In December of each year, the Secretary of Agriculture must determine the amount of sugar needed to meet the requirements of American consumers during the coming year. Actually, the requirements, or demand, of consumers will depend upon the price of sugar; and in estimating the requirements, the Secretary is directed to have in mind prices (1) "which will not be excessive to consumers" and (2) "which will fairly and equitably maintain and protect the welfare of the domestic sugar industry." The actual

formulation of such prices inevitably involves much guesswork and compromise.

After the Secretary of Agriculture determines the prospective consumption requirements, he establishes quotas for each supplying area—continental United States, Hawaii, Puerto Rico, the Virgin Islands, Cuba, the Philippines, and other foreign countries. Under the terms of the 1948 act, the Secretary is authorized to make subsidy payments to growers of sugar beets and sugar cane in the United States, Hawaii, Puetro Rico, and the Virgin Islands, on condition that they comply with the production quotas, as well as with other provisions specified in the act.

In order to finance the sugar program, the government imposes a special tax of 50¢ per hundred pounds, raw value, on all sugar processed in the United States and on all sugar imported for direct consumption. Subsidy payments to growers have been running about $60 million per year.

7. The imposition of import fees and total annual import quotas by Presidential proclamation. Whenever investigations by the Tariff Commission indicate that imports of agricultural products materially interfere with any price assistance program undertaken by the Department of Agriculture, the President is authorized to impose import fees not in excess of 50 percent *ad valorem* or such import quotas as he finds to be necessary. (Section 22 of the Agricultural Act of 1933, as amended.) Under this legislation, total annual import quotas have been established for raw cotton, wheat, oats, wheat flour, cheese and other dairy products, fats and oils.

8. The provision by Congress of *price-support* programs by which government attempts to establish a "floor" or minimum price for specified agricultural products. This feature of agricultural price assistance is the most controversial part of the total program. The controversy centers on (1) the commodities which are to be made subject to price support; (2) the minimum prices which government shall attempt to maintain; and (3) the extent to which the annual production of designated crops shall be restricted. Commodities covered, price-support levels, and acreage restrictions are likely to shift with changes in economic conditions, as well as with changes in the prevailing political climate. It is suggested that current information on "price floors" and commodities covered be secured by writing to the Department of Agriculture, Washington, D.C.

The principal mechanism which the federal government has employed in supporting the prices of designated commodities is the Commodity Credit Corporation (created in 1933). This agency seeks to establish minimum prices by making loans to farmers or by purchasing commodities at announced support prices. Under the loan operations, if the price of the commodity declines, the farmer keeps the loan money and the government takes the commodity and bears the loss. If, however, the price rises, the farmer is privileged to repay the loan and recover the commodity.

By terms of the Agriculture Act of 1938, as amended, the Secretary of Agriculture is authorized to establish *acreage allotments* for designated commodities when market supplies become excessive. The Secretary is also authorized to proclaim *marketing quotas* for designated commodities. These become applicable to all farmers if approved by two-thirds of those voting. Only those persons complying with acreage allotments or marketing quotas are eligible for commodity loans. Farmers producing in excess of their marketing quota, must also pay a penalty on sales of the excess production.

Commodities acquired by the C.C.C. are disposed of in a number of ways. Some have been sold in the United States at prices in line with support prices; some have been sold abroad at reduced prices; some have been donated in domestic and foreign relief programs; some have been disposed of as livestock feed; and some have been destroyed because of spoilage. During the period of October 1933 to June 1953, it is estimated, the C.C.C. realized losses of over $1 billion or about $55 million per year.

ALTERNATIVE MEASURES FOR PRICE ASSISTANCE
TO FARMERS

Flexible Price Supports. Critics of rigid price supports declare that the maintenance of high fixed prices during a period of prosperity stimulates production without regard to normal consumption requirements. Large surpluses develop, and government is forced to impose acreage restrictions and marketing quotas. Rigid supports, they believe, do not provide proper incentives for farmers to adjust the output of specific commodities to demand. As an alternative, they advocate flexible price supports by which support prices would be adjusted downward when supplies are above normal consumption requirements and adjusted upward when supplies are below normal requirements. Price, in this instance, would be used to guide the farmers on what to grow and how much to grow. Production would not be frozen in uneconomic patterns.

Two-Price Plans. The idea of two-price or multiple-price plans has strong support from many farm groups. Such plans call for the high-level support of product prices for specified domestic uses and the sale of quantities for other uses and for export at reduced prices. This is the monopoly principle of price discrimination. (See Chap. 9, pp. 181–184.) Price discrimination does serve to produce greater revenue from the sale of a given stock of goods. Its establishment as a national policy, however, is hardly in keeping with our declarations against cartels and price discrimination in international trade. Foreign nations selling agricultural products, such as cotton, in world market centers would suffer from the "dumping" of similar American products, and it is probable that they would resort to retaliatory measures.

Revision of Parity Concept. Many agricultural economists believe that the price parity formula should either be modernized or abandoned. Price parity, as we have seen, is the foundation upon which the American farm program has been built. Critics agree that farm products had certain empirical, per-unit price relationships with industrial products during the period 1909–1914, before the distortions of World War I and the postwar readjustments. However, during the years following this historical period, they state, improved equipment and new techniques in agriculture have made for greater abundance and hence for lower prices. Technical changes in production, they add, have operated differently in various agricultural activities, so that no single set of price relationships can be called normal.

Brannan Plan. The Brannan Plan (proposed in 1949 by Charles F. Brannan, Secretary of Agriculture), is a farm price support plan which seeks to provide a certain minimum income for the farm economy as a whole (not individual farmers), rather than parity prices for designated commodities. Loans and purchase agreements would continue to be used to support the prices of most storable products. Perishable commodities, such as milk, butter, eggs, poultry, meat, and potatoes, and possibly some storable products, too, would be allowed to move into consumption at whatever prices they would bring. If the resulting average prices were below official standards, the federal government would make compensatory payments to the producers of such products. The Brannan plan contemplates a much broader coverage for agricultural products, a free system of prices particularly for perishables, and the use of subsidy payments to bring farm income up to designated levels. Consumers would be given the benefits of abundant supplies, and burdensome surpluses of perishables and some storables would be avoided.

SOME CRITICISMS OF PRICE ASSISTANCE PROGRAMS

1. Price-support programs in agriculture apply the monopoly principle of creating *artificial* scarcity, as employed by various segments of private industry. They seek to remedy the problem of monopoly by creating more monopoly. An indispensable, *long-run* solution calls for the adoption of measures (antitrust and others) to remedy the problems of rigid prices and restraints on competition as they exist in the industrial and commercial areas of the economy.

A distinguished group of agricultural economists has said, "Since the agricultural depression of the twenties . . . some farmers seem to have adopted a defeatist attitude as to the growth of monopolistic positions in both industry and labor and to have decided to 'fight the devil with fire'. . . . This does not seem to us a sound economic philosophy. . . . Restrictionism in agriculture is not an effective and satisfactory way of compensating for the harm done to farmers by such price maintenance and restriction of production as exist in the industrial and labor segments of the economy." In recommending against acreage allotments, marketing quotas, and related devices to *restrict* output in agriculture, these economists "strongly recommend a carefully studied and vigorous attack by farmers, farm organizations, and farm statesmen upon those restrictionist policies or institutions of business, labor, or other parts of the economy which are designed to enhance the cost of goods or services for which the farmer must exchange his product."[16]

2. Price assistance programs for farmers seek to maintain the prices of various farm products not only during periods of industrial recession, but also during periods of full-capacity production in industry. Sagging agricultural prices during a period of high-level output in industry may well mean that more producers should move out of agricultural production.

Economists have long frowned upon government intervention to raise or maintain the prices of certain producers above the levels established by the interplay of demand and supply. The *increased income* given to certain groups, they point out, *is secured at the cost of other persons.* The process is simply one of transferring income from consumers to a favored group of producers. Artifically high prices in one segment of the economy also promote a maldistribution of resources. Production is maintained or encouraged without reference to demand, and burdensome surpluses develop which cannot be sold at the fixed prices.

3. The establishment of marketing quotas for designated commodities results in a percentage reduction of operations for each farm unit, whether it is efficient or inefficient and whether its land resources are class 1, 2, 3, or even poorer in quality. From the standpoint of economic efficiency, the goal should be one of getting the greatest results with the least cost. Present farm programs do not have this objective. Governmental policy should encourage the shifting of inferior land into other uses (such as grazing) and the transfer of low-income farmers into other employments.

4. In so far as price assistance programs involve direct payments to farmers, they serve to increase farm income in proportion to output. Owners and operators of large, fertile farms secure substantial cash benefits; whereas those on small farms and inferior land secure minor or zero benefits. Such a plan does not remedy the problem of low incomes which faces many thousands of tenant farmers and farmers with small-sized farms.

5. The present system of supporting farm prices—through loans, purchases, and the storage of products—provides a marvelous mechanism for *accumulating* farm products. It fails, however, to provide a method for moving them into consumption, either at home or abroad. Some plan, such as the Brannan plan, many agricultural economists believe, is needed for the disposal of farm products which are in large supply.[17]

INTERGOVERNMENTAL COMMODITY AGREEMENTS

In addition to the activity of government in controlling the domestic prices of various products, there is the joint activity of two or more governments to control the prices, exports, stocks, or production of certain

[16] *Turning the Searchlight on Farm Policy*, The Farm Foundation, Chicago, 1952, pp. 55–57, 65.

[17] J. K. Galbraith, "Economic Preconceptions and the Farm Policy," *American Economic Review*, March, 1954, p. 52.

commodities moving in international trade. An agreement made between two or more national governments with respect to the prices, production, or sale of a given product is called an "international commodity agreement." International commodity agreements are sometimes made for the purpose of curbing production in order to secure higher prices for domestic producers; and in such cases they are similar in nature to an international cartel—that is, a private agreement among businessmen in two or more countries on prices or output. In other cases, commodity agreements are made for the purpose of working out satisfactory arrangements with respect to (1) the disposal of agricultural surpluses; (2) the acquisition and development of resources which are becoming increasingly scarce—such as oil and the nonferrous metals; (3) the conservation of basic resources—as in fishing agreements; and (4) the promotion of health and morals—as in intergovernmental agreements on opium and narcotics.

In 1937 the United States entered into a sugar agreement with some twenty-one other nations for the purpose of "establishing and maintaining an orderly relationship between the supply and demand for sugar." This agreement has been renewed from time to time and will undoubtedly be continued in some form as long as the United States continues to plan the production and prices of its sugar supply. Other commodity agreements to which the United States is a party are concerned with fishing regulations and the sale of opium and other narcotics.

On July 1, 1949, some forty-one governments, including the United States, ratified and signed the International Wheat Agreement, to be effective for a period of four years. This agreement was revised and renewed in 1953 and will expire July 31, 1956. The agreement, Article I states, is intended "to assure supplies of wheat to importing countries and markets for wheat to exporting countries at equitable and stable prices." Exporting countries guarantee to sell specified quantities of wheat at prices no higher than designated *maximum* prices; and importing countries guarantee to buy specified quantities at prices no lower than stated minimum prices. Although transactions may be made at other prices, they will not count toward fulfilling the obligations assumed by the signatory countries.

During the four-year period of the initial agreement, the free-market price was consistently higher than the maximum price provided for in the agreement. In order to fulfill its contract to sell at the stated prices, therefore, the United States had to pay a subsidy to American exporters equal to the difference between market prices in the United States and the maximum price stated in the Wheat Agreement. This subsidy averaged 63 cents per bushel, and the total subsidy cost in four years was about $580 million. Thus far, the Wheat Agreement has been essentially a subsidy measure.

The United States is currently a member of international "study groups" on tin, rubber, and wool, which were formed to consider various problems connected with international trade in these commodities. There are no international agreements in these commodities, but there have been extensive discussions of possible international agreements. The Tin Study group, in particular, has been working actively on a draft agreement which provides for the stockpiling of surpluses. The Rubber Study group has also drafted an agreement for the establishment of a "buffer stock." The United States is also a member of the International Cotton Advisory Committee. A standing committee of this group meets periodically in Washington and keeps the world cotton situation under continuous review. If, and when, excessive supplies of cotton accumulate at existing prices, it is expected that an international cotton agreement will be formulated and submitted to the member countries for approval.[18]

AN APPRAISAL OF COMMODITY AGREEMENTS

In general, it may be said that most economists frown upon commodity agreements whenever they are restrictive in nature. Professor Edward S. Mason states a representative view in emphasizing that the making and administering of commodity agreements should always be directed toward an expansion of consumption rather than toward a restriction of production.[19] Professor Mason also declares that the United States should adopt a strong anticartel policy with respect to private commodity agreements. In so far as our government becomes a party to commodity agreements, he adds, it should be concerned with the proper policies to be followed in the production and sale of basic commodities.

Time alone will reveal whether or not cartel arrangements by governments will be, or can be, basically different from those managed by private industry. Price stabilization, in practice, typically means higher prices. Higher prices, in turn, unstabilize—that is, reduce—production and employment. Only those quantities must be produced which can be sold at the managed prices. A business recession brings problems of mounting surpluses, and demands are made for further restrictions on output in order to prevent a breaking of prices. Ultimately, the experience of the past indicates, agencies controlling commodity prices will be required to determine who shall produce, how much he shall produce, and the price at which he shall sell. In this process of control, it is possible that the influence of organized producers for continued restriction will outweigh that of consumers for abundance and plenty.[20]

THE PROPOSAL FOR A "CONTROLLED ECONOMY"

In view of the fact that the antitrust laws have not been adequately enforced during the past sixty years and private monopoly has been permitted

[18] Current material on developments in the field of international commodity agreements may be found in the reports of the Interim Co-ordinating Committee for International Commodity Arrangements, *Review of International Commodity Problems*, published by the United Nations, New York City, New York.

[19] Edward S. Mason, *Controlling World Trade* (New York, 1946), pp. 135–148.

[20] See also, Felix E. Wormser, "Recent Trends in Metal Controls," *The Commercial and Financial Chronicle*, December 25, 1952.

to develop over wide areas of the industrial field, it is frequently proposed that public-price and output control should be extended to the major industries. At the present time, it is said, "economic planning" is practiced by the heads of the giant monopolistic combinations. In the interest of the public, it is argued, this private control of the economy should be placed in public hands. Thus, Mordecai Ezekiel, a well-known agricultural economist, states, "The 'industry authority' should be an advisory committee, and the final decisions on programs should be made by a career government administrator responsible to legislative bodies and public opinion. Today many key economic decisions are made by business officials responsible to no one, not even to their stockholders, and able to intimidate legislatures or even national governments to their will. Planning, in the open, for the public interest and with public accountability, is far less likely to become fascistic than planning in the dark, for private monopolistic interests and with accountability to no one."[21]

Socialists, in particular, believe in planning, economic and social. Mr. Norman Thomas, for example, states: "For myself, socialism has always seemed primarily a doctrine and movement consciously concerned with the common good. Therefore, it requires planning. . . . Plans must be concerned with the directions in which we should go, the goals we should seek, and the roads toward them." Mr. Thomas believes, further, that the effective realization of planning requires a substantial amount of public ownership, but not the complete collectivization which exists in the Soviet Union. A considerable degree of control without ownership, he observes, would require the exercise of harsh and arbitrary directives. In his words, "If the state is not to be largely the tool of the great interests it nominally controls, it will be under grave temptation to develop extremely authoritarian attitudes and apparatus. For effective control over industries still legally owned by private individuals requires a more arbitrary exercise of political power than the state operation of these industries by public authorities under a system of social ownership."[22]

The prosecution of World War II brought a vast extension of direct governmental controls over prices, wages, rents, and the allocation of raw materials and labor, in the effort of government to restrict inflation and insure adequate supplies for the armed forces. The broad extension of direct controls to the price system generally, during World War II, was, in fact, an example of "overall" economic planning—for purposes of war. Professor E. S. Corwin expresses the opinion that the direct control over prices and outputs exercised by government in the name of the war powers could be reestablished at any moment under the "commerce clause" for purposes of overall economic planning, if the public should so demand.[23]

[21] Mordecai Ezekiel, "Is Government Intervention or Planning Consistent with Antitrust Policy?" *American Economic Review, Papers and Proceedings,* May, 1946, p. 201.
[22] Norman Thomas, *A Socialist's Faith* (New York, 1951), pp. 3, 185–186.
[23] E. S. Corwin, *Total War and the Constitution* (New York, 1947), p. 174.

As long as business activity continues at a high level and inflationary pressures do not get out of hand, it is unlikely that there will be any popular demand for overall economic planning by government. However, if a severe depression should develop, it is quite possible that a majority of people would turn to a plan of direct control of prices, incomes, and employment.

ECONOMIC PLANNING BY GOVERNMENT

The proposal to extend public control over prices, incomes, production, and uses of goods, generally, raises the question of the economic wisdom of "overall" planning. Almost everyone nowadays agrees that government must engage in a certain amount of economic planning. The main question is the kind and amount of planning to be undertaken. Let us consider a possible area of agreement. First, most people admit the need for planning a national minimum income. The Social Security Act of 1935, the Fair Labor Standards Act of 1938, and the various state minimum wage and old-age retirement laws are all examples of government planning for a minimum level of living for every citizen. Secondly, it is undoubtedly correct to state that everyone agrees to the need for control over the rates of public utility enterprises in which technical conditions make monopoly inevitable. Thirdly, a vast majority of the people are in favor of some form of government planning to maintain high-level employment. Fourthly, there is agreement on the need for government planning in the production of "public goods"—such as roads, parks, schools, public buildings, and defense facilities for national security. All of these forms of planning may be called "limited" economic planning.

"Overall" economic planning goes very much further. It consists in the determination or direct control by government of the prices, allocation, and output of what is commonly called "private goods"—namely, steel, copper, lead, zinc, coal, housing, flour, meat, clothing, automobiles, radios, and so forth, as well as the machinery, tools, and raw materials used in producing such goods. The controversial issue is whether the pricing and production of "private goods" should be determined (1) by governmental agencies—attempting to measure consumer choices—or (2) by the free play of the forces of demand and supply, with numerous independent enterprisers catering to the desires of millions of consumers. In the minds of many economists, either of these policies can be made effective if the public has the will and courage to do it. The issue is which *plan* in the long run is more likely to provide economic abundance and preserve a large measure of economic and political freedom.

In general, there is coming to be a sharper cleavage between economists who believe in the wisdom of overall economic planning and those who do not. Economists opposing comprehensive planning, moreover, are becoming more vehement in their opposition to it. In stating the case against price and output control, it is said that government intervention *to raise* particular prices—such as the prices of milk, coal, wheat, and cotton—involves essentially a transfer of income from consumers to the favored producers. At the same time, the higher product prices mean a reduction in sales and consumption. It is also possible that the increased profits in the favored industry may tend to attract new producers and cause a condition of "overproduction." Since the income of consumers available for other products is reduced by the higher prices, they find themselves unable to enjoy the same level of living. Other producers, too, find that their sales and incomes are correspondingly reduced.[24]

A transfer of income from one group to another may be justified on humanitarian grounds, as in the case of minimum wage legislation to provide basic subsistence. In other cases, however, there is little, if any, justification for a transfer of income except the doctrine that the political "might" of the favored economic groups makes right. It may be argued that if government raised the prices and incomes for *every* group of producers, all would gain. The error in this view, however, is the fact that the gain in purchasing power which each group gets is offset by the higher prices which it must pay. There is no economic magic in government price fixing.

Government price fixing may also seek to favor *consumers* by maintaining prices at levels *below* those established by the free play of demand and supply. In this case, consumers retain income at the expense of the producers. The artificially low prices, however, discourage production and promote black market activity. Since the supply of goods in the controlled industries which is available for consumption is curtailed, the welfare of consumers is injured. If price control to favor consumers is exercised over a wide area, the resulting discouragements on production may serve to bring about substantial reductions in the level of living.

Some economists believe that economic planning in industries which are *publicly owned* may be able to avoid the inequity of transferring income to a favored group at the expense of other groups, as discussed in the preceding paragraphs. With public ownership, it is said, government commissions will not be subject to the pressures typically exerted by the controlled industries. We shall give further consideration to public ownership in Chapter 25.

THE ECONOMIC BASIS FOR THE GROWTH OF A "CONTROLLED ECONOMY"

In the eyes of many people, the present growth of governmental price and output controls is an anathema which should immediately be swept away. The system of free enterprise and free markets, it is said, provides the best regulator of economic activity. Like most errors, this view contains an element of truth! A system of free and open markets is a highly effective

---

[24] See also Hubert Henderson, *The Uses and Abuses of Economic Planning* (Cambridge, 1947); John Jewkes, *Ordeal by Planning* (London, 1948); Lionel Robbins, *The Economic Problem in Peace and War* (London, 1947); and Ely Devons, "Economic Planning in War and Peace," *Manchester School*, January, 1948, pp. 1–28.

method of economic regulation. It is a mistake, however, to assume that the free-market economy still exists and continues to operate in most areas of private industry—as distinguished from agriculture and labor. In an earlier chapter we traced the rise of tariffs as a measure of restrictionism. Tariffs, most economists agree, result in an uneconomic allocation of resources and an overall lessening of productivity. Along with the growth of tariffs, there came the growth of pools, trusts, and finally the great financial mergers in which scores of formerly competing plants were united in single price-controlling units. The large monopolistic mergers early adopted the policy of curbing production in order to raise or maintain prices and maximize profits. Modern industry thereupon came to be characterized by "excess capacity," prolonged depressions, and chronic unemployment. When price competition does develop, it is largely discriminatory in nature. Such a condition of "competition" is not the type called for by the antitrust laws.

In part, at least, the demands for government to exercise direct controls —in such fields as agriculture and labor—have had their origin in the policies of restrictionism pursued by organized industry. Undoubtedly, industry's historic tariff grabs have served as a basic precedent for the "gimmes." The great depression, moreover, gave impetus to the demands of agricultural and labor interests for political favors to enhance their incomes. Further, the demands for controls have had their origin in the natural selfishness of people, as well as in the tendency of organized groups to look upon their immediate interests as the measure of the public good. *In yielding to the importunities of special interest groups, government has come to adopt a large measure of direct control over economic life, designed in many cases to restrict physical production rather than to increase it.*

Since a basic factor in the growth of authoritarian control in the fields of agriculture and labor has been the existence of private controls and public favors in industry, it follows logically that any effort to reduce authoritarian control should be accompanied by action to create effective price competition in industry. Until monopolistic mergers are dissolved and a system of properly functioning markets is created to serve as a pricing mechanism for the basic industrial commodities, there appears to be little hope or probability that direct control in other fields will be lessened. Over the past fifty years tariffs, mergers, and pricing formulas have enabled organized industry to rise on the teeter-totter in relation to agriculture and labor. The purpose of government intervention and "control" in other fields has largely been to create an approximate balance. Until all three groups slide off the teeter somewhat simultaneously, it is likely that government will have the continuing task of trying to keep them all in balance.

It does not seem likely that the United States will get away from planned restrictionism for some time. The fallacious notion that we can expect to have more of the good things for everybody by everybody's producing less is still widely prevalent. Much of the special-interest legislation benefits few people. Yet it is largely voted and supported by the general public which is disadvantaged the most. Economists since the days of Adam Smith have observed that this disheartening situation is to be explained largely by the prejudice and ignorance of the masses. If the nation is to strive in earnest for an economy of abundance, it will be necessary for citizens generally (1) to become better informed, (2) to learn to think objectively, and (3) to become politically active in their own behalf.

SUGGESTIONS FOR FURTHER READING

Benedict, M. R., *Farm Policies of the United States 1790–1950* (New York, 1953).
Davis, Joseph S., *International Commodity Agreements* (New York, 1947).
Halcrow, H. G., *Agricultural Policy of the United States* (New York, 1953).
Hardin, Charles M., *The Politics of Agriculture* (Glencoe, Ill., 1952).
Henderson, Hubert, *The Uses and Abuses of Economic Planning* (Cambridge, 1947).
Jewkes, John, *Ordeal by Planning* (London, 1948).
Lewis, W. Arthur, *The Principles of Economic Planning* (Washington, 1951).
Mason, Edward S., *Controlling World Trade* (New York, 1946).
Rose, J. K., *The Brannan Plan*, Public Affairs Bulletin 78, April, 1950, Legislative Reference Service, Library of Congress, Washington, D.C.
Schultz, T. W., *Production and Welfare of Agriculture* (New York, 1949); and *The Economic Organization of Agriculture* (New York, 1953).
Summers, R. E., *Subsidies for Farmers* (New York, 1951).
The Farm Foundation, *Turning the Searchlight on Farm Policy* (Chicago, 1952).

CHAPTER 24

Methods of Control for Public
Utility Enterprises

―――――――――

In the case of public utility enterprises, government accepts monopoly as being natural, inevitable, or desirable and imposes *maximum* rates to protect the public against unreasonable and arbitrary charges. Upon some occasions, the government may also establish *minimum* rates to protect the utilities from ruinous competition which would be of disadvantage to the public as well as to the enterprises concerned. The problem of competition between public utilities is entirely different from that found in manufacturing and merchandising activities. If two utilities in a given locality compete against each other on rates to attract customers, the rate reductions may become disastrous *to both*. The problem is not one of price cutting by a dominant firm and the elimination of a weaker one. Both firms stand to be ruined by rate reductions. This results from the fact that both plants usually have unused capacity, high fixed costs, high physical immobility, and a product which cannot be separated from the plant. In an effort to secure additional business, rates may be made which cover little more than the variable costs; and continued rivalry may make it impossible for either plant to secure sufficient revenue to maintain its equipment. Under such conditions, governmental commissions find it necessary to impose minimum rates.

In most cases, the control problem in public utilities centers on the establishment of maximum rates, for the utility or utilities concerned typically have substantial degrees of monopoly power. What procedures do the various commissions use in keeping down the prices of utility services in the interest of consumers and industrial users? What attitudes have the courts taken with respect to public control to prevent extortion?

THE RULE OF RATE MAKING IN MUNN v. ILLINOIS

The power of the legislature to impose price control on public utility enterprises, we have seen, was sanctioned by the Supreme Court in *Munn* v. *Illinois*. In that case the Court also held that the rates so established were not subject to judicial review or revision. "We know," the Court declared, "that this is a power which may be abused; but this is no argument against its existence. For protection against abuses by legislatures the people must resort to the polls, not to the courts."[1]

―――――
[1] *Munn* v. *Illinois*, 94 U.S. 113, 134 (1877).

The rule of rate making in *Munn* v. *Illinois* was maintained for more than a decade. Repeatedly, however, the railroad utilities were claiming in their litigations that the rates fixed by legislative action were confiscatory and illegal under the Fourteenth Amendment, which provides that no state shall "deprive any person of life, liberty, or property without due process of law." This argument had been presented in the *Munn* case, but the Court refused to give it application. The Fourteenth Amendment, the Court had earlier held, was enacted to protect the civil rights of the former slaves rather than of corporations.[2] By 1886, however, the Court had brought itself around to accepting the insistent view of the railroad attorneys that corporations are "persons" within the meaning of the Fourteenth Amendment.[3] In winning judicial review of legislative control, the public utility corporations secured a privilege of tremendous value. Henceforth, they would be entitled to protection in the federal courts against legislative enactments which might adversely affect their economic position.[4]

In 1890 the Supreme Court rendered a decision in the *Chicago, Milwaukee, and St. Paul* case which definitely established the principle of judicial review in the case of rate regulation.[5] The rates established by a legislative commission, the Court stated, are necessarily within the power of the courts to review, for otherwise a corporation will be denied the protection of due process of law. By this decision, the courts assumed final authority in the field of public utility rate making.

THE RULE OF SMYTH v. AMES

In the case of *Smyth* v. *Ames*, decided in 1898, the Supreme Court gave further sanction to its new doctrine that the rates established by government commissions are subject to judicial review. In doing so, the Court reasoned that if the rates established by legislative control do not provide the opportunity of a "fair return" on the "fair value" of the property which is devoted to a public use, there is confiscation of private property. Since corporations had come to be regarded as "persons" within the meaning of the Fourteenth Amendment, it followed, in the view of the Court, that the due process clause of the Constitution requires judicial review of the rates established for public utilities.[6]

[2] *Slaughter House Cases*, 16 Wall. 36 (1873).

[3] *Santa Clara County* v. *Southern Pacific Railroad*, 118 U.S. 394, 396 (1886). Chief Justice Waite declared, "The Court does not wish to hear the argument on the question whether the provision of the Fourteenth Amendment . . . applies to these corporations. We are all of the opinion that it does." The *Santa Clara* case involved the validity of certain state taxes.

[4] For a further discussion of the judicial extension of the Fourteenth Amendment to protect corporations, see W. P. Webb, *Divided We Stand* (New York, 1937), pp. 68–83.

[5] *Chicago, Milwaukee, and St. Paul Ry.* v. *Minnesota*, 134 U.S. 418 (1890).

[6] The rule of judicial review is also applicable under the Fifth Amendment to the regulatory activities of the federal government. Both state and national regulatory commissions must approve rates which give a utility a legal right to earn a "fair return" on the "fair value" of its property.

In affirming the principle of judicial review for rate making, the Court set forth the rules which it believed should be observed in setting rates. According to Justice Harlan, speaking for the Court,

> We hold . . . that the basis of all calculations as to the reasonableness of rates to be charged by a corporation maintaining a highway under legislative sanction must be the fair value of the property being used by it for the convenience of the public. And, in order to ascertain that value, *the original cost of construction*, the amount expended in permanent improvements, the amount and market value of its bonds and stock, *the present as compared with the original cost of construction*, the probable earning capacity of the property under particular rates prescribed by statute, and the sum required to meet operating expenses, are all matters for consideration, and are to be given such weight as may be just and right in each case. . . . *What the company is entitled to ask is a fair return upon the value of that which it employs for the public convenience.*[7]

Only two of the criteria suggested in *Smyth* v. *Ames* for the determination of "fair value" were found to be useful—namely, (1) original cost less depreciation and (2) reproduction cost new less depreciation. Which should be used? If both were used, should favor be given to one rather than to the other? Why? No answers to these questions were given by the Supreme Court, and the efforts of commissions to apply the rule of *Smyth* v. *Ames* gave rise to a continuous and stormy controversy over how the rate base should be determined.

COMMISSION CONTROL WITH JUDICIAL DOMINATION

The rule of rate making announced in *Smyth* v. *Ames* made it clear that public commissions, consisting of men who make the regulation of utilities their occupation, would have to be created to administer public utility rate making. Legislatures could not remain in session to apply the legal formulas of rate control and make adjustments in rates with changing economic conditions. The technical difficulties of valuation also required the employment of personnel with special economic and legal training. In consequence, the various state legislatures rapidly took steps to create special commissions. Year by year, moreover, the work of the commissions became more and more complex, for in a series of decisions following *Smyth* v. *Ames* the Supreme Court gave increasing consideration to the appropriateness of the rules followed by the commissions in calculating depreciation, going concern value, operating expenses, and a reasonable rate of return.

The orders made by the commissions were often challenged in the courts by the utility companies on the question of the determination of facts. "Due process of law," it was frequently claimed, required a different set of findings. The courts, in time, accepted the reasonableness of this view and thereupon undertook to examine for themselves the facts and the observance of the rules of rate making laid down, in particular, by the Supreme Court. As

[7] *Smyth* v. *Ames*, 169 U.S. 466, 546–547 (1898). Italics supplied.

a result, rate-making procedures came to be marked by expensive litigations and prolonged delays.

THE VALUATION OF PROPERTY FOR RATE REGULATION

Growing out of Smyth v. Ames there were two factors which the Supreme Court repeatedly held should be given appropriate weight by the commissions in approving public utility rates: (1) original cost less depreciation and (2) reproduction cost new less depreciation. The "original cost" procedure finds the appropriate rate base in the dollars which a company has actually invested in the utility presently used and useful, less an allowance for accrued (or total) depreciation. The reproduction cost procedure, on the other hand, finds the proper rate base in the cost of reproducing the specific plant or plants with reference to current prices, less an allowance for accrued depreciation. If the amount resulting from the depreciation charges is reinvested in productive facilities, it becomes a part of the rate base on which the utility is entitled to earn a "fair return."

Until about 1933, the majority of the Supreme Court accepted the principle of reproduction cost new less accrued depreciation. This method of valuation, it may be noted, was advantageous to owners during the era of rising prices. However, the many administrative difficulties involved in using the reproduction cost procedure, accentuated as they were by the depression, finally caused the Court (as well as public service commissions) to favor the original cost formula, provided the administrative agencies could show that they had given some consideration to present costs. In addition, with a falling level of prices the private utilities were more amendable to original cost in rate base determination. Thus, in the Los Angeles Gas case, decided in 1933, the Supreme Court supported the action of the California commission in basing rates largely upon original cost. The Court found that the company's estimates of reproduction cost were "too conjectural," and that the commission had given about as much attention to reproduction costs as could reasonably be done.[8]

THE HOPE NATURAL GAS DECISION

A marked change in the regulatory procedure which the courts had followed for years was made by the Supreme Court in 1944 in its decision in the Hope Natural Gas case. Experience with rate making had long shown the practical difficulties involved in trying to test the fairness of rates upon the basis of reproduction cost new less accrued depreciation. In addition to the technical administrative problems of regulation, there were also the many legal problems arising out of the exercise of judicial review by the courts. On the one hand, the commissions were placed in the difficult position of finding their work frequently cast aside by differences in judgment shown by the courts and by changes in the majority view of the Supreme Court. On the other hand, the courts, themselves serving as a final arbiter,

[8] Los Angeles Gas and Electric Co. v. California Commission, 289 U.S. 287, 304 (1933).

were faced with an almost impossible burden of trying to decide whether or not the rates were fair and reasonable.[9]

In the *Hope* case the Court apparently broke with the procedures of the past and shifted from the principle of judicial domination in the rate-making process to that of administrative domination. The Natural Gas Act of 1938 gave the Federal Power Commission authority to regulate companies selling natural gas at wholesale in interstate commerce. In the exercise of its powers, the Commission ordered the Hope Natural Gas Company to reduce its wholesale rates so as to bring about a reduction of not less than $3,609,857 in its operating revenues. In making this calculation, the Commission used the "actual legitimate cost" of some $33,000,000 as the rate base and allowed a return of 6½ percent on this investment. The company, however, claimed that it should be allowed to earn 8 percent on a cost-of-reproduction rate base of $66,000,000. The Court of Appeals set aside the order of the Commission on the principal grounds that the Commission had failed to consider the current or reproduction cost of the properties. Upon appeal, the Supreme Court in a five-to-three decision reversed the ruling of the Court of Appeals and upheld the order of the Federal Power Commission.

In summary form, the following important points were established by Justice Douglas in the majority opinion in the *Hope* case.

1. The Court will not review the rate orders of a commission or allow a utility to obtain a review except under the most extraordinary circumstances. In the words of the Court, "The Commission's order . . . is the product of expert judgment which carries a presumption of validity. And he who would upset the rate order under the Act carries the heavy burden of making a convincing showing that it is invalid because it is unjust and unreasonable in its consequences."

2. In order to secure a review of a commission's order the utility company must show that the "end result" of the order is unjust because it thwarts the successful operation of the company and restricts its ability to attract necessary capital. "Rates which enable the company to operate successfully, to maintain its financial integrity, to attract capital, and to compensate its investors for the risks assumed certainly cannot be condemned as invalid, even though they might produce only a meager return on the so-called 'fair value' rate base."

3. A review will not be allowed because a commission has used one particular method of valuation rather than another. The significant factor is the "end result." "It is not theory," the Court declared, "but the impact of the rate order which counts. If the total effect of the rate order cannot be said to be unjust and unreasonable, judicial inquiry under the Act is at an end. The fact that the method employed to reach that result may contain infirmities is not then important."

[9] By 1933 the Supreme Court began to recognize that it was in no position to substitute its judgment for that of a commission. See, for example, *Los Angeles Gas and Electric Co. v. California Commission*, 289 U.S. 287, 304 (1933); and *Federal Power Commission v. Natural Gas Pipeline Co.*, 315 U.S. 575, 586 (1942).

4. The Court recognized the practical difficulty of trying to set rates upon the basis of "costs of production." "Fair value," the Court observed, is the "end product of the process of rate-making not the starting point. . . . The heart of the matter is that rates cannot be made to depend upon 'fair value' when the value of the going enterprise depends on earnings under whatever rates may be anticipated."[10] As an alternative to the procedure of trying to set rates which will provide a fair return on the "value" of the property, the Court adopted the principle of examining the "total effect" or "end result" of the rates established by public control. This ruling, it may be noted, does not mean that "cost of production" is no longer a criterion of the reasonableness of rates. On the basis of the *Hope* case, both the commissions and the Court continue to discuss and rely upon cost of production as one of several tests of whether the "end result" is reasonable.

THE NEW PROCEDURE OF ADMINISTRATION DOMINATION

It is generally recognized that the effect of the *Hope Natural Gas* decision is to give federal and state utility commissions greater administrative freedom. Only in cases of extreme and arbitrary orders which threaten the financial integrity of a utility company, it appears, will the federal courts overrule the administrative agencies. The extent to which the state commissions and the state courts will follow the Supreme Court in cases involving state regulation of intrastate rates remains to be seen. In Wisconsin the commission made a bold attempt to take the language of the *Hope* case at its face value, but the state court rejected the new procedure.[11] Some of the other state courts have also refused to follow the broad language in the *Hope* case, and the expectations of those who felt that the *Hope* decision did in fact mark a general change in the scope of judicial review have not entirely materialized.[12]

The effect of the judicial policy of accepting administrative orders when there is substantial evidence to support them places new and significant responsibilities on the utility commissions. More than ever before, it is important for the commissions to be staffed with well-trained personnel who will make regulation their life career. The added power of control placed in the hands of the commissions is also certain to cause the utility companies to increase their political pressure on the legislatures and executive offices to secure the appointment of commissioners who are sympathetic to the industry and to obtain legislation on regulatory procedures which is advantageous to their economic position.

[10] *Federal Power Commission* v. *Hope Natural Gas Co.,* 320 U.S. 591, 601–605 (1944).

[11] See, for example, *City of Two Rivers* v. *Commonwealth Telephone Co., Public Utility Reports* (New Series), Vol. 70 (1947), pp. 5–17.

[12] See, for example, *Peoples Natural Gas Co.* v. *Pennsylvania Public Utility Commission,* 34 A (2d) 375, 382 (1943); *Northern States Power Co.* v. *Public Service Commission of North Dakota,* 13 N.W. (2d) 779, 785 (1944); and *Utah Power and Light Co.* v. *Public Service Commission of Utah,* 152 P. (2d) 542, 553 (1945).

STATE AND FEDERAL PUBLIC UTILITY COMMISSIONS

Public utility commissions have been established in the District of Columbia and in all states except Delaware. A state commission is usually called a public service or public utility commission, and its jurisdiction extends to designated utilities which conduct an intrastate business. Utility companies which are engaged in interstate commerce, on the other hand, are subject to control by one of the several commissions or agencies at the federal level. These consist of (1) the Interstate Commerce Commission, (2) the Civil Aeronautics Board, (3) the Secretary of the Army, (4) the Federal Communications Commission, (5) the Secretary of Agriculture, and (6) the Federal Power Commission.

ESSENTIAL FEATURES OF COMMISSION CONTROL

In the main, commission control is exercised with respect to "public utilities"—that is, enterprises which are "affected with a public interest" and which have an obligation to serve all customers at reasonable rates. The powers of control exercised by the federal commissions and by many state commissions typically take the following forms (see also Table 10, p. 80):

1. The power to prescribe and require the observance of uniform accounting systems and statistical regulations, including in certain instances prescription of amounts recorded on a utility's books (i.e., the classes of property for which depreciation charges may be included in operating expenses and the percentages of depreciation to be included on such property.)

2. The power to establish an appropriate rate base for use in testing the legitimacy of rates and charges.

3. The power to prescribe rates and charges—maximum, minimum, or both—after full opportunity for hearings. Many commissions have authority on their own motion *to initiate* proceedings for rate reductions or for rate increases.

4. The power to control entrance into or abandonment of service.

5. The power to pass upon applications to acquire the ownership or control of another company operating in the same line of business.

Upon the basis of the foregoing powers, it may be seen that the approach taken by a commission in controlling the rates of public utilities is that of (1) prescribing uniform systems of accounts and records, (2) scrutinizing and in some cases reviewing certain expenses incurred, and (3) approving or disapproving rates and charges in the light of the earnings which the records reveal.

The basic reasons underlying commission control are (1) the experience that the public interest is best served by having an enterprise operate in a monopolistic fashion and (2) belief that the service rendered is highly essential to the public. In controlling utility enterprises, commissions usually identify the public interest with rates of earnings on invested capital which are fair and reasonable. In some cases, however, the public interest is defined to include other factors, too. The Civil Aeronautics Board, for example, has the duty to subsidize the industry to the extent necessary for the development of a sound air transportation industry, not only for the purposes of commerce, but also for the national defense. The Interstate Commerce Commission, also, is charged with the duty of "developing, coördinating, and preserving a national transportation system."

In the following sections, we shall consider the activities of the federal commissions as they apply and give force to the main features of control.

1. THE INTERSTATE COMMERCE COMMISSION

The Interstate Commerce Commission was established in 1887 and is the oldest of the various federal commissions. It now consists of eleven members appointed by the President, with the "advice and consent" of the Senate, for terms of seven years. No more than six of the commissioners may be appointed from the same political party. The jurisdiction of the I.C.C., in general, extends to all forms of interstate public transportation, except air carriers, pipe lines for gas and water, and certain motor and water carriers operating in metropolitan areas.[13] In this capacity, the I.C.C. fixes rates for railroads in the United States, as well as for oil pipe lines, sleeping-car service, express service, motor carriers operating in interstate and foreign commerce, water carriers engaged in coastwise and intercoastal commerce and upon inland waters of the United States, and freight-forwarding companies. It also has certain jurisdiction over private car lines.

The act of 1887 was passed as a result of the Cullom Report of 1886, which revealed the widespread existence of railroad abuses.[14] These abuses included numerous examples of discriminatory pricing, resulting in large measure from a desire to maximize profits by "charging what the traffic will bear." Rates were made unreasonably higher at local, noncompetitive points (possibly nine-tenths of all stations) than on longer hauls to destinations and terminal points which were highly competitive. Startling discriminations were also practiced between persons and various classes of goods. Secret rebates were paid to favorite shippers, and monopolistic agreements were made to pool earnings and the volume of traffic.

In the same year that the Cullom Report was issued, the Supreme Court ruled that state regulation of interstate rates was unconstitutional.[15] Since most railroad transportation involved interstate hauls, Congress thereupon

---

[13] Air carriers are regulated by the Civil Aeronautics Board, while gas pipe lines are controlled by the Federal Power Commission. There is no federal control over water pipe lines.

[14] *Report of the Select Committee on Interstate Commerce*, 49th Congress, first session, Senate Report 46, Part 1, 1886.

[15] *Wabash, St. L. and P.R.R. v. Illinois*, 118 U.S. 557 (1886).

took steps to meet its responsibility by enacting the original "Act to Regulate Commerce" (1887).

The present Interstate Commerce Act, among other things, requires a publication of rates and prohibits "unjust and unreasonable rates." Discrimination between persons and unjust discriminations between places and goods are declared to be illegal. The act also outlaws higher charges for the transportation of passengers or property over a shorter than a longer distance, over the same line, the shorter being included within the longer distance, except where Commission approval is obtained. (See also Table 10, p. 80.)

The work of the Interstate Commerce Commission was long handicapped by a series of adverse Supreme Court decisions restricting its powers of control. A decision of 1897, for example, held that the I.C.C. could not fix rates, but only declare existing rates unreasonable.[16] Since a railroad could change its rates slightly upon getting an adverse decision, the ruling meant that a new complaint would have to be brought and again carried through the courts. It was not until 1906, when the act of 1887 was amended to give the Commission power to set maximum rates, that it could begin to exercise effective control over the railroad industry. The Commission's authority to control local discrimination was also nullified by adverse court decisions; and it was not until 1910 that it secured a revitalized power to prohibit, in most cases, the charging of a higher rate for a shorter than for a longer haul over the same route in the same direction. The Transportation Act of 1920 included a rule of rate making which provided for the control of rates by the Commission so that the carriers as a whole, or by various groups, would earn a "fair return" on the "fair value" of the property. The act of 1920 also gave the Commission the power to establish minimum rates and even specific rates.

Not long after the Commission began to exercise an effective control over the railroads, new forms of transportation began to develop—private automobiles, motor carriers, improved ships and tankers, and finally air carriers. Pipe lines, brought under regulation in 1906, also became increasingly important in this period. These new types of competition served to change the problems with which the I.C.C. had to deal. The business depression which began in 1929 also brought new problems and served to accentuate the difficulties involved in rate making. In the face of a general decline in prices, the Commission found that the fair-return-on-the-fair-value rule was no longer satisfactory as a pricing formula. Railroad managements and many investors, however, believed that they were entitled to earn a fair return on the past investment regardless of economic conditions or technological improvements.[17]

[16] *I.C.C.* v. *Cincinnati, New Orleans, and Texas Pacific Railway Co.*, 167 U.S. 479 (1897).

[17] National Resources Planning Board, *Transportation and National Policy* (Washington, 1942), pp. 102–103; and I. L. Sharfman, *The Interstate Commerce Commission*, (New York, 1936), Part 3, Vol. B, pp. 293–295.

NATIONAL TRANSPORTATION POLICY

At the present time, the control of the I.C.C. is directed to giving effect to the broad purposes of the Transportation Act of 1940. According to this act, a "national transportation policy" is established as follows:

It is hereby declared to be the national transportation policy of the Congress to provide for fair and impartial regulation of all modes of transportation subject to the provisions of this Act, so administered as to recognize and preserve the inherent advantages of each; to promote safe, adequate, economical, and efficient service and foster sound economic conditions in transportation and among the several carriers; *to encourage the establishment and maintenance of reasonable charges* for transportation services, *without unjust discriminations*, undue preferences or advantages, or unfair or destructive competitive practices; to coöperate with the several states and the duly authorized officials thereof; and to encourage fair wages and equitable working conditions; *all to the end of developing, coördinating, and preserving a national transportation system by water, highway, and rail, as well as other means, adequate to meet the needs of commerce of the United States, of the Postal Service, and of the national defense.*[18]

In applying the standard of reasonableness to rates and charges, the Commission is charged with the duty of carrying out the national transportation policy. This policy, in essence, is one of "developing, coördinating, and preserving a national transportation system," and commission control is to be directed to that end. At the same time, however, under the terms of the act, the Commission is not permitted to disregard the interests of the shippers.

In setting rates, the Commission is directed to give due consideration (a) "to the effect of rates on the movement of traffic by the carrier or carriers for which the rates are prescribed," (b) "to the need, in the public interest, of adequate and efficient railway transportation service at the lowest cost consistent with the furnishing of such service," and (c) "to the need of revenues sufficient to enable the carriers, under honest, economical, and efficient management to provide such service." Maximum, as well as minimum, rates may be prescribed. In rate cases decided during 1946 and subsequently, the Commission has discussed the rate of return being earned on the value of the railroad properties, but significant weight does not appear to have been given to this factor.[19] Greater emphasis appears to have been given to the increasing operating costs and the necessity of reimbursement of these costs in higher rates.

Customarily, the rates charged by common carriers are fixed by the car-

---

[18] *United States Statutes at Large,* 76th Congress, third session, Vol. 54 (Washington, 1940), Part 1, p. 899. Italics supplied.

[19] See *Increased Railway Rates, Fares, and Charges,* 1946, 264 I.C.C. 695 (June, 1946) and 266 I.C.C. 537 (December, 1946); *Increased Freight Rates,* 1947, 269 I.C.C. 33 (October, 1947) and 270 I.C.C. 403 (July, 1948).

riers themselves and simply filed with the I.C.C. As we have seen, the various carriers—rail, water, truck, and air—have secured exemptions from the antitrust laws with respect to their rate-making activities. In accordance with these privileges of legalized monopoly action, it is usual for the various companies in a given line of transportation—and sometimes in related lines —to meet together in rate-making conferences to fix rates by concerted action. These rates are thereupon submitted to the I.C.C. The Commission is empowered to investigate any and all rates proposed, either upon complaint or upon its own motion. It is also authorized to set aside proposed rates and to prescribe rates which it believes are in accordance with the act of 1940 and the orders of the Commission.

RAILROAD RATES IN A DEFENSE ECONOMY

Since World War II, the Interstate Commerce Commission has authorized a number of railroad rate increases in line with increased labor, material, and tax costs (see Fig. 45). The most important decision with respect to the

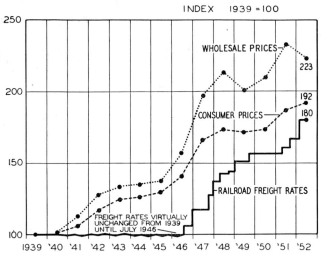

FIG. 45. Indexes of railroad freight rates, wholesale prices, and consumer prices. (Sources: Bureau of Labor Statistics and Interstate Commerce Commission.)

various rate increases was that of *Ex Parte 175, Increased Freight Rates, 1951*, decided April 11, 1952 (284 I.C.C. 589). In this decision, the Commission authorized a general increase of 15 percent in the basic rates and charges of railroads, water carriers, and freight forwarders, to continue until February 28, 1954. The decision of 1952 is important because in it the Commission ruled that the railroads, during a period of defense mobilization, should be permitted to charge rates which will provide revenue not only for operating costs, depreciation, and a reasonable rate of return, but also for some increase in capital investment. Said the Commission in support of its decision:

We believe at a time when the Nation is bearing arms against aggression and undertaking extraordinary efforts in the way of defense mobilization for peace, the developing of a transportation system by rail adequate to meet the needs of national defense, within the meaning of the national transportation policy, requires attention on our part in a proceeding of this kind, and warrants a degree of liberality in decision not otherwise to be taken into account. . . . We are not convinced that *money necessary for capital additions* to the railway systems should be derived wholly from income, but we must take note of the fact that many of these outlays are being made under the encouragement, if not the insistence, of the Government and the shipping public, with national defense primarily in mind. Such circumstances, therefore, bear upon our decision in this case.[20]

On July 29, 1953, the Commission extended the expiration date of the 1952 order to December 31, 1955, and it is possible that the 15 percent increase will subsequently be made permanent. In extending the rate order the Commission emphasized again that liberality in earnings would facilitate the maintenance of the carriers for meeting the needs of defense. "Our experience in the past," it was stated, "indicates that our transportation system may, without extensive notice, be called upon to make extraordinary exertions in behalf of national defense. There should be some insurance against any possible slowdown or breakdown in transportation service, and that fact may well resolve some doubts about the propriety of increases in rates which might otherwise prove insuperable."[21]

2. THE CIVIL AERONAUTICS BOARD

The Civil Aeronautics Act of 1938, as amended, provides for the establishment of the Civil Aeronautics Authority, a five-man administrative agency similar to the I.C.C., appointed by the President, with the advice and consent of the Senate, to prescribe economic regulations and safety rules for the air transportation industry. The Civil Aeronautics Authority (redesignated the Civil Aeronautics Board) is given jurisdiction over interstate rates (a) for the transportation of mail by aircraft and (b) for the transportation of persons and property. In practice, the Board also exercises a broad power over intrastate air commerce. This is in accordance with the decisions of the Supreme Court permitting Congress to regulate *intrastate* transportation in order to make effective its control over *interstate* transportation. Although the rates which are established are required to be fair and reasonable, the Board is directed to approve rates which will provide for the *development* of air transportation and the *needs* of commerce, the postal service, and national defense.

In addition to its control over rates, the Civil Aeronautics Board is given authority over other aspects of the inner workings of air transportation

[20] *Ex Parte 175, Increased Freight Rates, 1951*, 281 I.C.C. 557, 637 (1951). Italics supplied. See also 284 I.C.C. 589, 660 (1952).

[21] Interstate Commerce Commission, *Ex Parte 175, Increased Freight Rates, 1951*, Report of August 10, 1953, Mimeographed, p. 73.

companies. It is empowered to require annual, periodic, and special reports from any air carrier on any subject deemed necessary, including contracts, agreements, understandings, or other arrangements which a carrier may have with any other carrier or person with respect to air traffic. Air carriers are required to submit annually a list of stockholders owning more than 5 percent of their capital stock, and officers and directors are required to submit a report on any stock or interest which they hold in any phase of aeronautics. The Board is authorized to prescribe the form in which accounts are to be kept and to inspect all accounts, letters, records, and facilities. All rates, fares, and charges for air transportation must be filed with the Board and posted publicly. Rebating is prohibited. Unfair methods of competition, unjust discrimination, and unfair and deceptive practices are also prohibited, and the Board is given authority to issue cease-and-desist orders. (See also Table 10, p. 81.)

For purposes of regulation, air-lines companies are grouped into two categories: (a) certificated carriers and (b) noncertificated carriers. Certificated carriers are those which have been certified as being essential for the public convenience and necessity. Such companies are authorized to carry air mail and all other forms of revenue traffic between certain designated points. A noncertificated carrier, on the other hand, operates without a certificate of convenience and necessity from the Civil Aeronautics Board and is exempted from many of the regulations of the board.

MEASURES TO RESTRICT CONCENTRATION OF CONTROL

The act of 1938 prohibits consolidations, mergers, or contracts designed to give an air carrier a control over any other company or property in the field of aeronautics, unless such arrangements are approved by order of the Board. Interlocking directorships, likewise, are prohibited, unless they are given specific approval. In each instance, the Board is given authority to approve consolidations, mergers, or interlocking relationships if it finds that the public interest is not adversely affected. The act, however, expressly provides that the Board shall not approve a merger or acquisition which will result in creating a monopoly or monopolies. All agreements made between and among carriers with respect to rates, fares, classifications, the pooling of earnings, or other matters are required to be submitted to the Board for approval or disapproval. Finally, it is provided that if the Board issues an approval order with respect to mergers, acquisitions, interlocking relationships, or agreements on rates and other matters, the company or companies concerned will be exempted from the operation of the Clayton Act and the other antitrust laws.

At the time that the Board was established, a high degree of economic concentration and oligopoly had already come to exist in the air transport industry. In an effort to modify this condition, the Board stated in a decision rendered in 1940 that its policy would be one of developing and preserving a system of "balanced competition"—that is, a condition of numerous companies fairly evenly balanced in size. To this end, it declared that it would endeavor to strengthen the smaller carriers by granting them new routes and service extensions. The basic principle involved was stated to be that of seeking to provide a degree of competitive stimulus and to avoid granting a single company the exclusive right to exploit a specific sales area. In the words of the Board,

> It is the concentration of ownership and control which is fatal to the operation of a competitive economy. To allow one air carrier to obtain control of air transportation in the west coast area greatly in excess of that possessed by competitors would, in our opinion, seriously endanger the development of a properly balanced air-transportation system in this region; and the elimination of the only independent north and south air carrier west of the Rocky Mountains might be expected to retard the promotion of air travel in this direction.[22]

The policy of "balanced" or "constructive" competition, it may be noted, does not mean that the Board seeks to maintain price competition in the antitrust law sense. The Board, in fact, has declared that it will not employ the economic definition of monopoly as "restraint of competition" in its regulatory activity. It proposes rather to identify monopoly with that degree of ownership which it believes gives rise to a control of air transportation in the whole or any significant part of the United States.[23] In the eyes of the Board, the "competition" which is to maintained as far as possible is essentially a *service* or *sales* competition.

The declared goal of the Board to secure and maintain a condition of numerous, substantial, independent companies in the air industry is sound public policy, for it may help to limit the economic and political evils of economic concentration. At the present time, it is estimated that the Big Four account for about 50 percent of the commercial transport revenues. If mergers could be formed without restriction, it is most likely that the Big Four would further increase their percentage control.[24]

RATES AND SUBSIDIES

In exercising its rate-making powers and duties, the Board is directed to consider, among other factors:

> . . . the need of each such air carrier for compensation for the transportation of mail sufficient to insure the performance of such service, and, together with all other revenue of the air carrier, to enable such air carrier

[22] *United Air Lines Transport Corporation—Acquisition of Western Air Express Corporation,* 1 C.A.A. 739, 750–751 (1940).

[23] *United A.L.—Western A.E., Interchange Equipment,* 1 C.A.A. 723, 733 (1940).

[24] See also, Report of the Civil Aeronautics Board to the Select Committee on Small Business, *The Role of Competition in Commercial Air Transportation,* 82nd Congress, second session, 1952, especially pp. 47–51. The dominant companies consist of (1) American Airlines, (2) United Air Lines, (3) Trans World Airlines, and (4) Eastern Air Lines.

under honest, economical, and efficient management, to maintain and continue the development of air transportation to the extent and of the character and quality required for the commerce of the United States, the postal service, and the national defense. (Civil Aeronautics Act, Sec. 406-b.)

The Act states further that the Board may prescribe upon complaint, or upon its own initiative, the lawful rate, or the maximum and minimum rates, for the carriage or persons and property by air, whenever it finds that existing rates are unjust, discriminatory, or unduly preferential. Thus far the air lines have been able to work out satisfactory rate schedules with the Board, and no appeals on rates have been taken to the courts.

Upon the bases of the need or so-called "subsidy" provision, quoted in the preceding paragraph, the Board uses air-mail payments to provide total revenues which will permit a carrier to earn a fair return on operations required in the national interest. The principle followed in fixing mail pay has been to make up, under conditions of careful control, the difference between the operating revenue of a carrier and its operating expense and to provide a fair return on invested capital. The essential idea has been that a carrier should be allowed to "break even" and to have something left over to induce it to provide safe and adequate service.[25]

The air-mail payments established by the Board, in many cases, thus include not only compensation for carrying the mail, but also a subsidy to accomplish the broad purposes of the Civil Aeronautics Act. (See also Table

TABLE 35. Administrative Separation of Subsidy from Total Mail Payments for U.S. Certificated Air Carriers

	Fiscal Years				
	1951	1952	1953	1954	1955[a]
Net Service Mail Payments (000)					
Domestic Trunks	$25,432	$31,743	$32,355	$34,631	$36,370
Local Service	1,151	1,139	1,136	1,382	1,425
Helicopters	907	862	1,876	341	353
International, Overseas and					
Territorial	17,006	17,775	18,605	19,716	20,312
Total	$44,496	$51,519	$53,972	$56,070	$58,460
Subsidy Payments (000)					
Domestic Trunks	$18,881	$ 6,283	$ 4,210	$ 3,581	$ 3,566
Local Service	17,057	18,938	21,952	23,895	23,841
Helicopters	—	—	—	2,325	2,563
International, Overseas and					
Territorial	39,263	45,338	49,546	50,854	50,282
Total	$75,201	$70,559	$75,708	$80,655	$80,252

[a] Estimated.
(Source: Civil Aeronautics Board.)

[25] See, for example, Civil Aeronautics Board, *Braniff Airways, Inc.*, Docket 2680 (adopted September 2, 1948), pp. 29–30.

35.) At the present time, the Post Office Department makes the service mail payments to the air carriers, and the C.A.B. pays the outright subsidies.

3. THE JURISDICTION OF THE SECRETARY OF THE ARMY OVER THE CHARGES OF TOLL BRIDGES

The Secretary of the Army has been given jurisdiction by Congress, with certain exceptions, over the tolls charged for passage over bridges which span any of the navigable waters of the United States.[26] The tolls charged by the owners are required to be just and reasonable, but formal approval of proposed rates is not considered to be necessary. The Department of the Army may act in response to a complaint that tolls are unreasonable, on its own initiative, or at the request of the bridge owners. Where a controversy exists, the Secretary of the Army may determine the reasonableness of tolls only after full investigation and after giving all interested parties a reasonable opportunity to be heard.

It is the policy of the Department to act in complaint cases only upon receipt of specific information from which it can be reasonably inferred that existing rates are excessive. Complaints from municipal authorities, civic bodies, other organizations, or a substantial number of users of the bridge which make a strong preliminary showing that existing rates are unreasonable are preferred. Upon receipt of such a complaint the District Engineer, Corps of Engineers, is first directed to make a preliminary investigation with a view to determining whether a full investigation is justified. On the basis of his report the Department then determines whether a full investigation including public hearings should be made. Not until the completion of such an investigation is the Department in a position to decide that the existing tolls are proper or to prescribe such other rates as may be found reasonable.

According to the records of the Office, Chief of Engineers, rates of tolls have been prescribed by the Secretary of the Army for forty-two existing bridges, and investigations have been made by the Department in numerous other cases where no change in existing rates was found to be justified. After an order of the Secretary of the Army takes effect, it is unlawful to collect a toll in excess of that so prescribed.

4. THE FEDERAL COMMUNICATIONS COMMISSION

The Communications Act of 1934, as amended, provides for the creation of the Federal Communications Commission, an independent regulatory agency, composed of seven commissioners, appointed by the President, subject to confirmation by the Senate. The Commission has powers of regulation over (1) all interstate and foreign common carrier operations of domestic companies by wire and radio (telegraph, telephone, and submarine cable); (2) nonbroadcast radio facilities (safety and special); and (3) broadcast (program) stations, radio and television.

[26] 33 U.S.C. 494, 498 (a), 498 (b), 525–533.

The authority exercised over telephone, telegraph, and radio common carrier operations is principally concerned with rates and service. The regulation of radio and broadcasting facilities, on the other hand, consists of allocating radio bands for different services; the assigning of frequencies to individual stations; and the licensing of all radio transmitters and radio operators. In regulating radio broadcasting, the Commission has authority over commercial broadcasters, educational stations, police and fire stations, and facilities used in forestry, maritime activities, bus and taxi service, transportation, farming, and industry.

The Communications Act was adopted by Congress in 1934 after a Congressional committee had reported that "at the present time there is little, if any, federal regulation of the rates, practices, and charges of the several branches of the communications industry. . . . The American people are entitled to know if they are being overcharged for this service, though they may be satisfied with the quality of the service." With special reference to the telephone industry, the report declared that the "telephone business is a monopoly—it is supposed to be regulated. Thus far regulation, particularly by the federal government, has been nominal largely because Congress has not made appropriations sufficient to enable the Interstate Commerce Commission to give effect to existing statutes."[27]

THE CONTROL OF COMMON CARRIERS OF MESSAGES

The powers of the Federal Communications Commission with respect to the rates of communication carriers is concerned (a) with a division of the charges between the single domestic telegraph company and the several international carriers of messages sent outside of the United States, and (b) with the domestic rates charged the public for interstate wire and wireless communications.

The rates of common carriers of messages—telegraph and telephone—are required to be "just and reasonable"; and the Commission is empowered to set maximum and minimum rates, as well as the actual rates which may be charged. All rates must be filed with the Commission and posted for public inspection, and undue or unreasonable discrimination is prohibited. The Commission is authorized to prescribe uniform systems of accounts for use by telegraph and telephone carriers in interstate and foreign commerce. It also is required by law to approve the construction of new lines and the extension of interstate service; to regulate the interlocking of officers and directors; and to pass upon applications of communications companies for authority to merge or consolidate (see also Table 10, p. 81). A significant shortcoming of the act of 1934 is that no control was given to the Commission over the terms of purchase contracts made by operating companies and their affiliated companies. Also the Commission was given no control over the issuance of securities by the regulated companies.

Although the Communications Act of 1934 provides for the making of

[27] *Preliminary Report on Communication Companies*, 73rd Congress, second session, House Report 1273, 1934, Vol. 5, Part 1, pp. xvi–xxxi.

valuations of the property of companies subject to regulation, the Commission has not sought to set rates upon the basis of valuation standards. As a result of a Congressional investigation of the telephone industry in 1939, the Commission was able to secure several reductions in long-distance telephone rates by means of negotiation and agreement. No attempt, however, has been made to determine the "reasonableness" of interstate telephone rates by reference to the cost of the servics rendered.

The American Telephone and Telegraph Company, it may be noted, has an almost complete national monopoly of the telephone business. According to the Federal Trade Commission, "the Bell System," controlled by the American Telephone and Telegraph Company, is the "largest aggregation of capital and resources that has even been controlled by a single private company at any time in the history of business. The system consists of over 200 corporations directly and indirectly controlled by the American Telephone and Telegraph Company. This company controls between 80 and 90 percent of local telephone service and 98 percent of the long distance telephone wires of the United States, including practically all wire facilities used in radio program transmission."[28]

Intrastate telephone service is subject to state control by the several state commissions. Since substantially all telephone facilities are used in common in interstate and intrastate service, public regulation requires the separation of property and expense. The Supreme Court has ruled that separations should be based upon the relative use of property in the two different services.[29] The same principle, it may be noted, applies to the control of telegraph, railroad, motor carrier, air carrier, and gas and electric utilities. Not all states, however, control the various intrastate operations of interstate utilities. Only eighteen states, for example, undertake to regulate intrastate air transportation.

REGULATION OF RADIO BROADCAST SERVICES

The Federal Communications Act states that persons engaged in radio broadcasting shall not be deemed to be common carriers. The Commission, accordingly, does not have authority to control the rates charged for broadcasting services. It likewise has no *direct* power of broadcast censorship. The Act, however, specifically provides that the license of an operator may be suspended if he transmits any false or deceptive communications or any communications containing profane or obscene words, language, or meaning. Likewise, the Act provides that if a licensee permits any political candidate to use a broadcasting station, he shall afford equal opportunities to all other candidates.

Since all broadcast stations must secure a license, the Commission is in a position to make and enforce various rules with respect to the public interest as a condition for securing a license. Any person or company seeking to

[28] Federal Trade Commission, *Investigation of the Telephone Industry in the United States*, 76th Congress, first session, House Document 340, 1939, p. xxiii.
[29] See *Minnesota Rate Cases*, 230 U.S. 352 (1913).

operate a radio or television station must first apply for a construction permit. Then, if engineering and other conditions are met, he must apply for a license. The maximum license period prescribed in the Communications Act is three years. This statutory limitation enables the Commission to impose various regulations on the use of broadcasting time and secure compliance, for the companies are vitally concerned in securing a renewal of their licenses.

At the present time, there are over 3000 stations engaged in program broadcasting (see Table 36); some 214,000 nonbroadcast radio authoriza-

TABLE 36. The Number of Authorized and Licensed Stations at the Close of Each Fiscal Year.

	AM		FM		TV		Total	
	Author-ized	Li-censed	Author-ized	Li-censed	Author-ized	Li-censed	Author-ized	Li-censed
1943	912	911	48	37	6	6	966	954
1944	924	912	52	45	9	6	985	963
1945	955	931	53	46	25	6	1033	983
1946	1215	961	456	48	30	6	1701	1015
1947	1795	1298	918	48	66	6	2779	1352
1948	2034	1693	1020	142	109	7	3163	1842
1949	2179	1963	865	377	117	13	3161	2353
1950	2303	2118	732	493	109	47	3144	2658
1951	2385	2248	659	534	109	81	3153	2863
1952	2420	2333	648	582	108	96	3176	3011
1953	2584	2439	601	551	483	101	3668	3191
1954	2697	2565	569	529	573	104	3839	3198

(Source: Annual Reports of the Federal Communications Commission.)

tions, covering 2½ times as many transmitters, operating on land, sea, and in the air; and more than 1000 pickup and studio-transmitter links. The number of radio operator authorizations exceeds 800,000.

The act of 1934 provides that "all laws of the United States relating to unlawful restraints and monopolies and to combinations, contracts, or agreements in restraint of trade are declared to be applicable . . . to interstate or foreign radio communications." Moreover, the act provides, further, that if a broadcasting company is convicted of violating the antitrust laws the court may order a revocation of its license. To date, these two sections of the law have not been applied in the radio industry. In an effort to curb monopoly, the Commission itself has adopted rules barring the operation of more than one AM, FM, or TV station in the same locality by the same interests. A maximum limit of six FM or five TV stations in the country as a whole for a single interest has also been established. On December 23, 1953, the Commission announced a proposed rule increasing the maximum permissible ownership of television stations from 5 to 7. At the present time, newspapers or their owners control almost one-third of all television stations. Since the number of radio and TV stations which can be permitted to operate in the United States is limited by the available frequency range, it follows that in many areas the privilege of having a radio license is of great value. In practice, the established radio companies confidently expect their licenses to be renewed indefinitely. The result is that present station owners are proceeding to operate on the presumption that they have a vested interest in the airways of the nation—that is, in a particular frequency channel on the radio spectrum. In certain instances, radio stations have been sold at prices far above the value of the physical facilities; and in giving approval to transfers of licenses in such cases, the Commission has allowed private individuals to collect a capital gain from the use of a public resource. At various times the Commission, in the absence of statute provision, has asked Congress what policy it should follow in passing upon the transfer of stations where the sales prices are far in excess of the physical property values, but Congress has not replied.

5. CONTROL OF STOCKYARD CHARGES BY THE SECRETARY OF AGRICULTURE

The large combinations in the meat-packing industry, Armour, Swift, Wilson, and Cudahy, have long been under government scrutiny for possible collusive action with respect to prices and market sharing. In 1905, as we have seen, the federal government secured an injunction against various monopolistic practices carried on by the large packers in the meat industry.[30] Again, in 1919, the Federal Trade Commission reported that the large packers were not only continuing the collusive practices found in 1905 but were also controlling the stockyards in the principal market centers.

The investigations of the Federal Trade Commission led Congress to enact the Packers and Stockyards Act of 1921. This legislation combines the rate control features of the Interstate Commerce Act and the regulatory provisions of the Federal Trade Commission Act. (See also Tables 9 and 10, p. 81.) The main purposes of the legislation are (1) to provide patrons of the public stockyards with open competitive markets for livestock, free from collusion and unfair trade practices by those in livestock marketing or by the meat-packing industries; and (2) to require operators of public stockyards to furnish stockyard services at fair and nondiscriminatory rates to all patrons. In 1935 the act was amended to bring the handling of live poultry in large cities under the provisions of the law relating to services, facilities, rates, and charges, whenever the Secretary of Agriculture finds that "unfair, deceptive, and fraudulent practices" warrant such action.

At the present time, 66 terminal markets and 263 livestock auction markets are supervised by the Secretary of Agriculture. Some 2300 commission firms and 2700 dealers are registered for buying and selling in these markets.

[30] *Swift and Co. v. U.S.*, 196 U.S. 375 (1905).

More than 1900 packers are also subject to the provisions of the Act. The marketing of live poultry is supervised in seven major cities, and some 1500 licensees (commission merchants and dealers in poultry) are operating under the supervision of the Secretary of Agriculture.

The act of 1921 (a) forbids various commercial practices—such as apportioning supplies and manipulating or controlling prices—and (b) provides that the rates of public stockyards and market agencies "shall be just, reasonable, and non-discriminatory." The Secretary of Agriculture is given authority to supervise the business practices of packers, dealers, and market agencies; to prosecute alleged violations; and to obtain compliance with the law. A field supervisory force is maintained at 20 of the principal central markets. These marketing specialists observe the daily operations in the yards and market houses. Technical violations of a minor nature are disposed of by informal discussion. Violations which do not involve intentional dishonesty or an element of fraud are frequently settled by the signing of a stipulation—an agreement to discontinue the unlawful practice. More serious types of violations are handled by the issuance of formal complaints. Hearings are conducted, and cease-and-desist orders are issued if violations are found to exist. These orders may be appealed to the courts; but when they are approved or accepted, they serve as an injunction against the unlawful practices. In the case of violations by commission men and dealers, the order may provide for the suspension of an individual's registration or license.

To insure that the rates and charges of stockyard owners and market agencies (livestock commission men) are just, reasonable, and non-discriminatory, the act of 1921 provides that the Secretary of Agriculture may upon his own motion or upon complaint investigate the existing rates or charges and after a "full hearing" prescribe the specific rates which a stockyard or a market agency must charge. The act does not provide any formula for rate making, and the Secretary has not formally adopted any particular standard. However, stockyard rates have been set upon the basis of a fair return on the reproduction value of the stockyard facilities, and the Supreme Court has upheld this procedure.[31] In view of the *Hope Natural Gas* decision, it is possible that the Supreme Court will continue to limit the role of judicial review. This may mean that the Secretary of Agriculture will have greater discretionary authority in the determination of stockyard rates.

The task of setting a fair and just charge for the services of livestock commission agencies presents a problem which is different from that of other public utilities, for the amount of capital investment required in the business is negligible. Commission rates for selling livestock shipped in from the country have typically been set by the collective action of the commission men themselves, and government intervention is necessary to protect shippers from excessive charges. In setting the selling rates the Secretary of Agriculture endeavors to estimate the competitive salary which is paid for

[31] *Denver Union Stockyard Co.* v. *U.S.,* 304 U.S. 470 (1938).

competent employee salesmen for a reasonable year's work, as well as a reasonable sum for other salaries, travel, entertainment, advertising, office overhead, interest, and related expenses. Upon the basis of these data, the Secretary prescribes the rates to be charged for the sale of cattle, sheep, and hogs shipped in from the country districts.[32]

6. THE FEDERAL POWER COMMISSION

The Federal Power Commission was created in 1920 and is presently composed of five members appointed by the President. Its duties consist of administering the Federal Water Power Act of 1920, renamed the Federal Power Act and enlarged by amendment in 1935, and the Natural Gas Act of 1938.[33] The purposes of these statutes are (a) to control the nation's water-power resources subject to federal jurisdiction for the benefit of all the people and (b) to regulate *interstate* electric and natural gas utilities, so that their rates, services, and financing will be in the public interest.

The Federal Water Power Act of 1920 empowers the Commission to collect information on the water-power resources under the jurisdiction of the federal government and to grant licenses for their use and development. Under its power to regulate interstate commerce, Congress has jurisdiction over power sites on navigable waters and public lands of the United States. All such power sites may now be licensed for private use, but not sold.

The Act of 1920 gives the Commission authority to control rates for power from licensed projects under stated conditions. In 1935, these powers were extended to cover power transmitted in *interstate* commerce. The Commission may also provide for the control of *intrastate* rates involving power from a licensed project, if the state concerned does not have a utility commission. Companies granted licenses are required to agree to the use of original cost, less certain prescribed items, as the basis for rate making; and the Commission is given authority to demand cost records and to determine rates of depreciation.

Federal control of water-power resources seeks to limit the profits of interstate electric utilities *to a fair return on their net original investment,* and to prevent an inclusion in the rate base of a capitalized value on power sites which belong to the people. As early as 1909 President Theodore Roosevelt pointed out the need for federal control of power sites on streams subject to the jurisdiction of Congress. "To give away, without conditions, this, one of our greatest resources," he declared, "would be an act of folly. If we are guilty of it, our children will be forced to pay an annual return upon a capitalization based upon the highest prices which 'the traffic will

[32] G. N. Dagger and Howard D. Dozier, "Reasonable Livestock Commission Rates," *Journal of Land and Public Utility Economics,* February, 1931, pp. 45–51. The validity of this procedure was upheld in *Tagg Brothers and Moorhead* v. *U.S.,* 280 U.S. 420 (1930).

[33] In addition, the Commission has duties under certain sections of the Tennessee Valley Authority Act, the Bonneville Act, the Fort Peck Act, and the various Flood Control and River and Harbor Acts, beginning with the Flood Control Act of 1944.

bear.' They will find themselves face to face with powerful interests intrenched behind the doctrine of 'vested rights' and strengthened by every defense which money can buy and the ingenuity of able corporation lawyers can devise."[34]

In the discussions in Congress on proposals which led to the act of 1920 there was general agreement that "water-power opportunities are in a certain sense the property of all the people and should not be permitted to pass in perpetuity into private ownership."[35] By adopting a policy of licensing the power sites, it was believed, the public could take over the resources at a later date, if it so desired without payment for "water power rights" and other intangibles which in reality belong to the people. Water power is a perpetual resource, and the general view of Congress was that it should be reserved in perpetuity for the people.[36]

In 1935 the title of the act of 1920 was changed to the *Federal Power Act* (by Title II of the Public Utility Act of 1935), and the scope of the statute was enlarged to give the Federal Power Commission authority to fix the rates and charges for all electric energy sold at wholesale in *interstate* commerce, whether or not the utilities concerned are licensed by the Commission. This legislation was made necessary by several decisions of the Supreme Court holding that interstate wholesale rates could not be controlled by the states.[37] The investigations of the Federal Trade Commission also had revealed the existence of flagrant abuses in the management of many electric utilities, particularly the holding companies, which the state agencies were unable to correct.[38] Every utility subject to the act is now required to file with the Commission, when requested, "an inventory of all or any part of its property and a statement of the original cost thereof," and to "keep the Commission informed regarding the cost of all additions, betterments, extensions, and new construction." The Commission is also given authority to prescribe the accounting procedures which a utility must use and to determine and fix adequate rates of depreciation. Inasmuch as the act of 1935 provides for the reporting of original cost data, the Commission controls the

[34] *Special Message of the President of the United States,* House of Representatives, 60th Congress, second session, Document 1350, 1909, pp. 5–6.

[35] *Development of Waterpower,* House of Representatives, 63rd Congress, second session, Report 842, 1914, p. 10.

[36] *Development of Waterpower,* 64th Congress, first session, Senate Report 66, 1916, pp. 8–9.

[37] The decision of the Court in *Public Utilities Commission* v. *Attleboro Steam and Electric Co.,* 273 U.S. 83 (1927), made it clear that effective regulation required federal intervention in those instances where the energy moves across state lines.

[38] Some of the abuses reported by the Federal Trade Commission were (1) loading the capital accounts with arbitrary or imaginary amounts in order to establish a base for excessive rates; (2) writing up the valuations of the fixed assets without regard to their cost and the excessive issuance of securities; and (3) deceptive and unsound methods of accounting for assets, costs, and earnings. For a detailed discussion of these abuses, see James C. Bonbright and Gardiner C. Means, *The Holding Company* (New York, 1932), pp. 153–187.

rates of utilities subject to this act, as well as those subject to the act of 1920, upon the basis of original cost. (See also Table 10, p. 81.)

In addition to its control over the transmission and sale of electricity at wholesale in interstate commerce, the Commission has authority over mergers, the sale of properties, the issuance of securities, and interlocking directorates in the case of all electric utility *operating* companies engaged in interstate commerce. In each instance, no action can be taken without authorization by the Commission. The control of these matters in the case of electric utility *holding* companies, it will be remembered, is within the jurisdiction of the Securities and Exchange Commission (Chap. 19). Dissolution of most of the holding company systems has removed a large number of operating companies from supervision by the latter agency and placed them under the control of the Federal Power Commission. The Federal Power Commission is also directed to plan for the formation of regional power districts in which production and transmission facilities for electrical power can be coördinated and interconnected.

CONTROL OF NATURAL GAS RATES

The Natural Gas Act of 1938 authorizes the Federal Power Commission to control the rates of companies engaged in transporting natural gas in interstate commerce. The authority of the Commission is limited specifically to the *transportation* and *sale* of natural gas in interstate commerce and does not cover the production of gas or its local distribution. The interstate shipment of natural gas is a highly important business, and for many years various state commissions tried to regulate the large interstate companies to prevent unreasonable and discriminatory rates and excessive profits. In 1924, however, the Supreme Court held that a state could not regulate the business of transporting gas by pipe line from one state to another for sale to local distribution companies.[39] Thereupon, it took sponsors of regulation some fourteen years to secure the adoption of control by the federal government.

The act of 1938 gives the Federal Power Commission the authority, either upon its own motion or upon complaint, to determine just and reasonable rates for the transportation and sale of natural gas piped in interstate commerce. In setting such rates, the Commission is empowered to "investigate and ascertain the actual legitimate cost of the property of every natural gas company, the depreciation therein, and . . . other facts which bear on . . . the fair value of such property." A natural gas company, upon request, is required to furnish the Commission with an inventory of its property and a statement of its original cost. It is also required to provide information on the cost of all additions, betterments, and new extensions, and to use accounting procedures prescribed by the Commission. As in the case of electrical utilities, the procedure of the Commission is to provide for the determination of just and reasonable rates upon the basis of original cost.

[39] *Missouri v. Kansas Natural Gas Co.*, 265 U.S. 298 (1924).

The Natural Gas Act does not provide for the regulation of security issues, but it does require every company seeking to construct and operate interstate facilities to secure a certificate of public convenience and necessity.

Soon after the Natural Gas Act was passed, the cities of Cleveland and Akron brought complaints against the Natural Gas Pipeline Company of America and the Hope Natural Gas Company with respect to the rates being charged. The decision of the Supreme Court in the *Hope Natural Gas* case (1944), as we have seen, brought about a marked change in the scope of judicial review. In the *Hope* case, the Commission authorized rates exclusively upon the basis of original cost. The company, however, contended that weight should be given to reproduction cost. In settling the dispute, the Supreme Court announced the new rule that the orders of a commission will not be reviewed because it used one method of valuation rather than another. The significant factor is the "end result"; and if a company is able to operate successfully with the rates established by the Commission, no appeal can be made to the courts.

COMMISSIONS HANDICAPPED BY INADEQUATE FUNDS

During the postwar years of inflation, the regulatory commissions have not secured the additional appropriations which they have needed to perform their work effectively. Since 1948, in particular, the appropriations secured have not been adequate to maintain the staffs of the commissions. The annual appropriations have been about the same, but upward salary adjustments and higher costs for supplies and travel have considerably reduced effective regulation. (See Table 37.)

Some observers believe that the declining effective appropriations reflect economy attitudes in congress during a period when large expenditures have had to be made for defense and foreign-assistance programs. Others believe the restrictions and curtailments reflect pressure on Congress by organized producers in a subtle drive to curb the effectiveness of regulation and control. The basic statutes, it is said, cannot be changed, because public opinion will not support such drastic action. Indirectly, however, they can be changed by reducing the personnel engaged in regulation. Such an attack on the law is not visible, but it does have the result of providing "regulation which doesn't regulate." When staffs are reduced in size, certain activities must be curtailed; and an activity which is typically reduced or eliminated is that of making checks on compliance with orders and regulations.

The reasons for the failure of Congress to appropriate funds for the regulatory commissions commensurate with rising costs are complex. Undoubtedly, pressure for economy and lower taxes has been an important factor. An impartial student can only conclude that the actual appropriations have not made provision for rising costs, with the result that commission control has had to be curtailed or conducted in a less thoroughgoing way.

TABLE 37.   Independent Regulatory Commissions Appropriations and Employment, 1948–1955.

	Fiscal Year	Amount Appropriated	Positions Provided by Appropriations
Interstate Commerce Commission	1948	$10,713,000	2,409
	1949	11,300,317	2,293
	1950	11,416,700	2,216
	1951	11,408,200	2,146
	1952	11,298,535	1,995
	1953	11,003,500	1,888
	1954	11,284,000	1,881
	1955	9,816,000	1,682
Federal Power Commission	1948	$ 3,936,000	783
	1949	4,277,550	817
	1950	4,110,265	761
	1951	4,365,000	738
	1952	4,330,925	716
	1953	4,085,700	662
	1954	4,300,000	659
	1955	4,150,000	629
Federal Communications Commission	1948	$ 6,240,000	1,349
	1949	6,717,000	1,366
	1950	6,729,345	1,325
	1951	6,625,000	1,227
	1952	6,585,550	1,103
	1953	6,408,460	1,043
	1954	7,400,000	1,200
	1955	6,694,400	1,045
Civil Aeronautics Board	1948	$ 3,040,000	584
	1949	3,637,000	661
	1950	3,670,500	658
	1951	3,500,000	592
	1952	3,860,000	579
	1953	3,800,000	566
	1954	3,777,000	561
	1955	3,777,000	555

(Source: Bureau of the Budget.)

SUMMARY

The essential purposes of public utility control are (1) to prevent a utility enterprise from charging rates which yield a monopoly profit and (2) to prevent rates so low that the service suffers. The basic rule which the Supreme Court has established for rate regulation is that of permitting a utility to earn a "fair return" on the "fair value" of the property which is devoted to a public use. The judicial rule imposes a *ceiling* for preventing an excessive return and sets a *floor* below which rates may not be reduced by statutory or commission action. Utilities have protection under the due process clause against rates which are set too low by commission control.

Public utility control does not mean that a utility enterprise will always earn a fair return on the fair value of its property. A utility may actually find it necessary to establish rates which will yield less than the ceiling permitted by law. In some instances, moreover, the rates which a utility decides the "traffic will bear" may not even yield a profit at all, so that the company may face the prospect of bankruptcy or sale to a governmental agency.

SUGGESTIONS FOR FURTHER READING

Aitchison, Clyde B., *Fair Reward and Just Compensation, Common Carrier Service* (Washington, 1954).
Anshen, Melvin, and Wormuth, Francis D., *Private Enterprise and Public Policy* (New York, 1954).
Bauer, John, *Transforming Public Utility Regulation* (New York, 1950).
Clemens, E. W., *Economics and Public Utilities* (New York, 1950).
Dearing, Charles L., and Owen, Wilfred, *National Transportation Policy* (Washington, 1949).
Frederick, J. H., *Commercial Air Transportation* (Chicago, 1951).
Gray, Horace M., "Air Transportation," in *The Structure of American Industry* (New York, 1954).
Sharfman, I. L., *The Interstate Commerce Commission* (New York, 1931–1937), 5 vols.
Twentieth Century Fund, *The Power Industry and the Public Interest* (New York, 1944); and *Electric Power and Government Policy* (New York, 1948).
Welch, Francis, *Preparing for the Utility Rate Case* (Washington, 1954).
Westmeyer, R. E., *Economics of Transportation* (New York, 1952).

CHAPTER 25

Government Ownership as an Alternative to Commission Control

There is general agreement that some form of public control must be exercised over the prices charged by a private enterprise having the status of a public utility—that is, in a situation in which an essential service is rendered under conditions of monopoly control. Although certain administrative agencies have done effective work in preventing excessive charges, the record of most commissions on rate control has not been particularly successful from the standpoint of consumers. However, no one having the public interest in mind would propose to abandon such control as we have. Continued efforts must be made to improve the commission process; and if this cannot be done, some authorities suggest that steps should be taken to expand the area of public ownership in this field.

The principal problems in rate control by commissions are (1) the difficulties and complexities which the commissions have had in establishing rate or earnings levels, (2) the delay and time-consuming efforts which are involved in administering direct controls, and (3) the deleterious political influence which is often exerted by the large monopolistic utility organizations.

The purposes of the present chapter are (1) to review the main problems of commission control; (2) to consider the views of various authorities on the experience which the nation has had with commission control; and (3) to analyze proposals for extending public ownership to local and national industries which are monopolistic.

PRINCIPAL PROBLEMS OF COMMISSION CONTROL

1. TECHNICAL DIFFICULTIES IN RATE CONTROL

The policy of the Supreme Court, we have seen, has been to require public service commissions to give appropriate consideration (a) to reproduction cost new less accrued depreciation and (b) to original cost less accrued depreciation in determining the rate base for utility enterprises. Historically, the problem of deciding how much weight to give to one valuation procedure and how much to give to the other has given rise to a considerable amount of variation in calculations of the "fair value" of the property. In this process, the utilities frequently have reached one conclusion, the commissions a different conclusion, and the courts still another.

Even when the procedure of original cost less accrued depreciation is used, difficult administrative problems may arise because a utility may have paid more than the assets acquired were really worth, because its original cost records have been lost, or because its assets are not being fully utilized. It may also be that the original plant investment was a mistake, and the utility may not be able to establish rates which will earn a fair return on the fair value of its property. This situation has frequently arisen in the case of local street railway enterprises.

2. DELAY AND FRUSTRATION INVOLVED IN DIRECT CONTOL

A second difficulty in the direct control of business enterprises is the inevitable delay involved in the commission process. In investigating rates, it is often necessary for a commission to spend months, and sometimes years, in securing complete inventory records and in making appropriate valuation appraisals. Public hearings must be held to afford the parties due process, and opportunities must be given for filing reply briefs. A dozen or more years may be required in various stages of the investigation, hearing, and judicial review of a single case. The *Riss* case, for example, was originally filed with the Interstate Commerce Commission in 1935.[1] Some nineteen years later, in 1954, the case was finally terminated! Direct public control by commissions is necessary in certain fields, but it gets into problems of complexity and delay which serve to limit its effectiveness.

3. THE POLITICAL INFLUENCE EXERTED BY PRIVATE UTILITIES:

(a) *Influence on Legislation.* A third principal difficulty arising in the commission control of utility companies is found in the pressure and political influence which they exert (a) on the legislative and (b) on the administrative branches of government. Great wealth gives rise to undue political influence, and the general public has no counterbalancing organization to offset this evil. A special study prepared for the Temporary National Economic Committee on the lobbying activities of public utilities reports that "while paying lip service to the principal of public regulation, the railways and electrical utilities have done everything in their power to avoid it, or at least to control it in their own interest."[2] In the railroad field, it is reported that the Transportation Act of 1940, with its declaration of a national transportation policy, was developed by the organized railroads. Its final enactment by Congress is said to have represented "the successful termina-

[1] See Interstate Commerce Commission, *Performance of Motor Common Carrier Service by Riss and Co.*, Case No. MC–C–482, decided June 10, 1948. This case was originally initiated by Riss and Company in 1935. It involved the application of the Motor Carrier Act (1935) to certain operating rights which Riss had acquired from other motor carriers. After the decision of June 10, 1948, the company appealed various portions of the order. Finally, in February 1954 the case was settled. I am indebted to Mr. Wendell Berge for this example.
[2] *Economic Power and Political Pressures*, Monograph 26, Temporary National Economic Committee, 76th Congress, third session, 1941, p. 145.

tion of a long and costly propaganda and lobbying campaign by the railroads." The Reed-Bulwinkle Act (1948), exempting surface carriers from the antitrust laws in their rate-making activities, is a further example of legislation formulated by the organized railroads.

The electric utilities have been especially active in endeavoring to shape public policy along lines favorable to their interests. According to the study on political pressures prepared for the T.N.E.C., "Either through their trade association, the Edison Electric Institute, or through informal groups such as the Committee of Public Utility Executives, the electrical utilities have engaged in extensive legislative lobbying, have resorted to the courts when legislative lobbying failed, and, in addition, have made use of widespread propaganda for their general economic philosophy."[3] There is evidence to indicate that this extensive political activity is being continued. In 1953, for example, the National Association of Electric Companies, Washington, D.C., a lobbying organization, reported expenditures far greater than any other organization registered under the federal lobbying act. (See Table 7, p. 47.)

A special study by the Federal Trade Commission found that the electric utilities have actively endeavored to instill in the minds of the general public a point of view which is favorable to the private ownership of local utilities. Their objectives, the report declares, have been (a) "to inculcate in the public full belief in the right of the privately owned utilities exclusively to occupy the utility field," and (b) to oppose public ownership and operation "even to the point of characterizing . . . exponents as public enemies."[4]

In carrying out their propaganda activities, the Commission found that the utilities have conducted a great variety of public relations activities. These have included (a) the building up of good will and friendly relations with the press by means of "consistent and substantial advertising"; (b) an attempt to mold the minds of educators and students, from kindergarten to the college level, by giving endowments, scholarships, free books, payments to teachers and school officials, and by an editing of textbooks; and (c) an effort "to make impregnable the wall around private business" by selling securities to customers and employees. The general point of view taken in these activities, it is said, has been that if the public can be inculcated with ideas favorable to the industry, the political demand for more stringent regulatory control can be minimized or eliminated. In the words of Samuel Insull, an organizer of large utility holding companies, "The politician gets into office by attacking utilities. . . . He would not do that if the public was friendly to the utilities."

In concluding its report on the public relations work of the organized electric utilities, the F.T.C. states, "The total results which have been secured from all the various activities cannot be measured. But to such an extent has the utility program taken into consideration 'every public contact'

[3] *Ibid.*, p. 152.
[4] Summary Report of the Federal Trade Commission, *Utility Corporations*, 70th Congress, first session, Senate Document 92, 1934, Part 71A, p. 8.

that no campaign approaching it in magnitude has ever been conducted except possibly by governments in wartime. The various utility associations have collected and disbursed probably more money for good will publicity purposes than has been secured or paid out by any other group or organization. . . ."[5]

The T.V.A. program, in particular, has been, and still is, the target of special attack by the private utilities. In 1954, Mr. Purcell L. Smith, head of the private-power lobby, commenting on the large expenditures of his organization during 1953, is reported to have said that his organization "got its money's worth from the $547,789.32 spent on influencing legislation and other activities last year." Particularly, he is reported to have said, "I think we were effective in keeping T.V.A. appropriations to a reduced amount. . . . I think the results of our work have been reflected in the Interior Department appropriation's bill which included vast reductions for the Southeastern Power Administration, the Bonneville Power Administration, and the Southwestern Power Administration."[6]

(b) *Influence on the Commissions.* A further problem in commission control is the influence which private industry groups exert on the appointment, confirmation, and decisions of members of the commissions. Prospective members, first of all, are selected by politicians for political reasons, such as assistance in political campaigns, financial contributions, and the support of organized groups. Upon being nominated by the President, a commissioner must be confirmed by the Senate. It is at this stage, in particular, that organized producers bring their influence to bear against anyone who is, or who might be, unsympathetic to their interests. If a nominee is confirmed as a commissioner, he finds himself subject to continuing pressures from industry groups. Day after day he hears about *their plight*, and it is easy for him to lose perspective on the purpose of regulation. He quickly comes to realize that he is not smart enough to manage the regulated concerns, and he usually does not want to make a mistake with other people's money. Increasingly, experience shows, his concern shifts from the public interest to that of the well-being of the regulated industry.

Shippers and industrial users rarely provide much resistance to higher rates and charges. As long as their competitors must pay the same rates, and no one gets an advantage, they tolerate or accept the established rates. Their own pocketbook is not at stake, for their practice is to pass the higher charges on to consumers.[7]

[5] *Ibid.*, pp. 17–18.
[6] *Congressional Record*, May 3, 1954, p. 5547.
[7] Numerous authorities develop the thesis that there is a strong tendency for the utility commissions to become a defender of the industries controlled. See, for example, C. D. Edwards, *op. cit.*, p. 251. Professor S. P. Huntington, in a comprehensive study, concludes that the Interstate Commerce Commission has become an agency *for* the railroads and has turned more and more to the railroads *for its support.* In his view, the I.C.C. has lost its objectivity and its impartiality as a result. S. P. Huntington, "The Marasmus of the I.C.C.," the *Yale Law Journal*, April, 1952, pp. 467–509.

THE VIEW THAT COMMISSION CONTROL
HAS PROVED TO BE INEFFECTIVE

There is a considerable body of opinion that commission control has not proved to be an effective mechanism for protecting the public interest. The governmental agencies, it is pointed out, are frequently undermanned; suffer from an inadequate budget; are lacking in qualified personnel; and frequently appear to be more sympathetic to the company than to the consumer. Basically, the reasons for this situation, it is said, are to be found in the technical problems of control and in the political pressures which have been employed to weaken and, at times, to frustrate control.

A comprehensive study of the electric power industry, prepared under the auspices of the Twentieth Century Fund, a nonprofit foundation for economic research, concludes that under the state commissions many electric utilities have been permitted to earn unreasonably high profits. "There is a basis," declares the report, "for the widespread feeling (which reached a climax in several state legislatures about 1930) that state regulation in general has failed to achieve its primary purpose."[8]

Similarly, John Bauer and Peter Costello, recognized authorities on public utilities, conclude that, "Altogether state regulation has looked pretty hopeless as a means of holding private monopoly to its public functions. It has had to work under impossible restrictions and requirements, and under other strangling circumstances. Occasionally, some commission undertook to cut through the entanglements, but none ever succeeded in beating the system to which it was consigned. An occasional commissioner started with zeal to reform the methods, but his efforts were frustrated by the legal and procedural incrustations, the weight of inertia, utility influences, and the accumulations of resistance to public needs."[9]

GOVERNMENT OWNERSHIP AND OPERATION AS AN
ALTERNATIVE TO COMMISSION CONTROL

The economic and political difficulties involved in commission control, as well as in antitrust measures to maintain effective competition in the key industries, have caused various economists and statesmen to advocate public ownership and operation of the basic industries.[10]

[8] Twentieth Century Fund, *Electric Power and Government Policy* (New York, 1948), p. 244.

[9] John Bauer and Peter Costello, *Public Organization of Electric Power* (New York, 1949), p. 41.

[10] See, for example, Henry C. Simons, *Economic Policy for a Free Society* (Chicago, 1948), pp. 61–62, 195; Clifford L. James, "Commons on Institutional Economics," *American Economic Review*, March, 1937, pp. 61–75; Joseph B. Eastman, "A Plan for Public Ownership and Operation," *Annals of the American Academy of Political and Social Science*, January, 1932, pp. 112–119; and E. Davies, *National Enterprise* (London, 1946), p. 16. A list of arguments advanced in Great Britain for nationalization are presented by Ben W. Lewis in *British Planning and Nationalization* (New York, 1952), pp. 43–45.

In considering public ownership as a control device, it may be observed, first of all, that the proposal is exceedingly difficult to discuss without prejudice. Joseph B. Eastman, a long-time member of the Interstate Commerce Commission, has said,

> Aside from religion, there is perhaps nothing that so excites prejudice as the fear of being separated from the opportunity for profit. Under public ownership and operation of railroads and other public utilities, the field for profit on the part of bankers would unquestionably be curtailed very materially. The officers of the private companies fear that they would be displaced or their salaries reduced. Certain of the directors may fear the loss of the lucrative opportunities which grow out of advance knowledge of coming corporate events. Those who furnish the private companies with supplies or services, often under the generous guardianship of holding companies, fear interference with existing profitable relationships. . . . All of these, and many others which might be mentioned, are sources of prejudice, conscious or unconscious, against which those who wish to think soundly must be on their guard. . . . A belief or disbelief in public ownership and operation has in fact become a shibboleth by which the conservative test political and economic sanity.[11]

PUBLIC OPERATION NOT ALWAYS GUIDED BY YARDSTICK OF COMMERCIAL PROFIT

Secondly, in discussing the public ownership of essential utilities, it should be noted that government owns and operates a variety of productive undertakings *for reasons other than business profit*. Government ownership of forests, public lands, hydroelectric dams, and reclamation facilities is undertaken to conserve and develop our natural resources. Historically, the postal system has been operated to aid in developing the commercial and social life of the nation. During World War I, the federal government operated the railroads as a national defense measure, and from that standpoint the operation was eminently successful.

In certain instances, government ownership and operation are also adopted because of the inability of private enterprise to render an essential public service. The Alaska Railroad and numerous municipal electric, bus, and street railway systems, for example, were undertaken as private ventures and then taken over by government because they proved to be unprofitable. In some cases, with the growth of the community, such enterprises have become profitable. However, in other cases, such as the Alaska Railroad, the enterprises have continued to be unprofitable.

Since government operation in the foregoing situations, as well as in many others, is conducted for reasons other than profit, it follows that the success or failure of government operation cannot be measured only by the yardstick of commercial profit.

[11] National Association of Railroad and Utilities Commissioners, *Proceedings for 1927* (New York, 1928), pp. 365–366.

PUBLIC OWNERSHIP PROPOSALS USUALLY LIMITED TO AREAS OF PRIVATE MONOPOLY

Thirdly, in discussing public ownership, it may be noted that the principal area or segment of business activity which various economists, political scientists, and citizens believe should be placed in government hands consists of highly essential undertakings in which monopoly is found to be natural or strongly entrenched. In the case of public service enterprises, public ownership is usually proposed when it is believed that commission control is ineffective or where the enterprise under private ownership is a failing enterprise—such as a street railway. The particular utilities, it is said, which should be placed under government ownership and operation include electric power, gas (manufactured and natural), water, urban mass transportation, telephone communications, telegraph systems, railroads, and possibly intercity buses, motor transport, airlines, and oil pipe lines.

Some economists also propose that government ownership and operation be extended to other essential industries—such as the steel industry—in which monopoly has become firmly entrenched because of the inadequate enforcement of our antitrust laws. In such situations, it is believed, the conditions of free entry and price competition cannot or will not be created. Professor Ben W. Lewis, for example, declares, "I have come to believe . . . that these laws now represent a rear-guard (albeit, a very important rear-guard) action; and that in the years ahead a considerable and increasing portion of our economy will come to be controlled through conscious public action (probably public enterprise) rather than by the 'automatic' processes of competition bolstered by the Sherman Law."[12]

Professor Lewis further observes that the "dilution and weakening of competition as a compelling regulatory force" extends to a considerable area of our economy. In his words,

Some indication of the looseness of the regulatory force of competition in mass production industry is to be found in the exhortations increasingly being delivered by economists, public officials, and "enlightened" business leaders, urging managements to shape their price, output, wage and investment policies in accordance with long-run, over-all social considerations: increased purchasing power and consumption, full employment, an economy of plenty, etc. If competition, actual or potential, were really effective, these exhortations would be quite uncalled for and wholly useless. Need I add that as a prime regulatory instrument in our economy exhortations would seem to leave much to be desired? Something more certain in its promise and compelling in its force than an appeal to the good will and social consciousness of business leaders is called for in economic situa-

[12] "The Antitrust Laws: A Symposium," *American Economic Review*, June, 1949, p. 704. This point of view was reaffirmed by Professor Lewis in "Comments on the Teaching of Economics," *American Economic Review, Papers and Proceedings*, May, 1951, p. 714.

tions where sound criteria of individual and corporate gain run directly counter to sound criteria of general economic welfare.[13]

The *Committee on Cartels and Monopoly*, appointed by the Twentieth Century Fund, and composed of outstanding men in business, law, and economics, concludes that commission control "has not been so successful as to justify a similar prescription for all industries in which the degree of concentration destroys the effectiveness of competition." The *Committee*, in fact, frankly declares:

> If the state is to take over in large part the function of making managerial decisions, the question arises whether it would not be more efficient and economical to socialize the regulated enterprise. Duplication of functions could thus be avoided, the cost of litigation eliminated, and authority and responsibility combined. Where a high degree of concentration of control over physical operations is an accomplished fact, the most formidable obstacles to socialization have already been overcome. The transfer of control to public officials can be accomplished by the simple process of acquiring a majority of the voting stock. It is noteworthy that proposals for nationalization are more often concerned with industries in which firms are few in number and large in size than with those in which firms are numerous and small. It is a sound instinct that has led socialists consistently to oppose the policy of antitrust.[14]

THE VIEW THAT PRIVATE MONOPOLY LEADS TO NATIONALIZATION

The main idea underlying the thesis that public ownership sooner or later should—or probably will—be adopted to replace monopolistic control in various sectors of *general* industry is based upon the belief that government will not take significant action to dissolve economic concentration. In the words of Ben W. Lewis, "The way is effectively and permanently barred by the presence—the increasing presence—of large-scale industrial, marketing and labor units. We will not reduce their scale in any significant measure."[15]

Various reasons are suggested for the view that government will not act to dissolve the large financial combinations. They include (1) the political influence of the giant corporations and their lavish expenditures to defeat the enforcement of the Sherman Act; (2) the apathy of labor groups generally to a revitalization of the antitrust laws; (3) the general satisfaction of farm groups with subsidy and price-support plans to offset the disparity between farm and industrial prices; (4) the interest of many small business firms in seeking special monopolistic favors for themselves—such as resale price-maintenance laws and the unfair-practices acts; (5) the ignorance of many people with respect to the measures which government must adopt

[13] *Ibid.*, pp. 707–708.

[14] *Monopoly and Free Enterprise* (New York, 1951), p. 549.

[15] "The Antitrust Laws: A Symposium," *American Economic Review*, June, 1949, p. 705.

to implement a plan of competition; (6) the mistaken notion that monopoly is inevitable in the basic manufacturing industries because of technological factors; (7) the popular acceptance of the view that our present-day economy *is* a fully competitive system; and (8) the favorable attitude of the Army and Navy Departments toward big business.

In so far as Congress and the American people accept monopoly in an ever widening range of the American economy, it is believed by many economists and businessmen that capitalism will become increasingly unworkable. The experience of the great depression, following the extensive merger movement of 1920–1929, showed that monopolistic industry in a depression "stabilized" prices at high levels, despite the fact that other prices had generally fallen. Output and employment in the monopolistic industries were sharply curbed, and buying power was constricted. Serious price disparities developed between the monopolistic industries and those which were free, and the resulting maladjustments continued until World War II.

If a prolonged depression should occur, it is believed by some authorities that a large number of American people will increasingly look to government for jobs and security of income. In attempting to provide jobs, it is pointed out that government may be forced to take over several of the basic industries—such as steel, fuel, and transportation—for government has no authority to compel private enterprises to invest capital, employ men, or sell their products at low prices.

THE PROPOSAL SUGGESTED FOR OVERCOMING WEAKNESSES OF PUBLIC OWNERSHIP

In an effort to correct or overcome the shortcomings attributed to public enterprise, persons believing in that form of control propose that *government corporations* be created to own and operate the firms to be nationalized. Thus, Joseph B. Eastman, long-time advocate of public ownership of the railroads, states:

> It seems clear to me that public operation of an industry or business ought not to be handled in ordinary routine by a government bureau or department, nor should it be merged with the ordinary civil service. On the contrary, it should be kept separate and handled on a strict self-supporting basis by a business corporation organized in the usual way but controlled through stock ownership by the government. Its affairs should be directed, like those of any other business corporation, by a board of directors chosen by the government, as the controlling stockholder. . . . such a plan makes it possible to carry on the business in much the same manner as it would be carried on by a private business corporation.[16]

Government-owned corporations, in fact, have come to be extensively used for conducting various public enterprises. Important federal corporations include the Alaska Rural Rehabilitation Corporation, Commodity

[16] National Association of Railroad and Utilities Commissioners, *Proceedings for 1927* (New York, 1928), p. 371.

Credit Corporation, Federal Crop Insurance Corporation, Federal Deposit Insurance Corporation, Federal Farm Mortgage Corporation, Federal Savings and Loan Insurance Corporation, Home Owners' Loan Corporation, Inland Waterways Corporation, Virgin Islands Corporation, Tennessee Valley Authority, and Federal Prison Industries, Inc. Government corporations are initially financed by the issuance of capital stock to the Treasury Department in exchange for funds. The management of government corporations is vested in a board of directors appointed by the President by and with the consent of the Senate, and reports are made to Congress through the President.

Persons advocating public ownership of particular economic activities believe that public corporations are highly effective devices for conducting such enterprises. President Truman, in his message to Congress on January 3, 1947, for example, reported as follows: "Experience indicates that the corporate form of organization is peculiarly adapted to the administration of governmental programs which are predominantly of a commercial character—those which are revenue producing, are at least potentially self-sustaining, and involve a large number of business-type transactions with the public. In their business operations such programs require greater flexibility than the customary type of appropriation budget ordinarily permits. As a rule the usefulness of a corporation lies in its ability to deal with the public in the manner employed by private business for similar work."

THE T.V.A. EXPERIMENT IN PUBLIC ENTERPRISE

One of the most extensive and significant operations conducted by a public corporation is that of the Tennessee Valley Authority, which was created in 1933. During World War I, the federal government began to construct a power project at Muscle Shoals, Alabama, to provide power for making munitions. After the war, Senator George W. Norris and other public-minded citizens saw in the project an opportunity to develop the natural resources of the Tennessee River area. Political opposition to the project from private utilities, however, was very intense, and it was not until the election of President Roosevelt in 1932 that its sponsors secured substantial political support.

In a message to Congress on April 10, 1933, President Roosevelt asked for the creation of the Tennessee Valley Authority, a government corporation "possessed of the flexibility and initiative of a private enterprise," to engage in "planning . . . for the proper use, conservation, and development of the natural resources of the Tennessee River drainage basin and its adjoining territory for the general social and economic welfare of the nation."[17] The impact of the depression made the country ready to try an experiment in "national planning" and on May 18, 1933, Congress approved the Tennessee Valley Authority Act.

The T.V.A. is controlled by a board of three men appointed by the Presi-

[17] *Congressional Record*, April 10, 1933, p. 1423.

dent and confirmed by the Senate. Their terms of office run for nine years and expire at different times. The board directs the activities of the Authority and appoints the general manager who is in immediate charge of operations—very much like the hired manager of a business corporation. The Authority is authorized to develop and control the Tennessee River and

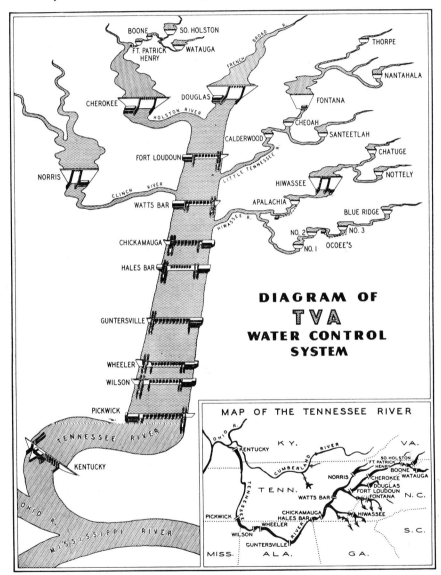

FIG. 46. Hydroelectric dams in the Tennessee River development. The TVA has transformed the Tennessee River from a destructive stream in flood time to a water system which yields year-round benefits in low power rates, increased economic opportunity, soil conservation, navigation, fish and wild-life development, and recreation. (Source: Tennessee Valley Authority.)

its tributaries for the purposes of flood control, the improvement of navigation, the generation of electric power, and the creation of recreational opportunities. It is also authorized to produce and sell nitrates and phosphates
for use as fertilizers and in making munitions, to sell surplus electric power,
to improve the utilization of land and prevent soil erosion, and to engage in
reforestation projects. In fulfillment of its duties, the Authority has presently
in operation nine major dams on the Tennessee River, with navigation locks
and power generation facilities at each location (see Fig. 46); a system of
28 storage dams on the tributary rivers, most of which have, or will have,
hydroelectric generating plants; a series of large steam plants for the generation of electricity by means of fuel; an extensive system of transmission
lines; chemical plants for the production of fertilizer; and nurseries for
growing seedling trees for reforestation and soil conservation purposes. The
main dams on the Tennessee River not only provide water for the generation of electricity but also make possible the maintenance of a navigable
channel along the entire 650-mile length of the river. In conjunction with
its various developmental activities, the Authority has also built camping,
fishing, boating, and other recreational facilities.

There is extensive evidence to indicate that T.V.A. is a successful project
measured in terms of resource conservation, chemical engineering development, and multiple-purpose benefits (flood control, navigation, malaria
control, electric power generation, and recreational development). Various
factors, without doubt, have contributed to the growing prosperity of the
region, but a considerable measure of the gain appears to have come as a
direct result of T.V.A. activities. Rural electrification, soil conservation, and
crop diversification have done much to improve the living conditions of
the people and the productivity of their farms. Large numbers of farmers
now have electric stoves, refrigerators, washing machines, and electrically
equipped barns with milking machines, water heaters, and milk coolers. The
typical Valley home uses twice as much electricity as the national average,
and the cost is about one-half of the average for the nation as a whole. The
T.V.A. sells fertilizer to farmers at cost, f.o.b. its huge phosphate plant at
Wilson Dam. It also employs county agricultural agents to aid farmers in
improving their land use. Two decades ago, some 30 percent of the population in various sections of the Valley had malaria. Today, the T.V.A. program of malaria control has practically eliminated this disease.[18] The T.V.A.
project was developed as a federal project, it may be noted, because private
enterprise believed that it could not be undertaken on a profitable basis.

The T.V.A. project also serves to promote the national interest. Its dams
helps to prevent the flood disasters which formerly occurred on the lower
Mississippi River. Its laboratories are developing new fertilizers and chemical processes. Many private corporations make use of its innovations. Some
5 million tourists from all parts of the nation annually enjoy its recreational

[18] For a detailed report on T.V.A. activities, see *Annual Reports of the Tennessee Valley Authority.*

facilities. The T.V.A. waterway system links the Tennessee Valley with the 8000-mile inland waterway system of the United States; and T.V.A. power, moreover, assists the national defense in providing energy for the atomic plants at Paducah, Kentucky, and at Oak Ridge, Tennessee.

The low rates for electricity which T.V.A. has pioneered in the Southwest have also served as a standard to moderate charges for electricity in other parts of the country. *Business Week* (5/30/'53), for example, reports that Mr. Hamilton Moses, President, Arkansas Power and Light Company, "has been afraid of something like an Arkansas T.V.A. for 20 years. He has fought it by pushing rural electrification, by selling power to rural coöperatives cheaper than the government's power systems could, and by building Arkansas." The dramatic success of T.V.A. has also had an international impact. Some eighteen projects, for example, have been built in underdeveloped countries largely upon the basis of T.V.A. experience.

The claim that T.V.A. is "creeping socialism" is a gross misstatement. Socialism, as an economic doctrine, means the uprooting of private ownership in the major industries and the imposition of direct controls, whereas T.V.A. and similar river-valley developments do not change the status of the major industries. They rather *promote* established capitalism by providing cheap power.

IS T.V.A. ELECTRICITY SUBSIDIZED BY TAXPAYERS?

Spokesmen for private utilities claim that since T.V.A. (1) pays no federal income taxes and (2) no interest on its appropriations from the federal treasury, consumers of T.V.A. power are not paying the full costs for benefits received. The Authority, in reply, declares that the facts point to a different conclusion. In the first place, it states, the records show that T.V.A. pays *tax equivalents* to state and local governments equal to about 6½¢ of each dollar of revenue. Privately-owned utilities in areas adjacent to T.V.A., by comparison, pay state and local taxes which range from 5.0¢ per dollar of revenue to 11.2¢; the median payment being 7.1¢. State and local tax payments by T.V.A., it is said, are thus in line with those of the private utilities.[19]

In the second place, the Authority points out, rates for its electricity provide not only for all costs of rendering the service and state and local tax equivalents, but also yield net earnings for the federal treasury of more than 4 percent (see Table 38). These net earnings give the federal government an interest return on the money appropriated for construction, as well as a return which is equivalent to federal income tax payments. Thus, according to Mr. Gordon R. Clapp, a former head of the Tennessee Valley Authority,

[19] O. S. Wessel, "Exploding 'Half-Truths' About TVA Taxes," *Public Power*, September, 1953, p. 22. For data on the cash payments, free services, and other contributions made by public systems, generally, see Twentieth Century Fund, *Electric Power and Government Policy* (Baltimore, 1948), pp. 407–408.

TVA is not required to pay Federal income taxes. All of TVA's income belongs to the Government. But if a share of TVA's power earnings, after setting aside the equivalent of interest, were earmarked for income taxes in the same proportion as for private utility companies, there would still be something left for a dividend to the taxpayers.

If you want a measure of what the consumer of TVA electricity pays toward the costs of running the Federal Government—that is, a tax equivalent—ponder this fact: In the past 12 years (since TVA began large-scale power operations), each consumer, on the average, has paid for the cost of producing the electricity and enough more to cover the Government's cost of money and, *in addition*, has paid about $13 each year, through TVA, to the Federal Government; this is to be compared with an average of about $10 per consumer paid to the Federal Government through private power companies in the form of income taxes.[20]

TABLE 38.   Statement of Income—T.V.A. Power Program.

	Millions of Dollars	
	Fiscal Year 1952	1933 Through 1952
Revenue	$ 95.0	$590.9
Expense:		
Operation and maintenance	52.4	230.4
Tax equivalent	3.0	26.3
Depreciation	13.8	118.2
Total expense	$ 69.2	$374.9
Net income before interest	$ 25.8	$216.0
Average investment assignable to power	$555.0	$264.0
Annual return on investment	4.7%	4.3%

(Source: Tennessee Valley Authority, Chattanooga, Tennessee. See also Comptroller General of the U.S., *Audit Report of Tennessee Valley Authority for the Fiscal Year Ended June 30, 1952.* 83rd Congress, first session, 1953.)

INTEREST IN PUBLIC OWNERSHIP NOW CENTERS IN ELECTRIC POWER

Throughout the nation there is a growing demand for abundant supplies of cheap electricity. In the opinion of some authorities, we have seen, commission control has failed to provide this end result. At the same time, particularly since 1935, publicly owned and consumer-controlled power systems have built an enviable record in providing plentiful supplies of electricity at rates which are typically below the rates of private utilities.[21] How is this to be explained? Is public power the appropriate alternative to commission control?

The relative importance of (1) *privately owned* power enterprises and

[20] Gordon R. Clapp, *Some Facts About the TVA* (Knoxville, Tennessee, September 30, 1953), p. 11.

[21] See Federal Power Commission, *Typical Electric Bills, Cities of 50,000 Population and More;* and *Typical Residential Electric Bills, Cities of 2,500 Population and More,* published annually.

(2) *publicly owned* systems and *consumer-controlled* local agencies (coöperatives) is shown in Table 39. Publicly owned power systems include (1) federal power projects, such as T.V.A., Bonneville Dam, and Grand Coulee Dam; (2) municipal corporations; (3) state-owned utilities, such as the Grand River Dam Authority in Oklahoma; and (4) public utility districts (public corporations) with authority to generate, transmit, and distribute electricity within designated areas. In addition to the publicly owned systems, there are the rural electric coöperatives in which ownership is credited to individuals. The Rural Electrification Act of 1936 authorizes the making of federal loans to farm coöperatives for the construction and operation of generating plants, transmission lines, and distribution systems. Rural electric coöperatives can borrow 100 percent of their investment capital from the federal government at 2% interest, with repayment to be made over a period of 35 years.

TABLE 39. Percentage of Electric Energy Generated and Sold by Privately-owned Enterprises and by Publicly-owned Systems and Coöperatives.

Year	Generation of Electric Energy Total kwh (Thousands)	Private	Public and Co-öperative	Sale of Electric Energy Total kwh (Thousands)	Private	Public and Co-öperative
1942	185,979,476	85.0%	15.0%	165,431,120	86.9%	13.1%
1947	255,738,984	81.4	18.6	223,688,095	83.2	16.8
1951	370,672,814	81.4	18.6	325,747,566	82.0	18.0
1952	399,223,620	80.7	19.3	350,384,865	81.5	18.5
1953	442,664,515	80.0	20.0	383,556,946	81.5	18.5

(Source: Federal Power Commission.)

THE CONTROVERSY OVER PUBLIC POWER

It is important to note that any comparison of public power with private power must be subject to numerous qualifications. Most publicly owned generating plants are based on water power; whereas privately owned plants are usually operated by steam power. Steam power is generally more expensive than water power. In making cost allocations for multiple-purpose projects, such as Bonneville and Grand Coulee moreover, controversy arises in the percentage of the cost (45, 50, or 90 percent) which should be charged to power. Some private and public plants serve cities in which population is dense and per capita distribution costs are low, while others serve rural areas in which distribution costs are high and customers are few. It may be noted also that supporters of public power believe that the case for publicly owned utilities cannot be stated solely in terms of comparative rates, taxes, and controversial financial issues. More fundamental points, they emphasize, are resource conservation, the development of multiple-purpose projects (flood control, navigation, and irrigation), and rural electrification. Whether or not public power measures up to the financial objectives of a private business, in their view, is a collateral issue.

Arguments Presented by
Public Power Advocates

1. Public power furnishes "the best possible electric service at the lowest possible rates." The rates of publicly owned utilities are typically below the rates of private utilities. Some 60 publicly owned utilities in the U.S. and Canada, in particular, sell electricity for residential use at rates under 1¢ per kilowatt-hour. This rate is fully 60 percent below the average residential rate in the U.S. The average consumer of public power also uses more electricity than the consumer of private power.

Public power, in general, is financed by the sale of revenue bonds. It stands on its own feet. Public power should also be given credit for contributions made to state and local governments in lieu of taxes. Available data indicate that contributions and free services are in line with state and local taxes paid by private utilities.

2. Publicly owned systems are able to borrow money at very low rates because the basic risks are less and the bonds are tax exempt. They retire their indebtedness, too, and do not continue paying interest to others. A private utility never pays off its investment. Its rates must support a return, after federal corporate income taxes, of 6–7½ percent forever.

Because of heavy investment in plant, the annual cost of capital is a substantial element in the cost of power. While the private companies are allowed a "fair return" of 6–7½ percent on the investment used and useful in the public service, public power pays interest only on its outstanding bonded indebtedness. Consequently, capital return requirements of a publicly owned system are at least 50 percent less than under private ownership.

Arguments Presented by
Private Power Advocates

1. Privately owned utilities provide electricity at the lowest possible rates in line with costs plus a fair profit. The lower rates charged by publicly owned utilities are to be explained primarily by special tax advantages. Public power has been able to secure favorable loans from the federal treasury, to avoid the payment of federal income taxes, and to issue tax-exempt securities. Such savings do not represent social gains. Rate comparisons are totally misleading, for all true costs are not considered.

State commissions control the rates of a privately owned utility, and private power pays its full share of taxes. Privately owned power stands on the principle that consumers of power should pay the cost of the benefit and carry their full share of the tax burden.

2. It is true that publicly owned utilities can borrow money at very low interest rates. State and local bodies are privileged to issue bonds which are exempt from federal and state income taxes. This is tax *avoidance*. It is an unfair tax advantage.

Any lower interest costs by reason of public ownership are purely the result of the avoidance of taxes which later must be made up by someone else. Persons benefited by public power do not pay for the full cost of the benefits, i.e., federal income taxes. They ride on the backs of others. Also, people who do not have the money to buy tax-exempt bonds pay higher taxes because the government receives less tax revenue from those who buy the bonds.

Public agencies typically finance normal plant expansion and retire debt out of earnings. In this way, bonded indebtedness is continually being decreased. Interest costs decline proportionately. When entirely debt-free, there are no interest charges at all; and rates can be reduced to cover only operating costs and depreciation.

3. The principal objective of publicly owned utilities is power at cost. Privately owned utilities, on the other hand, are operated to secure maximum profits, high dividends, high salaries for management, and generous management fees from subsidiary units.

A second objective is more democratic control over a basic utility service. Public ownership puts utility operations under the direction of commissions or boards elected directly by the people or appointed by their elected representatives. Policies pursued are thus better adapted to the needs and aspirations of the communities served. Under private ownership, the primary consideration must be profits, and policy is only incidentally concerned with community problems and development.

4. Publicly owned systems do not spend millions of dollars for propaganda, lobbying, and political activity, radio programs, and advertisements on the dangers of "creeping socialism," as have the private power companies. Much, if not all, of this cost is charged to the cost of service which consumers must pay. Publicly owned utilities also save the high costs of legal and other experts hired to fight rate increases through the commissions and courts.

5. Publicly owned systems do not have to pay federal corporate income taxes on business profits, because they do not seek to make an income return on capital investment.

3. The objective of privately owned utilities is the lowest possible rates consistent with good service and sound economic principles. Management ability is more truly reflected in private utilities where a reasonable profit motive acts as an incentive to reduce costs and to improve service.

Failure to provide good service at reasonable rates plus a regulated profit are accountable at once to the owners of the business (the stockholders). Public power has no such checks and balances. Public power decisions are too often made on the basis of political expediency with uneconomic decisions always backed by the power to tax.

4. Private power in its efforts to combat misleading public power propaganda is fighting for its very existence in attempting to halt the march of public power. In so doing, it is serving the public by providing factual information about political ownership and tax avoidance.

5. The exemption of public power from federal income taxes reduces the source of tax revenue. Consumers of public power avoid their share of the national tax burden.

Taxes are saved (not avoided) because public power is not operated for a return on equity capital.

In publicly owned enterprises, annual net earnings over costs, depreciation, and state and local taxes are used to retire debt and build new plant capacity. This in fact constitutes a contribution to the public which, in most cases, is greater than federal income tax payments.

Saving in federal taxes is further justified because public power provides *direct* public benefits (cheap electricity) to consumers. It promotes industry and employment. It also results in a greater tax base. This is shown by economic expansion in the Tennessee Valley, the Columbia Basin, and the Province of Ontario in Canada.

6. Publicly owned utilities have lower operating expenses. Operating costs are a basic measure of efficiency. Studies made by the Federal Power Commission and private experts show that unit costs for business expenses—accounting, collecting, advertising, sales promotion, and administration—are less for publicly owned utilities. Lower total costs also result from higher consumption due to lower rates.

There is no authoritative evidence that either public power or private power has an edge on the other with respect to the overall quality of service. In general, quality of service is more likely to be a function of size, natural conditions, and financial strength, rather than of ownership.

7. Public systems are coördinated much better than the private with the various other governmental activities—for example, the placing and maintenance of distribution facilities

This burden is transferred to all payers of federal taxes. The resulting loss of tax revenues must be made up by all the other taxpayers in the United States. This is unfair and inequitable.

Public power should carry its full share of the cost burden and pay its fair share of taxes. When we give special privilege in the avoidance of taxes to certain groups, we are furthering a policy of discrimination and preference which has no place in America today. Our economy cannot survive if certain groups avoid their fair share of the tax burden while others carry more than their share.

Public power should not be spread in order to try to make it fair. It should rather be curtailed and reduced. Otherwise, "creeping socialism" cannot help but continue to creep and spread faster.

6. The lower operating expenses of publicly owned utilities commonly reflect inferior service, poor voltage regulation, more frequent interruptions in service, and inattention to the needs of customers. Private utilities could reduce their operating costs, too, but they cannot take a chance in failing to serve the public or in failing to keep accurate cost and income records.

When one considers the generally better service, better voltage regulation, less frequent interruptions in service, and greater attention to the needs of customers, which are characteristic of private-utility operation, the small difference in *total* unit cost figures would seem to indicate greater efficiency on the part of private power companies.

7. Integration of generating and transmitting facilities, or power pooling, was first developed and made to work by the private electric utilities. Their objective was to shift

on the streets. They are also better integrated with other public power systems and so entail superior economy, both in capital requirements and operating expenses. In the T.V.A. program, for example, generation and distribution are directly integrated with the many municipal and coöperative distribution systems. The Bonneville and Grand Coulee power systems are also integrated with the Washington and Oregon public utility districts.

8. Unified *regional* development has maximum public advantages. Public hydro power is naturally a joint product of a comprehensive river-valley development that almost always combines flood control, soil conservation, reforestation, recreational facilities and sometimes river transportation, irrigation, and municipal water supplies. Power can thus be supplied most economically through unified multiple-purpose systems, planned and carried through by the federal government in close coöperation with state and local interests. No such overall economy or total public advantage is available through private power organization.

If power is separated from a multiple-purpose project and is turned over to private undertaking, there will be (1) enhanced capital outlays and operating costs not only for power but also for the other related functions continued under public organization and (2) reduced potentials for advantageous integration of power production with the other river-valley objectives. There will be a material loss of total regional and national benefits. This will be true of any large river system.

power over the transmission system from one locality to another to meet varying daily or seasonal needs and to back up loads in case of equipment failures. The result has been that all communities in the power pool have obtained better service at lower cost through the most efficient use of all equipment in the pool. The greatest percentage of federal power is hydroelectric power. This should be integrated into the established privately owned distribution systems to meet local requirements, without favor or discrimination.

8. In certain cases, there are river-valley developments which can be done better by federal agencies because they cannot be developed *economically* by private enterprise. They necessarily require government subsidy or guidance. Electric power from such developments, however, should be sold from the generators at the dams (at the "bus bar") to privately owned utilities. Private utilities should transmit and distribute this electricity to local consumers, subject to rate control by the regulatory commissions. Electric power facilities which *can* be built by private enterprise should be so constructed to avoid socialization of the industry.

Investor-owned utilities do and can exist and render valuable public service within the river-valley projects. In the Hoover Dam project, for example, private power distributes and provides a market for federal power.

Unified regional development presupposes overall control and domination by a superagency, inevitably political in origin and nature, which has the power of determining the use of natural resources as *it* believes to be best for the people. This is a departure from the principles of individual freedom which distinguish this nation's proud heritage.

SOME GENERALIZATIONS ON *PUBLIC* AND *PRIVATE* POWER

In comparing and evaluating public and private ownership in the utility field, it is important to note that the arguments for private ownership in the competitive segments of the economy do not fully apply to public utilities. The institutions of direct price competition and freedom of entry do not exist to protect consumers. Electric utilities provide a service essential to the public welfare under monopolistic conditions. Hence, if consumers are to be adequately protected, private companies must be placed under commission control or the service must be provided directly by government or by nonprofit coöperatives.

Public power, it may be noted, does not always mean lower rates. A municipal utility is commonly restricted by law in its operations to an area within the limits of a town. It is usually, moreover, not permitted to merge, acquire, or combine with other utility enterprises. Thus many municipal utilities are unable to secure the economies of large-scale generation and transmission. Isolated as they are, in a local community, they frequently are not in a position to take advantage of the best technology.

In general, however, the rates for public power are lower than those for private power. The cheaper rates for public power arise mainly (1) in the lower tax burden of public power, (2) in its lower interest cost on borrowed capital, and (3) in its use of net earnings to reduce indebtedness and rates. Should public power be privileged to enjoy a lower tax burden and a lower interest cost?

State and Local Tax Burdens. Private utilities contend that publicly owned enterprises do not pay their share of the state and local tax burden because their properties, in the main, are not assessed for property taxes. The facts are that often public power pays its full share of state and local taxes in other ways.

Municipal utilities and public utility districts typically pay state taxes on gross revenues from retail sales, state sales taxes, regular state business taxes, state gasoline taxes, state generating license fees, industrial insurance, and unemployment taxes, in line with those paid by privately owned utilities. They also usually pay local business and occupation taxes and local franchise taxes. It is common for publicly owned enterprises to furnish services, such as street lighting, at little or no cost. On some occasions, moreover, they pay special gross-revenue taxes or make cash contributions to state and local agencies in lieu of property taxes. The value of such payments and services may fully offset the property tax burden which privately owned utilities must pay.

Various economists have suggested that it would be desirable to prepare careful records of all state and local taxes paid by private and public enterprises, including all payments and services rendered in lieu of taxes. Such a practice would make it possible to compare costs and state and local tax burdens in a more accurate way.

Federal Income Tax Payments. Private utilities also complain that publicly owned systems do not have to pay federal corporate income taxes on business profits. Public power, it is said, thus avoids its share of the national tax burden as found in the corporate net income tax.

From an economic viewpoint, should the federal government impose a tax on the net earnings of publicly owned utilities? Some economists believe that if a public agency renders a *commercial-type* activity—i.e., the sale of electricity—the users should contribute to the cost of the national government. By equalizing the burdens of publicly and privately owned utilities, moreover, it is said, managerial efficiency and product rates can be more accurately compared. Other economists declare that under modern conditions the supplying of electric power has become basically a *governmental function.* The fundamental importance of electric power in modern life, together with its monopoly status, they affirm, places its production properly within the scope of government, like the provision of police and fire protection, water, streets, and sewers. Such activities, it is recognized, are not expected to contribute to the cost of the national government. As a further point, public power advocates declare that the social consequences of cheap power in making possible a higher level of living and a dynamic expanding capitalism are far more important than the possible payments of corporate net income taxes.

The Issuance of Tax-Exempt Securities. The main argument for the issuance of tax-exempt securities is that a governmental body is thereby able to borrow at lower rates of interest. This argument is undoubtedly true. With a system of progressive income taxes, however, the loss in tax revenue from persons with high incomes who buy such securities possibly is much greater than the saving in interest cost. A glance at the advertisements for tax-exempt securities will show that persons with high incomes investing in tax-exempt securities possibly are able to secure a higher net return on their capital than persons of moderate means who buy defense savings bonds. The practice of tax exemption may consequently serve to benefit persons of wealth more than the borrowing public. Tax exemption, therefore, does not appear to be a sound policy with the steep progressiveness in federal income tax rates which presently exist.

A CHOICE FOR THE PEOPLE

Public ownership of a monopolistic industry is neither economically sound in principle nor economically unsound. Each case must be judged on its merits. In some cases, public ownership may be selected as a means for securing what is hoped will be fair prices and incomes; and in other cases public ownership may serve as the most expedient way to conduct undertakings which private enterprise is unwilling or unable to assume. The experience with public ownership of essential utilities—as found in the Tennessee Valley Authority, the Canadian National Railway, the Seattle and Tacoma, Washington, municipal electric companies, and many similar public enterprises, shows that if a considerable public opinion wants public owner-ship, it can be made workable and efficient in given situations.

SUGGESTIONS FOR FURTHER READING

British Labour Party, *British Steel at Britain's Service* (London, 1948).

Davies, Ernest, *National Enterprise* (London, 1946).

Chamber of Commerce of the United States, *The Continuing Cost of TVA* (Washington, 1954).

Clegg, H. A., *The Future of Nationalization* (Oxford, 1953).

de Neuman, Andrew M., "Some Economic Aspects of Nationalization," *Law and Contemporary Problems*, Autumn, 1951, pp. 702–751.

Dimock, Marshall E., "Government Corporations; A Focus of Policy and Administration," *American Political Science Review*, October, 1949, pp. 899–921; and December, 1949, pp. 1145–1164.

Fienburgh, Wilfred, and Evely, Richard, *Steel Is Power: The Case for Na-tionalisation* (London, 1948).

Fuess, Claude M., *Joseph B. Eastman, Servant of the People* (New York, 1952).

Goodman, Edward, *Forms of Public Control and Ownership* (London, 1951).

Griffin, Clare E., *Britain: A Case Study for Americans* (Ann Arbor, 1950).

Laidler, Harry W., *Public Ownership Here and Abroad*, (New York, 1923); *A Program for Modern America* (New York, 1936).

Lewis, Ben W., *British Planning and Nationalization* (New York, 1952).

CHAPTER 26

The Relation of Government to Labor and Labor Organization

Government intervention to determine and supervise the methods of wage determination constitutes an important segment of government-and-business. A man's labor is usually all that he has to sell, and in a system of free contract his interest is centered on getting a "fair" price for services rendered to others. In relation to this area of buying and selling, government has the function of determining whether or not the prices and incomes which accrue to individuals are in accord with the public welfare. The importance of the "wage issue" is indicated by the fact that in the United States four out of every five persons who are gainfully engaged in productive activity live by selling their services for wages and salaries.

The purpose of the present chapter is to consider legislation pertaining to the establishment of wages, hours, and working conditions. What measures have been adopted by government to provide for a more equitable distribution of income? What social problems currently exist in the methods employed for determining wages, hours, and working conditions?

THE DEVELOPMENT OF COMPETITION AS A METHOD OF WAGE DETERMINATION

During the Middle Ages labor incomes were mainly based upon status. A person born as a serf secured a certain level of "living" which was determined largely by his minimum physical needs. Even free workers in the towns who worked for wages were paid a "customary rate" as determined "of old time." Any deviation from the customary rate was commonly regarded as excessive.

Gradually, periods of increasing labor scarcity brought the principle of competition into play, and wages were forced up from their customary levels by the bidding of employers seeking to get labor. The bubonic plague (called the Black Death) which swept over western Europe and England in 1348 and 1349, in particular, seriously depleted the labor supply. Workers, it is reported, thereupon were able to secure "double or treble of what they were wont to take."

In an effort to control the price of agricultural labor, the government in

England in 1351 enacted the Statute of Labourers. One of the various measures of control provided was the requirement that all rural laborers assemble
with their instruments in the market towns for hiring. Over the years these
gatherings of workers for hiring and wage-control purposes gradually developed into annual hiring fairs in which wages were determined by two-
sided wage competition. In some markets as many as two and three thousand
workers assembled each year for hiring. It was usual for workers in the
market gatherings to line up in rows and hold insignia to designate their
various trades. Prospective employers thereupon walked alongside the rows
of workers and negotiated wage rates for the ensuing year.

The rule of competition, it may be noted, means (1) that everyone is free
to select an occupation of his own choice and (2) that wages are determined
by price competition (a) among the workers seeking to get placed and (b)
among the employers desiring to hire labor. Two-sided wage competition
is an impersonal method of income determination which provides a return
based upon the estimated importance of labor's service in its various uses.
A wage so determined increasingly was looked upon as being "fair," because
it represented the common or public estimate of the "worth" of such services—determined without individual coercion or arbitrary compulsion.

The annual hiring fairs for agricultural labor flourished in England until
about 1850, after which time they declined rapidly. Employers had learned
that labor could be hired more cheaply by the method of private negotiation
"out of market." Increasingly, therefore, workers were hired at the farm or
in local villages without the concentrated hiring competition of many employers.

EARLY EFFORTS TO FORM LABOR UNIONS IN THE TOWNS

With the growth of monopolistic guilds around 1500, it was common for
the masters (guildsmen) to agree on rates to be paid journeymen and ap-
prentices. In order to offset this unified control, groups of journeymen made
determined efforts to agree on rates below which no one would work. These
efforts, however, were largely ineffective, for the English courts held that
collective action by workers to secure higher wages or shorter hours was an
illegal price-fixing conspiracy. Special statutes likewise prohibited collective
action by workers. Gradually, however, trade unions became accepted; and
in 1824 and 1825 the last of the combination acts were repealed. In 1871 and
in 1906 English workers were also able to secure legislation exempting labor
combinations from the common law against conspiracy.[1]

THE ACCEPTANCE OF COLLECTIVE BARGAINING IN
THE UNITED STATES

Upon the basis of the English common law against conspiracy, the courts
in the United States early held that labor combinations were unlawful
associations. In the famous *Cordwainers'* case, decided in Philadelphia in
1806, for example, it was held that a union of journeymen shoemakers was

[1] See also Adam Smith, *The Wealth of Nations*, Book I, chap. 8, pp. 68–69.

guilty of a conspiracy to fix rates in agreeing that none should work for less than another and in requiring others to join their association. The law against combinations, the court declared, is applicable to workers as well as to employers. In the view of the court, a combination of workers "is pregnant with public mischief and private injury . . . tends to demoralize the workmen . . . destroy the trade of the city, and leaves the pockets of the whole community to the discretion of the concerned. If these evils were unprovided for by the law now existing, it would be necessary that laws should be made to restrain them."[2]

Various groups of workmen continued their efforts to form unions, in spite of threats of criminal prosecution. Their belief was that employers commonly acted in concert to hold wages at low levels; and union activity was pressed in order to set a minimum rate which employers must meet. The position taken by union leaders was finally accepted in 1842 by the Supreme Court in Massachusetts. According to Chief Justice Shaw, speaking for the Court, labor unions are legitimate (1) if their purposes are "actually innocent" and (2) if the methods used are legal. An association of workers, he declared, is illegal only when "its powers are abused."[3] Following this decision, the mere fact of combination was no longer sufficient in Massachusetts to establish illegality; and the doctrine of criminal conspiracy was to that extent cut away by judicial action.

Although combinations of workmen came to be accepted in numerous other jurisdictions soon after 1842, their growth proceeded slowly. The doctrine of criminal conspiracy still continued to have some vitality, and public authorities and the courts continued to scrutinize the methods used by unions to achieve their ends. Union leaders who aggressively pushed the demands of labor were frequently given severe sentences for engaging in illegal activity. After 1880, moreover, the courts began the practice of granting injunctions against picketing, boycotting, and striking—the chief weapons which unions employ to make their demands effective. In such a climate, labor leaders found it difficult, if not impossible, to win economic gains and secure union members.

WAGE DETERMINATION UNDER CONDITIONS OF INDIVIDUAL BARGAINING

When a worker seeks employment or a wage increase, he commonly engages in *individual bargaining* with an employer. This means that he negotiates the terms individually and independently, without restraint by any agreement with others. In this process, an individual worker has little, if any, bargaining power unless there are employment opportunities elsewhere or a shortage of labor at existing rates. Labor economists point out that the term individual bargaining can be quite misleading. Usually, the employer offers a rate, and the worker's choice is to "take it or leave it."

[2] *Commonwealth v. Pullis* (1806), reported in John R. Commons and others, *A Documentary History of American Industrial Society* (Cleveland, 1910), Vol. 3, pp. 230–231.
[3] *Commonwealth v. Hunt,* 4 Metcalf (Mass.) 111, 129 (1842).

Bargaining power under competitive conditions may be defined as the power of a person to secure the equilibrium price of the services rendered (under existing conditions of demand and supply). Its basis exists in the opportunity which a person (or group) has to shift to some other employer or employment if such a return is not secured. When competitive forces are absent, bargaining strength tends to become simply a test of economic power to withhold supply from the employer, based upon endurance and financial resources. In the absence of competition among employers, the bargaining power of an individual worker is close to zero.

THE PROVISION OF EMPLOYMENT INFORMATION— PUBLIC EMPLOYMENT EXCHANGES

An employment exchange is an office—either public or private—for bringing together workers seeking jobs and employers desiring to employ labor. Its essential purpose is to serve as a market place for labor. An exchange is usually operated (1) by collecting and posting data on available jobs and (2) by registering applicants for placement in appropriate lines of work. When employment exchanges are properly supervised to provide full information on wage rates and job opportunities in local and adjacent labor market areas, and when they are actually utilized in placing a substantial part of a given supply of labor, they provide a desirable mechanism for the competitive determination of wage rates.

Employment exchanges have been established in the United States by numerous municipalities, by the state and federal governments, as well as by many private groups. The first state employment offices were set up by Ohio in 1890. In 1913 the newly created Department of Labor in the federal government established employment offices in eighteen designated areas throughout the nation to aid in the placement of immigrants. Subsequently, in 1916, the placement activities of the federal employment service were extended to all unemployed groups. During World War I, President Wilson made the federal agency and its branches the sole recruiting agency for civilian workers employed in the war industries.

The impact of the great depression beginning in 1929 and the unprecedented increase in unemployment brought demands for Congress to create an integrated system of labor exchanges, with units in every local labor market area in the nation. In order to meet the objections of states' rights advocates, Congress worked out a compromise plan in the Wagner-Peyser Act, which was adopted in June, 1933. This legislation provided for the creation of the United States Employment Service (U.S.E.S.) to integrate the work of all the state employment exchanges in a federal-state employment service system. The services offered by the state agencies were to be improved by the provision that their administrative costs would be matched dollar for dollar by the federal government. The purpose of the federal-state program was—and still is—to assist in achieving high-level employment, job continuity, and sustained purchasing power by providing local agencies throughout the nation for bringing workers and jobs together. The goal of a national employment plan was realized in 1937, when employment exchanges, affiliated with the United States Employment Service, came to be established in every state of the Union.

In order to meet the need for a centralized control over labor supplies in the prosecution of World War II, President Roosevelt on December 19, 1941, arranged for the transfer of all state employment service facilities to federal jurisdiction. The transfer was made in January, 1942, and thereupon the recruitment and placement of workers for all essential war activities were largely handled by the U.S.E.S. On November 16, 1946, following the end of World War II, the local public employment offices were returned to state control. Instead of matching state appropriations as it did before the war, the federal government adopted the plan of financing the entire cost of the state employment programs, provided that the state services maintain minimum standards which are acceptable to the Secretary of Labor.

In 1954, the federal-state system consisted of some 1627 full-time local offices and 2078 part-time offices maintained to meet seasonal needs. These various offices, in coöperation with the U.S.E.S., stand ready to provide (1) a placement service for all workers seeking employment and for all employers needing labor, (2) an employment counseling service, (3) special employment services to veterans, (4) assistance to employers in selecting, assigning, and transferring workers, (5) labor market information for all interested persons, and (6) assistance to community agencies in providing employment programs. A considerable number of local employment offices publish at regular intervals a labor market newsletter which indicates occupations in short supply and occupational fields in which shortages are developing. These "inventories" of the local labor market are generally described without reference to the average or going wage rate.

Although the duties of the U.S.E.S. have been considerably lessened since World War II, it still continues to be an important agency in the federal-state employment service program. Its main duty is to provide leadership, direction, and technical aid for the employment agencies in the forty-eight states, the District of Columbia, Alaska, Hawaii, Puerto Rico, and the Virgin Islands, which are affiliated with it. Employment reports are collected from each of the local offices and summaries are prepared for general use. The U.S.E.S. also has responsibility for organizing the recruitment and placement of farm labor. Approximately 18 percent of all hired farm workers in the United States are engaged on a migratory basis, and an important task of the federal service is to provide a clearing system for such workers. At the same time, the federal service is widely utilized in the recruitment and placement of year-round, general farm labor. The U.S.E.S. likewise maintains a job clearance system for persons with professional, technical, and managerial skills—such as store managers, architects, teachers, engineers, social workers, hospital technicians, and dentists—who commonly are willing to accept employment anywhere in the country. With the coöperation of the local offices, the U.S.E.S. prepares a file of job seekers in the special fields. When job openings are submitted from any one of the 1627 local offices, it endeavors to match the applications and the openings.

COLLECTIVE BARGAINING IN WAGE DETERMINATION AND THE RESTRICTION OF COMPETITIVE FORCES

Collective bargaining, in contrast with individual bargaining, means that a group of workers "act as one" in bargaining with an employer or group of employers. No individual worker in the group offers to work for less than another, and the "collective will" is presented in negotiation by a single person, or committee, chosen to represent the group. When workers join a union, they give up their right to bargain individually with the employer.

The power which a combination of workers exercises in wage negotiations is based (1) upon a unified, effective presentation of their case and (2) upon the power to inflict injury on an employer (or group of employers). A union—local, regional, or nation-wide—is in a position to inflict injury (a) by refusing to work (striking), (b) by keeping others from working (picketing), and (c) by getting ultimate consumers to refrain from purchasing the employer's products (consumer boycott). Although collective bargaining is primarily a mechanism for pricing labor, it is also a highly important means for giving workers some measure of control over their life in the industry, trade, or craft. By means of collective action, workers are able to secure protection against arbitrary discharge, demotion, layoff, unsafe working conditions, and so forth.

In economics and the law, collective action by labor is accepted as being necessary to offset the superior bargaining power of large corporations, monopolistic mergers, and unified groups of employers. The loss of a job is usually a serious matter for a worker, and he rarely is in a position to assert himself vigorously. The typical employer, on the other hand, can act directly in his own interest, for few if any individual workers are indispensable to him.

There is also a general recognition in economics and the law that labor on strike should be permitted to dissuade (but not coerce) others from taking their jobs (peaceful picketing). Employers, however, still possess the general right to break strikes by hiring nonunion men, if they are able to do so. They may also generally refuse to reëmploy strikers after a strike has been terminated, on the ground that the jobs have been filled. In general, whether or not an employer will be successful in breaking a strike by hiring replacements—and be able to retain such replacements after the strike is over—is a question which is resolved by the relative economic pressures brought to bear by the parties themselves.[4]

---

[4] An exception to the right of employers to break strikes is found in the Byrnes Act of 1936. This legislation prohibits the importing of strikebreakers across state lines (18 U.S.C. 407a).

THE APPLICATION OF THE SHERMAN ACT TO LABOR UNIONS

When the Sherman Act was being considered by Congress in the spring of 1890, several congressmen raised questions abouts its application to labor combinations and associations of agricultural producers. Senator Sherman took the position that the proposed legislation should not apply to organizations which seek to improve their bargaining position in dealing with corporations and combinations of capital. In order to clarify this point, Senator Sherman offered an amendment on March 25, 1890, to exclude labor and agricultural organizations from the application of the bill against restraint of trade and monopoly.[5] During the rewriting of the bill in the Senate Judiciary Committee, however, all reference to associations of workingmen and farmers was omitted. The bill was thereupon resubmitted for final voting on April 8, 1890, and adopted without any further mention of exemptions for associations of workingmen or farmers.

Senator Edmunds is usually considered to have been the person who had the leading role in redrafting the antitrust bill, and it was his view that special exemptions should not be granted to labor and farmers. In 1892 Senator Edmunds was asked in an interview whether or not there were any implied exemptions from the Sherman Act. He is reported to have replied that the act was "intended and I think will cover every form of combination that seeks to in any way interfere or restrain free competition, whether it be capital in the form of trusts, combinations, railroad pools or agreements, or labor through the form of boycotting organizations that say a man shall not earn his bread unless he joins this or that society. Both are wrong. Both are crimes, and indictable under the antitrust law."[6]

THE SUPREME COURT APPLIES THE SHERMAN ACT TO THE ACTIVITIES OF UNIONS

We have seen that the principle of collective bargaining acquired tentative acceptance in Massachusetts in 1842 in the case of *Commonwealth* v. *Hunt*. Thereafter, trade unions gradually secured recognition—that is, their mere formation and existence was not generally considered to be unlawful. Strikes for direct economic benefit to the strikers (e.g., wage and hour strikes) also gained a measure of freedom from the strictures of the law.

An important question following the enactment of the Sherman Act was whether or not the new legislation restricted the use of important union weapons—such as consumer boycotts and secondary striking by other union members. The Supreme Court answered the question of out-of-state consumer boycotts in the famous *Danbury Hatters'* case (1908). The facts of the case were that a local union of hat workers, affiliated with the United Hatters of North America, in the course of a strike against Dietrich Loewe,

---

[5] *Congressional Record*, March 25, 1890, p. 2612.
[6] Chicago *Inter-Ocean*, November 21, 1892, p. 1. Quoted by Edward Berman, *Labor and the Sherman Act* (New York, 1930), p. 6.

a manufacturer of hats in Danbury, Connecticut, called for a nation-wide consumer boycott of this employer. Members of the American Federation of Labor and consumers generally, everywhere in the country, were asked to refrain from buying hats made by the company.

The Loewe company sold hats in some twenty states other than Connecticut, and the boycott seriously crippled its sales. The Court found that the union had brought direct economic pressure to bear on Loewe's customers in out-of-state areas, and that this pressure had directly interfered with the flow of commerce between the states. In view of these facts, the Court held that the local union and its members as individuals were liable to pay the plaintiff treble damages which amounted to over $250,000.[7] The case of *Loewe v. Lawlor*, it may be noted, was not concerned with the legality of strikes, as such, or with whether or not competition was being destroyed from a public point of view. It was rather a *private* suit for damages under the Sherman Act, based upon the charge that the company had been injured by a monopolistic restraint.

The decision in the *Danbury Hatters'* case aroused a storm of protest from organized labor and led to demands for legislation to legalize unions and their activities. In response to this request, Congress provided in Sections 6 and 20 of the Clayton Act that labor unions and agricultural associations are not, in themselves, violative of the antitrust laws; and that no injunctions shall be issued to prohibit the quitting of work, the refusal to patronize or peaceful picketing, whether such acts are done "singly or in concert."

The gains which labor appeared to have secured in the Clayton Act proved to be somewhat illusory. In the *Duplex* case (1921) the Supreme Court held that secondary boycotts are illegal when the effect is to interfere with the movement of goods in interstate commerce. The opinion of the Court was that the Clayton Act exempted boycott activities only when they are practiced by workers who are directly involved in a dispute with their immediate employer.[8]

THE VIRTUAL EXEMPTION OF THE ACTIVITIES OF LABOR UNIONS FROM THE SHERMAN ACT

With the impact of the great depression, there occurred a transforming change in the economic thought of many public leaders. Strong and vigorous labor unions, exercising a considerable measure of economic power, it was believed, were a necessary counterbalance to the concentrations of capital found on the side of industry. Moreover, in the New Deal philosophy,

---

[7] *Loewe v. Lawlor*, 208 U.S. 274, 309 (1908).

[8] *Duplex Printing Press Co. v. Deering*, 254 U.S. 443 (1921). A secondary boycott is a situation in which a union puts pressure on an employer (A), with whom it has a dispute, by exerting economic pressure against another employer (B), to persuade him to cease doing business with employer A. This labor practice was made illegal in the Taft-Hartley Act (see below, p. 591).

deliberate action to increase wages was looked upon with favor as a means for increasing mass purchasing power and restoring prosperity. Many informed lawyers and judges believed that the interference-with-commerce rule was a misconception of the Sherman Act, and that the prohibitions of the act should be applied only to activity designed to restrict production or fix prices in interstate business. In the light of these various factors, the Court switched its economic thinking on labor unions and largely retracted its view that the Sherman Act applies to the activity of unions which is interruptive of commerce among the states.

The view that the Sherman Act permits a union to pursue its economic interests, even though interstate commerce is adversely affected, was first developed in the *Apex Hosiery* case (1940). The *Apex* case involved a suit for treble damages which grew out of a sit-down strike called in an effort to unionize a hosiery plant. Some 80 percent of the employer's product was shipped in interstate commerce, and the strikers refused to permit any orders for hosiery to be filled. Numerous acts of violence were also committed by the union in enforcing its seizure of the plant.

The Supreme Court in a six-to-three decision held that the activities of the union were not subject to the Sherman Act because they did not substantially affect market supplies or prices. In the words of Justice Stone, "The Sherman Act was directed only at those restraints whose evil consequences are derived from the suppression of competition in the interstate market, so as 'to monopolize the supply, control its price or discriminate between its would-be purchasers.' "[9] Conspiracies which obstruct the flow of commerce, the Court observed, are violations of the Sherman Act only when they affect product prices to the detriment of purchasers or consumers.

Subsequently, in the *Hutcheson* case (1941), the Supreme Court virtually exempted labor unions and their activities from the application of the Sherman Act. The *Hutcheson* case involved a jurisdictional dispute between the carpenters' union and the machinists over certain jobs in the Anheuser-Busch brewery in St. Louis. The carpenters called a strike, established picket lines, and requested affiliated union members and their friends to refrain from buying Anheuser-Busch beer (consumer boycott). Although the union's activities were interruptive of interstate commerce, the Court declined to declare them illegal. In its view, "So long as a union acts in its self-interest, and does not combine with non-labor groups, the licit and the illicit . . . are not to be distinguished by any judgment regarding the wisdom or unwisdom, the rightness or wrongness, the selfishness or unselfishness of the end of which the particular union activities are the means."[10] The *Hutche-*

[9] *Apex Hosiery Co.* v. *Leader*, 310 U.S. 469, 511 (1940).
[10] *U.S.* v. *Hutcheson*, 312 U.S. 219, 231–232 (1941). For illustrations of what Justice Frankfurter meant in the *Hutcheson* case by "so long as a union . . . does not combine with non-labor groups," see *U.S.* v. *Brims*, 272 U.S. 549 (1926); *Allen-Bradley* v. *I.B.E.W.*, 325 U.S. 797 (1945); and *U.S.* v. *Carpenters' Union*, 330 U.S. 395 (1947). These cases hold that collusive action between a union and an employer to fix the prices of the product sold in commerce is violative of the Sherman Act.

son decision removed labor unions from the restrictions of the Sherman Act except in the situation in which a union collusively agrees with an employer or an association of employers in order to restrain competition to the detriment of consumers. Any substantial federal regulation of strikes, boycotts, and related weapons of economic force after 1941 required further action by Congress.

GOVERNMENT INTERVENTION TO AID COLLECTIVE BARGAINING

At the present time, some 17.5 million workers belong to trade unions in the United States (see Table 40). Among labor economists, it is estimated that this number represents about one-half of the total number of workers who are potentially organizable into trade unions.

What forces have brought about the large percentage of organized labor in our country? Basically, the growth of trade unions is to be explained (1) by the development of large-scale methods of production and (2) by the rise of an expanding employee class whose economic life is dependent upon a job. The widespread existence of unions is thus a product of mass-production industry and large corporate size. In a summary statement of this development, Dr. Clark Kerr has stated, "Among other things, the growth of the large corporation brought modern industrial unionism."[11]

In the environment of modern industry, unions have emerged to meet the needs of a large and growing class of employees. As employees in a mass-production industry, workers have found that it is essential to have an agency to represent them on such matters as wages and hours, working conditions, and the prevention of arbitrary discharge. Some formalized mechanism, they have learned, is needed to replace the personal relationships between management and labor which operate in a two-man shop or small-scale enterprise.

TABLE 40.   Membership in Labor Unions
(thousands)

1930	3,632	1942	10,762
1931	3,526	1943	13,642
1932	3,226	1944	14,621
1933	2,857	1945	14,796
1934	3,249	1946	14,974
1935	3,728	1947	15,414
1936	4,164	1948	14,000–16,000
1937	7,218	1949	14,000–16,000
1938.	8,265	1950	14,000–16,000
1939	8,980	1951	16,500–17,000
1940	8,944	1952	16,500–17,000
1941	10,489	1953	17,000–17,500

(Source: Bureau of Labor Statistics.)

[11] Clark Kerr, *Industrial Peace and the Collective Bargaining Environment* (Berkeley, 1954), p. 48.

In the development of the trade-union movement, government itself has intervened to promote the use of collective bargaining. Its purpose has been to encourage collective bargaining as a method of self-government in which the parties themselves make rules and settle issues in the area of employment relationships.

The first important step taken by government to aid the formation of labor unions came during World War I. Prior to that time, government accepted the principle of collective bargaining, but adopted no positive measures to promote it. During World War I, however, the Wilson administration gave dignity to the labor movement by placing representatives of organized labor on important governmental committees. The National War Labor Board, a federal agency established to handle wage problems in war industries, moreover, declared in 1918 that it was the policy of the federal government to recognize "the right of workers to organize in trade unions and to bargain collectively, through chosen representatives." Labor unions quickly utilized the advantage of the recognition granted to them, and the rising demand for labor made many employers willing to bargain collectively. By 1920 the total membership of all trade unions had reached an estimated total of more than 5,000,000 persons.

During the recession period which followed World War I, employers, generally, launched a drive for the return of the "open shop," and union membership fell to a low of about 3,500,000 workers by 1924. This small membership was further reduced by the great depression, and by 1933 the total membership in unions included less than 3,000,000 persons. Many employers not only adopted a policy of refusing to bargain with labor unions but also took active means to discourage workers from joining unions. Workers were often fired as soon as they joined a union; and in numerous cases they were required to sign a "yellow-dog" contract in which they agreed, as a condition of employment, not to join a union.

The Railway Labor Act of 1926 marks the beginning of intervention by government to establish the right to form unions without interference by employers. For many years railroad workers and the organized railroads had found that collective bargaining provided a peaceful and effective means for adjusting their conflicts of interest, and both groups supported a proposal to give each other the legal right of self-organization without interference by the other party. In large measure, the Railway Labor Act of 1926 became the forerunner of the Wagner Act of 1935 and the general acceptance of the principle of self-organization throughout industry. The act of 1926 forbids any "interference, influence, or coercion exercised by either employers or employees over the self-organization or designation of representatives by the other."

In 1932 Congress made yellow-dog contracts unenforceable and restricted the issuance of labor injunctions by the federal courts. The Norris-La Guardia Act, passed in that year, provides that the federal courts shall not (1) enforce contracts whereby employees agree not to join a union or (2) issue injunctions in labor disputes, except in cases of fraud or violence. By freeing unions (in large part) from federal injunctions, the Norris-La Guardia Act greatly increased trade-union power. This power, moreover, was further enhanced by the action of some seventeen states in passing anti-injunction statutes. In effect, the Norris-LaGuardia Act amounted to strong governmental encouragement of trade-union activity.

Section 7 (a) of the National Industrial Recovery Act (1933), enacted during the great depression, guaranteed workers the right to form unions of their own choice and provided another stimulus to the growth of organized labor. If the workers were encouraged in the formation of unions to bargain for higher wages, the New Dealers believed, purchasing power could be increased, and the nation could be placed on the road to recovery. Minimum wages were also fixed for many thousands of unorganized workers. Section 7 (a) of the N.I.R.A. provided that "employees shall have the right to organize and to bargain collectively through representatives of their own choosing, and shall be free from the interference, restraint, or coercion of employers . . . in the designation of such representatives."

THE NATIONAL LABOR RELATIONS ACT (1935)

Shortly after the N.I.R.A. was declared to be unconstitutional, Congress reaffirmed and strengthened the principle of collective bargaining by enacting the National Labor Relations Act (also called the Wagner Act) of 1935. This act has been called the Magna Charta of American labor, for it provided the basis for the large membership in labor unions which now exists in the United States. In adopting the Wagner Act, Congress continued to be influenced by the thought that national prosperity could be promoted by increasing the purchasing power of an important group of consumers. It was also believed by many congressmen that the growing economic concentration in industry should be counterbalanced by the rise of a strong labor movement.

Senator Wagner, the principal sponsor of the act which bears his name, urged the adoption of the bill on the ground that the alternative to the plan of "give and take" collective bargaining, in the present stage of our industrial development, "would be for the government to invoke compulsory arbitration, or to dictate the terms of settlement whenever a controversy develops."[12] The concentrated power of organized industry, he believed, had become so great that it was necessary for government either to fix wages by authority or to legalize collective action by labor.

Leon H. Keyserling has summarized the underlying purposes of the Wagner Act as follows: "The Wagner Act was pointed toward more than strengthening labor or bettering its economic position. It was founded upon the proposition that the whole economy would prosper through a better distribution of the Nation's goods. It also evaluated collective bargaining as

[12] *Congressional Record*, May 15, 1935, p. 7573.

an essential attribute of a free society—and as the only alternative to an intensely contralized economy in the modern industrial state."[13]

The essential functions of the Wagner Act are (1) to provide by federal law that employees shall have the right to join a union of their own choice and through it to bargain with management on wages, hours, and working conditions, (2) to require management to bargain with a union duly certified by the National Labor Relations Board, and (3) to establish an orderly procedure for resolving the bitterest of all industrial conflicts, the strike for recognition. In place of strikes to force union recognition, the Wagner Act provides that employees shall determine by means of an election which union, if any, they desire as their bargaining representative. Employers are not required to reach an agreement with union officers, but they are required in good faith to try to do so. By the terms of the act, the National Labor Relations Board was established as a permanent administrative agency charged with the duty of administering the law and protecting the collective bargaining rights of employees. (See also Table 9, p. 81.) The Wagner Act is applicable to all firms, except railroads, which are engaged in interstate commerce or whose activities affect such commerce.

The rights of labor to organize under the Wagner Act are protected by specific provisions which declare that it shall be an unfair labor practice for an employer (1) to interfere with or restrain employees in the exercise of their rights to organize; (2) to dominate a labor organization or to set up a company union; (3) to discriminate against union members or to discourage or encourage membership in any union; and (4) to discharge or discriminate against an employee for filing charges or testifying under the Act.

THE GROWTH OF LABOR UNIONS SINCE 1935

The Wagner Act made possible a tremendous growth in organized labor. From 1935 to 1940, the number of union members increased from some 3,700,000 to almost 9,000,000. By 1947, there were more than 15,000,000. It is likely that the number of persons in unions will continue to increase, for numerous industries   such as the wholesale and retail trades—are still largely unorganized.

As a counterpart to the large growth in union membership, there has come an increase in the geographical area of collective bargaining. When once started, the process of collective action among employees and among employers tends to become ever wider in scope. Workers in one plant striking for a higher wage, for example, may find that employees in another plant are willing to make a contract to work for less. The control of competition thus requires that more and more workers be included in the area of collective action. Likewise, a group of employers holding out for a low wage may find that it must yield because some employer has agreed to pay more. Employers, thereupon, seek to widen their area of collective action. As long as

[13] Louis G. Silverberg (ed.), *The Wagner Act: After Ten Years* (Washington, 1945), p. 12.

substantial competitive forces continue to operate outside of the area of collective action, each side finds that it must moderate its demands in some degree and yield to competitive forces. In view of this fact, national unions, as well as organized employer groups, since 1935 have increasingly sought to fix uniform wage scales within an entire industry or within an important geographical area.

Industry-wide bargaining means that various local unions within a given industry act together through their national union in bargaining with a national employers' association consisting of all or nearly all of the employers in that industry. The wage contract so determined thereupon becomes applicable to all employees and employers in the industry. Industry-wide bargaining arrangements are found in the railroad and bituminous coal industries. Closely related to industry-wide bargaining is the bargaining conducted by large national unions with a few large corporations which dominate an industry. The contract terms so determined typically set a pattern which is largely followed by the smaller companies in the industry. Collective bargaining by organized labor and organized employers on a regional or local basis is also a growing and highly important form of multiple-employer bargaining.

THE "LABOR MONOPOLY" ISSUE

The development of regional and industry-wide collective bargaining systems, particularly since 1935, has given rise to the charge that many national unions and regional union groups have become labor monopolies. Is it possible for a labor union to become a monopoly? What is a labor monopoly?

Strictly speaking, every restraint by a union or an employers' association on the independent action of individual members is a restraint on competition. Such a restraint on the part of organized workers *in a single plant or in a limited locality*, however, is not likely to give them an appreciable degree of monopoly power, for there are usually competing groups of workers in nearby plants. The employer (or employers) engaged in bargaining with a local union, moreover, is usually not in a position to exert monopoly power over product prices. The small degree of monopoly power which may be secured by a union in such cases is generally accepted today as being a necessary and desirable means for improving the bargaining position of labor groups, so that wage rates will more closely reflect the valuation of labor's services.

The labor monopoly issue involves more than the concept of collective bargaining. It is rather concerned with the organization of *all* employees in an industry or an important regional area to bargain collectively with *all* employers in that area. In so far as competitive forces on the side of employees (as well as employers) are eliminated, it is quite likely that a substantial degree of monopoly power will be secured.

Various economists have reasoned that from the standpoint of public policy it is desirable to maintain and preserve a considerable measure of competitive pressure in the sale *and* purchase of labor services, for otherwise wage settlements in a particular industry will turn largely on economic pressure and endurance. The method of *force* alone, it is emphasized, is not likely to make for a determination of fair wages and working conditions.

Economists proposing that the government should preserve some measure of competition in wage determination do not recommend that the principle of collective bargaining should be abandoned. They do suggest, however, that the government should place limitations on industry-wide and regional bargaining systems—applicable to union groups as well as to employers—in order to provide competitive forces to moderate the extreme demands made on either side.

Many specialists in the field of labor economics, on the other hand, believe that the conventional monopoly analysis is not properly applicable to the labor market. Experience has shown, they state, that unions are not really successful in controlling the supply of labor in the same way that an industrial monopoly controls supply. In many areas, from coal mining to plumbing, labor is available on a contract or wage basis outside of union control.

Many labor economists argue, moreover, that industry-wide bargaining has contributed to stability in labor relations. It is said that a union is inclined to accept a greater measure of responsibility for its acts when it has achieved the security and status which usually accompany an industry-wide bargaining structure.

EFFORTS IN CONGRESS TO REDUCE THE SCOPE OF COLLECTIVE BARGAINING

The paralyzing, nation-wide strikes in the coal, steel, automobile, and railroad industries following the close of World War II gave rise to many demands in Congress for the placing of limitations on "monopolistic strikes" and "monopolistic concentrations of bargaining power." In the 80th Congress (1947–1948) the Hartley bill, which was passed by the House of Representatives, prohibited collective bargaining involving two or more competing employers unless such competing plants were located within a radius of fifty miles and together employed fewer than a hundred employees. The Senate likewise considered proposals to restrict bargaining by national unions, as well as the exertion of pressure by national unions on the wage negotiations conducted by their local unions. The Ball amendment, designed to restrict the scope of collective bargaining, in fact, was defeated in the Senate by the close margin of a 44-to-43 vote.

The various efforts made in the 80th Congress to prevent "monopolistic concentrations of bargaining power," it is generally agreed by labor economists, were poorly drafted and based upon an insufficient study of the operation of industry-wide and regional bargaining systems.[14] The restrictions

[14] See, for example, Richard A. Lester, "Reflections on the 'Labor Monopoly' Issue," *Journal of Political Economy*, December, 1947, pp. 532–533.

proposed on common collective bargaining, moreover, were designed to prevent monopolistic action by groups of local unions without reference to organized employer associations. This aspect of the proposals made them manifestly unfair and did much to defeat their adoption.

A strong case can be made for restricting multiple-employer bargaining on the grounds that it is socially desirable to maintain competitive pressures on each side of the bargaining process. In practice, however, the prospects of securing independent action on the part of local unions or industry members are not bright. The various local unions in a regional or national area are closely affiliated with their national union and look to it for leadership in making wage demands. Business firms in a given locality, moreover, are frequently subsidiaries of large corporations operating on a nation-wide basis. Smaller independents commonly "follow the leader" on prices, as well as wages. Any effort to apply the Sherman Act to break national unions into small bargaining units—or otherwise to limit the scope of the bargaining unit—would be unfair unless it were also applied to secure a divestiture of the scores of branch plants and subsidiaries, located from coast to coast, which make up the giant corporations. Application of the antitrust laws should also be made to interlocking arrangements, the use of patents to control an industry, and the concerted use of pricing formulas. The many segments of the economy enjoying antitrust exemptions should also be modified.

For the present, there appears to be no ready alternative but to permit multiple-unit bargaining by national unions. At the same time, however, efforts should be made to shape national policy along lines of limiting centralization of power in all segments of the economy. Professor George W. Stocking has wisely observed, "Power which impedes market forces should be curtailed, not strengthened. Limiting the power of trade unions is a delicate task of political surgery and, if the power of corporations is not similarly curtailed, it might endanger the health of the economy. Limiting the power of big business is equally delicate and more complex. An indiscriminate program of disintegration is neither economically feasible nor politically expedient."[15]

GOVERNMENT INTERVENTION TO REGULATE CONTRACT TERMS AND THE BARGAINING PROCESS

Under the Wagner Act the government, in substance, (1) guaranteed employees the legal right to join a union and select representatives of their own choice to sit at the bargaining table and (2) required the employer to sit down at the other side of the table to bargain with these representatives. No effort was made by government to tell the parties what they could or could not include in their agreement, or how they should bargain collectively on wages and working conditions.

[15] George W. Stocking, "Saving Free Enterprise From Its Friends," *The Southern Journal*, April, 1953, p. 443.

The Taft-Hartley Act, adopted in 1947, amended the Wagner Act of 1935. It continued the principle of collective bargaining. In addition, it introduced some degree of government regulation over (1) the collective bargaining process, (2) the terms of the agreement, and (3) the internal conduct of the union, itself. Under the new law, in effect, the government not only brought the parties to the bargaining table but also sat down with them to supervise the collective bargaining process. In exercising this supervisory function, the law provided that government shall take action,

1. To limit the contract provisions which labor and management may legally adopt—(a) by outlawing the closed shop, (b) by permitting the parties to agree to a union shop provision only when a majority of eligible employees vote their approval, (c) by limiting the scope of health and welfare plans and by requiring that such plans be administered jointly by the parties, and (d) by outlawing the automatic deduction ("checkoff") of union dues from the earnings of employees unless each employee tells his employer to do so.
2. To require unions to conduct their relationships with employers in certain prescribed ways—(a) by denying unions the right to employ a secondary boycott (b) by prohibiting jurisdictional strikes, (c) by placing numerous restrictions on the right to strike, (d) by prohibiting strikes by federal employees, and (e) by requiring unions as well as employers to bargain in good faith.
3. To require unions to meet certain conditions before they can secure the services of the National Labor Relations Board—(a) by requiring all officers of every local or international union to sign non-Communist affidavits, (b) by providing that unions shall send copies of their constitutions and by-laws to the Secretary of Labor, as well as reports on the compensation of officers, initiation fees, and methods of union operation, and (c) by requiring that periodic reports of a union's financial affairs be given to every member and filed with the U.S. Department of Labor.
4. To require unions to observe certain rules in the conduct of their organizations—(a) by providing that employers cannot be forced to discharge employees who lose "good standing" in the union as long as such employees pay their dues, (b) by forbidding trade unions to make expenditures and contributions in any national election, (c) by forbidding excessive initiation fees, and (d) by making it unlawful for unions or employers to interfere with, coerce, or restrain employees in exercising their rights under the act.

The adoption of the Taft-Hartley Act was vigorously opposed by all organized labor; and since 1947, labor unions in general have spared no effort in working for its repeal. The disposition of the postwar Congress, however, is to write a labor code which imposes federal restrictions on labor as well as employers. Today the real question is not one of government regulation versus self-regulation of the bargaining process but rather one of the kinds and amount of federal regulation to be imposed. It is likely that the issues of regulation in the labor field will continue to be the subject of political argument for many years to come.

STATE LAWS REGULATING LABOR UNIONS

Most states have adopted some form of regulatory legislation with respect to labor unions and their activities.[16] Following the national pattern, some seventeen states have enacted laws restricting the use of injunctions in labor disputes. Some twelve states have adopted laws which provide assistance to employees engaged in intrastate commerce in forming labor unions. Almost all the states have adopted procedures for the submission of labor disputes to voluntary arbitration.

As a result of the numerous strikes which occurred soon after the close of World War II, many states enacted legislation to curb union activities. Some eight states prohibit or strictly regulate strikes in public utilities. A number of states include hospitals and medical services in this category. Seven states have provided that if disputes in public utilities cannot be settled by agreement, they must be submitted to arbitration. Strikes by public employees are forbidden in eight states (Michigan, Minnesota, Nebraska, New York, Ohio, Pennsylvania, Texas, and Virginia). In 1953 Alabama adopted a statute which denies public employees (except teachers, employees of cities and towns, and a few other groups) the right to belong to unions.

About one-third of the states have banned or restricted the use of the secondary boycott. About one-third also have outlawed or greatly restricted closed-shop or union-shop arrangements. Other regulations extend to the checkoff of union dues by employers, the use of coercive action, picketing, jurisdictional disputes, strikes and lockouts, and the filing of reports and financial statements by unions.

GOVERNMENTAL DETERMINATION OF MINIMUM WAGES

It has been found by experience in numerous industries and localities that the principle of competition does not always operate effectively to develop the worth of labor's services. Frequently groups of workers have had no bidding competition among employers for their services. Publicity on actual wage rates, moreover, has commonly been lacking; and employers have been able to offer low rates to persons in urgent need of work without fear of losing their services. Women and children, in particular, in mill, factory, and cannery operations have been willing to work for what was offered.

The great depression beginning in 1929 brought further pressure on wage scales for persons with poor bargaining power. The New York *Times* for December 18, 1932, for example, reported that women and girl operatives in the Connecticut textile trades received "actual wage payments of 2 cents for a day's work, 40 cents for 120 hours, 65 cents for fifty-eight hours, $1.08

---

[16] See Charles C. Killingsworth, *State Labor Relations Acts* (Chicago, 1947), and the current reports of the Commerce Clearing House, Inc. and Prentice-Hall, Inc., on *State Labor Laws*.

for eighty hours." On August 1, 1936, the New York *Times* gave a report on the settlement of a strike of silk mill workers in Paterson, New Jersey, the silk center of America. According to the spokesman for labor, "We did not ask for much. Where our men made $6 a week, they will now make $9.50 or $10." Again, on December 26, 1937, the New York *Times* reported that women cigar workers in the state of New York received as little as $5.35 per week.

It has long been held by labor economists that the poor bargaining power of various groups of workers, particularly women and children, and the lack of competition for their services make it necessary for government to intervene and establish a "floor" for wages below which no employer can go in hiring labor. At the present time most of the states, as well as the national government, have enacted minimum wage legislation covering various classes of workers.

The Fair Labor Standards Act of 1938 (also known as the Wage and Hour law) is the principal national legislation on minimum wages. By its terms, Congress made provision for minimum wages, overtime pay, and the abolition of child labor in private employment. The minimum wage and overtime provisions of the Wage and Hour law, as amended, apply to all employees engaged in interstate commerce or in the production of goods for interstate commerce, as well as to employees in any "closely related process or occupation directly essential" to such activity. The prohibitions on child labor apply to all firms which ship goods in interstate commerce or which produce goods for interstate commerce. A minimum age of 16 years for general employment is specified. It is estimated that some 550,000 business establishments—about one out of every six in the United States —have employees covered by the Fair Labor Standards Act.

The goal of the Wage and Hour law is to remedy "labor conditions detrimental to the maintenance of the minimum standard of living necessary for health, efficiency, and general well-being of workers." In the application of this principle, the law provided for the establishment of a minimum wage of 30¢ per hour until October 24, 1945, and a rate of 40¢ per hour thereafter. It is estimated that approximately 1.7 million workers received wage increases as a result of the enactment of the Wage and Hour law. On October 26, 1949, the basic law was amended to provide a new wage floor of 75 cents an hour. The coverage of the law was also restricted somewhat. It is estimated that under the new law some 1.5 million workers secured wage increases which amounted to about $300 million a year. The maximum work period beyond which pay at not less than one and one-half times the regular rate is obligatory is forty hours.

Additional minimum wage provisions are provided by the federal government in the Walsh-Healy Public Contracts Act of 1936. This act applies to all contracts awarded by the federal government which amount to more than $10,000. Contractors accepting such contracts must observe overtime pay requirements, prohibitions on child labor, safe and sanitary working conditions, and minimum wage rates as prescribed by the Secretary of Labor.

THE PROBLEM OF MAJOR WORK STOPPAGES

Growth of the regional areas covered by collective bargaining has greatly aggravated the impact of strikes on the general public. Major stoppages in coal, oil refining, steel, automobile manufacturing, shipping, longshoring, and telephone communications, in particular, have brought demands for some form of remedial legislation to settle labor-management strife. Continuing international tensions have also generated a belief that crippling strikes cannot be permitted in industries related to our defense and foreign-aid programs.

In an effort to assist in the settlement of industrial disputes, the federal government provides a mediation and conciliation service for any dispute which significantly affects interstate commerce. The Federal Mediation and Conciliation Service, an independent agency, was created in 1947 to unite the formerly existing mediation and conciliation functions of the Secretary of Labor and the U.S. Conciliation Service. The agency has a staff of some 240 experienced personnel whose services are available upon request or upon the initiative of the agency, itself.

Conciliation is the attempt of a neutral person to bring the parties together after they have broken off negotiations. Frequently, in negotiations feeling runs high, and one side or the other may walk out and close the door. The task of the conciliator is to try to bring the parties back into conference. *Mediation*, on the other hand, is the attempt of a neutral person to secure agreement by narrowing the issues and by seeking to find terms acceptable to both parties. Mediation proceeds without resort to publicity, fact finding, or governmental pressure. It is an aid to collective bargaining, and it is effective as long as the parties are amenable to compromise. When a dispute involves sharp differences, however, the parties may forego mediation and resort to a strike or lockout.

Local strikes in public utility enterprises—telephone communications, urban transportation, electric power, and gas—have long been recognized as calling for special forms of public intervention, and a number of states have enacted legislation outlawing strikes in this field. Strikes on the railroads and airlines have also been singled out for special forms of settlement machinery.

The Virginia antistrike law for public utilities marks a significant attempt by a state to outlaw strikes and at the same time to encourage compromise and settlement by collective bargaining. The Public Utilities Labor Act, passed in 1947, prohibits strikes in public utilities and authorizes the governor to seize the facilities of a utility if the public welfare is seriously affected. The law places pressure on the parties to settle the dispute themselves by providing (1) that the state shall take 15 percent of the net revenues during the period of seizure and (2) that the terms of employment for labor shall continue without change.

FEDERAL INTERVENTION TO PREVENT "NATIONAL EMERGENCY" STRIKES

The Taft-Hartley Act of 1947 sought to provide procedures for handling national emergency strikes in industry, but it is generally agreed that its methods have proved to be unsatisfactory. By the terms of the act, the President is empowered to appoint a board of inquiry to study a dispute whenever an impending or actual strike or lockout, affecting an entire industry or a substantial segment of the economy, threatens the national health or safety. Subsequently, the President may direct the Attorney General to seek an injunction delaying the strike or lockout for a period not to exceed 80 days. Experience under the law has been that the 80-day injunction period operates to delay settlement by collective bargaining, discourages compromise, and serves to solidify the differences of the parties.[17] When the 80-day period has elapsed, moreover, the law provides no further remedy for settlement.

PROPOSALS FOR HANDLING EMERGENCY DISPUTES

There is general agreement that new legislation is required for handling industry-wide strikes. In the main, the proposals take two forms, namely, (1) the adoption of procedures to promote and foster voluntary settlements by improving the operation of collective bargaining and (2) the adoption of some form of compulsory arbitration.

The proposal to promote the voluntary settlement of disputes by improving the operation of collective bargaining has been given careful statement by Professor Richard A. Lester. In his words,

The lessons of long experience with major disputes can be summed up in this way: First, the handling of labor disputes is an art. Consequently the executive [the President] should not be hamstrung by one set procedure, but should have at hand alternatives and a variety of combinations so that his actions may be adjusted to the peculiarities. Second, executive flexibility enhances the risks to management and labor if government intervention occurs, and thus directs them away from reliance on the government and toward voluntary settlements. *Ad hoc* boards have the advantage over a continuing board that they do not establish precedents for themselves and, therefore, create greater uncertainties for the parties in any government action. Third, federal use of injunction or seizure should be a measure of last resort, coupled with some penalties on both parties for as long as the injunction, seizure, or both, last. If one side or the other is definitely aided by government injunction or seizure, it is thereby encouraged . . . to be uncompromising during the period of government intervention.[18]

[17] Richard A. Lester, *Labor and Industrial Relations* (New York, 1951), pp. 338–340.
[18] Richard A. Lester, "How to Handle Crippling Strikes," *New Republic*, June 16, 1952, pp. 10–11.

Professor Lester finds merit in providing sanctions for use in emergency disputes which operate to encourage the parties to make voluntary settlements. Such sanctions include not only government seizure and operation of plant facilities, but also the taking by government of a percentage of net revenues from the business for its service, as well as a provision that the terms of employment for labor shall remain unchanged during the period of government operation. Professor Lester believes, however, that these extreme remedies should be used only when all other measures have failed.

Federal seizure of plants, mills, or mines, made idle by crucial disputes, is an expedient within the powers of Congress to authorize, if it desires to do so. The attempt of President Truman to provide for Government seizure of the steel mills in April, 1952, in an effort to prevent an industry-wide strike of steel workers, was held by the Supreme Court to be invalid. In the view of the Court, Congress *alone* has power to authorize seizure. Without prior authorization by Congress, the President, himself, is powerless to seize strike-bound facilities. The reasoning of the Court in affirming this principle was stated by Justice Black as follows:

> The Founders of this Nation entrusted the law-making power to the Congress alone in both good and bad times. It would do no good to recall the historical events, the fears of power and the hopes for freedom that lay behind their choice. Such a review would but confirm our holding that this seizure order [by the President] cannot stand.[19]

In addition to the enactment of new legislation for handling emergency disputes, it has been proposed that unions and managements themselves be encouraged to develop their own private procedures for emergency stoppages. Thus, Professor John T. Dunlop states, "The interposition of further private machinery, or quasi-public machinery, is desirable between the initial breakdown of collective bargaining and emergency dispute procedures. The parties can help to develop 'another place to go' before resort to generalized emergency procedure. . . . I have great confidence in the ingenuity of the parties to develop such procedures. They can develop their own conciliation steps; they may decide to limit stoppages to some fraction of the total production of the industry; they may mutually select new wage leaders more apt to reach agreement; they may declare in advance their willingness to handle any vital cargo or production. In brief, the subject of emergency disputes should itself become a subject of bargaining between the parties. . . ."[20]

Whether or not the operation of collective bargaining by two monopolistic groups can be improved by private and public action can only be determined by time and experience. Surely, every effort should be made to promote the effectiveness of collective bargaining, for compulsion has its limits in a society of free people.

[19] *Youngstown Sheet and Tube Co.* v. *Sawyer*, 343 U.S. 579, 589 (1952).
[20] John T. Dunlop, "The Settlement of Emergency Disputes," *Proceedings of the Fifth Annual Meeting, Industrial Relations Research Association*, December, 1952, pp. 122–123.

THE SETTLEMENT OF EMERGENCY DISPUTES BY COMPULSORY ARBITRATION

The development of industry-wide and regional collective bargaining systems in essential industries—such as bituminous coal and steel—has given rise to demands for compulsory arbitration to settle the prolonged strikes or lockouts which involve industry shutdowns. Since the public cannot turn to an alternative source of supply, it is believed that government intervention is necessary to protect the public interest. International tensions and the "cold war" create a situation, it is also believed, in which the nation cannot afford to permit protracted interruptions in the production of essential supplies.

As long ago as 1902, J. B. Clark, an eminent American economist, proposed that a plan of compulsory arbitration be established for the settlement of all strikes which threaten to tie up an entire industry. According to Clark, "Let a competent tribunal decide what rate of pay is just and at the rate of pay that is thus fixed let the workmen already in the positions have the first option of keeping them. If on fair terms they refuse to keep them, let them go where they will, but let the State see to it that they do not interfere with men who are willing to work at the just rate."[21]

Today, various economists continue to advocate the use of compulsory arbitration for settling wage disputes in essential industries. They point out that the cost *to the public* of local and national strikes runs into many hundreds of millions of dollars. In allowing strikes to run their course, moreover, the public cannot be certain that fair principles will be employed in reaching a settlement. There is also a possibility that the industry and the union will join in a plan of wage and price fixation which is disadvantageous to the nation as a whole.

Professor Sumner H. Slichter proposes that workers in essential industries be denied the right to strike by federal and state law. If unresolved issues develop, he would require that they be referred to arbitration. Thereupon, if one party or both reject the recommendations, Professor Slichter proposes that the government require them to accept the award for a period of time. In his words, "The most appropriate arrangement would be to authorize the President (or the governor) to require the parties to try out the recommendations of the emergency arbitration board for a limited period—say not less than six months or more than a year—unless they agree to different terms."[22]

One standard for wage determination is the rate which is developed in the "general market" by competitive forces. In so far as substantial competitive forces are not at work in any of the principal industries, there is little objective material available for use in the determination of wages.

[21] J. B. Clark, "Do We Want Compulsory Arbitration?" *Independent*, November 13, 1902, pp. 2681–2682.

[22] Sumner H. Slichter, "To End Strikes in Essential Industries," New York *Times*, January 12, 1947, sec. vi, p. 7; and *The American Economy* (New York, 1949), pp. 46–48.

Under such conditions, a public tribunal would frequently be forced to resort to compromise and political expediency.

Whether or not compulsory arbitration will be established in the United States for handling national emergency disputes is likely to depend upon our success in providing new legislation to foster settlements by collective bargaining. At present, most organized business and labor groups oppose the adoption of compulsory arbitration. Most economists also appear to favor plans to preserve and encourage settlement by collective bargaining. It is possible, however, that the tremendous cost of nation-wide strikes in the loss of employment and production, in public inconvenience, and in jeopardizing our national security will bring increasing public demands for the establishment and compulsory use of public arbitration tribunals. Maximum rates for public utility enterprises are fixed by regulatory commissions, and it is quite possible that the same or related commissions will be given jurisdiction over wage rates, as well as product prices, in highly essential monopolistic industries.

SUGGESTIONS FOR FURTHER READING

Bakke, E. W., and Kerr, Clark, *Unions, Management, and the Public* (New York, 1948).

Barbash, Jack, *Taft-Hartley Act in Action* (New York, 1954).

Gregory, Charles O., *Labor and the Law* (New York, 1946).

Hopkins, William S., "Employment Exchanges for Seamen," *American Economic Review*, June, 1935, pp. 250–258; *Labor in the American Economy* (New York, 1948).

Kerr, Clark, *Factors in Achieving Industrial Harmony*, Institute of Industrial Relations, University of California (Berkeley, 1948).

Millis, Harry A., and Brown, Emily C., *From Wagner Act to Taft-Hartley* (Chicago, 1950).

National Emergency Labor Disputes Act, Committee on Labor and Public Welfare, U.S. Senate, Report 2073, 82nd Congress, second session, 1952.

Lester, Richard A., *Economics of Labor* (New York, 1941); and *Labor and Industrial Relations* (New York, 1951).

Lester, Richard A., and Shister, J., (eds.), *Insights into Labor Issues* (New York, 1948).

Reynolds, L. G., *The Structure of Labor Markets* (New York, 1949); and *Labor Economics and Labor Relations* (New York, 1954).

Sanford, W. V., "Strikes by Government Employees," *Vanderbilt Law Review*, April, 1949, pp. 441–450.

Toner, Jerome L., O.S.B., "Union Shop Under Taft-Hartley," *Southern Economic Journal*, January, 1954, pp. 258–273.

Witte, E. E., *The Government in Labor Disputes* (New York, 1932).

Wollett, Donald H., *Labor Relations and Federal Law* (Seattle, 1949).

CHAPTER 27

The Legal Responsibility of Government to
Maintain High-Level Output and Employment

The basic functions of government in the control of business, we have seen, are (1) to promote the maximum production of goods and services and (2) to provide for a determination of prices and incomes which is in harmony with the public interest. For the most part, government in the United States has pursued these objectives by adopting measures to maintain and restore the institutions of free enterprise and price competition. Historically, the general assumption has been that if government provides a fair and open field for private investment, private enterprise will invest capital and provide maximum employment opportunities.

During the course of our economic development, however, as we have seen in the preceding chapters, the federal and state governments have largely failed to maintain the necessary conditions for effective competition in important sectors of the economy. In place of many independent concerns in the various lines of business, a few corporations have come to dominate each major industrial field. Primary and central markets for the basic commodities—such as pig iron, steel, copper, lead, zinc, and sugar—have been largely or entirely destroyed by the action of mergers in controlling supplies and in eliminating competitors by outright purchase or by stock ownership. Under such conditions, the effective operation of the institutions of free enterprise and price competition has been, and continues to be, largely frustrated.

Entry into important fields is frequently restricted by the inability of newcomers to secure basic resources and the latest technology, by the need to expend large sums in advertising, and by the fear of the discriminatory pricing policies which may be employed by large rivals. Large, oligopolistic firms, moreover, produce only those amounts which they can sell at "stabilized" prices. When demand declines, the large producers place further restrictions on output and employment in order to maintain the prices they would like to get. It is in a period of depression, in particular, that "stabilized" or "administered" prices serve to accentuate unemployment and unused capacity (see Fig. 54, p. 656).

Since restrictions on competition, oligopoly, and monopolistic pricing methods hamper a free play of the forces of demand and supply, it follows in the view of various economists that plans to provide full employment should include an intensified program of antitrust law enforcement. Efforts should be made, it is said, to create numerous independent firms in the various fields of industry (1) by preventing the continuing corporate acquisition of independent and competing firms and (2) by adopting positive action to dissolve existing mergers of formerly independent (or potentially competing) plants.

FISCAL POLICY AS A REMEDY FOR CHRONIC UNEMPLOYMENT

In recent years many economists, under the leadership of the late Lord Keynes, have developed the hypothesis that a chronic condition of unemployment may develop not only from restrictions on competition but also from a deficiency in total demand. Keynes reasoned that the amount of spending—consumer spending plus private and public investment—determines the level of employment. In his view, the amount that the public tends to spend for consumption out of any given level of income is relatively stable, and the dynamic factor affecting the level of employment is investment. If the rate at which the public desires to accumulate savings is not offset by actual investment, the level of spending declines and a chronic condition of unemployment develops. Keynes believed that when persistent unemployment develops, government spending should be increased to compensate for the decline in private investment. It follows from the Keynesian analysis that the fiscal policy of government should be directed toward providing a rate of total spending which will maintain a satisfactory level of employment.

Many of the followers of Keynes agree that competition (freedom of entry and price competition) is an essential corollary to an effective policy for promoting a full utilization of resources. In their view, competition operates to moderate excessive demands, to prevent coercion, and to provide for a proper utilization of resources in the various lines of business activity. They believe, however, that the history of antitrust law enforcement during the past sixty years indicates that government is not likely to take the necessary action to create effective price competition. "The therapy is sound," says Professor Seymour Harris, "but will the patients accept it?" Upon the basis of this judgment, they declare that major reliance must be placed upon monetary and upon fiscal policy *to avoid depressions and keep output high.* Indeed, they reason that the more monopolistic the economic system, the greater is the work for fiscal policy to do.

In the present chapter we shall consider the use of fiscal policy as a remedy for chronic, or mass, unemployment. Fiscal policy, it may be noted, relates to the procedures followed by government in its financial operations. It is concerned with (1) taxation and borrowing, (2) the management of the public debt, and (3) public expenditure. Fiscal policy, as an instrument of control, is designed to create, or to remove, a sufficient money demand for goods and services to provide a satisfactory and stable level of employment and prices, regardless of the degree of monopoly or competition.

THE USE OF MONETARY-FISCAL POLICY
TO COMBAT DEPRESSION

The substantial rise in unemployment during the great depression led the federal government to experiment with monetary control as a means for promoting recovery. In 1933 the Treasury, upon the basis of new legislation enacted by Congress, began manipulating the money supply in an effort to bring about an increase in internal prices. Gold was devalued, and increased amounts of silver were purchased for monetary use. Large quantities of government bonds were also sold to the commercial banks, and the proceeds were used to finance a government spending program. Following the lead of the Treasury, the central banks adopted an aggressive policy of making credit supplies freely available throughout the country at low rates of interest. Rediscount rates were sharply reduced, and government bonds were purchased in the open market.

Experience during the great depression indicated that monetary management can contribute to economic revival, but that its use alone cannot be relied upon to bring recovery. In general, it may be said that the monetary authorities found that although bank rates of interest could be maintained at low levels, and credit supplies could be made freely available, businessmen could not be induced to expand their borrowing and investment activity. The public, moreover, could not be made to spend its deposits. Low rates of interest, it was found, are only one factor influencing business profits and the volume of investment. Other factors, such as wages, taxes, and monopolistic restrictions on prices and business enterprise, experience indicated, may offset any inducement to expand production which might be provided by a low rate of interest.

In as much as the results of monetary management in combating depression proved to be largely disappointing, the government turned to *fiscal policy* as a mechanism for stimulating employment and output. In utilizing fiscal measures, the federal government undertook large-scale borrowing and spending activities. Budget deficits were incurred; and vast programs of public works, subsidy payments, and make-work schemes were undertaken.

The government financed its expenditures by heavy borrowing from the banking system, for the view of its experts was that deficit financing, in itself would not help much, if at all, if the government borrowed from the public, because the result might well be to reduce spending by the public. In the plan of deficit financing, government bonds were sold to the commercial banks, and new money in the form of bank deposits was created and added to the monetary supply.[1] Monetary management and supply thus came to involve not only (1) the currency and credit policies of the mone-

---

[1] "Deficit financing" means government cash disbursement in excess of cash receipts (including cash on hand) which is financed by borrowing.

tary authorities but also (2) the fiscal policy of the federal government. As a result of government borrowings to finance public works and military expenditures, the gross public debt of the federal government rose from some $22 billion in 1933 to nearly $43 billion in 1940 (see Fig. 47). Thereafter, with the entrance of the United States into World War II, the national debt increased rapidly and by the close of the war it had reached a total of over $258 billion. Although some of the borrowed funds were secured from the savings of individuals, a very large part was secured by the sale of government bonds to the commercial banks and the creation of bank deposits and Federal Reserve notes.

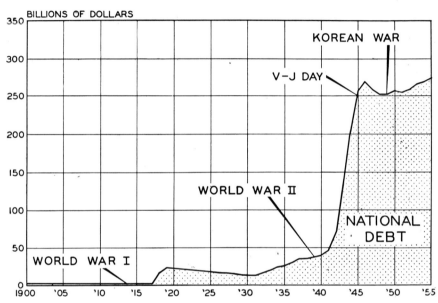

FIG. 47. Total gross public debt of the federal government. The financing, management, and perhaps eventual repayment of the huge debt which arose in consequence of World Wars I and II and depression budgetary deficits presents a national problem of major significance. For the future, moreover, the assumption by the federal government of a responsibility for contributing to the maintenance of high employment and high national income promises to make government borrowing and debt management an extremely important factor in the economy. (Source: Treasury Department.)

Budget deficits incurred during eight years of depression and four years of war gave rise to an enormous increase in the money supply. The supply of Federal Reserve notes outstanding in 1933, for example, was $3 billion, and by 1945 it had increased to $26 billion. Currency of all kinds in circulation was less than $6 billion in 1933, but by 1945 it had increased to $29 billion. Demand deposits, too, increased from some $15 billion in 1933 to $94 billion in June, 1945. Never before in the history of the United States had the supply of money been so greatly increased in relation to the physical volume of goods. Since no effective action was taken by Congress to reduce the enormous supply of currency and bank deposits, it was all but inevitable for the country to experience a serious period of postwar price inflation (see Fig. 48).

During the period which followed World War II, the Federal Reserve authorities failed to restrict credit in any substantial way to curb inflationary forces which were then threatening. This policy reflected, in large measure, an inability to act because of pressure from Treasury officials; and in some degree, an unwillingness to act because of opposition from important pressure groups to any effective measures of inflation control. Higher interest costs, the Treasury officials believed, would seriously affect the federal budget and rates of taxation. Open market activity *in selling* government securities to diminish the reserves of commercial banks, it was also believed, would injuriously affect the prices of government bonds, as well as the market for new issues of securities. As an alternative policy, the Federal Reserve banks, in order to maintain the prices of government securities, bought bonds on the open market from the public and from the commercial banks. The use of the traditional credit-control devices to check inflation was thus largely nullified by the consideration which governmental authorities felt obliged to give to the management of the national debt.

In March 1951, the Federal Reserve and Treasury authorities reached an accord on the responsibility of the Federal Reserve System to support the prices of government securities. By this accord, the policy of rigidly supporting the prices of government bonds was abandoned. Support activity of the Federal Reserve was limited to that of providing assistance to the Treasury in its refunding operations. These changes have made it possible for the Federal Reserve authorities to have a considerable range of independence in exercising a flexible credit policy.

THE LEGAL RESPONSIBILITY OF GOVERNMENT TO PROVIDE MAXIMUM EMPLOYMENT AND HIGH-LEVEL PRODUCTION

The close of World War II brought growing fears of a business depression and a return to the conditions of mass unemployment which characterized the great depression. These fears led to a widespread demand for government to assume a direct responsibility in providing sustained employment. The high level of employment reached during the war period, it was declared, showed that the economic system could be made to operate effectively.

In response to the public demand for government to assume a responsibility for insuring "full employment," Congress enacted the Employment Act of 1946. This act declares in Section 2 that:

> It is the continuing policy and responsibility of the Federal Government to use all practicable means consistent with its needs and obligations and other essential considerations of national policy, with the assistance and coöperation of industry, agriculture, labor, and State and local governments, to coördinate and utilize all its plans, functions, and resources for

the purpose of creating and maintaining . . . conditions under which
there will be afforded useful employment opportunities, including self-
employment, for those able, willing, and seeking to work, and to promote
maximum employment, production, and purchasing power.[2]

In general, it may be said that the Employment Act confers upon the
federal government the obligation to use all its powers to provide and maintain (1) a *maximum volume* of employment, (2) a maximum volume of output, and (3) price stability within the limits necessary to bring about high-
level employment and production. The act does not mention any specific
means for the government to use in accomplishing these objectives. Instead,
the President and Congress are charged with the duty of finding and adopting means which, under the circumstances, appear to be sound. Groups outside of government are also called upon to participate in carrying out the
program formulated by the federal government.

The act provides for a Council of Economic Advisers, composed of three
members, which has the tasks (1) of making studies of the current economic
situation and (2) of preparing recommendations to the President on what
needs to be done to maintain economic stability. In particular, it is provided
that the Council is "to develop and recommend to the President national
economic policies to foster and promote free competitive enterprise, to avoid
economic fluctuations or to diminish the effects thereof, and to maintain
employment, production, and purchasing power." The law states that members of the Council shall be persons "exceptionally qualified to analyze and
interpret economic developments." They are appointed by the President
and serve at his pleasure.

The Employment Act of 1946 further provides that the President shall
transmit to Congress at the beginning of each regular session an "Economic
Report." This report, it is stated, shall (1) describe the economic conditions
currently prevailing in the United States and (2) present "a program for
carrying out the policy declared in Section 2, together with such recommendations for legislation as he [the President] may deem necessary or desirable."

Provision is also made in the law for the creation of a Joint Committee on
the Economic Report, to be composed of seven members from the Senate
and seven members from the House. The committee is bipartisan and has
the functions (1) of making continuing studies on matters pertaining to the
Economic Report and (2) of preparing reports on the main recommendations submitted by the President. The Joint Committee, like the Council of
Economic Advisers, is an advisory body. Its task is to advise Congress on the
economic outlook and on proposed economic legislation. The Council of

[2] 15 U.S.C. 1021. The policy of full employment is an essential provision of the United
Nations Charter (1945). The Charter provides that the United Nations "shall promote
. . . full employment"; and declares that "all members pledge themselves to take joint
and separate action" for its attainment. Chapter IX, Article 55.

Economic Advisers, on the other hand, advises and assists the President on the Economic Report.

During March of each year the Joint Economic Committee submits to Congress an annual report advising the Congress on "the main recommendations made by the President in the Economic Report." The Committee also publishes each month *Economic Indicators*, a publication containing some 33 charts and tables on prices, employment, wages, business activity, money, credit, and federal finance. This publication, as well as the annual *Joint Economic Report* and the *Economic Report of the President* can be secured from the Superintendent of Documents.

THE COUNCIL OF ECONOMIC ADVISERS AND PUBLIC POLICY

Basic and unresolved problems with respect to the functioning of the Council of Economic Advisers are (1) whether its activity should be limited to economic analysis which is as objective as trained economists can make it; (2) whether *in its confidential dealings* with the President and Cabinet, the Council should take sides on controversial matters of public policy; and (3) whether the Council should express policy positions to the public in a printed report of its own or through participation in Congressional hearings.

During the period of July 1948 to January 1953, the Council's activity included all three of its possible functions—the preparation of objective reports, the making of policy determinations with the President, and the outright support of Administration policies. Public criticism of this blending of economics and politics was sharp, and various demands were made that the Council should be abolished.

Many economists believe that the Council should confine its activities to (1) "economic analysis" and (2) *confidential* reports on policy. Dr. Edwin G. Nourse, a former chairman of the Council, for example, believes that the *published* reports of the Council should be limited to an analysis of economic problems. At no time, he declares, should the Council be forced to publish reports which make a case for particular Administration policies, for such policies are necessarily shaped by political considerations. It is his belief, however, that the Council should take a *confidential* policy position with the President and Cabinet as to what would be sound, but realistic or "practical" *economic* policy, recognizing at the same time that the course adopted by the Executive Office will, in the typical situation, be modified by considerations of political expediency, however much it may agree with the Council's analysis of economic soundness.[3]

Other economists believe that the Council should confine its activities *solely* to a reporting of facts, to an explanation of economic data, and to analysis of alternative courses of action. The formulation, choice, or outright support of particular party policies, it is believed, should be avoided. Economists selected for the Council, it is also believed, should be given

[3] Edwin G. Nourse, *Economics in the Public Service* (New York, 1953), pp. 398–407.

specific or permanent tenure and should not be swept out *en toto* with a change of administration. Presumably, Council members should be capable of serving *either* political party. There are always "two sides" to questions of public policy, but there should not be two sides to economic analysis itself as an explanation. If there are, the analysis is incomplete and faulty. By limiting the function of the Council to analyses which satisfy professional standards of objectivity, it is believed that Congress and national leaders will have a better basis upon which to formulate public policy.

An example of a governmental economic institute which confines its activities to economic analysis, is found in the *Konjunkturinstitutet*, Stockholm, Sweden. This institute is an independent governmental agency under the Department of Finance. Its chairman, Dr. Erik Lundberg, is also a professor at the University of Stockholm. Staff members have continuous tenure, and there is no change in personnel when another political party comes into power.

The *Konjunkturinstitutet*, the law provides, shall limit its activities to economic research of a nonpolitical character. Its tasks include making national accounts, the preparation of semiannual economic reports, and the conduct of scientific research on business cycle theory and related subjects. In attending Parliamentary hearings, staff members sit as technical experts. They provide national accounting materials and alternative forecasts for the coming year, but they advance no policy decisions and *give no advice*.

The reports of the Institute sometimes indicate support and sometimes disapproval of the government's economic policy. In the opinion of Dr. Lundberg, advising on policy is dangerous for research. There is a strong tendency, he observes, for one, consciously or unconsciously, to come to the position of rationalizing and interpreting the statistical material to support the advice once given.

MEASURES TO PROMOTE ECONOMIC STABILITY

The goal of economic stability is usually defined to include (1) a high and rising level of production with an increasing output per man-hour of work; (2) a minimum amount of unemployment; and (3) a reasonably stable price level.[4] Many monetary and fiscal authorities believe that government should try to maintain a level of prices close to the level of the recent past in its efforts to achieve "reasonable price stability" (see Fig. 48). If a major deflation were permitted to develop, they reason, the reductions in prices would operate unevenly and inequitably throughout the economy (see Chap. 29, p. 655).

Experience has shown that in industries with "stabilized" prices, a decline in demand usually gives rise to unused capacity and mass unemployment. With competitive, flexible prices, on the other hand, a decline in demand typically results in lower prices which provide a selling outlet for available

[4] Committee on Economic Stabilization, Federal Reserve Bank of Boston, *Report on Steps to Maintain Economic Stability* (Boston, 1953), p. 9.

supplies. Experience has shown also that enterprisers who sell at low prices and buy at rigid, "pegged" prices suffer a serious disadvantage—a price-cost "squeeze"—in the ensuing distortion of the price system.

Since a spontaneous, competitive lowering of prices does not now occur in many industries, government, today, is faced with the problem of stabilizing employment and prices *in all sectors*. The objective of government in

WHOLESALE PRICES

FIG. 48. Wholesale prices in the United States, 1800 to 1954. Many monetary and fiscal authorities believe that the general price level should probably be stabilized as closely as possible to the level of prices prevailing during the past decade. Deflation, in their opinion, would cause sharp declines in industrial output and employment. (Source: U.S. Department of Agriculture.)

this undertaking is (1) to prevent the development of unused capacity and mass unemployment in industries of rigid prices and wages, (2) to support prices in other industries and occupations, and (3) to restrict or curb the inflationary forces which may develop from its own monetary and fiscal activities.

Basically, the measures available to government for maintaining economic stability are (1) instruments of control and influence designed to make free enterprise and price competition function more effectively or (2) controls by which wages, prices, and quantities produced are actually determined by or through governmental organisms ("economic planning"). Both sets of measures constitute a "plan," but in the first set the government does not attempt to take over, or make, detailed entrepreneurial decisions.

1. POLICIES TO MAKE A PRIVATE-ENTERPRISE ECONOMY FUNCTION MORE EFFECTIVELY

Measures designed to promote the operation of a private-enterprise economy include (a) the use of monetary and fiscal controls and (b) the application of the antitrust laws, including the Federal Trade Commission Act.

Monetary-fiscal controls include the following:

1. Programs of public works, federal housing, and public health. The Public Works Administration (1933) and the Works Progress Administration (1935), for example, were created to sponsor and finance public works projects and to provide useful work for the unemployed. In using fiscal policy as a tool for maintaining economic stability, government acts (a) *to decrease* income and spending during a boom period and (b) *to stimulate* the flow of income and expenditure during a period of depression.

2. The adjustment of taxes (a) to discourage or (b) to encourage consumption and private capital investment.

3. The direct extension of credit and the provision of credit guarantees to help corporations and persons who are unable to borrow from established banking firms. Federal agencies to provide credit and credit guarantees include the Federal Home Loan Bank System (1932), the Farm Credit Administration (1933), the Federal Housing Administration (1934), the Veterans Administration (G.I. housing loans and G.I. business loans under the Servicemen's Readjustment Act of 1944), the Farmers Home Administration (1946), and the Small Business Administration (1953). Governmental credit agencies stimulate the *demand* for credit by offering easy terms, such as lower rates, smaller down payments, and longer maturities, and they increase the *supply* of credit by making direct loans and by guaranteeing loans made by private lenders.

4. The use of subsidies to provide higher prices and incomes to certain groups. In recent years, federal subsidy payments to support the various agricultural programs have been amounting to more than $800 million per year. Total federal subsidies for all purposes, chiefly to provide higher farm incomes, to stimulate the production of scarce metals and other materials, and to provide subsidies for the U.S. shipping companies, have been costing the federal government about a billion dollars each year.

5. The stimulation of foreign investment and exports by government loan guarantees, subsidies, direct foreign loans, foreign-aid programs, and related measures. The Export-Import Bank (1934) was created to lend money to exporters, importers, and foreign governments; the Reciprocal Tariff Act of 1934 was enacted to stimulate foreign trade; and various subsidy and foreign-aid programs have been used since 1946 to provide an outlet for agricultural products and strengthen domestic agricultural prices.

6. The exercise by the Federal Reserve authorities of various measures of control over the amount of credit and the interest rate (or price of credit) to promote spending by business and the public. In using the tool of monetary management, money and credit are made relatively tight during a period of high employment and relatively easy during a period of substantial unemployment.

7. The provision of unemployment compensation and public assistance payments to the needy.

The policy of competition, in contrast to monetary-fiscal policy, consists of measures which must be *continuously* applied and implemented. Competition provides a mechanism for the determination of prices and incomes. Its operation, we have seen, promotes a full utilization of resources by providing a selling outlet for available goods and services. With a free play of the forces of demand and supply, supplies find a selling outlet, and prices are established at which business can be done.

During a period of business recession, excess capacity and persistent unemployment typically develop in areas of administered prices. When producers in such areas cannot sell all the goods which they can or do produce, they commonly cry "overproduction" and call for public spending programs. Government, in other words, is called upon to make it possible for producers of steel, copper, lead, and so forth to sell all which they would like to produce at the prices they would like to get! This, it appears, is an impossible burden for government to assume.

Monetary-fiscal policy and the maintenance of competition are two separate and distinct approaches which may be followed by government in providing high-level employment. Each has a particular role to play; and the two policies, it is suggested, should be considered *complementary* measures of control.

A properly planned monetary-fiscal policy makes it possible to avoid extreme fluctuations in prices, output, and employment. Its use during depressions helps to promote full employment by creating and maintaining the total rate of money spending. In providing for reasonable stability *in the price level*, government also promotes the effective functioning of markets and independent enterprise. Inflationary forces stimulate speculative dealings, especially by nonprofessional trade interests, and give rise to extreme price swings and unhealthy boom conditions. A general price deflation, on the other hand, brings the threat of bankruptcy and makes business survival depend more upon large financial resources than upon productive efficiency.

At any given time, the use which is made of particular monetary-fiscal measures depends upon the severity of the unemployment problem. If the volume of unemployment is high, the most effective measure for speedy relief is the creation of deficits through *tax reduction and increased government spending*. Both of these policies involve a minimum of interference with business enterprise and are politically expedient, for they do not require the taking of any direct action against organized pressure groups in industry, labor, or agriculture.

2. "ECONOMIC PLANNING" FOR MAXIMUM EMPLOYMENT

The use of extreme forms of economic control to achieve maximum employment, in which government actually takes over the determination of wages, prices, and quantities produced, is currently advocated mainly by the socialists.[5] If the country should lapse into a severe economic depression, it is possible that "economic planning" would rapidly gain additional supporters. In so far, moreover, as monopolistic combinations exercise private controls over important segments of the economy, it is possible that many leaders will increasingly favor the imposition of direct governmental controls. Professor Jacob Viner, for example, has said, "And, in so far as our economy is now in a position where either the Iron and Steel Institute or the Government must make important decisions, I am afraid I am for the Government."[6]

THE CONCEPT OF FULL EMPLOYMENT

The Employment Act of 1946, it may be noted, does not define the objective of "maximum employment." From the standpoint of economic analysis, what meaning can be given to the term? Sir William Beveridge, an English advocate of full employment policies, takes the position that "full employment" means "having always more vacant jobs than unemployed men." In his view, "Full employment, in any real sense, means that unemployment in the individual case need not last for a length of time exceeding that which can be covered by unemployment insurance. . . . Those who lose jobs must be able to find new jobs at fair wages within their capacity, without delay."[7] Similarly, Bent Hansen, a Danish economist, defines full employment as a situation in which "the individual worker always sells that quantity of labour he wishes to sell and expects to sell."[8]

Full employment, in brief, is a condition in which all persons desiring work at the going rates for their skill and ability can find it without considerable delay. When workers cannot sell all the services they desire and expect to sell, there is unemployment; and the advocates of full employment believe that this condition should be remedied at once by some sort of government intervention (see Fig. 49).

It may be noted that in discussions of full employment, there is rarely if ever any mention made of the adjustment of wages downwards to stimulate the demand for labor. The general view is that in a monopolistic economy product prices are rigid and sticky during a recessionary period and that wage rates should accordingly be maintained, or even increased, in order to maintain consumer spending. A transfer of income to employers, it is reasoned, would have little effect on their consumption, but it would diminish sharply the consumption by wage earners.

---

[5] "Economic planning," in itself, is not socialism. Socialists believe in a broad extension of economic planning *plus* an expansion of direct public ownership. (See also Chap. 23, p. 521.)

[6] Jacob Viner, "The President's Economic Program," *Current Business Studies*, Trade and Industry Law Institute, June, 1949, p. 41.

[7] William H. Beveridge, *Full Employment in a Free Society* (New York, 1945), pp. 18–20.

[8] Bent Hansen, *The Theory of Inflation* (London, 1951), p. 33.

5.0 MILLION PERSONS

FIG. 49. Estimates of total unemployment. The figures for unemployment are estimated on a sampling basis and are subject to some error. (Source of data: Bureau of the Census, *Monthly Report on the Labor Force.*)

Special antidepression measures, some economists believe, should be adopted by the government when unemployment reaches 2.5 million. Others place the level at 5 million. A "normal" amount of unemployment is accepted on the ground that it reflects seasonal factors, temporary layoffs, and a general switching from one job to another. Too much "full employment," it is believed, promotes inflationary wage increases, excessive absenteeism, and unwarranted job switching.

SOME CONSEQUENCES OF FULL EMPLOYMENT POLICIES

Following World War II and the subsequent period of rearmament for defense, the strong demands for consumer goods, capital equipment, and military supplies gave rise in many Western nations to sustained periods of full employment. With full employment, however, there developed many curious and uneconomic consequences. Various studies indicate that in a period of "full employment" there occurs (1) an increase in absenteeism; (2) a greater amount of declared sickness; (3) an increase in labor turnover; (4) a higher rate of accidents resulting from the employment of workers having inferior mental and physical dexterity; (5) a shifting of workers away from "dirty" jobs; and (6) a persistent tendency toward wage and price inflation. A larger total employment, it has been found, may actually result in a very small increase in total output or in no increase at all. Employment can be "too high" as well as "too low."

The principal economic problem arising in a full-employment program is the consequence of a tendency towards price and wage inflation. Public spending programs to fight depressions usually involve "deficit financing" (cash disbursements in excess of cash receipts) and the creation of new supplies of money. Demand is bolstered, and the drop in prices is checked. Gradually, over time, the policies of public works, cheap credit, and deficit spending may cause an upward pressure on prices, particularly if they are continued after the need subsides.

With the strengthening of demand, various industry groups act in concert to raise product prices. Labor unions, moreover, make periodic demands for higher wages. Since the fear of unemployment is largely removed, wage demands are pressed aggressively; and it is likely that wages and insurance benefits will rise more rapidly than technological progress. Many employers voluntarily raise wages in order to hold existing workers and to recruit new ones, for they know that in a period of high demand they can easily add new wage costs to their selling prices. This also makes for higher wages and labor costs.

Higher labor and raw material costs create a need for larger loans at the banks. The credit authorities (the Federal Reserve Board and the Treasury) are thereupon placed under a compulsion to expand the money supply to support the level of employment at the higher plateau of costs and prices. Restrictive credit policies decrease employment and production; and the political officials, experience has shown, are not willing to choose this alternative. Since it is likely that the money supply will be increased to permit a higher level of employment, a continuous rise in prices over the long run is to be expected. "It is high time," observes Professor Sumner H. Slichter, "that the public understand that . . . we can have maximum employment only at the cost of some long-run rise in the price level. Perhaps advances in economic knowledge or changes in institutions will eventually enable us to escape this dilemma, but that day has not yet arrived."[9]

THE GREATER RESISTANCE OF THE AMERICAN ECONOMY TO DEPRESSION

A growing number of economists believe that in the coming years recurrent inflation, rather than chronic depression, is likely to be the main source of economic difficulty in the United States. Governmental activity to provide for defense, maximum employment, an expanded program of social services, and various welfare measures, we have seen, usually involves budgetary deficits, government borrowing, and the maintenance of low interest rates; and these policies make for inflationary tendencies. At the same time, the adoption of various antidepression measures following the great depression, it is believed, will likely prevent the recurrence of any serious or prolonged depression. These measures include (1) the Employment Act of 1946 and the present-day use of monetary and fiscal measures to promote and maintain high-level employment; (2) a widespread social security program which serves to maintain consumer demand; (3) an agricultural price-support program which will probably prevent any serious decline in agricultural prices; (4) a system of insurance for deposits in banks and savings and loan associations; and (5) a more stable flow of American loans and financial aid to foreign nations.

The greater resistance of the American economy to depression does not mean that there will be no periods of recession or unemployment—that would be a utopian dream. Business activity is still subject to booms arising from the excesses of credit and speculative investment. If certain segments of the economy—consumer credit, bank loans, and speculative buying—should get badly out of balance, a marked recession is likely to occur. Dr.

[9] *The Journal of Commerce*, New York, September 2, 1952.

Arthur F. Burns, reporting on our knowledge of business cycles, concludes: "The only things we can be reasonably certain of in the proximate future are, first, that our economic system will continue to generate cyclical tendencies, second, that the government will at some stage intervene to check their course. . . . Our limited experience with contracyclical policy does not provide strong support for the belief, so often expressed by theoretical writers, that the government is capable of adjusting its spending, taxing, and regulatory policies with the fine precision and promptness needed to assure virtually full employment and a virtually stable price level at all times."[10]

During a period of recession, it is probable that industry groups and labor unions will be permitted to use whatever monopoly power they have to maintain prices and wages; and that governmental intervention will consist largely of measures to provide selling outlets and jobs *at existing prices and wages*. Significant fields for public investment include housing, highway construction, schools, and other public buildings.

INFLATION ACCENTUATED BY REARMAMENT AND WAR

With the outbreak of war in Korea in 1950, the United States and her Western allies found themselves compelled to mobilize man power, equipment, and productive capacity for use against Communist aggression. This mobilization greatly accentuated the already existing inflationary pressures of a full employment economy. Men and women in the military services and defense industries earn dollars, but they do not add to the supplies of goods and services at the consumer level. The purchasing power which flows into their hands thus operates directly to force up prices of available supplies. Military procurement also increases the demand for raw materials and exerts an upward pressure on basic prices. Further inflationary pressures arise from the demands of employers in defense and munitions trades for available labor supplies, as well as from the activity of labor unions themselves in pressing for higher wages.

The strong inflationary pressures generated by defense expenditures during 1950–1953 led to the formulation by the President and Congress of comprehensive plans for maintaining economic stability. Considerable reliance was placed upon "indirect" measures to reduce excess demand. Action was taken (1) to increase taxes, (2) to stimulate savings, and (3) to restrict the volume of bank credit. Direct controls were also placed for a time upon prices, rents, wages, and the uses of certain materials.

THE CONTROL OF INFLATION

The chief objection to inflation is that it reduces, to the advantage of favored groups, the real incomes of a large part of the population. Debtors, private and corporate, gain from rising prices, for inflation diminishes the

[10] Arthur F. Burns, *Business Cycle Research and the Needs of Our Times* (New York, 1953), pp. 8–9.

burden of repaying their loans. Inflation also places a premium on speculation, property ownership, hoarding, and manipulation, for dollar incomes in
such activities usually rise rapidly and provide extra claims for available
goods. A large part of the population, however, typically finds that their
incomes rise less rapidly than prices. Those, especially, who suffer include
pensioners, holders of fixed-interest securities, government employees,
creditors, persons having savings and insurance, salaried workers, and wage
earners whose bargaining power is relatively weak. Some of these groups
are injured much more than others, because of variations in the extent to
which their incomes are fixed, or nearly fixed, in money terms.

With the spread of inflation, class conflicts grow; and wage disputes become sharper and more bitter. Many persons become disillusioned with the
virtues of hard work, increased productivity, and the development of personal skills. Those who have been able to accumulate government bonds,
savings, life insurance, and retirement annuities, discover that the value of
their savings is frittered away by rising prices. All of such groups provide a
reservoir of discontent which may give rise to unwise measures of social
reform. Sound public policy thus demands that effective controls be adopted
to prevent inflation and to provide for price level stability.

Inflation is defined as a situation in which there is extensive *excess demand*
for available goods and services (at noninflationary prices). The procedure
taken by government in controlling inflation is that of preventing excess
demand from finding expression in rising prices. This may be done (1) by
reducing or neutralizing the excess of purchasing power in the hands of
buyers; (2) by directly controlling prices and wages to repress their upward movement; and (3) by increasing, when possible, supplies of goods
and services. In summary form, the main weapons available to government
for carrying out these activities are as follows:

1. FISCAL CONTROLS (INDIRECT CONTROL)

Fiscal controls to prevent inflation consists of governmental financial
measures designed to bring and keep the total demand for goods and services
in balance with available supplies. They include increased taxation for individuals and corporations, an improved system of tax collection and enforcement, governmental economy, an increased sale of government bonds to the
public, the postponement of public works which are not urgent and essential, such as certain public buildings and roads. Higher rates of taxation are,
in particular, a major weapon for use against inflation because they can be
used to cut deeply into the excess demand which generates higher prices.

2. MONETARY CONTROLS (INDIRECT CONTROL)

Monetary controls are an ingenious instrument for checking inflation.
They operate to prevent higher prices by making bank credit scarce. The
Federal Reserve authorities have power to restrict the volume of credit (1)
by raising the discount rate, (2) by selling government securities in the open

market to reduce the money supplies of member banks, (3) by making regulations which restrain the extension of credit on real estate, securities, and installment buying, (4) by increasing the reserve requirements of member banks, and (5) by encouraging banks, insurance companies, and investment bankers to follow a voluntary, self-imposed policy of restricting the amount of credit granted to their customers.

Credit controls can be, and have been, used with considerable success in slowing down and checking inflation. The principal factor making for their success is the courage and vigor with which they are applied. If there is a *will* to use them, civilian expenditures can be quite effectively restrained. A weakness of credit controls is that they do not affect (a) business concerns which are self-financing or (b) consumers who hold large amounts of cash. A policy of raising interest rates also has the disadvantage of making for an increase in the cost of financing the federal debt. Experience has shown, however, that credit controls can and should be made a principal instrument for controlling *inflation*.

3. Increased Supplies as a Remedy for Inflation (Indirect Control)

Contrary to the popular view, private and public investment to expand productive facilities does not provide a ready answer to inflation. An expansion of facilities creates new demands for available supplies, and frequently these demands are financed by bank credit. Such investment aggravates inflation, at least in the short run. During a period of inflation, the most desirable way to increase output is to increase the productivity and efficiency of existing resources, for the additional purchasing power so released is matched by a rise in output.

If Congress were willing to reduce tariffs and encourage imports, it could frequently do much to increase supplies and reduce inflationary pressures. In most cases, however, the vigorous opposition of domestic producers and labor groups prevents the making of significant changes in our tariff policies.

4. Price and Wage Control (Direct Control)

A further weapon for limiting inflation consists of direct controls to "repress" demands for available supplies. Such controls include wage and price fixation; rationing of consumer goods; and the allocation of raw materials to avoid congestion in markets for durable goods.

The imposition of direct wage and price controls, it may be noted, does not immediately reduce excess purchasing power which is the basic cause of inflation. With price control *and* excess purchasing power, there develop acute shortages of goods and a large inflationary potential in the form of idle cash balances and government bonds. Experience has shown that if direct controls are to be effective, there must also be the vigorous use of fiscal and monetary weapons to reduce or neutralize excess demand. Further measures which may be used to strengthen a program of wage and price control are (a) consumer rationing to achieve an equitable distribution of available consumer goods and (b) a plan of allocations (or priorities) to channel short supplies of raw materials into uses of greatest national urgency.

Although price and wage controls are not alone sufficient to cope with inflationary pressures, they have an essential role to play in a program of inflation control, particularly during war emergencies. Their particular function is to provide a measure of protection against *an upward spiral* of wages, raw material prices, and product prices. During a period of full employment, strong unions are able to force wage increases, which in turn are used by business firms to justify price increases. Acute scarcities of raw materials also make for higher prices. Such price increases thereupon permeate the price structure and provide the basis for further wage demands. It is desirable to permit some flexibility of particular wages and prices, to stimulate output and to direct the flow of resources, but the dangerous spiralling of costs and prices should be prevented. Fiscal and monetary measures are an overall type of control and do not provide protection against particular price rises and the exploitation of particular shortages. It is for this reason that direct controls have a specific, though limited, function to perform in restraining inflation.

5. CONTROL OF INVESTMENT (DIRECT CONTROL)

A considerable measure of control over the level of investment is exercised by government through fiscal and monetary policies. In addition, government may exercise a direct physical investment control by licensing new construction and modifications of existing construction. With a plan of investment control, private enterprise develops and initiates plans for investment projects; and the government decides which projects are most useful. It thereupon selects some and forbids others.

Physical investment control is a highly effective way to curb investment and inflationary pressures. It is more restrictive than the policy of controlling interest rates, for many firms are self-financing and do not have to borrow money. The use of physical investment control, moreover, does not raise the cost of financing government debt, as does the plan of raising interest rates. The danger in using investment control is the possibility that government will take a short-term view on public needs and conserve established enterprises to the disadvantage of new firms seeking to enter the field.

Physical investment control has been extensively used by various foreign nations, notably Sweden and England, in their programs of planning and inflation control. During the Korean War (1950–1953), the United States placed restriction on the use of steel, copper, and aluminum in new construction and in modification of existing construction. Regulations formulated by the National Production Authority specified that any construction project which was to use more than certain specified quantities of "controlled materials"—steel, copper, and aluminum—had to be carefully scanned and its relative essentiality determined before an authorization to commence construction could be granted.

OPPOSITION TO EFFECTIVE INFLATION CONTROL

Despite resulting injuries and inequities, governments, at home and abroad, typically have operated quite ineffectively in controlling inflation. Millions of people enjoy the prosperity which comes from rising prices for salable goods, and efforts to curb inflation meet the organized opposition of powerful groups. The business community, in general, has shown itself unwilling to restrain a gradually rising price level; and industrial and agricultural leaders alike oppose policies which are deflationary. Vast debts are incurred during an inflationary period, and the debtor classes want to pay their debts in cheap dollars. (See also Fig. 50.)

The strongest opposition to effective price control comes from the large pressure groups in industry, labor, and agriculture. Large combinations in industry are opposed to any form of direct control which will curb their profits and prevent the transfer of higher costs to users and consumers. Labor groups likewise are unwilling to accept effective measures of control for wages. In their view, legislation to control the cost of living is not likely to be effective, and they want to be in a position to protect themselves. Industry and labor groups, moreover, are rarely, if ever, satisfied with the balance of power between them, and each seeks to jockey for individual advantage over the other. Farmers, too, strive to benefit fully from rising prices for agricultural products; and the large farm organizations vigorously resist the placing of curbs on agricultural prices.

The very real difficulty which government encounters in controlling inflation is clearly expressed in a statement by Mr. Charles E. Wilson, Director of Defense Mobilization during the Korean War, and formerly president of the General Electric Company. According to Mr. Wilson,

> The most unpleasant aspect of the fight against the controls program has to do with greed and selfishness and high pressure by powerful groups. Lobbies of all kinds have been at work either to kill controls completely or else to wring the law to their own particular advantage. They don't object to controls—for the other fellow. None will accept graciously the thought of sacrificing any part of his own substance for the common welfare. . . .
>
> Price controls would not deny to these groups their fair and reasonable profits. In fact, the pricing systems are worked out with the advice and assistance of representatives of various producing groups so as to give them a fair return for their investment or labor. The shameful picture is one of pressure groups not accepting a fair slice out of the nation's pocketbook but insisting upon inordinate profit. . . . Powerful interests fight the Government because they want only outsized profits. Lives can be sacrificed, dollars never![11]

[11] The New York *Times*, August 26, 1951.

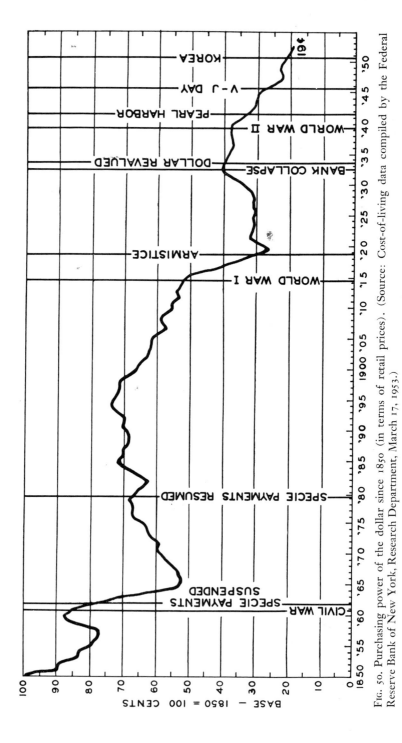

Fig. 50. Purchasing power of the dollar since 1850 (in terms of retail prices). (Source: Cost-of-living data compiled by the Federal Reserve Bank of New York, Research Department, March 17, 1953.)

The debt management and fiscal policies of the federal government also have operated to favor and promote inflation. The federal government is the world's largest debtor, and treasury officials have had a strong incentive for maintaining low interest rates to hold down the interest burden. As we have seen, the maintenance of a cheap money policy by the Treasury has seriously impaired the effectiveness of the Federal Reserve authorities in checking inflation.

THE DILEMMA IN GOVERNMENTAL POLICY

We have indicated reasons for believing that a policy of maintaining high-level employment is inherently inflationary. Apparently we can have maximum employment, with our present institutions, only at the cost of some inflation and some injustice to those receiving fixed incomes. The alternative of mass unemployment, however, means injustice, too. As is true in many situations, one must choose the lesser of two evils. A substantial economic opinion is that injustice caused by slowly rising prices is preferable to the injustice of widespread unemployment. The policies of full employment, moreover, it is said, result in more output and a higher level of living. The really critical problem of governmental policy in this field, many economists believe, is that of guarding against inflationary policies which go beyond those necessary to maintain high-level employment.

SOME CONCLUSIONS ON FULL EMPLOYMENT POLICIES

1. In fulfilling the legal obligation to provide high-level employment, governmental authorities have come to place major reliance upon monetary-fiscal measures to keep output high. Government spending, as the principal fiscal instrument, is an effective means for providing sales outlets and jobs. Its extensive use, however, typically results in budgetary deficits, increased governmental debt, and the maintenance of artificially low interest rates. These conditions create a base for, and a bias toward, inflation. The resulting expansion of the money supply becomes a "time bomb" which is likely to explode in higher prices in a subsequent upswing of business activity.

2. Inflationary tendencies are likewise generated by the efforts of business, labor, and farm groups to secure higher incomes. Large pressure groups in these sectors, moreover, are vigorously opposed to effective measures of inflation control. The result is that the economy faces the prospect of a continuing rise in general prices.

3. The antidepression measures adopted by the federal government after 1929, it is generally agreed, have done much to provide the economy with a greater resistance to severe depressions. Recessions and deflationary tendencies will undoubtedly recur, but it is unlikely that they will be as prolonged or as aggravated as during 1929–1940. In place of more serious depressions, it appears that the nation will experience recurrent periods of inflation and recession. *The main source of economic difficulty is likely to be unsatisfactory levels of persistent unemployment.* It is also probable that

there will be continued long-run inflation growing out of the efforts of government to combat recessions and to remedy persistent unemployment.

4. Excessive uses of full-employment policies, or attempts to secure too high a level of full employment, tend to create a condition in which the price mechanism works ineffectively in stimulating production and in distributing available supplies of labor and materials. Experience has shown that the price mechanism does not work effectively (a) when there is too much "full employment" and (b) when reserves of productive facilities are too low. The effect of higher prices is only to pull up other prices and wages. Supplies do not answer rising demand.

5. It is possible that the inflationary pressures generated by too much full employment will give rise to a more or less continuous system of price, wage, and output controls. Since 1941, the American economy has come to be more and more subject to a centralized direction and control. This development has largely been the result of specific needs to curb inflationary pressures, arising from war and rearmament for defense.

6. Employment, experience indicates, can be too high as well as too low. It is probable that something less than full employment will prove to be the desirable goal or target. Additional time and experience, however, will be needed to determine the optimum degree of employment which government should seek to maintain.

SUGGESTIONS FOR FURTHER READING

Bresciani-Turroni, C., *The Economics of Inflation* (London, 1937).

Chandler, Lester V., *Inflation in the United States* (New York, 1951).

Douglas, Paul H., *Controlling Depressions* (New York, 1935).

Galbraith, John K., *A Theory of Price Control* (Cambridge, 1952).

Hald, Earl C., *Business Cycles* (Boston, 1954).

Harris, Seymour E., *The Economics of Mobilization and Inflation* (New York, 1951).

Hart, Albert G., *Defense Without Inflation* (New York, 1950).

Keynes, John M., *General Theory of Employment, Interest and Money* (London, 1936).

Monetary Policy and the Management of the Public Debt. Replies to questions and other material for the use of the Subcommittee on General Credit Control and Debt Management, Joint Committee on the Economic Report (Washington, 1952), 2 vols.

National and International Measures for Full Employment, Report by a Group of Experts appointed by the Secretary-General (United Nations, Lake Success, New York, 1949).

Poole, Kenyon E. (ed.), *Fiscal Policies and the American Economy* (New York, 1951).

United States Chamber of Commerce, *Economic Policies for National Defense* (Washington, 1951).

CHAPTER 28

The Relation of Government to the Use and Conservation of Natural Resources

Today, the nation is faced with a growing scarcity of many basic resources. In numerous fields we are depleting resources faster than they are being discovered or renewed. Authorities in the field of conservation are in general agreement that, unless measures are adopted (1) to conserve (not waste) our mineral resources and (2) to provide for a continual renewal and maintenance of our forests, fisheries, water supplies, fertile soil, and grasslands, we shall not be able to maintain our present high level of living. A growing realization of this fact on the part of business leaders, statesmen, and citizens generally is placing conservation in the forefront as a highly important economic function of government.

The nation's zinc, lead, and silver deposits, it is estimated, could be depleted at present rates of utilization in twenty years or less. Gold production reached a peak in 1915, and present reserves may last for only a few decades. High-grade iron ore on the Mesabi range, which was opened in 1893, is more than one-half exhausted, and the remainder may not last for another forty years. It is estimated that the anthracite fields in Pennsylvania are now about one-third exhausted. The proved domestic reserves of petroleum in 1953 were estimated at about 12½ times the annual production.

During the period 1900 to 1950, the nation used up 40 billion barrels of petroleum, 26 million tons of coal, 3 billion tons of iron ore, 33 million tons of copper, 26 million tons of zinc, and 22 million tons of lead. The amounts of copper, lead, zinc, and oil which have been mined during the past 50 years, it is estimated, are considerably larger than present known reserves.[1]

Foodstuffs, forage, hydroelectric power, and such raw materials as wool, cotton, hides, and vegetable oils are all dependent upon water. In many areas, water shortages and a lowering of water tables are creating serious problems. Water supplies are dependent upon the preservation of extensive grassland and forest areas. At the present time, both of these primary resources are rapidly being depleted—one by overgrazing and the other by poor cutting and management practices. According to the U.S. Forest Service, present stands of "saw timber" are being reduced by cutting, fire,

[1] The President's Materials Policy Commission, *Resources for Freedom* (1952), Vol. 1, p. 25.

insects, and disease at a rate which is 50 percent greater than the annual growth.

One of the most serious threats to our material prosperity is found in the erosion and exhaustion of the soil. H. H. Bennett, recent chief of the U.S. Soil Conservation Service, estimates that at least 100 million acres of our formerly cultivated land—enough to care for 33 million people—have been ruined by erosion. Nearly a third of our original supply of topsoil, he judges, has been blown away or washed into the sea. Fortunately, fertile topsoil is one resource which can be maintained by proper use and care. Only a beginning has been made, however, in the adoption of such measures. At present, it is estimated that not more than 15 percent of our croplands are being worked in accordance with scientific soil practices.

The problem of resource depletion is made even more critical by the rapid increase in the nation's population. In 1954 there were over 160 million people in the United States. The annual rate of increase is close to 3 million. By 1975, it is estimated by the Census Bureau, our total population will range between 198 and 221 million persons. A mid-point figure of about 210 million will mean an increase of 50 million persons.

What will be the impact of our future population growth on the resources problem? Some authorities believe that our increasing population and the growing scarcity of resources point to a coming crisis. In the years ahead, it is said, Americans will have to forego the widespread use of automobiles, tractors, and gasoline. Urban population will need to be concentrated in large apartment houses, and recreation will have to be found in the garden and library. Others take a more optimistic view and predict that science, new discoveries, and increasing imports will enable the United States to grow and prosper as in the past. In each of these points of view there is a common area of agreement. As expressed by the President's Materials Policy Commission, it is this: "one point of overriding significance stands out . . . that demand can be expected to rise substantially."

The purpose of the present chapter is to present a survey of the main policies which have been adopted by government with respect to the ownership and use of natural resources. Consideration will also be given to the various efforts being made to correct (1) our spendthrift use of minerals and (2) our failure to renew those resources which can be renewed.

THE PUBLIC DOMAIN

The area of the continental United States comprises some 1,904 million acres of land. About 70 percent of this land (1342 million acres) is in private ownership. Some 3 percent (57 million acres) is land reserved for the Indians and administered by the Bureau of Indian Affairs. The remaining 27 percent (505 million acres) is publicly owned and administered by the federal, state, and local governments. Approximately four-fifths of the *public* land in the continental United States is owned by the federal government (see Table 41).

TABLE 41.   Distribution of public land ownership.

	Acres (000,000)	Percent
Federal land	398	79
State land	80	16
County and municipal	17	3
Not allocable	10	2
Total	505	100

(Source: Mid-Century Conference on Resources for the Future, "Competing Demands for Use of Land" (Washington, 1953), Section 1.

Soon after the Revolutionary War, the original thirteen states conveyed to Congress control over the western lands to which they claimed title. This area became the original part of the public domain. Thereafter, by a series of acquisitions, the federal government secured title to vast areas in the West (see Fig. 51). By 1853 the total public domain consisted of some 1442 million acres. The purchase of Alaska in 1867 gave the federal government title to 378,165,760 additional acres of land, approximately 365 million acres of which are still retained under public ownership. The term "public domain" is used to mean public land under the direct control of the federal government.

Lands in the public domain do not include lands lying within our insular possessions. The territories of Hawaii and Puerto Rico each have their own public lands, administered by their own agencies.

DISPOSAL OF THE PUBLIC DOMAIN

The federal government made provision for the sale of public land to settlers as early as 1784 in an effort to stimulate settlement in the West and also to secure revenue. Most of the early sales were made at 75¢ per acre. The policy of sale was continued, and by 1841 the minimum sale price was fixed at $1.25 per acre. The land laws usually provided that a given individual could secure not more than 160 acres at the minimum price, and at all times the laws specified that the land was to be sold only to "heads of families" and for purposes of "settlement and cultivation." Actually, however, many wealthy individuals and corporations were able to acquire large holdings of land by employing special agents to make "dummy entries" and thereafter to transfer the land to the persons employing them.[2]

After 1830, the federal government made enormous grants of land to railroads as a means of encouraging their development. Large areas were also given to the states for the support of education and for use in promoting internal improvements—such as roads, bridges, canals, and railroads. In 1862 the first of a series of federal homestead laws was passed. By the terms of this legislation any citizen twenty-one years of age or over was given the right to secure title to 160 acres of land by occupation and cultivation for a period

[2] C. R. Van Hise, *The Conservation of Natural Resources* (New York, 1913), p. 281.

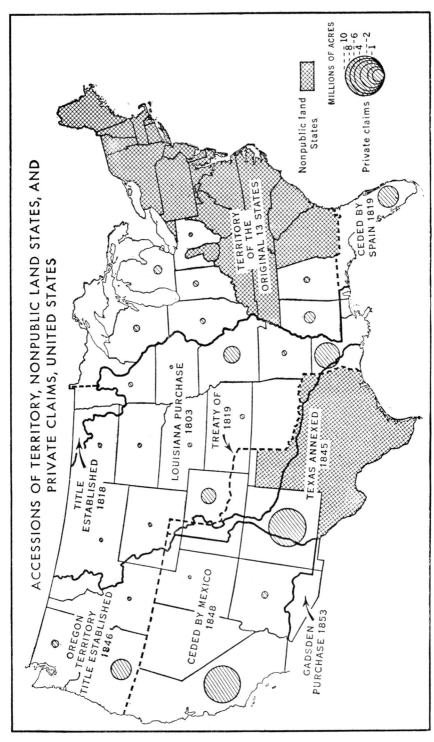

ACCESSIONS OF TERRITORY, NONPUBLIC LAND STATES, AND PRIVATE CLAIMS, UNITED STATES

FIG. 51. The original public domain in the continental United States. The unshaded area indicates the original public domain—the area which was once publicly owned and under the direct control of the federal government. (Source: U.S. Department of Agriculture, *Federal Rural Lands*, Washington, 1947.)

of five years.[3] A provision of the law of 1862 also made it possible to secure title to the 160 acres within a few months by paying $1.25 per acre for the land. Although the Homestead Act of 1862 was designed to benefit individual settlers, its provisions were also widely abused. By employing agents to make dummy entries, large mining, lumber, and railroad corporations secured vast tracts of the nation's finest timber and land resources for the nominal price of $1.25 per acre.[4]

The Timber and Stone Act of 1878 (43 U.S.C. 311–313) provided that timberlands and stone deposits in the states of California, Oregon, Nevada, and in Washington Territory could be sold at a minimum price of $2.50 per acre. This legislation also specified (1) that not more than 160 acres could be sold to any one person or association of persons and (2) that persons acquiring timber and stone lands did so in good faith for their own use. Here, again, vast timber holdings were acquired by large corporations through the method of hiring dummy claimants. For an investment of $400, a corporation could secure a quarter-section of timberland which was frequently worth from $10,000 to $20,000 and more. By multiplying this process many times, it became possible for corporations and persons of modest wealth to secure large fortunes within a few years. A government official has estimated that the Timber and Stone Act resulted in the sale of over 12 million acres of timberland (to June, 1909), of which at least 10 million acres were acquired by corporations and individual investors.[5] The Act of 1878 is still in existence, but the resources available for selection are remotely located or poor in quality.

As a result of the various laws which have been passed to provide for a disposal of the public domain, the original public domain in the continental United States has been reduced from some 1400 million acres to approximately 400 million acres (see Table 42). The federal government, however, continues to be the largest owner of real estate in the nation.[6]

TABLE 42.   Disposition of the Original Public Domain.

Item	Acres
	(000,000)
Granted to homesteaders	285
Granted to states	225
Granted to railroad corporations	90
Sales and other disposals	392
Total land disposed of	992

(Source: U.S. Dept. of Agriculture, *Federal Rural Lands*, Washington, 1947.)

[3] Present-day rules on homesteading (1) in the continental United States and (2) in Alaska may be secured from the Bureau of Land Management, U.S. Department of the Interior, Washington, D.C. Almost all publicly owned land suitable for agriculture has been sold or homesteaded.

[4] C. R. Van Hise, *op. cit.*, pp. 282–283.

[5] *Ibid.*, p. 285.

[6] See also Committee on Public Lands, *Interim Report*, 78th Congress, second session, House Report 1884, 1944, p. 3.

About one-half of the land which remains in public ownership is arid or semiarid land which individuals and corporations have shown little interest in owning. Some 40 percent of the federal land is wooded, and most of this area has been made a part of the national forests. Other tracts of the public domain are utilized for Indian reservations, national defense, national parks, soil conservation, and public recreation. In addition to public-domain lands, the federal government has acquired in recent years, by gift, purchase, or exchange, some 50,000,000 acres for forestry, national defense, and soil conservation purposes.

OWNERSHIP OF THE SUBMERGED COASTAL LANDS

In the Presidential campaign of 1952, a major issue was whether or not the submerged coastal lands adjoining the continental United States should be given to the respective coastal states. These lands are a part of the continental shelf, a submerged, comparatively shallow land surface which extends, on the average, about 30 miles from the low-water mark along the open coast out into the sea. It is estimated that this land area is one-tenth the size of the United States. The Republican candidate, Dwight D. Eisenhower, declared his belief that the offshore lands belonged to the adjacent states. The Democratic candidate, Adlai E. Stevenson, on the other hand, upheld ownership by the federal government for the benefit of all the states.

The idea that each littoral nation owns, or at least has the right of control over, a three-mile ocean belt adjacent to its coastline appears to have developed from the efforts of maritime nations to protect their shores. A cannon shot, it is said, would carry for three miles (one league), and the rule became established that each nation exercises jurisdiction over a three-mile water area extending into the sea.[7]

For many years, the states and the federal government, relying upon cases by the Supreme Court and upon political history, thought that the coastal states had rights to the resources found over the shelf within the seaward boundary. Various coastal states, such as California, Washington, and Florida, adopted rules to regulate the taking of oysters, shrimps, crabs, sponges, and other marine life within the three-mile limit; and the federal government accepted the exercise of such local police power functions.[8] The discovery of oil on the ocean lands in 1920 led numerous states to take an active interest in asserting their ownership claims over the tidelands up to three miles and beyond.[9] In 1938 Louisiana enacted a statute which extended its ownership claims to the submerged lands for a distance of twenty-seven miles from its shore; and in 1947 Texas extended its boundary to the "outer limits of the continental shelf."

[7] Gordon Ireland, "Marginal Seas Around the States," *Louisiana Law Review*, January, 1940, pp. 252–293; *ibid.*, March, 1940, pp. 436–478; and *U.S. v. California*, 332 U.S. 19, 32–33 (1947).

[8] *Skiriotes* v. *Florida*, 313 U.S. 69 (1941).

[9] Robert E. Hardwicke, "The Tidelands and Oil," *Atlantic*, June, 1949, pp. 21–22.

With the discovery and production of oil and gas on the submerged shelf lands off the coasts of California and Louisiana—sometimes as far as twelve miles out into the sea—the federal government began to assert its ownership claims to the continental shelf. In 1937 Senator Nye introduced a bill in Congress providing that "all submerged lands lying under the high seas off the coasts of the continental United States between the low-water mark and the three-mile limit [shall be] part of the public domain." Several similar bills were introduced between 1937 and 1945, but none was adopted. Finally, in October, 1945, the U.S. Attorney General filed suit against the state of California, claiming title to the belt of submerged land extending for three miles into the sea.

On June 23, 1947, the Supreme Court, in a six-to-two decision, upheld the federal government in its claim over the land in dispute off the California coast. The conclusion of the Court was "that California is not the owner of the three-mile marginal belt along its coast, and that the Federal Government rather than the state has paramount rights in and power over that belt, an incident to which is full dominion over the resources of the soil under that water area, including oil."[10] In the view of the majority, the federal government has "paramount rights" in the seaward areas (1) because of its duty to protect the peace and commerce of the nation and (2) because of its responsibility to conduct our relations with foreign nations.

Following the Supreme Court decision of 1947, several states and many oil companies made vigorous efforts in Congress to secure legislation granting the continental shelf to the coastal states. The state governments had a real interest in securing royalties from the utilization of the oil lands. The interest of the oil companies, on the other hand, was that of desiring to have the states as lessors rather than the federal government (see below pp. 643–644). From a financial standpoint, it is doubtful whether it made any difference to the companies whether the lessor was the federal government or a state.

In 1953, following the victory of the Republican party in the national elections, legislation was enacted establishing in the states the right to develop the resources of the shelf. On May 22, 1953, President Eisenhower signed the tidelands oil bill, Public Law 31, giving the coastal states title to the submerged lands three miles out to sea, except for Texas and Florida where the historic boundaries were deemed to extend 10½ miles into the Gulf of Mexico. Beyond these boundaries the federal government retained paramount rights in the continental shelf.

In signing the tideland's legislation, President Eisenhower stated: "I am pleased to sign this measure into law recognizing the ancient rights of the states in the submerged lands within their historic boundaries. As I have said

---

[10] *U.S.* v. *California*, 332 U.S. 19, 38–39 (1947). For a comprehensive account of the federal-state controversy, see Robert E. Hardwicke, Carl Illig, and C. P. Patterson, "The Constitution and the Continental Shelf," *Texas Law Review*, April, 1948, pp. 398–439.

many times I deplore and I will always resist federal encroachment upon rights and affairs of the states. Recognizing the states' claim to these lands is in keeping with basic principles of honesty and fair play."

Upon the basis of the new legislation, the states can now authorize the development for oil and gas as to that part of the shelf within the boundary of the state; and the federal government has similar rights to the area beyond the state boundary.

GOVERNMENTAL POLICY ON MINERAL RIGHTS—THE COMMON LAW ON MINERALS

A principle of the early common law in England, as well as on the Continent, was the doctrine that government has the "right to mines." The important minerals of the Middle Ages were gold and silver, and the rule established by the courts was that the ownership of all gold and silver mines resides in the king. In justifying this rule, the English courts held that the sovereign should have the gold and silver in order to provide coined money to promote commerce.[11] Subsequently, the rule of ownership was extended by the English courts to all mineral deposits which contained gold or silver. The right to mines applied to mineral deposits on any land within the realm. Since the mines were usually developed by private enterprisers, the king secured compensation in the form of "royalties." A royalty payment was a payment to the king of a certain portion of the subsoil products.

In granting charters to the colonists coming to America, it was usual for the English rulers to require "royalty payments" of a certain fraction of the value of any gold, silver, copper, or precious gems which might be found in the New World. The same system of mineral law was instituted by Spain in its control of Mexico, California, and South America. Private enterprise was invited to develop the mines, and royalty payments were levied by the government.[12]

Following the American Revolution, the original thirteen states acquired the royal right to mines in their respective areas. New York State has continued to exercise its sovereign rights, and its land laws today provide that "The following minerals are the property of the people of the state of New York in their right of sovereignty: (a) All deposits of gold and silver in or upon private lands and lands belonging to the state heretofore or hereafter discovered within the state, [and] (b) all deposits of minerals and fossils heretofore or hereafter discovered in or upon any lands belonging to the people of the state of New York" (Public Lands Law, chap. 872).

[11] William Blackstone, *Commentaries on the Laws of England*, 3rd ed. (Chicago, 1884), Vol. 1, chap. 8, p. 293.

[12] The Constitution of Mexico adopted in 1917 provides that "In the Nation is vested direct ownership of all minerals . . . precious stones, rock salt and salt lakes . . . phosphates which may be used for fertilizers, solid mineral fuels, petroleum, and all hydrocarbons."

MINERAL POLICY OF THE FEDERAL GOVERNMENT TO 1866

The idea that government should retain the royal right to mines was adopted by the federal government with respect to (1) the western lands which it secured from the thirteen states and (2) all the territory which it acquired in rounding out the continental United States (see Fig. 51). In selling tracts of this land to individuals and corporations, the general rule was to reserve all "lands on which are situated any known salines or mines." Provision was made for the development of mineral lands by private enterprise under a system of leasing. A system of leasing, it was believed, would provide not only maximum revenue for the government but also the best security against monopolistic control of essential minerals.

In 1807 the leasing plan was applied to the lead mines which were then being developed in the area of Missouri and Illinois. It is reported that royalty payments were made for some years with tolerable regularity. After 1834, however, the mining companies in the lead district refused to make further payments because of "the immense number of illegal entries of mineral land at the Wisconsin land office."[13] By means of dummy entries and fraud, it was alleged, other companies had been able to secure the outright ownership of mineral lands and were not obliged to pay royalties. Difficulties in collecting royalties continued, and in 1846 Congress authorized the sale of lead deposits in Missouri, Illinois, and Arkansas, as well as in the territories of Wisconsin and Iowa, at a minimum price of $2.50 per acre. A related law made provision for the sale of copper mines in the Lake Superior region at the same price. In 1864 the policy of sale was extended to coal lands at the nominal price of $2.50 per acre.

THE GRANTING OF PRIVATE RIGHTS TO MINERALS

The continued pressure of organized mining groups to secure private ownership of mineral resources finally led in 1866 to the adoption of a new federal policy on mineral lands. A statute passed in that year declared (1) that all mineral lands on the public domain were to be free and open to exploration and occupation; (2) that mineral rights which had been acquired by direct appropriation in accordance with local rules should be accepted and confirmed; and (3) that titles to deposits of gold, silver, cinnabar, and copper could be secured by improvement work and the filing of claims in a local land office. As a result of this legislation, Congress abandoned the idea of retaining title to, or of securing royalties from, minerals located in those parts of the public domain upon which individuals and corporations might file claims.

The legislation of 1866 was supplemented and amended by the Mineral Act of 1872, which still constitutes the basic federal law on the disposition of

[13] Committee on Public Lands, *Exploration for and Disposition of Coal, Oil, Gas,* 63rd Congress, second session, House Report 668, 1914, Part 2, p. 18.

minerals. By the terms of the act of 1872 "All valuable mineral deposits in lands belonging to the United States . . . are hereby declared to be free and open to exploration and purchase." Persons desiring to possess and occupy a particular tract of land must first make a valid "discovery" of minerals. Secondly, they must perform a certain amount of development work—such as marking out the boundaries of the claim. Thirdly, they must record the land claimed with local authorities—usually the county auditor. Upon taking these three steps, any citizen is given the privilege of developing the mineral deposit without a payment of royalties to the government. The claim may be held and utilized year after year by doing annual improvement work.

If a person enjoying possessory occupation desires to acquire title to the land—called a patent—he must apply to the local land office of the U.S. Department of the Interior. Upon meeting various requirements, he may purchase the land at the nominal price of $2.50 per acre for placer claims and $5.00 for lode claims. The principal minerals now controlled by the legislation of 1872 are (1) the metals—gold, silver, copper, lead, zinc, cinnabar, manganese, molybdenum, tungsten, chrome, antimony, arsenic, nickel, and iron; and (2) the nonmetals—magnesite, talc, clays, marble, limestone, gypsum, bauxite, feldspar, sand, gravel, and building stone.

On August 1, 1946 (the date of the Atomic Energy Act), the federal government reserved to itself all uranium deposits which may be found on public lands. This means that all such deposits must be transferred to the federal government. However, individual prospectors and mining corporations are encouraged to search for new deposits of uranium on the public domain. Prospectors and mining companies may also locate claims over uranium deposits in the same manner as in the case of other ores—such as lead, copper, or gold. The Atomic Energy Commission stands ready to pay guaranteed ten-year minimum prices for all domestic refined uranium and high-grade uranium ores—supplied from either public or private lands. In general, deposits of uranium discovered by the Atomic Energy Commission on public lands will be made available for development by private operators. Uranium deposits located on lands under private ownership to which title was granted by the federal government prior to August 1, 1946, belong to the private owners of the land.

REËSTABLISHMENT OF THE PRINCIPLE OF LEASING

The principle of leasing, as applied to the lead mines in 1807, was revived by Congress in 1914 in legislation providing for the leasing of coal lands in Alaska. In 1917 the leasing plan was also applied to potash deposits on all lands held by the federal government. The principle was further extended in the Mineral Leasing Act of 1920 to coal, oil and gas, phosphate, oil shale, and sodium deposits on lands owned by the United States. In 1927 the principle was applied to sulfur, and also to gold, silver, and mercury deposits which had been reserved to the federal government in certain prior land grants.

The principle of leasing mineral lands has proved to be very advantageous for the public. Substantial royalty payments are secured from the private development of publicly owned mineral deposits, and rules are provided to prevent physical waste, especially in the unitization of oil lands. Approximately 5 percent of the domestic production of oil, it is estimated, comes from federal lands administered under the Mineral Leasing Act of 1920. The Act of 1920 provides that substantial portions of the royalty payments accruing to the federal government shall be paid to the states within which the income is produced, to be used for public roads, parks, the school system, and other improvements. Certain authorities believe that it would be desirable to extend the principle of leasing to all mineral deposits which may henceforth be found on lands owned by the federal government.

OWNERSHIP OF LAND AND MINERAL RIGHTS IN THE UNITED STATES

At the present time, land surface and mineral rights in the United States are owned in four principal ways (see Fig. 52). First, there is the situation (case No. 1) in which the government owns the land surface and the minerals. Private individuals may utilize large portions of our public lands for grazing purposes by paying nominal rentals. In the case of a number of minerals—such as petroleum (gas and oil), coal, potash, and sulfur—the government leases the lands to private enterprisers for exploration and development in accordance with the mineral leasing law of 1920. If minerals are found, the government secures royalty payments. Royalty payments in modern usage mean the payments made to the owner of land for the right to remove exhaustible materials.

A portion of the publicly owned land surface is still available for private ownership under the homestead laws. Numerous minerals—such as lead, copper, and gold—may also be developed privately (without royalty payments) under the mineral legislation of 1872. Private claims may be located over the mineral deposits, and an outright ownership of the minerals may be secured by purchase, except in the case of uranium ore.

Secondly, there is the situation (case No. 2) in which private individuals own the land surface, and the government owns the mineral rights (see Fig. 52). This situation exists with respect to sales of public lands with a reservation of minerals by the federal government. If minerals are found, the government is paid royalties for their utilization. There is only a small amount of land under private ownership with a reservation of minerals to the government.

Thirdly, there is the condition (case No. 3) in which individuals or corporations own the land surface and also the mineral rights. This is generally the situation in the United States. As a rule, there has been no reservation of minerals when lands have passed from the public domain. In this situation, the owner of the land gets the royalties if oil or other minerals are found and developed by other persons.

Fourthly, there is the situation (case No. 4) in which one person owns the

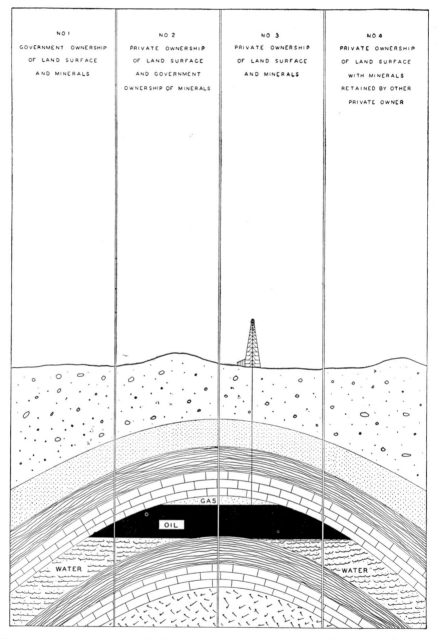

Fig. 52. A cross-section sketch illustrating the various ways in which land surface and minerals (including oil) are owned in the United States.

land surface and some other individual or corporation owns the mineral rights. This is not a prevalent condition. In most cases, separate private ownership of land surface and minerals comes about through the practice of certain large timber and railroad companies to reserve mineral rights whenever plots of land are sold to individual settlers. If oil or other minerals are subsequently found, the timber company or railroad—and not the surface owner—secures the royalty payments. The owner of minerals has the right to do what is reasonably necessary to develop the minerals, regardless of damage.

THE CONSERVATION MOVEMENT

The many frauds which were practiced under the early land laws led to growing public demands that something be done to stop the plundering of the public domain. In response to these demands, Congress has adopted numerous measures to retain, preserve, and develop resources under public control. The principal actions taken will be summarized in the following paragraphs.

1. Natural resources of great value have been retained in the public domain by the creation of national parks and monuments. The creation of Yellowstone National Park in 1872 established the principle of reserving important areas for the nation as a whole. Altogether, twenty-eight national parks have now been created by special acts of Congress.

In 1906 Congress passed the Act for the Preservation of American Antiquities. By the terms of this legislation, the President, by proclamation, is authorized to establish as national monuments any areas in the public domain which contain historic landmarks or objects of scientific interest. Eighty-five national monuments thus far have been created. National parks and national monuments are administered by the National Park Service. At the present time, more than 20 million acres of the public domain have been reserved under the National Park Service.[14]

2. In 1891 Congress enacted a law stating that the President of the United States could set aside, from time to time, public reservations of timberland from the public domain. Upon the basis of this legislation, our present system of national forests has been developed. The most important withdrawals have been the following:[15]

President Harrison (1889–1892)	13,416,710 acres
President Cleveland (1893–1896)	25,686,320 acres
President McKinley (1897–1901)	7,050,089 acres
President Roosevelt (1901–1908)	148,346,925 acres
Total	194,500,044 acres

[14] Unless otherwise indicated, figures on the total number of acres in the various classes of public land reservations are from the *Task Force Report on Natural Resources*, prepared for the Commission on Organization of the Executive Branch of the Government (Washington, 1949).

[15] C. R. Van Hise, *op. cit.*, p. 215.

Some of the reserved forest land has been set aside for national parks, national monuments, and other uses, but most of it has been placed in a system of national forest reserves. The total amount of forest land in the national forests is approximately 180 million acres.

3. Under the leadership of President Theodore Roosevelt, Congress authorized a reservation to the people of 1.5 million acres of land for water-power sites, 30,000 acres of coal land, 5 million acres of phosphate land, 5 million acres of oil lands, 4 million acres of oil-shale lands, and 9 million acres of potash lands. In all, more than 200 million acres of the public domain were reserved for public use under the administration of President Roosevelt.[16]

4. The Reclamation Act of 1902 provided that money secured from the sale of public land in the West should be set aside in a reclamation fund for use in developing irrigation projects. Nearly 10 million acres of the public domain have been set aside for management and development by the Bureau of Reclamation.

5. The Water Power Act of 1920 created the Federal Power Commission and gave it authority to regulate the development of all water-power resources on navigable streams.[17] Private companies are granted licenses to develop water-power sites, but ownership of the sites is retained by the federal government in perpetuity for the people. All licenses expire at the end of fifty years, and at that time the federal government may acquire the hydroelectric plants by purchase.

6. By 1934 most of the unreserved lands of the public domain consisted of arid, semiarid, and brush lands in the West which were generally unsuited for agriculture. These lands had long been used by stockmen for the grazing of cattle and sheep, and years of unregulated use had resulted in a serious condition of overgrazing. In many areas the more valuable grasses were entirely destroyed, and widespread erosion had developed. The Taylor Grazing Act of 1934 was enacted by Congress in an effort to correct this situation. More than 132 million acres of the public domain have now been reserved in grazing districts under the Taylor Act for improvement and management by the Department of the Interior.

7. The Bankhead-Jones Farm Tenant Act of 1934 authorized the Secretary of Agriculture to acquire submarginal agriculture lands for purposes of soil conservation. Submarginal land is land which does not yield enough to pay for the expenses of cultivation. In accordance with this legislation, some 11.3 million acres have been purchased. The land so acquired is managed by the Soil Conservation Service, the Forest Service, and various other federal agencies.

8. With the development of the public domain, many wild animals and birds have had their natural habitats destroyed. Many, also, have been over-

---

[16] A. F. Gustafson, C. H. Guise, W. J. Hamilton, Jr., and H. Ries, *Conservation in the United States* (Ithaca, 1949), pp. 18–19.

[17] See also chap. 24.

hunted, and some—such as the passenger pigeon—have been completely destroyed by unrestricted hunting. In order to conserve and perpetuate our wild-life resources, numerous measures of game control have been adopted, including the creation of federal and state game refuges. At the present time, some 10 million acres of land have been reserved by special acts of Congress as federal game refuges. Federal aid is also currently being given to the states for use in establishing wild-life conservation areas. The funds for this assistance are raised from excise taxes on the sale of guns and ammunition. Authorities on wild-life conservation declare that many additional reservations are still needed to insure the survival and maintenance of many species of birds, big game, and the fur-bearing animals.[18]

PHYSICAL WASTE IN NATURAL RESOURCE UTILIZATION

The various reservations of land for purposes of national forests, national parks and monuments, reclamation projects, grazing districts, land conservation areas, and wild-life refuges help, in part, to redress the past despoiling of the public domain by large commercial interests. In addition to these measures, the federal government and many states have undertaken conservation programs to prevent soil erosion, to restore and preserve the fishery resources, to prevent forest fires, and to reforest logged-off areas. A further problem of conservation is that of preventing outright physical waste in the utilization of a resource. This problem has arisen particularly in the case of timber and oil resources.

It is estimated that about 75 percent of the commercial forest land is in private ownership, 20 percent in federal ownership, and 5 percent in state and local ownership. Forest land under private ownership is subject to regulation by the states in which the land is located. Some 19 states now regulate the use of private forest lands within their borders. The national forests are managed by the Forest Service in the Department of Agriculture, and the national park lands are administered by the Department of the Interior.

The general view of forestry authorities is that state regulation of cutting practices is quite inadequate. The state laws, it is said, are either too vague or lack provision for enforcement. As a result of inadequate regulations, a large part of the cutting operations on private forest lands is characterized by wasteful methods which leave the land unproductive (see Fig. 53). Some two-thirds of the private forest lands, it is estimated, are being operated without management plans for maintaining or increasing forest production.[19]

At present, there are strong demands from various labor and conservation groups for Congress to give the U.S. Forest Service a control over the cutting practices employed on private forest lands within the various states. As an alternative approach, a number of states in coöperation with industry

[18] See Ira N. Gabrielson, *Wildlife Conservation* (New York, 1941).

[19] Mid-Century Conference on Resources for the Future, "Utilization and Development of Land Resources" (Washington, 1953), Section II, p. 15.

groups are now sponsoring educational programs on sound cutting methods. It is the feeling of many that educational programs of this type and improved state regulation will provide an adequate remedy for private abuses and wasteful methods without federal regulation.

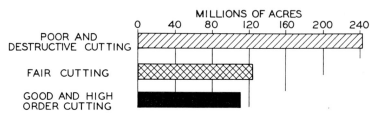

Fig. 53. Present cutting practices on U.S. commercial forest acreage. U.S. Forest Service officials report that cutting practices on most private forest lands are "poor." This means that cutting practices are employed which leave the land unproductive. Young trees are destroyed in the logging process, seed trees are cut or otherwise destroyed, and little or no effort is made to replant the cut-over area. Frequently the land is left covered with debris which constitutes a serious fire hazard. "Good" cutting practices mean that timber is cut and the forest land is administered so that forest trees will reproduce themselves. The goal is a "sustained yield" of forest products. (Source: President's Materials Policy Commission, Resources for Freedom, June 1952, Vol. 1, p. 43.)

FEDERAL SUSTAINED-YIELD LEGISLATION

In an effort to encourage the use of sustained-yield methods of forestry, Congress in 1944 enacted Public Law 273 (16 U.S.C. 583), which is known as the "Sustained-Yield Law." Its purpose, the title states, is to promote sustained-yield forest management in order "(a) to stabilize communities, forest industries, employment, and taxable forest wealth; (b) to assure a continuous and ample supply of forest products; and (c) to secure the benefits of forests in regulation of water supply and stream flow, prevention of soil erosion, amelioration of climate, and preservation of wildlife."

Section 2 of the legislation provides that the Secretary of Agriculture or the Secretary of the Interior is authorized to enter into coöperative sustained-yield agreements with owners of private forest lands by which privately owned and federal forest lands are combined into "sustained-yield units." In agreeing to manage his forest land on a sustained-yield basis, a private owner is privileged to purchase the contiguous federal timber which is included in the sustained-yield unit. The owner, in turn, places all his included lands under the direct supervision of the Secretary of Agriculture or Interior as the case may be. By 1954, only one sustained-yield agreement had been made under the provisions of Section 2. This project is located on the Olympic Peninsula in the state of Washington, and the parties to the agreement are the Forest Service and the Simpson Logging Company.

Some small-scale operators in the forest industries are very much opposed to the provisions and application of Section 2. First, it is said, this part of the law provides no standard or guide for the federal agencies to use in making contracts with private operators. Vast areas of federal land, it is said, may be set aside in sustained-yield units for the exclusive use of particular private coöperators. In principle, critics declare, the Secretary of Agriculture or the Secretary of the Interior could make an agreement with *a single* operator to purchase and use timber on *all* federal lands *forever*.

Secondly, it is said that the provisions of Section 2 are unsound because they exclude potential competitors from the purchase and use of federally owned timber resources. Sustained-yield operations normally extend over a period of 100 years or more. During this period of time, private operators who enter into the agreements have the exclusive right to buy and utilize federally owned timber included within the sustained-yield unit. Such operators are thus given the privilege of an assured supply of timber for long periods of time, without the expense of taxes, carrying charges, or fire prevention. Under coöperative agreements, moreover, public timber must be sold at appraised prices rather than by competitive bidding.

The reports of the Forest Service (Department of Agriculture) and the Bureau of Land Management (Department of the Interior) indicate that these agencies realize fully their responsibility in administering the law. Each agency has been leaning over backward (1) in limiting the amount of federal forest land which may be allocated to any single owner and (2) in reserving other timber for sale at competitive bidding. The standards they have established to minimize the tendency toward one-company towns and local vertical monopolies, in fact, have been a factor limiting the application of the sustained-yield legislation. A second factor has been the unwillingness of some large operators to place their forest lands under the direct supervision of the federal government. A final factor has been the strong opposition to Section 2 of many small-scale logging companies who are unwilling to see tracts of federal timber set aside for the exclusive use of a particular co-operator.

Whether or not the federal government should enter into a long-term contract with an individual company or group of companies to work out a coöperative sustained-yield program is a matter of policy. Congress in enacting Public Law 273 came to the conclusion that the advantages of sustained-yield operations outweigh their disadvantages. Thus far, neither Congress nor any one of the state legislatures has been willing to carry regulation of private cutting to the point of requiring sustained-yield management.

Section 3 of Public Law 273 provides for the creation of sustained-yield units consisting entirely of federal forest lands which are to be managed for the benefit of communities primarily dependent upon timber. By 1954 five sustained-yield units had been established under Section 3. These are as follows: Vallecitos Unit, New Mexico; Flagstaff Unit, Arizona; Grays Harbor Unit, Washington; Big Valley Unit, California; and the Lakeview Unit, Oregon. Federal sustained-yield units are favored by independent forest operators provided the timber is sold competitively to industries located within the area to be stabilized. Section 4 of the law provides further that the Secretaries of Agriculture and Interior may enter into coöperative agreements with each other or with any federal *or state* agency having jurisdiction over forest land. The formation of such units is also generally favored by industry, provided the permissible annual cut of timber is sold by competitive bidding.

PHYSICAL WASTE IN THE PETROLEUM INDUSTRY

Problems of physical waste are also found in the production of petroleum (oil and gas). In order to explain the measures which have been adopted to prevent a wastage of oil and gas, we shall first examine the conflict existing between our land laws and the facts of geology. Petroleum is found in underground pools or reservoirs which consist of a mixture of oil and gas and usually water (see Table 18). The pools are of variable extent and typically underlie the land surface controlled by numerous owners. When a well is drilled into the pool, a low-pressure point is created, and oil and gas are drawn into the well without regard to the lines which mark the surface boundaries.

The general rule applied by the courts to the ownership of oil and gas is that of the "law or rule of capture." This rule means that the owner of a tract of land surface acquires title to all the oil or gas secured from wells on his land, even though a part or all of the oil or gas migrates from the reservoir under adjoining lands.[20] The rule of capture was developed years ago by the courts as a matter of convenience and expediency, on the finding that the underground migration of oil could not be accurately measured or traced, much less be blocked off. The courts took the view that a surface owner was entitled to keep whatever amount was secured from wells on his land.

What can an owner do to prevent the oil or gas which is under his land from coming under another's control? In answering this question, the courts developed the rule of "offset drilling." Since, it was reasoned, underground movements of oil and gas cannot be traced, adjoining land surface owners must find protection in drilling offsetting wells on their own tracts in an effort to get a share of the oil or gas. Thus, the Supreme Court of Pennsylvania, in the *Barnard* case of 1907, declared: "What, then, can the neighbor do? Nothing; only go and do likewise. He must protect his own oil and gas. He knows it is wild and will run away if it finds an opening and it is his business to keep it at home. *This may not be the best rule; but neither the Legislature nor our highest court has given us any better.*"[21]

SOME CONSEQUENCES OF THE LAW OF CAPTURE

As a result of the court-made "law of capture" and the "go-and-do-likewise" rule, each surface owner was impelled to drill as many wells as possible

[20] Robert E. Hardwicke, "The Rule of Capture and Its Implications as Applied to Oil and Gas," *Texas Law Review*, June, 1935, pp. 391–422.

[21] *Barnard* v. *Monongahela Natural Gas Co.*, 65 Atl. 801, 802 (1907). Italics supplied.

to get the oil and gas before someone else could get it. Large supplies of oil were accordingly produced and offered for sale without regard to waste or to prices; unnecessary wells were dug; much oil was wasted on the ground because of inadequate storage facilities; and large quantities of natural gas were blown off into the air as total waste. It is estimated that, with a proper control of pressure in an oil reservoir, oil wells can be made to flow over a long period of years, yielding in many instances from 80 to 90 percent of the oil originally in place. As a result of the unregulated methods employed in the United States prior to about 1930, however, from 75 to 90 percent of the oil was left underground in most fields. Even with the improved methods of control which have been increasingly adopted in recent years, it was believed as late as 13 years ago that in most fields from 55 to 60 percent of the oil was left unrecovered.[22] In recent years, reports indicate, the percentage of recovery has been materially increasing.

PRODUCTION CONTROL IN THE OIL INDUSTRY

In an effort to prevent the many evils resulting from the "rule of capture" and the "go-and-do-likewise" rule, most states and the federal government have enacted various statutes to regulate the way in which oil reservoirs are produced.

Nearly all the principal oil-producing states have established petroleum commissions with power to limit the production of oil and gas. In exercising this control, the commissions usually determine (1) the daily allowable production for each field and (2) the daily quota for each well or unit area. In the case of old or stripper fields, with small average daily production per well, the state authorities usually set a blanket quota for an entire field which represents the maximum amount it can produce, for it is a near-marginal affair with no need for production control.

In establishing state-wide output quotas, a state agency may consider the monthly forecasts or estimates of "market demand" which are prepared by the Bureau of Mines (U.S. Department of the Interior). This agency has been preparing such estimates since 1935. These are forecasts of the amount of production in various states or areas that will be needed to supply current consumptive uses, considering probable imports, withdrawals from storage, and other factors. There is no legal compulsion for a state agency to follow the forecasts or estimates of the Bureau of Mines, and frequently a commission arrives at an entirely different decision.

The estimate supplied to each state agency by the Bureau of Mines is only a part of the evidence considered by a state commission in regulating production. The "nominations" of the purchasers of crude oil, representing their views of the amounts they need for current use and are willing to buy over the next period—usually one month—are also considered by some of

[22] H. C. Miller and G. B. Shea, "Gains in Oil and Gas Production, Refining, and Utilization Technology," Technical Paper 3, National Resources Planning Board (Washington, 1941), pp. 1, 5–9.

the state commissions as a factor in market demand. Increases and decreases in above-ground storage are another important factor in the decision reached. In the view of the state commissions, if the storage of oil that was produced from a particular state or area is materially increasing, the production allowable is too high. The demand is less than the production. If the storage is decreasing below proper levels, on the other hand, more production is needed. Production control exercised in relation to the estimates of the Bureau of Mines, the nominations of purchasers, and the stocks of oil and products in storage is a control exercised to prevent production in excess of "market demand" and to prevent physical waste.

FEDERAL INTERVENTION IN PRODUCTION CONTROL

In order to strengthen the control exercised by the states, the federal government enacted the Connally "Hot Oil" Act of 1935. Hot oil is that produced, or withdrawn from storage, in excess of valid orders of the state. The act of 1935 prohibits the use of interstate commerce facilities in moving illegally produced oil or oil withdrawn from storage in excess of state regulations. The act also provides for the forfeiture to the federal government of the oil so shipped. In actual practice, the custom has been to proceed against violators by means of criminal proceedings. Administration of the Connally Act is under the Department of the Interior, but enforcement is handled by the Department of Justice, through local federal district attorneys or special assistants.

The Connally Act provides that the President may suspend its operation whenever he finds that the amount of petroleum and petroleum products moving in interstate commerce is so limited as to result in "an undue burden on or restriction of interstate commerce." Although the President's Office has been called upon to suspend the operation of the act in the interest of consumers, it has thus far taken no action to interfere with the control exercised by the states.

MARKET DEMAND AS A STANDARD
FOR CONTROLLING OUTPUT

Since a considerable part of the petroleum output is controlled to conform to "reasonable market demand," it is important to consider the meaning of this term. In an economic sense, market demand means the amount, or number of units, which will be taken at a given price. Critics of the state programs point out that to the extent that market demand is used as a guide in curbing output, the Bureau of Mines and the state agencies must necessarily take into account the amounts which it is believed can be sold *at given prices*. They further point out that there is substantial evidence to indicate that the prices for petroleum products are "administered" or "managed" prices, established by "price leaders." In part, therefore, it is said, the control plan exercised in petroleum is one in which the state and federal governments limit oil production to the outputs which the large refiners can sell at managed prices. Although state control of production undoubtedly does result in preventing physical waste, its concomitant purpose is said to be economic.[23]

Advocates of market-demand limitation, on the other hand, maintain that limitation of production to reasonable current needs is an effective way to prevent physical waste that always results when production materially exceeds the current consumptive needs. Such limitation is also a reasonable and effective way to protect the rights of owners of oil and gas lands, giving each the opportunity to produce and market his share of the common supply. The basic and principal purpose of state regulation, they contend, is conservation. In the words of Robert E. Hardwicke, "The limitation of the production of oil so that it will not exceed the reasonable market demand in substantial amounts for an extended period is a practical and necessary method of preventing physical waste and protecting correlative rights. It increases the ultimate recovery of oil and gas, thereby providing more not less for trade and commerce. . . . The reasonable market demand statutes and the restrictions contemplated thereby are clearly necessary to prevent physical waste, whether or not that element is necessary to their validity."[24]

In *Parker* v. *Brown*, 317 U.S. 341, 350–351 (1943), the Supreme Court held that a plan for restricting the marketing of raisins, directed and required by a state government, for the expressed purpose of reducing competition and maintaining prices, is not in violation of federal antitrust laws, as the regulation is accomplished by command of the state, not by agreement of private persons. Said Chief Justice Stone, "We find nothing in the language of the Sherman Act . . . which suggests that its purpose was to restrain a state or its officers or agents from activities directed by its legislature. . . . The Sherman Act makes no mention of the state, as such, and gives no hint that it was intended to restrain state action or official action directed by a state." Since the restriction of oil production is accomplished by statutory power, not by voluntary agreements of producers, compliance with orders controlling production does not violate antitrust laws.[25]

UNITARY OPERATION AS A REMEDY FOR PHYSICAL WASTE IN THE OIL INDUSTRY

Many petroleum authorities declare that our efforts to control physical waste in oil production have not been so effective as they might have been.

---

[23] George W. Stocking, "Stabilization of the Oil Industry: Its Economic and Legal Aspects," *American Economic Review, Papers and Proceedings*, March, 1933, pp. 55–70; and E. V. Rostow, *A National Policy for the Oil Industry* (New Haven, 1948), pp. 70–87.

[24] Robert E. Hardwicke, "Antitrust Laws and the Conservation of Oil and Gas," *Tulane Law Review*, December, 1948, pp. 198–199.

[25] Robert E. Hardwicke, "Antitrust Laws and the Conservation of Oil and Gas," *Tulane Law Review*, December, 1948, pp. 183–208; also *Antitrust Laws, et al. v. Unit Operation of Oil or Gas Pools* (New York, 1948), pp. 169–173.

What additional remedy can be utilized? The proposal recommended is that of "unitary operation," or "unit operations." By this method, an oil reservoir is treated as a single entity and operated without regard to property lines, as if owned by one person. Usually the operator is responsible to a committee on which all royalty owners and lessees are represented. Each royalty owner and lessee receives a share of the oil and gas produced. In most instances, unit operation of an oil reservoir makes it possible to secure the maximum recovery of oil and gas at the lowest possible cost. A minimum number of wells needs to be drilled; the wells can be properly located; and gas reserves can be conserved by reinjection into the reservoir, if that is a practical and proper practice under the prevailing, individual conditions.

Although most engineers and many economists and lawyers have advocated the use of unit operations, it is doubtful that the method has been adopted as widely as it should have been. The Mineral Leasing Act provides for the unitization of federal oil resources, and unit plans have largely been formed in conjunction with the use of federal land. Mr. C. E. Hinkle, a legal expert on unit operations, states, "The Department of the Interior has been the foremost advocate of unitization, and most unit plans have revolved around the federal laws and regulations rather than the laws and regulations of any particular state."[26]

What explanation can be given for the unwillingness of private owners to adopt, and of states to require, the unit operation of oil pools? One factor, undoubtedly, is ignorance and misunderstanding. Many people apparently fail to realize the long-run advantages to be secured from unitized operations. In some cases, failure to unitize operations is to be explained by the selfishness of certain producers. Another factor which has retarded the use of unit operations by voluntary agreement is the fact that nearly all the owners must coöperate in making a pooling arrangement, if it is to be successful. Much time and money are required to secure agreements from all the surface owners, and not infrequently the adoption of unit plans is prevented by the complete unwillingness of a few parties to coöperate. It is sometimes said that producers have been unwilling to participate in voluntary agreements for unit operations because of possible antitrust prosecution. This has prompted the legislatures in several states to pass statutes under which unit operation would be brought about by orders of a state agency. The fear of possible prosecution has also prompted legislation authorizing some administrative agency or some official to approve *voluntary* agreements, and thereby remove any question of violation of antitrust laws. The constitutionality of the Oklahoma Compulsory Unitization Law has been upheld.[27] A state may therefore, by a proper statute, now compel unitization as a conservation measure.

[26] C. E. Hinkle, "Some Legal Aspects of the Unitization of Federal, State, and Fee Lands," *Montana Law Review*, Spring, 1953, p. 50.
[27] *Palmer Oil Corp.* v. *Amerada Petroleum Corp.*, 343 U.S. 390 (1952).

FEDERAL VERSUS STATE REGULATION
OF NATURAL RESOURCES

Oil, gas, and lumber producers, as well as political leaders in states with such resources, are typically much opposed to the exercise of conservation measures by the federal government on private lands or on public lands of the states. Instead of federal regulation, it is believed that the states themselves should regulate the use of resources within their borders. The principal arguments in favor of state regulation, as presented by industry groups in oil, gas, and lumber, and by various state officials, are shown in the left-hand column. Arguments in favor of federal regulation, advanced mainly by civic, labor, and congressional leaders interested in problems of conservation, are shown in the right-hand column.

Arguments for State Regulation of Natural Resources	Arguments for Federal Regulation of Natural Resources
1. State regulatory agencies are better acquainted with the local problems which require regulation. Federal commissions in Washington, D.C., are far removed from the site of operations and make for delay, uncertainty, and added cost in the handling of administrative matters. Planning by private operators is made most difficult.	1. State regulatory agencies frequently do not have the personnel, funds, or facilities for exercising effective regulation. All federal regulatory activity must of necessity be conducted at a distance from the site of operations. Local and regional offices and local advisory committees help to overcome the distance factor.
2. The regulation of productive activity in accordance with conservation practices has been exercised by state governments for more than twenty-five years. Although state administration may have been inadequate in the early years, it has constantly been improved with experience and education.	2. The federal government has been engaged in extensive conservation programs—forests, wild life, and scenic areas—for more than fifty years. The fact that state governments have not gone further in requiring the sustained-yield development of forest resources and the unitary development of oil reservoirs points unmistakably to the need for federal intervention.
3. Federal regulation imposes many obligations which most private operators consider to be unnecessary and unreasonable. State regulation is much less restrictive and provides for greater flexibility. Private enterprisers are given more freedom to explore and develop natural resources. Production is stimulated and a rapid discovery of natural resources is promoted.	3. Conservation measures are more actively sponsored and applied by the federal government. Experience shows that private operators are eager to get federal leases even with their more restrictive provisions.

4. Great centralization of power in the federal government increases the possibility of autocratic, arbitrary control. If we wish to preserve democracy and a free way of life, we must maintain a decentralization of political power as contemplated in our federal-state system of government. Governmental power must be made responsive to the local communities which it serves.

4. Citizens in all the forty-eight states are materially affected by the wasteful or the wise use of oil, forest, and land resources, whether or not they are owned privately or by the state and federal governments. The extension and growth of centralized power in the federal government are the responses to the national scope of these problems.

The problem of federal versus state regulation of the use of natural resources—particularly the forest and oil resources—promises to be an issue of increasing importance in Congress, as well as in the legislatures of the several states. There is evidence to indicate that the regulations on resource utilization exercised by various states fail to make adequate provision for conservation. At the present time, cutting practices on many private forest lands continue to be "poor." Progress continues in the prevention of waste of both gas and oil. The production of petroleum in many situations, however, still involves the drilling of unnecessary wells and the wastage of much gas. If the extension of federal control is to be avoided, it would appear that citizens generally will need to take a greater interest in the utilization of resources located in their respective communities. It is also possible that regulatory procedures can be developed by which both the state and federal interests can be represented and harmonized.

RESTRICTIVE TARIFFS AND THE CONSERVATION OF EXHAUSTIBLE RESOURCES

To an increasing degree, the United States is coming to depend upon foreign supplies of minerals. At present, for example, we produce only a part of our requirements of a wide variety of items: iron ore (93%), petroleum (88%), zinc (78%), copper (69%), lead (48%), bauxite (33%), mercury (15%), manganese (4%), and mica (1%). In the case of many primary materials, we have virtually no production at all. These include chrome, tin, cobalt, nickel, graphite, quartz crystals, tantalum, platinum, industrial diamonds, and asbestos. Out of 38 principal industrial minerals it is estimated that the United States produces only 9 in quantities sufficient to meet our needs.

What commercial policy should the United States pursue with respect to the importation of minerals? Should there be an elimination of all tariffs and other impediments on imports? Or, should the present restrictive tariffs on many critical items be maintained or even increased?

Advocates of high tariffs declare that restrictions should be placed on the importation of minerals in order (1) to encourage the development of mining and oil production and (2) to protect established domestic producers from the output of newer countries. Foreign products, they say, should not be imported to the extent that they would materially weaken the domestic industry and retard the discovery of new resources. Abundant domestic capacity, it is emphasized, should be available in case of an emergency.

Experience has shown that the placing of restrictive tariffs on such products as manganese, mercury, tungsten, copper, and lead has not brought about the development of new supplies. In a careful study of this problem as to these materials, the National Resources Board concluded, "The encouragement of tariffs has not greatly aided exploration, discovery, and research; on the contrary, the stimulus of a protected market of uncertain duration has merely accelerated the depletion of the few high-grade deposits we have at a time when consideration for national defense requires that such limited supplies be conserved for emergency use."[28]

At the present time, the United States has protective tariffs on the importation of a wide variety of highly critical minerals. In many instances, the domestic reserves of these materials are scarce. The protected minerals include barium, boron, bauxite, bismuth, copper, fluorspar, graphite, lead, magnesium, manganese, mercury, mica, molybdenum, petroleum, strontium, thorium, titanium, tungsten, uranium, vanadium, and zinc. The *Buy American Act of 1933* also imposes restraints on the importation of minerals. This legislation requires the government and suppliers on government contracts to purchase domestically produced materials unless the domestic cost is "unreasonable" or the product is not obtainable in the United States in adequate quantity or quality. "Unreasonable cost" has been interpreted to mean a cost more than 25 percent above the delivered cost of foreign materials.

In the near future, as domestic mining and oil companies are forced to utilize thinner beds, leaner ores, and poorer wells, and to extend their shafts to greater depths, it is likely that demands will be made for an even greater amount of tariff protection. Tariffs on nonrenewable resources mean their more rapid exhaustion; and if the people are really interested in conservation, they will strongly resist all such efforts. The depletion of domestic mineral resources also makes our nation more vulnerable in the event of war, for it means that we shall be dependent upon foreign or water-borne supplies.

The Paley Commission in its report *Resources for Freedom* (1952) recommends the enactment of permanent legislation "authorizing unilateral elimination of import duty on any industrial material in either crude or refined form whenever it is determined that the United States is, or is expected to become, substantially dependent on imports of the material, and that such action is in accord with the national interest." It also recommends the outright repeal of the *Buy American Act*.[29] Other authorities believe that there should be a complete elimination of all protection to the domestic producers of ex-

---

[28] National Resources Board, *Report of the Planning Committee for Mineral Policy* (Washington, 1934), Part 4, p. 416.
[29] The President's Materials Policy Commission, *Resources for Freedom* (1952), Vol. 1, p. 79.

haustible natural resources.[30] In their view, the adoption of stock-piling measures for strategic minerals and the maintenance of tariff-protected oil and mining industries are forms of government intervention which must find their justification in military expediency rather than in economic wisdom.

THE BASIC IMPORTANCE OF A CONSERVATION PROGRAM

The adoption of a consistent conservation program by government is an essential condition for maintaining and increasing the real income of our nation. Fertile soil, large stands of timber, productive fisheries, and plentiful supplies of minerals provide the very foundation for our economic life. In order to preserve and maintain the basic elements of our economic strength, government has the highly important tasks (1) of managing our public resources to provide for their efficient use and development and (2) of providing rules for the use of privately owned resources, so as to secure sustained yields of forest products, the adoption of soil-conserving practices, and the efficient utilization of mineral deposits.

In the case of inorganic, or nonrenewable, resources, such as oil, coal, iron, copper, lead, and zinc, the term "conservation" is used to mean (1) prevention of waste *and* sparing use in order to delay inevitable exhaustion *or* (2) simply prevention of outright physical waste. As applied to renewable resources, such as fisheries, timber, fertile soil, and grasslands, conservation means the use of resources in a way which will insure continued renewal.

Some authorities disagree vigorously with the idea that it is good public policy to provide that nonrenewable resources shall be used sparingly so that future generations may enjoy their benefits. Why should the owner of oil lands, it is said, forego a reasonable present use on the theory that his grandchildren might need some of the oil? Other authorities believe that national interests demand that thought be given for tomorrow. Since most landowners have a high preference for present income, it appears that it will largely be up to the government to buy and hold reserves of nonrenewable resources for future generations, if such is to be done at all.

Conservation measures have their greatest potential in the case of renewable resources. In this area, it is possible for government to aid in restoring, maintaining, and increasing the supply of most of the essential means of living. Forest areas can be made to yield sustained outputs; fishery resources can be rebuilt; and large areas of land can be made more productive by drainage, irrigation, and the use of soil-conserving practices. The population of the world needs more and better food, clothing, and basic commodities such as hides, fats, cotton, wool, linen, vegetable oils, and wood products. Through the exportation of renewable resources it may be possible for the United States to secure many of the minerals which we shall increasingly need from abroad in order to maintain our great industrial economy.

---

[30] Mid-Century Conference on Resources for the Future, "U.S. Concern with World Resources" (Washington, 1953), Section VI, pp. 16–17.

SUGGESTIONS FOR FURTHER READING

Bennett, Hugh H., *Soil Conservation* (New York, 1939).

Davis, Joseph S., "The Population Upsurge and the American Economy, 1945–1980," *Journal of Political Economy*, October, 1953, pp. 369–388.

Hardwicke, Robert E., "Antitrust Laws and the Conservation of Oil and Gas," *Tulane Law Review*, December, 1948, pp. 183–208; and "Adequacy of Our Mineral Fuels," *Annals of the American Academy of Political and Social Science*, May, 1952, pp. 55–72.

Johnson, V. Webster, and Barlow, Raleigh, *Land Problems and Policies* (New York, 1954).

McKinley, Charles, *Uncle Sam in the Pacific Northwest* (Berkeley, 1952).

Mid-Century Conference on Resources for the Future, *Proceedings, 1953,* (Washington).

Moulton, H. G., *Controlling Factors in Economic Development* (Washington, 1951).

Ordway, S. H., *Resources and the American Dream* (New York, 1953).

President's Materials Policy Commission, *Resources for Freedom* (Washington, 1952), Vols. 1–5.

Wooten, Hugh H. *Major Uses of Land in the United States,* United States Department of Agriculture, Technical Bulletin 1082 (Washington, 1954).

Woytinsky, W. S. and E. S., *World Population and Production* (New York, 1953).

Zimmermann, Erich W., *World Resources and Industries* (New York, 1951).

CHAPTER 29

The Optimum Adjustment of Government to Business

In concluding our study of the many ways in which business and economic life are shaped and directed by government, we come face to face with the problem of the optimum amount of government in business. A large amount of historical experience points, on the one hand, to the fallacy of "the law of the jungle"—that is, business rivalry which admits no rules of fair play and in which only the strongest and most ruthless survive. On the other hand, there is a growing amount of evidence which points to the futility of the "law of the jail"—namely, widespread authoritarian control with restrictions on free choice and initiative and with a multitude of regulations which invite evasion and disregard for the law.

The negative doctrine of a minimum amount of government intervention in business has been abundantly proved by experience to be fallacious. When business is left alone to do as it pleases, it invariably develops all sorts of monopolistic devices to exclude competitors, curb production, and enhance the prices charged consumers. At the other extreme, too much government in business restricts freedom of choice and initiative. It means a stifling of individual enterprise with its emphasis on efficiency, economy, vigorous selling, and imaginative planning. Too much government also carries with it the evils of centralized administration (bureaucracy). These include (1) an unresponsiveness of employees in dealing with the public, (2) cumbersome and irritating rules, and (3) the tendency of bureau chiefs to spend time in expanding their own importance. Finally, substantial intervention in the form of direct control over prices, wages, and output, provides a means and a temptation for private groups to influence governmental policy in their own behalf.

In some sectors of the economy, the federal and state governments have adopted commission control or public ownership in an effort to secure fair prices and incomes and to aid in developing economic resources. It is possible that in some areas public ownership will be extended in the years ahead. In other sectors, experience indicates that regulated competition can be made a workable method for directing production and determining prices and incomes, if ample appropriations and an intelligent administration of the antitrust laws are provided. Our experience with antitrust law enforcement shows that the policy of maintaining competition requires much more government intervention than Congress and the courts have thought to be necessary. The alternative of public price and output control by commissions, however, requires an even greater application of government to business.

What the optimum adjustment of government to business is—or should be —will vary from time to time and from industry to industry as conditions change and emergent needs arise. As in the recipe of an experienced cook, there should be "enough and not too much." Government is an indispensable instrument of control, and the basic rule for its application should be that of promoting "the greatest good of the greatest number."

REASONS FOR THE INCREASE IN GOVERNMENT INTERVENTION

At the present time, large corporate mergers, with considerable degrees of monopoly power, have come to dominate the principal fields of business. This condition—directly and indirectly—has called forth a greatly increased application of government to business. Many new federal commissions have been established to exercise direct control in areas in which monopoly has been accepted. Government intervention—in the form of minimum wages, "parity" prices, and enforced collective bargaining—moreover, has been extended to numerous lines of activity which have been disadvantaged as a result of monopolistic control in other segments of industry. A management of prices to enhance business income usually involves a curbing of production; and artificial restraints on production have been an important factor in causing the rise of unemployment which persists year after year, except during periods of vast public spending. The problem of persistent (chronic) unemployment, in turn, has brought forth need for further applications of government to business.

In the United States, in particular, many people are dismayed and alarmed by the growing intervention of government in business. It is a trend, however, which will probably strengthen in the years ahead. A few thousand corporations largely dominate the various industries. The leading corporations, moreover, are getting larger through acquisitions, the creation of subsidiaries, and the building of branch plants. Our economic history shows that big business has called forth big government to curb its abuses. It is unlikely that concentrated governmental power over business can be—or will be—diminished until concentrated economic power is lessened or reduced. The really important question about "big government" is whether the power will be used (a) to provide the essential conditions for competition or (b) to inaugurate a program of direct control.

Government reports are filled with factual information demonstrating that a large part of our present economic ills are traceable to the concentration of economic power in the hands of a few corporations in each industry. These reports and the records in court cases provide sad commentaries on the way in which many corporate giants have utilized the economic power in their hands to practice price fixing, discriminations, boycotts, elimination of competitors, and the like. It is because of the record of such abuse of economic power that there is today the hue and cry for antimonopoly action.

ALTERNATE POLICIES TOWARD PRIVATE PROPERTY AND PRIVATE ENTERPRISE

Experience has shown that a policy of "self-government" in business cannot be relied upon to provide fair prices and full employment. In the view of many economists and legal authorities, government must either (1) maintain the policy of price competition or (2) undertake directly to fix the prices which are managed by large industrial combinations. General William J. Donovan, a leading corporation lawyer in New York City, has stated the problem as follows:

> Those who would remove the inhibitions of existing law must recognize that the alternative is not between the Sherman Act on the one hand and the regulation of industry by industry on the other. The alternative is between the continuance of the competitive system as a proper safeguard to the public, and the closest supervision and control of industry by the Government. The self-interest of business in such matters would often be antagonistic to the interest of the public as a whole. The recent experience under the N.R.A. shows the abuses that may arise by vesting in business the power of self-regulation without at the same time providing for adequate and capable supervision and control by a governmental agency.[1]

Numerous economic and legal authorities also agree that any extension of public price fixing to the basic industries would place an impossible task upon governmental agencies. At best, we have seen, administrative regulation of private monopoly power is a means of control for only a few limited fields—such as transportation, electric utilities, and related industries in which price competition is not feasible. It follows that if we are to avoid succumbing to private monopoly power we shall need to reduce the present extent of monopoly control in industry through a dissolution of the larger financial mergers. This we have never really tried, except in a very limited way.

THE GENERAL PREVALENCE OF MONOPOLY CONTROL

Many people continue to look upon and describe our present system of price and output determination in industry as a "free market" economy. "Markets," it is said, are buyers and sellers; and "market prices" are simply prices on which buyers and sellers "get together." The fact, moreover, that there are several sellers actively soliciting a customer's business, even though at identical delivered prices, is said to provide "competitive" market prices. Such descriptions of "markets," "market prices," and "competitive market prices," we have seen in the course of our present study, are incomplete and inaccurate concepts which have no basis in economics or the law.

[1] William J. Donovan, address before the Commerce Committee of the American Bar Association, Boston, Mass., August 26, 1936, p. 15.

Frequently it is said that the presence of substitute products means that there is no monopoly in a given industry. Substitute competition, in fact, is hailed as the "new competition." The experience of many centuries, however, is that substitute competition does not, in itself, provide adequate protection against extortion. Private monopoly is never an absolute power to set any price desired. At all times, there are limits to "what the traffic will bear." Even so, moderate price increases may be very profitable to sellers and highly burdensome to the public. It is for this reason that legislative bodies have found it necessary to enact statutes against monopolistic conduct among sellers (or among buyers) *within* a given industry.

Many eminent economists have recognized that the concentration of economic power in the hands of a few in each of our important industries has led to the advent and maintenance of "administered prices." In a study of industrial prices made in 1938, Dr. Edwin G. Nourse and H. B. Drury concluded that in important areas the pricing of our industrial products is no longer accomplished in the process of sale by "the unseen hand." No longer is it true that "the market is the birthplace of prices." Instead, "the office of the industrial executive has now become the center of significant action." Today, an executive "sets a price objective and directs a controlled productive mechanism toward attainment of that price level." Thereupon, "If goods do not sell at this price, two courses are open. One is to intensify promotional effort. This in essence means stimulating demand, a procedure which itself adds further to costs and works only within the limits set by consumers' purchasing power. The other is to curtail supply."[2]

Other authorities, including Edward H. Chamberlin, C. D. Edwards, Joan Robinson, Clair Wilcox, George Stigler, and G. W. Stocking, point out that when a small group of sellers make up an industry, coördination, and in fact, concert of action are not only possible but expected, even though the course of action rests only upon quasi understandings. Large firms may be capable of holding small business units in line with noncompetitive price behavior by punishing violators economically, chiefly by discriminatory pricing and by refusing to sell essential supplies. If the small business firms recognize the probability and go along, the result is noncompetitive price fixing. In each of these instances, the present antitrust laws do not afford much opportunity of relief for the public interest or for the small business firms.

WHY DO BUSINESS ENTERPRISERS SEEK MONOPOLY POWER?

Although private monopoly power has stood condemned in the law and in economics from earliest times, it still continues to be actively and earnestly sought by many businessmen who are honest and upright citizens. How is this anomaly to be explained? The purpose of a business enterprise, we have seen, is the making of profit; and since monopolistic selling brings in more

[2] Edwin G. Nourse and H. B. Drury, *Industrial Price Policies and Economic Progress* (Washington, 1938), p. 256.

profit, some businessmen are led to identify monopolistic action with sound business policy.

After many years of service as an economist in the Department of Justice, Dr. George P. Comer observed that monopolies are formed

> not because business-men are criminals, but because the reports from the bookkeeping department indicate, in the short run at least, that monopoly and restraints of trade will pay if you can get away with it. It will pay a large corporation to agree with its competitors on price fixing. It pays to operate a basing-point or zone-price system. If patent pools can be organized, especially with hundreds or thousands of patents covering a whole industry, the profits will be enormous. If an international cartel can be formed which really works, the very peak of stabilization and rationalism is reached. If the management of all the large units in an industry can get together with the labor unions in the industry, a number of birds can be killed with one stone. And finally, if the government can be persuaded to legalize the restrictive practices, the theory of "enlightened competition" is complete.[3]

It is sometimes said that businessmen adopt "coöperative pricing" because price competition tends to become cutthroat and chaotic. Discriminatory price cutting is employed primarily by large multiple-plant firms operating in several sales areas. Such concerns are in a position to cut prices in one area while maintaining them elsewhere, and the resulting competition on price may prove to be highly unstable. It is doubtless this sort of condition which causes some businessmen and trade association executives to declare that "competition is war and war is hell," and to urge that coöperation on price be adopted in lieu of senseless competition. The fact of the matter is, however, that discriminatory pricing is a monopolistic type of competition. It is not the uniform, aboveboard type of price competition found in central and primary markets. If geographic price discrimination were completely outlawed, the claim of various business leaders that competition is inherently chaotic and destructive would largely lose its validity.

SOME ECONOMIC CONSEQUENCES OF PRIVATE MONOPOLY

1. *Monopoly Promotes Artificial Scarcity and Economic Stagnation.* The fact that monopoly enables a unified group to secure higher prices and incomes makes it seem to some businessmen like a desirable method for determining prices. This, however, is only one side of the coin. On the other side, as the inevitable concomitant of monopoly, is the fact that production is curbed to secure the higher prices. Higher prices and incomes do not just come naturally by coöperation. Supply must be restricted in order to enhance scarcity and thus to force prices to the higher levels of buyers' valuations. Monopoly, therefore, means the creation of artificial scarcity. It also means lower levels of real income for the masses of people.

[3] George P. Comer, "The Outlook for Effective Competition," *American Economic Review, Papers and Proceedings*, May, 1946, pp. 154–155.

A buying monopoly (monopsony) makes it possible for a unified group of buyers to "put the squeeze" on price and force down buying prices without fear of being unable to buy. The complaints of farmer and labor groups on inequitable returns is to be explained, in large measure, by the existence of large industrial combinations which exercise monopoly buying power. This condition, it may be added, has been a principal factor promoting the growth of powerful labor and farm organizations to secure subsidies and monopoly favors of their own.

A further criticism of monopoly is the fact that monopolistic sellers have little or no competitive motive to reduce their prices in response to declining demand or to lower costs resulting from increases in technical efficiency. Without the stimulus of price competition, an oligopolistic group is led to maintain its prices when sales decline or when output per man-hour is increased. A unified group, moreover, may have little competitive incentive to try new methods or to introduce new products which would require a scrapping of existing equipment.

Restrictive controls in industry not only prevent the full use of resources in a given industry, but also the absorption of the displaced labor and materials into other sectors. As a result, monopolistic controls aggravate the problem of economic readjustment. In the words of A. G. B. Fisher, "It has become fashionable in many quarters in recent years to take a favourable view of 'controlled' monopoly as a factor making for 'stability,' but when we consider the immense power of monopoly influences in checking the structural adjustments necessary both for raising income levels and for assuring steady growth to an economy as a whole, the weight of the argument seems to be on the other side."[4]

2. *Monopoly Promotes Cost-Raising Methods of Doing Business.* Under conditions of effective competition, business makes profits by lowering prices to increase sales volume, by increasing efficiency to secure lower unit costs, and by producing more and better products. Although monopoly sellers may seek profits by these methods, they typically seek gains in curbing production to raise or maintain prices. At the same time, they are led to adopt "cost-raising" methods of doing business in order to stimulate and induce buying at the prices which they would like to get. In the words of Professor Viner, "The cost-raising methods of increasing profits can take the form of increased sales effort, or of false differentiation of product, promoted by advertising which may contain no useful information and some misinformation and, as in one of its notorious manifestations, may contribute to the demoralization of modern capitalism by printing in large type and blaring over the radio day-after-day statements and testimonials which everybody knows are fakes."[5] The plight of the businessman himself, selling in a regime of administered prices, is indicated in a statement made by the president of a

[4] A. G. B. Fisher, *Economic Progress and Social Security* (London, 1945), p. 81.
[5] Jacob Viner, "The Role of Costs in a System of Economic Liberalism," *Wage Determination and the Economics of Liberalism* (Washington, 1947), pp. 26–27.

leading brass and copper company: "To sell my customers I've got to have an advertising agency, a public relations firm, a direct-mail expert, charge accounts at all the restaurants, tickets for 'South Pacific,' sales analysts and boxes at Yankee Stadium and Ebbets Field. God forbid I should take a Yankee fan to a Dodger game. I'd have to go out of business. My reputation would be ruined." In the business world, it may be noted, such forms of non-price competition are sometimes called "commercial massage."

3. *Monopoly Control in General Industry Has Not Shown Public Benefits.* In manufacturing industries there is little, if any, proof that a large combination of formerly independent and competing plants gives rise to lower unit costs of production. The economies of mass production—such as a continuous utilization of specialized machines and assembly line methods of production—apply to a *single plant* rather than to a chain of mills. The economies which do arise in large business size are mainly *commercial* (not technological)—such as the power to control the flow of products from raw materials to finished products and the ability to buy supplies and secure credit more cheaply than smaller competitors. Continued study is required to determine whether or not, on balance, there are public benefits in such private advantages. In so far as monopolistic control results from large business size, arguments on the "economy" of monopoly control are largely beside the point, for competitive pressures to force such economies on to the public are weakened or nonexistent.

Many large industrial corporations maintain extensive research laboratories, and their research activities have contributed substantially to the development of new products and processes. At the same time, there are numerous giant industrial combinations which do not have a distinguished record in research progressiveness. There are few facts to indicate that research is a basic cause of extremely large company size or that monopolistic mergers are essential for leadership in the field of research. Indeed, studies in business histories lead to the conclusion that "a quiet life" rather than extraordinary innovation is frequently the road taken by monopolistic enterprise. All available evidence points to the conclusion that an indispensable condition for progressiveness in research is the maintenance of competitive pressures.

Professor J. Jewkes, an English economist, in a penetrating study of private monopoly and innovation concludes that monopolistic enterprises "look askance at revolutionary ideas" and are notably "sluggish" and "resistant" to new methods. He states, "In conditions so rapidly changing as those of the dynamic economies to which we have become accustomed in the past two centuries, the prime defects of monopoly may well have been not that they were wicked or extortionate, deliberately restrictive or blindly predatory, but simply that they were there, blocking the ground and finding it impossible to generate sufficient energy to do continually, or even to do more than once, what they had originally performed in breaking new ground, in pursuing innovations. In that sense the waste of monopoly would lie, not in depriving the community of what it now has or what it might have in the immediate future, but of what it might have in the longer future."[6]

4. *Monopoly Control Aggravates and Prolongs Depressions.*   As long as the volume of sales is expanding, as it typically is during a period of prosperity or wartime boom, the influence of monopoly on the level of employment is not immediately felt. New facilities may not be expanded to any great extent in various monopoly fields, but labor and materials are in general demand for other uses. With a strong and seemingly insatiable demand for goods at high prices, monopolistic industries are able to operate at high levels of output. It is for this reason that monopoly is sometimes called a "fair weather sailor."

It is when depression strikes that monopoly tends to promote a condition of chronic or persistent unemployment (see Fig. 54). Since consumers have reduced incomes, they can buy in volume only at low prices. Industries and trade groups having monopoly power, however, find that their maximum net profits are obtained by raising prices or by holding prices up. This action tends to check consumers' demand and to frustrate recovery. The result is a continuing condition of unused capacity and unemployment. As the Federal Trade Commission has said of the maintenance of high and inflexible prices in the steel industry, "The ability to decide on a price and hold to it regardless of demand, which is the essence of monopoly, is a prime factor in establishing the vicious circle of high prices, restricted production, and reduced employment so widely condemned as 'scarcity economics.' " And further, "High prices, not in conformity with the law of supply and demand, place unreasonable limitations on use of the material. The effect, when combined with that of similar artificial prices in many other lines of production, is a depressed condition which can be kept from utter collapse only by repeated doses of public subsidy."[7]

Persons seeking to restrict the operation of price competition in the downswing of the business cycle generally overlook the fact that price competition is *not* the *cause* of economic recession and falling sales. Price competition is rather a means by which adjustments are made to economic change. If a nation is in a business depression, a basic way to bring about expanding sales and increased employment is to allow price competition to operate freely to determine the prices and wages at which business can be done.

5. *Monopoly Makes for an Inequitable Distribution of Income.*   The monopoly principle, we have seen, means that the stronger party—the one with monopoly power—gets the better of the deal. Thus, monopoly control gives sellers the power to get the most that buyers will pay by concerted action in withholding supplies and in eliminating alternative sources of supply.

[6] J. Jewkes, "Monopoly and Economic Progress," *Economica*, August, 1953, pp. 213–214.

[7] *The Basing Point Problem*, Monograph 42, Temporary National Economic Committee, 76th Congress, third session, 1941, pp. 4, 5.

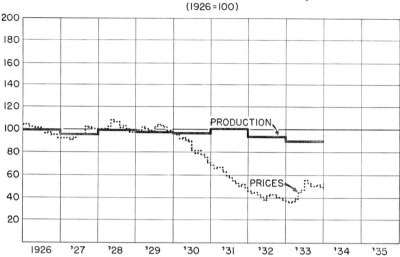

PRICES AND PRODUCTION FOR AGRICULTURE, 1926-1933
(1926 = 100)

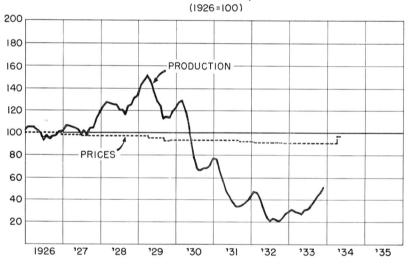

PRICES AND PRODUCTION FOR THE AGRICULTURAL
IMPLEMENTS INDUSTRY, 1926-1933
(1926 = 100)

FIG. 54. Rigid versus flexible prices in a depression period. Rigid prices are closely cor-
related with fewness of sellers and managed prices (basing-point and zone pricing systems; industry-wide wage contracts; and public utility rates). Competitive industries
reduce prices to find selling outlets. Oligopolistic industries, on the other hand, peg prices
in the face of declining demand in their attempts to maximize profits. Industries able to
peg their prices during a depression gain at the expense of the rest of the community.
(Source: U.S. Department of Agriculture.)

Since monopoly gives one class of people higher prices and incomes at the expense of others, it gives rise to inequalities in the distribution of income which have no social justification. It has been observed that the difference between a monopolist and a pickpocket is that the monopolist takes a great deal more money from the pockets of the people!

The inequality of incomes promoted by monopoly control is accentuated in the American economy by the fact that the ownership of the large corporations which enjoy and exercise monopoly power is vested in the hands of very few people. It is estimated that only about 8 percent of the families or other "spending units" in the United States own stock in publicly held corporations.[8] Thus, 92 percent of American families own none whatever. One-half of American families owning publicly held stock valued their stock at less than $1000, and one-fifth (about 2 percent of all family units in the nation) estimated their holdings to be worth $5000 or more. Also, it is estimated, 0.6 percent of American families own 80 percent of the publicly held stock. The evils of monopoly control would exist even if corporate stock were widely held. The fact, however, that the ownership of monopoly enterprises is concentrated in the hands of very few people makes for an extreme degree of inequality in the distribution of income. In the words of Professor Clair Wilcox, "A more nearly perfect mechanism for making the poor poorer and the rich richer could scarcely be devised."[9]

6. *Monopoly is Hostile to Economic and Political Freedom.* In a system of monopoly control, individual businessmen find many restrictions placed upon the custom of free enterprise. The restrictions may be either legal or economic. Under the N.R.A. program of legalized cartels (1933–1935), for example, it was made illegal in the United States for any firm in the steel industry to "initiate the construction of any new blast furnace or open hearth or Bessemer steel capacity" (Iron and Steel Code). Steel fabricators were thus denied the right to become producers of basic steel products. The prices of steel, too, were fixed by an industry committee controlled by the major producers. Any person failing to comply with these prices was subject to a government fine of $500 for each offense and for each day of the violation.

Today, in numerous industries, economic restraints imposed by firms controlling the basic sources of supply determine who shall buy, when they shall buy, and how much they shall buy. Independent concerns desiring to compete on price, moreover, find themselves repressed through fear that major firms will "cut" delivered prices in particular local areas, or to particular customers, *in a discriminatory way*, expressly to injure those showing an independence on price.

Monopoly likewise means restrictions on the free choice of consumers to

[8] "1949 Survey of Consumer Finances," *Federal Reserve Bulletin*, October, 1949, p. 1183.

[9] *Competition and Monopoly in American Industry*, Monograph 21, Temporary National Economic Committee, 76th Congress, third session, 1940, pp. 17–18.

determine the kinds and quantities of goods which shall be produced. In a free economy, every day is election day for consumers, and every dollar spent is a vote for one product or one producer rather than another. With monopoly, however, decisions on kinds and qualities of goods produced are made by dominant enterprisers in terms of materials controlled, facilities at hand, and established product forms. Prices, moreover, are controlled by producers alone.

The experience of Europe shows that when monopoly becomes widespread, there is a public demand for direct control or public ownership. Indeed, when the industries of a nation become centralized in the hands of a few, there is little choice, for there is no middle class of business enterprise into which industrial ownership can be diffused by dissolution and divestiture proceedings. Direct control or public ownership becomes the favored method for protecting the public interest. When business units are in numerous hands and freedom of entry is a reality, there is rarely, if ever, a demand for nationalization and socialization.

Perhaps the greatest evil of widespread monopoly is the threat which it presents to the operation and survival of our democratic form of government. Concentrated wealth makes it possible for a relatively few persons to provide generous campaign funds, to finance influential lobbies in the legislative process, and to engage in subtle public relations to shape the thinking of the people, themselves. Such a regime of government means the frustration of democracy as "rule by the majority."

Many persons are now asking if political democracy can survive without a diffusion of property ownership and the presence of competitive enterprise. When a few powerful interests control the sources of employment, they are in a position to coerce those who might oppose their will. The existence of many opportunities for employment in competing enterprises, it is believed, is essential if individuals are to feel free to speak for themselves on issues of public policy.

THE NEED TO FORMULATE A NATIONAL POLICY ON CORPORATE CONCENTRATION

In large measure the economic problem of monopoly in the United States centers around the several large companies (the "Big Threes" and the "Big Fours") which have become dominant in the various industrial fields. It is in this area that the antitrust laws have not been applied to remedy the problems of price leadership and unified selling. As we have seen, the antitrust laws *could be* applied to the condition of oligopoly (a) on the ground of implied conspiracy or (b) on the principle that the larger companies jointly or collectively possess the power to control prices (Chap. 11). At the present time, however, it appears that neither the antitrust agencies nor the courts will act in a positive way to reduce the great amount of economic concentration which has been allowed to develop under the antitrust laws.

The passage of the Antimerger Act in December 1950 indicates that there is a considerable public opinion agitated for action against monopoly and the continuing rise in concentration of economic power. Gradually, the public and Congress may come to realize that if it is detrimental to our economic health to permit new concentration, it is also detrimental to permit those few which have grown too big to be frozen in their present position of dominance.

The development of a standard for the percentage of production or sales which a concern may be permitted to control is one of the vital tasks in present-day antimonopoly work. The standard need not contemplate the so-called atomization of industry. Crossroad forges need not be substituted for modern steel plants. It is clear that the American economic system must be made to accommodate itself to the largest *physical plant* that is necessitated by the existing or any future technology.

PUBLIC POLICY AND THE GROWTH OF MONOPOLY AND SPECIAL PRIVILEGE

During our history as a nation, the relations of government to business have been a strange mixture (1) of policies designed to promote the common interest and (2) of grants of special favor to organized interest groups. Few people realize the extent to which business groups (including labor and farm groups) have gone into politics to secure special economic privileges in order to increase their incomes at the expense of other citizens (see Fig. 55).

The process of granting special favors began with tariffs. Then special advantages were secured by commercial groups in the disposal of the public domain. Within a few decades large railroad, mining, lumber, and other corporations secured much of the nation's finest mineral, forest, and agricultural land either as a gift or for a nominal price. As a result of a deliberate change in our statute laws—sponsored by business itself—corporations secured the right to acquire and vote the stock of other corporations. Thereupon, the corporation, as a creation of government, became the most effective method for securing monopoly control which has ever been devised.

Although the antitrust laws were enacted to curb monopoly in all fields of business, exemptions have now been granted by Congress to producers in many important areas. The federal courts, too, following a fallacious notion of laissez faire, have given approval to the formation of giant mergers, and to the right of corporations to sell if they please, when they please, and to whom they please. Outright immunity from antitrust prosecution has been granted by Congress only during periods of national emergency. However, during most of the years since 1890 a large measure of de facto immunity has been enjoyed as a result of the small appropriations which have been made for enforcement purposes.

With the impact of the great depression, organized labor and farm groups were able to secure special legislation to enhance their incomes. In granting this legislation, government itself undertook to give favors to agriculture (by direct action) and to labor (by more or less indirect action), in part, at least,

FIG. 55. Special interest groups typically identify with the public good the laws which are best for their immediate interest. Economic theories are also developed to aid and strengthen their claims. Sound public policy, however, may require the adoption of rules which restrict and limit the immediate gain of various groups. The "national interest" is not the sum of all the special economic greeds. (Fitzpatrick in the St. Louis *Post-Dispatch*.)

to offset the monopolistic (or restrictive) power of industry. Today, as Dr. Leverett S. Lyon has said, "there is a growing tendency in the United States for special groups to identify their limited good with the national good and to ask government for subsidy, support, or special protection rather than for laws which increase competitive opportunity."[10]

[10] Leverett S. Lyon, "Government and American Economic Life," *Journal of Business*, April, 1949, pp. 89–90.

In a regime of special privilege, large numbers of consumers and workers—the white-collar, middle-class, and professional groups—find themselves defenseless against organized capital, labor, and agriculture. Thousands of small business enterprisers, moreover, find that they do not have equality of opportunity in relation to giant mergers which are in a position to restrict the expansion of independents by spending large sums on advertising, by engaging in prolonged patent litigation, and by quoting discriminatory prices. What can forgotten consumers, workers, and independent businessmen do to protect themselves? The spirit of the times is "Organize," "Get a public favor, too, if you can." By raising prices and producing less, it is erroneously believed, everybody can have more of the good things. The forces involved in this point of view are deep-seated and have their roots in our political and economic psychology and in the workings of our economic system.

THE CONSEQUENCES OF A CONTINUING GROWTH OF MONOPOLY AND SPECIAL PRIVILEGES

In considering the exercise of regulatory functions by government, it is important to realize that the recipients of special privilege are not passive or inactive on the matter of public policy. Having worked to secure monopolistic privileges, they are not prepared to see their control weakened if they can prevent it. The efforts of government agencies to maintain and restore competition, therefore, are made increasingly difficult as monopoly grows and expands its area of control. Legal proceedings become prolonged and inconclusive. More and more pressure is exerted on Congress to legalize the monopolistic practices which the established law will not permit. Since Congress has complete and absolute power to regulate interstate commerce, a determined effort is made to shape governmental policies along the lines of the commercial interest by means of lobbying activities, substantial campaign contributions, and the use of the press for propaganda purposes.

It is possible that the next step in the evolving pattern of economic control will be one in which the federal government is called upon and given authority to supervise price and output behavior in industry. The Spence bill, introduced in Congress in 1949, indeed, sought to give the President power to supervise *industrial* prices which are "too high" or outputs which are "too low." It was not proposed that the President should directly fix prices and outputs. Rather it was provided that he should be given discretionary powers to authorize voluntary allocations; to impose mandatory allocations and priorities; to scrutinize wage increases which are to be made the basis for price increases; to buy, sell, store, and refine essential raw materials; to make loans for expanding productive capacity; and to construct new plant facilities.

Public pressure for the adoption of direct controls in industry is likely to come with a severe depression and mass unemployment. Under these conditions, it is possible that influential business groups themselves may join in a plan for relaxing the antitrust laws and establishing public commissions to fix prices and outputs. The idea of N.R.A. still lurks in some important business circles. As we have seen, the great danger in plans for the direct control of prices and output is the opportunity which they provide for organized groups to influence public policy in their own behalf.

A chief weakness of organized producers is their failure to have an idea of the economy *as a whole*. Each operates in an atmosphere of getting more for itself. The higher prices or wages secured by unified action mean a transfer of income to the favored groups from others. The increased gains for some result in increased burdens for other producers and the general public.

EXPERIENCE WITH CARTEL CONTROL IN EUROPE

A basic problem encountered when the principle of price competition is abandoned is whether *organized industry* or *the people* will "call the tune" for authoritarian control. Some evidence on this question may be secured by considering the attempts of various governments in western Europe—particularly Germany, Austria, and Italy—to control cartels. In accepting monopoly in industry generally, the view of politically important groups in Europe was that business had advanced beyond the stage of "competition" and that "control" was the realistic and practical approach to take. With control, it was held, monopolistic abuses may be discouraged and industry can be maintained in a strong and adequate manner.

The common testimony of neutral observers is that the attempts of European governments to regulate cartels up to World War II, as well as during the postwar period, have failed to prevent (1) high prices, (2) restricted production, and (3) the wide disparities in prices existing between industries organized in cartels and the few continuing to operate under conditions of free entry and price competition. When price competition and free enterprise are not operative, someone must determine prices, incomes, and the allocation of resources. Some commission, for example, must decide whether to set low prices on fertilizer to favor the farmers or high prices to enable the chemical companies to expand their research activities. What is the public interest? How can it be identified? The experience in Europe with cartel control has been that the criteria with respect to "public interest" in the economic sphere of man's activities are determined principally by the shifting commercial interests of the cartels and large combinations (mergers). The concentrated economic wealth of the cartels and combinations has enabled them to exercise a dominant political influence in government, and public policy has largely been shaped along the lines of their commercial interest.[11]

[11] Heinrich Kronstein and Gertrude Leighton, "Cartel Control: A Record of Failure," *Yale Law Journal*, February, 1946, pp. 297–335. See also Wendell Berge, *Cartels, Challenge to a Free World* (Washington, 1944); Joseph Borkin and Charles A. Welsh, *Germany's Master Plan* (New York, 1943); G. W. Stocking and M. W. Watkins, *Cartels in Action* (New York, 1946); and Walter Eucken, "On the Theory of the Centrally Administered Economy," *Economica*, May, 1948, pp. 79–100; and August, 1948, pp. 173–193.

PLANNING FOR ECONOMIC ABUNDANCE AND
INDIVIDUAL FREEDOM

The maintenance of a system of private property, free initiative, and competitive enterprise does not mean a policy of leaving things as they are. Rather it involves and requires vigorous and far-reaching measures of intervention to break and dissipate monopoly power and to end monopolistic practices. This action will not be easy, for in taking it government will have to step on some toes.

REMEDIES PROPOSED

1. *Federal Charters with Strictly Limited Powers for all Corporations Engaging in Interstate Commerce.* The chief obstacles to the attainment of a fully competitive economy are to be found in the gaps, vagaries, and laxity of present-day corporation law. Although we now have a national economy, we leave to forty-eight charter-granting states the prescription of rules and standards for the organization and internal government of interstate business units. Rivalries for fees have made it impossible for the states to adopt and enforce rules and standards in the public interest. There is substantial agreement among economists and legal experts that the remedy for this condition is (1) the adoption of federal incorporation or licensing legislation for all corporations engaging in interstate commerce and (2) the formulation of rules and standards for corporate behavior which will remedy the recognized evils. (See Chap. 19.)

As soon as the rights and duties of corporations are carefully defined, business regulations will, in considerable degree, be self-enforcing. Stockholders will have clear ideas of their rights against management, and the public will know the standards of performance which corporate managements are pledged to render. The self-interest of majority and minority stockholders, as well as the general public, in pursuing their individual rights and claims, will thus be enlisted to see that corporate managements comply with federal rules and standards.

2. *A Basic Antitrust Program.* If the Department of Justice and the Federal Trade Commission are to make their contribution to the creation of a competitive economy, it will be necessary for them to fulfill certain standards of accomplishment. Assaults upon the growth of monopoly and monopolistic practices which fall short of these standards will probably prove to be futile. The two antitrust agencies, it is suggested, should include in their programs:

1. Efforts to eliminate all price fixing which is found to result from any action other than the impersonal forces of demand and supply operating in competitive markets.
2. Unstinted efforts to halt the abuse of economic power as manifested through acts and practices of discrimination; blacklisting; boycotting; disparagement; and agreements which seek to restrict the production, sale,

and distribution of any particular product to one or a few individuals or corporations.

3. Efforts to halt the trend toward concentration of economic power through full use of Section 7 of the Clayton Act to condemn acquisitions in a given market whenever a large company having a substantial share of the sales in that market acquires another company also having a substantial share in that market, regardless of possible justification by the rule of reason.

4. Efforts to break up existing concentrations of economic power. Corporate giants which have already grown too big should be reorganized to meet the same standard on size which is imposed for new growth. The formulation of an appropriate standard for size will probably require the adoption of additional legislation by Congress. One proposal is that the Sherman Act be amended to provide that a *prima facie* case shall exist against any concern which controls more than a specified percentage of the production or sales of a given product, or related group of products, *in its area of practical shipment.* Concerns seeking to control more than the specified limit (for example 20 percent) would be forced to bear the burden of proof in rebutting the presumption of illegal size. If they could demonstrate that such a degree of concentration was in the public interest, they could be permitted to retain their existing control of production or sales. However, if not, the size of the company could be reduced, and the right to expand by acquisition or by building branch plants could be denied.[12]

Until Congress acts to provide new legislation, it is unlikely that really effective assaults on corporate concentration will be taken by the Department of Justice, for neither the Department nor the courts have a clear-cut idea on an appropriate standard for use in dissolution proceedings.

3. Further Measures for Strengthening a Policy of Competition. Additional measures which, it is believed, are essential for the maintenance and preservation of a system of free enterprise include the following:

1. A requirement that industrial corporations controlling major sources of supply sell their products at posted prices to all customers offering cash or approved credit.

2. The provision of publicity on prices, sales, and supplies of the basic industrial commodities by some quasi-public organization—such as a commodity exchange—or by the government itself.

3. The reduction of restrictive tariffs—a monopolistic measure—in order to promote domestic abundance and to achieve a more balanced world economy.

4. An informed and purposeful use of monetary and fiscal policies to aid in stabilizing income and employment levels.

5. A continuing effort by officials in defense agencies, as well as by Congress, itself, to spread defense contracts and accelerated amortization privileges

[12] See also the "Report of the Committee on Cartels and Monopoly" in George W. Stocking and Myron W. Watkins, *Monopoly and Free Enterprise* (New York, 1951), p. 553.

equitably among small and large business firms. The nation is largely dependent upon small business for competitive pressures, and it is highly important that small business be given a fair chance to survive upon the basis of its efficiency.

6. The abolition of all special privileges and exemptions granted to organized business groups which cannot be defended on the principle of "the greatest good of the greatest number."

7. (a) The provision of rules for trade-union activity by legislative action (in lieu of antitrust prosecution) prohibiting uneconomic and restrictive abuses—such as limitations on the use of more efficient methods, materials, and equipment; restrictions on the entry of new firms and products; and the enforcement of illegally established product prices; (b) the requirement of some form of compulsory arbitration in key industries if voluntary arrangements fail; and (c) the making of continuing studies in the field of labor with respect to the development of effective institutions of control.

8. The adoption of sound measures of conservation to prevent physical waste in the use of nonrenewable resources—such as petroleum (oil and gas)—and to provide for the continual renewal of all other resources.

A policy of individual enterprise and price competition is a highly elaborate and complex plan for organizing the conduct of economic activity. It is a plan, however, which is not self-enforcing. When the policy of competition is accepted, it must be implemented by positive measures to provide for its creation, maintenance, and preservation. Competition is a form of human behavior; and like other behavior it should be conducted according to good manners and morals. The big mistake which government has made with respect to economic regulation is in thinking that in the absence of direct price control (as in the case of public utilities) government intervention is not necessary. The lessons of history clearly show that we cannot have fair competition unless positive measures are taken to create and maintain it. Government regulation is necessary to prevent profit-seeking activity from expressing itself in predatory acts, monopolistic practices, and other injustices.

The alternative to a plan of fair and orderly competition is the adoption of some form of authoritarian control over prices and outputs. Direct control and public ownership provide essential protection for the public interest in fields in which monopoly has been found by experience to be inevitable or economically desirable—i.e., public utilities. However, when the areas of private monopoly are widened by acceptance and choice, there is increasing danger that public control will be bent from considerations of the public interest to a concern for the selfish interests of the groups to be regulated. The very fact of competition itself helps to offset and diffuse the power of business groups to determine prices to their own advantage. Each competitor helps to moderate the excessive demands of others. When this moderating influence is removed and the power of business is concentrated in unified control, experience indicates that it is exceedingly difficult for democratic government to prevent organized groups from getting essentially what they want.

How is a policy of effective price competition and freedom of enterprise to be attained? How are larger appropriations for antitrust law enforcement to be secured? What steps are necessary to secure the adoption of federal incorporation legislation? How can a more effective control be exercised over public utility enterprises? What, in brief, is the starting point in a consistent program of government intervention to promote the common interest?

It is to Congress and the Chief Executive, in the main, that the nation must look for positive leadership in adopting measures to promote the economic welfare of the nation. Typically, congressmen want to do what is right and best for the entire country. However, each one knows that he has little chance to be reëlected if he incurs the displeasure of special interests "back home." Organized minorities and pressure groups—such as the silver bloc, the wool bloc, the tobacco bloc, the coal bloc, the sugar bloc, and the basing-point industry bloc—have funds, newspaper influence, and votes which can be used to defeat a person seeking reëlection. As a result, congressmen commonly find themselves swayed and guided by the wishes of the dominant interest groups in their respective constituencies rather than by a regard for the national economic interest—that is, the interest of consumers collectively. Under our democratic form of government, where representation is by geographic districts—and hence, largely by less-than-national interest groups—it does not seem likely that we shall work toward an economy of abundance in earnest until citizens generally become (1) better informed and (2) more disposed to become politically active in their own behalf.

Table of Landmark Cases

INTRODUCTION: SUGGESTIONS FOR USING CASE MATERIAL

In reading and studying the actual court decisions, it is suggested that
students endeavor to develop "opinions" and "judgments" on the following
questions:

1. What is the main problem or issue?
2. What is the position (a) of the government and (b) of the defendant?
3. What alternatives does the court face?
4. What action was taken?
5. What are some of the consequences of the action taken?
6. What might be some of the consequences if an alternative action had
   been taken?
7. How would I have decided the case? Why?
8. Did the court utilize economic analysis in reaching its decision? If so,
   what appraisal can you make of its economic analysis?

After each decision, there are included additional questions for discussion.
These bear directly upon the interpretation of the decision of the court.

For the most part, answers to questions on court decisions can be given
only as an expression of "opinion." The purpose of the case method is served,
however, in grappling with real problems and in applying concepts, principles, and "common sense" to the solution of these problems.

A. SCOPE OF THE REGULATORY POWER OF CONGRESS

1. THE DARBY CASE

Note:

Prior to the so-called "New Deal Constitutional Revolution," the Supreme Court, following its laissez-faire principles, held that the "commerce clause" *did not* give the federal government power to regulate "production," including agriculture, mining, manufacturing, and the employer-employee relationship. In *Hammer* v. *Dagenhart*, 247, U.S. 251 (1918) for example, the Court denied Congress the power to prohibit the interstate shipment of goods made by child labor, on the ground that Congress was invading "the reserved powers of the states," namely, the power to regulate "the making of goods." (See E. S. Corwin, *Commerce Power versus States Rights* (1936), pp. 175–209.) All this was changed, however, with the impact of the great depression and the coming of the New Deal. Today Congress has the power to regulate manufacturing, mining, agriculture, and the employer-employee relationship whenever the products enter into interstate commerce, are a part of commerce, or "affect" such commerce.

A landmark decision extending the scope of federal regulatory power is found in *U.S.* v. *Darby* (1941). Here the Court held that Congress could reach directly into the area of manufacturing activity and fix minimum wages and the method of overtime compensation for workers whose products move in interstate commerce or whose products are "intended" for such commerce.

The Darby case is also notable because it affirmed the power of Congress to restrict freedom of contract in order to attain objectives which it deems important. This power may be exercised to *regulate* business, as well as to *control* it.

Decision:

U.S. v. DARBY, 312 U.S. 100 (1941)

Supreme Court of the United States

Mr. Justice STONE delivered the opinion of the Court:

[This case involves the constitutionality of the Fair Labor Standards Act of 1938. By its terms Congress imposed prohibitions on (1) the shipment in interstate commerce of goods produced by labor whose wages are less than a prescribed minimum or whose compensation for overtime is at a rate less than time and one-half for hours in excess of forty a week, and (2) the employment of workmen in industrial production for interstate commerce at other than the prescribed wages and overtime rates of pay. Appellee, a Georgia lumber producer, failed to conform with the law, claiming that the law sought to regulate manufacturing rather than interstate commerce.]

While manufacture is not of itself interstate commerce, the shipment of manufactured goods interstate is such commerce and the prohibition of such shipment by Congress is indubitably a regulation of the commerce. The power to regulate commerce is the power "to prescribe the rule by which commerce is to be governed." *Gibbons* v. *Ogden*, 9 Wheat. 1, 196.

It extends not only to those regulations which aid, foster and protect the commerce, but embraces those which prohibit it. . . .

The power of Congress over interstate commerce "is complete in itself, may be exercised to its utmost extent, and acknowledges no limitations, other than are prescribed by the constitution." *Gibbons* v. *Ogden*, supra, 9 Wheat. 196. That power can neither be enlarged nor diminished by the exercise or nonexercise of state power. . . .

The motive and purpose of the present regulation are plainly to make effective the Congressional conception of public policy that interstate commerce should not be made the instrument of competition in the distribution of goods produced under substandard labor conditions, which competition is injurious to the commerce and to the states from and to which the commerce flows. The motive and purpose of a regulation of interstate commerce are matters for the legislative judgment upon the exercise of which the Constitution places no restriction and over which the courts are given no control. . . .

The conclusion is inescapable that *Hammer* v. *Dagenhart* was a departure from the principles which have prevailed in the interpretation of the commerce clause both before and since the decision and that such vitality, as a precedent, as it then had, has long since been exhausted. It should be and now is overruled. . . .

As appellee's employees are not alleged to be "engaged in interstate commerce" the validity of the prohibition turns on the question whether the employment, under other than the prescribed labor standards, of employees engaged in the production of goods for interstate commerce is so related to the commerce and so affects it as to be within the reach of the power of Congress to regulate it. . . .

Without attempting to define the precise limits of the phrase, we think the acts alleged in the indictment are within the sweep of the statute. The obvious purpose of the Act was not only to prevent the interstate transportation of the prescribed product, but to stop the initial step toward transportation, production with the purpose of so transporting it. Congress was not unaware that most manufacturing businesses shipping their product in interstate commerce make it in their shops without reference to its ultimate destination and then after manufacture select some of it for shipment interstate and some intrastate according to the daily demands of their business, and that it would be practically impossible, without disrupting manufacturing businesses, to restrict the prohibited kind of production to the particular pieces of lumber, cloth, furniture or the like which later move in interstate rather than intrastate commerce. . . .

There remains the question whether such restriction on the production of goods for commerce is a permissible exercise of the commerce power. The power of Congress over interstate commerce is not confined to the regulation of commerce among the states. *It extends to those activities intrastate which so affect interstate commerce or the exercise of the power of Congress over it as to make regulation of them appropriate means to the attainment of a legitimate end, the exercise of the granted power of Congress to regulate interstate commerce.* . . . [Italics supplied.]

Congress, having by the present Act adopted the policy of excluding from interstate commerce all goods produced for the commerce which do not conform to the specified labor standards, it may choose the means reasonably adapted to the attainment of the permitted end, even though they involve control of intrastate activities. Such legislation has often been sustained with respect to powers, other than the commerce power granted to the national government, when the means chosen, although not themselves within the granted power, were nevertheless deemed appropriate aids to the accomplishment of some purpose within an admitted power of the national government. . . .

The means adopted . . . for the protection of interstate commerce by the suppression of the production of the condemned goods for interstate commerce is so related to the commerce and so affects it as to be within the reach of the commerce power. Congress, to attain its objective in the suppression of nationwide competition in interstate commerce by goods produced under substandard labor conditions, has made no distinction as to the volume or amount of shipments in the commerce or of production for commerce by any particular shipper or producer. It recognized that in present day industry, competition by a small part may affect the whole and that the total effect of the competition of many small producers may be great. . . .

The Act is sufficiently definite to meeet constitutional demands. One who employs persons, without conforming to the prescribed wage and hour conditions, to work on goods which he ships or expects to ship across state lines, is warned that he may be subject to the criminal penalties of the Act. No more is required. . . .

Dissenting opinion by Mr. Justice McReynolds in which Justices Van Devanter, Sutherland, and Butler concurred.

QUESTIONS FOR DISCUSSION

1. On what grounds has Congress historically been prevented from regulating the manufacturing of products within states? See also *Sugar Trust* case, Chap. 10, pp. 204–205.

2. Does the power to regulate interstate commerce include the power to prohibit such commerce? What if the prohibition affects manufacturing? How did the Court reason that the power of Congress over commerce extends to manufacturing?

3. What motive and purpose did Congress have in establishing standards for wages and hours of work in manufacturing industries making products for commerce. Is there any constitutional restraint on the motive or purpose which Congress may have in regulating commerce?

4. When a plant is making products for interstate and local commerce, are all its employees subject to federal regulation? What if the production of goods for interstate commerce constitutes only a small fraction of total output? What if the production of goods is wholly for intrastate use?

5. Discuss the implications of the *Darby* case in extending the scope and area of federal regulation. What types of business activity, in your opinion, remain clearly within the jurisdiction of state regulation and control?

6. Upon the basis of the present powers of control residing in the federal government, do you think that Congress could undertake a broad program of "economic planning"—i.e., to fix wages, prices, and output in manufacturing—either to combat depression or to control industrial monopolies?

B. AGREEMENTS NOT TO COMPETE: MULTIPLE-FIRM MONOPOLY CONTROL

2. ADDYSTON PIPE AND STEEL CASE

Note:

The *Addyston Pipe* case stands for the rule that the Sherman Act calls for independent *price* competition. An agreement among six pipe foundries operating in four states, fixing prices and dividing sales territory, declared the Court, is a restraint on interstate commerce and illegal under the Sherman Act. Evidence presented at the trial indicated that in many cases the prices of pipe were raised a third more than they might have been with independent price competition. The decision in the case, however, did not turn on whether or not the "managed prices" were reasonable or unreasonable. In the opinion of the Court, an agreement to fix prices is, in itself, a restraint on interstate commerce and illegal.

Decision:

ADDYSTON PIPE AND STEEL COMPANY v. U.S.,
175 U.S. 211 (1899)
Supreme Court of the United States

Mr. Justice PECKHAM delivered the opinion of the Court:

We are thus brought to the question whether the contract or combination proved in this case is one which is either a direct restraint or a regulation of commerce among the several states or with foreign nations contrary to the act of Congress. It is objected on the part of the appellants that even if it affected interstate commerce the contract or combination was only a reasonable restraint upon a ruinous competition among themselves, and was formed only for the purpose of protecting the parties thereto in securing prices for their product that were fair and reasonable to themselves and the public. It is further objected that the agreement does not come within the act because it is not one which amounts to a regulation of interstate commerce, as it has no direct bearing upon or relation to that commerce. . . .

Referring to the first of these objections to the maintenance of this proceeding, we are of opinion that the agreement or combination was not one which simply secured for its members fair and reasonable prices for the article dealt in by them. Even if the objection thus set up would, if well founded in fact, constitute a defense, we agree with the circuit court of appeals in its statement of the special facts upon this branch of the case and with its opinion thereon as set forth by Circuit Judge Taft, as follows:

[The six conspiring firms, stated Judge TAFT, were located in Ohio, Kentucky, Alabama, and Tennessee. Their area of practical shipment—called "pay territory"—extended west and south of New York, Pennsylvania, and Virginia. In this area the six firms were protected from distant competition by the high freight costs which local buyers would have had to pay in buying pipe elsewhere. The six manufacturers controlled some 30 percent of the national production of cast-iron pipe.]

672

"The freight upon cast-iron pipe amounts to a considerable percentage of the price at which manufacturers can deliver it at any great distance from the place of manufacture. Within the margin of the freight per ton which eastern manufacturers would have to pay to deliver pipe in pay territory the defendants . . . were practically able to fix prices. The competition of the Ohio and Michigan mills of course somewhat affected their power in this respect in the northern part of the pay territory, but the further south the place of delivery was to be the more complete the monopoly over the trade which the defendants were able to exercise within the limits already described. Much evidence is adduced upon affidavit to prove that defendants had no power arbitrarily to fix prices and that they were always obliged to meet competition. To the extent that they could not impose prices on the public in excess of the cost price of pipe with freight from the Atlantic seaboard added this is true, but within that limit they could fix prices as they chose. . . .

The defendants were by their combination therefore able to deprive the public in a large territory of the advantages otherwise accruing to them from the proximity of defendants' pipe factories, and, by keeping prices just low enough to prevent competition by eastern manufacturers, to compel the public to pay an increase over what the price would have been if fixed by competition between the defendants, nearly equal to the advantage in freight rates enjoyed by defendants over eastern competitors. The defendants acquired this power by voluntarily agreeing to sell only at prices fixed by their committee, and by allowing the highest bidder at the secret auction pool to become the lowest bidder of them at the public letting. Now the restraint thus imposed on themselves was only partial, it did not cover the United States, there was not a complete monopoly. It was tempered by the fear of competition and it affected only a part of the price. But this certainly does not take the contract of association out of the annulling effect of the rule against monopolies. . . ."

It has been earnestly pressed upon us that the prices at which the cast-iron pipe was sold in pay territory were reasonable. A great many affidavits of purchasers of pipe in pay territory, all drawn by the same hand or from the same model, are produced, in which the affiants say that in their opinion the prices at which pipe has been sold by the defendants have been reasonable. We do not think the issue an important one, because, as already stated, we do not think that at common law there is any question of reasonableness open to the courts with reference to such a contract. Its tendency was certainly to give to the defendants the power to charge unreasonable prices, had they chosen to do so. But if it were important we should unhesitatingly find that the prices charged in the instances which were in evidence were unreasonable. . . .

As has frequently been said, interstate commerce consists of intercourse and traffic between the citizens or inhabitants of different states, and includes not only the transportation of persons and property and the navigation of public waters for that purpose, but also the purchase, sale, and exchange of commodities. . . . If, therefore, an agreement or combination directly restrains not alone the manufacture, but the purchase, sale, or exchange of the manufactured commodity among the several states, it is brought within the provisions of the statute. The power to regulate such commerce, that is, the power to prescribe the rules by which it shall be governed, is vested in Congress, and when Congress has enacted a statute such as the one in question, any agreement or combination which directly operates, not alone upon the manufacture, but upon the sale, transportation, and delivery of an article of interstate commerce, by preventing or restricting its sale, etc., thereby regulates interstate commerce to that extent, and to the same extent trenches upon the power of the national legislature and violates the statute. We think it plain that this contract or combination effects that result. . . .

We have no doubt that where the direct and immediate effect of a contract or combination among particular dealers in a commodity is to destroy competition between them and others, so that the parties to the contract or combination may obtain increased prices for themselves, such contract or combination amounts to a restraint of trade in the commodity, even though contracts to buy such commodity at the enhanced price are continually being made. Total suppression of the trade in the commodity is not necessary in order to render the combination one in restraint of trade. It is the effect of the combination in limiting and restricting the right of each of the members to transact business in the ordinary way, as well as its effect upon the volume or extent of the dealing in the commodity, that is regarded. . . . The views above expressed lead generally to an affirmance of the judgment of the court of appeals.

QUESTIONS FOR DISCUSSION

1. In the opinion of the Court, is the legality of concerted action on price to be tested by the reasonableness of the prices? What precedent did the Court have for this rule of law?
2. Did the Court relate "monopoly" to the percentage controlled by the combination in the entire United States? In an important regional sales area?
3. Did the conspirators have an absolute power to manage prices? How was their area of "local monopoly" limited?
4. Upon the basis of the *Addyston Pipe* case, how should business firms act, in relation to competitors, in conducting their buying and selling activities? What kind of competition is called for by the Sherman Act?
5. Is the power of Congress to regulate commerce limited, in any way, with respect to the purposes for which it is exercised? In your opinion, could the power to regulate commerce be used to authorize or permit agreements instead of prohibiting them?
6. Attorneys for various industries—such as the petroleum industry—frequently urge that the Sherman Act be construed administratively and judicially to permit agreements which impose only a reasonable restraint on price competition. Do you think that price agreements should be considered with reference to facts as to the reasonableness of private restraints?
7. *Note:* The general rule followed by the courts since the *Addyston Pipe* case is that collusive arrangements among competitors are unreasonable and illegal, *per se.* Examples of such illegal restraints are price fixing, pro-

duction control, division of sales areas, allocation of customers, and sharing of business done.

Justice DOUGLAS in the *Socony Vacuum Oil* case, 310 U.S. 150 (1940), footnote No. 59, gives a clear statement of present-day law on collusive arrangements:

Price-fixing agreements may or may not be aimed at complete elimination of price competition. The group making those agreements may or may not have power to control the market. But the fact that the group cannot control the market prices does not necessarily mean that the agreement as to prices has no utility to the members of the combination. The effectiveness of price-fixing agreements is dependent on many factors, such as competitive tactics, position in the industry, and the formula underlying price policies. Whatever economic justification particular price-fixing agreements may be thought to have, the law does not permit an inqury into their reasonableness. They are all banned because of their actual or potential threat to the central nervous system of the economy.

C. THE RULE OF REASON

3. AMERICAN TOBACCO CASE

Note:

The "rule of reason" was originally announced in the *Standard Oil* case (1911) and was reaffirmed in the *American Tobacco* case decided two weeks later. In the *Standard Oil* decision, the Court was very much preoccupied with seeking to justify its action in changing its former decisions on the Sherman Act, and its opinion is long and confusing (see text pp. 208–211). It is for this reason that the American Tobacco decision is included here.

Summarizing its view that the Sherman Act should be construed in "the light of reason," the Court declared in the *Standard Oil* decision: "As the contracts or acts embraced in the provision [of the Sherman Act] were not expressly defined . . . it inevitably follows that the provision necessarily called for *the exercise of judgment* which required that some standard should be resorted to for the purpose of determining whether the prohibition contained in the statute had or had not in any given case been violated." 221 U.S. 1, 60 (1911). [Italics supplied.]

In essence, the "rule of reason" means that a commission or court, in applying a statute condemning restraints on trade or competition, applies it not in a rigid "thou-shalt-not" fashion, as written, but rather (1) by considering the impact of the particular situation under examination (i.e., a merger) in the light of its particular market setting (whether *some* competition still flourishes), and (2) by looking at the particular situation under examination in the light of a factual showing of illegality (whether there are specific evils, overt acts, or illegal motives).

Basic to the rule of reason is the idea that monopoly is limited and relative (not absolute). The rule makes possible the acceptance of a degree of monopoly which—in the eyes of the judges—is tolerable.

Some conduct—such as collusion on price—is considered to be illegal, *per se* (taken by itself). The rule of reason means that particular conduct—such as acquisition of competitors—which the statute declares is monopolistic and illegal—may be excused by the Court if it thinks that the public interest—on balance—is served.

It is doubtful that Congress intended to outlaw *all* restraints on trade and commerce. An agreement not to practice a trade for a limited time, made in selling out one's business, for example, had long been accepted by the law. Lawmakers and the courts, moreover, had long recognized the legal maxim *de minimis non curat lex* (the law does not concern itself with trifles). Taking into account *economic results*, it would seem that a sound interpretation of the Sherman Act would bar the merger of two large corporations—or a large corporation and a small one—which are in direct competition, whenever the resulting restraint in a given sales area is substantial (not trivial).

Decision:

U.S. v. AMERICAN TOBACCO COMPANY, 221 U.S. 106 (1911).

Supreme Court of the United States

Mr. Chief Justice WHITE delivered the opinion of the Court:

Thus, the government, for the purpose of fixing the illegal character of the original combinations which organized the old American Tobacco Company, asserts that the illegal character of the combination is plainly shown because the combination was brought about to stay the progress of a flagrant and ruinous trade war. In other words, the contention is that, as the act forbids every contract and combination, it hence prohibits a reasonable and just agreement made for the purpose of ending a trade war. . . .

So as to the defendants. While it is argued on the one hand that the forms by which various properties were acquired, in view of the letter of the act, exclude many of the assailed transactions from condemnation, it is yet urged that, giving to the act the broad construction which it should rightfully receive, whatever may be the form, no condemnation should follow, because, looking at the case as a whole, every act assailed is shown to have been but a legitimate and lawful result of the exertion of honest business methods, brought into play for the purpose of advancing trade, instead of with the object of obstructing and restraining the same. . . .

[In the *Standard Oil* case] it was held, without departing from any previous decision of the Court, that as the statute had not defined the words "restraint of trade," it became necessary to construe those words—a duty which could only be discharged by a resort to reason. We say the doctrine thus stated was in accord with all the previous decisions of this Court, despite the fact that the contrary view was sometimes erroneously attributed to some of the expressions used in two prior decisions (the *Trans-Missouri Freight Assn.* and *Joint Traffic* cases, 166 U.S. 290, and 171 U.S. 505. . . .

Applying the rule of reason to the construction of the statute, it was held in the *Standard Oil* case that, as the words "restraint of trade" at common law and in the law of this country at the time of the adoption of the anti-trust act only embraced acts or contracts or agreements or combinations which operated to the prejudice of the public interests by unduly restricting competition, or unduly obstructing the due course of trade, or which, either because of their inherent nature or effect, or because of the evident purpose of the acts, etc., injuriously restrained trade, that the words as used in the statute were designed to have and did have but a like significance. It was therefore pointed out that the statute did not forbid or restrain the power to make normal and usual contracts to further trade by resorting to all normal methods, whether by agreement or otherwise, to accomplish such purpose. . . .

The soundness of the rule that the statute should receive a reasonable construction, after further mature deliberation, we see no reason to doubt. Indeed, the necessity for not departing in this case from the standard of the rule of reason which is universal in its application is so plainly required in order to give effect to the remedial purposes which the act under consideration contemplates, and to prevent that act from destroying all liberty of contract and all substantial right to trade, and thus causing the act to be at war with itself by annihilating the fundamental right of freedom to trade which, on the very face of the act, it was enacted to preserve, is illustrated by the record before us. In truth, the plain demonstration which this record gives of the injury which would arise from, and the promotion of the wrongs which the statute was intended to guard against which would result from, giving to the statute a narrow, unreasoning, and unheard-of construction, as illustrated by the record before us, if possible serves to strengthen our conviction as to the correctness of the rule of construction—the rule of reason—which was applied in the *Standard Oil* case, the application of which rule to the statute we now, in the most unequivocal terms, re-express and re-affirm. . . .

Dissenting Opinion:

Mr. Justice HARLAN, dissenting in part:

But my objections have also reference to those parts of the Court's opinion reaffirming what it said recently in the *Standard Oil* case, 220 U.S. 1, about the former decisions of this Court touching the anti-trust act. We are again reminded, as we were in the *Standard Oil* case, of the necessity of applying the "rule of reason" in the construction of this act of Congress—an act expressed, as I think, in language so clear and simple that there is no room whatever for construction.

Congress, with full and exclusive power over the whole subject, has signified its purpose to forbid *every* restraint of interstate trade, in whatever form, or to whatever extent; but the Court has assumed to insert in the act, by construction merely, words which made Congress say that it means only to prohibit the "undue" restraint of trade.

If I do not misapprehend the opinion just delivered, the Court insists that what was said in the opinion in the *Standard Oil* case was in accordance with our previous decisions in the *Trans-Missouri* and *Joint Traffic* cases, 166 U.S. 290, 171 U.S. 505, if we resort to *reason*. This statement surprises me quite as much as would a statement that black was white or white was black. . . . One thing is certain, "rule of reason," to which the Court refers, does not justify the perversion of the plain words of an act in order to defeat the will of Congress.

By every conceivable form of expression, the majority, in the *Trans-Missouri* and *Joint Traffic* cases, adjudged that the act of Congress did not allow restraint of interstate trade to any extent or in any form, and three times it expressly rejected the theory, which had been persistently advanced, that the act should be construed as if it had in it the word "unreasonable" or "undue." But now the Court, in accordance with what it denominates the "rule of reason," in effect inserts in the act the word "undue," which means the same as "unreasonable," and thereby makes Congress say what it did not say; what, as I think, it plainly did not intend to say; and what, since the passage of the act, it has explicitly refused to say. It has steadily refused to amend the act so as to tolerate a restraint of interstate commerce even where such restraint could be said to be "reasonable" or "due." In short, the Court now, by judicial legislation, in effect amends an act of Congress relating to a subject over which that department of the government has exclusive cognizance.

QUESTIONS FOR DISCUSSION

1. What reason did the Court give for construing the Sherman Act in "the light of reason"—that is, what reason did the Court give for looking at the restraints on competition not by themselves, but in the light of a factual showing of illegality?

2. In your opinion, does the inclusion of the "rule of reason" in the Sherman Act make the language of the statute more certain or less certain?

3. What is meant by the term "judicial legislation"? At whose behest did the Court write the "rule of reason" into the statute?

4. Discuss the view that "the public policy of the government is to be found in its statutes" in the light of the *Standard Oil* and *American Tobacco* cases.

5. Distinguish between (a) the application of the rule of reason to private restraints made in selling out one's business, as recognized in the common law; and (b) its application to mergers.

6. It has been said that if only those contracts which "unreasonably" restrain trade are illegal, the question of reasonableness is substantially left to the private companies, themselves. Discuss.

7. In your opinion, what is the possibility that Section 1 of the Sherman Act may be construed to bar the merger of any two corporations which are in direct competition with each other when the resulting restraint in a given sales area is substantial?

D. MERGERS AND THE ANTITRUST LAWS

4. The Steel Corporation Case

Note:

The law against conspiracy can be effectively circumvented by the merging of competing plants. One might expect the Supreme Court to scrutinize mergers with the same concern as agreements on prices. Actually, however, it has treated mergers with much tolerance. The decisions in this field have failed to establish any clear-cut rules on the permissive limits of acquisitions and capital aggrandizement. How the Court will weigh and judge various business acts and practices in given instances cannot be answered with any degree of confidence.

The *U.S. Steel* decision (1920) formally adopted the "abuse theory of mergers." In a four-to-three decision, the Court indicated that it would not dissolve a giant corporation—built by acquisitions—in the absence of unworthy motives, predatory acts, conspiracy, and an overwhelming percentage control of the industry. This standard is called the Sherman Act test for the legality of mergers. The Court declined to hold that "every contract, combination in the form of trust or otherwise" is illegal on the ground that "it [the Court] is not expected to enforce abstractions" and that it should have "flexibility of discretion" (to use the rule of reason).

The majority refused to find that the Corporation was a "monopoly." In its view, the Corporation had sought and secured the coöperation of other sellers in fixing prices, so that others were guilty, too. The Corporation, "in and of itself" did not achieve monopoly. Further, the majority added, the public welfare would be served by a combination which represented "integration." The minority rejected this reasoning, as well as the contention that the combination was a product of industrial progress.

Decision:

U.S. v. U.S. STEEL CORPORATION, 251 U.S. 417 (1920)
Supreme Court of the United States

Mr. Justice McKenna delivered the opinion of the Court:

[In its brief, the government charged the existence of a monopolistic combination which suppressed competition among the parties themselves. It requested dissolution. The Corporation contended that whether a combination of competitive units "constitutes *an undue restriction* depends not upon the amount of competition suppressed, but upon the amount which remains." As long as *some* competitors remain in the field "to maintain reasonably competitive conditions," it urged, a combination should not be condemned. In addition, the Corporation stressed its record in expanding foreign trade, in fulfilling the wartime demands of the government, and in treating its competitors as gentlemen.]

The case was heard in the District Court by four judges. They agreed that the bill should be dismissed; they disagreed as to the reasons for it. One opinion . . . expressed the view that the Steel Corporation was not formed with the intention or purpose to monopolize or restrain trade, and did not have the motive or effect "to prejudice the public interest by unduly restricting competition or unduly obstructing the course of trade." The corporation, in the view of the opinion, was an evolution, a natural consummation of the tendencies of the industry. . . . The tendency of the industry and the purpose of the corporation in yielding to it was expressed in comprehensive condensation by the word "integration," which signifies continuity in the processes of the industry from ore mines to the finished product. . . .

The other opinion [expressed the view that] . . . the organizers of the corporation and the preceding companies had illegal purpose from the very beginning, and the corporation became "a combination of combinations by which, directly or indirectly, approximately 180 independent concerns were brought under one business control," which, measured by the amount of production, extended to 80 percent or 90 percent of the entire output of the country, and that its purpose was to secure great profits. . . .

We have seen, that the judges of the District Court unanimously concurred in the view that the corporation did not achieve monopoly, and such is our deduction, and it is against monopoly that the statute is directed; not against an expectation of it, but against its realization, and it is certain that it was not realized. The opposing conditions were underestimated. The power attained was much greater than that possessed by any one competitor—it was not greater than that possessed by all of them. Monopoly, therefore, was not achieved, and competitors had to be persuaded by pools, associations, trade meetings, and through the social form of dinners, all of them, it may be, violations of the law, but transient in their purpose and effect. They were scattered through the years from 1901 (the year of the formation of the corporation) until 1911, but, after instances of success and failure, were abandoned nine months before this suit was brought. There is no evidence that the abandonment was in prophecy of or dread of suit; and the illegal practices have not been resumed. . . .

What, then, can now be urged against the corporation? . . . The company's officers, and, as well, its competitors and customers, testified that its competition was genuine, direct, and vigorous and was reflected in prices and production. No practical witness was produced by the government in opposition. . . . But this absence of complaint counsel urge against the corporation. Competitors, it is said, followed the corporation's prices, because they made money by the imitation. Indeed, the imitation is urged as an evidence of the corporation's power. "Universal imitation," counsel assert, is "an evidence of power." In this concord of action, the contention is, there is the sinister dominance of the corporation—"its extensive control of the industry is such that the others [independent companies] follow. . . ."

But there are other paradoxes. . . . In one, competitors (the independents) are represented as oppressed by the superior power of the corporation; in the other, they are represented as ascending to opulence by imitating that power's prices, which they could not do, if at disadvantage from the other conditions of competition, and yet confederated action is not asserted. If it were, this suit would take on another cast. The competitors would cease to be the victims of the corporation, and would become its accomplices. And there is no other alternative. The suggestion that lurks in the government's contention that the acceptance of the corporation's prices is the submission of impotence to irresistible power is, in view of the testimony of the competitors, untenable. They, as we have seen, deny restraint in any measure or illegal influence of any kind. The government, therefore, is reduced to the assertion that the size of the corporation, the power it may have, not the exertion of the power, is an abhorrence to the law, or, as the government says, "the combination embodied in the corporation unduly restrains competition by its *necessary effect*, and therefore is unlawful regardless of purpose. . . ."

The corporation is undoubtedly of impressive size, and it takes an effort of resolution not to be affected by it or to exaggerate its influence. But we must adhere to the law, and the law does not make mere size an offense, or the existence of unexerted power an offense. It, we repeat, requires overt acts, and trusts to its prohibition of them and its power to repress or punish them. It does not compel competition, nor require all that is possible. . . . We have seen whatever there was of wrong intent could not be executed; whatever there was of evil effect was discontinued before this suit was brought, and this, we think, determines the decree. We say this in full realization of the requirements of the law. . . .

And it is certainly a matter for consideration that there was no legal attack on the corporation until 1911, 10 years after its formation and the commencement of its career. We do not, however, speak of the delay simply as to its time, or say that there is estoppel in it because of its time, but on account of what was done during that time—the many millions of dollars spent, the development made, and the enterprises undertaken; the investments by the public that have been invited and are not to be ignored. And what of the foreign [trade]. . . . In conclusion, we are unable to see that the public interest will be served by yielding to the contention of the government respecting the dissolution of the company or the separation from it of some of its subsidiaries; and we do see in a contrary conclusion a risk of injury to the public interest, including a material disturbance of, and, it may be serious detriment to, the foreign trade. . . .

Mr. Justice McReynolds and Mr. Justice Brandeis took no part in the consideration or decision of the case.

Dissenting Opinion:

Mr. Justice Day, dissenting:

This record seems to me to leave no fair room for a doubt that the defendants, the United States Steel Corporation and the several subsidiary corporations which make up that organization, were formed in violation of the Sherman Act. . . .

This record shows that the power obtained by the corporation brought under its control large competing companies which were of themselves illegal combinations, and succeeded to their power; that some of the organizers of the Steel Corporation were parties to the preceding combinations, participated in their illegality, and by uniting them under a common direction intended to augment and perpetuate their power. It is the irresistible conclusion from these premises that great profits to be derived from unified control were the object of these organizations. The contention must be rejected that the combination was an inevitable evolution of industrial tendencies compelling union of endeavor. . . .

For many years, as the record discloses, this unlawful organization exerted its power to control and maintain prices by pools, asssociations, trade meetings, and as the result of discussion and agreements at the so-called "Gary Dinners". . . . It inevitably follows that the corporation violated the law in its formation and by its immediate practices. . . .

As I understand the conclusions of the court, affirming the decree directing dismissal of the bill, they amount to this: That these combinations, both the holding company and the subsidiaries which comprise it, although organized in plain violation and bold defiance of the provisions of the act, nevertheless are immune from a decree effectually ending the combinations . . . because of some reasons of public policy requiring such conclusion. I know of no public policy which sanctions a violation of the law, nor of any inconvenience to trade, domestic or foreign, which should have the effect of placing combinations, which have been able to thus organize one of the greatest industries of the country in defiance of law, in an impregnable position above the control of the law forbidding such combinations. Such a conclusion does violence to the policy which the law was intended to enforce, runs counter to the decisions of the court, and necessarily results in a practical nullification of the act itself. . . .

If the plan were followed, as in the *American Tobacco* case, of remanding the case to the District Court, a decree might be framed restoring competitive conditions as far as practicable. . . . Mr. Justice PITNEY and Mr. Justice CLARKE concur in this dissent.

QUESTIONS FOR DISCUSSION

1. The entire Supreme Court agreed that the Corporation had openly violated the Sherman Act over a period of ten years—from 1901 until nine months before the suit was brought. In your opinion, what sort of penalty should have been given for this illegal action?

2. Discuss the view that the Corporation was not "in and of itself" a monopoly: (a) Consider the restraint on competition between and among the many firms combined in the Corporation? Compare, also, with the rule of law in the *Addyston Pipe* case in which six defendants controlled *by agreement* some 30 percent of the national production of cast-iron pipe. (b) Whose power was instrumental in *effecting* "unified selling" with the remaining independents? (c) Why, in your opinion, were the independents "willing" accomplices?

3. According to Justice McKenna, what does the word "integration" signify? Does the argument of Justice McKenna in favor of integration really apply to a horizontal merger of many formerly *competing* plants—as the Corporation preëminently was?

4. What, in your opinion, were the reasons or beliefs which probably caused the Court not to dissolve the Corporation? Consider (1) the view that the Corporation "in and of itself" did not restrain trade, (2) the "exemplary" conduct of the Corporation, (3) disturbance to the Company and its foreign trade, (4) the discontinuance of "trade meetings" nine months before the suit was brought, (5) the "advantages of integration." Appraise these reasons.

5. In the *Steel* case was the Sherman Act construed to fit the needs and desires of the Corporation? Could the Act have been construed to make the Corporation fit the pattern of the Sherman Act? How?

6. What action might the Court have taken if the government had included the independents in its suit and charged "unified action"?

7. Upon the basis of the *Steel* case, how would you summarize the "Sherman Act test" for determining the legality of mergers? Is this test based upon the rule of reason?

8. Compare (a) Justice McKenna's statement in 1920 that the government had not called one customer to testify against the price policies of the Corporation with (b) the complaints by customers from the Middle West in 1924 on Pittsburgh-Plus pricing which the Corporation had instituted in 1901 (see Chap. 17). Basing-point pricing was not fully understood by the government prior to 1924 and was not an issue in the *Steel* case.

5. The Columbia Steel Case

Note:

In the Columbia Steel decision (1948) the Supreme Court stated that the test governing the legality of horizontal and vertical combinations is the same. This test, in the main, Justice Reed declared, speaking for the majority, is whether or not the merger involves "unreasonable restraint." What is "unreasonable" depends upon the judgment of a majority of the justices. Here, again, it may be noted, the Court did not provide any clear-cut rules for testing the legality of mergers except its own weighing and judging of the particular business situations presented to it.

The suit was brought by the United States against the U.S. Steel Corporation and its subsidiaries, including the Columbia Steel Co., to enjoin the purchase of the Consolidated Steel Corporation, the largest independent steel fabricator in the West.

Decision:

U.S. v. COLUMBIA STEEL CO. *et al.,* 334 U.S. 495 (1948)
Supreme Court of the United States

Mr. Justice REED delivered the opinion of the Court:

Consolidated Steel, the sale of whose assets the government seeks to enjoin, is engaged only in structural fabrication and plate fabrication. . . . Consolidated has structural fabricating plants near Los Angeles and at Orange, Texas, and plate fabricating facilities in California and Arizona. Consolidated has sold its products during the past ten years in eleven states, referred to hereafter as the Consolidated market: Arizona, California, Idaho, Louisiana, Montana, Nevada, New Mexico, Oregon, Texas, Utah and Washington. It is that market which the government views as significant in determining the extent of competition between United States Steel and Consolidated. . . .

The theory of the United States in bringing this suit is that the acquisition of Consolidated constitutes an illegal restraint of interstate commerce because all manufacturers except United States Steel will be excluded from the business of supplying Consolidated's requirements of rolled steel products, and because competition now existing between Consolidated and United States Steel in the sale of structural fabricated products and pipe will be eliminated. . . . The appellees contend that the amount of competition which will be eliminated is so insignificant that the restraint effected is a reasonable restraint not an attempt to monopolize and not prohibited by the Sherman Act. . . .

It seems clear to us that vertical integration, as such without more, cannot be held violative of the Sherman Act. . . . The extent of permissible integration must be governed, as other factors in Sherman Act violations, by the other circumstances of individual cases. Technological advances may easily require a basic industry plant to expand its processes into semi-finished or finished goods so as to produce desired articles in greater volume and with less expense.

It is not for courts to determine the course of the Nation's economic development. . . . If businesses are to be forbidden from entering into differ-

ent stages of production that order must come from Congress, not the courts.
. . . We conclude that the so-called vertical integration resulting from the
acquisition of Consolidated does not unreasonably restrict the opportunities
of the competitor producers of rolled steel to market their product. . . .

We turn now to a discussion of the significance, as to possible violation
of the Sherman Act, of the fact that Consolidated has been a competitor of
United States Steel in structural steel fabrication and in the manufacture of
pipe. The same tests which measure the legality of vertical integration by
acquisition are also applicable to the acquisition of competitors in identical
or similar lines of merchandise. It is first necessary to delimit the market in
which the concerns compete and then determine the extent to which the concerns are in competition in that market. If such acquisition results in or is
aimed at unreasonable restraint, then the purchase is forbidden by the
Sherman Act.

In determining what constitutes unreasonable restraint, we do not think
the dollar volume is in itself of compelling significance; we look rather to
the percentage of business controlled, the strength of the remaining competition, whether the action springs from business requirements or purpose to
monopolize, the probable development of the industry, consumer demands,
and other characteristics of the market. We do not undertake to prescribe
any set of percentage figures by which to measure the reasonableness of a
corporation's enlargement of its activities by the purchase of the assets of a
competitor. The relative effect of percentage command of a market varies
with the setting in which that factor is placed. . . .

We conclude that in this case the government has failed to prove that the
elimination of competition between Consolidated and the structural fabricating subsidiaries of United States Steel constitutes an unreasonable restraint. . . .

We turn last to the allegation of the government that United States Steel
has attempted to monopolize the production and sale of fabricated steel
products in the Consolidated market. . . . The reasons given by Consolidated and United States Steel for the purchase and sale of the assets here involved seem not to involve any action condemned by the Sherman Act.
Granting that the sale will to some extent affect competition, the acquisition
of a firm outlet to absorb a portion of Geneva's rolled steel production seems
to reflect a normal business purpose rather than a scheme to circumvent the
law. . . .

The judgment of the District Court is affirmed.

Dissenting Opinion:

Mr. Justice DOUGLAS, with whom Mr. Justice BLACK, Mr. Justice MURPHY,
and Mr. Justice RUTLEDGE, concur, dissenting:

This is the most important antitrust case which has been before the Court
in years. It is important because it reveals the way of growth of monopoly
power—the precise phenomenon at which the Sherman Act was aimed. Here
we have the pattern of the evolution of the great trusts. Little, independent
units are gobbled up by bigger ones. At times the independent is driven to
the wall and surrenders. At other times any number of "sound business
reasons" appear why the sale to or merger with the trust should be made. If

the acquisition were the result of predatory practices or restraints of trade, the trust could be required to disgorge. *Schine Chain Theaters, Inc.* v. *U.S.,* 334 U.S. 110. But the impact on future competition and on the economy is the same though the trust was built in more gentlemanly ways.

We have here the problem of bigness. Its lesson should by now have been burned into our memory by Brandeis. The *Curse of Bigness* shows how size can become a menace—both industrial and social. It can be an industrial menace because it creates gross inequalities against existing or putative competitors. It can be a social menace—because of its control of prices. Control of prices in the steel industry is powerful leverage on our economy. For the price of steel determines the price of hundreds of other articles. Our price level determines in large measure whether we have prosperity or depression—an economy of abundance or scarcity. Size in steel should therefore be jealously watched.

In final analysis, size in steel is the measure of the power of a handful of men over our economy. That power can be utilized with lightning speed. It can be benign or it can be dangerous. The philosophy of the Sherman Act is that it should not exist. For all power tends to develop into a government in itself. Power that controls the economy should be in the hands of elected representatives of the people, not in the hands of an industrial oligarchy. Industrial power should be decentralized. It should be scattered into many hands so that the fortunes of the people will not be dependent on the whim or caprice, the political prejudices, the emotional stability of a few self-appointed men. The fact that they are not vicious men but respectable and social minded is irrelevant. That is the philosophy and the command of the Sherman Act. It is founded on a theory of hostility to the concentration in private hands of power so great that only a government of the people should have it. The Court forgot this lesson in *U.S.* v. *U.S. Steel Corporation,* 251 U.S. 417, and in *U.S.* v. *International Harvester Co.,* 274 U.S. 693. The Court today forgets it when it allows United States Steel to wrap its tentacles tighter around the steel industry of the West.

QUESTIONS FOR DISCUSSION

1. In your opinion, which is the more significant indicator of monopoly: (a) the percentage of sales controlled by a seller or (b) the existence of a price leader who establishes or fixes the "going price" which as an actual fact is largely observed in a given sales area?

2. Appraise the "restraint of trade" involved in the purchase of Consolidated Steel by Columbia Steel, a subsidiary of U.S. Steel: (a) To what extent is it likely that Consolidated Steel (a fabricator) will now be free to buy primary supplies from independent suppliers? (b) What recourse is there for such suppliers when an important customer is eliminated from the market? (c) Whose "interest" is served by denying "competitors presently selling to Consolidated" a sales outlet for their products? (d) Were U.S. Steel *and its subsidiaries* formerly in competition with Consolidated in the sale of fabricated products? Discuss consequences of the horizontal aspects of the merger by which U.S. Steel increased its sales of fabricated steel in the Western area from 13 to 24 percent.

3. According to Justice Reed, what factors are to be considered in de-

termining "unreasonable restraint"? Compare these "judge-made" standards with the prohibition in Section 1 of the Sherman Act.

4. Appraise the view that monopolistic mergers should be accepted if the
business management is "socially minded." According to Justice Douglas,
what is the philosophy of the Sherman Act.

5. Is vertical integration, as such, illegal? How about vertical integration
which restrains trade?

6. Appraise Justice Reed's statement "It is not for courts to determine the
course of the Nation's economic development" in light of (1) the "rule of
reason" which the Court "added" to the Sherman Act, and (2) the effects
of the rule of reason on the merger movement.

E. EXPANDED SCOPE OF DOCTRINE OF CONSPIRACY— CONSCIOUS PARALLEL ACTION

6. INTERSTATE CIRCUIT CASE

Note:

Since the decision of Justice Stone in the *Interstate Circuit* case (1939), the participation of businessmen in a common course of action on prices or sales policies, each with a knowledge of the similar conduct of others, has been held to justify a finding of conspiracy. Conspiracies to restrain trade are illegal in the common law, as well as by statute law (the Sherman Act). Proof of conspiracy, however, is a judge-made doctrine which has never been formulated by the legislature. The judicial finding of conspiracy, the courts now hold, may be made (1) upon proof of explicit (overt) agreement or (2) upon proof of conscious parallel action. See also Chap. 10, pp. 217–219.

The extent to which the "circumstantial-evidence" doctrine of conspiracy will be employed in bringing cases will depend upon the *attitudes* of the men in the antitrust agencies.

Decision:

INTERSTATE CIRCUIT, INC. v. U.S., 306 U.S. 208 (1939)

Supreme Court of the United States

Mr. Justice STONE delivered the opinion of the Court:

On July 11, 1934, following a previous communication on the subject to the eight branch managers of the distributor appellants [Interstate, a large exhibitor] asked compliance with two demands as a condition of Interstate's continued exhibition of the distributors' films in its "A" or first-run theatres at a night admission of 40 cents or more. One demand was that the distributors "agree that in selling their product to subsequent runs, that this 'A' product will never be exhibited at any time or in any theatre at a smaller admission price than 25¢ for adults in the evening." The other was that "on 'A' pictures which are exhibited at a night admission of 40¢ or more—they shall never be exhibited in conjunction with another feature picture under the so-called policy of double features."

The trial court found that the distributor appellants agreed and conspired among themselves to take uniform action upon the proposals made by Interstate, and that they agreed and conspired with each other and with Interstate to impose the demanded restrictions upon all subsequent-run exhibitors in Dallas, Fort Worth, Houston and San Antonio . . . that the effect of the restrictions upon "low-income members of the community" patronizing the theatres of these exhibitors was to withhold from them altogether the "best entertainment furnished by the motion picture industry"; and that the restrictions operated to increase the income of the distributors and of Interstate and to deflect attendance from later-run exhibitors who yielded to the restrictions to the first-run theatres of Interstate.

The court concluded . . . that the agreement of the distributors with each other and those with Interstate . . . constituted a combination and conspiracy in restraint of interstate commerce in violation of the Sherman Act. . . . It accordingly enjoined the conspiracy. . . .

689

As is usual in cases of alleged unlawful agreements to restrain commerce, the government is without the aid of direct testimony that the distributors entered into any agreement with each other to impose the restrictions upon subsequent-run exhibitors. In order to establish agreement it is compelled to rely on inferences drawn from the course of conduct of the alleged conspirators.

The trial court drew the inference of agreement from the nature of the proposals made on behalf of Interstate and Consolidated; from the manner in which they were made; from the substantial unanimity of action taken upon them by the distributors. . . . This conclusion is challenged by appellants because not supported by subsidiary findings or by the evidence. We think this inference of the trial court was rightly drawn from the evidence. . . .

Each was aware that all were in active competition and that without substantially unanimous action with respect to the restrictions for any given territory there was risk of a substantial loss of the business and good will of the subsequent-run and independent exhibitors, but that with it there was the prospect of increased profits. There was, therefore, strong motive for concerted action, full advantage of which was taken by Interstate and Consolidated in presenting their demands to all in a single document. . . .

It taxes credulity to believe that the several distributors would, in the circumstances, have accepted and put into operation with substantial unanimity such far-reaching changes in their business methods without some understanding that all were to join, and we reject as beyond the range of probability that it was the result of mere chance. . . .

We think that in the circumstances of this case . . . agreement for the imposition of the restrictions upon subsequent-run exhibitors was not a prerequisite to an unlawful conspiracy. It was enough that, knowing that concerted action was contemplated and invited, the distributors gave their adherence to the scheme and participated in it. Each distributor was advised that the others were asked to participate; each knew that coöperation was essential to successful operation of the plan. They knew that the plan, if carried out, would result in a restraint of commerce, which, we will presently point out was unreasonable within the meaning of the Sherman Act, and knowing it, all participated in the plan. The evidence is persuasive that each distributor early became aware that the others had joined. With that knowledge they renewed the arrangement and carried it into effect for the two successive years.

It is elementary that an unlawful conspiracy may be and often is formed without simultaneous action or agreement on the part of the conspiritors. . . . Acceptance by competitors, without previous agreement, of an invitation to participate in a plan, the necessary consequence of which, if carried out, is restraint of interstate commerce, is sufficient to establish an unlawful conspiracy under the Sherman Act. . . .

Affirmed.

Mr. Justice FRANKFURTER took no part in the consideration or decision of this case.

Mr. Justice ROBERTS wrote a dissenting opinion, concurred in by Justices McREYNOLDS and BUTLER.

QUESTIONS FOR DISCUSSION

1. Distinguish between "conscious" parallel action on prices and parallel action.

2. Do you think that in the prosecution of business firms for alleged conspiracy on prices or sales policies, the courts should require explicit proof of agreement?

3. Upon the basis of the *Interstate Circuit* case, *could* the federal government attack price identity, production control, division of territories, price leadership, and refusals to sell on the part of an industry group, without presenting proof of actual agreement? What acts and practices might the government present to prove its claim that a common course of action is "planned" or "conscious?"

4. "Enforcement," it has been said, "is the life of the law." What are some of the factors which will determine the extent to which the antitrust agencies will utilize the doctrine of "conscious parallel action."

F. TRADE ASSOCIATIONS AND THE ANTITRUST LAWS
7. TAG MFRS. CASE

Note:

Basic problems with respect to trade associations are (1) whether or not "open-price" reporting plans should be carried on *openly* and *publicly*, as in a central market or exchange; and (2) whether or not the activity should be limited to the collection and dissemination of *impersonal* data—i.e., actual prices on closed transactions, quantities sold, production, and inventories, *without* the names of buyers or sellers—as in a central market or exchange.

A leading Supreme Court decision (*Sugar Institute* case, 1936) established the rule that the "market information" collected from refiner members should be "fully and fairly" made available *to all*—i.e., to buyers and distributors of sugar. The unresolved problem is whether a trade association should be permitted to collect and disseminate *personal* and *intimate* data on prices and sales, such as list prices for *future* sales, the purchases and sales of *particular* persons, and the actual prices received and paid by *designated* persons.

The public exchanges—such as the security and commodity exchanges—disseminate prices on actual, *closed* transactions. No names, either of buyers or sellers, are made available. Bid and ask prices, moreover, are reported *without* the names of prospective buyers or sellers. It is this kind of market information which unquestionably facilitates the operation of price competition without leading to restraints or coercion.

The *Tag Institute* case is significant because it indicates the acceptance of an open-price association which collected (1) *list* or asking prices used by *designated members;* (2) the actual prices, terms, and conditions of each sale or contract and the *name of the member* making the sale; and (3) duplicates of *every invoice*, showing all pertinent information, including the *buyer's name*. The association disseminated (1) the list or asking prices of members identified by *name of member;* (2) data in the form of "pink sheets" on all "off-list" transactions, showing *name of seller*, description of product, quantity, list price, actual list price, and *the state* in which *the buyer* resided; and (3) summary data compiled from the invoice sheets on quantities sold and total sales receipts. The data so disseminated were made available to all interested persons upon payment of a reasonable fee.

The Federal Trade Commission in 1941 charged that the open-price plan of the Tag Institute was being used to restrain price competition, and subsequently (1947) a cease-and-desist order was issued. The Tag Institute carried the order to the Court of Appeals and the court ruled against the Commission. Subsequently, the Solicitor General declined to appeal the case to the Supreme Court.

Decision:

TAG MFRS. INSTITUTE v. F.T.C., 174 F. 2d 452 (1949)
Court of Appeals, First Circuit

Chief Judge MAGRUDER:

The manufacturing petitioners sell and distribute approximately 95 percent of the tag products purchased and used in the United States, with 55 percent of the business of the industry shared by the four largest manufacturers.

Certain standardized tags are made in advance of sale and sold out of stock, such as plain unprinted stock shipping tags. However, over 80 percent of the business is in made-to-order tags, the varieties of which are almost unlimited, representing as they do selective combinations of materials and processes, or component elements, in various sizes and shapes. . . .

The 1940 agreement [on price reporting] is stated to be between certain manufacturers and distributors of tag products, thereinafter called the "Subscribers," and Frank H. Baxter Associates, thereinafter called the "Associates." The agreement recites the desire of the Subscribers "by voluntary action to foster fair competitive opportunities in the public interest, by gathering and disseminating information regarding the essential factors entering into their commercial transactions, and to preserve and maintain a free and open market for the sale and distribution of their products. . . ."

Under the Tag Industry Agreement, a manufacturer may put into effect a new price list without prior notice to Baxter, and, though leaving unchanged his filed price list, he may make off-list sales also without prior notice to Baxter. The commitment is to report such transactions to Baxter after the event. . . . They all made off-list sales, and reported them to Baxter as required by the agreement. Off-list pricing has occurred without discernible territorial pattern, with no apparent correlation between the frequency of off-list sales and the size of the companies, or the types of tag products, or the size of the orders, or the classes of customers. . . .

Despite the fact that the Tag Industry Agreements have been in effect for a number of years, the Commission has produced no evidence indicating that the percentage of adherence to list prices has been on the increase. . . . Nor is there evidence of "retaliatory action" by any Subscribers to coerce other Subscribers into adherence to list prices. They all engaged in off-list pricing to such an extent that it would be wholly irrational to infer that the essence of their agreement was that they would all adhere to their current price lists on file with Baxter. The Commission argues in its brief that the requirement of disclosure of off-list sales "exposed the manufacturer who reduced his price to the odium of being a 'price cutter' or 'chiseler.' " Petitioners have aptly replied: "Someone has said that an odor which is common to all is offensive to none."

We quote now another important finding by the Commission:

"The effect of the operation of the open price-reporting plan under the agreements and in the manner hereinabove described has resulted in a substantial uniformity of prices for tags and tag products among the respondent members. . . ."

We think the evidence does warrant a finding that during the life of the Tag Industry Agreements there has from time to time been considerable list price uniformity with respect to types of tags constituting a large portion of the industry's business. Such a finding, in conjunction with the unchallenged finding that on the average 75 percent of the industry's business is done at list, would warrant the inference that during the years in which the Tag Industry Agreements have been in effect there has been a considerable uniformity of actual selling prices. The evidence does not, however, warrant the Commission's finding [of restraint on competition]. . . . In the first place, this implies that the instances of departure from uniformity are insignificant and unsubstantial—which certainly cannot be said. In the second place, there is no evidence that such uniformity as has existed is a result of the operation of the Tag Industry Agreements, for it does not appear whether there has been an increase or decrease of uniformity either in list prices or in actual selling prices since the agreements have been in operation. . . .

We have come to the conclusion that the reporting agreements herein, and the practices of petitioners thereunder, are lawful under the controlling authorities. In the sense indicated earlier in this opinion, the issuance of a price list may be said to be an "announcement of future prices." The nature of price lists has not changed under the Tag Industry Agreements from what it has historically been in the industry. The price list is subject to change without notice, and may be freely revised at any time. Even while a particular price list is extant, the manufacturer is free to make sales at off-list prices. . . .

The Tag Industry Agreement merely facilitates the assembling of such data. As to the obligation of Subscribers to report off-list sales and to furnish copies of all invoices, that is no more than the reporting of past transactions. The Commission has endeavored to show that the agreement was something more than this, that it was a price-fixing agreement having the purpose and actual effect of restraining and preventing price competition. We believe that such findings are unsupported by the evidence or by any reasonable inferences to be drawn therefrom. . . .

QUESTIONS FOR DISCUSSION

1. Why, in your opinion, was the Federal Trade Commission opposed to the filing and reporting of the *asking* (list) prices *of particular* sellers?

2. Why, in your opinion, did the Commission oppose the filing and reporting of "off-list prices" showing the *name* of the seller and the general *location* of the buyer?

3. Compare the price reporting activities of the Tag Mfrs. Institute with those of an exchange—such as the New York Stock Exchange—on the following points:
   (a) *Asking* prices of *designated sellers*
   (b) Prices on *closed* transactions
   (c) Name of *particular seller* and price received
   (d) Location of *buyer*

4. Assume (a) that a trade association collects and reports the production statistics of its members and (b) that the data on production are used by individual members to restrict output to amounts which can be sold at the established prices. In your opinion, is this a legitimate function of a trade association?

5. What arguments can you develop for and against the proposal to have the government engage in the collecting and reporting of prices for the principal industries?

G. SINGLE-FIRM MONOPOLY CONTROL

8. THE ALCOA CASE

Note:

The significance of the *Alcoa* decision lies in its identification and condemnation of monopoly without reference to abuses, predatory acts, injury to competitors, acquisition of competitors, or intent to monopolize. With the exception of monopoly arising "by force of accident," Judge Hand ruled, monopoly is illegal, *per se*. The test of monopoly, emphasized Judge Hand, is that size which gives a concern power to affect prices by a restriction of production.

What percentage of control of production or sales *in a nation* is necessary to constitute monopoly? Judge Hand wrestled with this question, but gave no clear-cut answer. Percentage figures are useful, but they should be considered in light of the principle that "monopoly is relative to place and limited by distance." The important question is the percentage of production or sales of a concern *in its area of practical* shipment. *Above all, the key factor is whether or not the firm is able to establish or make the "going price" which other firms regularly follow.*

Decision:

U.S. v. ALUMINUM CO. OF AMERICA *et al.*, 148 F. 2d 416 (1945)
Court of Appeals, Second Circuit

L. HAND, Circuit Judge:

[Alcoa had patents on the production of virgin ingot until 1909. Thereafter, it continued its monopoly position through the control of bauxite, high protective tariffs, denial of supplies to others, and cutthroat pricing. A decree of 1912 condemned Alcoa's unfair practices. In the present case, the government (as plaintiff) alleged that Alcoa continued to be the single producer of virgin ingot in the U.S. and that it had maintained this position by the use of "exclusionary practices." The government asked for dissolution of Alcoa. The Company denied that it was a monopoly, stating that it was always subject to the competition of imports and secondary ingot made from scrap.]

There are various ways of computing "Alcoa's" control of the aluminum market. . . . The percentage we have already mentioned—over ninety—results only if we both include all "Alcoa's" production [of ingot] and exclude "secondary." That percentage is enough to constitute a monopoly; it is doubtful whether sixty or sixty-four percent would be enough; and certainly thirty-three percent is not. . . . That part of its production which "Alcoa" itself fabricates, does not of course ever reach the market as ingot; and we recognize that it is only when a restriction of production either inevitably affects prices, or is intended to do so, that it violates Sec. 1 of the Act. *Apex Hosiery Co. v. Leader*, 310 U.S. 469, 501. However, even though we were to assume that a monopoly is unlawful under Sec. 2 only in case it controls prices, the ingot fabricated by "Alcoa," necessarily had a direct effect upon the ingot market. . . .

We conclude therefore that "Alcoa's" control over the ingot market must be reckoned at over ninety percent; that being the proportion which its production bears to imported "virgin" ingot. . . . There are indeed limits to its power; substitutes are available for almost all commodities, and to raise the price enough is to evoke them. . . . But these limitations also exist when a single producer occupies the whole market: even then, its hold will depend upon its moderation in exerting its immediate power. . . . Within the limits afforded by the tariff and the cost of transportation, "Alcoa" was free to raise its prices as it chose, since it was free *from domestic competition,* save as it drew other metals into the market as substitutes. . . .

It is no excuse for "monopolizing" a market that the monopoly has not been used to extract from the consumer more than a "fair" profit. The Act has wider purposes. . . . Many people believe that possession of unchallenged economic power deadens initiative, discourages thrift and depresses energy; that immunity from competition is a narcotic, and rivalry is a stimulant, to industrial progress; that the spur of constant stress is necessary to counteract an inevitable disposition to let well enough alone. Such people believe that competitors, versed in the craft as no consumer can be, will be quick to detect opportunities for saving and new shifts in production, and be eager to profit by them. . . . True, it might have been thought adequate to condemn only those monopolies which could not show that they had exercised the highest possible ingenuity, had adopted every possible economy, had anticipated every conceivable improvement, stimulated every possible demand. No doubt, that would be one way of dealing with the matter, although it would imply constant scrutiny and constant supervision, such as courts are unable to provide. Be that as it may, that was not the way that Congress chose; it did not condone "good trusts" and condemn "bad" ones; it forbade all. Moreover, in so doing it was not necessarily actuated by economic motives alone. It is possible, because of its indirect social or moral effect, to prefer a system of small producers, each dependent for his success upon his own skill and character, to one in which the great mass of those engaged must accept the direction of a few. These considerations, which we have suggested only as possible purposes of the Act, we think the decisions prove to have been in fact its purposes. . . .

Starting . . . with the authoritative premise that all contracts [agreements] fixing prices are unconditionally prohibited, the only possible difference between them and a [single-firm] monopoly is that while a monopoly necessarily involves an equal, or even greater, power to fix prices, its mere existence might be thought not to constitute an exercise of that power. That distinction is nevertheless purely formal; it would be valid only so long as the monopoly remained wholly inert; it would disappear as soon as the monopoly began to operate; for, when it did—that is, as soon as it began to sell at all—it must sell at some price and the only price at which it could sell is a price which it itself fixed. Thereafter the power and its exercise must needs coalesce. Indeed it would be absurd to condemn such contracts unconditionally, and not to extend the condemnation to monopolies; for the contracts are only steps toward that entire control which monopoly confers: they are really partial monopolies. . . .

We have been speaking only of the economic reasons which forbid monopoly; but, as we have already implied there are others, based upon the belief that great industrial consolidations are inherently undesirable, regardless of their economic results. In the debates in Congress Senator Sherman himself . . . showed that among the purposes of Congress in 1890 was a desire to put an end to great aggregations of capital because of the helplessness of the individual before them. . . . Throughout the history of these statutes it has been constantly assumed that one of their purposes was to perpetuate and preserve, for its own sake and in spite of possible cost, an organization of industry in small units which can effectively compete with each other. We hold that "Alcoa's" monopoly of ingot was of the kind covered by Sec. 2.

It does not follow because "Alcoa" had such a monopoly, that it "monopolized" the ingot market: it may not have achieved monopoly; monopoly may have been thrust upon it. . . . Persons may unwittingly find themselves in possession of a monopoly, automatically so to say: that is, without having intended either to put an end to existing competition, or to prevent competition from arising when none had existed; they may become monopolists by force of accident. Since the Act makes "monopolizing" a crime, as well as a civil wrong, it would be not only unfair, but presumably contrary to the intent of Congress, to include such instances. A market may, for example, be so limited that it is impossible to produce at all and meet the cost of production except by a plant large enough to supply the whole demand. Or there may be changes in taste or in cost which drive out all but one purveyor. A single producer may be the survivor out of a group of active competitors, merely by virtue of his superior skill, foresight and industry. . . .

It would completely misconstrue "Alcoa's" position in 1940 to hold that it was the passive beneficiary of a monopoly, following upon an involuntary elimination of competitors by automatically operative economic forces. Already in 1909, when its last lawful monopoly ended, it sought to strengthen its position by unlawful practices, and these concededly continued until 1912. . . .

We need charge it with no moral derelictions after 1912; we may assume that all it claims for itself is true. The only question is whether it falls within the exception established in favor of those who do not seek, but cannot avoid, the control of a market. It seems to us that that question scarcely survives its statement. It was not inevitable that it should always anticipate increases in the demand for ingot and be prepared to supply them. Nothing compelled it to keep doubling and redoubling its capacity before others entered the field. It insists that it never excluded competitors; but we can think of no more effective exclusion than progressively to embrace each new opportunity as it opened, and to face every newcomer with new capacity already geared into a great organization, having the advantage of experience, trade connections and the elite of personnel. . . . [Although Judge Hand found that Alcoa had "monopolized" the aluminum ingot market, he postponed remedial action until after the federal government had disposed of its wartime aluminum plants.]

QUESTIONS FOR DISCUSSION

1. Do you agree with the court's analysis of the aluminum ingot market—"virgin" and "secondary"—and Alcoa's share of it? Note: The figure of

"90 percent" of primary or ingot aluminum was obtained by taking all "virgin" aluminum ingot *sold* and *fabricated* by Alcoa and its subsidiaries (including the production of its Canadian subsidiary sold in the United States). Ingot fabricated by Alcoa was included on the ground that all ingot is eventually used for fabrication, and its control affects the total market for ingot. The competition of "secondary" was disregarded because its supply was indirectly subject to Alcoa's control.

2. What limits were there to Alcoa's power to raise the price of ingot by restricting its own production? Did Judge Hand accept the view that the competition of substitutes—stainless steel, nickel, tin, zinc, copper, lead—prevented a monopoly of aluminum ingot in the United States?

3. How can monopoly power be identified? Consider Judge Hand's reference to the *Apex Hosiery* case and his sentence following it commenting on what it is that monopoly does. Which is the better clue to monopoly—the percentage control of an industry or the power to make the "going price"?

4. Appraise Judge Hand's reasoning that since "all contracts fixing prices are unconditionally prohibited," condemnation should also extend to large single-firm size which involves an equal or greater power to fix prices. Do you think that the *Alcoa* decision provides a basis for reconsidering large mergers—such as U.S. Steel—which are "price leaders"—i.e., which make the "going price" that, as an actual fact, is largely observed in the industry?

5. In prosecuting monopoly, is it necessary for government to show that monopoly abused its power? In your opinion, should monopoly be tolerated if it can show that it has not abused its power? That it has made only a "fair" return on invested capital?

6. According to Judge Hand, what are the main objectives of the Sherman Act? Is the condemnation of monopoly based solely upon economic grounds?

7. Discuss Judge Hand's statement that "the power and its exercise must need coalesce" in relation to his ruling that, in principle, single-firm monopoly is always an unreasonable restraint of trade.

8. Under what conditions might a producer declare that "monopoly may have been thrust upon it"? How may persons "unwittingly find themselves in possession of monopoly"? Is monopoly, in such a situation, condemned by the law? Did Alcoa qualify for this exemption? Why?

9. THE ALCOA CASE: DETERMINATION OF RELIEF

Note:

The *Alcoa* case was remanded to a District Court for the formulation of relief to be granted the government. Following the disposal of the government's wartime plants to Reynolds and Kaiser, Alcoa in 1947 petitioned the court for a decree (1) that the company had ceased to be a monopoly and (2) that effective competition prevailed. The government, however, denied these allegations and asked the court to carve from Alcoa's facilities a new competitor and to provide other relief.

Judge Knox refused to create a new company from Alcoa's physical resources. However, he did require the common control of Alcoa and Aluminum Limited (Canada) to be eliminated, and he retained jurisdiction of the case for five additional years (until 1955).

Decision:

U.S. v. ALUMINUM COMPANY OF AMERICA, 91 F. Supp. 333 (1950)
U.S. District Court (New York)

Chief Judge KNOX:

The precise ingredients of "effective competition" cannot be said to have been a static concept under the Sherman Act. Their applications, as well as their implications, have varied with changes in judicial thought with respect to economic and legal philosophies. . . . Courts formerly looked to an overt misuse of a defendant's dominant competitive position as a *sine qua non* of illegality. But this is no longer true. The more recent authoritative precedents indicate that the mere existence of what is denominated "monopoly power," irrespective of its exercise, may be the focal element that will resolve the outcome of a particular suit. . . . In considering the matter of monopoly power, two ingredients are of outstanding significance: viz., the power to fix prices and the power to exclude competitors. . . .

The criteria [of effective competition] applicable to this case . . . necessitate two basic inquiries: (1) whether competitors flourish, and the extent to which they flourish, and whether they do so at the sufferance of Alcoa; (2) whether a foreseeable change in market conditions can secure an alteration in Alcoa's present condition, either by expansion where any competitor cannot, or by perseverance where any competitor would fail.

In determining the extent of permissible power that is consistent with the antitrust laws in a particular industry, the following factors are relevant: the number and strength of the firms in the market; their effective size from the standpoint of technological development, and from the standpoint of competition with substitute materials and foreign trade; national security interests in the maintenance of strong productive facilities, and maximum scientific research and development; together with the public interest in lowered costs and uninterrupted production. . . .

The government urges that Alcoa's monopolistic power is manifest in its control over the price of aluminum pig and ingot as reflected in price uniformity; in price leadership on the part of Alcoa; and in the inability of the other producers to deviate for a protracted period from the prices charged by Alcoa.

Assuming the truth of these assertions, the criteria advanced in describing the aluminum market suggest the fallacy in the plaintiff's position. The reasons that convince me that the sales of primary pig and ingot do not measure market position, lead me to conclude that the price of pig and ingot is not the critical factor. . . . As has previously been noted, Alcoa's percentage of primary sales to other fabricators completely overshadows its competitors. . . . It is not surprising that Alcoa's commanding position in this phase of the market is accompanied by prime responsibility for prices. However, the extent to which prices can be raised is undoubtedly limited by the potential competition of the other two primary producers, a condition quite different from that existing when Alcoa, as the sole American producer, was adjudicated to be a monopoly.

Any price control presently exercised by Alcoa is merely a facet of its concededly dominant position in this phase of the aluminum market. . . . The government has not demonstrated that Alcoa enjoys price leadership with regard to fabricated products, a matter which would have to be included if a true representation of the industry were sought. Nor has the United States established that post-war pig and ingot prices, when compared to costs, are so unreasonably low as to preclude Reynolds and Kaiser from this business. Accordingly, I hold that price domination on the part of Alcoa has not been established. . . .

While I am firmly convinced that the government is entitled to some relief, I am as strongly persuaded that, for the present at least, the organization of Alcoa's physical properties should not be disturbed.

In the first place, it is my considered and firm judgment that a strong and resourceful domestic aluminum industry is a vital necessity, not alone from the standpoint of national security, but also for the peacetime welfare of the general public. . . . One must constantly remember that aluminum products are in fierce rivalry with articles composed of other materials, and which are manufactured and sold by concerns that, in size, are fully equal to Alcoa. Indeed, in some instances, the resources of such competing firms far exceed those of all three domestic aluminum producers. . . . Rightly or wrongly, from an economic and social standpoint, big business in many industries is an actuality, and if such enterprises are to be subjected to effective competition, their trade rivals must be of somewhat comparable strength. This situation imposes a minimum effective size on any aluminum producer if it be a real contributor to the growth of the industry, and be, as well, a lively competitor with the producers of other metals.

The insurance of successful competition by any dissociated portion of Alcoa would depend upon the ability of the new corporation to supply itself with efficient and experienced management. Since Alcoa, for so long, was the only domestic producer of aluminum, there is but a limited number of persons outside of its staff. . . .

When account is taken of the personnel and equipment presently employed in research, an equally grave problem must be faced. It would be a singular disservice to the public if the skill and technique of Alcoa's research department were impaired. . . . Furthermore, serious problems are created as a result of the financial benefits that were received by Reynolds and Kaiser under the government's disposal program. The capital structure of a new company would have to be consistent with the low investment bases of these two producers. Otherwise, a disproportionate strain might soon wreck the competitive opportunities of the newcomer.

The Reynolds and Kaiser organizations are operating successfully and profitably, and there is little or no reason to think that either of them will be unable, under existing trade circumstances, to continue to thrive, and even to prosper. . . . Moreover, if the common control of Alcoa and Limited be eliminated, it is fairly possible, and even probable, that there will be introduced into the domestic market, a rival that is fully worthy. . . . The competitive potential of Limited could not be duplicated in this country by the organization of an additional producer, except at the risk of serious danger and disruption to the present effectiveness of the industry. Today, the United States provides a natural and ample market for part of the huge surplus of metal produced in Canada. . . .

These possibilities, plus the fact that there has been such a short time over which the operations of Reynolds and Kaiser are open to appraisal, require that, for another five years, jurisdiction of this case shall be retained by the Court.

QUESTIONS FOR DISCUSSION

1. How far, in your opinion, did Judge Knox actually go in delineating the "ingredients" or standards for "effective competition"? Consider his standards (1) whether competitors flourish and (2) whether the dominant firm expands over a period of years and others cannot. Are these elements adequate? Compare with the requisites of "effective competition" from the standpoint of economics. See Glossary of Terms, p. 104.

2. According to Judge Knox, what are the two main ingredients of monopoly?

3. What factors—in the view of Judge Knox—should be considered "in determining the extent of permissible power?" What factors, that is, should the court consider in limiting the power of a dominant producer to fix prices?

4. (a) Upon the basis of what evidence (or behavior) did the government charge that Alcoa still possessed monopolistic power? (b) Consider also the pricing formulas used in the sale of aluminum pig and ingot (see Chap. 17).

5. How did Judge Knox rationalize and come to accept Alcoa's "prime responsibility for prices" in the sale of pig and ingot?

6. In accepting Alcoa's "power to fix prices" for pig and ingot, did Judge Knox, in fact, fail to take remedial action against monopoly?

7. Why, in your opinion, did Judge Knox decide that "the organization of Alcoa's physical properties should not be disturbed." Consider (a) national defense, (b) large financial size of producers of copper and other substitutes, (c) the capability of undertaking extensive research, and (d) the problem of finding experienced personnel for a new concern.

8. In your opinion, did Judge Knox believe that substitute products make for "effective competition." What protection does the consuming public have if there is the "power to fix prices" in the aluminum industry *and* in the copper industry?

9. Do you think that Judge Knox provided significant relief in requiring the common control of Alcoa and Aluminum Ltd. (Canada) to be eliminated? What relief is afforded if Aluminum Ltd. sells aluminum in the United States (a) by matching Alcoa's prices and (b) by adopting Alcoa's pricing formulas?

10. In your opinion, do farmers now enjoy independent price competition in the sale of aluminum products? If not, what sort of an attack can farmers take toward price leadership in the aluminum industry?

11. If dissolution and divestiture cases are to be developed by government, do you think that the appropriate decree should be formulated, in the first instance, by a commission of experts rather than by a federal judge? See also Chap. 11, p. 239, for a reference to Section 7 of the F.T.C. Act.

Note:

The problem of refusal to sell does not ordinarily arise in a competitive market. In a central or terminal market for such products as wheat, potatoes, apples, or mill-feed, a buyer can count on buying at the current price. Any given seller could refuse to sell, but he has no motive to do so, unless his supplies are exhausted or ready payment cannot be secured. If he did refuse to sell, a prospective buyer could quickly turn to another seller.

When sellers begin to acquire degrees of control over supply, however, they frequently sell only to certain buyers, in specified quantities, at certain times, and with various stipulations on resale. Degrees of monopoly power may arise from patents, trademarks, control of raw materials, collusion, or geographic location. By refusing to sell in certain situations, a monopolistic seller or group of sellers is able to restrict supply, exercise greater control over prices, and enhance profits. *At the present time, the antitrust agencies report that "refusal to sell" is one of the most frequent complaints which they receive.*

In so far as refusal to sell reflects an industry-wide policy and the prosecution can show proof of conspiracy, the courts will readily condemn the practice. The troublesome situations are those of oligopoly in which proof of conspiracy is difficult to secure.

In the case of *U.S. v. Colgate*, 250 U.S. 300 (1919), the Court gave limited approval to the right of a *single seller* to refuse to sell (see text, p. 231). Since 1919, however, the doctrine of the Colgate ruling has been severely restricted by subsequent decisions. *Today, in so far as refusal to sell can be shown to have trade-restraining effects, there is a probability that the courts will condemn it under the Sherman Act or the Federal Trade Commission Act.* It is impossible, however, to predict in advance of a Supreme Court decision how the Court will decide!

Decision:

EASTMAN KODAK CO. v. SOUTHERN PHOTO MATERIALS CO.,
273 U.S. 359 (1927)
Supreme Court of the United States

Mr. Justice SANFORD delivered the opinion of the Court:

This suit was brought by the Southern Photo Materials Company, a Georgia corporation . . . against the Eastman Kodak Company, a New York corporation to recover damages for injuries sustained by the plaintiff through the defendant's violation of the Sherman Antitrust Act. . . . The trial to the court and jury resulted in a verdict for the plaintiff assessing its actual damages at $7,914.66. Judgment was entered against the defendant for triple this amount and an attorney's fee. This was affirmed by the Circuit Court of Appeals. . . .

The plaintiff operates a photographic stock house in Atlanta and deals in photographic materials and supplies, which it sells to photographers in Georgia and other Southern States. The defendant is a manufacturer of photographic materials and supplies, which it sells to dealers throughout the United States.

The case made by the allegations of the complaint was, in substance, this: The defendant, in violation of the Antitrust Act, had engaged in a combination to monopolize the interstate trade in the United States in photographic materials and supplies, and had monopolized the greater part of such interstate trade. This had been brought about by purchasing and acquiring the control of competing companies engaged in manufacturing such materials, and the businesses and stock houses of dealers; by restraining the vendors from reëntering these businesses; by imposing on the dealers to whom it sold goods restrictive terms of sale fixing the prices at which its goods could be resold and preventing them from handling competitive goods; and by other means of suppressing competition.

Prior to 1910 the plaintiff had dealt with the defendant and purchased its goods on the same terms as other dealers, with whom it was enabled to compete; but in that year the defendant, having acquired the control of the stock houses in Atlanta which were in competition with the plaintiff and unsuccessfully attempted to purchase the plaintiff's business, had, in furtherance of its purpose to monopolize, thereafter refused to sell the plaintiff its goods at the dealers' discounts, and would no longer furnish them except at the retail prices at which they were sold by other dealers . . . with whom the plaintiff could no longer compete. And, the plaintiff being thus deprived, by reason of the monopoly, of the ability to obtain the defendant's goods and supply them to its trade, its business had been greatly injured and it had sustained large damages in the loss of the profits which it would have realized in the four years covered by the suit had it been able to continue the purchase and sale of such goods. . . .

Although there was no direct evidence—as there could not well be—that the defendant's refusal to sell to the plaintiff was in pursuance of a purpose to monopolize, we think that the circumstances disclosed in the evidence sufficiently tended to indicate such purpose, as a matter of just and reasonable inference, to warrant the submission of this question to the jury. "Clearly," as was said by the Court of Appeals, "it could not be held as a matter of law that the defendant was actuated by innocent motives rather than by an intention and desire to perpetuate a monopoly. . . ." The defendant further contends that, apart from this question the plaintiff's damages were purely speculative, not proved by any facts from which they were logically and legally inferable, and not of an amount susceptible of expression in figures. . . .

As to this question the Court of Appeals—after stating that in its opinion the plaintiff's evidence would have supported a much larger verdict than that returned by the jury—said:

"The plaintiff had an established business, and the future profits could be shown by past experience. It was permissible to arrive at net profits by deducting from the gross profits of an earlier period an estimated expense of doing business. Damages are not rendered uncertain because they cannot be calculated with absolute exactness. It is sufficient if a reasonable basis of computation is afforded, although the result be only approximate."

This, we think, was a correct statement of the applicable rules of law.

Furthermore, a defendant whose wrongful conduct has rendered difficult the ascertainment of the precise damages suffered by the plaintiff, is not entitled to complain that they cannot be measured with the same exactness and precision as would otherwise be possible. . . . Affirmed.

QUESTIONS FOR DISCUSSION

1. Under what conditions is refusal to sell unlawful?
2. The Eastman Kodak Company had a *national* monopoly of photographic supplies. Do you think that a company exercising monopoly power, but controlling only a fraction of the national market, stands subject to the *Eastman Kodak* decision?
3. What relief did the plaintiff secure in the *Kodak* case? Did the Court order Eastman Kodak to sell to anyone offering cash?
4. Does a dealer or large customer have the right to stop *buying* from a supplier? What if the act contains elements of monopoly or oppression?
5. Under what conditions do you think that a large corporation, controlling substantial percentages of *primary* supplies, should be required by law to sell to all persons desiring to buy and offering cash?
6. Assume a period of extreme scarcity of primary raw materials—such as pig lead, copper ingots, or steel ingots. A primary producer refuses to sell you the supplies which you have been purchasing. In fact, he declines to sell you at all on the ground that he needs the products for his own fabricating plants. If you can show that it is impossible to secure supplies elsewhere, except at a prohibitive price, do you think that the courts might afford relief under the Sherman Act?
7. Assume that you are a retailer and that your supplier refuses to sell you needed supplies—such as gasoline. What reasons can you suggest for his action? (See also Chap. 16, p. 355.) What relief does the law afford? Under what conditions is it possible that you might secure relief?

I. EXCLUSIVE DEALING AND TYING CONTRACTS

11. STANDARD OIL OF CALIFORNIA CASE

Note:

Section 3 of the Clayton Act condemns tying arrangements which compel a buyer to engage in other transactions with a seller where the effect "may be to substantially lessen competition." The Act makes no distinction among the various kinds of agreements. All are violative of the Clayton Act, as well as the Sherman Act, when they have the specified effect on competition.

The *Standard Oil of California* decision (1949) is a landmark in the field of tying arrangements in that it establishes a single criterion for testing the legality or illegality of such contracts, namely, whether or not a substantial amount of the trade in a sales area is covered by such contracts.

Decision:

STANDARD OIL CO. OF CALIFORNIA v. U.S., 337 U.S. 293 (1949)
Supreme Court of the United States

Mr. Justice FRANKFURTER delivered the opinion of the Court:

The Standard Oil Company of California . . . owns petroleum-producing resources and refining plants in California and sells petroleum products in what has been termed in these proceedings the "Western area"—Arizona, California, Idaho, Nevada, Oregon, Utah and Washington. It sells through its own service stations, to the operators of independent service stations, and to industrial users. It is the largest seller of gasoline in the area. . . .

Exclusive supply contracts with Standard had been entered, as of March 12, 1947, by the operators of 5,937 independent stations, or 16% of the retail gasoline outlets in the Western area, which purchased from Standard in 1947 $57,646,233 worth of gasoline and $8,200,089.21 worth of other products. Some outlets are covered by more than one contract so that in all about 8,000 exclusive supply contracts are here in issue. These are of several types, but a feature common to each is the dealer's undertaking to purchase from Standard all his requirements of one or more products. . . .

The District Court held that the requirement of showing an actual or potential lessening of competition or a tendency to establish monopoly was adequately met by proof that the contracts covered "a substantial number of outlets and a substantial amount of products, whether considered comparatively or not." Given such quantitative substantiality, the substantial lessening of competition—so the court reasoned—is an automatic result, for the very existence of such contracts denies dealers opportunity to deal in the products of competing suppliers and excludes suppliers from access to the outlets controlled by those dealers. Having adopted this standard of proof, the court excluded as immaterial testimony bearing on "the commercial merits or demerits of the present system as contrasted with a system which prevailed prior to its establishment and which would prevail if the court declared the present arrangement [invalid]."

The issue before us, therefore, is whether the requirement of showing that the effect of the agreements "may be to substantially lessen competition" may be met simply by proof that a substantial portion of commerce is affected or

706

whether it must also be demonstrated that competitive activity has actually diminished or probably will diminish. . . .

Requirements contracts may well be of economic advantage to buyers as well as to sellers, and thus indirectly of advantage to the consuming public. In the case of the buyer, they may assure supply, afford protection against rises in price, enable long-term planning on the basis of known costs, and obviate the expense and risk of storage in the quantity necessary for a commodity having a fluctuating demand. From the seller's point of view, requirements contracts may make possible the substantial reduction of selling expenses, give protection against price fluctuations, and—of particular advantage to a newcomer to the field to whom it is important to know what capital expenditures are justified—offer the possibility of a predictable market. . . .

[The Court concedes that it might consider] evidence that competition has flourished despite use of the contracts, and under this test much of the evidence tendered by appellant in this case would be important. . . . Still another test would be the status of the defendant as a struggling newcomer or an established competitor. Perhaps most important, however, would be the defendant's degree of market control. . . .

Yet serious difficulties would attend the attempt to apply these tests. . . . Moreover, . . . to require firm prediction of an increase of competition as a probable result of ordering the abandonment of the practice would be a standard of proof if not virtually impossible to meet, at least most ill-suited for ascertainment by courts. . . .

Congress has authoritatively determined that those practices are detrimental where their effect may be to lessen competition. It has not left at large for determination in each case the ultimate demands of the "public interest. . . ." Though it may be that such an alternative to the present system as buying out independent dealers and making them dependent employees of Standard Stations, Inc., would be a greater detriment to the public interest than perpetuation of the system, this is an issue, like the choice between greater efficiency and freer competition, that has not been submitted to our decision. We are faced, not with a broadly phrased expression of general policy, but merely a broadly phrased qualification of an otherwise narrowly directed statutory provision. . . .

We conclude, therefore, that the qualifying clause of Sec. 3 is satisfied by proof that competition has been foreclosed in a substantial share of the line of commerce affected. It cannot be gainsaid that observance by a dealer of his requirements contract with Standard does effectively foreclose whatever opportunity there might be for competing suppliers to attract his patronage, and it is clear that the affected proportion of retail sales of petroleum products is substantial. . . . Standard's use of contracts creates just such a potential clog on competition as it was the purpose of Sec. 3 to remove wherever, were it to become actual, it would impede a substantial amount of competitive activity. . . . The judgment below is affirmed.

QUESTIONS FOR DISCUSSION

1. What single criterion or rule did the Court affirm for testing the legality or illegality of exclusive dealing contracts?

2. (a) What kinds of considerations bearing on "substantial lessening of competition" did the District Court exclude from consideration?
   (b) Did the Supreme Court concur in the exclusion of these tests? Why?
3. Spokesmen for large petroleum companies condemn the Standard Oil of California decision on the ground that the Court departed from the "rule of reason." The rule of reason, they declare, "is being strangled." In your opinion, should the courts construe the legality of exclusive dealing arrangements (1) by looking at tying arrangements in the light of a factual showing of illegality—such as specific evils, overt acts, or illegal motives and (2) by considering the impact of the tying arrangements in the light of the particular market setting (i.e., whether some competition still flourishes).
4. To what extent under Section 3 of the Clayton Act does a buyer (wholesaler or retailer) have "freedom to buy" without being compelled to engage in other transactions with the seller?
5. Can you give examples of "tie-in" arrangements which exist in your community? Consider the provision of expensive ice-cream cabinets on condition that a retailer will buy all of his ice cream from a given supplier. How about the provision of coffee makers to eating houses on condition that all coffee and spices will be purchased from a given supplier?
6. What reason, or reasons, can you give for adopting legislation which would provide that tying restrictions shall be illegal, *per se* (by themselves or standing alone) without the qualification "where the effect . . . may be to substantially lessen competition."

J. SECTION 7 OF THE CLAYTON ACT, AS AMENDED, AND THE PREVENTION OF MERGERS

12. THE PILLSBURY CASE

Note:

In 1950 Congress passed the Antimerger Act, amending Section 7 of the Clayton Act (1914). The new legislation prohibits the acquisition of assets, as well as stock, "where in any line of commerce in any section of the country, the effect of such acquisition may be substantially to lessen competition, or to tend to create a monopoly."

Construing the new Section 7 in the *Pillsbury* case (see text, p. 359), the Federal Trade Commission rejected the proposal of its own attorneys that the proper Clayton-Act test for condemning acquisitions in a given market area is whether a large company "having a substantial share of that market, acquires another . . . [company] in that market also having a substantial share of that market." The Commission also rejected the "Sherman Act test" —whether a large acquiring firm secures an overwhelming percentage control of the total market—*U.S. Steel* and *Columbia Steel* cases. In particular, the Commission made it clear that it would not adopt a *"per se* test" for Section 7—that is, a clear-cut rule which condemns certain conduct by itself— standing alone—without regard to evidence of effects. The *per se* doctrine, it may be noted, stands in opposition to the rule of reason.

In place of the tests mentioned, the Commission formulated the "Clayton-Act test" as a case-by-case testing of acquisitions which fall short of over-whelming control "in order to ascertain probable economic consequences." This test is the rule of reason approach. It considers whether the restraints involve undue harm to competition.

Antitrust experts believe that the opinion of the Federal Trade Commission in the *Pillsbury* case will set a landmark for future merger cases coming before it. See also S. Chesterfield Oppenheim, "Federal Antitrust Legislation: Guideposts to a Revised National Antitrust Policy," *Michigan Law Review,* June, 1952, pp. 1181–1197.

Opinion of the commission:

IN THE MATTER OF PILLSBURY MILLS, INC., DOCKET NO. 6000 FEDERAL TRADE COMMISSION, 1953.

. . . One of the purposes of amended Section 7 was to re-establish the dif-ference between Sherman Act and Clayton Act violations and to restate the legislative view . . . that the tests of the Sherman Act have no proper place in the application of Section 7. . . .

Putting aside the broad concepts of competition and monopoly, the essen-tial difference seems to be that the Clayton Act requires a lower standard of proof of the same kind of facts. . . . More specifically, the merger in *U.S. v. Columbia Steel Co.,* 334 U.S. 495 (1948), which was examined under the Sherman Act, would probably not have been approved had new Section 7 been in existence and invoked against it. . . .

As we see it, amended Section 7 sought to reach the mergers embraced within its sphere in their incipiency, and to determine their legality by tests of its own. These are not the [Sherman Act test] . . . nor are Section 7 prohibtions to be added to the list of *per se* violations. Somewhere in between is Section 7, which prohibits acts that "may" happen in a particular market, that looks to "a reasonable probability," to "substantial" economic consequences, to acts that "tend" to a result. Over all is the broad purpose to supplement the Sherman Act and to reach incipient restraints.

While these are far from specific standards—specificity would in any event be inconsistent with the "convenient vagueness" of antitrust prohibitions—they can, we believe, be applied on a case-by-case basis.

K. PRICE DISCRIMINATION UNDER THE CLAYTON ACT, AS AMENDED BY THE ROBINSON-PATMAN ACT

13. MORTON SALT CASE

Note:

The Morton Salt case considers (a) the application of Section 2 of the Clayton Act, as amended, to quantity discounts and (b) the question of whether the defendant has the burden of showing that his quantity discounts are justified by cost savings.

The Federal Trade Commission argued that price differentials to large purchasers under the Robinson-Patman Act should be no greater than are justified by cost savings. Beyond this point, they would be discriminatory. It contended (1) that Morton's quantity discounts were discriminations; (2) that the effect of the price differences *may be* to injure competition; (3) that respondent did not show that its price differences were justified by cost savings; and (4) that respondent did not show that the lower prices were made in good faith to meet competition.

The Company contended (1) that its quantity discounts, openly available to all, were not discriminatory under the Act; and (2) that the Commission had the burden of proving an absence of cost justification for the price differences.

The Supreme Court held for the Commission. To the argument that the discounts were not discriminatory because they were openly available to all, the Court replied that, in fact, only four or five large buyers were in a position to utilize the largest discount. The purpose of the Robinson-Patman Act, it declared, was "to deprive a large buyer" of any competitive advantage it might secure in lower cost prices, except where the lower prices can be justified by a savings in cost or by a seller's effort to meet a competitor's price. The Court also stated that the burden of justifying the lower sale price rests with the defendant.

Decision:

F.T.C. v. MORTON SALT CO., 334 U.S. 37 (1948)
Supreme Court of the United States

Mr. Justice BLACK delivered the opinion of the Court:

Respondent manufactures several different brands of table salt and sells them directly to (1) wholesalers or jobbers, who in turn resell to the retail trade, and (2) large retailers, including chain store retailers. Respondent sells its finest brand of table salt, known as Blue Label, on what it terms a standard quantity discount system available to all customers. Under this system the purchasers pay a delivered price and the cost to both wholesale and retail purchasers of this brand differs according to the quantities bought. These prices are as follows, after making allowance for rebates and discounts:

	Per case
Less-than-carload purchases	$1.60
Carload purchases (approx. 1035 cases)	1.50
5,000-case purchases in any consecutive 12 months	1.40
50,000-case purchases in any consecutive 12 months	1.35

Only five companies have ever bought sufficient quantities of respondent's salt to obtain the $1.35 per case price. These companies could buy in such quantities because they operate large chains of retail stores in various parts of the country. As a result of this low price these five companies have been able to sell Blue Label salt at retail cheaper than wholesale purchasers from respondent could reasonably sell the same brand of salt to independently operated retail stores, many of whom competed with the local outlets of the five chain stores. . . .

Respondent's basic contention, which it argues this case hinges upon, is that its "standard quantity discounts, available to all on equal terms, as contrasted for example, to hidden or special rebates, allowances, prices or discounts, are not discriminatory, within the meaning of the Robinson-Patman Act." Theoretically, these discounts are equally available to all, but functionally they are not. For as the record indicates, no single independent retail grocery store, and probably no single wholesaler, bought as many as 50,000 cases or as much as $50,000 worth of table salt in one year. Furthermore, the record shows that, while certain purchasers were enjoying one or more of respondent's standard quantity discounts, some of their competitors made purchases in such small quantities that they could not qualify for any of respondent's discounts, even those based on carload shipments. The legislative history of the Robinson-Patman Act makes it abundantly clear that Congress considered it to be an evil that a large buyer could secure a competitive advantage over a small buyer solely because of the large buyer's quantity purchasing ability. The Robinson-Patman Act was passed to deprive a large buyer of such advantages except to the extent that a lower price could be justified by reason of a seller's diminished costs due to quantity manufacture, delivery or sale, or by reason of the seller's good faith effort to meet a competitor's equally low price. . . .

The Committee considered the present Robinson-Patman amendment to Sec. 2 "of great importance." Its purpose was to limit "the use of quantity price differentials to the sphere of actual cost differences. Otherwise," the report continued, "such differentials would become instruments of favor and privilege and weapons of competitive oppression. . . ."

The government interprets the opinion of the Circuit Court of Appeals as having held that in order to establish "discrimination in price" under the Act the burden rested on the Commission to prove that respondent's quantity discount differentials were not justified by its cost savings. . . . We agree that it does not. First, the general rule of statutory construction that the burden of proving justification or exemption under a special exception to the prohibitions of a statute generally rests on one who claims its benefits. . . . Secondly, Sec. 2 (b) of the Act specifically imposes the burden of showing justification upon one who is shown to have discriminated in prices. And the Senate committee report on the bill explained that the provisos of Sec. 2 (a) throw "upon any who claims the benefit of those exceptions the burden of showing that their case falls within them." We think that the language of the Act, and the legislative history just cited, show that Congress meant . . . that in a case involving competitive injury between a seller's customers the Commission need only prove that a seller had charged one purchaser a higher price for like goods than he had charged one or more of the purchaser's competitors. . . . It is argued that the findings fail to show that respondent's discriminatory discounts had in fact caused injury to competition. There are specific findings that such injuries had resulted from respondent's discounts although the statute does not require the Commission to find that injury has actually resulted. The statute requires no more than that the effect of the prohibited price discriminations "may be substantially to lessen competition . . . or to injure, destroy, or prevent competition." After a careful consideration of this provision of the Robinson-Patman Act, we have said that "the statute does not require that the discriminations must in fact have harmed competition, but only that there is a reasonable possibility that they 'may' have such an effect." *Corn Products Co.* v. *F.T.C.*, 324 U.S. 726, 742. Here the Commission found what would appear to be obvious, that the competitive opportunities of certain merchants were injured when they had to pay respondent substantially more for their goods than their competitors had to pay. The findings are adequate. . . .

Congress intended to protect a merchant from competitive injury attributable to discriminatory prices on any or all goods sold in interstate commerce, whether the particular goods constituted a major or minor portion of his stock. Since a grocery store consists of many comparatively small articles, there is no possible way effectively to protect a grocer from discriminatory prices except by applying the prohibitions of the Act to each individual article in the store.

Furthermore, in enacting the Robinson-Patman Act Congress was especially concerned with protecting small businesses which were unable to buy in quantities, such as the merchants here who purchased in less-than-carload lots. . . . Since there was evidence sufficient to show that the less-than-carload purchasers might have been handicapped in competing with the more favored carload purchasers by the differential in price established by respondent, the Commission was justified in finding that competition might have thereby been substantially lessened or have been injured within the meaning of the Act. . . .

The judgment of the Circuit Court of Appeals is reversed and the proceedings are remanded to that court to be disposed of in conformity with this opinion. Reversed.

QUESTIONS FOR DISCUSSION

1. Under the Clayton Act, as amended, the F.T.C. in a complaint has the burden of showing that (a) differences exist in the prices which a seller charges customers in competition with one another—and (b) that these differences may have injurious effects on competition. What defenses are available to the defendant seller? Who has the burden of proving the cost defense? The "good faith" defense?

2. For what business reason, or reasons, might a seller grant large-scale buyers substantial discounts which are not related to cost savings?

3. In your opinion, should government take action "to deprive a large buyer" of competitive advantages which he gains in being able to force down his buying prices, except when the seller can justify the lower prices by (a) cost savings or (b) the claim that lower prices were made in good faith to meet competition?

4. If the "lower" discriminatory price to certain distributors is "passed on," in some measure, to consumers, do you think that fact justifies the practice of discrimination? What weight do you attach to the view that "the price cutter of today [the company getting the benefits of discrimination] may be the monopolist of tomorrow"?

Note:

The *Staley* case involved the sale of glucose by the defendant at its mill in Decatur, Illinois, at delivered prices determined by a base price in Chicago, Illinois, plus freight from Chicago. The F.T.C. contended that Staley's pricing system resulted in systematic discriminations, as measured by variations in its mill net returns, which injured competition among its customers (candy and syrup manufacturers). Some buyers (in Chicago), it found, did not pay the actual cost of delivery (freight absorption); while others (in Decatur, Kansas City, Dallas, Sioux City, St. Louis, and Shreveport) paid substantial amounts of "phantom" freight. Staley contended that when it entered the industry, it adopted the basing-point system used by the industry leader (the Corn Products Company); and that its divergent mill nets were justified as discriminations to meet the equally low prices of a competitor.

The Court condemned Staley's pricing system on the ground that it resulted in injurious discrimination among Staley's customers. In reaching this decision, the Court looked to the differences in Staley's mill-net returns (i.e., mill-net prices) in determining that discriminations existed and in measuring those that were found to exist. The defendant, it held, did not discriminate in good faith in adopting and "slavishly" following the pricing system of another seller. If discrimination is to be justified, the Court declared, it must be made to meet "individual competitive situations."

The *Staley* decision is a landmark because (1) it sets out a definition of price discrimination (variations in a seller's mill-net returns); (2) it holds that systematic price discrimination to match another's delivered price is not discrimination "in good faith"; and (3) it condemns systematic price discrimination whenever there is injury to competition.

Decision:

F.T.C. v. A. E. STALEY MFG. CO. 324 U.S. 746 (1945)
Supreme Court of the United States

Mr. Chief Justice STONE delivered the opinion of the Court:

The principal question for decision is whether respondents, who adopted the discriminatory price system of their competitors, including the Corn Products Refining Company, have sustained the burden of justifying their price system under Sec. 2(b) of the Clayton Act, as amended, by showing that their prices were made "in good faith" to meet the equally low prices of competitors. . . .

The Decatur price, as well as the delivered price at all points at which the freight from Decatur is less than the freight from Chicago, includes an item of unearned or "phantom" freight, ranging in amount in instances mentioned by the Commission, from 1 cent per hundred pounds at St. Joseph, Missouri, to 18 cents at Decatur. The Chicago price, as well as that at points at which the freight from Decatur exceeds freight from Chicago, required respondents to "absorb" freight, varying in instances cited by the Commission from 4 cents per one hundred pounds at St. Louis, Missouri, to 15½ cents per hundred pounds at Chicago.

The Commission found that this inclusion of unearned freight or absorption of freight in calculating the delivered prices operated to discriminate against purchasers at all points where the freight rate from Decatur was less than that from Chicago and in favor of purchasers at points where the freight rate from Decatur was greater than that from Chicago. It also made findings comparable to those made in the *Corn Products Refining Company* case that the effect of these discriminations between purchasers, who are candy and syrup manufacturers competing with each other, was to diminish competition between them.

The sole question we find it necessary to discuss here is whether respondents have succeeded in justifying the discriminations by an adequate showing that the discriminations were made "in good faith" to meet equally low prices of competitors.

We consider first respondents' asserted justification of the discriminations involved in its basing point pricing system. As we held in the *Corn Products Refining Company* case with respect to a like system, price discriminations are necessarily involved where the price basing point is distant from the point of production. This is because, as in respondents' case, the delivered prices upon shipments from Decatur usually include an item of unearned or phantom freight or require the absorption of freight with the consequent variations in the seller's net factory prices. Since such freight differentials bear no relation to the actual cost of delivery, they are systematic discriminations prohibited by Sec. 2(a), whenever they have the defined effect upon competition. . . .

Respondents argue that they have sustained their burden of proof, as prescribed by 2(b), by showing that they have adopted and followed the basing point system of their competitors. . . .

But Sec. 2(b) does not concern itself with pricing systems or even with all the seller's discriminatory prices to buyers. It speaks only of the seller's "lower" price and of that only to the extent that it is made "in good faith to meet an equally low price of a competitor." The Act thus places emphasis on individual competitive situations, rather than upon a general system of competition. . . .

Respondents have never attempted to establish their own non-discriminatory price system, and then reduced their price when necessary to meet competition. Instead they have slavishly followed in the first instance a pricing policy which, in their case, resulted in systematic discrimination. . . .

In none of the markets in which respondents had a freight advantage over their Chicago competitors did respondents reduce their prices below those of their competitors. Instead they met and followed their competitors' prices by prices rendered artificially high, by the inclusion of unearned freight proportioned to the amount by which their competitors' delivered costs exceeded their own.

We cannot say that a seller acts in good faith when it chooses to adopt such a clearly discriminatory pricing system, at least where it has never attempted to set up a non-discriminatory system, giving to purchasers, who have the natural advantage of proximity to its plant, the price advantages which they are entitled to expect over purchasers at a distance.

The Commission's order will be sustained. The judgment below will be reversed, and the cause remanded with instructions to enforce the Commission's order.

So ordered. Reversed and remanded.

TABLE 43. The Basing-Point System Condemned in the *Staley* Case.

Mill Nets of Chicago

$2.	2.	2.	2.	2.	2.	2.	2.	2.	2.	2.	2.	2.	2.

Freight Cost

Chicago   Decatur

.	0.01	0.02	0.03	0.04	0.05	0.06	0.07	0.08	0.09	0.10	0.11	0.12	0.13	0.14

Base
Price

Delivered Prices

$2.00	2.01	2.02	2.03	2.04	2.05	2.06	2.07	2.08	2.09	2.10	2.11	2.12	2.13	2.14

Mill Nets of Staley

$1.86	1.88	1.90	1.92	1.94	1.96	1.98	2.00	2.02	2.04	2.06	2.08	2.10	2.12	2.14

The Court held that regular and systematic price discrimination in matching another's delivered prices is illegal when there is injury to competition.

TABLE 44. The Multiple Basing-Point System in Which Each Seller Quotes (a) His Own F.O.B. Mill Price Plus Freight in His Adjacent Area and (b) Another Seller's Mill Price Plus Freight in Distant Areas.

Mill Nets of Chicago
Systematic Freight Absorption

$2.	2.	2.	2.	2.	2.	2.	1.98	1.96	1.94	1.92	1.90	1.88	1.86

Freight Cost

Chicago   Decatur

.	0.01	0.02	0.03	0.04	0.05	0.06	0.07	0.06	0.05	0.04	0.03	0.02	0.01	.

Base   Base
Price   Price

Delivered Prices

$2.00	2.01	2.02	2.03	2.04	2.05	2.06	2.07	2.06	2.05	2.04	2.03	2.02	2.01	2.00

Mill Nets of Staley
(Systematic Freight Absorption)

$1.86	1.88	1.90	1.92	1.94	1.96	1.98	2.	2.	2.	2.	2.	2.	2.	2.

Since the *Staley* decision, numerous industries have been shifting over to this method of pricing—i.e., the multiple basing-point system of pricing. Whether or not new legal attacks will be made on pricing systems which continue to involve systematic freight absorption will depend upon the *attitudes* of the antitrust agencies. If there is direct evidence of conspiracy, cases will most likely be brought. Usually, industry members allege that they are using a given pricing system "independently and innocently." Whether the doctrine of conscious parallel action or implied conspiracy will be applied to an industry group will depend on the views of the enforcement officers.

QUESTIONS FOR DISCUSSION

1. Appraise the argument that a mill (such as Staley) does not engage in price discrimination when it cuts its mill-net prices (by absorbing freight) to sell to distant buyers (at Chicago), for all buyers at a given destination point pay the same delivered prices. See Table 43. How in the words of the Court, is price discrimination to be determined and measured?

It may be noted that variations in a seller's mill-net returns through time ("in response to changing conditions affecting the market") are not illegal. In an economic sense, they are not discriminations at all.

2. When a mill (such as Staley) regularly cuts its mill-net returns on distant sales *to meet* the delivered prices of a distant competitor (a Chicago mill), is it *competing* on price? Discuss.

3. When a local mill (Staley at Decatur) sells basic products at a price determined by a distant base (Chicago) plus freight from that base to local destinations (at or near Decatur), are local fabricators or users placed at a competitive disadvantage in relation to those located at or near a base? Discuss.

4. Following the Supreme Court decision, it is reported that corn syrup producers adopted the plan (a) of quoting f.o.b. mill prices plus actual freight for local and nearby sales and (b) of quoting the lower delivered prices of distant competitors on distant sales (by absorbing freight). Assume that Staley adopts an f.o.b. mill price of $2.00 (see Table 44).

(a) In selling in the Chicago area, does Staley now "slavishly adopt and follow" the prices of another seller? Discuss.

(b) Does Staley engage in systematic freight absorption in selling in the Chicago area?

(c) In your opinion, can systematic price discriminations which "injure" competition (by avoiding price competition through price matching) be justified?

5. Distinguish between (a) price reductions "to meet competition" in basing-point pricing and (b) the price reductions "to meet competition" which occur in a central market (such as the Boston wool market or the Chicago Board of Trade).

15. Standard Oil of Indiana Case

Note:

The *Standard Oil of Indiana* case considers the question of whether a seller charged with selling at a lower discriminatory price which actually injures competition, can make a complete defense by showing that the lower price was made in good faith to meet the equally low price of a competitor. There is general recognition that the Robinson-Patman Amendment made the "good faith proviso" a "procedural aid" and not a complete defense. This means that an accused can answer a charge of alleged discrimination by saying that it was done in good faith. Thereupon, it is up to the prosecution to prove injury; and if injury can be proven, the good faith excuse ceases to be a defense.

The Court of Appeals in 1949 upheld the F.T.C. in its contention that if discrimination results in injury, the good faith proviso ceases to be a defense. Standard appealed the decision. During the trial before the Supreme Court, the Commission changed its attitude toward price discrimination. A majority of the Commission adopted the view that although good faith *in the statute* was only a "procedural aid," it *should* be made a complete defense. In the Commission's view, the quoting of discriminatory "lower" prices to some buyers is, itself, a kind of competition which should be permitted.

A majority of the Supreme Court similarly adopted the view that discrimination is a kind of competition which should be permitted under the law. A seller practicing discrimination, the Court held, has an absolute defense if he can show that he met in good faith the equally low price of a competitor.

Justice Reed wrote a vigorous dissent, joined by the Chief Justice and Justice Black. In their view, the legislative history of the statute and the wording of the statute, itself, show clearly that meeting the price of a competitor *is not* a defense to a charge of price discrimination.

Decision:

STANDARD OIL CO. v. F.T.C., 340 U.S. 231 (1951)
Supreme Court of the United States

Mr. Justice BURTON delivered the opinion of the Court:

In this case the Federal Trade Commission challenged the right of the Standard Oil Company, under the Robinson-Patman Act, to sell gasoline to four comparatively large "jobber" customers in Detroit at a less price per gallon than it sold like gasoline to many comparatively small service station customers in the same area. The company's defenses were that (1) the sales involved were not in interstate commerce and (2) its lower price to the jobbers was justified because made to retain them as customers and in good faith to meet an equally low price of a competitor. . . .

For the reasons hereinafter stated, we agree with the court below that the sales were made in interstate commerce but we agree with petitioner that, under the Act, the lower price to the jobbers was justified if it was made to retain each of them as a customer and in good faith to meet an equally low price of a competitor. . . .

Each of petitioner's so-called "jobber" customers has been free to resell its gasoline at retail or wholesale. Each, at some time, has resold some of it at retail. One now resells it only at retail. The others now resell it largely at wholesale. As to resale prices, two of the "jobbers" have resold their gasoline only at the prevailing wholesale or retail rates. The other two, however, have reflected, in varying degrees, petitioner's reductions in the cost of the gasoline to them by reducing their resale prices of that gasoline below the prevailing rates. The effect of these reductions has thus reached competing retail service stations. . . . The Commission found that such reduced resale prices "have resulted in injuring, destroying, and preventing competition between said favored dealers and retail dealers in respondent's gasoline. . . ."

Petitioner presented evidence tending to prove that its tank-car price was made to each "jobber" in order to retain that "jobber" as a customer and in good faith to meet a lawful and equally low price of a competitor. . . .

There is no doubt that under the Clayton Act, before its amendment by the Robinson-Patman Act, this evidence would have been material and, if accepted, would have established a complete defense to the charge of unlawful discrimination. . . . The question before us, therefore, is whether the amendments made by the Robinson-Patman Act deprived those facts of their previously recognized effectiveness as a defense. . . .

The defense relating to the meeting of the price of a competitor appears only in subsection (b). There it is applied to discriminations in services or facilities as well as to discriminations in price. . . . In its opinion in the instant case, the Commission recognizes that it is an absolute defense to a charge of price discrimination for a seller to prove, under Sec. 2 (a), that its price differential makes only due allowances for differences in cost or for price changes made in response to changing market conditions. Each of these three defenses is introduced by the same phrase "nothing . . . shall prevent" and all are embraced in the same word "justification" in the first sentence of Sec. 2 (b). It is natural, therefore, to conclude that each of these defenses is entitled to the same effect. . . . The Commission says, however, that the proviso in Sec. 2 (b) as to a seller meeting in good faith a lower competitive price is not an absolute defense if an injury to competition may result from such price reduction. We find no basis for such a distinction between the defenses in Sec. 2 (a) and Sec. 2 (b).

The defense in subsection (b), now before us, is limited to a price reduction made to meet in good faith an equally low price of a competitor. It thus eliminates certain difficulties which arose under the original Clayton Act. . . . It also excludes reductions which undercut the "lower price" of a competitor. None of these changes, however, cut into the actual core of the defense. That still consists of the provision that wherever a lawful lower price of a competitor threatens to deprive a seller of a customer, the seller, to retain that customer, may in good faith meet that lower price. Actual competition, at least in this elemental form, is thus preserved. . . .

The heart of our national economic policy long has been faith in the value of competition. In the Sherman and Clayton Acts, as well as in the Robinson-Patman Act, "Congress was dealing with competition, which it sought to protect, and monopoly, which it sought to prevent." *A. E. Staley Mfg. Co.* v. *F.T.C.* 135 F. 2d 453, 455. . . .

It is enough to say that Congress did not seek by the Robinson-Patman Act either to abolish competition or so radically to curtail it that a seller would have no substantial right of self-defense against a price raid by a competitor. . . . We may, therefore, conclude that Congress meant to permit the natural consequences to follow the seller's action in meeting in good faith a lawful and equally low price of its competitor. . . .

The judgment of the Court of Appeals, accordingly, is reversed and the case is remanded to that court with instructions to remand it to the Federal Trade Commission to make findings in conformity with this opinion. It is so ordered.

QUESTIONS FOR DISCUSSION

1. Is the privilege of discrimination in good faith to meet a competitor's price wherever you find it, good or bad for competition? Does it promote fair price competition among resellers?
2. Distinguish between the price reduction of a seller in an open central market—such as the Boston wool market—to meet the lower price of a competitor and the price reduction made in the *Standard Oil* case.
3. Do you think that it is sound public policy to permit a seller to favor customer A (fabricator, wholesaler, or retailer) over other customers who are in direct competition with A, even when it can be shown that competition is injured, if the seller can show that the lower price was made to meet a quotation which someone else had offered the favored buyer?
4. Discrimination involves a "higher" price and a "lower" price, without a corresponding difference in quality, service, or conditions in the terms of sale. Consider the higher price. Why is it, in your opinion, that a seller can regularly get a higher price from some buyers than from others? Why do not the buyers paying the higher price turn to the seller offering to sell for less?
5. Can a seller on a public exchange—such as the New York Stock Exchange, the Cotton Exchange, or the Chicago Board of Trade—make some buyers pay more than the "going" price to others for the same commodity? Why or why not?
6. Consider the case of a small seller who tries to attract new customers by offering a low, nondiscriminatory price, rather than by heavy advertising. A large competitor may readily block this expansion by offering *those customers* low discriminatory prices. In your opinion, is this "fair" competition?
7. Assume that you are a seller charged with discriminating in price among your customers who are in competition with one another (in the resale market). The Commission has established a *prima facie* case against you, showing injury to competition at the secondary level. If you seek to rely on the good faith defense, you must bear the burden of proving it. How would you go about establishing your defense?
8. In the *Standard Oil* case, the company argued that " 'actual' or 'reasonably possible' injury to competition must be present *in every price discrimination case*. If injury to competition rebuts the affirmative defense of meeting a competitor's price in good faith, it necessarily follows that the affirmative defense is unavailable in any case and that the proviso to Sec-

tion 2(b) is without meaning." (a) Distinguish between (1) the injury to competition—i.e., to a rival in the same line of business—which flows from a uniform reduction in a seller's f.o.b. mill price and (2) that which flows from a discriminatory reduction in price. (b) Which type of reduction (and effects) did Congress seek to preclude in 1936? (c) If a business practice injures competition, should the practice be permitted? Why or why not?

9. The attorneys for Standard Oil argued that "The right in good faith to meet the lower price of a competitor in order to keep a customer is of first significance in our competitive system." Discuss in light of the efforts of Congress to curb price discrimination.

L. DIRECT PRICE CONTROL BY GOVERNMENT

16. THE NEBBIA CASE

Note:

Prior to the great depression, the Supreme Court followed the general rule that "freedom of contract" must be preserved in the making of prices and wages. The word "liberty" in the Fourteenth Amendment, it declared, protects "freedom of contract" from direct control. Only in a small category of "business affected with a public interest"—narrowly defined as public utilities—did the Court permit price fixing by public authority. In *Nebbia* v. *New York* (1934), however, the Court set aside its past decisions and affirmed the power of a state government to control prices in a line of business characterized by competition (not monopoly) whenever it is "reasonably necessary" to do so in the public interest. Freedom of contract, it held, must give way to public price fixing if the legislature finds that such is necessary for the public good.

The Fifth Amendment, applicable to the federal government, provides, "No person shall be . . . deprived of life, liberty, or property, without due process of law." The Fourteenth Amendment declares, "Nor shall any state deprive any person of life, liberty, or property, without due process of law; nor deny to any person within its jurisdiction the equal protection of the laws."

Decision:

NEBBIA v. NEW YORK, 291 U.S. 502 (1934)

Supreme Court of the United States

Mr. Justice ROBERTS delivered the opinion of the Court:

The Legislature of New York established by chapter 158 of the Laws of 1933, a Milk Control Board with power, among other things, to "fix minimum and maximum . . . retail prices to be charged by . . . stores to consumers for consumption off the premises where sold." The board fixed nine cents as the price to be charged by a store for a quart of milk. Nebbia, the proprietor of a grocery store in Rochester, sold two quarts and a 5-cent loaf of bread for 18 cents; and was convicted for violating the board's order. At his trial he asserted the statute and order contravene the equal protection clause and the due process clause of the Fourteenth Amendment, and renewed the contention in successive appeals to the county court and the Court of Appeals. Both overruled his claim and affirmed the conviction. . . .

Under our form of government the use of property and the making of contracts are normally matters of private and not of public concern. The general rule is that both shall be free of governmental interference. But neither property rights nor contract rights are absolute; for government cannot exist if the citizen may at will use his property to the detriment of his fellows, or exercise his freedom of contract to work them harm. Equally fundamental with the private right is that of the public to regulate it in the common interest. . . .

These correlative rights, that of the citizen to exercise exclusive dominion over property and freely to contract about his affairs, and that of the state to regulate the use of property and the conduct of business, are always in collision. . . . But subject only to constitutional restraint the private right must yield to the public need.

The Fifth Amendment, in the field of federal activity, and the Fourteenth, as respects state action, do not prohibit governmental regulation for the public welfare. They merely condition the exertion of the admitted power, by securing that the end shall be accomplished by methods consistent with due process. And the guaranty of due process, as has often been held, demands only that the law shall not be unreasonable, arbitrary, or capricious, and that the means selected shall have a real and substantial relation to the object sought to be attained. . . .

The Constitution does not guarantee the unrestricted privilege to engage in a business or to conduct it as one pleases. . . . The public policy with respect to free competition has engendered state and federal statutes prohibiting monopolies, which have been upheld. On the other hand, where the policy of the state dictated that a monopoly should be granted, statutes having that effect have been held inoffensive to the constitutional guarantees. Moreover, the state or a municipality may itself enter into business in competition with private proprietors, and thus effectively although indirectly control the prices charged by them. . . .

We are told that because the law essays to control prices it denies due process. . . . The appellant urges that direct fixation of prices is a type of regulation absolutely forbidden. His position is that the Fourteenth Amendment requires us to hold the challenged statute void for this reason alone. The argument runs that the public control of rates or prices is *per se* unreasonable and unconstitutional, save as applied to businesses affected with a public interest; that a business so affected is one . . . as is commonly called a public utility; or a business in its nature a monopoly. The milk industry, it is said, possesses none of these characteristics, and therefore, not being affected with a public interest, its charges may not be controlled by the state. Upon the soundness of this contention the appellant's case against the statute depends.

We may as well say at once that the dairy industry is not, in the accepted sense of the phrase, a public utility. We think the appellant is also right in asserting that there is in this case no suggestion of any monopoly or monopolistic practice. . . . But if, as must be conceded, the industry is subject to regulation in the public interest, what constitutional principle bars the state from correcting existing maladjustments by legislation touching prices? We think there is no such principle. . . .

The phrase "affected with a public interest" can, in the nature of things, mean no more than that an industry, for adequate reason, is subject to control for the public good. . . . There can be no doubt that upon proper occasion and by appropriate measures the state may regulate a business in any of its aspects, including the prices to be charged for the products or commodities it sells.

So far as the requirement of due process is concerned, and in the absence of other constitutional restriction, a state is free to adopt whatever economic policy may reasonably be deemed to promote public welfare, and to enforce that policy by legislation adapted to its purpose. The courts are without

authority either to declare such policy, or when it is declared by the legislature, to override it. If the laws passed are seen to have a reasonable relation
to a proper legislative purpose, and are neither arbitrary nor discriminatory,
the requirements of due process are satisfied. . . . With the wisdom of the
policy adopted, with the adequacy of practicability of the law enacted to
forward it, the courts are both incompetent and unauthorized to deal. . . .

Price control, like any other form of regulation, is unconstitutional only
if arbitrary, discriminatory, or demonstrably irrelevant to the policy the
Legislature is free to adopt, and hence an unnecessary and unwarranted
interference with individual liberty.

Tested by these considerations we find no basis in the due process clause
of the Fourteenth Amendment for condemning the provisions of the Agriculture and Markets Law here drawn into question.

The judgment is affirmed.

QUESTIONS FOR DISCUSSION

1. What basic restrictions do the Fifth and Fourteenth Amendments place
   upon government regulation and control for the public welfare? Explain.
2. Upon the basis of the *Nebbia* case, what limitations may government impose on the privilege of private enterprise to conduct a business as it
   pleases?
3. In promoting the public interest according to Justice Roberts, may the
   state enter a line of business in competition with private enterprise? Under
   what conditions might it choose to do so?
4. Did the Court hold that the milk industry in the state of New York is a
   public utility in the accepted sense of the term? On what principle did the
   Court permit public price control?
5. Compare the purpose of government control in the case of a public utility
   with the purpose which the state legislature had with respect to the milk
   industry.
6. Is it legally possible for government—state or federal—to adopt any economic policy—such as public price fixing in place of competition—if it
   deems that such a policy is in the public interest? In other words, could
   public price fixing be applied to the steel industry? The petroleum industry? The bread industry? Any industry? if reasonably related to a
   public policy?
7. Upon the basis of the "commerce clause," do you think that government
   could extend public ownership to industries which the public might desire to nationalize? What restrictions apply to the taking of private property for public use?

Index of Cases

References are to pages in the text and the Appendixes. Cases with asterisks are presented in the Appendixes with study questions for class discussion.

Index of Subjects and Names

1504